TWELFTH EDITION

Business Communication

CAROL M. LEHMAN
Professor of Management
Mississippi State University

DEBBIE D. DUFRENE
Professor of General Business
Stephen F. Austin State University

South-Western College Publishing
an International Thomson Publishing company I(T)P®

Cincinnati • Albany • Boston • Detroit • Johannesburg • London • Madrid • Melbourne • Mexico City
New York • Pacific Grove • San Francisco • Scottsdale • Singapore • Tokyo • Toronto

Publishing Team Leader:	John Szilagyi
Acquisitions/Developmental Editors:	Susan Freeman Carson, Amy Villanueva
Production Editor:	Kelly Keeler
Production House:	DPS Associates, Inc.
Internal Design:	Carolyn Deacy Design, San Francisco
Internal Icon Illustrations:	© 1998 Roger Xaiver, Torrance, California
Cover Design:	Barbara Matulionis, Matulionis Photography and Design, Cincinnati
Cover Illustration:	© 1998 Lisa Ballard, Cincinnati
Marketing Manager:	Sarah Woelfel

Copyright ©1999
by SOUTH-WESTERN COLLEGE PUBLISHING
Cincinnati, Ohio

2 3 4 D2 1 0 9 8

Printed in the United States of America

ISBN: 0-538-87520-8

Library of Congress Cataloging-in-Publication Data

Lehman, Carol M.
    Business communication / Carol M. Lehman, Debbie D. DuFrene. —
12th ed.
      p.   cm.
    Includes biblographical references and index.
    ISBN 0-538-87520-8
    1. Commerical correspondence.   2. Business report writing.
3. Business communication.   I. DuFrene, Deborah Daniel, 1954-
II. Title.
HF5721.L44   1998
648.4'5—DC21   98-22969
                                                  CIP

I⟨T⟩P®

International Thomson Publishing
South-Western College Publishing is an ITP Company.
The ITP trademark is used under license.

Brief Contents

PART FOUR

Communicating Through Reports and Business Presentations / 303

PART FIVE

Communicating About Work and Jobs / 477

Appendices

Contents

CHAPTER TWO

Organizational Setting for Business Communication / 45

PART TWO

The Writing Process / 79

CHAPTER THREE

Organizing and Composing Messages / 81

PART THREE

Communicating Through Letters, Memorandums, and E-Mail Messages / 155

CHAPTER SEVEN

Writing Memos and E-Mail Messages / 231

PART FOUR

Communicating Through Reports and Business Presentations / 303

CHAPTER NINE

Understanding the Report Process and Research Methods / 305

PART FIVE

Communicating About Work and Jobs / 477

Photo Credits

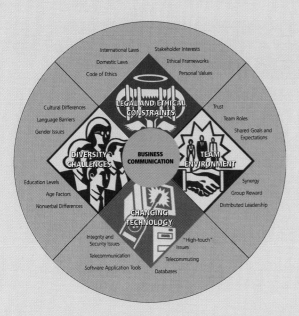

The Strategic Model for Communication

The Twelfth Edition of **Himstreet & Baty's**

Business Communication

Carol M. Lehman, *Mississippi State University*
Debbie D. DuFrene, *Stephen F. Austin State University*

Established as a classic and known for its strong
theoretical base, this text has maintained its relevance
in the dynamic environment of contemporary business! The
hallmarks of each edition—impeccable research, comprehensive
coverage, and excellent writing—are not only continued in this
Twelfth Edition, but improved upon.

What's more, the authors brought a **dynamic new focus** to the text, one that
reflects the growing integration within the field of Business
Communication. **The Strategic Model for Communication** teaches
students how communication is influenced by dynamic environmental forces!

NEW!

Strategic Model for Communication

LEGAL AND ETHICAL
CONSTRAINTS

DIVERSITY
CHALLENGES

TEAM
ENVIRONMENT

CHANGING
TECHNOLOGY

*S*tudents learn how communication is influenced by dynamic environmental forces . . . *diversity, technology, legal and ethical constraints,* and *team environment.*

This model appears in Chapter One and is integrated throughout the text via new "Strategic Forces" features.

Strategic Forces Influencing Business Communication

Communication is often a complicated process. Furthermore, communication does not take place in a vacuum, but rather is influenced by a number of forces at work in the environment. The effective communicator carefully considers each of these influences and structures communication responsively. Various forces influence the communication process and help to determine and define the nature of the communication that occurs, as shown in Figure 1-5.

How would you rank the four strategic forces in terms of magnitude of importance to business communication? Why?

3 Explain how legal and ethical constraints act as a strategic force to influence the process of business communication.

Legal and Ethical Constraints as a Strategic Force Influencing Communication

Legal and ethical constraints act as a strategic force on communication in that they set boundaries in which communication can occur. International, federal, state, and local laws affect the way that various business activities can be conducted. For instance, legislation controls can and must be stated in letters that reply to credit applications and those dealing with collection of outstanding debts. Furthermore, one's own ethical standards will often influence what he or she is willing to say in a message. A system of ethics built on honesty may require that the message provide full disclosure, for instance, rather than a shrouding of the truth. Legal responsibilities, then, are the starting point for appropriate business communication. One's ethical beliefs, or personal sense of right and wrong behavior, provides further boundaries for professional activity.

The press is full of examples of unethical conduct in the business and governmental communities:

● Allegations that the tobacco industry added higher levels of nicotine to its product with knowledge that nicotine is addictive.

NEW! Business Technologies

Up-To-Date Topics

In-depth coverage includes electronic job searches, scannable and on-line résumés, e-mail, Internet search engines, electronic meetings, multimedia presentations, etc. Students benefit from gaining a working knowledge of these critical business communication resources for effective use in the technology-driven workplace.

NEW! Real-Time Internet Cases

make students think critically and communicate complex ideas while strengthening their Internet skills.

Part V / Communicating About Work and Jobs

520

FIGURE 13-9
On-line résumé posted to personal web site.

Jeanne Fulton

89 Lincoln Street
San Antonio, TX 78285-9063
(512) 555-9823

❶ Begins with her name, address, and objective just as her traditional résumé.

❷ Includes a link to an ASCII version of her résumé (no special formatting) that an employer can download into an electronic database.

❸ Includes a link to a copy of a résumé that is formatted professionally and can be read by scrolling down the screen and printed with one command.

❹ Makes it easy for an employer to communicate with her by providing a link directly to her e-mail address.

Includes links to additional information with titles that employers will recognize as sections typically found in a traditional résumé.

Objective

First-year audit staff with an international accounting firm; interest in work with information systems.

ASCII Résumé
Download a text version of my resume. Use the "Save" command in your browser to save to a disk.

Complete Résumé
View or print a fully formatted copy of my resume.

Feedback
www.netdoor/

Additional information to support my qualifications:
- Education
- Computer skills
- Work experience
- Leadership activities

42

Chapter 1 / A Framework for Business Communication

e. An employee in another division office has requested that you send a spreadsheet that you have prepared so that he can manipulate the data to produce a report.

12. **Team Environment as a Strategic Force (Obj. 6)**
Using the Internet, locate an article that covers how a company or organization is using teams in its operation. Write a one-page abstract of the article.

E-MAIL APPLICATION

Read an article from a current magazine or journal about how technology is impacting communication. Send your instructor a brief e-mail message discussing the major theme of the article. Include a complete bibliographic entry so that the instructor could locate the article (refer to Appendix B for examples for formatting references).

REAL-TIME INTERNET CASE

Can the United States Succeed Without Rewarding Rugged Individuality?

A basic element of the fabric of U.S. entrepreneurship is the faith in the ingenuity of the individual person's ability to conceive, develop, and profit from a business endeavor. The frontier spirit and triumph of the individual over looming odds have been a predominant force in the development of the United States. Such individualism has also been recognized by organizations, with reward going to those who contribute winning ideas and efforts.

The recent shift in organizational structures toward team design has caused management to reassess reward systems that focus on individual recognition and to consider rewards that are based on team performance. Some fear that removing individual incentive will lead to mediocrity and a reduction in personal effort. They argue that while the team model might work in other cultures, it is inconsistent with the U.S. way of thinking and living. According to Madelyn Hochstein, president of DYG Inc., a New York firm that researches corporate trends, America is moving away from the model of team building in which everyone is expected to do everything and toward focusing on employees who are the best at what they do. She describes this change as a shift toward social Darwinism and away from egalitarianism, in which everyone has equal economic, political, and social rights.[33]

Team advocates say that teams are here to stay and liken those who deny that reality to the proverbial ostrich with its head in the sand. They stress the need for newly structured incentive plans to reward group effort. Visit the following Internet sites for information on the issue and respond to one or more of the following activities as directed by your instructor.

Internet sites

http://lionhrtpub.com/apics/apics-3-96/motivating.html/
http://www.tpcorp.com/fed/library/articles/scholtes.html
http://www.gainshare.com/cmnts.html

Activities

1. How would you respond to those with concerns about loss of individual incentive? Argue for or against the increased emphasis on team reward, using either personal examples or examples from business.

2. Structure a reward system that would recognize both individual and team performance. You may use an organization of your choice to illustrate.

3. Select a specific corporation or nation that has implemented the team model. Describe the transition away from a hierarchical structure and the consequences that have resulted from the shift, both positive and negative.

NEW FEATURES!

Team Building Projects

While the process by which a group of individuals becomes an effective, functioning team is somewhat different in each situation, it follows a fairly predictable pattern. Experts in team development define four stages of progression: (1) forming, or cautious affiliation; (2) storming, or competitiveness; (3) norming, or harmonious cohesion; and (4) performing, or collaborative teamwork. The phases are described more fully below:

Forming

This stage is an exploration period, in which members' attachment to the team is tentative. Most of the time, members are anxious about what the team and they, as individual members, are supposed to do. Team members assess other team members' abilities and attitudes and try to determine how and where they fit into the group. They are worried about the team's ability to cope with group problems and conflicts. Little is accomplished during this stage. Productivity is low, and working relationships are guarded, cautious, and noncommittal.

toward the leader and each other decreases significantly. Previously warring factions mellow into normal, healthy, interpersonal patterns. Competitive relationships become cooperative, close, and mutually supportive. Communication channels open, and feelings of mutual trust develop. During this stage, individuals discover that they are proud to be associated with the team. The quantity and quality of work slowly increase.

Performing

A group of individuals becomes a truly collaborative team during this stage. Structured processes and procedures resources, resolve personal conflicts, give warranted positive behav-

Team Building Applications

Ross's **doctrine of prima facie duties** include (1) not harming innocent people, (2) keeping promises, (3) showing gratitude, (4) acting in a just way, and (5) providing reparations to those who have been harmed by one's actions, and (5) providing should be honored whenever possible. To apply this doctrine, you must consider the organization's major stakeholders and determine which of Ross's five duties are relevant to the decision under consideration, and of those, which may be violated for any of the stakeholders.

As these assessments show, applying ethical theories is not an easy task. Such analytical processes, however, enhance your critical thinking about the consequences of any action.

Which of the ethical frameworks do you find most appropriate for you personally? Why?

4 *Explain how diversity challenges act as a strategic force to influence the process of business communication.*

Diversity Challenges as a Strategic Force Affecting Communication

Diversity in the workplace is another strategic force influencing communication. Differences between the sender and the receiver in areas such as culture, age, gender, and education require a sensitivity on the part of both the sender and receiver so that the intended message is the one that is received.

Understanding how to communicate effectively with people from other cultures is becoming more integral to the work environment as many U.S. companies increasingly conduct business with international companies or become multinational. Successful communication must often span barriers of language and almost always requires a person to consider differing world views resulting from societal, religious, or other cultural factors. If a person fails to consider these factors, communication suffers, and the result is often embarrassing and potentially costly.

McDonald's is an example of a large U.S. company that has expanded its operations to include most major the world. To be successful on an international

Critical Thinking Marginal Notes

Integrated Learning Approach

Chapter 4 / Revising and Proofreading Messages

VIDEO CONNECTION

Amatulli & Associates, Inc.

Developing effective training programs for organizations (skill development and employee awareness programs) involves thorough planning, articulate writing and editing, and meticulous proofreading.

The planning process involves (1) identifying the audience, the purpose, and the outcome expected by the client; (2) selecting the appropriate media (written, video, computer interactive) for presenting the message; and (3) identifying and understanding the message to be communicated.

After considering the crucial issues, the writer(s) develop(s) a first draft using the style, language, tone, and approach that is appropriate for the audience and the specific content to be communicated. Finally, the writer(s) and others edit for accuracy, consistency in style among collaborative writers, format, and mechanics.

Discussion Questions

1. According to Jim Amatulli, what information must a writer identify before writing the first

does he offer the reliability of electronic spell check?

6. Study carefully the writing project Jo Huntington described. (1) Identify the audience, the purpose and intended outcome, and the media combination selected; (2) describe the content of the message and the specific approach used to present the message, and (3) discuss how collaborative writing enhanced this project.

7. What does Jim Amatulli mean when he describes the objective and subjective nature of communication?

Applications

As a senior writer in a business communication consulting firm, your task is to *plan* a message that will increase the membership of a student organization of your choice or increase involvement in a community organization such as the United Way, Scouts, and so forth. Your preliminary planning involves providing answers to the following questions:

Video Connection Features

MORE NEW FEATURES!

NEW!
Communication in Action Cases

address communication dilemmas of real companies, challenging students to think through these real-life situations and formulate a plan.

COMMUNICATION IN ACTION
Lonny Uzzell, Southside Bank

When Southside Bank opened its doors in November, 1960, as an independent and locally owned bank, its founders knew that responsiveness to customers was crucial to its success. Today, the bank has a strong community reputation for responsiveness to customers. Having kept the same name for more than 37 years, the bank has maintained stability and demonstrated steady growth. The bank employs more than 300 personnel and manages assets of over $400 million. What elements have been key to this success? What role does business communication play in the bank's stability and growth?

Lonny Uzzell, executive vice president of Southside, believes key elements in Southside's success are responsiveness to customers...

It is essential to the bank's profitability. Bank employees demonstrate responsiveness in other ways. When Uzzell meets someone in the lobby, telephones a customer, or responds to a bank customer through a letter, he listens and treats customers as if they are special. In doing so, he knows that customers receiving any less than special treatment may choose a competitor. When Uzzell talks with customers, he fully understands the concept of "relationship marketing." Personalized service at Southside is as important to customers as interest rates and investments. Today's bank clients demand better, more personalized service.

Not only must Uzzell listen well to customers, he must listen and respond to other bank employees. During a normal work day, he interacts with and listens to employees in different departments and throughout all levels of the bank's organization. Without good listening skills, he would not be successful at his work. Uzzell develops good relationships and quality service through good listening.

Applying What You Have Learned

During the working day, how does Mr. Uzzell experience listening in the four levels of communication?

...tify various directions in the flow of listening in the bank. How does good listening and accurate feedback facilitate communication when a new computer system is installed?

...on your own experiences with a bank, your interpersonal communication employees make that experience negative?

...ganization chart for Citizens' Bank ...d in Figure 2-2 as a sample, distin...formal and informal communi...side Bank. Provide several

---

COMMUNICATION MENTOR

The mistake we often make in our approach to diversity is to focus on the differences. I have discovered that when I search for common ground, the differences become less of an obstacle and more of an opportunity to learn and develop. Each individual is diverse; that diversity should be seen as an untapped resource that has the ability to enrich a company's mission and

business strategies. At the core of diversity is the goal that every employee feels valued and is provided the opportunity to excel. The success of business today is strengthened by diversity. When diversity is embraced as a vital part of the corporate culture, the result is a more productive workforce.

Marquette L. Wilson
Manager, Human Resources
G.E. Capital Commercial Finance

Culture and Communication. Managers with the *desire* and the *skill* to conduct business in these new international markets and to manage a diverse workforce effectively will confront problems created by cultural differences. The way messages are decoded and encoded is not just a function of the experiences, beliefs, and assumptions of the person sending or receiving those messages but also are shaped by the society in which he or she lives. The **culture** of a people is the product of their living experiences within their own society. Culture could be described as "the way of life" of a people and includes a vast array of behaviors and beliefs. These patterns affect how people perceive the world, what they value, and how they act. Differing patterns can also create barriers to communication. Culture has three key characteristics.

- **Culture is learned by people over time.** Individuals are not born knowing their culture but acquire it through interactions with others. Social institutions such as churches, clubs, businesses; the family; schools; as well as the media, all play a part in teaching each member of a society the expectations and norms of behavior.

- **Components of culture are interrelated.** In the United States, for instance, the high value placed on material goods is related to the use of economic well-being as a measure of success and happiness. These values provide support for the approval placed on independence of mind and action, which in turn is connected to the existence of a relatively fluid class structure. The list of connections could go on, but these examples alone make it clear that each of these components of American culture is connected to other components.

- **Culture is shared.** That is, the various aspects of culture are common to many individuals. No country has one unified culture, however. Modern societies are so large and diverse that many different cultures can exist within them; these are called **subcultures**. Although each subculture differs from others, they often share some traits that derive from the main or dominant culture.

Each society exhibits its culture in many ways. Certainly customs, the accepted way of interacting with others, are expressions of the culture. The North American

What are some examples in your own community of culture-oriented activities?

UPDATED!
Communication Mentor Panel

of corporate leaders is introduced at the beginning of the text, illustrating for students how this material is relevant to their future.

Additional Learning Tools . . .

Instructor's Resource Guide

ISBN: 0-538-87521-6

- Suggestions for organizing the course for both a semester and a quarter system, administering the course, managing collaborative writing projects, and integrating the six videotapes.
- Guidelines for grading letters, reports, and oral presentations.
- Chapter learning objectives, an outline, teaching suggestions, and a reduced copy of each acetate and master with teaching notes for each chapter.
- Answers to end-of-chapter review questions.
- Extensive coverage of grammar, writing, style, and usage, with exercises and solutions.

Transparency Acetates

ISBN: 0-538-87524-0

Over 100 color transparencies are available to adopters. They are also available in PowerPoint.

PowerPoint Slides

ISBN: 0-538-87525-9

The concepts in the text are professionally rendered in PowerPoint. Instructors can use slides to fit their lectures or to produce elaborate classroom presentations with ease.

Test Bank

ISBN: 0-538-87523-2

Over 1,000 questions are also available in printed form.

Study Guide

ISBN: 0-538-87522-4

The study guide reinforces learning and includes three types of exercises:
- Review Questions
- Practical Applications
- Comprehensive review of major grammatical principles with exercises

World Class Testing Tools™

ISBN: 0-324-00061-8

Organized by the integrated learning system, each test bank chapter begins with a correlation table that classifies each question according to type and learning objective. The electronic test bank allows instructors to edit and customize tests.

MicroExam, 3.5

ISBN: 0-538-87526-7

MicroExam 3.5 provides World Class Testing Tools™ in DOS format.

BusinessLink Video

ISBN: 0-538-87527-5

Students are exposed to communication problems experienced by real companies. Teaching/learning materials are provided to maximize the effectiveness of this learning aid. These videos explore listening, diversity, ethics, persuasion, report writing, interviewing, and other important topics in business communication.

Part Opener Videos

ISBN: 0-538-87530-5

Videos are included that allow students to go inside real companies, meet business executives, and learn effective communication strategies.

More Learning Tools . . .

South-Western Web Site
http://www.swcollege.com/BookTour

Visit us on the Web. On-line textbook resources in business communication are available at your fingertips.

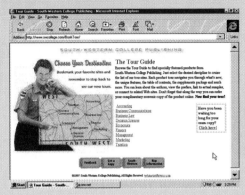

Wired Resumes
http://www.wired-resumes.com

The first and only web site with everything you need to teach on-line résumé creation in your classroom—lesson plans, samples, graphics, resources, discussion lists, résumé posting, etc.

PoWER—Professional Writer's Electronic Resource

by Guffey, Clark, and Clark

This software serves as an on-line reference tool and electronic workbook. It references and reinforces business English skills—grammar, punctuation, usage—plus business communication skills—letter, memo, report, and résumé writing.

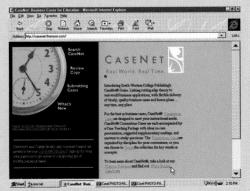

CaseNet
Real World. Real Time.
http://casenet.thomson.com

Visit our web site and access relevant leading-edge cases written by the top researchers in business communication.

Preface

For years, *Business Communication* has inspired students to improve communication skills as a key ingredient in career success. This respected text has pioneered many of the widely accepted strategies for understanding important communication principles and developing writing and speaking proficiency that have become standard. Before-and-after examples of documents, marginal notes and checklists that help students identify important concepts and evaluate their understanding, and strong emphasis on planning and outlining before writing are among these timeless learning strategies.

While known for its strong theoretical base, this text has maintained its relevance in the dynamic environment of contemporary business. Carol Lehman, professor of Management in the College of Business and Industry at Mississippi State University, joined William Himstreet and Wayne Baty in the Tenth Edition to bring expertise in communication technology, ethics, and diversity, and continued commitment to fundamental writing and speaking skills. Joining for the Twelfth Edition is Debbie DuFrene, professor of General Business at Stephen F. Austin State University, who has been a valuable part of this team for several years as a user, valuable reviewer, and contract writer.

Both Lehman and DuFrene had taught from numerous editions of this text before their involvement as authors, and are committed now to building on the proven strengths of this text and ensuring its relevance in today's dynamic workplace. They bring broad experience in team building, multimedia presentations, law and ethics, diversity, and technology. The Twelfth Edition has been carefully revised to prepare students to meet the new and increasing demands of today's workplace: to communicate effectively with a widely diverse work force, to work as a team player, to think critically, and to use advanced technology to communicate effectively and productively. The result, we believe, is a classic text with an exciting contemporary edge.

Introducing a New Strategic Model for Business Communication

The Twelfth Edition presents a strategic model for business communication that integrates some newly identified topics into traditional business communication subject matter, underscoring the impact that each of these forces has on effective communication. The strategic model reflects four forces that have an inevitable impact on business communication effectiveness: changing technology, legal and ethical constraints, diversity challenges, and team communication.

Students who learn to communicate using this strategic forces approach will:

- Understand the interrelationship of business communication with each identified force.
- Appreciate the dynamic environment in which business communication occurs.
- Be able to analyze business communication situations that take into account the complexities of today's workplace.

- Be able to design business communication documents that are reflective of the strategic forces that impact effectiveness.

The model is presented in Chapter 1 where students are introduced to the four major forces that influence the communication process and help determine and define the nature of the communication that occurs. The strategic forces model is integrated into the remaining chapters; distinctive strategic forces icons focus the students' attention on this integration. Additionally, two new feature boxes in each chapter and new Real-Time Internet Cases address pertinent strategic forces affecting the communication topic under discussion.

Hallmark Features Continued Through the Editions

- **Provides a strong theoretical foundation.** Students build a strong theoretical foundation for writing (Chapters 1–4) before encountering the writing applications (Chapters 5–14). Part One, "Communication Foundations," establishes a framework for communicating in an organizational setting with a focus on the communication process, strategic forces influencing business communication, and various levels of communication (interpersonal, group, and organizational). In Part Two, "The Writing Process," students develop skill in the process of writing—determining the purpose and channel, envisioning the audience, adapting the message to the audience, organizing the message, writing the first draft, and revising and proofreading. Additionally, Appendix C provides an extensive grammar and mechanics review—explanations of major grammar rules and self-check quizzes help students see where grammar review is needed.

- **Facilitates powerful writing proficiency.** Important techniques that assist students in grasping important concepts and evaluating their own work include:
  - *Before-and-after writing examples.* Numerous examples of poor and revised documents include targeted annotations that help students understand specific applications of effective writing principles. A new visual design for good examples highlights key organizational points, provides specific comments about the revision, and addresses strategic forces and format considerations.
  - *Model documents presented in full-document format.* The format adds realism to letters, memos, and résumés, and reinforces students' understanding of standard business formats. These documents, complete with letterheads, add visual appeal to the regular text discussion. Comprehensive appendixes also provide visual models and detailed explanations of document formats.
  - *Evaluative checklists.* "General Writing Guidelines" and "Check Your Writing" checklists enable students to evaluate their documents.

- **Includes extensive end-of-chapter activities.** Students solve realistic, challenging problems. Included are review questions, exercises, and e-mail and other applications. Activities require students to revise poorly written documents, compose documents based on the information provided in the problems, conduct library research to locate relevant information needed to solve a problem, or analyze a complex issue that may require extensive research in order for an informed decision to be reached. (Answers to questions and applications appear in the *Instructor's Resource Guide*.)

Some **e-mail applications** require students to send the instructor responses to cases, an outline and bibliography of an upcoming oral or written report, or minutes of group meetings. Others ask that students message one another to apply specific communication theory and facilitate collaborative writing projects. Several new e-mail applications have been added to the Twelfth Edition.

- **Develops critical-thinking skills.** The ability to analyze complex issues, organize thoughts logically, and communicate these complex ideas concisely is essential for career success. The pedagogy of previous editions, and continued in this edition of *Business Communication* involves teaching students to analyze and organize before beginning to write. Other features that foster the development of critical thinking are (1) marginal notes that require students to apply information presented to reach an appropriate conclusion or action, (2) an ethical framework to teach students to analyze ethical dilemmas from multiple perspectives and to identify solutions that conform to personal values, (3) the new Real-Time Internet Cases that require students to complete a series of critical-thinking activities after exploring a topic using the Internet, and (4) the practical applications in the *Study Guide*.

- **Equips students to communicate with advanced technology.** This up-to-date revision reflects the skills needed to communicate using today's advanced technology: production and visual enhancement of documents using word processing, desktop publishing, spreadsheet, and presentation graphics software; use of collaborative software and videoconferencing to facilitate teamwork; expanded understanding of efficient and courteous use of e-mail; effective Internet search skills; electronic job search methods; and highly professional electronic presentations to support oral presentations.

- **Exposes students to communication challenges in real-world companies.** Several features of the text are designed to help students understand the relevance of effective oral and written communication in their career success by exposing them to real companies facing real communication challenges. Students are required to apply specific communication principles to these companies and situations.
  - The *Communication Mentors* features give students a priceless opportunity to "look over the shoulders" of a panel of communication mentors. These corporate leaders represent numerous disciplines and various levels of management. As students study a particular principle, one or more of the communication mentors discuss how the principle actually works in today's dynamic business environment. A special format alerts students that they are learning from the real-life experiences of corporate executives.
  - A *Communication in Action* (CIA) case for each chapter is built around an executive who addresses a communication dilemma in a real company. Cases are based on personal interviews with the executives. Each CIA case includes critical-thinking questions and legitimate writing assignments (in chapters where writing has been introduced) that allow students to apply what they have learned.
  - Chapter openers, photographs, and extensive text discussion highlight communication issues in real companies.
  - Videotapes take students inside real companies to learn how business executives solve communication problems. Teaching and learning materials in the

textbook and *Instructor's Resource Guide* help you use these videos to enliven your classroom presentation.

- **Provides comprehensive, concise coverage.** This comprehensive textbook addresses all major business communication issues with thorough explanations and sufficient examples in as concise a manner as possible. The number of chapters in this edition has been reduced from 18 to 14 in response to feedback from a large number of business communication instructors who feel that the number of chapters should conform more closely to the number of weeks of instruction in a semester.

Exciting Features New to the Twelfth Edition

- **Integration of strategic forces influencing business communication in new feature boxes and text discussion.** The strategic forces model for communication is integrated throughout this edition with in-depth looks at the four strategic forces: legal and ethical constraints, changing technology, diversity challenges, and team environment. Additionally, two new feature boxes in each chapter and many of the Real-Time Internet Cases address the pertinent strategic forces affecting the communication topic under discussion.

- **Expanded team skills.** As one of the four strategic forces influencing business communication, team environment becomes an integral part of this edition. Numerous strategic forces feature boxes examine issues related to team skills (e.g., groups vs. teams, using groupware software to enhance the effectiveness of work teams, collaborative skills for team writing, and team job interviews) and Real-Time Internet Cases (for example, "Can the United States Succeed Without Rewarding Rugged Individuality?" in Chapter 1).

  Five new **team-building applications** provide an exciting, effective method for developing team skills. These applications focus students' attention first on the concept of team building and then each of the four phases of team building: forming, norming, storming, and performing. Students read a brief overview of the team building phase provided in the text, and are then directed to printed sources and Internet sites to explore the concept more fully, to learn about team experiences—good and bad—in real companies, and to complete selected activities that require reflection and critical thinking about the phase. The *Instructor's Resource Guide* includes an array of processes, handouts, evaluation forms, and suggestions needed to facilitate team building development.

- **Critical thinking cases using the Internet.** New Real-Time Internet Cases provide critical-thinking activities as well as experience using the Internet as a research tool. Students explore a timely, thought-provoking topic using Internet sites listed in the case and must present two or more sides of the issue, present a logical argument for a particular viewpoint, or describe an aspect of the issue, using pertinent examples to illustrate. These cases represent the type of critical thinking and analysis required in the GMAT Analytical Writing Assessments (AWA); specifically, tasks designed to assess the ability to think critically and communicate complex ideas. The *Instructor's Resource Guide* contains guidelines for scoring the AWA following the holistic scoring methods used by GMAT graders to rate analytical writing.

- **Critical thinking marginal notes.** These critical thinking questions require the student to apply information presented to reach an appropriate conclusion or action. These notes replace standard summary comments and simple questions.

- **Updated integration of real companies and events.** New chapter openers focusing on companies such as Southwest Airlines, Nike, Steak and Ale, MTV, The Gap, and Campbell Soup Company, as well as numerous examples integrated into the text discussion. These provide students with exposure to communication challenges in real companies. Two new communication mentors join the communication mentor panel, which is composed of executives who supplement the text's concepts with specific advice based on their experiences. Three completely new Communication in Action cases give students a glimpse of communication challenges faced by Gary Lopez, Southwest Airlines; Steve Wolff, JCPenney; and Pamela Plager, Allen & Company.

- **Expanded coverage of e-mail and memorandums (new chapter).** An entire chapter with numerous examples devoted to content and formatting guidelines, etiquette, and ethical and legal implications of technology has been added. The popular e-mail applications at the end of each chapter have been updated.

- **Expanded coverage of multimedia presentations.** The chapter on "Public Speaking and Oral Reporting" in the Eleventh Edition was updated significantly to provide a chapter on designing and delivering a business presentation and developing highly professional presentation media to support a presentation. The new coverage includes detailed discussion of the steps involved in developing an electronic presentation, basic presentation design principles, and the creation of effective audience handouts and speaker notes. The chapter also addresses the important issue of adapting a presentation to an intercultural audience.

- **New, comprehensive coverage of electronic job searches.** New coverage includes a model scannable résumé with specific guidelines for writing and formatting a résumé to be read by an electronic résumé tracking system, detailed discussion of electronic job search methods (career guidance, job listings, and résumé posting), and a model on-line résumé. The employment portfolio and video are presented as alternate tools for capturing career accomplishments.

- **Expanded coverage of documentation for electronic sources.** Because business writers must know how to cite electronic sources, a new appendix has been added to provide direction in citing electronic sources from the Internet, discussion groups, CD-ROM, e-mail messages, etc. The use of footnotes/endnotes is illustrated using the *Chicago Manual of Style*.

Exceptional Instructional Resources

A complete package of instructional resources complements the textbook as well as your classroom presentations. An instructor's resource guide, study guide, test bank, transparency acetates, PowerPoint slides, videos, and web sites can be used to simplify and strengthen the study of business communications to make both in- and out-of-class time more effective. A description of each resource is included in the Additional Learning Tools feature on pages xxii and xxiii.

Acknowledgments

The authors express their sincere appreciation to all persons who have contributed to this textbook. These include:

- The many faculty members with whom we have worked and the many professional educators who have reviewed, critiqued, and made significant contributrion to each edition, and particularly to this one. These truly professional educators include:

  Carol Barnum, Southern Polytechnic State University
  Dr. Beverly Block, Professor, Missouri Southern State College, Joplin, MO
  Doris A. Christopher, Ed.D., California State University–Los Angeles
  Dr. Sidney W. Eckert, Appalachian State University, Boone, NC
  Mohan R. Limaye, Boise State University, Boise, ID
  Dr. James A. Manos, California State University–Northridge, Irvine, CA
  Jeanette S. Martin, Ed.D., University of Mississippi, University, MS
  Paul H. Martin, Aims Community College, Greeley, CO
  Paula J. Pomerenke, Illinois State University, Normal, IL
  Dr. Carolyn Mae Rainey, Southeastern Missouri State University,
     Cape Girardeau, MO
  Dr. Ruth D. Richardson, University of North Alabama, Florence, AL
  Dr. Jean Anna Sellers, Fort Hays State University, Hays, KS
  Gayle J. Vogt, California State University–Fullerton, Fullerton, CA
  Brenna Best Weller, Oregon State University, Corvallis, OR
  Dr. Myron D. Yeager, Chapman University, Orange, CA

- Instructors and other professionals who prepared ancillary materials that coordinate with the content of the text. These individuals are Susan Petersen (*Test Bank*), Corinne Livesay (*Study Guide*) and Diana McKowen (selected solutions).

- Students in Dr. Lehman's and Dr. DuFrene's classes, who completed many of the new exercises and suggested desirable changes.

We also appreciate the invaluable assistance provided by the various members of the South-Western College Publishing staff that made this edition possible. Our sincere thanks go to Susan Freeman Carson, our creative developmental editor, who adeptly coordinated the many intricate details of this project, Steve Momper, Kelly Keeler, Jennifer Mayhall, and Amy Villanueva. Lastly, we express genuine thanks to our spouses and our children for their constant support throughout such a lengthy and demanding project.

Carol M. Lehman

Debbie D. DuFrene

COMMUNICATION MENTOR

As head of the Investor Relations and Corporate Communications Division at California Federal Bank, one of the nation's largest savings institutions, I was responsible for investor relations, financial public relations, and general media communications. My duties also included membership on the Bank's Management Committee and the Community Development Committee. Oral and written communication skills are an important part of my current responsibilities as the head of a consulting firm.

James F. Hurley
Principal, Hurley Advisors

COMMUNICATION MENTOR

As an investment planner, my responsibility is to be knowledgeable of the latest developments in the fast-changing world of finance and then present my clients with the financial options that work best for them throughout their lives. I must access and transmit time-sensitive information quickly and communicate complex financial information orally and in writing. More importantly, my commitment to build strong long-term relationships with clients requires strong interpersonal communication skills.

Ernest T. George, III
Certified Financial Planner,
Registered Principal

COMMUNICATION MENTOR

I direct the communications effort of the Professional Golfers' Association of America, the world's largest working sports organization. My responsibilities include (1) supervising public relations efforts to promote the association; (2) coordinating media relations programs to assist the nation's media in their coverage of the PGA; and (3) overseeing internal and external communications vehicles such as books, programs, magazines, news releases, and speeches. I am also responsible for developing an effective corporate identification program.

Terrence E. McSweeney
Director of Communications,
PGA of America

COMMUNICATION MENTOR

I oversee all banking relationships, bonding, and insurance, Developing, implementing, and updating the strategic plan is another important part of my responsibilities. In my work in community relations, I am required to speak publicly for civic and non-profit organizations.

Shirley F. Olson
President,
J. J. Ferguson Prestress-Precast Co., Inc.

COMMUNICATION MENTOR

In my role as president of a full-service public relations firm, I develop communication strategies for our clients, manage a firm composed of professional communicators, lead new business development activities, and provide senior-level counsel to executives.

Cynthia Pharr
President,
C. Pharr & Company

COMMUNICATION MENTOR

I currently am working for a small family-owned investment banking firm and am responsible for searching for potential clients, This field is highly competitive; therefore, communication is key to my success. My communication skills are constantly at work on the telephone, writing letters, giving presentations to companies and other audiences, serving on panels, and entertaining. My ultimate goal is to assist managements of companies in understanding the firm's capability to give investment advice, raise capital, and to provide all other related investment banking services.

Pamela M. Plager
Vice President & Director
Allen & Company, Incorporated.

COMMUNICATION MENTOR

As a corporate financial officer, my responsibilities range widely, including financial reporting, banking relations, assessing financial aspects of strategic business matters, and evaluating economics of internal operations. Overall, my goal is to bring a financial perspective to corporate affairs to preserve and enhance the company's financial health. Previous experience includes independent consulting, developing professional staff at Price Waterhouse and other companies, including the supervision of over 300 people in a multi-location retail corporation.

R. D. Saenz
Chief Financial Officer,
Snider Communications Corporation.

COMMUNICATION MENTOR

My responsibilities are to manage and oversee the firm's practice of accounting, audit, and business advisory services in Former Soviet Union, now referred to as the Confederation of Independent States (CIS). Our present offices include Moscow and St. Petersburg in Russia, Kiev in the Ukraine, an Almaty in Kazakhstan. I am responsible for the quality and development of our overall practice and serve numerous clients as engagement partner. I am involved in all areas of recruiting and training local personnel with the objective of eventually turning the practice over to national personnel.

Lawrence E. Wilson
Partner,
Arthur Andersen, Moscow

COMMUNICATION MENTOR

I have worked in a variety of industries ranging from entertainment to financial services where my challenge has been to understand a company's mission and business strategies and to communicate that information to prospective new hires. My current position as a staffing and human resources consultant involves my serving as a resource for internal employees and for external marketing. My goal is to aid in identifying candidates for future employment while developing relationships with external service providers.

Accomplishing this goal provides many opportunities to communicate effectively with individuals at all levels of the organization. I frequently write company-wide correspondence and public relations announcements, present at company events, participate on councils and project teams, spearhead program development, represent a company at community functions, and implement training. Sometimes the messages I deliver are sensitive and confidential in nature and always involve communicating sensitively to a diverse audience. When necessary, I assume the roles of negotiator and facilitator, which require good listening skills—a critical communication skill.

Marquette L. Wilson
Manager, Human Resources,
GE Capital Commercial Finance

Communication Foundations

CHAPTER ONE

A Framework for Business Communication

LEARNING OBJECTIVES

When you have completed Chapter 1, you will be able to:

1 Define communication and describe the main purposes for communication in business.

2 Explain the communication process model and the ultimate objective of the communication process.

3 Explain how legal and ethical constraints act as a strategic force to influence the process of business communication.

4 Explain how diversity challenges act as a strategic force to influence the process of business communication.

5 Explain how changing technology acts as a strategic force to influence the process of business communication.

6 Explain how team environment acts as a strategic force to influence the process of business communication.

A team of computer programmers at Tsinghua University in Beijing, China, is writing software for IBM using Java technology. At the end of the day, they send their work over the Internet to an IBM facility in Seattle. There, programmers refine it and use the Internet to zap it more than 5,000 miles to the Institute of Computer Science in Belarus and Software House Group in Latvia. From there, the project is sent east to India's Tata Group, which passes the software back to Beijing by morning. The great global communication relay doesn't cease until the project is completed.

Companies have been going global for more than a decade. Nike makes shoes in Asia; McDonald's sells burgers from Moscow to Beijing and gets more than half its revenue from outside the USA. Coca-Cola sells 48 percent of the world's soft drinks. But in hundreds of companies large and small, simply going global isn't enough anymore. Communications technology is changing the rules as companies are realizing they have to embrace the world as their workplace and marketplace.

International businesses have long been able to connect by telephone or electronic data networks, but the Internet and its subset, the World Wide Web, create new possibilities. More people in diverse places want world-class goods and services, opening new markets for companies. The North Atlantic Free Trade Agreement and the General Agreement on Tariffs and Trade are helping to overcome economic and legal barriers to international business activity and easing trade in much of the industrialized world. The Internet also allows the internationalization of team formation, enabling firms to draw on the particular strengths of personnel from around the world. This new phase of globalization will soon bring the day when work and trade happen seamlessly, around the world, around the clock. Global operations will be as common a part of life as long-distance telephone calls or delivered pizza.[1]

Globalization of business has enhanced the need for effective communication between individuals and teams from around the world. While technology has provided the means for accurate, virtually instant transmission of electronic messages and images, the process of communication continues to pose challenges due to its complexities. To be effective in any business setting, you will need to understand the process of communication and the dynamic environment in which it occurs.

1 *Define communication and describe the main purposes for communication in business.*

In what ways will communication be important in the career field you have chosen?

Purposes of Communication

What is communication? For our purposes, communication is the process of exchanging information and meaning between or among individuals through a common system of symbols, signs, and behavior. Other words often used to describe the communication process are expressing feelings, conversing, speaking, corresponding, writing, listening, and exchanging.

People communicate to satisfy needs in both their work and nonwork lives. People want to be heard, appreciated, and wanted. They also want to accomplish tasks and achieve goals. Obviously, then, a major purpose of communication is to help people feel good about themselves and about their friends, groups, and organizations. Generally people communicate for three basic purposes: to inform, to persuade, and to entertain.

Studies have shown that managers spend approximately 60 to 80 percent of their time involved in some form of communication, including

- Attending meetings and writing reports related to strategic plans and company policy.

- Presenting information to large and small groups.
- Explaining and clarifying management procedures and work assignments.
- Coordinating the work of various employees, departments, and other work groups.
- Evaluating and counseling employees.
- Promoting the company's products/services and image.

The Communication Process

2 *Explain the communication process model and the ultimate objective of the communication process.*

Effective communicators realize that communication is not an automatic process. That is, the message is not interpreted correctly just because the manager transmitted it. Rather than thinking, "*Anybody* could understand these instructions; they're crystal clear," the prudent manager anticipates possible breakdowns in the communication process—the unlimited ways the message can be misunderstood. This mind-set motivates the manager to design the initial message effectively and to be prepared to intervene at the appropriate time to ensure that the message received is as close as possible to the message sent.

Consider the simplified form of the communication process model presented in Figure 1-1. The stages of the model are as follows:

1. The sender encodes a message.
2. The sender selects an appropriate channel and transmits the message.
3. The receiver decodes the message.
4. The receiver encodes a message (feedback) to clarify any part of the message not understood. Feedback involves (a) the receiver encoding a message, (b) the

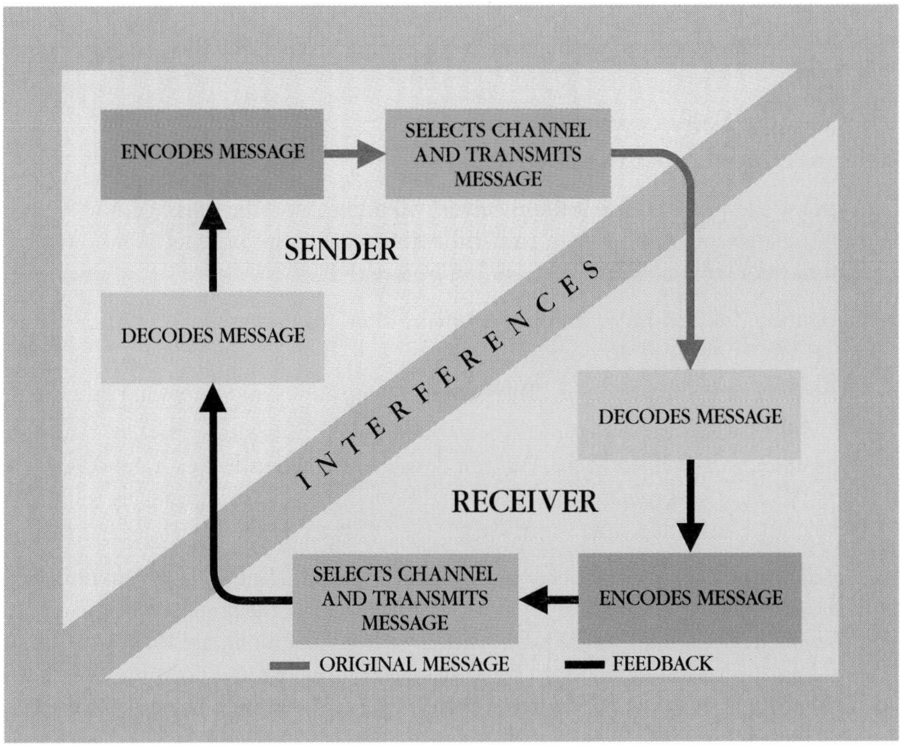

FIGURE 1-1
The communication process model.

receiver selecting a channel and transmitting the message, and (c) the sender decoding the message. The sender and receiver continue to reverse roles until the message is understood.

5. The sender and receiver remove or minimize interferences that hinder the communication process.

The Sender Encodes the Message

The message originates with the sender who transmits it to the receiver. The sender carefully designs a message by selecting (1) words that clearly convey the message and (2) nonverbal signals (gestures, stance, tone of voice, and so on) that reinforce the verbal message. The process of selecting and organizing the message is referred to as **encoding**. The sender's primary objective is to encode the message in such a way that the message received is as close as possible to the message sent. Knowledge of the receiver's educational level, experience, viewpoints, and other information aids the sender in encoding the message. If information about the receiver is unavailable, the sender can put himself or herself in the receiver's position to gain fairly accurate insight for encoding the message. Chapters 3 and 4 provide guidance in using words effectively; nonverbal communication is covered in greater detail in Chapter 2.

Obvious breakdowns in the communication process at the encoding stage occur if the sender uses

- words not present in the receiver's vocabulary.
- ambiguous, nonspecific ideas that distort the message.
- nonverbal signals that contradict the verbal message.
- expressions such as "uh" or grammatical errors, mannerisms (excessive hand movements, jingling keys), or dress that distract the receiver.

Of course, this list is only a beginning of possible problems at the encoding stage.

List three breakdowns in the encoding process that you have experienced.

The Sender Selects an Appropriate Channel and Transmits the Message

To increase the likelihood that the receiver will understand the message, the sender carefully selects an appropriate channel for transmitting the message. Three typical communication channels are illustrated in Figure 2–2.

Which channel would be the most appropriate for communicating the following messages? Justify your answer.
- Request from a client additional information needed to provide requested services.
- Inform a customer that an order cannot be delivered on the date specified in the contract.
- Inform the sales staff of a special sales incentive (effective six weeks from now).

- ***Two-way, face-to-face.*** Informal conversations, interviews, oral reports, speeches, and teleconferences.
- ***Two-way, not-face-to-face.*** Telephone conversations and intercompany announcements.
- ***One-way, not-face-to-face.*** Written documents such as letters, memos, reports, and press releases prepared traditionally or sent electronically (electronic mail, facsimile, voice-mail).

Selecting an inappropriate channel can cause the message to be misunderstood and can adversely affect human relations with the receiver. For example, for a very complex subject, a sender might begin with a written document and follow up with a face-to-face discussion after the receiver has had an opportunity to study the document. Written documents are required when legal matters are involved and written records must be retained.

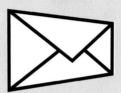

TWO-WAY, FACE-TO-FACE

- Instant feedback
- Nonverbal signals

TWO-WAY, NOT FACE-TO-FACE

- Instant feedback
- Limited Nonverbal signals

ONE-WAY, NOT FACE-TO-FACE

- No Instant feedback
- Minimal nonverbal signals

FIGURE 1-2
Channels of communication.

A face-to-face meeting is a more appropriate channel for sending sensitive, unpleasant messages. For example, consider a supervisor calling an employee into a private office to discuss the employee's continual violation of safety regulations. A face-to-face meeting provides two distinct benefits: (1) The manager can solicit immediate feedback from the receiver to clarify misunderstandings and inaccuracies in the message. (2) The manager can "read" equally important nonverbal cues (tone of voice, body movements, and so on) in addition to hearing what the receiver is saying (the verbal message). The manager may feel comfortable with the verbal message, but the nonverbal message may indicate that the receiver is overamplifying the problem or is underestimating the importance of the warning. The manager's discerning choice of a channel—meeting with the employee face-to-face rather than calling or writing a disciplinary memo—marks this manager as sensitive and empathetic, qualities that foster trust and open communication.

The Receiver Decodes the Message

The receiver is the destination of the message. The receiver's task is to interpret the sender's message, both verbal and nonverbal, with as little distortion as possible. The process of interpreting the message is referred to as **decoding**. Because words and nonverbal signals have different meanings to different people, countless problems can occur at this point in the communication process. Obvious breakdowns in communication occur at this stage in the following circumstances:

- The sender inadequately encodes the original message. For example, the sender may use words not present in the receiver's vocabulary; use ambiguous, nonspecific ideas that distort the message; or use nonverbal signals that distract the receiver or contradict the verbal message.

- The receiver is intimidated by the position or authority of the sender. This tension may prevent the receiver from concentrating on the message effectively enough to understand it clearly. Furthermore, an intimidated receiver may be

Give examples of nonverbal gestures that have different meanings among generations or cultures.

afraid to ask for clarifications because of the perceived fear that questions might be associated with incompetence.

- The receiver is unwilling to attempt to understand the message because the topic is perceived to be too difficult to understand. Regardless of the clarity of a message explaining procedures for operating a computer software program, a receiver terrified of computers may be incapable of decoding the message correctly.

- The receiver is unreceptive to new and different ideas; that is, stereotypical visions and prejudices prevent the receiver from viewing the message with an open mind.

The infinite number of breakdowns possible at each stage of the communication process makes us marvel that mutually satisfying communication ever occurs. The complexity of the communication process amplifies the importance of the next stage in the communication process—feedback to clarify misunderstandings.

The Receiver Encodes a Message to Clarify Any Misunderstandings

When the receiver responds to the sender's message, the response is called **feedback**. The feedback may prompt the sender to modify or adjust the original message to make it clearer to the receiver. Feedback may be verbal or nonverbal. A remark such as "Could you clarify . . ." or a perplexed facial expression provides clear feedback to the sender that the receiver does not yet understand the message. Conversely, a confident "Yes, I understand," and an upward nod of the head likely signal understanding or encouragement.

Interferences Hinder the Process

What is meant by the terms *internal barriers* and *external barriers*? How can each type be overcome?

Senders and receivers must learn to deal with the numerous factors that interfere with the communication process. These factors are referred to as **interferences** or **barriers** to effective communication. Previous examples have illustrated some of the interferences that may occur at various stages of the communication process. For example,

- Differences in educational level, experience, and culture and other characteristics of the sender and the receiver increase the complexity of encoding and decoding a message.

- Physical interferences occurring in the channel include loud talking near an area where a supervisor is explaining a work assignment, distracting and annoying static on a telephone line, or an overly warm room used for a lengthy staff meeting. Many companies schedule officer retreats at hotels or remote lodges to eliminate physical and mental interferences such as constant interruptions and other distractions present in workday surroundings. These retreats allow employees to disconnect themselves from routine responsibilities enough to participate effectively in strategic planning sessions, leadership development, cultural awareness workshops, and other executive meetings.

- A supervisor too rushed or too insecure to allow subordinates to ask questions or offer suggestions (feedback) creates a formidable barrier to effective communication. This supervisor loses time and money from errors made because unclear messages are not clarified and also generates negative feelings because employees perceive their opinions to be unwelcome.

Study carefully the barriers listed in Figure 1-3, and compile a list of other barriers that affect your ability to communicate with friends, teachers, coworkers, supervisors, and others. By being aware of them, you can make concentrated efforts to remove these interferences whenever possible.

Consider another example to illustrate the stages in the communication process. While reading the following scenario, notice that the sender and receiver function in dual roles. That is, they both serve as sender and receiver, giving and receiving feedback (encoding and decoding messages) until the original receiver understands the message.

John, an irate audit partner, barges into a senior accountant's work area (located in the center of a large, open office) wildly waving a file in his hand. Not seeming to notice that several others were standing nearby and

Consider a situation in which you have experienced a communication breakdown. What factor(s) was/were responsible for the miscommunication? What could have been done to assure successful communication?

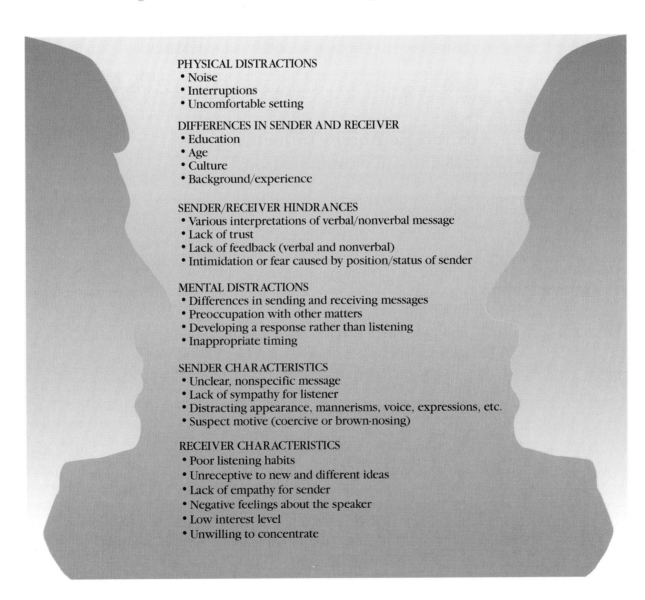

PHYSICAL DISTRACTIONS
• Noise
• Interruptions
• Uncomfortable setting

DIFFERENCES IN SENDER AND RECEIVER
• Education
• Age
• Culture
• Background/experience

SENDER/RECEIVER HINDRANCES
• Various interpretations of verbal/nonverbal message
• Lack of trust
• Lack of feedback (verbal and nonverbal)
• Intimidation or fear caused by position/status of sender

MENTAL DISTRACTIONS
• Differences in sending and receiving messages
• Preoccupation with other matters
• Developing a response rather than listening
• Inappropriate timing

SENDER CHARACTERISTICS
• Unclear, nonspecific message
• Lack of sympathy for listener
• Distracting appearance, mannerisms, voice, expressions, etc.
• Suspect motive (coercive or brown-nosing)

RECEIVER CHARACTERISTICS
• Poor listening habits
• Unreceptive to new and different ideas
• Lack of empathy for sender
• Negative feelings about the speaker
• Low interest level
• Unwilling to concentrate

FIGURE 1-3 Communication barriers.

without giving a greeting, John rudely throws a report on the desk. He says, "Just look at this report, Michele! Haven't you read any accounting pronouncements during the last two years?"

Startled at first, Michele takes just a few seconds to gain her composure and then replies, "Obviously, John, you have a major concern with the Krause report. Could you tell me exactly what the difficulty is?"

A little calmer now, John answers, "I've read through this report several times, and I just don't understand. Why doesn't the report contain a disclosure of market risks as required by SFAS No. 105?"

With a quiet sigh, Michele answers, "The industry specialists in our New York office assured me that a market risk disclosure is unnecessary in this case. I included their explanation with complete documentation in a memo placed in the Krause audit file."

Nodding his head, John says, "Fine; that particular disclosure was my only concern. Prepare the report for my signature, and let's try to get it to the client by tomorrow at the latest. Good work, Michele."

The communication process model will help identify the problems that the partner and accountant dealt with to finally reach an understanding, as shown in Figure 1-4.

Strategic Forces Influencing Business Communication

How would you rank the four strategic forces in terms of magnitude of importance to business communication? Why?

Communication is often a complicated process. Furthermore, communication does not take place in a vacuum, but rather is influenced by a number of forces at work in the environment. The effective communicator carefully considers each of these influences and structures communication responsively. Various forces influence the communication process and help to determine and define the nature of the communication that occurs, as shown in Figure 1-5.

Legal and Ethical Constraints as a Strategic Force Influencing Communication

3 *Explain how legal and ethical constraints act as a strategic force to influence the process of business communication.*

Legal and ethical constraints act as a strategic force on communication in that they set boundaries in which communication can occur. International, federal, state, and local laws affect the way that various business activities can be conducted. For instance, legislation controls can and must be stated in letters that reply to credit applications and those dealing with collection of outstanding debts. Furthermore, one's own ethical standards will often influence what he or she is willing to say in a message. A system of ethics built on honesty may require that the message provide full disclosure, for instance, rather than a shrouding of the truth. Legal responsibilities, then, are the starting point for appropriate business communication. One's ethical beliefs, or personal sense of right and wrong behavior, provides further boundaries for professional activity.

The press is full of examples of unethical conduct in the business and governmental communities:

- Allegations that the tobacco industry added higher levels of nicotine to its product with knowledge that nicotine is addictive.

FIGURE 1-4 The communication process in action.

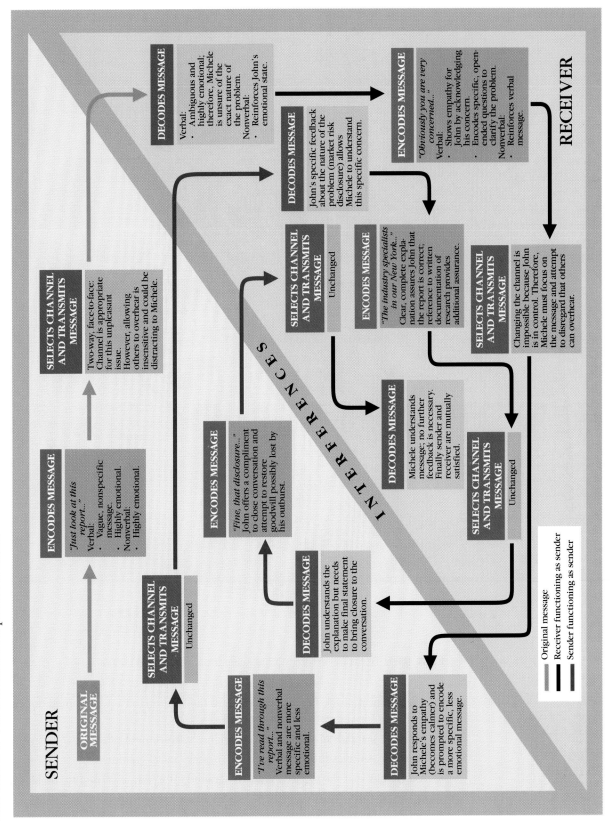

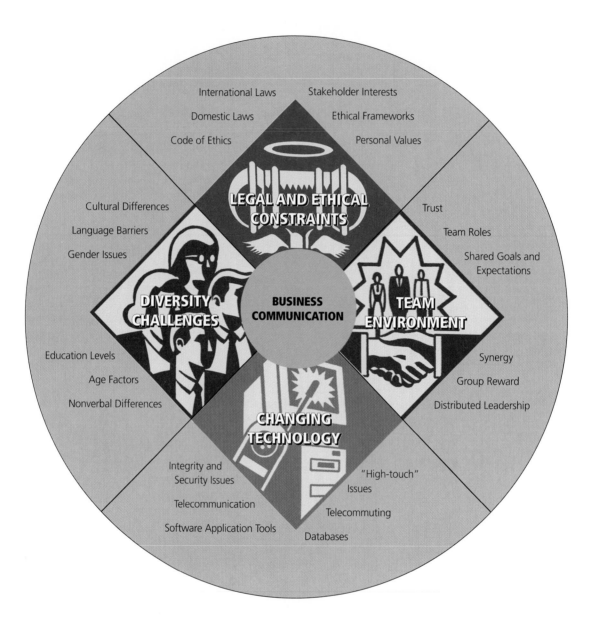

FIGURE 1-5 Strategic forces influencing business communication.

- Allegations that the Lincoln Bedroom of the White House was "rented out" in exchange for campaign contributions.[2]
- Multiple scandals in federal, state, and local government offices.
- Texaco executives fired for making derogatory racial comments.
- Allegations that the tobacco industry ignored information related to the health risks associated with its product.
- Sexual harassment charges abound in the branches of the armed forces.

COMMUNICATION MENTOR

Many of today's generation are learning cynicism from political leaders. Often it seems that those who lie, cheat, steal, deceive, and mock others have short-term successes at the expense of those who try to do everything "by the book."

When considering decisions that could possibly compromise my personal values, I recall my grandfather's simple wisdom, "If you never tell a lie, you won't have to worry about or remember what you said." Likewise, I urge my children to live their lives as if everything they say and do will be reviewed for 60 Minutes by Mike Wallace (or your favorite news magazine).

Clients depend on me to keep their investment strategies up to date and their futures financially secure so they can concentrate on their own careers. While technical expertise is important, I am convinced that strong client relationships are the most critical ingredient in the success of any business. The important factor is "Who you are" not "what you say." Ethics is an extension of who you are—a visible indication of your principles and values. Once a client's trust is lost, seldom can you regain it.

Your word—written or spoken—establishes a binding contract. Sincere, ethical actions are the foundation of strong client relationships and successful businesses. What is your word worth? Who are you?

Ernest T. George, III
Certified Financial Planner
　and Registered Principal
Investment Management & Research, Inc.

These are just a few of the numerous unethical acts reported by the press almost daily. Concern exists about the apparent erosion of ethical values in society. Indeed, one research study revealed that six out of ten Americans surveyed admitted that they would probably trade six months' probation for an illegal $10 million.[3] Compounding the issue of ethical behavior is that matters of ethics are seldom clear-cut issues of right versus wrong and often contain many ambiguous elements. In addition, the pressure appears to be felt most strongly by lower-level managers who are least experienced doing their jobs. Many of these managers are recent business school graduates.

What can you do now to prepare for dealing with pressure to compromise personal values? First, remember that only if you have definite beliefs on a variety of issues and the courage to practice them will you be able to make sound ethical judgments. Putting ethical business practices first will also benefit the company for whom you work as its reputation for fairness and good judgment retains long-term clients or customers and brings in new ones. Second, learning to analyze ethical dilemmas (identify the consequences of your actions) will help you make decisions that conform to your own value system. Thus, unless you know what you stand for and how to analyze the ethical issue, you become a puppet, controlled by the motives of others, too weak to make a decision on your own. What will you do?

> What other recent events can you think of that have ethical themes?

The Foundation for Legal and Ethical Behavior. Although ethics is a common point of discussion, many find defining ethics challenging. Most people immediately associate ethics with standards and rules of conduct, morals, right and wrong, values, and honesty. Dr. Albert Schweitzer defined *ethics* as "the name we give to our concern for good behavior. We feel an obligation to consider not only our own personal well-being, but also that of others and of human society as a whole."[4] In other words, **ethics** refers to the principles of right and wrong that guide you in making decisions that consider the impact of your actions on others as well as yourself.

Although the recorded accounts of legal and ethical misconduct would seem to indicate that businesses are dishonest and unscrupulous, keep in mind that millions of business transactions are made daily on the basis of honesty and concern for the welfare of others. Why should a business make ethical decisions? What difference will it make? James E. Perrella, executive vice president of Ingersoll-Rand Company, has a powerful reply to these questions:[5]

> Our question of today should be, what's the right thing to do, the right way to behave, the right way to conduct business? Don't just ask, is it legal? Have you ever considered what business would be like if we all did it? If every businessman and businesswoman followed the Golden Rule? Many people, including many business leaders, would argue that such an application of ethics to business would adversely affect bottom-line performance. I say nay. . . . Good ethics, simply, is good business. Good ethics will attract investors. Good ethics will attract good employees.
>
> You can do what's right. Not because of conduct codes. Not because of rules or laws. But because you know what's right.

Identifying ethical issues in typical workplace situations may be difficult, and coworkers and superiors may apply pressure for seemingly logical reasons. To illustrate, examine each of the following workplace situations for a possible ethical dilemma:

What situations have you faced as a worker or student that caused ethical dilemmas?

- Corporate officers deliberately withhold information concerning a planned sell-out so as to not affect stock prices negatively.

- A salesperson who travels extensively feels cheated that personal telephone calls are not reimbursed travel expenses. Consequently, the salesperson overstates car mileage to cover the cost of the telephone calls.

- To protect his job, a product engineer decides not to question a design flaw in a product that could lead to possible injuries and even deaths to consumers because the redesign would cause a delay in product introduction.

- To stay within the departmental budget, a supervisor authorizes that a software program be installed on fifty office computers when only one legal copy was actually purchased.

- Angry at a superior for an unfavorable performance appraisal, an employee leaks confidential information (e.g., trade secrets such as a recipe or product design, marketing strategies, or product development plans) to an acquaintance who works for a competitor.

Your fundamental morals and values provide the foundation for making ethical decisions. However, as the previous examples imply, even minor concessions in day-to-day decisions can gradually weaken an individual's ethical foundation.

Causes of Illegal and Unethical Behavior. Understanding the major causes of illegal and unethical behavior in the workplace will help you become sensitive to signals of escalating pressure to compromise your values. Research on unethical corporate behavior has identified several potential causes of unethical behavior.

- ***Excessive emphasis on profits.*** Business managers are often judged on their ability to increase business profits. The salaries of business managers are often based on the amount of profits earned. This emphasis on profits may send a message that the end justifies the means. In other words, if only the amount of earnings per share matters in assessing managerial performance, the message to managers is "Do whatever is necessary to increase the bottom line." Thus, managers justify unethical acts because they are in the "best interest" of the company.

- **Misplaced corporate loyalty.** A misplaced sense of corporate loyalty may cause an employee to do what seems to be in the best interest of the company, even if the act is illegal or unethical.

- **Obsession with personal advancement.** Employees who wish to outperform their peers or are working for the next promotion may feel that they cannot afford to fail. They may do whatever it takes to achieve the objectives assigned to them. To ensure favorable measures of success, for instance, managers may attempt to minimize controllable expenses long enough to earn a promotion. A manager may neglect preventive maintenance of equipment, reduce or postpone essential research and development, or bypass selected quality control points. These actions may make the manager (and even the company) look good in the short run, but continued disregard for these critical factors is detrimental to the long-term well-being of a company.

- **Expectation of not getting caught.** Employees who believe that the end justifies the means often believe that the illegal or unethical activity will never be discovered. Unfortunately, a great deal of improper behavior escapes detection in the business world. Therefore, this cause of inappropriate behavior is difficult to correct. Believing no one will ever find out, employees are tempted to falsify records such as expense accounts. They may overstate the cost of meals to compensate for unauthorized expenses (telephone calls, entertainment, laundry service) or include expenses not incurred (meals paid for by others or nonexistent taxi fares). Similarly, sales representatives may overreport the number of sales contacts made during a certain period if they believe no control measure will reveal the true effort they expended. Employees who call in sick and spend the day conducting personal business or enjoying an extra-long weekend have little fear that management will discover this unethical activity.

- **Unethical tone set by top management.** If top managers are not perceived as highly ethical, lower-level managers may be less ethical as a result. Employees have little incentive to act legally and ethically if their superiors do not set an example and encourage and reward such behavior. The following action by top management clearly sets the tone for unethical behavior: A staff development director routinely copies articles, entire software documentation manuals, training guides, and preview copies of training films for distribution at staff development seminars. Although several employees have brought these infringements of copyright laws to the attention of the company president, no action has been taken. A similar message is sent when management reports that only undeliverable e-mail will be read, yet managers routinely access and read employees' e-mail messages.

- **Uncertainty about whether an action is wrong.** Many times, company personnel are placed in situations in which the line between right and wrong is not clearly defined. When caught in this gray area, the perplexed employee asks, "How far is too far?" The following situation poses such a dilemma: A company bids for a job that requires expertise the company does not have but would acquire if the bid is ultimately received. For example, a computer systems company bids to install a sophisticated network system even though the company has no experience in installing networks; or a construction company with no experience in building high-security correctional facilities bids to build a jail or state prison.

Consider the following saying: The speed of the leader is the speed of the pack. What other adages might be used to enforce the importance of leading by example?

- *Unwillingness to take a stand for what is right.* Often employees know what is right or wrong but are not willing to take the risk of challenging a wrong action. Furthermore, employees may lack the confidence or skill needed to confront others with sensitive legal or ethical issues. They may remain silent and then justify their unwillingness to act. Consider the risk involved in speaking out on coworker's personal use of the company long-distance telephone service and computer (including expensive on-line information services).

Framework for Analyzing Ethical Dilemmas. Determining whether an action is ethical is difficult. In many business situations, the line between right and wrong is not clear. Learning to analyze an ethical dilemma from multiple perspectives will help you find a solution that conforms to your own personal values. The flow chart shown in Figure 1-6 represents a framework for making an ethical decision and for supporting that decision in a written or oral message. The framework instructs you (the decision maker) to complete the following four-step process after you have identified a possible course of action:

What is meant by the term "situational ethics?"

1. *Identify the legal implications of the alternative and determine whether the alternative adheres to contractual agreements and company policy.* In other words, is the alternative legal? The law specifically outlines the "black" area—those alternatives that are clearly wrong. Your employer will require you to become an expert in the laws that affect your particular area. When you encounter an unfamiliar area, you must investigate any possible legal implications. Obviously obeying the law is in the best interest of all concerned: you as an individual, your company, and society. In addition, contractual agreements between the organization and another group provide explicit guidance in selecting an ethically responsible alternative. If the action is legal, then . . .

2. *Determine whether the alternative violates any company or professional codes of ethics.* If the alternative is legal and complies with relevant contractual agreements and company policy, your next step is to consult your company's or profession's **code of ethics**. This written document summarizes the company's or profession's standards of ethical conduct. Some companies refer to this document as a *credo* or *standards of ethical conduct*. If the behavior does not violate the code of ethics, then . . .

3. *Use ethical principles and theories to assess whether the alternative judged to be legal (Step 1) and in compliance with codes of ethics (Step 2) is ethical.* The final—and extremely important—test your alternative must satisfy is the test of integrity. Is it ethical? If, after careful analysis, you judge the alternative to be ethical, you may implement it; otherwise, you must evaluate another alternative. If you feel the alternative is ethical, then . . .

4. *Implement the alternative and communicate ethical decisions to appropriate individuals inside or outside the organization.*

Note the three decision points in the framework shown in Figure 1-6. Any one of the following criteria would be required to reject the alternative being considered and select another one: (1) The alternative is illegal or does not comply with relevant contractual agreements and company policy, (2) the alternative is not consistent with the company's and/or the profession's code of ethics, or (3) the alternative violates your personal code of ethics.

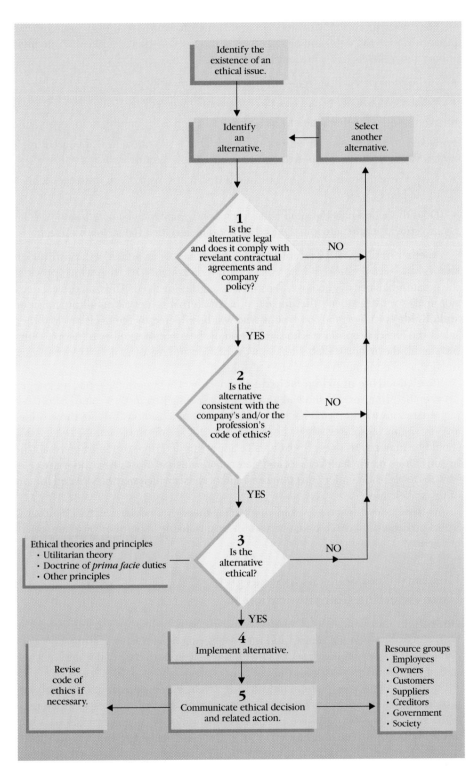

FIGURE 1-6
Framework for analyzing ethical issues.

Somewhat more sophisticated but still straightforward are the six points in the Pagano Model for determining whether a proposed action is ethical.[6] You must answer the following six questions honestly:

- Is the proposed action legal—the core starting point?[7]
- What are the benefits and costs to the people involved?
- Would you want this action to be a universal standard, appropriate for everyone?
- Does the action pass the light-of-day test? That is, if your action appeared on television or others learned about it, would you be proud?
- Does the action pass the Golden Rule test? That is, would you want the same to happen to you?
- Does the action pass the ventilation test? Ask the opinion of a wise friend with no investment in the outcome. Does this friend believe that the action is ethical?

Another framework for examining the correctness of an action is the **utilitarian theory**. Its basic premise is that in all situations one ought to do that which provides the greatest balance of good over harm for all parties involved. Thus, an ethical decision maker must estimate the impact of each alternative action on all organization **stakeholders** (the persons or groups who will be affected by the decision) and then select the one that optimizes the satisfaction of the greatest number of people. Simply stated, the major stakeholders consist of five groups: owners, employees, customers, local communities, and society at large.

Ross's **doctrine of prima facie duties** include (1) not harming innocent people, (2) keeping promises, (3) showing gratitude, (4) acting in a just way, and (5) providing reparations to those who have been harmed by one's actions.[7] While these duties are not moral absolutes, they are considered highly desirable moral tenets that should be honored whenever possible. To apply this doctrine, you must consider the organization's major stakeholders and determine which of Ross's five duties are relevant to the decision under consideration, and of those, which may be violated for any of the stakeholders.

As these assessments show, applying ethical theories is not an easy task. Such analytical processes, however, enhance your critical thinking about the consequences of any action.

> Which of the ethical frameworks do you find most appropriate for you personally? Why?

4 *Explain how diversity challenges act as a strategic force to influence the process of business communication.*

Diversity Challenges as a Strategic Force Affecting Communication

Diversity in the workplace is another strategic force influencing communication. Differences between the sender and the receiver in areas such as culture, age, gender, and education require a sensitivity on the part of both the sender and receiver so that the intended message is the one that is received.

Understanding how to communicate effectively with people from other cultures is becoming more integral to the work environment as many U.S. companies increasingly conduct business with international companies or become multinational. Successful communication must often span barriers of language and almost always requires a person to consider differing world views resulting from societal, religious, or other cultural factors. If a person fails to consider these factors, communication suffers, and the result is often embarrassing and potentially costly.

McDonald's is an example of a large U.S. company that has expanded its operations to include most major countries in the world. To be successful on an international scale, McDonald's managers had to be aware of cultural differences and be willing to work to ensure that effective communication occurred despite these barriers. The results so far have been overwhelmingly positive for McDonald's; for example, their store in Moscow reports healthy sales despite the ailing economy in the former Soviet Union.

Occasionally, however, a whopper of an intercultural communication faux pas occurs. That is what happened when McDonald's began their promotional campaign in Britain for the World Cup soccer championship. It seemed like a clever (and harmless) idea to reproduce the flags of the 24 nations participating in the event and print them on packaging—two million Happy Meal bags, to be exact. What marketing personnel failed to consider was that words from the *Koran* are printed on the Saudi flag. The *Koran*, the holy book of Islam, which contains the teaching of Mohammed, is viewed as sacred by Muslims. The idea that these words were mass-printed to sell a product with the knowledge that the packages would be thrown into the trash angered and offended many Muslims, who immediately complained. McDonald's apologized for the gaffe and agreed to cooperate with the Saudis in finding a solution to the problem.[8] U.S. software giant Microsoft faced a similar dilemma when it shipped a batch of Arabic-language Microsoft Office software to the United Arab Emirates with labels written in Hebrew. A spokesman for the company expressed Microsoft's regret: "If it had arrived in the U.K. labeled in French, it wouldn't have been a big deal," he said, speculating that the reason the mistake attracted such attention was the long-standing strife between Israel and many Arab nations.[9]

These errors serve as examples of how much "homework" is involved in maintaining good relations with customers or clients from other cultures. The potential barrier of language is obvious; however, successful managers know that much more is involved in communicating with everyone—across cultures, genders, ages, abilities, and other differences.

> In groups, discuss other intercultural communication mistakes made by U.S. companies doing business in another country. Conduct an on-line search if necessary.

Communication Opportunities and Challenges in Diversity. As world markets expand, U.S. employees at home and abroad will be doing business with more people from other countries. You may find yourself working abroad for a large American company, an international company with a plant in the United States, or a company with an ethnically diverse workforce. Regardless of the workplace, your **intercultural communication** skills, that is, your ability to communicate effectively with both men and women of all ages and with people of other cultures or minority groups, will affect your success in today's culturally diverse, global economy.

- *International issues.* Worldwide telecommunications and intense international business competition have forced many industries to expand into world markets. During the past four decades, U.S. firms have established facilities in Europe, Central and South America, and Asia. At many U.S. corporations, such as Dow Chemical, Gillette, and IBM, more than 40 percent of total sales in recent years has come from international operations. Over the past decade, Asians (primarily Japanese) and Europeans have built plants in the United States. Many U.S. workers are now employed in manufacturing plants and facilities owned and operated by foreign interests. Understanding a person of another culture who may not speak your language well or understand your culturally based behaviors is a daily challenge faced by many.

- *Intercultural issues.* Changing demographics in the United States are requiring businesses to face ethnic diversity in the workplace. The United States

Managing a diverse workforce requires cultural understanding, as well as superb communication skills. What are the possible consequences if these qualities are lacking?

traditionally has accepted individuals from other lands. Rather than being a melting pot, the United States created an environment in which people of varying cultures could live and practice their cultural heritage. People with a common heritage generally formed their own neighborhoods and worked intently at retaining their traditional customs and language, while still sharing in the common culture. Consequently, *mosaic* seems to be a more accurate term than *melting pot* to reflect the changing demographics.[10] As in a mosaic, small, distinct groups combine to form the pattern or design of the U.S. population and workforce. Ethnic issues can complicate the communication process.

What impact will the "greying of America" have on the workplace?

- *Intergenerational issues.* While age diversity has always been present in the workplace, recent trends have made it a more important issue than ever. The so-called "greying of America" has changed the age distribution in the U.S. population. The older segment of the population is larger today than at any time previously. The maturing of the "baby-boom" generation (those born between 1946 and 1964), a relatively low birthrate, and increasing life spans have led to a higher average age in the population. Today's workforce has proportionately more older workers than in the past, because many older workers choose to continue in their professional activities and because of changes in laws affecting retirement benefits. Predictions are that by the year 2020, more than one-third of the total population will be older than 50.[11] Because the broadening of the age span in the workplace, businesses will be faced with new challenges related to differences in perceptions, values, and communication styles of the generations.

- *Gender issues.* The flood of women entering the job market has substantially changed the American workforce. Old social patterns of behavior that defined the appropriate roles for men and women do not fit in a work environment free from discrimination. While Civil Rights laws prohibiting sex discrimination and pay equity requirements have been in place for more than 30 years, charges continue to be filed by individuals who feel that their rights have been violated. The number of sexual harassment cases has increased in recent years, resulting from a broader-based definition of what indeed constitutes sexual harassment. Although a charge of sexual harassment may certainly be based on actions with sexual overtones, it has also been interpreted to include comments, visual images, or other conditions that create a hostile working environment. One result of the increased focus on sexual harassment in the workplace is the reluctance of some to communicate with other workers for fear that their actions or words might be misconstrued. Both men and women confront workplace communication challenges.

According to the U.S. labor statistics, the proportion of white males in the labor force continues to decline.[12] The workforce pool of the future will consist primarily of minorities, including women, African Americans, Latin Americans, and Asian Americans. The demographics illustrated in Figure 1-7 show that the makeup of the workforce, once dominated by white males, is changing. People from such different backgrounds as today's workers invariably bring different values, attitudes, and perceptions to the workplace. This diversity can lead to misunderstandings, miscommunications, and missed opportunities to improve both the workers and the organizations. Thus, managers must be prepared to communicate effectively with workers of different nationalities, genders, races, ages, abilities, and so forth.

Managing a diverse workforce effectively will require you to communicate with *everyone* and to help all employees reach their fullest potential and contribute to the company's goals. When miscommunication occurs, both sides are frustrated and often angry. To avoid such problems, increasing numbers of companies are providing diversity training seminars to help workers understand and appreciate gender differences and the cultures of coworkers.

Several generations will undoubtedly be required for us to learn to deal effectively with an ethnically diverse workforce. As the workforce evolves, subtle changes will probably occur in the dominant culture as well. Such changes have occurred throughout America's history as people of different backgrounds have joined and contributed to the culture.

> What other aspects of diversity can influence communication?

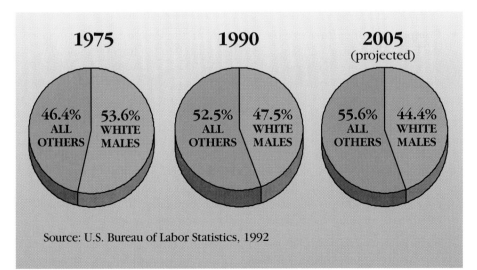

FIGURE 1-7
A shift in U.S. workforce demographics has occurred as white males make up a smaller proportionate share when compared to women and minorities.

Source: U.S. Bureau of Labor Statistics, 1992

The mistake we often make in our approach to diversity is to focus on the differences. I have discovered that when I search for common ground, the differences become less of an obstacle and more of an opportunity to learn and develop. Each individual is diverse; that diversity should be seen as an untapped resource that has the ability to enrich a company's mission and business strategies. At the core of diversity is the goal that every employee feels valued and is provided the opportunity to excel. The success of business today is strengthened by diversity. When diversity is embraced as a vital part of the corporate culture, the result is a more productive workforce.

Marquette L. Wilson
Manager, Human Resources
GE Capital Commercial Finance

Culture and Communication. Managers with the *desire* and the *skill* to conduct business in these new international markets and to manage a diverse workforce effectively will confront problems created by cultural differences. The way messages are decoded and encoded is not just a function of the experiences, beliefs, and assumptions of the person sending or receiving those messages but also are shaped by the society in which he or she lives.

People learn patterns of behavior from their culture. The **culture** of a people is the product of their living experiences within their own society. Culture could be described as "the way of life" of a people and includes a vast array of behaviors and beliefs. These patterns affect how people perceive the world, what they value, and how they act. Differing patterns can also create barriers to communication. Culture has three key characteristics.

- *Culture is learned by people over time.* Individuals are not born knowing their culture but acquire it through interactions with others. Social institutions such as churches, clubs, businesses; the family; schools; as well as the media, all play a part in teaching each member of a society the expectations and norms of behavior.

- *Components of culture are interrelated.* In the United States, for instance, the high value placed on material goods is related to the use of economic well-being as a measure of success and happiness. These values provide support for the approval placed on independence of mind and action, which in turn is connected to the existence of a relatively fluid class structure. The list of connections could go on, but these examples alone make it clear that each of these components of American culture is connected to other components.

- *Culture is shared.* That is, the various aspects of culture are common to many individuals. No country has one unified culture, however. Modern societies are so large and diverse that many different cultures can exist within them; these are called **subcultures**. Although each subculture differs from others, they often share some traits that derive from the main or dominant culture.

Each society exhibits its culture in many ways. Certainly customs, the accepted way of interacting with others, are expressions of the culture. The North American

What are some examples in your own community of culture-oriented activities?

practice of shaking hands reflects the value that is placed on the individual. Indians greet each other with a slight bow to honor the divine spark that they believe resides in each person. Each culture has certain objects, gestures, sounds, or images that contain special meaning. The American flag symbolizes the nation's independence and strength; a red, white, and blue package tries to associate itself with those meanings. Advertising, which in some respects is the use of cultural symbols, requires sensitivity to the specific meanings of the symbols employed.

How people communicate in speaking and writing as well as nonverbally is shaped by culture. Culture enables people to acquire a language that they may use in common with others of the same culture and as a medium for passing culture from one generation to the next. The language also reflects cultural values and norms. English is the language of Australia, Jamaica, and South Africa, as well as Great Britain, Canada, and the United States. However, all of these cultures are very different; in fact, even their forms of English differ.

Culture provides individuals with standards for behavior and gives them a feeling of identification and belonging; they feel a part of something larger than themselves. Problems occur between people of different cultures primarily because people tend to assume that their own cultural norms are the right way to do things. They wrongly believe that the specific patterns of behavior desired in their own cultures are universally valued.

Barriers to Intercultural Communication. Because cultures give different definitions to such basics of interaction as values and norms, people raised in two different cultures may clash. Some of the main areas in which cultures clash are explored below:

- *Stereotypes.* One group often forms a mental picture of the main characteristics of another group, creating preformed ideas of what people in this group are like. These pictures, called **stereotypes**, influence the way members of the first group interact with members of the second. When members of the first group observe a behavior that conforms to that stereotype, the validity of the preconceived notion is reinforced. They view the other person as a representative of a class of people rather than as an individual. All cultures have stereotypes about other cultures they have encountered. These stereotypes can get in the way of communication when people interact on the basis of the imagined representative and not the real individual.

  Give several examples of stereotypes that prevail concerning certain cultural groups.

- *Interpretation of time.* The study of how a culture perceives time and its use is called **chronemics**. In the United States, we have a saying that "time is money." North Americans, like some northern Europeans who are also concerned about punctuality, make appointments, keep them, and do not waste time completing them. In some other cultures, time is the cheapest commodity and an inexhaustible resource; time represents a person's span on earth, which is only part of eternity. For instance, in Latin America, the language of time says that important things take longer than unimportant ones. An interesting thing about cultures that pay little attention to appointment keeping is that once the appointment begins, the host will probably spend more than the agreed-on time and show more hospitality and generosity than North Americans generally expect. The next visitor may be kept waiting interminably, but that visitor will also receive the same cordial, considerate treatment.

- ***Personal space requirements.*** Space operates as a language just as time does. The study of cultural space requirements is known as **proxemics**. In North America, large offices frequently are reserved for executives as status symbols. In many parts of the world, large offices are for clerical workers and smaller ones for executives, since minimal space is required for thinking and planning. In all cultures, the distance between people functions in communication as "personal space" or "personal territory." In the United States, for example, for intimate conversations with close friends and relatives, individuals are willing to stay within about a foot and a half of each other; for casual conversations, up to two or three feet; for job interviews and personal business, four to twelve feet; and for public occasions, more than twelve feet. However, in many cultures other than the United States, close personal contact is accepted. Men customarily kiss each other on the cheek when they are introduced or when they meet. To many North Americans, this situation is embarrassing; to the international, it is no more personal than shaking hands.

Do differences exist in the non-verbal communication of people of different generations? Justify your answer.

- ***Body language.*** The study of body language is known as **kinesics**. Body language is not universal, but instead is learned from one's culture. The familiar North American symbol for "okay" or "everything is all right" means zero in France, money in Japan, and an expression of vulgarity in Brazil. North Americans nod their heads up and down to indicate agreement or "yes." In much of Asia, the nod indicates only that the person heard what was said. In Bulgaria and some other Eastern European countries, the up-and-down head motion means "no" and the side-to-side motion "yes"—just the opposite of the meanings for North Americans. Other cultures indicate "no" by a jerk of the head or a back-and-forth waving of a finger, as people sometimes do when saying "no" to a child. You can have your appointment or interview cut short in most Arabian countries if you sit in such a way that the sole of your shoe is visible—an insulting gesture. The solution is to sit with feet flat on the floor. Men and women from the same culture typically exhibit different body language. For instance, North American men make less body contact with other men than do women with women. Acceptable body contact for men might include a handshake or a pat on the back. Women in our culture are afforded more flexibility in making body contact with each other.

Talk with international students at your college and generate a list of words commonly used in business that have no equivalents in their language.

- ***Translation limitations.*** Words in one language do not always have an equivalent meaning in other languages, and the concepts the words describe are often different as well. A study of how Japanese and North American business students understood the concept of profit concluded this way: "It is important for the American to understand that his definition of *profit* as solely corporate gain—involving as it will the maximization of short-term gains—conflicts with the Japanese definition, which necessarily involves a long-term view of things."[13] When the meaning of a word is not agreed on in advance, later misunderstanding is a strong possibility. Translators can be helpful, but keep in mind that a translator is working with a second language and must listen to one language, mentally cast the words into another language, then speak them. This process is difficult and opens the possibility that the translator will fall victim to one or more of the cultural barriers. Knowing the language of the host country demonstrates your sincere interest in the culture. Learning the language will provide insight into some of the culture's central concepts embedded in the language. For example, knowing that the Japanese concept of "indebtedness" is expressed in a word that has no direct English equivalent will help a stranger understand this important concept in the context of the Japanese language.[13] Recent attention on Ebonics has emphasized the presence of cultural language subsets even among speakers of English within the same country.

- *Lack of language training.* The following is an anecdote that speaks to the need for language training:

What do you call someone who speaks two languages? (Reply: bilingual)
What do you call someone who speaks three languages? (Reply: trilingual)
What do you call someone who speaks one language? (Reply: an American)

This tongue-in-cheek humor reinforces the language illiteracy of most U.S. citizens. Carroll Perkins, the general manager of the Salt River Project, in Phoenix, Arizona, makes an interesting observation and recommendation about the need to learn a second language: "We recruit employees who can conduct conversations in Spanish and translate written materials from Spanish to English or English to Spanish. However, many of our applicants place little emphasis on their knowledge of a second language." So that you can compete for the many jobs that involve communication with people of different cultures, reserve some of your elective courses for taking a series of foreign language courses (enough to gain some degree of fluency) or a refresher course in the foreign language you studied in high school. Then, above all, when preparing your resume, be certain to exploit your ability to communicate in other languages—especially if you know the job sought requires such skills. In some situations, learning a second language may not be feasible—you are completing a short-term assignment, you must leave immediately, or the language is extremely difficult to learn (e.g., Japanese and Arabic) and you have no previous training. However, even if you cannot speak their language fluently, people from other cultures will appreciate simple efforts to learn a few common phrases. Suggestions for overcoming the barriers created by differences are discussed in the accompanying Strategic Forces Box.

Changing Technology as a Strategic Force Influencing Communication

5 *Explain how technology acts as a strategic force to influence the process of business communication.*

Electronic tools have not eliminated the need for basic communication skills. If anything, electronic tools, like all new tools and techniques, create new obstacles or barriers to communication that must be overcome. These tools, however, also create opportunities, which range from the kinds of communications that are possible to the quality of the messages themselves. Electronic tools for communication can help people in various ways, such as (1) collecting and analyzing data, (2) shaping messages to be clearer and more effective, and (3) communicating quickly and efficiently with others over long distances.

Tools for Data Collection and Analysis. Knowing how to collect information and communicate in a networked world is critical if you and your company are to be competitive. The "information superhighway," a part of the National Information Infrastructure, is predicted to bring vast amounts of data into our homes and businesses. However, on-line information services currently available provide a wide range of sources and services to facilitate our research. Generally, electronic communication provides researchers with two distinct advantages: (1) Electronic searches of organizational databases and electronic networks can be done in a fraction of the time required to conduct manual searches of printed sources, and (2) the vast amount of information available allows researchers to develop better solutions to problems.

In your opinion, what communication technology has most changed the way business is conducted? Why?

Strategic Forces: Diversity Challenges

Viva la Difference!

With so many barriers to communication, communicating with people of another culture is difficult. Communicating between genders, through the generation gap, among races, and through other differences present unique challenges as well. Anyone who enters the business world today must be aware of these potential trouble spots and of ways to avoid them. Application of some common-sense guidelines can help to overcome intercultural barriers.

- **Learn about that person's culture.** Many sources of useful information are available. University courses in international business communication are increasing,[14] and experienced businesspeople have written books recounting some of the subtle but important ways that people from other cultures communicate. Networking can generate the names of other businesspeople who have made successful contact with another culture. A telephone conversation or a lunch meeting may provide useful pointers on proper and improper behavior. Large corporations with frequent and extensive dealings in other countries often establish workshops in which employees receive briefing and training before accepting overseas assignments. Learning the language is an invaluable way of becoming more familiar with another culture.

- **Have patience—with yourself and the other person.** Conversing with someone from another culture, when one of you is likely to be unfamiliar with the language being used, can be difficult and time consuming. By being patient with mistakes, making sure that all questions are answered, and not hurrying, you are more likely to make the outcome of the conversation positive. You must also learn to be patient and

tolerant of ambiguity. Being able to react to new, different, and unpredictable situations with little visible discomfort or irritation will prove invaluable. The author Howard Schuman writes that "a sense of humor is indispensable for dealing with the cultural mistakes and faux pas you will certainly commit."[15]

- **Get help when you need it.** If you are not sure what is being said—or why something is being said in a certain way—ask for clarification. If you feel uneasy about conversing with someone from another culture, bring along someone you trust who understands that culture. You will have a resource if you need help.

You will certainly work in a culturally diverse workplace, and perhaps for a multinational firm. Your success will likely depend on your ability to communicate effectively across cultures, genders, ages, abilities, and other differences. Language, values, attitudes, and other cultural traits change very slowly. Therefore, communicating interculturally requires you to recognize the cultural elements that cause people to view things differently and thus create barriers to communication. Instead of ignoring cultural factors, workers and employers can improve communication by recognizing them and by considering people as individuals rather than as members of stereotypical groups.

Application

Interview a person from a cultural group other than your own. Include the following questions: (1) What examples can you give of times when you experienced discrimination or isolation? (2) What information can you provide to aid other groups in understanding your cultural uniqueness? (3) What advice would you give for improving intercultural understanding?

Internal databases enable decision makers to obtain information from their own company records quickly and accurately. Databases offer these advantages:

- **Data organization,** the ability to organize large amounts of data.
- **Data integrity,** assurance that the data will be accurate and complete.
- **Data security,** assurance that the data are secure because access to a database is controlled through several built-in data security features.

You must never assume that your messages are interpreted the same way by everyone. Instead, anticipate possible breakdowns in communication and try to overcome these gaps.

External databases (networks) allow users to access information from remote locations literally around the world and in an instant transfer that information to their own terminals for further manipulation or storage. The **Internet** is a loose collection of millions of computers at thousands of sites around the world (universities, government offices, and businesses) whose users can pass along information and share files. For example, users have access to NASA-funded computers, transcriptions of the U.S. Supreme Court opinions, software, card catalogs from many libraries, immense archives of indexed materials, and the list goes on and on. The Internet was intended to be used for academic and research purposes; however, about 63 percent of the networks worldwide are registered to corporations whose primary use is electronic mail. The Internet is growing phenomenally, from about 1,000 systems in 1984[16] to over 9.5 million systems[17] and 50.6 million individual users in January 1997.[18] An estimated 650,000 web sites existed in January 1997,[19] and that number is doubling every 53 days.[20]

Many people as well as organizations subscribe to an on-line service to assist them in using Internet resources effectively. The computer screen in Figure 1-8 shows typical options available to subscribers when they access their Internet provider. Through membership with such an on-line service, subscribers can (1) send electronic messages and computer files across the world, (2) participate in discussion groups (forums) to get answers to questions and to benefit from the information generated by a group interested in a specific topic, (3) browse occasionally through the "network news" generated by other discussion groups to read the latest discussions in these areas, (4) download software available on the service, and (5) access vast amounts of information from a wide range of sources. Information is available on general news, stocks, financial markets, sports, travel, weather, and a variety of publications (some allow you to retrieve the full text). An on-line encyclopedia is a standard service; one service updates its encyclopedia quarterly to keep it current. A clipping service that finds all articles on a specific topic from the various news services is a time-efficient way to stay abreast of important topics.

Lack of Internet access is causing some nations to be classified as information "have-nots." What international problems could result?

FIGURE 1-8
Internet subscription services provide access to a wealth of information.

Using a modem, the appropriate communication software, and an assigned password, you can obtain information from around the world by subscribing to the Internet via a commercial on-line service. Obviously, using on-line services can provide valuable information for making informed decisions quickly. However, knowing which service is likely to contain the information you need and then learning to "tunnel" through the vast amount of irrelevant information to find what you want can be overwhelming. The experience can also be expensive in terms of time spent and charges incurred for on-line time. Locating information from electronic sources requires that you know the search procedures and methods for constructing an effective search strategy. You will develop these skills when studying the research process in Chapter 9.

For preparing reports containing any analysis of numbers, an electronic spreadsheet is invaluable. An **electronic spreadsheet** is a forecasting and decision-making tool that can manipulate and analyze data easily, as shown in Figure 1-9. The spreadsheet's forecasting ability allows the user to ask, for instance, how profits would change if costs and sales were reduced by 10 percent or increased by 5 percent. The ability to calculate quickly these variable forecasts—called "what-if" questions—is one of the main benefits of spreadsheets. Spreadsheets can transform a vast amount of numerical data into information that can be used in decision making. By condensing data into organized tables, the spreadsheet greatly assists the manager in meaningfully interpreting the data. Once it has been created, a spreadsheet can be inserted into a word processing file. To depict complex data more clearly, the manager can also quickly construct a graphic using the prepared spreadsheet.

How can spreadsheet usage be abused?

Tools for Shaping Messages to Be Clearer and More Effective. Another significant benefit to communication offered by technology is message clarification and refinement. Documents that took days to produce during the b.c. (before computers) era can now be created in hours. Perhaps the greater benefit, however, is the advent of whole new possibilities for document preparation and presentation.

Campbell, Smith & Winter
Projection of Year 2000 Revenues
January 12, 2000

Level	1999 Actual			2000 Projected			Percent Change in Revenue
	Hours (000s)	Average Billing Rate/Hour	Revenue ($000s)	Hours (000s)	Average Billing Rate/Hour	Revenue ($000s)	
Staff	346	$55	$19,030	280	$60	$16,800	-11.7%
Senior	268	$80	$21,440	245	$90	$22,050	2.8%
Manager	142	$140	$19,880	160	$150	$24,000	20.7%
Partner	66	$220	$14,520	90	$240	$21,600	48.8%
Totals	**822**	**$91**	**$74,870**	**775**	**$109**	**$84,450**	**12.8%**

FIGURE 1-9
A spreadsheet simplifies computing of a projected change in composition of billable hours.

Word processing software expedites the production of a document and also improves the quality of the message. Other electronic tools that improve writing are electronic spell check, thesaurus, and writing analysis software. Using word processing, you can draft a document, store it on magnetic medium, and retrieve and revise it as many times as necessary to produce a clear, understandable document. Word processing software also allows you to format the document using print features, graphic and layout features, and various typefaces, and then print a highly professional copy. Reports and longer documents become less tedious to produce because of features that facilitate writing and editing. Most of the sophisticated word processing programs include a feature that generates a contents page, index, and document references automatically. This feature saves time in the initial creation of these pages and in their updating if pagination changes during editing. The mail-merge feature facilitates large-scale mailings of personalized form letters.

Collaborative software programs that assist groups in writing collaboratively are also available. Each author marks revisions and inserts document comments in much the same way as with word processing software and then sends the computer file to the coauthor. Some collaborative software programs allow multiple authors to work on documents at the same time when they are placed on an electronic whiteboard. Drawings or information written on its surface can be displayed simultaneously on the computer monitors of others in the work team.

Desktop publishing software helps managers and other workers surpass simple word processing capabilities by using typography, design elements, and even graphic images to create communications that are persuasive and professional looking. Using desktop publishing software and a high-quality printer, a person can create important publications such as prospectuses, annual reports, and newsletters. When printed on a laser printer, the result can be visually convincing, as shown in Figure 1-10.

In what way has word processing software become more and more like desktop publishing software?

Graphics are available from several sources:

- Electronic spreadsheet and presentation graphics software are used to generate graphics.

FIGURE 1-10
Desktop publishing creates highly professional business documents.

- Clip art (predrawn graphics stored on disk) comes with top-of-the-line word processing software, and additional disks can be purchased separately.

- Drawing software allows desktop publishers to draw their own images (flowcharts, pictograms, scaled drawings of products, and so on).

- Scanners convert images (graphics, photos, signatures, letterhead, and text) to electronic files that can be integrated into a document.

Decision makers who do not have the time to wade through pages of written text searching for key information are among the primary beneficiaries of graphic presentations. A manager may win the day by supporting a case for expansion with a line graph showing the resulting increase in profits. A salesperson might close a deal by backing up a proposal with five bar graphs illustrating the superiority of a product over the competition's version.

Tools for Communicating Quickly and Efficiently Over Long Distances. Computer networks have placed the world at our fingertips. To exploit the possibilities, whole new channels for communication have emerged. The businessperson is no longer limited to paper-copy letters and memos, the telephone, and face-to-face meetings; rather, exciting new methods for sending and receiving messages are available.

Will e-mail replace the telephone and postal mail? Justify your answer.

Electronic mail, or **e-mail**, as it is often called, is most commonly defined as person-to-person communication in which the transmission and receipt of the message take place through a computer. Electronic mail can be used to distribute memos, reports, and documents without sending them through the mail. E-mail helps solve the problem of "telephone tag." Approximately 70 percent of business telephone callers *do not* reach the person they called on the first try. The result is a game of tag, as the caller and the person called keep trying to reach the other unsuccessfully. With electronic mail, the caller simply keys a message and sends it to an electronic mailbox. Receivers are notified that a message awaits them, and they respond to the caller as soon as the message is read. When it is delivered and read quickly, electronic mail can be almost as convenient and articulate as a personal conversation.

E-mail systems that operate on a company's existing computer system are relatively inexpensive. When a single message is sent to several recipients, the savings are even greater compared to the cost of traditional communication methods. E-mail will continue to gain widespread use, especially as it becomes the foundation for more advanced corporate applications. One such application is the *forms definition feature*. For example, this feature would allow a sales rep to select an expense form, complete it, and send it to his/her supervisor, who will electronically sign it and send copies to the appropriate persons. Additionally, intelligent rules based on content can be encoded, which will instruct the form to route itself automatically. For example, if a claim is more than $10,000, the form will forward itself to a senior bank officer.[21]

Voice mail allows you to use your telephone to dial a voice mail service and store an oral message. The message is then delivered to the person or list of persons you are calling. Recipients can retrieve messages when they return to the office or dial in from remote locations to listen to their messages. Voice mail provides many of the benefits of e-mail but does not require a computer.

A **facsimile**, or **fax**, is a flexible and inexpensive form of electronic mail. A fax machine reads a document that has been inserted into the machine and transmits the document (text, pictures, and graphics) over telephone lines to another fax machine that receives the message and prepares a printed copy of the document. Because increasing numbers of companies of all sizes are using fax machines, entrepreneurs are putting fax machines that take credit cards into airport lounges, hotel lobbies, and convention centers. To use them, you simply insert your credit card, dial the number you want to reach, and send your document.

The advantage of fax transmission is speed. For example, a high-speed fax machine can transmit a page in about twenty seconds. Improved machines offer print quality comparable to that of a copy machine. In addition, fax machines are easy to operate. Because they can be programmed, the cost of transmission can be cut by sending a message in evening hours to take advantage of lower telephone rates. Sending faxes also facilitates communicating with people in different time zones.

Telecommuting allows individuals to work in their homes and use electronic mail to transmit work from home to the office. The major advantages of telecommuting are the reduced time and expense of commuting and the increased flexibility of working hours. Rather than spending two to three hours a day commuting to work in an urban area, for example, employees use a modem, telephone lines, and a remote workstation to transmit their work electronically. Memos, reports, even entire books can be transmitted in this way.

> How would telecommuting affect the social dynamics of the worker, colleagues, and family?

Transmitting information and computing from remote locations have become more prevalent because of the availability of *laptop* and *notebook computers*. These smaller computers give professionals access to computing power regardless of where they are—hotel room, airplane, taxi, or client's office, and so on. Such portable systems are battery-operated and generally contain secondary storage (a floppy disk drive, a hard disk drive, or both), a screen, and a keyboard. Newer innovations include palmtop computers, tiny hand-held computers that rest on the palm of the hand, lapbody computers that can drape from the neck, and "wearable" computers (e.g., computers that wrap around the forearm to facilitate recording inventory).

Desktop videoconferencing allows users to hold electronic meetings and share and annotate files and images across LANs and telephone lines in real time.

In your opinion, what does the future hold for business travel?

Cellular telephones, often called *mobile phones*, are cellular radios that transmit messages over airways. Cellular telephones are a powerful communication tool, especially for managers who are on the move (those who spend several hours commuting to and from work, travel from one meeting or work site to another, or work at sites with no access to a telephone) and must stay in immediate reach of the home office at all times. The increased productivity resulting from the more efficient use of time justifies the use of cellular service. Cellular telephones also help managers stay in closer contact with coworkers and with current and prospective clients and customers. Quick, courteous responses build strong interpersonal relations, which in turn lead to increased employee commitment and an edge over competitors. As cellular service expands to reach remote areas, cellular telephones are quickly becoming a standard business tool.

Electronic conferencing via teleconferencing and videoconferencing are alternatives to face-to-face meetings that allow several people at different locations to communicate electronically. **Teleconferencing** allows several persons in different geographic locations to be on the same line at the same time. **Videoconferencing** takes advantage of all media—audio, graphics, and video. Speakers provide the audio feedback, facsimile devices send graphics, and cameras transmit the video portion of the conference in a specially equipped room. Participants engage in group discussions while observing one another's facial expressions and gestures. **Electronic conferences** can eliminate or reduce the high costs of face-to-face meetings: travel, hotels, food, and time lost in transit.

Some personal computer companies have introduced inexpensive and personal **desktop videoconferencing systems** that allow users to hold electronic meetings and share and annotate files and images across existing local area networks and telephone lines in real time. Desktop videoconferencing restores the nonverbal elements of interpersonal communication that are lost over the telephone and, thus, is more personal than a "disembodied" voice at the other end of a telephone line. More important than the visual dimension, however, is the ability to "document conference." Using collaborative software with the desktop technology, users in remote locations can see each other as they work together on computer files (share text files, graphics, and images) at the same time. As the cost of videoconferencing capability declines, electronic meetings will become a common communication medium. Oral communication, especially within small groups, will be critical to interacting effectively in this environment.

Legal and Ethical Implications of Technology. In addition to its many benefits, technology poses some challenges for the business communicator. According to one writer, "computer technology, like any other invention, has the potential to exalt or debase the people who use it."[22] However, it is our responsibility to insure that information technology and the information it handles are used to enhance the dignity of mankind. Technology raises issues of ownership, as in the case of difficulties that arise in protecting the copyright of documents transmitted over the Internet. Technology poses dilemmas over access, that is, who has the right to certain stored information pertaining to an individual or a company.

Technology threatens our privacy, our right to be left alone, free from surveillance, or interference from other individuals or organizations. Common invasions of privacy caused by technology include collecting excessive amounts of information for decision making and maintaining too many files, monitoring the exact time employees' spend on a specific task and between tasks and the exact number and length of breaks, and supervisors' or coworkers' reading another employee's electronic mail and computer files. Integrating computer files containing information collected from more than one agency without permission is a major threat to privacy. Although an individual may have authorized the collection of the individual information, merging the information may reveal things the individual may want to remain private.[23] The privacy issue is explored further in the accompanying Strategic Forces Box.

Have you personally been affected by a loss of privacy because of technology? How?

Team Environment as a Strategic Force Influencing Communication

6 *Explain how team environment acts as a strategic force to influence the process of business communication.*

A team-oriented approach is replacing the traditional top-down management style in today's organizations. Firms around the world are facing problems in decreasing productivity, faltering product quality, and worker dissatisfaction. Work teams are being examined as a way to help firms remain globally competitive. Although worker involvement in the management process has long been the hallmark of Japanese business, a significant portion of U.S. businesses, as well as those of other countries, is experimenting with self-directed work teams.[27] The list of companies using self-directed work teams is diverse, including such firms as Hunt-Wesson, the Internal Revenue Service, and the San Diego Zoo. Other companies using the team concept include Toyota, Motorola, General Electric, Hewlett-Packard, and Corning.

Work Team Defined. The terms *team, work team, group, work group, cross-functional team* and *self-directed team* are often used interchangeably.[28] Whatever the title, a **team** is a small number of people with complementary skills who work together for a common purpose. Team members set their own goals, in cooperation with management, and plan how to achieve those goals and how their work is to be accomplished. The central organizing fact of a team is that it has a common purpose and measurable goals for which the team can be held accountable, independent of its individual members. Employees in a self-directed work team handle a wide array of functions and work with a minimum of direct supervision.[29] Some major strengths of teams are as follows:[30]

Considering the four strategic forces discussed, how is business communication today different from that of 30 years ago? In what ways is it easier? In what ways is it more difficult?

Strategic Forces: Legal and Ethical Constraints

Is Anything Private Anymore?

Despite the passage of federal legislation and additional state laws designed to enhance and strengthen electronic privacy, most Americans feel they have less privacy today than ever. According to a recent Harris poll, 76 percent of Americans believe they have lost all control over personal information, and 67 percent believe that computers must be restricted in the future to preserve privacy.[24] Workplace privacy has also become an area of concern, as computer monitoring and surveillance capabilities expand.

George Orwell, in his classic novel *1984*, described what many believe to be the ultimate in privacy-shattering totalitarianism as he offered a foreboding look at future society. In his fictitious account *". . . there was of course no way of knowing whether you were being watched at any given moment. . . . It was even conceivable that they watched everybody all the time. . . . You had to live—did live—, from habit that became instinct in the assumption that every sound you made was overheard, and, except in darkness, every movement scrutinized."*[25] We have now advanced technologically to the point that, if desired, this kind of surveillance is easily possible.

An important aspect of technology is its seductive power: If a technology exists, it must be used. Where does this principle leave the individual regarding privacy needs in a highly automated world? Experts in the area of individual privacy have suggested three key aspects in the ethical management of information and protection of privacy:[26]

- **Relevance.** An inquiring party should have a clear and valid purpose for delving into the information of an individual.

- **Consent.** An individual should be given the right to withhold consent prior to any query that might violate privacy.

- **Methods.** An inquiring party should distinguish between methods of inquiry that are reasonable and customary and those that are of questionable ethical grounding.

While technology offers tremendous advantages and endless possibilities for enhancing communication, it poses challenges for both individuals and organizations in the maintenance of a proper degree of privacy. Most of us are not ready for the all-seeing eye of Orwell's "Big Brother."

Application

Read a book review of George Orwell's *1984*. In a two-page written summary, cite instances in which Orwell described technological capabilities that have been realized in recent years. How has society's response to these capabilities differed from the fictional plot?

- Teams make workers happier by causing them to feel that they are shaping their own jobs.

- Teams increase efficiency by eliminating layers of managers whose job was once to pass orders downward.

Explain the significance of 1+1=3.

- Teams enable a company to draw on the skills and imagination of a whole workforce. A key element in team success is the concept of **synergy**. Synergy is defined as a situation in which the whole is greater than the sum of the parts. Teams provide a depth of expertise that is unavailable at the individual level, as illustrated in the cartoon on p. 36. Teams open lines of communication that then lead to increased interaction among employees and between employees and management. The result is that teams help companies reach their goals of delivering higher-quality products and services faster and with more cost-effectiveness.

COMMUNICATION IN ACTION

Gary Lopez, Southwest Airlines

Southwest Airlines began operating in 1971 with three planes serving three cities and with annual revenues of $2 million. In 1997, the company had 261 planes serving 51 cities and revenues of $317.8 million. Of importance is the fact that the airline has made a profit every year since 1973, the only airline to do so. At the heart of this success story is a work culture where employees are treated as the company's number one asset, according to Herb Kelleher, the president, chief executive officer, and chairman of the board for Southwest Airlines.

The backbone of this employee-oriented company is its team orientation. Southwest Airlines has a "people department," not a personnel or human resources department. Teamwork is built through the Crew Resource Management program. Southwest focuses on crews, not individuals, as the driving force behind the company. Pilots serve as team leaders in the 25,000-employee company. Gary Lopez, flight attendant base manager, the main Southwest hub in Dallas, Texas, says that use of teams enhances team members' job satisfaction and helps meet many of their other needs; the result is increased productivity.

According to Lopez, Southwest starts by hiring the right people. They hire first for attitude, and second for skills. Southwest Airlines doesn't think of itself as an airline, but rather as a service business that happens to fly airplanes. A second strategy is based on an ironclad rule: if you treat your employees like dogs, they are going to bite the customer. Southwest tries to maintain as few rules and regulations as possible, and the overriding one is to have employees use common sense. When employees make mistakes, they ask them to learn from their mistakes. The company recognizes that happy people make better employees; creating such an environment works to build mutual trust. A third success strategy focuses on team rewards. To build a team-oriented culture, Southwest Airlines avoids individual merit pay in favor of profit sharing and stock ownership, with emphasis on the welfare of the organization. Employees have benefited significantly from this team strategy, as every $1,000 worth of stock issued in the 1970s is worth $1.5 million today.

Lopez believes that a major reason for ineffective teams is that leaders are often more focused on themselves than on their people and what they are doing right. "People excel, overachieve, and produce results when they are appreciated, listened to, and supported. It is very simple!"

Applying What You Have Learned

1. Summarize Southwest Airlines' approach to building successful teams.

2. Refer to Lopez's comment about the use of teams helping to meet many needs of employees. To what needs might he be referring?

Communication Differences in Work Teams. In the past most businesses were operated in a hierarchical fashion, with most decisions made at the top. Communication followed a top-down/bottom-up or lateral pattern. Communication patterns are different in successful team environments as compared to traditional organizational structures. Trust building is the primary factor that changes the organization's communication patterns. Open meetings are an important method for enhancing communication, as they educate employees about the business while building bridges of understanding and trust. A second trust-building structure is shared leadership, which involves more direct and effective communication between management and its internal customers. Listening, problem solving, conflict resolution, negotiation, and consensus become important factors in group communication.

The concept of synergy is that the whole is greater than the sum of the parts.

Ziggy

Many of us are more capable than some of us...

..but none of us is as capable as all of us !!

©1994 Ziggy and Friends, Inc./Dist. by Universal Press Syndicate

Communication is perhaps the single most important aspect of successful teamwork. Open lines of communication increase interaction between employees and management. Information must flow vertically up to management and down to workers, as well as horizontally among team members, other teams, and supervisors. All affected parties should be kept informed as projects progress.

Maximization of Work Team Effectiveness. Grouping employees into a team structure does not mean that they will automatically function as a team. A group must go through a developmental process to begin to function as a team. Members need training in such areas as problem solving, goal setting, and conflict resolution. Teams must be encouraged to establish the "three R's"—roles, rules, and relationships.[31]

Provide other examples of emotional barriers, process barriers, and cultural barriers that deter team function.

The self-directed work team can become the basic organizational building block to best ensure success in dynamic global competition. Skills for successful participation in team environments are somewhat different from those necessary for success in old-style organizations. Effective communication skills include the ability to give and take constructive criticism, listen actively, clearly impart one's views to others, and provide meaningful feedback. Emotional barriers, such as insecurity or condescension, can limit team effectiveness. Process barriers, such as prevailing policies and procedures, can also interfere by stifling effective team functioning. Cultural barriers, such as role assignment and perceived responsibilities, can separate workers from management. Effective team communication will involve overcoming all of these barriers.[32]

Perhaps the greatest requirement for successful teams is the ability to understand the feelings and needs of coworkers. Members must feel comfortable stating their opinions and discussing the strengths and weaknesses of the team. The ability to experience this openness is largely dependent on the level of trust workers have in one another and in management. Team members must also develop leadership skills that apply to a dynamic group setting. In dynamic team leadership, which is referred to as *distributed leadership*, the role of leader may alternate among members, and more than one leadership style may be active at any given time.[33]

To improve group communication, time needs to be set aside to assess the quality of interaction. Questions to pose about the group process might include the following:

- What are our common goals?
- What roles are members playing? For instance, is one person dominating while others contribute little or nothing?
- Is the group dealing with conflict in a positive way?
- What in the group process is going well?
- What about the group process could be improved?

Research on communication patterns in mixed-gender work groups shows that the traditional behaviors of men and women may restrict the richness of discussion and limit the productivity of the group. These dynamics are often so subtle that group members may not be aware of what is happening. Here is a partial listing of these differences:[34]

What do you see as the three major challenges to the success of work teams?

- Men are, for example, more likely to control discussion through introducing topics, interrupting, and talking more than women.
- Women not only talk less, but often assume supportive rather than leadership roles in conversation and receive less attention for their ideas from the group.
- Both men and women may expect group members to follow gender stereotyped roles that can limit each individual's contributions (for example, always selecting a man as leader or a woman as note taker).
- Either women or men may use exclusionary language that reinforces gender stereotypes and that others in the group find offensive.
- Women may exhibit verbal or nonverbal behavior characteristic of submissiveness (twirling their hair or using self put-downs) while men communicate with words and actions in ways that restrict and control a group (treating a woman with a good idea like a rarity or touching in a way that can be perceived as condescending).
- Men and women may sit separately, thereby limiting cross-gender interaction.
- Men's nonverbal behavior (eye contact, touching, gestures) may convey messages of dominance while women's nonverbal behavior (smiling, eye contact, deference) may suggest a lack of self-confidence and power.

Cultural or age differences among members of a team may also be barriers to team communication. Knowing what behaviors may limit the group process is imperative to maximizing results. Team members may need awareness training to assist in recognizing behaviors that may hinder team performance and in overcoming barriers that may limit the effectiveness of their communication. You can explore the team model versus reward for individual effort by completing the Real-Time Internet Case at the end of this chapter.

SUMMARY

1. **Define communication and describe the main purposes for communication in business.** Communication is the process of exchanging information and meaning between or among individuals through a common system of symbols, signs, and behavior. Managers spend most of their time in oral and written communication.

2. **Explain the communication process model and the ultimate objective of the communication process.** People engaged in communication encode and decode messages while simultaneously serving as both senders and receivers. In the communication process, feedback helps people resolve possible misunderstandings and thus improve communication effectiveness. Feedback and the opportunity to observe nonverbal signs are always present in face-to-face communication, the most effective of the three communication levels.

3. **Explain how legal and ethical constraints act as a strategic force to influence the process of business communication.** Communication occurs within an environment of strategic forces that includes legal and ethical constraints. Pressures to succeed often place individuals in difficult legal and ethical dilemmas. International, federal, state, and local laws impose legal boundaries for business activity. Ethical boundaries are determined by personal analysis that can be assisted by application of various frameworks for decision making.

4. **Explain how diversity challenges act as a strategic force to influence the process of business communication.** Communication occurs within an environment of strategic forces that includes diversity in nationality, culture, age, gender, and other factors. Such diversity offers challenges for the business communicator in interpretation of time, personal space requirements, body language, translation limitations, and lack of language training. Through diversity, the organization and the individual are provided with tremendous opportunities to maximize talent, ideas, and productivity.

5. **Explain how technology acts as a strategic force to influence the process of business communication.** Communication occurs within an environment of strategic forces that includes changing technology. Significant strides have occurred in the development of tools for data collection and analysis, tools for shaping messages to be clearer and more effective, and tools for communicating quickly and efficiently over long distances. The use of technology also raises various legal and ethical concerns in regard to ownership, access, and privacy.

6. **Explain how team environment acts as a strategic force to influence the process of business communication.** Communication occurs within an environment of strategic forces that includes team environment. Communicating in teams differs from communication in traditional organizational structures. Team orientation focuses on group synergy rather than on individual effort. The result of effective teams is better decisions, more creative solutions to problems, and higher worker morale.

REFERENCES

[1]Maney, K. (1997, April 24). Technology is 'demolishing' time, distance. *USA Today*, pp. 1B–2B.

[2]Isokoff, M. (1997, February 10). The White House shell game: How the Clinton campaign's frantic fund raising may have crossed the line. *Newsweek*, pp. 34–35.

[3]Reinemund, S. S. (1992). Today's ethics and tomorrow's work place. *Business Forum*, 17(2), 6–9.

[4]Slayton, M. (1980). *Common sense & everyday ethics.* Washington, DC: Ethics Resource Center.

[5]Slayton, M. (1991, May–June). Perspectives. *Ethics Journal.* Washington, DC: Ethics Resource Center.

[6]Mathison, D. L. (1988). Business ethics cases and decision models: A call for relevancy in the classroom. *Journal of Business Ethics*, 10(7), 781.

[7]Freeman, R. E., & Gilvert, D. R. (1988). *Corporate strategy and the search for ethics.* Englewood Cliffs, NJ: Prentice Hall.

[8]McGarry, M. J. (1994, June 9). Short cuts. *Newsday*, p. A50.

[9]Microsoft investigating software labeling problem. (1977, July 11). *The Dallas Morning News*, p. 11D.

[10]Solomon, J. (1990, September 12). Learning to accept cultural diversity. *The Wall Street Journal*, p. B1.

[11]Holland, J. R. (1991, May). Reaching older audiences: Aging America presents communications challenges and opportunities. *Public Relations Journal*, 14–15, 20–21.

[12]Miller, W. H. (1991, May 6). A new perspective for tomorrow's workforce. *Industry Week*, 6.

[13]Sullivan, J. H., & Kameda, N. (1982). The concept of profit and Japanese-American business communication problems. *Journal of Business Communications, 19*(1), 33–39.

[14]Green, Diana J. & Scott, J. C. (1996).The status of international business communication courses in schools accredited by the American Assembly of Collegiate Schools of Business. *The Delta Pi Epsilon Journal 39*(1), 43–62.

[15]Marquardt, M. J., & Engel, D. W. (1993). HRD competencies for a shrinking world. *Training and Development, 47*(5), 59–64.

[16]Grant, G. (1996). Emerging platforms for commerce over the Internet. *The Internet strategy handbook.* In Cronin, M. J. (Ed.). Boston: Harvard Business School Press.

[17]Gray, M. (1996). Internet Growth Summary. [Online]. http://www.mit.edu/people/mkgray/net/web-growth-summary.html [1997, October 17].

[18]Third age media secures second round financing. (1997, October 7). *Business Wire.*

[19]Gray, M. (1996). Internet Growth Summary. [Online]. http://www.mit.edu/people/mkgray/net/web-growth-summary.html [1997, October 17].

[20]Bollier, D. (1996). *The future of electronic commerce.* Washington, DC: Aspen Institute.

[21]Shannon, J. H., & Rosenthal, D. A. (1993). Electronic mail and privacy: Can the conflicts be resolved? *Business Forum, 18*(1,2), 31–34.

[22]Connell, J. (1993, December 10). Cyberethics: Innovations raise questions about who should be allowed to do what with the information superhighway. *The San Diego Union-Tribune,* pp. 1–9.

[23]Mason, R. O. (1986). Four ethical issues of the information age. In Dejoie, R., Fowler, G., & Paradice, D. (1991). *Ethical issues in information systems* pp. (46–55). Boston: Boyd & Fraser.

[24]Equifax report on consumers in the information age, a national survey. (1992). In Laudon, K. C., & Laudon, J. P. (1994). *Management information systems: Organization and technology.* (3rd ed.). New York: MacMillan.

[25]Orwell, G. (1949). *1984.* New York: Signet Classics. [6-7].

[26]Brown, W. S. (1996). Technology, workplace privacy, and personhood. *Journal of Business Ethics, 15* (11), 1237-1248.

[27]Felts, C. (1995). Taking the mystery out of self-directed work teams. *Industrial Management, 37*(2), 21–26.

[28]Miller, B. K., & Butler, J. B. (1996, November/December). Teams in the workplace. *New Accountant,* 18–24.

[29]Ray, D., & Bronstein, H. (1995). *Teaming up.* New York: McGraw Hill.

[30]The trouble with teams. (1995, January 14). *Economist,* 61.

[31]Frohman, M.A. (1995, April 3). Do teams . . . but do them right. *Industry Week,* 21–24.

[32]Zuidema, K. R., & Kleiner, B. H. (1994). New developments in developing self-directed work groups. *Management Decision, 32*(8), 57–63.

[33]Barry, D. (1991). Managing the Baseless Team: Lessons in distributed leadership. *Organizational Dynamics, 20*(1), 31–47.

[34]Kaser, J. S. (1985). *Count me in: Guidelines for enhancing participation in mixed-gender work groups.* Su. Doc. # FD 1.310/2:29Y996. Washington, D.C.: U.S. Government Printing Office.

[35]Pounds, M. H. (1996, April 12). New breed of executive is ruthless, highly paid. *Sun-Sentinel* (Fort Lauderdale), p. 1F.

Note: Selected portions of the discussion of ethical constraints were adapted with permission from Spencer, B. A., & Lehman C. M. (1990). Analyzing ethical issues: Essential ingredient in the business communication course. *Bulletin of the Association for Business Communication, 53*(3), 7–16.

REVIEW QUESTIONS

1. What are the three purposes for which people communicate? What percentage of a manager's time is spent communicating? Give examples of the types of communication managers use. (Obj. 1)

2. What are some communication activities in which managers are typically engaged? (Obj. 1)

3. List the five stages in the communication process using the following terms: (a) sender, (b) encode, (c) channel, (d) receiver, (e) decode, (f) feedback, and (g) interferences or barriers. (Obj. 2)

4. What are the three channels typically used to transmit messages? Provide several examples of each channel. (Obj. 2)

5. What types of differences between sender and receiver create barriers to communication? (Obj. 2)

6. Discuss four strategic forces that influence business communication? (Obj. 3, 4, 5, 6)

7. Give two definitions for ethics. (Obj. 3)

8. What are some common causes of unethical behavior in the workplace? (Obj. 3)

9. What are some aspects of diversity that pose communication challenges? (Obj. 4)

10. Describe several intercultural communication barriers and how they might be overcome. (Obj. 4)

11. Describe several ways that communication technology can assist individuals and organizations. (Obj. 5)

12. What concerns are raised over the use of technology? (Obj. 5)

13. Explain the concept of synergy. (Obj. 6)

14. How does communication in work teams differ from that of traditional organizations? (Obj. 6)

15. Why has communication been identified as perhaps the single most important aspect of team work? (Obj. 6)

EXERCISES

1. **Communication Activities (Obj. 1)**
   Shadow a business manager for a day. Keep a log of his/her communication activities for the time period you are observing. Divide the communication activities into the following categories: (1) attending meetings; (2) presenting information to groups; (3) explaining and clarifying management procedures and work assignments; (4) coordinating the work of various employees, departments, and other work groups; (5) evaluating and counseling employees; (6) promoting the company's products/services and image; (7) other activities. Calculate the percentage of time spent in each activity.

2. **Communication Barriers (Obj. 2)**
   In groups of three, develop a list of 12 to 15 annoying habits of yours or of others that create barriers (verbal and nonverbal) to effective communication. Be prepared to present the list to the class.

3. **Communication Interferences (Obj. 2)**
   In groups assigned by your instructor, develop a list of possible interferences (barriers) that may occur at each stage of the communication process. You may refer to the list of annoying habits generated in Exercise 2.

   Stages of Communication

Process	Inference	Suggestions for Improvement
Encoding	_____	_____
Channel	_____	_____
Decoding	_____	_____
Feedback	_____	_____

4. **Communication Process (Obj. 2)**
   Recall a recent conversation that you have had with a friend, teacher, coworker, supervisor, or some other person. Write a brief scenario including the dialogue between the sender and receiver. Analyze the effectiveness of this conversation using the communication process model in Figure 1-1 as a guide. Identify problems (interferences or barriers) occurring at each stage of the communication process and provide suggestions for improvement. Be prepared to discuss your analysis with the class or in small groups assigned by your instructor.

5. **Communication Activities (Obj. 2)**
   Prepare a record of your listening, speaking, reading, and writing activities and time spent in each during the hours of 8 a.m. to 5 p.m. for the next two days. You should attempt to record the time spent doing each activity for each one-hour time block in such a way that you obtain a total time for each activity. Be prepared to share your distribution to the class.

6. **Legal and Ethical Constraints as a Strategic Force (Obj. 3)**
   Read *The Power of Ethical Management* by Kenneth Blanchard and Norman Vincent Peale, a short, engaging story about a sales manager's attempt to make an ethical decision. Write a brief report summarizing the ethical principles presented in the book.

7. **Identifying Ethical Dilemmas (Obj. 3)**
   Locate in a current newspaper or magazine an example of an illegal or an unethical act by a business organization or its employee(s). Choose an incident as closely related as possible to your intended profession. Prepare a written summary of the article.

8. **Analyzing an Ethical Dilemma (Obj. 3)**
   Over the past two years, the salaries and bonuses of top management at Golden Value Stores have increased over 50 percent—an increase consistent with management compensation levels of similar companies. Much of this increase resulted from management's achieving a variety of non-income-related goals such as the number of retail outlets opened during the year. During the same period, however, Golden Value Stores' stock and company earnings have increased at an annual rate of four percent, and dividends have increased only seven percent.

   A stockholder has submitted a proposal to eliminate all management bonuses if the company does not achieve a 10 percent growth rate. You are an assistant manager of a stock mutual fund that owns 100,000 shares of Golden Value stock. You have been asked to determine how the mutual fund should cast its votes on the proposal.

Use the ethical framework in Figure 1-6 to analyze whether the following action demonstrates ethical behavior. Consider the costs and benefits of the action on each of the company's stakeholders (persons who will be affected by the decision): Golden Value Stores, management, stockholders, and employees. Consider which of Ross's five duties are relevant and which may be violated for any of the stakeholders. Use the following tables as a guide for your analysis.

Decision: Restrict Management Compensation		
Stakeholder	*Cost*	*Benefit*
Golden Value Stores	Proposal (restricting compensation) could encourage managers to take risks or unethical actions to achieve goals	Will relate compensation costs more directly to company operating results. Attaining 10 percent growth would improve market position.
Stakeholder	*Obligation*	
Stockholders	Meets obligation to provide a fair return on their investment in the short-term. Restricting salary could have a long-term negative impact on the company's ability to attract and retain quality managers.	

9. **Diversity as a Strategic Force (Obj. 4)**
   Describe a situation you have encountered in which international, intercultural, intergenerational, or gender issues affected communication. How did the involved parties deal with the issue? What was the result?

10. **Understanding Diversity Issues (Obj. 4)**
    In groups of three, discuss each of the following critical incidents. Identify how you think the different cultures will interact.
    a. A U.S. engineer working with a subsidiary in Asia begins a general meeting of the professional staff by praising one manager for outstanding work on a report.
    b. A U.S. manager sees two Arab-American employees arguing and decides to stay out of it.
    c. While the American supervisor waits, a Latino manager starts a budget-planning meeting by chatting casually and taking care of other formalities.
    d. After carefully presenting the benefits of the company's product, a sales representative from the United States presses on an Indonesian buyer for a sales decision and eventually asks directly whether the buyer wishes to place an order.

e. A human resources manager becomes irate when an Asian woman does not maintain direct eye contact during a performance appraisal interview—or at any other time.

f. Two managers have applied for an overseas assignment in Asia. One is a highly aggressive marketing expert with proven managerial experience; the other is a good team worker with a high degree of interpersonal skill. Which one would you choose and why?

g. As negotiations with Malaysian business executives become quite lengthy, a group of U.S. businesspersons becomes less formal, repeatedly crossing their legs in such a way that the soles of their shoes are visible.

h. A U.S. executive, committed to preparing reports with the most up-to-date information possible, required that all periodic reports be submitted approximately two days before the composite report was to be submitted to the president. The executive has been transferred to the Mexican operation and plans to follow the same procedure.

i. Discouraged about the slow pace of negotiations with the Japanese, a U.S. manager suggests that the senior-level people from each side meet alone to attempt to work out the differences.

j. A female executive is being considered for transfer to a Middle Eastern country to negotiate the location of a new plant.

11. **Technology as a Strategic Force (Obj. 5)**
    Indicate which of the following communication mediums would be most appropriate for sending the following messages: e-mail, fax, telephone, or face-to-face communication. Justify your answer.
    a. The company is expecting a visit from members of a committee evaluating your bid for this year's Malcolm Baldridge National Quality Award. All employees must be notified of the visit.
    b. After careful deliberation, the management of a mid-sized pharmaceutical company is convinced the only way to continue its current level of research is to sell the company to a larger one. The employees must be informed of this decision.
    c. Lincoln Enterprises is eager to receive the results of a drug test on a certain employee. The drug testing company has been asked to send the results as quickly as possible.
    d. The shipping department has located the common carrier currently holding a customer's shipment that should have been delivered yesterday. Inform the customer that the carrier has promised delivery by tomorrow morning.

e. An employee in another division office has requested that you send a spreadsheet that you have prepared so that he can manipulate the data to produce a report.

12. **Team Environment as a Strategic Force (Obj. 6)**
Using the Internet, locate an article that covers how a company or organization is using teams in its operation. Write a one-page abstract of the article.

E-MAIL APPLICATION

Read an article from a current magazine or journal about how technology is impacting communication. Send your instructor a brief e-mail message discussing the major theme of the article. Include a complete bibliographic entry so that the instructor could locate the article (refer to Appendix B for examples for formatting references).

REAL-TIME INTERNET CASE

Can the United States Succeed Without Rewarding Rugged Individuality?

A basic element of the fabric of U.S. entrepreneurship is the faith in the ingenuity of the individual person's ability to conceive, develop, and profit from a business endeavor. The frontier spirit and triumph of the individual over looming odds have been a predominant force in the development of the United States. Such individualism has also been recognized by organizations, with reward going to those who contribute winning ideas and efforts.

The recent shift in organizational structures toward team design has caused management to reassess reward systems that focus on individual recognition and to consider rewards that are based on team performance. Some fear that removing individual incentive will lead to mediocrity and a reduction in personal effort. They argue that while the team model might work in other cultures, it is inconsistent with the U.S. way of thinking and living. According to Madelyn Hoshstein, president of DYG Inc., a New York firm that researches corporate trends, America is moving away from the model of team building in which everyone is expected to do everything and toward focusing on employees who are the best at what they do. She describes this change as a shift toward social Darwinism and away from egalitarianism, in which everyone has equal economic, political, and social rights.[35]

Team advocates say that teams are here to stay and liken those who deny that reality to the proverbial ostrich with its head in the sand. They stress the need for newly structured incentive plans to reward group effort.

Visit the following Internet sites for information on the issue and respond to one or more of the following activities as directed by your instructor.

Internet sites

http://lionhrtpub.com/apics/apics-3-96/motivating.html/

http://www.tpcorp.com/fed/library/articles/scholtes.html

http://www.gainshare.com/cmnts.html

Activities

1. How would you respond to those with concerns about loss of individual incentive? Argue for or against the increased emphasis on team reward, using either personal examples or examples from business.

2. Structure a reward system that would recognize both individual and team performance. You may use an organization of your choice to illustrate.

3. Select a specific corporation or nation that has implemented the team model. Describe the transition away from a hierarchical structure and the consequences that have resulted from the shift, both positive and negative.

Pacific Bell Directory

The United States is a nation of cultural diversity. Each wave of immigration, whether prompted by religious, political, or economic reasons, has added new facets to our distinct culture. The term *eclectic* has been used to describe this diversity; it refers to that which is made up of components from various sources and implies that the result is the sum of many perspectives.

As businesses attempt to serve the diverse needs of an eclectic community, recognizing and respecting cultural differences becomes increasingly important. The management of Pacific Bell Directory discusses this vital concept in terms of the unique characteristics of the Southern California intercultural environment. While the particular cultural components may vary, the same communication challenges exist.

Discussion Questions

1. Stephanie Dollschnieder refers to an important ingredient in successful intercultural communication as "cutting each other slack." What does she mean? Give examples of how this strategy can be accomplished.

2. What part do respect and trust play in intercultural communication? How are they related concepts?

3. To what extent is courtesy a universal concept?

4. How does the "salad bowl" concept of culture differ from the traditional "melting pot" idea?

5. Jan Birkelbach discusses the wide array of behavior within cultural groups and cautions against generalizing that all members of a specific group fit a certain stereotype. Give examples of several such stereotypes.

Application

You must make a short presentation to your company's staff concerning the cultural diversity of your community and the importance of effective intercultural communication.

1. Determine what cultural groups are present in your community and in what proportions. (Your chamber of commerce or city offices may be of help.)

2. Interview one or more persons from each of the major cultural groups in your community. Identify what is unique about their language, nonverbal communication, perception of time, customs, family life, and so on.

3. Prepare an outline for your talk, emphasizing the importance of intercultural communication and including several suggestions for improving intercultural communication in your community.

CHAPTER TWO

Organizational Setting for Business Communication

LEARNING OBJECTIVES

When you have completed Chapter 2, you will be able to:

1 Identify the four levels of communication.

2 Explain how behavioral theories (Maslow's human needs, stroking, and the Johari Window), nonverbal communication, and listening affect group communication.

3 Identify factors affecting group communication.

4 Identify factors leading to the need for formal organizations.

5 Discuss how information flows within an organization (formally and informally; and downward, upward, and horizontally).

*A*n organization's balance sheet may fail to reflect its most important asset—its people. To remain viable and profitable in today's complex and turbulent business environment, organizations need to be rich, not only in terms of dollars but also in human resources. Peter Drucker, the renowned management expert, says that today's business environment requires a flexible, creative, autonomous, speedy, and entrepreneurial workforce. To be successful, organizations must create an environment that energizes and provides intrinsic encouragement to employees to accomplish tasks by encouraging genuine openness and communication.

Eugene Chen, a corporate training specialist in Malaysia, sees empowerment as the means for building a successful workforce. Empowerment is a new way of working together to gain the maximum synergy from all levels in an organization. Empowerment begins with management's trust in employees, which provides freedom to people to do successfully what they want to do. Sharing of information is important if people are to be empowered, and this process can only occur in an organization that believes in and practices open and honest communication. Chen's research on empowerment has revealed that empowered employees are more productive, satisfied, and innovative, and more likely to create high-quality products and services, than are nonempowered employees. Empowered individuals tend to form natural teams and serve as role models for others.

Organizational movement toward empowerment has its challenges. According to Chen, the evolving organization typically goes through stages of trial and error, inertia, skepticism, pain, anger, and chaotic moments prior to achieving a truly empowered workforce. The change, however, is worth the effort, as rewards to the organization can be immense in terms of worker satisfaction and, ultimately, in corporate profits.[1]

Organizational communication is concerned with the movement of information within the company structure. Regardless of your career or your level within an organization, your ability to communicate will affect not only the success of the organization but also your personal success and your advancement within that organization.

1 *Identify the four levels of communication.*

What is the difference between a task goal and a maintenance goal?

Levels of Communication

The primary function of communication is to convey information and meaning through words, symbols, signs, or actions. People form messages by combining pieces or bits of information. This communicative process takes place on four levels:

- **Intrapersonal communication** occurs when an individual processes information based on his or her own experiences. It is, in a sense, communication within one person.

- **Interpersonal communication** takes place primarily when two people are involved in the process. As mentioned, they have two goals: (1) They want to accomplish whatever task confronts them, and (2) they want to feel better about themselves as a result of their interaction. These two goals are commonly referred to as **task goals** and **maintenance goals**, respectively, and they exist side by side in varying degrees in most of our daily activities.

- **Group communication** occurs among more than two people: a committee, a club, or all the students enrolled in a class. Groups are formed usually because the combined efforts of a number of people result in greater output than the individual efforts of the same number of people. In other words, groups can do more for the individuals than the individuals can do for themselves.

- **Organizational communication** arises when groups discover that they are unable to accomplish their goals without some kind of organization. Thus, organizations are combinations of groups formed in such a way that large tasks may be accomplished. Despite the differences in size and complexity, each of these levels of communication continues to have task and maintenance goals. The idea of maintenance goals can be divided into two distinct goals—self-maintenance and group maintenance:

  - A **self-maintenance goal** describes an individual's need to maintain his or her personal worth or psychological well-being. An example of a self-maintenance goal would be a group member's striving to be liked by every member of the team.
  - A **group maintenance goal** describes a group's need to maintain the non-task relationships they have developed through interacting with one another as a team. An example would be a team's effort to promote empathetic listening among all members.

A corporate study by the Ford Foundation found that productivity is increased in companies who show concern for employees' personal lives and needs.[2] How do you explain this finding?

Communicating Intrapersonally

All interpretation of information ultimately takes place in the individual mind. *Self-talk* is the term used to describe conversation that takes place within a person. Self-talk may be either positive and constructive, or negative and destructive. People's self-talk influences the communication with others that they initiate and receive, since attitudes and mind-sets have already been formed prior to the exchange of ideas between individuals.

Communicating Interpersonally

Most of your communication in business will occur in various one-to-one relationships. Behavioral scientists working in the fields of sociology and psychology have strongly influenced business management by stressing interpersonal communication problems in the business environment. Understanding these behavior patterns provides supervisors valuable insights that facilitate communication with employees in today's information age.

Recognizing Human Needs. Psychologist Abraham Maslow developed the concept of a hierarchy of needs through which people progress. In our society, most people have reasonably satisfied their lower-level physiological needs and their security and safety needs (food, shelter, and protection from the elements and physical danger). Beyond these two basic need levels, people progress to satisfy three upper levels: (1) social needs for love, acceptance, and belonging; (2) ego needs to be heard, appreciated, and wanted; and (3) self-actualizing needs, including the need to achieve one's fullest potential through professional, philanthropic, political, educational, and artistic channels.

2 *Explain how behavioral theories (Maslow's human needs, stroking, and the Johari Window), nonverbal communication, and listening affect group communication.*

As people satisfy needs at one level, they move on to the next. The levels that have been satisfied still are present, but their importance diminishes. Effective communicators are able to identify and appeal to need levels in various individuals or groups. Advertising is designed to appeal to need levels. Luxury-car ads appeal to ego needs, toothpaste and deodorant ads appeal to social needs, and cellular telephone and home

Think about the types of information you (1) share freely, (2) share only with close friends, and (3) keep hidden. How do these decisions affect your interpersonal communication?

To which need level would each of the following apply? penthouse office; years of service award; expanded retirement program; employee lounge.

security system ads appeal to security and safety needs. In business, efforts to help people satisfy needs are essential, since a satisfied worker is generally more productive than a dissatisfied one. In communication activities, a sender is more likely to structure the message to appeal to the receiver if the receiver's need can be identified.

Stroking and the Johari Window. People engage in communication with others in the hope that the outcome may lead to mutual trust, mutual pleasure, and psychological well-being. The communication exchange is a means of sharing information about things, ideas, tasks, and selves.

When two strangers first meet, their knowledge about each other might be nil. Assume, for example, that two employees meet at the vending machine in the company break room. After an introduction—"Hello, I'm John Robbins"; "Hello, I'm Susan Smith"—they know something about each other, if only the other's name and gender. They probably also gain an impression about the other person through appearance and dress. At this point, they know only superficial things about each other.

As the exchange continues, the two learn more and more about each other. Susan soon learns that John is the recently hired human resources manager. She says, "Yes, I'd heard that you were joining the company. Welcome aboard. I'm a data-entry operator in inventory control." John continues, "I'm glad to know you, Susan. If you have a couple of minutes, could you tell me how you feel about the current flexible scheduling? Do you have any suggestions for making it work better?" As a result of this exchange, John learns a little more about Susan—her knowledge and commitment to the company—as well as valuable information about a company procedure. Susan has learned that management cares about her opinion of a work-related issue.

This casual interaction becomes a definite **stroke** that is likely to enhance Susan's feelings about her work. Getting a pat on the back from the supervisor, receiving a congratulatory telephone call or letter, and taking the time to listen to another person are other examples of everyday positive stroking. By paying attention to the importance of strokes, managers can greatly improve communication and people's feelings about their work.

As the relationship between John and Susan develops, they continue to learn more about each other. Their behavior leads to trust, and this trust leads to freer conversation. Sharing also allows people to learn about themselves. The Johari Window, shown in Figure 2-1, illustrates this concept. The upper left area, labeled "I," or "free area," represents what we know about ourselves and what others know about us. Area II, the blind area, designates those things others know about us but that we don't know about ourselves; for example, you are the only person who can't see your physical self as it really is. Things we know about ourselves but that others don't know about us occupy the hidden or secret area, III. Area IV includes the unknown: things we don't know about ourselves and others don't know about us, such as our ability to handle emergency situations if we've never been faced with them.

Each of these areas may vary in size according to the degree that we can learn about ourselves from others and to the degree that we are willing to disclose things about ourselves to others. Only through reciprocal sharing can people learn about themselves and about others. In communication practice, such sharing occurs only when people develop *trust* in each other. Trust is something that must be earned. We are usually willing to tell people about our school records, our jobs, and other things that aren't truly personal. But we share personal thoughts, ambitions, and inner feelings only with selected others—those whom we have learned to trust. Trust is a quality we develop from experience with others. Through performance, we earn the trust of others. The relationships existing between supervisor and employee, doctor and

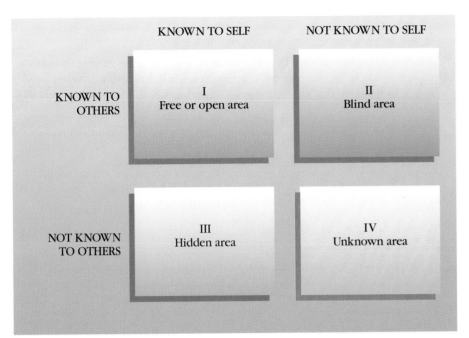

FIGURE 2-1
The Johari Window.

patient, and lawyer and client are those of trust, but only in specific areas. In more intimate relationships—wife and husband, brother and sister, parent and child—deeper, personal feelings are entrusted to each other. When a confidant demonstrates that he or she can be trusted, trust is reinforced and leads to an expansion of the open area of the Johari Window. In business, the supervisor-employee relationship is often strengthened to the point where nonwork elements can be discussed freely.

What can an employer do to increase trust among employees?

The idea that trust and openness lead to better communication between two people also applies to groups. People engaged in organizational development (OD) are concerned with building large organizations by building effective small groups. They believe effectiveness in small groups evolves mostly from a high level of mutual trust among group members. The aim of OD is to open emotional as well as task-oriented communication. To accomplish this aim, groups often become involved in encounter sessions designed to enlarge the open areas of the Johari Window.

Nonverbal Communication. Managers use verbal and nonverbal messages to communicate a message to a recipient. Verbal means "through the use of words," either written or spoken. Nonverbal means "without the use of words." Although most concern in communication study is given to verbal messages, studies show that nonverbal messages account for approximately 93 percent of the total meaning.[3] Nonverbal communication includes *metacommunication* and *kinesic* messages.

- ● ***Metacommunication.*** A metacommunication is a message that, although *not* expressed in words, accompanies a message that *is* expressed in words. For example, "Don't be late for work" communicates caution; yet the sentence may imply (but not express in words) such additional ideas as "You are frequently late, and I'm warning you," or "I doubt your dependability" (metacommunication). "Your solution is perfect" may also convey a metacommunication such as "You are efficient," or "I certainly like your work." Whether you are speaking or writing, you can be confident that those who receive your messages will be sensitive to the messages expressed in words and to the accompanying messages that are present but not expressed in words.

- **Kinesic communication.** People constantly send meaning through kinesic communication, an idea expressed through nonverbal behavior. In other words, receivers gain additional meaning from what they see and hear—the visual and the vocal:

  - Visual—gestures, winks, smiles, frowns, sighs, attire, grooming, and all kinds of body movements.
  - Vocal—intonation, projection, and resonance of the voice.

Some examples of kinesic messages and the meanings they may convey follow:

Action	Possible Kinesic Message
A wink or light chuckle follows a statement.	*"Don't believe what I just said."*
A manager is habitually late for staff meetings.	*"My time is more important than yours. You can wait for me."*
A supervisor lightly links his arm around an employee's shoulders at the end of a formal disciplinary conference.	*"Everything is fine; I'm here to help you solve this problem."* Alternatively, the action may be considered paternalistic—a parent comforting a child after necessary discipline.
An employee smokes in areas other than those designated for smoking.	*"I don't have to obey company rules that infringe on my personal rights. A little smoke won't hurt anyone."*
A job applicant submits a résumé containing numerous spelling and grammatical errors.	*"My spelling and grammar skills are deficient."* An alternative meaning is *"For you I didn't care to do my very best."*
The supervisor looks up but then returns her attention to a current project when an employee arrives for a performance appraisal interview.	*"The performance appraisal interview is not an important process. You are interrupting more important work."*
A group leader sits at a position other than at the head of the table.	*"I want to demonstrate my equality with other members."*

What non-verbal messages might be conveyed by a job applicant? A customer? A salesperson?

Overcoming Barriers Created by Nonverbal Messages. Metacommunications and kinesic communications have characteristics that all communicators should take into account:

- **Nonverbal messages cannot be avoided. Both written and spoken words convey ideas in addition to the ideas contained in the words used.** All actions—and even the lack of action—have meaning to those who observe them.

- **Nonverbal messages may have different meanings for different people.** If a committee member smiles after making a statement, one member may conclude that the speaker was trying to be funny; another may conclude that

COMMUNICATION MENTOR

Whether you are the sender or receiver, one skill will help you more than any other. Unfortunately, this skill comes only from experience. We're talking about developing an "ear" for nuance. Most of us say as much indirectly—through inflection, pauses, accelerations, and volume changes—as we do directly.

Learning from these subtle suggestions is not analytical detective work but requires making the extra effort to lean mentally into what the other person is saying or asking and truly participating in the feeling being expressed. Also you must block out your own agenda for the time being. You will learn more from this skill than you will ever learn from so-called "body language."

James F. Hurley
Principal
Hurley Advisors

the speaker was pleased about having made such a great contribution; another may see the smile but have no reaction to it.

- **Nonverbal messages may be intentional or unintentional.** "You are right about that" may be intended to mean "I agree with you" or "You are right on *this* issue, but you have been wrong on all others discussed." The sender may or may not intend to convey the latter and may or may not be aware of doing so.

- **Nonverbal messages can contradict the accompanying verbal message, and affect whether your message is understood or believed.** If the verbal and nonverbal messages contradict, which do you suppose the receiver will believe? Exactly; the old adage "Actions speak more loudly than words" is correct. To illustrate the impact of the nonverbal message, Decker,[4] a leading communication consultant, calls to mind a person who says, "'I'm happy to be here,' but looks at the floor, talking in a halting, tremulous voice, clasping his hands together in front of his body in an edgy, inhibited 'fig-leaf' posture." His verbal and nonverbal messages are contradictory; consequently, his audience may not trust his words. Likewise, consider the detrimental effect spelling and grammatical errors in job credentials might have on a job applicant's success in an interview. The verbal message communicates impeccable qualifications. However, the interviewer receives the contradictory nonverbal message that implies the applicant is careless or has inadequate language skills. Likewise, a reader might react speculatively to "We appreciate your writing to us when you have a problem" when nothing has been done to solve the problem or to explain the lack of action.

- **Nonverbal messages may get more attention than verbal messages.** If a supervisor rhythmically taps a pen while making a statement, the words may not register in the employee's mind. An error in basic grammar may get much more attention than does the idea that is being transmitted.

- **Nonverbal messages provide clues about the sender's background and motives.** For example, excessive use of big words may suggest that a person reads widely or has an above-average education; it may also suggest a need for social recognition or insecurity about social background.

What non-verbal messages did you convey today through your attire, posture, gestures, etc.?

Strategic Forces: Diversity Challenges

Cultural Differences in Nonverbal Messages

Although no one can give a set of rules for interpreting nonverbal messages, being aware of their presence and impact will improve chances of encoding nonverbal messages effectively. International communication poses particular challenges for proper use of nonverbal signals. At the opening session of Bangladesh's new parliament in July 1996, legislators reacted with fury to a gesture by U.S. Shipping Minister A. S. M. Abdur Rob. "This is a dishonor not only to parliament but to the nation," said Dr. A. Q. M. Badruddoza Chowdhury, the Bangladesh Nationalist Party's deputy leader.

What Rob had done to provoke such anger was to give the thumbs up sign. In the United States, the gesture means "good going!" But in Bangladesh, it is a taunt; in other Islamic countries, it is an obscenity. This example is only one of the huge array of cross-cultural gaffs a naive U.S. businessperson could make on an overseas assignment.[5]

Becoming familiar with subtle and not so subtle differences in nonverbal communication in other cultures can avoid the creation of barriers to effective communication. Some cultural examples of nonverbal behavior include the following:

- The Japanese greet with a respectful bow rather than the traditional handshake. Middle Easterners may exchange kisses on the cheek as the preferred form of greeting.
- While North Americans believe that eye contact is an indicator of interest and trust, Japanese believe that lowering the eyes is a sign of respect. Asian females and many African Americans listen without direct eye contact.
- The time-conscious North American can expect to be kept waiting for an appointment in Central America, the Middle East, and other countries where the North American sentiment that "time is money" is not accepted.
- North Americans, who often slap each other on the back or put an arm around the other as a sign of friendship, receive disapproval from the Japanese, who avoid physical contact. Japanese shopkeepers place change on a plastic plate to avoid physical contact with customers.[6]

Cultural awareness includes both education and sensitivity concerning behaviors, expectations, and interpretations of persons with different backgrounds and experiences.

Application

Interview a person from another culture or subculture to determine how his or her expectations for nonverbal behavior differ from your own. Prepare a chart that shows three to five particular nonverbal actions and their meanings in each of the two cultures.

- **Nonverbal messages are influenced by the circumstances surrounding the communication.** Assume that two men, Ganesh and Sam, are friends who work for the same firm. When they are together on the job, Ganesh sometimes puts his hand on Sam's shoulder. To Sam, the act may mean nothing more than "We are close friends." But suppose Ganesh becomes a member of a committee that subsequently denies a promotion for Sam. Afterward, the same act could mean "We are still friends," but it could also arouse resentment. Because of the circumstances, the same act could now mean something like "Watch the hand that pats; it can also stab."

- **Nonverbal messages may be beneficial or harmful.** Words or actions can be accompanied by nonverbal messages that help or hurt the sender's purpose. Metacommunications and kinesic communications can convey something like "I am efficient in my business and considerate of others," or they can convey the opposite. They cannot be eliminated, but they can be made to work for communicators instead of against them.

Have you ever experienced a situation in which the verbal and nonverbal message did not agree? Describe it. Which message did you believe? Why?

Listening as an Interpersonal Skill. Most managers spend a major part of their day listening and speaking with supervisors, employees, customers, and a variety of business or industry colleagues and associates. Listening commonly consumes more of business employees' time than reading, writing, and speaking combined. Listening is an interpersonal skill as critical as the skill of speaking. Effective listening habits pay off in several ways:

How can improving your listening benefit you in your career advancement?

- Good listeners are liked by others because they satisfy the basic human needs of being heard and being wanted.
- Job performance is improved when supervisors receive and understand oral messages from their employees.
- Accurate feedback from employees provides evidence of job performance.
- Both supervisors and employees may acquire greater job security from fewer mistakes or ignored messages.
- People who listen well are able to separate fact from fiction, to cope effectively with false persuasion, and to avoid having others use them for personal gain. In other words, good listeners don't "get taken" very often.
- Listening opens doors for ideas and thus encourages creativity.
- Effective listeners are constantly learning—gaining knowledge and skills that lead to increased job performance, advancement, and satisfaction.
- Job satisfaction increases when people know what is going on, when they are heard, and when they participate in the mutual trust that develops from good communication.

Listening depends on your abilities to receive and decode both verbal and nonverbal messages. The best-devised messages and sophisticated communication systems will not work unless people on the receiving end of oral messages actually listen. Senders of oral messages must assume their receivers can and will listen, just as senders of written messages must assume their receivers can and will read.

Bad Listening Habits. Physicians must first diagnose the nature of a person's medical problems before prescribing treatment. In the same way, you can't improve your listening unless you understand some of the nonphysical ailments of your own listening. Most of us have developed bad listening habits in one or more of the following areas:

- *Faking attention.* Have you ever had an instructor call on you to respond to a question in class only to find you weren't listening? Have you ever had a parent, friend, or fellow worker ask you a question and find you weren't listening? Have you ever left a classroom lecture and later realized that you had no idea what went on? Have you ever been introduced to someone only to realize 30 seconds later that you missed the name? If you had to answer "yes" to any of these questions, join the huge club of "fakers of attention." The club is rather large because almost all people belong. Isn't it wonderful that we can look directly at a person, nod, smile, and pretend to be listening? We even fake giving feedback.
- *Allowing disruptions.* Listening properly requires both physical and emotional effort. As a result, we welcome disruptions of almost any sort when we are engaged in somewhat difficult listening. The next time someone enters your classroom or meeting room, notice how almost everyone in the room turns away from the speaker and the topic to observe the latecomer. Yielding to such disruptions begins early in life. Perhaps it is a form of curiosity.

- *Overlistening.* Overlistening occurs when listeners attempt to record in writing or in memory so many details that they miss the speaker's major points. Overlisteners "can't see the forest for the trees." An illustration of bad listening habit is the old story about college freshmen who, on the first day of class when the professor began with "Good morning," put it in their notes.

- *Stereotyping.* Most people use their prejudices and perceptions of others as a basis for developing stereotypes. As a result, we make spontaneous judgments about others based on their appearances, mannerisms, dress, speech delivery, and whatever other criteria play a role in our judgments. If a speaker doesn't meet our standards in any of these areas, we simply turn off our listening and assume the speaker can't have much to say.

- *Dismissing subjects as uninteresting.* People tend to use "uninteresting" as a rationale for not listening. Unfortunately, the decision is usually made before the topic is ever introduced. A good way to lose an instructor's respect is to ask, "Are we going to do anything important in class today?" if you have to (or want to) miss that day's class.

- *Failing to observe nonverbal aids.* Good listening requires use of eyes as well as ears. To listen effectively you must observe the speaker. Facial expressions and body motions always accompany speech and contribute much to messages. Unless you watch the speaker, you may miss the meaning.

In addition to recognizing bad listening habits and the variety of barriers to effective listening, you must recognize that listening isn't easy. Many bad listening habits develop simply because the speed of spoken messages is far slower than our ability to receive and process them. Normal speaking speeds are between 100 and 150 words a minute. The human ear can actually distinguish words in speech in excess of 500 words a minute, and many people read at speeds well beyond 500 words a minute. Finally, our minds process thoughts at thousands of words a minute.

Because individuals can't speak fast enough to challenge our ability to listen, listeners have the primary responsibility for making oral communication effective. People do seem to listen to gifted speakers, but they are rare. In everyday activities, good listening requires considerable mental and emotional effort.

Suggestions for Effective Listening. Because feedback and nonverbal signs are available, you can enhance the effectiveness of your face-to-face listening by following these suggestions:

- *Watch the speaker.* Gestures, facial expressions, and eye movements can add much to the words used and the meaning intended. If the speaker can't look you in the eye, the sincerity of the remarks may be questioned. Of course, the opposite is probably true: steady eye contact may indicate added sincerity or firmness.

- *Provide feedback.* You can acknowledge understanding, agreement, disagreement, and a variety of other feedback responses through facial expressions, sounds, and gestures. This feedback allows the speaker to provide whatever restatement or added information may be necessary or continue with the discussion.

- *Take time to listen.* Because people in face-to-face communication are serving as senders and receivers simultaneously, they may become so preoccupied with thoughts about what to say that they fail to listen.

What is your own worst listening habit? What can you do to eliminate it?

- *Use your knowledge of speakers to advantage.* In most jobs, face-to-face oral communication occurs between people who already know each other. Through experience, you will begin to recognize others' speaking and organizing traits. Some people simply seem to run on and on with details before making their point. Ask them what they had for dinner, and in reply you will probably be given recipes for each item and a description of the dining room's decor. With this type of speaker, you will learn to anticipate the major point but not pay much attention to the details. Other speakers give conclusions first and perhaps omit support for them. In this case, you will learn to ask feedback questions to obtain further information.

Listening for a Specific Purpose. Individuals listen to (1) interact socially, (2) receive information, (3) solve problems, and (4) share feelings with others. Each reason may call for a different style of listening or for a combination of styles.

- *Casual listening.* Listening for pleasure, recreation, amusement, and relaxation is casual listening. Some people have the radio on all day long; it provides background music and talk during daily routines and work periods, just as the car radio provides companionship for most commuters. Casual listening provides relaxing breaks from more serious tasks and supports our emotional health. An interesting concept about all listening, but particularly true of casual listening, is that people are selective listeners. You listen to what you want to hear. In a crowded room in which everyone seems to be talking, you can block out all the noise and engage in the conversation you are having with someone. Casual listening doesn't require much emotional or physical effort, which is one of the reasons people engage in small talk.

- *Listening for information.* Listening for information is restricted to the search for data or material. In the classroom, for example, the instructor usually has a strategy for guiding the class to desired goals. The instructor will probably stress several major points and use supporting evidence to prove or to reinforce them. When engaged in this type of listening, you could become so engrossed with recording every detail that you take copious notes without using an outline. The end result is a set of detailed notes without any organization. Understand the outlining process. When you take notes, use a logical system such as the Roman-numeral outline that uses I-A-1-a schemes to carry an outline to four levels (one major item with three degrees of subitems). If you find yourself with a lot of information beyond I-A levels, you are probably making notes of detailed information that is not essential to your success in the course.

    In the process of listening for information, watch the speaker. Most speakers have developed a set of mannerisms composed of gestures and vocal inflections to indicate the degree of importance or seriousness they attach to portions of their presentation. Above all else, listening for information requires that listeners be able to separate fact from fiction, comedy from seriousness, and truth from untruth.

    How have your class notes changed during your college career?

- *Intensive listening.* When you listen to obtain information, solve problems, or persuade or dissuade (as in arguments), you are engaged in intensive listening. Intensive listening involves greater use of your analytical ability to proceed through problem-solving steps. You should have an understanding of the problem, recognize whatever limitations are involved, and know the implications of possible solutions. Intensive listening can be achieved by following these suggestions:

- *Try to become involved in the material.* Make written or mental notes that should be introduced as feedback to the speaker. Doodling can help you assemble your ideas for drawing a meaningful solution to the problem.
- *Attempt to predict or anticipate the speaker's future points.* Listen with the speaker but try to think ahead at times as well. Thinking ahead can help you develop a sense of the speaker's logic and future points.
- *Watch speakers for any nonverbal clues.* These clues will help you understand the speaker's point of view and emotional state.
- *Try to avoid yielding to stereotypes, personal judgments, and distractions.*
- *Provide feedback to the listener.* You may give oral or nonverbal feedback, such as nods, facial expressions, or body movements to encourage further speaker comments and behavior adjustment.
- *Become a good summarizer.* When your turn comes to respond, trace the development of the discussion and then move from there with your own analysis. Feel free to "tailgate" on the ideas of others. Creative ideas are generated in an open discussion related to problem solving.

- **Empathetic listening.** Empathy occurs when a person attempts to share another's feelings or emotions. Counselors attempt to use empathetic listening in dealing with their clients. Good friends listen empathetically to each other. Empathy is a valuable trait developed by people skilled in interpersonal relations. The interesting thing about empathetic listening is that it more often than not results in reciprocal listening. When you take the time to listen to another, the courtesy is usually returned. Empathy leads to sharing.

> How would you score yourself as an empathetic listener? How can you improve? How will empathetic listening be important in your career?

Many people in positions of authority have developed excellent listening skills that apply to gaining information and to problem solving. However, an equal number of people have failed to develop good listening practices that work effectively in listening for feelings. For example, a meeting between a supervisor and an employee might go something like this:

"Stephanie, I really need to talk with you about something important."

"That so, Maria? Well, take a seat and let me hear about it," the supervisor says in a friendly tone as she continues to stare in a perplexed way at a stack of papers on her desk.

As Maria takes a seat, Stephanie continues, "Maria, you think you have a problem, eh? How would you like to have the ones I'm faced with now? First, I'm right in the middle of union negotiations for the new three-year contract; I've had several problems with our supervisory crew in the Midland plant; and somebody has botched up our inventory procedure so we're running short and will have to back-order with several customers."

Finally Stephanie asks hastily, "Well, what's your problem, Maria?"

Intimidated by her supervisor's preoccupation with her own problems and her abrupt manner, Maria decides today is not an appropriate time to get any assistance. To end the conversation without looking foolish, she quickly decides to ask a few questions about a routine procedure.

Before Maria has a chance to speak, however, the supervisor suddenly signals the end of the discussion by saying, "Maria, I have another appointment now. If you'd like, we can continue our discussion later. I want to be of help, and my door is always open to you." She returns her attention to her work before Maria moves from her chair.

Maria leaves completely frustrated, her problem still on her mind and unresolved.

Because of the supervisor's poor listening habits, Maria likely feels worse after the meeting than she did before. The supervisor learned nothing from the exchange. What if Maria's problem were company related? Good listening might have resulted in information helpful to solving the supervisor's own problems.

What specific effective listening techniques did the supervisor violate? First, the supervisor was too preoccupied with her own problems to take the time to listen for Maria's message—not to mention her feelings. Talking too much and giving strong nonverbal signals that she was not interested in what Maria had to say destroyed Maria's desire to talk. Despite the rough beginning, a gentle, empathetic, open-ended question might have encouraged Maria to share her information. Instead, the abrupt, emotion-laden question ("Well, what's your problem?") resembled a drilling question-and-answer session. (Remember, Maria did not use the word "problem" in her initial approach.)

Total empathy can never be achieved simply because no two people are exactly alike, and one can never really become the other person. The more similar our experiences, however, the better our opportunity to put ourselves in the other person's shoes. If two people have been skydiving, for example, one can appreciate how the other felt the first time. Listening with empathy involves some genuine tact along with other good listening habits. Remember that listening for feelings normally takes place in a one-to-one situation. Close friends who trust each other tend to engage in self-disclosure easily. Empathetic listening is enhanced when the participants exhibit trust and friendship. Here are some suggestions for empathetic listening:

> Can empathy be carried too far? Explain.

- *Get in step with the speaker.* Try to understand the speaker's background, prejudices, and points of view. Listen for emotionally charged words and watch for body language as clues to the speaker's underlying feelings.

- *Do not interrupt the speaker.* Try to understand the speaker's full meaning, and wait patiently for an indication that you should enter the conversation. In addition, minimize environmental and mental distractions that serve as barriers to effective listening. For example, a supervisor's closing the office door to reduce distracting noise and refusing to accept telephone calls during a performance appraisal interview enable the speaker and listener to concentrate more fully on the message.

- *Let the speaker know you are interested in listening and are an active partner in the exchange of information.* Show genuine interest by remaining physically and mentally involved; for example, avoid daydreaming, yawning, frequently breaking eye contact, looking at your watch or papers on your desk, whispering to a person nearby, and allowing numerous interruptions (telephone calls or others breaking in to ask questions). Praise the speaker for his or her willingness to share information. As a result, you can realistically expect to receive additional information from this individual. Supervisors who show genuine interest will find that they receive valuable feedback from employees. In addition, the open, trusting work environment increases employee morale and productivity.

- *Encourage the speaker to continue by providing appropriate, supportive feedback.* Develop your own encouraging signs, such as a nod of the head, a throat-clearing sound, a smile, and even an encouraging grunt.

- *Take advantage of your opportunity to speak to evaluate your understanding of the message and the speaker's feelings.* One way to check your level of understanding is to make reflective statements—an important part of effective listening. You simply restate in your own words what you think the other person has said. This paraphrasing will reinforce what you have heard and allow the speaker to correct any misunderstanding. For example, when Marcos says, "I really dislike the new production supervisor," an empathetic coworker might summarize or reflect Marcos's message by saying, "You think he isn't a nice person?" Then Marcos might say, "Oh, I don't dislike him as a person, and as supervisor he's quite good at giving instructions. The problem is he never stops long enough to find out whether I understand anything he's said. Then he's furious when the job isn't done correctly the first time." The reflective statement confirms that the listener has understood the message correctly. The statement also elicits a response that helps reveal the true source of the problem: frustration that the supervisor's communication style does not allow for feedback.

- *Use probing prompts to encourage the speaker to discuss a particular aspect of the message more thoroughly.* These prompts (statements or questions) help speakers define their problems more concretely and specifically. In the previous example of the disgruntled employee, the coworker might say, "I realize that you aren't getting along with the new production supervisor, but I'm not entirely sure what Sam does that makes you so irritated." Like the reflective statement used previously, this probing prompt summarizes Marcos's message, but it also encourages him to explore his feelings and to identify the true source of the problem—inadequate feedback.

Give other examples of situations in which combined listening is required.

Frequently you may have to combine listening intensively and listening for feelings. Performance appraisal interviews, disciplinary conferences, and other sensitive discussions between supervisors and employees require listening intensively for accurate understanding of the message and listening empathetically for feelings, preconceived points of view, and background. The interviewing process also may combine the two types of listening. Job interviewers must try to determine how someone's personality, as well as skill and knowledge, will affect job performance. You can learn more about developing effective listening skills by completing the Real-Time Internet Case at the end of this chapter.

3 *Identify factors affecting group communication.*

Communicating in Groups

Although most of your oral communication in business will occur in one-to-one relationships, your second most frequent oral communication activity will likely occur when you participate in groups, primarily groups within the organizational work environment. Group and committee work have become crucial in most organizations. Group meetings can be productive when members understand something about groups and how they operate.

Purposes of Groups. Groups form for synergistic effects; that is, through pooling their efforts, group members can achieve more collectively than they could individually. At the same time, the social nature of groups contributes to the self-maintenance goals of members. Communication in small groups leads to group decisions that are generally superior to individual decisions. The group process can motivate members, improve thinking, and assist attitude development and change. The emphasis that groups place on task and maintenance activity is based on several factors in group communication.

Factors in Group Communication. As you consider the following factors in group communication, try to visualize their relationship to some groups to which you have belonged in school, religious organizations, athletics, and social activities.

- **Common goals.** In effective groups, participants share a common goal, interest, or benefit. This focus on goals allows members to overcome individual differences of opinion and to negotiate acceptable solutions.

- **Role perception.** People who are invited to join groups have perceptions of how the group should operate and what it should achieve. In addition, each member has a self-concept that dictates fairly well how he or she will behave. Those known to be aggressive will attempt to be confrontational and forceful, and those who like to be known as moderates will behave in moderate ways by settling arguments rather than initiating them. In successful groups, members play a variety of necessary roles and seek to eliminate nonproductive ones.

- **Longevity.** Groups formed for short-term tasks such as arranging a dinner and program will spend more time on the task than on maintenance. However, groups formed for long-term assignments such as an audit of a major corporation by a team from a public accounting firm may devote much effort to maintenance goals. Maintenance refers to division of duties, scheduling, record keeping, reporting, and assessing progress.

- **Size.** The smaller the group, the more its members have the opportunity to communicate with each other. Conversely, large groups often inhibit communication because the opportunity to speak and interact is limited. When broad input is desired, large groups may be good. When expert opinion is the goal, smaller groups may be more effective. Interestingly, large groups generally divide into smaller groups for maintenance purposes, even when the large group is task oriented. Although much research has been conducted in the area of group size, no optimal number of members has been identified. Groups of five to seven members are thought to be best for decision-making and problem-solving tasks. An odd number of members is preferred because deciding votes are possible, and tie votes are infrequent.

- **Status.** Some group members will appear to be better qualified than others. Consider a group in which the chief executive of the organization is a member. When the chief executive speaks, members agree. When members speak, they tend to direct their remarks to the one with high status—the chief executive. People are inclined to communicate with peers as their equals, but they tend to speak upward to their supervisor and downward to lower-level employees. In general, groups require balance in status and expertise rather than homogeneity.

- **Group norms.** A **norm** is a standard or average behavior. All groups possess norms. An instructor's behavior helps establish classroom norms. If an instructor is generally late for class, students will begin to arrive late. If the instructor permits talking during lectures, the norm will be for students to talk. People conform to norms because conformity is easy and nonconformity

Recall a group of which you were a member. Why was the group formed? Was more time spent on task or maintenance goals? Why? How effective was the leader in facilitating the group's success (accomplishing the task and developing each individual's and the group's maintenance goals)? Explain.

What is the ideal size group? What factors would affect your response?

Often when someone in the workplace is ready to tell you something, you are not ready to listen. If the subject is important enough, don't hesitate to say, "Before I can pay full attention to you, I really need to finish this report (or whatever is distracting)." After clearing the decks, then give the communicator your full attention and listen intently.

When hearing a complex message, you may want to use the technique of "playing back" to the speaker what you have understood. When you can restate what you think someone said in your own words, you can be assured you have both heard and understood the message.

Cynthia Pharr, President
C. Pharr & Company, Inc.

is difficult and uncomfortable. Conformity leads to acceptance by other group members and creates communication opportunities.

- *Leadership.* The performance of groups depends on several factors, but none is more important than leadership. Some hold the mistaken view that leaders are not necessary when an organization moves to a group concept. The role of leaders changes substantially, but they still have an important part to play. The ability of a group leader to work toward task goals while contributing to the development of group and individual maintenance goals is often critical to group success. In these group activities, leadership activities may be shared among several participants. Leadership may also be rotated, formally or informally. The leader can establish norms, determine who can speak and when, encourage everyone to contribute, and provide the motivation for effective group activity.[7]

Group Roles. Groups are made up of members who play a variety of roles, both positive and negative. Negative roles detract from the group's purposes and include the following:

Which role do you view as being most destructive to group function?

- *Isolated*—one who is physically present but fails to participate
- *Dominator*—one who speaks too often and too long
- *Free rider*—one who does not do his/her fair share of the work
- *Detractor*—one who constantly criticizes and complains
- *Digresser*—one who deviates from the group's purpose
- *Airhead*—one who is never prepared
- *Socializer*—one who pursues only the social aspect of the group

Perhaps you recognize one or more of the negative roles, based on your personal group experiences. Or perhaps your group experiences have been positive as a result of members' playing positive group roles that promote the group's purposes:

- *Facilitator (also known as gatekeeper)*—one who makes sure everyone gets to talk and be heard
- *Harmonizer*—one who keeps tensions low
- *Record keeper*—one who maintains records of events and activities and informs members

Strategic Forces: Team Environment

From Groups to Teams

While some use the terms *group* and *team* interchangeably, others distinguish between the terms. The major distinction between a group and a team is in members' attitudes and level of commitment. A team is typified by a clear identity and a high level of commitment on the part of members. A variety of strategies have been used for organizing workers into teams. Task forces are generally given a single goal with a limited time to achieve it. Quality assurance teams, or quality circles, focus on product or service quality, and projects can be either short- or long-term. Cross-functional teams bring together employees from various departments to solve a variety of problems, including productivity issues, contract estimations and planning, and multidepartment difficulties. Product development teams concentrate on innovation and the development cycle of new products and are usually cross-functional in nature. Work teams are typically given the authority to act on their conclusions, although the level of authority varies, depending on the organization and the purpose of the team. Typically, the group supervisor retains some responsibilities, some decisions are made completely by the team, and the rest are made jointly.[7]

Merely placing workers into a group does not make them a functional team. A group must go through a developmental process to begin to function as a team. To begin, team members need training in such areas as problem solving, goal setting, conflict resolution, risk taking, active listening, and recognizing the interests and achievement of others. The three basic needs of any team member are belonging, personal recognition, and support. The successful team member exhibits the following 4 C's:[8]

- **Commitment.** He or she is focused on the mission, values, goals, and expectations of the team and the organization.
- **Cooperation.** He or she has a shared sense of purpose, mutual gain, and teamwork.
- **Communication.** Information must flow smoothly between top management and workers. Team members must be willing to face confrontation and unpleasantness when necessary.
- **Contribution.** All members share their different backgrounds, skills, and abilities with the team.

Organizational changes are also often necessary since teams are a systems approach to an organization. Support must be in place through the performance evaluation recognition, communication, and training systems. Strategies for bringing about needed change might include arranging site visits to similar organizations that already have teams, bringing a successful team to speak to the organization, and bringing in consultants to discuss the team development process.

Teams have existed for hundreds of years throughout many countries and cultures. Teams are more flexible than larger organizational groupings because they can be assembled, deployed, refocused, and disbanded more quickly, usually in ways that enhance rather than disrupt more permanent structures and processes. Most models of the "organization of the future" are networked, clustered, nonhierarchical, and horizontal. They are organized on the idea that teams surpass individuals as the primary performance unit in the organization.

Application

Locate articles on the use of teams in business and industry. Write a short report that presents the advantages of using teams in organizations. Then include a discussion of the challenges associated with the use of teams. Conclude with a list of recommendations for using teams effectively.

- *Reporter*—one who assumes responsibility for preparing materials for submission
- *Leader*—one who assumes a directive role

In healthy groups, members may fulfill multiple roles, which rotate as the need arises. Negative roles are extinguished as the group communicates openly about its goals, strategies, and expectations. The opinions and viewpoints of all members are encouraged and expected. The Strategic Forces box on page 61 explores the differences between groups and teams.

What group roles have you played? What is the result?

Communicating in Organizations

4 *Identify factors leading to the need for formal organizations.*

A formal organization and a group are made up of individuals, and both have goals. However, organizations can accomplish some things individuals and groups cannot do by or for themselves. For example, the task goals of individuals and groups may generate such complicated and sizable endeavors that a more formal organizational structure is necessary to accomplish them.

Organizational structure is the overall design of an organization, much like a blueprint developed to meet the company's specific needs and to enhance its ability to accomplish goals. A company's organizational structure is depicted graphically in an organization chart. It helps define the scope of the organization and assists people in getting a total view of a large, formal organization with employees performing specialized tasks yet working interdependently to accomplish common goals.

Consider the example of a small community bank that expands beyond the current management's ability to cope with it. In this case, the community bank concentrates on providing personal loan and mortgage financing. Suddenly this sleepy little town is awakened by an outburst of expansion—amusement parks, restaurants, hotels, outlet malls, and modern shopping centers. Soon, the bank is issuing multimillion dollar commercial loans. An in-house investment brokerage service is added to provide customers a convenient vehicle for investing in the stock market. Because customers are demanding service at other locations, the bank opens a full-service branch in a newly developed shopping center in the center of the new-growth area.

Specialization of Individuals and Units. The expanded bank needs more employees and skills not currently available to handle the expanded business. Bank employees must be equipped to evaluate and manage corporate loans; provide up-to-the-minute, accurate investment advice; develop effective advertising campaigns for the bank's expanded services and new locations; and exercise control over a variety of other activities.

To exercise the necessary control over the wide range of activities, management has reorganized the large organization into a **functional organizational structure** as shown in Figure 2-2. Employees are grouped into smaller, separate departments on the basis of common tasks: lending and trust, operations, and fund-raising. Within these departments, further specialization of labor occurs. Lending and trust, for example, has specialists in three areas: commercial loans and mortgages, personal loans, and trusts. As the complexity of the undertaking increases, employees continue to become even more specialized.

How does communication change as an organization grows and alters its internal structure?

Independence of Units and Individuals. Because of the specialization in a large, functional organization, each of the smaller departments is dependent on the other units to some extent. Efforts by the lending and trust staff are very much dependent on the level of funds raised by the fund-raising department. A high degree of the bank's

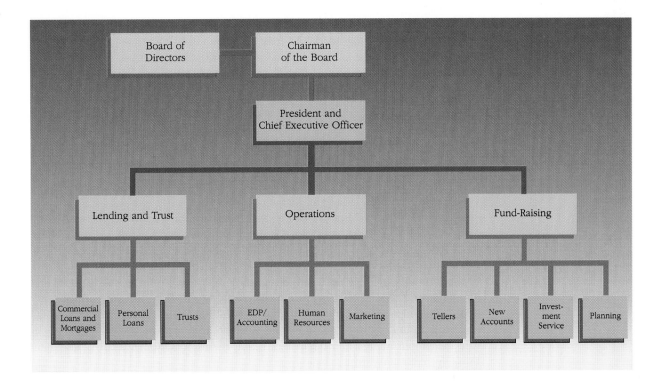

FIGURE 2-2 Organizational Chart: Citizens' Bank.

success rests on these departments' maintaining an appropriate spread between the interest rates charged on loans issued by the lending and trust department and interest earned on moneys raised by the fund-raising department. Regular reports from these units provide the basis for an efficient record keeping system that can, in turn, provide information to assist management in planning and decision making.

Within each of these departments, specialization of people leads to interdependence of individuals and among departments. All, however, are organized so that the goals of the organization can be achieved. In the everyday work of the organization, the task goals of the total organization exist side by side with the group maintenance goals of the departmental units and the self-maintenance goals of the individuals involved. The interdependence of units and individuals applies equally to both task goals and maintenance goals.

To achieve its goals, the organization needs to direct and coordinate the interdependent units and individuals. The organizational structure develops to facilitate the communication networks needed to accomplish the goals. The original community bank in our example needs the functional organizational structure now that it has grown into a large full-service bank with numerous *specialized, interdependent* departments.

Many companies have realized that the traditional hierarchy organized around functional units is inadequate for coping or competing in the increasingly competitive global markets. Companies are organizing work teams that integrate work-flow processes rather than having specialists who deal with a single function or product. These cross-functional work teams break down the former barriers between isolated functional departments. Each employee, from the president to the custodian, is empowered to make decisions that will improve the quality of the company's products and services to satisfy the customer.

How can an organization empower its employees?

Implementation of Management Styles. Douglas McGregor, a management theorist, attempted to distinguish between the older, traditional view that workers are concerned only about satisfying lower-level needs and the modern view that production can be enhanced by assisting workers in satisfying higher-level needs. Under the older view, management exercised strong control, emphasized the job to the exclusion of concern for the individual, and sought to motivate solely through external incentives—a job and a paycheck. McGregor labeled this management style Theory X. Under the modern style, Theory Y, management strives to balance control and individual freedom. By treating the individual as a mature person, management lessens the need for external motivation: treated as adults, people will act as adults. Combining Maslow's and McGregor's ideas leads to the conclusion that "the right job for the person" is a better philosophy than "the right person for the job."

The Total Quality Management movement draws on McGregor's assumptions about Theory Y management, thus creating a more responsible role for the worker in an organization. In a Total Quality Management environment, decision-making power is distributed to the people closest to the problem, those who usually have the best information sources and solutions. Each employee, from the president to the custodian, is expected to solve problems, participate in team-building efforts, and expand the scope of his or her role in the organization. The goal of employee empowerment is to build a work environment in which all employees take pride in their work accomplishments and begin motivating themselves from within rather than through traditional extrinsic incentives.[9]

Earlier efforts to develop greater job satisfaction have involved workers in "team" and "quality circle" programs. Voluntary groups of workers met periodically with supervisors or management to identify production problems and propose solutions. Many quality circles did not receive support from top management, and employees were not empowered to carry through with their solutions. In contrast, today the top managers of many companies understand that empowering employees to initiate continuous improvements is critical for survival. Only companies producing quality products and services will survive in today's world market.

Communication Barriers Caused by a Functional Organizational Structure.
Management designs organizational structures as a means of coordinating and controlling the behavior of members and units. However, communication problems are introduced by rigid organizational structure.

Does position on the organizational chart indicate an employee's power in the organization? Why?

- *Unclear indication of role vs. status.* Traditionally, organization charts have been used to describe the authority structure of the organization. People in higher positions on the chart appear to have greater authority (status) than those at lower levels. If used to describe communication in the organization, however, the chart may be entirely inadequate in revealing communication roles. May people communicate only with those immediately above or below them; that is, only with those employees whose positions on the chart are connected to theirs by an uninterrupted line? Is each department on the chart autonomous and shielded from relationships with other departments? If units and individuals depend on one another, the chart does not define the communication structure.

    The organization chart does not necessarily define the relative importance of each department or individual participating in the organization. The chairman of the board occupies the highest spot on the chart, but the actual role may have little to do with the success or failure of the organization. The administrative assistant to an executive or someone in human resources, for example, may play a role considerably more authoritative and powerful than the position's status on the chart would indicate. **Role** is an informal part; **status** is a formal position based on the organization chart or other prescribed functions.

- *Excessive competition.* Organizational structure affects the behavior of individuals and units within the organization. Traditionally, organizations have had tall, pyramid-shaped organizational structures. The higher a person is on the pyramid, the greater the apparent authority and rewards. Most people probably strive for a higher position on the pyramid. This striving may determine relationships with peers, lower-level employees, and supervisors. Competition has become a characteristic of the way of life in U.S. companies. People and organizations compete for a greater share of scarce resources, for a limited number of positions at the top of organizations, and for esteem in their professions. Such competition is a healthy sign of the human desire to succeed, and, in terms of economic behavior, competition is fundamental to the private enterprise system. At the same time, when excessive competition replaces the cooperation necessary for success, communication may be diminished, if not eliminated.

What places do competition and cooperation have in contemporary organizations?

Just as you want to look good in the eyes of your peers, lower-level employees, and supervisors, units within organizations want to look good to one another. This attitude may cause behavior to take the competitive form, a "win/lose" philosophy. When excessive competition has a negative influence on the performance of the organization, everyone loses.

Most conflict among people and groups results from a lack of understanding. When one unit is uninformed about the importance or function of another, needless conflicts may occur as groups attempt to better themselves at the expense of others. Interestingly enough, a group engaged in competition tends to solidify and become cohesive with great internal group morale. As a consequence, the competitive spirit of the group may intensify and lead to further deterioration of communication with other groups.

Stephen Covey's experience with a company president illustrates this point. The president described his employees as selfish, uncooperative, and not as productive as he believed they could be. He insisted they had no reason not to cooperate. However, Covey found a chart behind a curtain on a wall of the president's office that contained a number of racehorses with the faces of the managers superimposed on the racehorses. At the end of the racetrack was a picture of Bermuda. Once a week the president would bring the managers in and ask them, "Now which of you is going to win a trip to Bermuda?"[10] He wanted his people to benefit from working together, but he set them up in competition with one another so that one manager's success meant failure for the others.

Although competition is appropriate and desirable in many situations, management must take steps through open communication and information and reward systems to reduce competition and to increase cooperation. Cooperation is more likely when the competitors (individuals or groups within an organization) have an understanding of and appreciation for others' importance and functions. This cooperative spirit is characterized as a win/win philosophy. One person's success is not achieved at the expense or exclusion of another. Employees need to identify a solution that everyone finds satisfactory and is committed to achieving. Reaching this mutual understanding requires a high degree of trust and effective interpersonal skills, particularly empathetic and intensive listening skills and the willingness to communicate long enough to agree on an action plan that is acceptable to everyone.

Businesses today are streamlining their operations, often referred to as downsizing, rightsizing, or reengineering. How is this process affecting organizational charts? The communication process?

- *Flat organizational structures.* Businesses today are downsizing and eliminating layers of management. Companies implementing Total Quality Management programs are reorganizing to distribute the decision-making power throughout the organization. As mentioned, the trend is to eliminate functional or departmental boundaries (e.g., lending and trust and fund-raising). Instead, work is reorganized in cross-disciplinary teams that perform broad core processes (e.g., product development and sales generation) and not narrow tasks such as forecasting market demand for a particular product. In a flat organizational structure, communicating across the organization chart (among the cross-functional teams) becomes more important than communicating up and down in a top-heavy hierarchy. Communication is enhanced because the message must travel shorter distances. Much of the communication involves face-to-face meetings with team members rather than numerous, time-consuming "handoffs" as the product moves methodically from one department to another.

    The time needed to design a new card at Hallmark Cards decreased significantly when the company adopted a flat organizational structure. Team members representing the former functional areas (graphic artists, writers, marketers, and others) now work in a central area, communicating openly and frequently, solving problems and making decisions about the entire process as a card is being developed. For example, a writer struggling with a verse for a new card can solicit immediate input from the graphic artist working on the team rather than finalizing the verse and then "handing it off" to the art department.[11]

5 *Discuss how information flows within an organization (formally and informally; and downward, upward, and horizontally).*

Communication Flow in Organizations

Communication occurs in a variety of ways in an organization; some communication flow is planned and structured; some is not. Some communication flow can be formally depicted, while some defies description.

Formal and Informal Channels

The flow of communication within an organization follows both formal and informal channels. The **formal communication** channel is typified by the formal organization chart, which is created by management to control individual and group behavior and to achieve the organization's goals. Essentially, the formal system is dictated by the technical, political, and economic environment of the organization. Within this system, people are required to behave in certain ways simply to get the work done. Because it is dictated by environmental forces existing outside the needs of the individuals in the organization, the formal communication channel system is also called an *external system.*

The **informal communication** channel develops as people interact within the formal, external system, and certain behavior patterns emerge—patterns that accommodate social and psychological needs. To distinguish between the two systems, return to Citizens' Bank and its organization chart. After the bank expansion, the president chose to continue working in the personal loan department, which is subordinate to and apparently has a reporting relationship to the operations department. Quite likely, however, the people in the operations department do not give the president a bad time. The behavior of these employees in the external system is minimal

Businesspeople often speak informally about on-the-job issues. This communication network is referred to as "the grapevine"—a valuable source of accurate information as well as rumor.

and just enough to get the work done. In the internal system, or informal, however, their behavior is adapted, depending on their personal perceptions of the president.

Communication Flow in Action

When employees rely almost entirely on the formal external communication system as a guide to behavior, the system might be identified as a *bureaucracy*. Procedures manuals, job descriptions, organization charts, and other written materials dictate the required behavior. Communication channels are followed strictly, and red tape is abundant. Procedures are generally followed exactly; terms such as *rules* and *policy* serve as sufficient reasons for actions. Even the most formal organizations cannot function long without an internal communication system emerging. As people operate within the external system, they must interact on a person-to-person basis and create an environment conducive to satisfying their personal emotions, prejudices, likes, and dislikes.

In the college classroom, for example, the student behavior required to satisfy the external system is to attend class, take notes, read the text, and pass examinations. On the first day of class, this behavior probably is typical of almost all students, particularly if they did not know one another prior to attending the class. As the class progresses, however, the internal system emerges and overlaps the external system. Students become acquainted, sit next to people they particularly like, talk informally, and may even plan ways to beat the external system. Cutting class and borrowing notes are examples. Soon, these behaviors become norms for class behavior. Students who do not engage in the internal system may be viewed with disdain by the others. Obviously, the informality of the internal system is good for people because it helps satisfy maintenance goals. At the same time, it affects communication.

The Grapevine as an Informal Communication System

The **grapevine**, often called the *rumor mill*, is perhaps the best-known internal communication system. It is actually a component of the internal system. As people talk casually during coffee breaks and lunch periods, the focus usually shifts from topic to topic. One of the topics most certainly would be work—job, company, supervisor,

Managers who ignore the grapevine have difficulty achieving organizational goals. Think about a situation you have experienced in which an instructor/ adviser/employer used the grapevine effectively or ineffectively. What was the result?

fellow employees. Even though the external system has definite communication channels, the grapevine tends to develop and operate within the organization.

As a communication channel, the grapevine is reputed to be speedy but inaccurate. In the absence of alarms, the grapevine may be the most effective way to let occupants know that the building is on fire. It certainly beats sending a written memorandum.

While the grapevine often is thought of as a channel for inaccurate communication, in reality, it is no more or less accurate than other channels. Even formal communication may become inaccurate as it passes from level to level in the organizational hierarchy. The inaccuracy of the grapevine has more to do with the message input than with the output. For example, the grapevine is noted as a carrier of rumor, primarily because it carries informal messages. If the input is rumor, and nothing more, the output obviously will be inaccurate. But the output may be an accurate description of the original rumor.

For a college student, the grapevine carries much valuable information. Even though the names of the choice instructors may not be published, students learn those names through the grapevine. How best to prepare for certain examinations, instructor attitudes on attendance and homework, and even future faculty personnel changes are messages that travel over the grapevine. In the business office, news about promotions, personnel changes, company policy changes, and annual salary adjustments often are communicated by the grapevine long before being disseminated by formal channels.

A misconception about the grapevine is that the message passes from person to person until it finally reaches a person who can't pass it on—the end of the line. Actually, the grapevine works through a variety of channels. Typically, one person tells two or three others, who each tell two or three others, who each tell two or three others, and so on. Thus, the message may spread to a huge number of people in a very short time. Additionally, the grapevine has no single, consistent source. Messages may originate anywhere and follow various routes. More will be said about sources and routes later in this chapter.

An informal, internal communication system will emerge from even the most carefully designed formal, external system. Managers who ignore this fact are attempting to manage blindfolded. Carroll M. Perkins, general manager of the Salt River Project in Phoenix, recommends that managers "learn to *use* the informal communication network rather than condemn or resist it. After two major workforce reductions at the Salt River Project, a rumor spread that a third layoff was imminent. The grapevine was as useful in counteracting the rumor as it was in spreading false information."[12]

Yet some managers do try to work exclusively with the external system. Achieving organizational goals must be extremely difficult for them. As long as people interact, the organization will have both systems.

> Share a personal communication experience that involved the grapevine as an information source. How reliable was the message you sent or received? How time-efficient was the message transmission?

Directions for Communication Flow

The direction in which communication flows in an organization may be downward, upward, or horizontal, as shown in Figure 2-3. Because these three terms are used frequently in communication literature, they deserve clarification. Although the concept of flow seems simple, direction has meaning for those participating in the communication process.

Downward Communication. **Downward communication** flows from supervisor to employee, from policy makers to operating personnel, or from top to bottom on the organization chart. As messages move downward through successive levels of

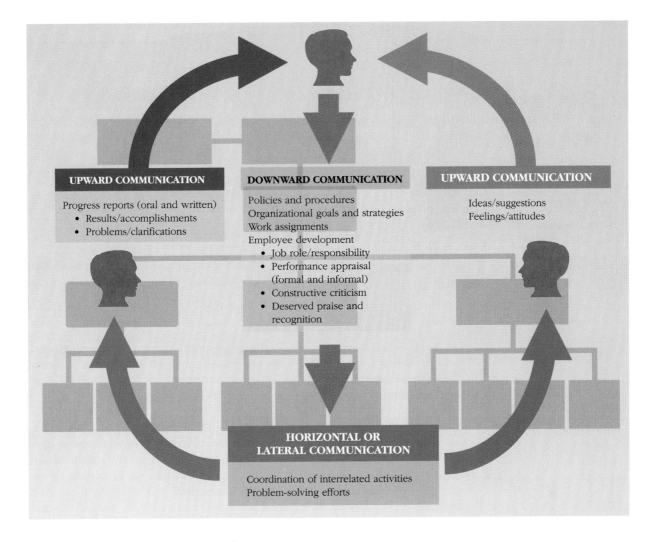

FIGURE 2-3 Flow of information within an organization.

the organization, they seem to get larger. A simple policy statement from the top of the organization may grow into a formal plan for operation at lower levels.

Teaching people how to perform their specific tasks is an element of downward communication. Another element is orientation to a company's rules, practices, procedures, history, and goals. Employees learn about the quality of their job performance through downward communication.

Downward communication normally involves both written and oral methods and makes use of the following guidelines:

- People high in the organization usually have greater knowledge of the organization and its goals than do people at lower levels.

- Both oral and written messages tend to become larger as they move downward through organizational levels. This expansion results from attempts to prevent distortion and is more noticeable in written messages.

- Oral messages are subject to greater changes in meaning than are written messages.

What would be an appropriate "rule of thumb" for a manager in deciding whether to send a written message to subordinates?

In the Soviet/Russian culture, communication flowed only one way—down. Our challenge has been to reverse this pattern, teaching our Russian staff that to provide quality service to our customers, we must communicate with each other at least as much, if not more, than with our clients. This open communication flow (upward and downward) also builds trust and confidence, which are important as we develop this practice.

The "open-door" policy was also alien to the Russian culture; young staff would not consider walking into their Russian General Director's (similar to a president in the West) office to discuss a problem. In the former U.S.S.R., knowledge/information was power. Knowledge was shared only when doing so was personally beneficial—compartmentalization in its most specific and detailed form.

Lawrence E. Wilson, Partner
Arthur Andersen, Moscow

As discussed in Chapter 1, the receiver's reaction to a message is called *feedback*. When a supervisor sends a message to a lower-level employee who then asks a question or nods assent, the question and the nod are signs of feedback. Feedback may flow both downward and upward in organizational communication.

Upward Communication. Upward communication generally is feedback to downward communication. Although necessary and valuable, upward communication does contain risks. When management requests information from lower organizational levels, the resulting information becomes feedback to that request. Employees talk to supervisors about themselves, their fellow employees, their work and methods of doing it, and their perceptions of the organization. These comments are feedback to the downward flow transmitted in both oral and written form by group meetings, procedures or operations manuals, company news releases, and the grapevine.

Accurate upward communication keeps management informed about the feelings of lower-level employees, taps the expertise of employees, helps management identify both difficult and potentially promotable employees, and paves the way for even more effective downward communication. Employees reporting upward are aware that their communications carry the risk of putting them on the spot. They might commit themselves to something they cannot handle, or they might communicate incorrectly.

Employees appreciate and welcome genuine opportunities to send information to management. They are likely to feel better about themselves and their purpose in the organization. On the other hand, they will likely resent and perhaps react harshly to any superficial attempt to provide an open communication network with management.

These factors, then, are important to consider when upward communication flow is involved.

What do you believe would be the typical communication patterns of a manager working under a win/lose philosophy? Under a win/win philosophy?

- Upward communication is primarily feedback to requests and actions of supervisors.

- Upward communication may be misleading because lower-level employees often tell the superior what they think the superior wants to hear. Therefore, their messages might contradict their true observations and perceptions.

COMMUNICATION IN ACTION

Lonny Uzzell, Southside Bank

When Southside Bank opened its doors in November, 1960, as an independent and locally owned bank, its founders knew that responsiveness to customers was crucial to its success. Today, the bank has a strong community reputation for responsiveness to customers. Having kept the same name for more than 37 years, the bank has maintained stability and demonstrated steady growth. The bank employs more than 300 personnel and manages assets of over $400 million. What elements have been key to this success? What role does business communication play in the bank's stability and growth?

Lonny Uzzell, executive vice president at Southside, believes key elements underlie Southside's success: responsiveness and sensitivity to customers' needs through effective listening and accurate feedback. Uzzell recounts the recent updating of the bank's computer system as an example. The system has undergone several major changes in recent months, requiring bank officers to inform customers of changes. Uzzell stated, "As a result of the transition between computer systems, customers received two bank statements one month; one from the old system and one from the new system. These changes created many questions and made communication with the customer extremely important." Letters were sent to customers about the change. Then, in response to questions, Southside organized incoming calls that allowed customers to talk with individual officers about their accounts. As a bank officer who helps train and develop Southside employees, Uzzell knows well that good listening with customers is not just important to his work. It is essential to the bank's profitability.

Bank employees demonstrate responsiveness in other ways. When Uzzell meets someone in the lobby, telephones a customer, or responds to a bank customer through a letter, he listens and treats customers as if they are special. In doing so, he knows that customers receiving any less than special treatment may choose a competitor. When Uzzell talks with customers, he fully understands the concept of "relationship marketing." Personalized service at Southside is as important to customers as interest rates and investments. Today's bank clients demand better, more personalized service.

Not only must Uzzell listen well to customers, he must listen and respond to other bank employees. During a normal work day, he interacts with and listens to employees in different departments and throughout all levels of the bank's organization. Without good listening skills, he would not be successful at his work. Uzzell develops good relationships and quality service through good listening.

Applying What You Have Learned

1. During the working day, how does Mr. Uzzell experience listening in the four levels of communication?

2. Identify various directions in the flow of listening at the bank. How does good listening and timely, accurate feedback facilitate communication when a new computer system is installed?

3. Reflect on your own experiences with a bank. How did your interpersonal communication with bank employees make that experience positive or negative?

4. Using the organization chart for Citizens' Bank of Springfield in Figure 2-2 as a sample, distinguish between formal and informal communication at Southside Bank. Provide several examples to illustrate the two distinct systems.

- Upward communication is based on trust in the supervisor.
- Upward communication frequently involves risk to an employee.
- Employees will reject superficial attempts by management to obtain feedback from employees.

How can a manager maximize the effectiveness of horizontal communication among subordinates?

Horizontal Communication. Horizontal, or lateral, communication describes interactions between organization units on the same hierarchical level. These interactions reveal one of the major shortcomings of organizational charts. Charts do not allow much room for horizontal communication when they depict authority relationships by placing one box higher than another and define role functions by placing titles in those boxes. Yet horizontal communication is the primary means of achieving coordination in a functional organizational structure.

Management must recognize that informal, horizontal communication takes place in any system or organization where people are available to one another. The informal communication and behavior that is not task oriented develop alongside formal task communication and behavior, contributing to morale, to improvements in ways to accomplish tasks, and to clarification of upward and downward communication. Formal horizontal communication serves a coordinating function in the organization. Units coordinate their activities to accomplish task goals just as adjacent workers in a production line coordinate their activities.

In an organization divided into cross-functional teams, horizontal communication among the team members is extremely important to achieve individual and team goals. Total Quality Management experts emphasize that honest, open communication is the single most important factor in successfully creating a Total Quality Management environment. Hunt, a TQM author, emphasizes, "If people keep talking to one another, they can work through their problems, overcome barriers, and find encouragement and support from others involved in quality efforts." [13]

SUMMARY

1. **Identify the four levels of communication.** Communication takes place at four levels: intrapersonal (communication within one person), interpersonal (communication between two people), group, and organizational. Appropriate nonverbal behavior and effective listening are important elements in interpersonal communication. Groups and organizations exist because people working together can accomplish more and make better decisions than can the same people working individually.

2. **Explain how behavioral theories (Maslow's human needs, stroking, and the Johari Window), nonverbal communication, and listening affect interpersonal communication.**

   - Human needs theory, nonverbal communication, and listening are essential aspects of interpersonal communication. The needs of all individuals to be heard, appreciated, wanted, and reinforced significantly affect their interpersonal communications.

   - Nonverbal communication conveys a significant portion of meaning and includes metacommunications, which are wordless messages that accompany words and kinesic communications that are expressed through body language.

   - Effective listening, which requires effort and discipline, is crucial to effective interpersonal communication and leads to career success.

3. **Identify factors affecting group communication.** Effective group communication results from shared purpose, constructive activity and behaviors, and positive role fulfillment among members. A team is a special type of group that is typified by strong commitment among members; this commitment results in behaviors that produce synergy.

4. **Identify factors leading to the need for formal organizations.** As tasks increase in size and complexity, specialization is required and interdependence of individuals and departments is critical. These elements are coordinated through application of an appropriate management style in order to control and coordinate the work of the organization. Communication barriers arise from functional organizational structures that must be successfully overcome.

5. **Discuss how information flows within an organization (formally and informally; and downward, upward, and horizontally).** Both formal (external) and informal (internal) communication systems exist in every organization. The formal system exists to accomplish

tasks, and the informal system serves a personal maintenance purpose that results in people feeling better about themselves and others. Because these systems operate simultaneously, a modified system emerges that combines qualities of both. Communication flows upward, downward, and horizontally or laterally. These flows often defy the ability of management to describe them graphically, yet each should be viewed as a necessary part of the overall communication activity of the organization.

REFERENCES

[1]Chen, E. (1996, December 10). Empowerment as a source of motivation. *New Straits Time (Malaysia)*, p. 11.

[2]Kleiman, C. (1997, February 16). Concern for workers' private lives is just good business. *Chicago Tribune*, Jobs, p. 1.

[3]Mehrabian, A. (1971). *Silent messages.* Belmont, CA: Wadsworth.

[4]Decker, B. (1992). *You've got to be believed to be heard.* NY: St. Martin's Press.

[5]Axtell, R. E. (1997, April). Watch what you say: Hand gestures mean different things to different people. *Reader's Digest*, 71–72.

[6]Flannigan, T. (1990), Successful negotiating with the Japanese. *Small Business Reports*, 15(6), 47–52.

[7]Zuidema, K. R., & Kleiner, B. H. (1994, October). Self-directed work groups gain popularity. *Business Credit*, 21–26.

[8]Hunt, V. D. (1993). *Managing for quality: Integrating quality and business strategy.* Homewood, IL: Business One Irwin. [p. 121].

[9]Felts, C. (1995). Taking the mystery out of self-directed work teams. *Industrial Management*, 37(2), 21–26.

[10]Covey, S. (1989). *The seven habits of successful people: Powerful lessons in personal change.* New York: Simon & Schuster. [206].

[11]Hillkirk, J. (1993, November 9). More companies reengineering: Challenging status quo now in vogue. *USA Today*, p. 1b.

[12]Himstreet, W. C., Baty, W. M., & Lehman, C. M., (1993). *Business communications* (10th ed.) Belmont, CA: Wadsworth. [p. 17].

[13]Hunt, V. D. (1993). *Managing for quality: Integrating quality and business strategy.* Homewood, IL: Business One Irwin. [p. 37].

[14]Bly, A., & Bly. R. W. (1997). Improving your listening skills. [On-line]. Available http://www.smartbiz.com/sbs/arts/bly55.htm [1998, February 16].

REVIEW QUESTIONS

1. What is the difference between interpersonal and intrapersonal communication? (Obj. 1)

2. Why are four levels of communication necessary in a healthy organization? (Obj. 1)

3. How can managers use Maslow's need levels, stroking, and the Johari Window to improve interpersonal communication with employees? (Obj. 2)

4. When a manager says to the sales staff, "Let's try to make budget this year," what are some of the possible metacommunications? (Obj. 2)

5. What is meant by stroking? How does it affect interpersonal communication in the workplace? (Obj. 2)

6. Discuss six bad listening habits. Which do you think is the biggest challenge for you personally? (Obj. 2)

7. Synergy results from effective group work. What is synergy? (Obj. 3)

8. Why is an odd number of group members frequently desirable? (Obj. 3)

9. How might the pyramid shape of an organization chart affect individual and group performance? (Obj. 3)

10. What is a possible cause of most conflict between or among groups? (Obj. 3)

11. How are a group and a team different? (Obj. 3)

12. What four factors combine to characterize large, formal organizations? (Obj. 4)

13. How has the Total Quality Management movement extended the work of McGregor? How does this movement differ from the use of quality circles to increase job satisfaction popular in the 1980s? (Obj. 4)

14. List three barriers caused by formal organizational structure. (Obj. 4)

15. How might an organization chart fail to indicate the relative importance of positions or individuals on the chart? (Obj. 4)

16. Discuss how a flat organizational structure affects communication. (Obj. 4)

17. What is the system of organizational communication called when it relies on rules, procedures, and formalities? (Obj. 5)

18. Explain how the grapevine in an organization can be both a positive and a negative channel for information. (Obj. 5)

19. Why do downward messages tend to become larger as they travel through upward-downward communication channels? (Obj. 5)

20. Discuss the benefits and risks inherent in upward communication. (Obj. 5)

EXERCISES

1. **Depicting Levels of Communication (Obj. 1)**
   Visually depict the relationship between the four levels of communication.

2. **Recognizing Events that Involve Metacommunication (Obj. 2)**
   Keep a journal over the next two to five days that records events that involve metacommunication. Describe how each incident influences the understanding of the verbal message involved.

3. **Locating Information on Nonverbal Communication in Other Cultures (Obj. 2)**
   Locate one or more articles in the library or over the Internet that discuss nonverbal communication in various cultures. Compile a list of gestures that have different meanings among cultures. Discuss how ignorance of these differences might affect interpersonal communication.

4. **Analyzing Group Experiences (Obj. 3)**
   Analyze a group experience you have had in the past; it might be a class project, club activity, or other situation. What were the strong factors of the group? What were the weak factors of the group? What roles, both positive and negative, were played out in the group?

5. **Discussing the Impact of Flat Organizational Structure on Communication (Obj. 4)**
   Using the on-line database in your library, locate an article about a company that has adopted a flat organizational structure. Write a brief summary emphasizing the effect this change in organizational structure has had on the communication process.

6. **Understanding the Grapevine's Effect on Communication (Obj. 5)**
   In groups assigned by your instructor, complete the following activity: (a) Select one group member to develop a short message (instructor may provide one). The first member whispers this message to the second member, the second member to the third member, and so on. Finally, the first member repeats the original message. (b) As a group discussion, offer a few suggestions to managers for dealing with the grapevine. (Obj. 5)

7. **Recognizing Differences Between a Formal and an Informal Communication System (Obj. 5)**
   Draw an organization chart to depict the formal system of communication within an organization with which you are familiar. How is the informal system different from the organization chart?

E-MAIL APPLICATION

Working with a student that your instructor designates, send your instructor a brief e-mail message that (a) provides a list of guidelines for effective group communication, or (b) discusses the role of e-mail in organizational communication. Elaborate on how e-mail is different from and superior or inferior to other means of communication, such as memos, face-to-face meetings, telephone, and so on. Discuss the factors that would lead you to select e-mail as an appropriate channel for a message.

REAL-TIME INTERNET CASE

Is Anyone Listening?

The ability to listen effectively is consistently rated as one of the most important skills necessary for success in the workplace. Effective listening is crucial to providing quality service, facilitating groups, training staff, improving teamwork, and supervising and managing for improved performance. In times of stress and change, effective listening is the cornerstone of workplace harmony, since it furthers interpersonal and intercultural understanding. Listening is more than just hearing. It is an interactive process that takes concentration and commitment.

Although listening is critical to our daily lives, it is taught and studied far less than the other three basic communication skills: reading, writing, and speaking. Much of the trouble we have communicating with others is because of poor listening skills. Studies show that we spend about 80 percent of our waking hours communicating, and at least 45 percent of that time listening. Most people, however, are not good listeners. The Sperry Corp., a company that has built its corporate identity around the theme of good listening, reports that 85 percent of all people questioned rated themselves average or less in listening ability. Fewer than 5 percent rated themselves either superior or excellent.[14]

You can come up with a fairly accurate idea of where you fall in this spectrum by thinking about your relationships with the people in your life—your boss, colleagues, best friends, family. If asked, what would they say about how well you listen? Do you often misunderstand assignments, or only vaguely remember what people have said to you? If so, you may need to improve your listening skills.

Visit the following Internet sites and respond to one or more of the activities, as directed by your instructor.

Internet Sites

http://www.smartbiz.com/sbs/arts/bly55.htm
http://www.listen.org/
http://www.smartbiz.com/sbs/arts/wwt3.htm

Activities

1. Tell why you are either a good or poor listener. Support your conclusion with reasons and/or evidence.

2. One of the sites you visited identified a plan for improving the listening skills of a negotiator. Prepare a similar plan for a position in your chosen career field (human resources manager, auditor, salesperson, etc.), adapting the points to fit the activities and expectations of the position.

3. Outline and implement a plan for improving your own listening skills. Your plan should include the following: (1) identification of your major listening weaknesses; (2) one or more strategies for overcoming each of the stated weaknesses; (3) activities or occasions in which you applied the corrective strategies, with dates and times; and (4) outcomes of your corrective strategies. Implement your plan for one week, or some other time period as specified by your instructor. Summarize in writing the results of your self-improvement project.

Team Building Projects

hile the process by which a group of individuals becomes an effective, functioning team is somewhat different in each situation, it follows a fairly predictable pattern. Experts in team development define four stages of progression: (1) forming, or cautious affiliation; (2) storming, or competitiveness; (3) norming, or harmonious cohesion; and (4) performing, or collaborative teamwork. The phases are described more fully below:

Forming

This stage is an exploration period, in which members' attachment to the team is tentative. Most of the time, members are anxious about what the team and they, as individual members, are supposed to do. Team members assess other team members' abilities and attitudes and try to determine how and where they fit into the group. They are worried about the team's ability to cope with group problems and conflicts. Little is accomplished during this stage. Productivity is low, and working relationships are guarded, cautious, and noncommittal.

Storming

In this stage, members grow impatient with the team's lack of progress and become overly zealous. Finally, they realize that the team's job is different and more difficult than they had initially imagined. The gap between expectations and reality leads to frustration and anger. As a result, blaming, defensiveness, destructive disagreement, and confrontations occur—especially with the team leader or those vying for dominant positions. Subgroups may form, with factions competing for influence. While struggling over mission, goals, tasks, roles, and responsibilities, the group makes some progress toward accomplishing its objectives.

Norming

During this stage, members have discovered that they, in fact, like the team as an entity, the members as individuals, their social encounters, and the sense of belonging they are beginning to feel. With the urgent issues of mission, goals, tasks, roles, and standards at least partially resolved, members become less dissatisfied. Animosity toward the leader and each other decreases significantly. Previously warring factions mellow into normal, healthy, interpersonal patterns. Competitive relationships become cooperative, close, and mutually supportive. Communication channels open, and feelings of mutual trust develop. During this stage, individuals discover that they are proud to be associated with the team. The quantity and quality of work slowly increase.

Performing

A group of individuals becomes a truly collaborative team during this stage. Structured processes and procedures emerge to allocate resources, resolve personal conflicts, deal with the larger organization, give warranted positive feedback, and discipline members for unacceptable behavior. Members begin to define high standards for evaluating team and individual performance. The team makes diagnoses and solves (or foresees and prevents) problems. Members freely share and pool viewpoints and information to make sound decisions. Team members are motivated by pride in their accomplishments and a sense of ownership and belonging. Individual and coordinated task expertise leads to peak performance levels.

Many so-called teams never achieve optimal performance. Some stall and others regress to earlier stages. Of the teams that do reach the fourth stage, many do so only after many painful months or years of hit-or-miss struggle and fluctuation. Understanding the normal progression of stages and the strategies and behaviors that are appropriate for each can help to hasten the movement to the advanced stages. Future team builders located at the end of each section of the text will focus on the individual stages and provide insight for advancing your team effectiveness.

Exploration

Visit the following website to gain further understanding of the characteristics of a successful team:

http://members.amaonline.com/d&wweb/grian1/teams/tsld002.htm

Companies that have experienced positive results from teams include General Mills, Ingersoll-Rand, Federal Express, Kodak, General Electric, and AT&T Credit Corporation. Select one of these companies and locate one or more articles that discuss how teams have been used. Compose a short summary of the organization's use of teams, giving reasons why you feel teams succeeded in that company.

Application

Visit the following web site to obtain helpful suggestions concerning team meetings and performance contracts:

http://www.cbdcom.apgea.army.mil/Staff/quality/
integration/funbook/page16.html

Schedule your initial meeting with your team. At that meeting, complete the following activities:

- Introduce yourselves to each other; discuss the strengths and experiences that each of you can offer to completing your team assignment.
- Exchange contact information and determine the times in a typical week that you all could meet together if necessary.
- Prepare a team performance contract that states the terms you all agree to honor. Submit a copy to your instructor, with each member's signature affixed.

Source: Montebello, A. R. & Buzzotta, V. R. (1993, March). Work teams that work. *Training and Development*, 47(3), 59–64.

The Writing Process

CHAPTER THREE

Organizing and Composing Messages

When you have completed Chapter 3, you will be able to:

1 *Identify the purpose of the message and the appropriate channel.*

2 *Envision the audience so you can adapt messages to the audience.*

3 *Apply techniques for adapting messages to the audience.*

4 *Apply the guidelines for communicating ethically and responsibly.*

5 *Recognize the importance of organizing a message before writing the first draft.*

6 *Select the appropriate outline (deductive or inductive) for developing messages by identifying the central idea and the likely receiver reaction.*

7 *Apply techniques for developing effective sentences and unified and coherent paragraphs.*

*M*anagers and employees who strive for success must first master the basics of written and oral communication. Building good communication skills is like acquiring athletic skills. Successful athletes first envision their goals and work hard to master the basics of their sports. Their practice often involves repeating and practicing fundamental tasks a dozen times or more. Becoming an effective communicator, too, requires practice, patience, and a willingness to continue to learn effective writing strategies.

If you have ever felt that writing is especially difficult for you, you might draw some inspiration from the stories of determined people who have overcome formidable obstacles. Likely, you remember the amazing fortitude of Dan Jansen, the American speed skater, who continued his quest for an Olympic gold medal after a series of personal losses and ego-crushing falls. Additionally, Christopher Reeve, renowned for his role in several films, including the Superman series, was paralyzed after being thrown from a horse while participating in an equestrian event. Despite his personal tragedy, Reeve has refused to give up. In addition to directing films and writing an autobiography, he is a spokesperson for those with spinal cord injuries and is working to increase funding for spinal cord research.

Although your challenge to learn to write effectively is *certainly* not on the scale of Jansen and Reeve, you can draw inspiration from their determination. As you tackle each phase of the writing process—researching, organizing, writing, revising, proofreading—recognize that the process cannot be avoided or rushed. Stay focused until you reach your goals and reap the rewards of communicating effectively.

1 *Identify the purpose of the message and the appropriate channel.*

It has been said that all business messages have some persuasive intent. Do you agree or disagree?

In a small group, identify the appropriate channel for (a) telling a customer damaged merchandise will be replaced, (b) notifying a sales rep his or her job has been eliminated because of reorganization, or (c) informing sales reps of annual bonuses.

Determining the Purpose and Channel

Before beginning to compose the first draft of a message, you must first think about the reason for writing the message. Is the purpose to get information, to answer a question, to accept an offer, to deny a request, to seek support for a product or idea? If a message were condensed into a one-sentence telegram, that sentence would be the purpose for writing or the **central idea** of the message. Later you will learn that the central idea is used to determine the appropriate organizational pattern for achieving the results you desire.

The major purpose of many business messages is to have the receiver understand a body of information and concentrate on the logical presentation of the content. Messages *to inform* are used to convey the vast amounts of information needed to complete the day-to-day operations of the business—explain instructions to employees, announce meetings and procedures, acknowledge orders, accept contracts for services, and so forth. Some messages are intended *to persuade*—to influence or change the attitudes or actions of the receiver. These messages might include letters promoting a product or service and seeking support for ideas and worthy causes presented to supervisors, stockholders, customers/clients, and others. You will learn to compose messages written for each of these purposes.

Selecting an appropriate channel of communication increases the likelihood that the receiver will understand and accept your message. Recall the typical communication channels discussed in Chapter 1. For example, a written document (letter/memo, e-mail, or voice mail message) is appropriate for routine or pleasant information. Complex information may require a written document and follow-up with a face-to-face meeting. A face-to-face meeting is appropriate for sending unpleasant or highly emotional messages that may be subject to misinterpretation. E-mail is especially effective when sending the same message to many people and communicating with people in different time zones but should *never* be used to send confidential information because the security of e-mail is low. E-mailing or leaving a voice mail message eliminates time-consuming games of telephone tag. Detailed messages enable the receiver to reply with timely answers to your questions.

Envisioning the Audience

2 *Envision the audience so you adapt messages to the audience.*

A good writer has a strong mental picture of the audience. To help you envision the audience, first focus on relevant information you know about the receiver. The more familiar you are with the receiver, the easier this task will be. When communicating with an individual, you immediately recall a clear picture of the receiver—his or her physical appearance, background (education, occupation, religion, culture), values, opinions, preferences, and so on. Most important, your knowledge of the receiver's reaction in similar, previous experiences will aid you in anticipating how this receiver is likely to react in the current situation. Add to your mental picture by thoughtfully considering all you know about the receiver and how this information might affect the content and style of your final message.

To help you tailor your message to fit your audience, consider the following major areas:

- **Age.** A letter answering an elementary-school student's request for information from your company would not be worded the same as a letter answering a similar request from an adult.

- **Economic level.** A banker's collection letter to a customer who pays promptly is not likely to be the same form letter sent to clients who have fallen behind on their payments for small loans.

- **Educational/occupational background.** The technical jargon and acronyms used in a financial proposal sent to bank loan officers may be inappropriate in a proposal sent to a group of private investors. Similarly, a message to the chief executive officer of a major corporation may differ in style and content from a message to a stockholder.

- **Culture.** The vast cultural differences between people (language, expressions, customs, values, religions) increase the complexity of the communication process. A memorandum containing typical American expressions such as "The proposal was *shot down*," "projections are *way off base*, *off target*, *right on the mark*," "the prices are *out of our ballpark*," and "the *competition is dropping like flies*" would likely confuse a manager from a different culture. Thinking and learning patterns also vary among cultures. For example, clarity is important to American readers; whereas Japanese readers value beauty and "flow."[1] Americans expect a user's manual to contain an overview and then a step-by-step tutorial; however, Japanese readers are "frightened off by seeing the big picture right way. They prefer to be introduced to the parts one at a time before encountering the whole."[2]

- *Rapport.* A sensitive letter written to a long-time client may differ significantly from a letter written to a newly acquired client. The rapport created by previous dealings with this client aids understanding in this new situation.

- *Expectations.* Because accountants, doctors, and lawyers are expected to meet high standards, a letter from one of these professionals containing errors in grammar or spelling would likely cause a receiver to question the credibility of the source.

- *Needs of the receiver.* Just as successful sales personnel begin by identifying the needs of the prospective buyer, an effective manager attempts to understand the receiver's frame of reference as a basis for organizing the message and developing the content.

You may find that envisioning an audience you know well is often such a conscious action that you may not even recognize that you are doing it. On the other hand, envisioning those you do not know well requires additional effort before you are prepared to adapt the message to your audience.

---

3 *Apply techniques for adapting messages to the audience.*

How are empathy and sympathy different?

Adapting the Message to the Audience

After you have envisioned your audience, you are ready to adapt your message to fit the specific needs of your audience. Adaptations include assuming an empathetic attitude, focusing on the receiver's point of view, using bias-free language, avoiding statements that destroy goodwill, and projecting a positive, tactful tone.

Assume an Empathetic Attitude

Empathy is the ability to identify another's frame of reference (knowledge, feelings, and emotions) and to project or communicate understanding back to the person. The phrases "walking a day in your moccasins" or "putting myself in your shoes" imply that empathy requires you to experience another person's situation firsthand. Sharing an experience does make empathy easier. For example, a person who has recovered from a life-threatening disease can more easily understand the emotions and feelings of a person who has just received a similar diagnosis. The power of empathy is central to the success of self-help groups such as Narcotics Anonymous, Mothers Against Drunk Drivers (MADD), and many support groups.

Fortunately, relying on firsthand experience is not necessary to be able to provide genuine empathy. In situations when you cannot "walk in another's shoes," you can empathize by mentally projecting how you believe you would feel if that situation had happened to you. To illustrate this mental projection, Jess Lair once said, "Empathy is your pain in my heart."[3]

How can being in touch with someone's feelings assist in business-related situations? First, trying to understand the situation from another's point of view makes sense. Your receivers will appreciate your attempting to understand their feelings, that is, your being in touch with them. The outcome may be mutual trust, which can greatly improve communication and people's feelings about you, your ideas, and themselves (as shown in the discussion of the Johari Window in Chapter 2). In other words, empathy is an excellent way to establish rapport and credibility and to build long-lasting personal and business relationships.

Second, seeing a situation or problem from the receiver's perspective not only will permit you to address the receiver's needs and concerns but will also enable you to anticipate the receiver's possible reaction to the message. For example, from your knowledge of yourself and from your experiences with others, you can predict (with reasonable accuracy) receivers' reactions to various types of messages. To illustrate, ask yourself these questions:

- Would I react favorably to a message saying my request is being granted?

- Would I experience a feeling of disappointment upon learning that my request has been refused?

- Would I be pleased when an apparently sincere message praises me for a job well done?

- Would I experience some disappointment when a memo reveals that my promised pay increase is being postponed?

Now, reread the questions as though you were another person. Because you know *your* answers, you can predict *others'* answers with some degree of accuracy. Such predictions are possible because of commonality in human behavior. Of course, each individual is unique; but each has much in common with others. Otherwise, psychology, psychiatry, and sociology would not have survived as disciplines. Asking yourself how you would react if you were in the other person's position *before* you write a message greatly simplifies the task of *organizing* your message. Your knowledge of the receiver's likely reaction enables you to select relevant content, to determine the appropriate sequence of ideas, and to write in a suitable style.

In today's competitive environment, no company can afford to alienate talented workers, and empathy helps companies create environments supportive of the needs of diverse groups. For instance, recent efforts to involve workers in continuous improvement teams allow management to see production through the eyes of the worker, the person closest to the operation, and give the worker an opportunity to be heard and appreciated. Because of increased foreign competition, companies must learn to use empathy to understand people who may not speak the same language; do not understand the culture's jargon, expressions, or nonverbal language; practice a different religion and customs; support a different political system; and apply entirely different management practices.

Empathy is especially important when communicating with other cultures. Generate a list of phrases and nonverbal expressions peculiar to your culture that a person from another culture might not understand.

To illustrate empathy for the needs of dual-career and single-parent homes, some companies are introducing flexible work schedules, strong family-benefit policies, extended leaves for parents of newborns, assistance with child and elder care, and reductions in travel and relocations. More companies are offering employee services such as work/family seminars on various topics, tutoring for children, free shuttles for long-distance commuters, and on-site services (e.g., fitness center, repair service, pharmacy, subsidized cafeteria with take-out dinners). For example, the corporate concierge at PepsiCo makes employees' lives "a little easier" by arranging for theater tickets, picking up a birthday cake, hiring someone to wait in an employee's home for a repair or delivery person, and other similar requests. Many companies believe that helping employees manage their personal lives will increase productivity.[4]

Use an on-line database or the Internet to locate articles describing companies' efforts to stay in touch with and meet employee concerns. Share personal experiences from your workplace.

Consider the use (or lack) of empathy in the following workplace example:

Sample Message	*Problem Analysis*
Example 1: Hurriedly as the store closed on Thursday evening, the store manager told sales clerks, "Oh, by the way, it's time for our annual inventory. I want you here Sunday at 7a.m. sharp and plan to stay until . . . And one other thing. Don't bother embarrassing yourself by giving me some flimsy excuse for not being able to work. I don't want to hear it. If I don't have this job done by Monday morning, the district manager will have my head. End of conversation."	• *Overuse of the pronoun I emphasizes the manager's self-centered attitude. Tactless, intimidating, and overly demanding tone eliminates the possibility of feedback.* • *Insistence on one-way communication and the timing of the message highlight lack of consideration for individual needs (arrangements for child or elder care and other extenuating circumstances).*
Example 2: A U.S. manager's instructions to a new employee from an Asian culture: "Please get to work right away on <u>inputting</u> the financial data for the Collier proposal. Oh, I need you to get this work out <u>ASAP</u>. Because this proposal is just a <u>draft</u>, why don't you just plan to give me a <u>quick-and-dirty</u> job. You can clean it up after we <u>massage the stats</u> and get <u>final blessings</u> from the <u>top dog</u>. Do you have any questions?"	• *Creation of confusion and intimidation caused by the acronyms and expressions peculiar to the U.S. environment.* • *Final open-ended question indicates the writer does not understand the importance of saving face to a person from an Asian culture.* • *Deep cultural influences may prevent this employee from asking questions that might indicate lack of understanding.*
Example 3: An excerpt from a letter sent to Ms. Kelly Lazzara: Dear <u>Mr. Lazarra</u>: The desktop publishing software and the laser printer that you expressed an interest in <u>is</u> now available in our local stores. Both can be demonstrated at <u>you convience</u>. Please call your local sales representative to schedule <u>a</u> appointment. <u>I remain</u> Respectfully yours, *Hugh Washam* Hugh Washam District Manager	• *The misspelling of the receiver's name, use of Mr. to refer to a woman, and the grammatical and spelling errors are unforgivable. They confirm incompetence (or carelessness) and disrespect for the receiver.* • *The outdated closing reduces the writer's credibility further. Although the writer is claiming expertise in a technological field, the communication does not reflect modern conventions.* • *Omission of the sales representative's name and telephone number indicates the writer's failure to anticipate and adapt the message to meet the receiver's needs.*

In communicating with someone of another culture, how can we effectively focus on similarities while being aware of differences?

Today's workforce is diverse, filled with people from many differing racial or ethnic groups, people of all ages, abilities, and genders. Because of this great diversity, you must be very careful to use language that shows your sensitivity toward and recognition of these various groups.

Focus on the Receiver's Point of View

Ideas are more interesting and appealing if they are expressed from the receiver's viewpoint. Thus, develop a "you attitude," which involves thinking in terms of the other person's interests and trying to see a problem from the other's point of view. A letter or memo reflecting a "you attitude" sends a direct signal of sincere concern for the receiver's needs and interest.

You (appropriately used) conveys to receivers a feeling that messages are specifically for *them*. However, if the first-person pronoun *I* is used frequently, the sender may impress others as being self-centered—always talking about self. *I* used as the subject receives significant emphasis. Compare the following examples of writer-centered and receiver-centered statements:

How can the following statement be revised to be more receiver-centered? "I'm asking all work teams to generate a list of innovative product ideas."

I- or Sender-Centered	*Receiver-Centered*
<u>I</u> want to take this opportunity to offer <u>my</u> congratulations on your recent promotion to regional manager.	Congratulations on <u>your</u> recent promotion to regional manager.
<u>We</u> have two laser printers compatible with your software.	<u>Your</u> software is compatible with two of our high-quality laser printers.
<u>I</u> am interested in ordering . . .	Please send me . . .
<u>We</u> allow a 2 percent discount to customers who pay their total invoices within ten days.	Customers who pay within ten days may deduct 2 percent from their total invoice. (<u>You</u> could be the subject in a letter to a customer.)

To cultivate a "you attitude," concentrate on the following questions:

- Does the message address the receiver's major needs and concerns?
- Would the receiver feel this message is receiver-centered? Is the receiver kept clearly in the picture?

COMMUNICATION MENTOR

Written communication is required in any corporation. While a meeting can be an effective communication tool, written correspondence is more effective—and permanent. A turn-off in any type of written communication is use of the word *I* and its sister words *me* and *us*. Try to eliminate these words from your writing to prevent an *us* vs. *them* attitude.

Terence E. McSweeney
Director of Communications
PGA of America

- Will the receiver perceive the ideas to be fair, logical, and ethical?

- Are ideas expressed clearly and concisely (to avoid lost time, money, and possible embarrassment caused when messages are misunderstood)?

- Does the message serve as a vehicle for developing positive business relationships—even when the message is negative? For example, are *please*, *thank you*, and other courtesies used when appropriate? Are ideas stated tactfully and positively and in a manner that preserves the receiver's self-worth and cultivates future business?

- Is the message sent promptly to indicate courtesy?

- Does the message reflect the high standards of a business professional: quality paper, accurate formatting, quality printing, and absence of misspellings and grammatical errors?

Concentrating on these points will boost the receiver's confidence in the writer's competence and will communicate nonverbally that the receiver is valued enough to merit the writer's best effort. For people who practice courtesy and consideration, the "you attitude" is easy to incorporate into a written message.

Use Bias-Free Language

In today's competitive workplace, a writer or a speaker cannot afford the risk of sending an insensitive message. In addition, managers in today's highly competitive, diverse workforce cannot afford to alienate employees and customers. Therefore, select words carefully to eliminate any trace of insensitivity regarding gender, race or ethnicity, religion, age, or disability.

Avoid Gender Bias. The following guidelines will help you avoid gender bias:

Give examples of words and phrases that can be used to avoid race, ethnicity, or disability bias.

1. **Avoid referring to men and women in stereotyped roles and occupations.** The use of *he* to refer to a group was once standard and accepted; however, this usage is considered insensitive and to some offensive. Therefore, do not use the pronoun *he* when referring to a group of people that may include women or the pronoun *she* to refer to a group that may include men. Otherwise, you may unintentionally communicate an insensitive message that "only women or men serve in certain professions," diverting the receiver's attention from the message to a stereotypical attitude and insensitivity. In the following examples, gender-neutral terms replace gender-biased expressions.

Gender-Biased	Improved
When your accountant completes year-end financial statements, ask <u>him</u> to send a copy to the loan officer.	When accountants complete year-end financial statements, ask <u>them</u> to send a copy to the loan officer. (*Uses plural noun*)
The human resources manager must evaluate <u>his</u> employees' performance at least twice a year.	The human resources manager must evaluate employees' performance at least twice a year. (*Omits pronoun*)
A nurse must complete in-service training to update <u>her</u> certification.	Nurses must complete in-service training to update <u>their</u> certification. (*Uses plural noun*)

Follow these guidelines for using gender-neutral language:

- Avoid using a pronoun.
  Not: When your auditor arrives, <u>he</u> is to go . . .
  Instead: Upon arrival, <u>your auditor</u> is to go . . .

- Repeat the noun.
  Not: . . . the courtesy of your guide. Ask <u>him</u> to . . .
  Instead: . . . the courtesy of <u>your guide</u>. Ask the guide to . . .

- Use a plural noun.
  Not: If a supervisor needs assistance, <u>he</u> can . . .
  Instead: If supervisors need assistance, <u>they</u> can . . .
  (Because "they" can refer to men only, women only, or both, using "they" avoids implying that supervisors can be men only.)

- Use pronouns from both genders (when necessary, but not repeatedly).
  Not: Just call the manager. <u>He</u> will in turn . . .
  Instead: Just call the manager. <u>He</u> or <u>she</u> will in turn . . .

2. **Be certain to use occupational titles that reflect genuine sensitivity to gender.** In the following examples, substituting "sales representative" or "fire-fighter" for "fireman" is a simple way to eliminate gender bias. Note the other gender-free titles in these examples.

Gender-Biased	Gender-Free
salesmen	sales representatives
firemen	fire fighters
policeman, policewoman	police officers
businessman	executive, manager, businessperson
career woman	professional
foreman	supervisor
bag boy, stock boy	courtesy clerk, stock clerk
working mother	working parent

3. **Avoid designating an occupation by gender.** For example, why include "woman" in "A woman doctor is opening a hematology clinic next month"? The doctor's profession, not the gender, is the point of the message. Similarly, avoid using the *-ess* ending to differentiate genders in an occupation:

Rewrite the following sentences to reflect more sensitive wording: "Managers and their wives are invited to a weekend retreat at Lake Lawrence" and "Ross Industries is the corporate sponsor of this year's Father and Son Camporee."

What other examples of gender-biased terms and appropriate gender-free alternatives can you give?

Gender-Biased	Gender-Free
steward or stewardess	flight attendant
waiter or waitress	server
hostess	host
authoress	author
poetess	poet

4. **Avoid using expressions that may be perceived to be gender-biased.**
   Avoid commonly used expressions in which "man" represents all humanity, such as "Man does not live by bread alone," and stereotypical characteristics, such as "man hours," "man and wife," "man-made goods," and "work of four strong men." Note the improvements made in the following examples by eliminating the potentially offensive words.

Gender-Biased	Improved
Preparing the company's annual report is a <u>man-sized</u> task.	Preparing the company's annual report is an <u>enormous</u> task.
Sid Paradiso is the best <u>man</u> for the job.	Steve is the best <u>person</u> for the job.
This estimate of the <u>manpower</u> needed to install this information system is quite conservative.	This estimate of the <u>number of workers</u> needed to install this information system is quite conservative.

Avoid Race and Ethnicity, Age, Religion, and Disability Bias. Changes in the demographics of the workforce are requiring managers to design bias-free messages in terms of race and ethnicity, age, religion, and disability. In fact, companies are investing in diversity workshops designed to raise awareness of racial and gender bias and to seek ways to change.

The guidelines for writing gender-sensitive messages also apply to writing messages sensitive to race and ethnicity, age, religion, and disability:

1. **Avoid referring to these groups in stereotypical ways, and avoid emphasizing age, ethnicity, religion, or disability when these factors are not relevant.** In the following examples, the references to race or ethnic group in the first three sentences are irrelevant, just as gender is immaterial in "woman doctor" or "male nurse." Eliminating the individual's race, ethnicity, age, or religion will not alter the meaning of the last sentence.

   The <u>black</u> mayor of Aberdeen has announced his bid for reelection.

   Alfonso Perez, the <u>Spanish</u> clerk in the Quality Control Division, immediately identified the discrepancy in the raw materials.

   Dan's <u>Irish</u> temper flared today when we learned of the new production quotas.

   Russell Payne, the <u>55-year-old</u> president of Norton Bank, has resigned to accept a position with another company.

   The <u>Jewish</u> account executive has designed a creative point-of-sale display for the Milton campaign.

2. **Use people-first language when communicating about people with disabilities.** Using people-first language simply means referring to the person

Identify methods used by companies to raise employee awareness of diversity issues.

COMMUNICATION MENTOR

Think before you speak. If you believe you have been insensitive, be careful not to make the issue bigger by your explanation. I once heard a seminar speaker use the phrase "as clear as black and white." Then, thinking that she might have offended members of the audience, she spent 15 minutes nervously explaining the terminology. This behavior only exaggerated a statement that likely would have been ignored.

Shirley F. Olson, President
J. J. Ferguson Prestress-Precast Co., Inc.

first and the disability second; thus, the emphasis is appropriately focused on the person's ability rather than on the disability.[5] Additionally, avoid words with negative or judgmental connotations, such as *handicap, unfortunate, afflicted,* and *victim*. When describing people without disabilities, use the word *typical* rather than *normal*; otherwise, you may inadvertently imply that people with disabilities are abnormal. Consider these more sensitive revisions:

Insensitive	*Sensitive (People-First)*
<u>Blind</u> employees will receive company memorandums by voice mail.	<u>Employees with vision impairments</u> will receive company memorandums by voice mail.
The new elevator is for the exclusive use of <u>handicapped</u> employees and should not be used by <u>normal</u> employees.	The new elevator is for the exclusive use of <u>employees who have disabilities</u>.

Talk with a person with a disability to find out ways to communicate acceptably using bias-free language.

To communicate that you are responsive to the differences of others, you must make a conscious effort to use bias-free (nondiscriminatory) language. Taking even a remote chance of offending someone is too great a risk. Using bias-free language permits the receiver to focus on your message rather than to raise serious questions about your sensitivity. Your concerted efforts to be caring and sensitive will yield tangible results: increased clarity and strong, lasting relationships—both measuring sticks for effective communication.

Avoid Statements that Destroy Goodwill

Tone is the way a statement sounds. The tone of a message conveys the writer's or speaker's attitude toward the message and the receiver. Chances for achieving good human relations are diminished when the tone of a message is condescending, overly euphemistic or flattering, demeaning, or presumptuous.

Eliminate Condescension. Condescending words seem to connote that the communicator is temporarily coming down from a level of superiority to join the receiver on a level of inferiority. To build strong goodwill, avoid condescending words. Note how the reminders of inequality in the following examples seriously hamper communication:

As director of marketing, I will decide whether your product proposal has any merit.

As a retired editor of best sellers, I could assist you in editing your PTA newsletter.

Use Euphemisms Cautiously. A **euphemism** is a term that makes an unpleasant idea seem better than it really is. For example, the idea of picking up neighborhood garbage does not sound especially inviting. Someone who does such work is often referred to as a *sanitation worker*. This term has a more pleasant connotation than *garbage collector*. Business writers prefer the euphemistic terms in the right column to the negative terms in the left column:

Negative Tone	*Euphemistic Tone*
died	passed away
aged or elderly	senior citizen
secretaries	office support staff
line worker	production associate
bagger	courtesy clerk
Complaint Department	Customer Service
Repair Department	Maintenance Department
Inspection Department	Quality Control
Housekeeping	Environmental Services

Generally, you can recognize such expressions for what they are—unpleasant ideas presented with a little sugar coating. Knowing that the sender was simply trying to be polite and positive, you are more likely to react favorably than unfavorably. Yet you should avoid euphemisms with excess sugar coating or those that appear to be deliberate sarcasm. For example, to refer to a janitor as a *maintenance engineer* is to risk conveying a negative metacommunication, such as "I wish this janitor held a more respectable position, but I did the best I could by making it sound good." To the receiver (and to the janitor), just plain *janitor* would sound better.

When using euphemisms, be sure your motive is to cushion the blow of the negative information and not to ridicule the receiver or prompt the receiver to misconstrue the true message. For example, is it ethical for a politician to talk about *tax*

In groups, identify two additional euphemisms you have heard recently. Do you believe their use is acceptable?

Is pre-owned an acceptable euphemism for used cars? Explain.

BEETLE BAILEY

It's all in a name, or is it?

enhancements rather than *tax increases* if the intent is to distort the voters' perceptions? Is it truthful for a military spokesperson to speak of *friendly casualties* to minimize and, in some cases, avoid the negative publicity inherent in reporting the number of soldiers killed accidentally by the military's own weapons? Use euphemisms when the purpose is to present unpleasant thoughts politely and positively. Avoid euphemisms when they could mislead the receiver.

Avoid a Flattering Tone. Compliments (words of deserved praise) normally elicit favorable reactions. They can increase a receiver's receptivity to subsequent statements. Yet even compliments can do more harm than good if paid at the wrong time, in the wrong setting, in the presence of the wrong people, or for a suspicious motive.

Flattery (words of *un*deserved praise) may be accepted gracefully, but the net result is almost always negative. Although flattery *can* be accepted as a sincere compliment, the recipient is more likely to interpret undeserved praise as an attempt to curry favor. Suspicion of motive makes effective communication less likely. Give sincere compliments judiciously; avoid flattery.

Avoid Demeaning Expressions. An expression that is designed to make an idea seem negative or disrespectful (sometimes called a *dysphemism*) is a **demeaning expression**. Many demeaning expressions are common across regions and perhaps even cultures. The following examples can be taken as contempt for an occupation or a specific job/position. Like words that attack races or nationalities, words that ridicule occupations work against a writer's purpose. Many demeaning expressions are common across regions and perhaps even cultures. Some demeaning expressions belong to a particular company. For example, "turtles" in the following examples was coined in one firm to mock first-year employees for the slow pace at which they completed their work. Because such expressions divert attention from the real message to emotional issues that have little to do with the message, avoid demeaning expressions.

In groups, generate a list of demeaning expressions for each career field represented in the group or those used in companies with which members have experience (e.g., shrinks, techies/nontechies). Discuss how these expressions can harm human relations.

Demeaning Expression	*Respectful Expression*
The <u>pencil pushers</u> (or <u>bean counters</u>) require that all requisitions be approved by the inventory manager.	The <u>accountants</u> require that all requisitions be approved by the inventory manager.
Be sure the <u>turtles</u> understand the importance of meeting next week's deadline.	Be sure the <u>management trainees</u> understand the importance of meeting next week's deadline.
Coach Roberts intends to concentrate on recruiting <u>skilled players</u> this season.	Coach Roberts intends to concentrate on recruiting <u>quarterbacks, running backs, and receivers</u> this season.

Use Connotative Tone Cautiously. Human relations can suffer when connotative words are inadvertently used instead of denotative words. The **denotative meaning** of a word is the literal meaning that most people assign to it. The **connotative meaning** is the literal meaning plus an extra message that reveals the speaker's or writer's qualitative judgment. Here is an example:

Connotative Meaning with Negative Meaning	Denotative Meaning (Preferred)
Another <u>gripe session</u> has been scheduled for tomorrow.	Another <u>employee forum</u> has been scheduled for tomorrow.

The first message contains a connotative meaning and an additional message: The writer has a bias for or against employee forums. The connotation may needlessly introduce thoughts about whether employee forums are beneficial. While thus occupied, the receiver may not pay sufficient attention to the statements that follow.

Note the commonality between connotations and metacommunications. Both involve messages that are implied. In the preceding example, the connotation seems to be more harmful than helpful. At times, however, connotations can be helpful:

Denotative Meaning	Connotative with Positive Meaning
<u>Research and Development</u> has developed yet another outstanding production process.	Our <u>corporate think tank</u> has developed another outstanding production process.
John's likable personality <u>is beneficial</u> when he negotiates labor contracts.	John's likable personality <u>has made him a miracle worker</u> when he negotiates labor contracts.

Compared with denotative words, connotative words invite a wider range of interpretation. Words that elicit a positive reaction from one person could elicit a negative reaction from another. The appropriateness of connotations varies with the audience to which they are addressed and the context in which they appear. For example, referring to a car as a "foreign job" might be received differently by a group of teenagers and a group of senior citizens. The expression is less appropriate in a research report than in a popular magazine.

In business writing rely mainly on denotative words or connotative words that will elicit a favorable reaction. By considering the audience, the context, and the timing, you can usually avoid connotative words that elicit unfavorable reactions.

Avoid Statements of Surprise, Doubt, and Judgment. Phrases that reveal a writer's surprise about a receiver's behavior can cause problems in human relations. "I am surprised" risks conveying the idea "I am accustomed to normal behavior. Yours is abnormal and therefore bad or totally unjustified." "I cannot understand" takes the same risks. Such expressions are particularly offensive to receivers because they seem to place them in a position of recognized inferiority.

Similarly, expressions that reveal judgment of recipients' emotional state are very risky. "I am so sorry you are upset" may be intended as a heart-felt apology, but the "I am sorry" can be completely overshadowed by "you are upset." This statement could mean, "Your conduct is such that I recognize your lack of self-control. Because of your condition, you could not be thinking rationally." Avoid expressions of surprise, doubt, and judgment when they would be interpreted as insults.

Avoid Statements of Certainty. Avoid the expressions of certainty when you cannot be certain the statement is accurate. In the following examples, the writer seems to be making a declaration of certainty when certainty is hardly possible. If the writer *can* be sure of agreement, the expression is unnecessary. If the writer truly *knows* the idea presented in the sentence, the words are inaccurate.

Is an extra message conveyed in *"Have you read the latest commandment from above?"* How might you rewrite the sentence using the literal meaning? Label the two sentences denotative or connotative.

Statement of Certainty	*Improved Statement*
<u>I am sure</u> you will agree that the instructions are clear.	Reexamine the instructions to see that they are clear.
<u>I know</u> you will understand the importance of completing the designs by Friday.	The designs must be completed by Friday if we are to meet the final deadline.

When the phrases "I know" and "I am sure" *cannot* be true, the writer conveys a lack of empathy and respect for the receiver. If the writer stretches the truth in this way often enough, the receiver may question whether other statements are accurate or exaggerated too. Avoid expressions of certainty when certainty is hardly possible.

Project a Positive, Tactful Tone

Being adept at communicating negative information will give you the confidence you need to handle sensitive situations in a positive, constructive manner. You will find that stating unpleasant ideas tactfully and positively preserves the receiver's self-worth and builds future relationships. The following suggestion can reduce the sting of an unpleasant thought:

State Ideas Using Positive Language. For good human relations, rely mainly on positive words—words that speak of what can be done instead of what cannot be done, of the pleasant instead of the unpleasant. In each pair, both sentences in the following examples are sufficiently clear, but the positive words in the improved sentence make the message more diplomatic and promote positive human relations.

Negative Tone	*Positive Tone*
<u>Don't forget</u> to submit your time and expense report by noon on Friday.	Remember to submit your time and expense report by noon on Friday.
We <u>cannot</u> ship your order until you send us full specifications.	You will receive your order as soon as you send us full specifications.
Our new electronic mail system will <u>not</u> be installed by the first of the year.	Our new electronic mail system will be installed by February 1.
You <u>neglected</u> to indicate the specifications for Part No. 332-3.	Please send the complete specifications for Part No. 332-3 so we can complete your order quickly.

Positive words are normally preferred, but sometimes negative words are more effective in achieving the dual goals of *clarity* and positive *human relations*. For example, addition of negative words can sharpen a contrast (and thus increase clarity):

> Use an oil-based paint for this purpose; *do not use* latex.

> Final copies are to be printed using a laser printer; dot-matrix print is *not* acceptable.

When pleasant, positive words have not brought desired results, negative words may be justified. For example, a supervisor may have used positive words to instruct an accounts payable clerk to verify that the unit price on the invoice matches the unit price on the purchase order. Discovering later that the clerk is not verifying the invoices correctly, the supervisor may use negative words such as "*No*, that's the *wrong way*," demonstrate once more, and explain. If the clerk continues to complete

Many people describe themselves as optimists; however, their language contradicts their statements. Think of examples of negative language you have heard (or used) that could easily be stated using positive words.

the task incorrectly, the supervisor may feel justified in using even stronger negative words. The clerk may need the emotional jolt that negative words can provide. Thus, when the purpose is to sharpen contrast or when positive words have not evoked the desired reaction, use negative words.

Avoid Using Second Person when Stating Negative Ideas. For better human relations, avoid second person for presenting unpleasant ideas, but use second person for presenting pleasant ideas. Note the following examples:

Pleasant idea	*You* keyed a perfect copy.	*The person will appreciate the emphasis placed on his/her excellent performance.*
Unpleasant idea	This page contains numerous mistakes.	*"You made numerous mistakes on this page" would direct attention to the person who made the mistakes and would not be diplomatic.*

However, use of second person with negative ideas *is* an acceptable technique on the rare occasions when the purpose is to jolt the receiver by emphasizing a negative.

Use Passive Voice to Convey Negative Ideas. Presenting an unpleasant thought emphatically (as active verbs do) makes human relations difficult. Compare the tone of the following negative thoughts written in active and passive voices:

Active Voice	*Passive Voice Preferred for Negative Ideas*
<u>Saburo</u> did not proofread this bid proposal carefully.	The bid proposal was not proofread carefully.
<u>Saburo</u> completed the job two months behind schedule.	The job was completed two months behind schedule.

Because the subject of each active sentence is the doer, the sentences are emphatic. Because the idea is negative, Saburo probably would appreciate being taken out of the picture. The passive voice sentences place more emphasis on the job than on who failed to complete it. When passive voice is used, the sentences retain the essential ideas, but the ideas seem less irritating. For negative ideas, use passive voice. Just as emphasis on negatives hinders human relations, emphasis on positives promotes human relations. Which sentence makes the positive idea more vivid?

Passive Voice	*Active Voice Preferred for Positive Ideas*
The job was completed ahead of time.	Saburo completed the job ahead of schedule.

Because "Saburo" is the subject of the active-voice sentence, the receiver can easily envision the action. Pleasant thoughts deserve emphasis. For presenting positive ideas, use active voice. Active and passive voice are discussed in greater detail in the "Write Powerful Sentences" section later in this chapter.

Use the Subjunctive Mood. Sometimes, the tone of a message can be improved if the writer switches to the subjunctive mood. **Subjunctive sentences** speak of a wish, necessity, doubt, or conditions contrary to fact and employ such conditional

---

What advice would you give a businessperson for balancing tact and assertiveness?

expressions as *I wish, as if, could, would, might,* and *wish*. In the following examples, the sentence in the right column conveys a negative idea in positive language, which is more diplomatic than negative language.

Negative Tone	Subjunctive Mood Conveys Positive Tone
I <u>cannot</u> approve your transfer to overseas operation.	If positions <u>were</u> available in our our overseas operation, I <u>would</u> approve your transfer.
I am <u>unable</u> to accept your invitation to speak at the November meeting.	I <u>could</u> only accept your invitation to speak at the November meeting if I <u>were</u> to miss the annual stockholders' meeting.
I <u>cannot</u> accept the recommendation of the site-selection committee	I <u>wish</u> I <u>could</u> accept the recommendations of the site-selection committee.

Compose another sentence that uses subjunctive mood to de-emphasize a negative idea.

The revised sentences also include a reason. Because a reason is included, the negative idea seems less objectionable, and the tone is thus improved. Tone is important, but clarity is even more important. The revised sentence in each of the preceding pairs sufficiently *implies* the unpleasant idea without stating it directly. If for any reason a writer suspects the implication is not sufficiently strong, a direct statement in negative terms is preferable. For tactful presentation of an unpleasant thought, consider stating it in the subjunctive mood.

Include a Pleasant Statement in the Same Sentence. A pleasant idea is included in the following examples to improve the tone:

Negative Tone	Positive Tone
Your personnel ratings for communication ability and interpersonal skills were satisfactory.	Your personnel ratings for communication ability and interpersonal skills were satisfactory, but <u>your rating for technical competence was excellent</u>.
Because of increased taxes and insurance, you are obligated to increase your monthly payments by $50.	Because of increased taxes and insurance, your monthly payments will increase by $50; however, <u>your home has increased in value at the monthly rate of $150</u>.

Communicating Ethically and Responsibly

4 *Apply the guidelines for communicating ethically and responsibly.*

An effective communicator will reap unlimited benefits: (1) increased likelihood that the message will yield the desired response from the receiver, (2) courage to deal with ethical issues otherwise ignored because of insecurity in communicating about sensitive or unpleasant issues, (3) positive business relationships built on honest disclosure of information, and (4) justified respect from superiors as an honest, sensitive, highly effective communicator worthy of challenging and rewarding opportunities.

The familiar directive "with power comes responsibility" applies especially to your use of communication skills. Because effective communication is such a powerful tool, you must accept responsibility for using it for *one and only one purpose*:

COMMUNICATION IN ACTION

Cynthia Pharr, C. Pharr and Company, Inc.

Receiving attention from a respected national newspaper presents a challenge for most business organizations, even when the news is positive. When negative comments are printed, however, the challenge can become daunting. Any financial analyst's comments in the national media about the book value of a company's stock can have a tremendous impact on the price of the stock.

Cynthia Pharr, president of C. Pharr & Company, Inc. recently faced a challenge in her role of handling public relations for a large corporation. *The Wall Street Journal* printed an article in which a financial analyst made negative comments about the stock price of Showbiz Pizza Time, Inc., a restaurant for which Cynthia Pharr serves on the Board of Directors. Well-written responses to such analysts can "turn that analyst around" and potentially change his or her attitude toward a company.

In the newspaper article, the analyst had "turned up his nose" at Showbiz's stock because he was not enamored with the concept of the restaurant and believed "they serve rubber pizza." Rebuttal letters to such negative comments often include numbers and harsh logic, focusing on economic reasons in an attempt to change the financial analyst's thinking. Instead, Pharr chose a lighter theme, more in line with the company's fun-loving slogan, "Where a Kid Can Be a Kid!" Note how the letter written and signed by Chuck E. Cheese, Showbiz's large rodent icon, addresses the analyst's key points in a positive, fun-loving way.

June 2, 19--
Mr. Roland Whitridge
David L. Babson & Company
One Memorial Drive, Suite 1100
Cambridge, MA 02142-3123

Dear Mr. Whitridge:

I am happy you mentioned my company in *The Wall Street Journal* on May 18 but very sad you don't know us very well.

You say we serve rubber pizza. The enclosed sample of rubber pizza is definitely not what we serve. Please be our guest at Showbiz and see what we're really serving. Be very careful if you go during prime birthday party time because hundreds of excited little consumers who still think Chuck E. Cheese is the best place to spend their most special day of the year are running around.

Oh, yes, you said you think we have a "faddy thing." One of my fans of over ten years is pictured in the enclosed photos. This young man and his friends thought we were pretty neat in the early 80s, and they're all grown up now. When you come to see us, you won't see the same kids running around, and thank goodness—they're too big for the rides! However, you will see lots of little guys who still think we're pretty special.

Let's get re-acquainted and be friends.

Your pal,

Chuck E. Cheese

Enclosures

Reprinted with permission by Cynthia Pharr, C. Pharr & Company, Inc.

Applying What You Have Learned

1. Why was the lighter theme of Pharr's letter to the financial analyst appropriate for a rebuttal?

2. Assume that you are the financial analyst. What impact do you believe the letter and its enclosures would have on you?

to uphold your own personal values and your company's standards of ethical conduct. Before speaking or writing, use the following guidelines to help you filter your message to ensure that you are using effective communication skills responsibly and ethically.

- **Is the information stated as truthfully, honestly, and fairly as possible?** Have you included all information relevant to the receiver even if it is contrary to your argument? Consider the enticing error of omission in the following workplace dilemma: In a letter to an investor, an investment manager enthusiastically reports that the client's stock portfolio has experienced 24 percent growth but does not reveal the stock market as a whole has increased 32 percent in the same period. Is it ethical for the stock investor to withhold the overall stock market growth so that the client is unable to compare his or her stock growth to a standard? Likewise, when writing the company's annual report to the stockholders, a company president disclosed the financial benefits of a plant closing but omitted reporting that 3,000 employees were laid off in a town where the plant was the primary employer. Is that omission ethical? Gaining a reputation for sending messages that disclose complete and accurate information (regardless of whether it supports your views) builds a solid foundation for strong, long-lasting relationships.

Were you ever the recipient of an unethical business practice? Describe the incident, your feelings, and the outcome.

- **Are the ideas expressed clearly and understandably?** If a message is to be classified as honest, you must be reasonably confident that the receiver can understand the message accurately. Ethical communicators select words that convey the exact meaning intended and that are within the reader's vocabulary. Consider a plumber's frustration with the following responses to his query: "The effect of HCL is incompatible with the metallic piping" and "We cannot assume responsibility for the production of toxic and noxious residues with HCL." Finally the Bureau of Standards wrote a message the plumber could understand: "Don't use HCL. It eats the heck out of pipes!"[6] Communicators who intentionally obscure meaning are being unethical. For example, is a CEO unethical when he states, "We conclusively consolidated our endeavors to revoke the capitulation in earnings," if his intention is to create confusion about the company's poor performance? To protect consumers, some states have passed "Plain English" laws that require businesses to write policies, warranties, and contracts in language an average reader can understand. You can learn more about the importance of Plain English laws by completing the Real-Time Internet Case at the end of this chapter.

- **Are unpleasant ideas stated tactfully and positively to preserve the receiver's self-worth and to build future relationships?** Becoming adept at communicating negative information will give you the confidence needed to handle sensitive situations in a positive, constructive manner rather than ignoring them until they get out of control. For example, a supervisor, uncertain how to approach an employee about low productivity, may (1) intimidate or antagonize the employee if the negative information is not carefully presented or (2) continually postpone the confrontation until the only recourse is to terminate the employee. Consider the negative tone reflected in the following memorandum:

TO: Owen Herren
FROM: Sandra Chesser *SC*
DATE: January 5, 1999
SUBJECT: ACCOUNTS RECEIVABLE MUST BE CONTROLLED

Accounts receivable are out of control.

What has happened to the credit checks that are supposed to control such grotesque delinquency? The company has provided you with staff to perform these credit checks and to contact overdue accounts. Maybe it would be a good idea if you started using them.

Owen, this problem is inexcusable, and I expect to see improvement right away.

Even though Owen is clearly responsible for the problem, the revised memo is more tactful and offers suggestions for solving the problem. The memo ends with a final offer of help rather than a threat.

TO: Owen Herren
FROM: Sandra Chesser *SC*
DATE: January 5, 1999
SUBJECT: STRATEGIES FOR EVALUATING COLLECTION
                PROCEDURES

Accounts receivable continue to grow. Because this rising delinquency rate is approaching an alarming level, I believe we must evaluate our current procedures to identify a viable solution. Therefore, please begin a full-scale evaluation of the collection process immediately. Specifically, you might begin by

1. Scheduling a meeting with the sales staff to discuss our current credit limits and our methods of granting credit. Based on this input, make the necessary changes.

2. Evaluating the effectiveness of the procedures used to collect past-due accounts. Could you revise the collection letters so that they appeal more effectively to the needs of specific customers? Should we consider modifying the time intervals between collection notices?

As you evaluate the collection process, call me if you need additional input. I look forward to seeing the results of the plans you initiate.

Obviously, being able to say "no" without alienating everyone is a priceless tool when you must take a stand on a difficult ethical issue. Chapter 6 will help you gain skill in conveying negative information while retaining the goodwill of the receiver.

- **Does the message embellish or exaggerate the facts?** Legal guidelines related to advertising provide clear guidance for misrepresentation of products or services; however, overzealous sales representatives or imaginative writers can use language skillfully to create less-than-accurate perceptions in the minds of the readers. Businesses have learned the hard way that overstating the capabilities of a product or service (promising more than can be delivered) is not good for business in the long run. *Persuading* the reader to take a particular action

In small groups discuss the ethics of inflating a résumé to increase the chances of getting a job interview (e.g., applicants' suggesting they graduated from college when they never completed the degree, fudging on the grade point average, being creative with job responsibilities and titles).

(buy a product or service, provide an adjustment on a nonroutine claim, or agree to grant a favor) is covered in Chapter 8. Developing skill in writing persuasively will be important throughout your profession. Using effective persuasion techniques to write a winning resume and application letter, the topic of Chapters 13 and 14, will be especially helpful as you begin your career. These techniques should *not* be used, however, if your motive is to exploit the receiver.

- ***Is your viewpoint supported with objective facts?*** Are facts accurately documented to allow the reader to judge the credibility of the source and to give credit where credit is due? Can opinions be clearly distinguished from facts? Do you have a conflict of interest that will prevent you from preparing an unbiased message? Suppose a company has determined it must close one of its plants because of excess capacity. The controller has been appointed to a committee to evaluate the plant sites and determine which should be closed. Questions such as these must be answered: Which plant is least efficient? Which plant closing will have the least negative impact on the community? Which plant is least desirably located? Which plant is least adaptable to future product changes? Before coming to corporate headquarters, the controller managed one of these plants and still knows many of the management team and workers at the plant. The controller must explain the exact nature of the potential bias to the project superiors so they can determine whether the controller should be removed from the committee to protect the usefulness of the recommendation. Chapters 9–12 will guide you in learning to write objective, well-documented reports.

- ***Are graphics carefully designed to avoid distorting facts and relationships?*** For example, is it ethical for a company to overstate an insignificant change in unit sales by using confusing graphic styles to hide negative information deliberately or by using a graph with inappropriate scales? The Strategic Forces box in Chapter 10 presents the principles of creating graphics that show information accurately and honestly.

How bound is a business professional to "tell the truth, the whole truth, and nothing but the truth"?

Organizing the Message

5 *Recognize the importance of organizing a message before writing the first draft.*

After you have identified the specific ways you must adapt the message to your specific audience, you are ready to organize your message. In a discussion of communication, the word **organize** means "the act of dividing a topic into parts and arranging them in an appropriate sequence." Before undertaking this process, you must be convinced that the message is the *right* message—that it is complete, accurate, fair, reasonable, ethical, and logical. If it doesn't meet these standards, it should not be sent. Good organization and good writing or speaking cannot be expected to compensate for a bad decision.

If you organize and write simultaneously, the task seems hopelessly complicated. Writing is much easier if questions about the organization of the message are answered first: What is the purpose of the message, what is the receiver's likely reaction, and should the message begin with the main point? Once these decisions have been made, you can concentrate on expressing ideas effectively.

Outline to Benefit the Sender and the Receiver

When a topic is divided into parts, one part will be recognized as a central idea and the others as minor ideas (details). The process of identifying these ideas and arranging them in the right sequence is known as **outlining**. Outlining *before* writing provides numerous benefits:

How can the business writer make sure the message outline is a time saver and not a time waster?

- *Encourages brevity and accuracy.* Outlining reduces the chance of leaving out an essential idea or including an unessential idea.

- *Permits concentration on one phase at a time.* Having focused separately on (a) the ideas that need to be included, (b) the distinction between major and minor ideas, and (c) the sequence of ideas, the writer is now prepared for total concentration on the next problem—expressing.

- *Saves time in writing.* With questions about which ideas to include and their proper sequence already answered, little time is lost in moving from one point to the next.

- *Provides a psychological lift.* The feeling of success gained in preparing the outline increases confidence that the next step—writing—will be successful, too.

- *Facilitates emphasis and de-emphasis.* Although each sentence makes its contribution to the message, some sentences need to stand out more vividly in the receiver's mind than others. An effective outline ensures that important points will appear in emphatic positions.

The preceding benefits derived from outlining are writer oriented. Because a message has been well outlined, receivers benefit, too:

- The message is more concise and accurate.

- Relationships between ideas are easier to distinguish and remember.

- Reaction to the message and its writer is more likely to be positive.

Receiver reaction to a message is strongly influenced by the sequence in which ideas are presented. A beginning sentence or an ending sentence is in an emphatic position. (Other emphasis techniques are explained later in this chapter.) Throughout this text, you will see that outlining (organizing) is important.

Sequence Ideas to Achieve Desired Goals

6 *Select the appropriate outline (deductive or inductive) for developing messages by identifying the central idea and the likely receiver reaction.*

When planning your writing, you should strive for an outline that will serve you in much the same way a blueprint serves a builder or an itinerary serves a traveler. Organizing your message first will ensure that your ideas are presented clearly and logically and all vital components are included. To facilitate your determining an appropriate sequence for a business document, follow the three-step process illustrated in Figure 3-1. This process involves your answering the following questions in this order:

1. **What is the central idea of the message?** Think about the *reason* you are writing—the first step in the writing process. What is your purpose—extend a job offer, decline an invitation, seek support for an innovative project? The purpose is the central idea of your message. You might think of it as a message condensed into a one-sentence telegram.

2. **What is the most likely receiver reaction to the message?** Ask, "If I were the one receiving the message I am preparing to send, what would *my* reaction be?" Because you would react with pleasure to good news and displeasure to bad news, you can reasonably assume a receiver's reaction would be similar. Recall the dual goals of a communicator: clarity and effective human relations. By considering anticipated receiver reaction, you build goodwill with the receiver. Almost every letter will fit into one of four categories of anticipated receiver reaction: (1) pleasure, (2) displeasure, (3) interest but neither pleasure nor displeasure, or (4) no interest, as shown in Figure 3-1.

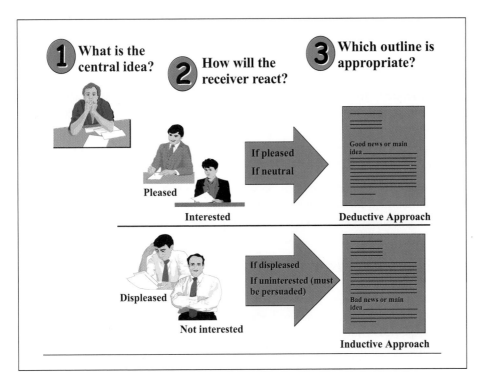

FIGURE 3-1
Process for selecting an appropriate outline.

3. **In view of the predicted receiver reaction, should the central idea be listed *first* in the outline; or should it be listed as one of the *last* items?** When a message begins with the major idea, the sequence of ideas is called **deductive**. When a message withholds the major idea until accompanying details and explanations have been presented, the sequence is called **inductive**.

Consider the receiver to determine whether to use the inductive or deductive paragraph. If a receiver might be antagonized by the main idea in a deductive message, antagonism can be avoided by leading up to the main idea (making the message inductive). If a writer wants to encourage receiver involvement (to generate a little concern about where the details are leading), the inductive approach is recommended. Inductive organization can be especially effective if the main idea confirms the conclusion the receiver has drawn from the preceding details—a cause is worthy of support, an applicant should be interviewed for a job, a product/service should be selected, and so on. As you write letters, memorandums, and e-mail messages in Chapters 5-8, you will comprehend the benefits of using the appropriate outline for each receiver reaction:

When is the deductive sequence recommended? The inductive?

Write Deductively (main idea first)	*Write Inductively (details first)*
When the message will *please* the receiver	When the message will *displease* the receiver
When the message is *routine* (will not please nor displease)	When the receiver *may not be interested* (will need to be persuaded)

For determining the sequence of minor ideas that accompany the major idea, the following bases for paragraph sequence are common:

In groups, discuss whether a deductive or an inductive outline is appropriate for a message (a) accepting an invitation to speak, (b) denying credit to a customer, and (c) commending an employee for exemplary performance.

• **Time.** When reporting on a series of events or a process, paragraphs proceed from the first step through the last step.

- **Space.** If a report is about geographic areas, paragraphs can proceed from one area to the next until all areas have been discussed.
- **Familiarity.** If a topic is complicated, the report can begin with a point that is known or easy to understand and proceed to progressively more difficult points.
- **Importance.** In analytical reports in which major decision-making factors are presented, the factors can be presented in order of most important to least important, or vice versa.
- **Value.** If a report involves major factors with monetary values, paragraphs can proceed from those with greatest values to those with least values, or vice versa.

Although the principal focus is on writing, the same sequence-of-idea patterns are recommended for *oral communication*. These patterns are applicable in memorandums, e-mail messages, and reports as well as in letters.

7 *Apply techniques for developing effective sentences and unified and coherent paragraphs.*

Writing the First Draft

Once you have determined whether the message should be presented deductively (main idea first) or inductively (explanation and details first) and have planned the logical sequence of minor points, you are ready to begin composing the message.

Normally, writing rapidly (with intent to rewrite certain portions if necessary) is better than slow, deliberate writing (with intent to avoid any need for rewriting portions). The latter approach can be time-consuming and frustrating. Thinking of one way to express an idea, discarding it either before or after it is written, waiting for new inspiration, stopping to read and reread preceding sentences—these time-consuming habits can reduce the quality of the finished work.

Recall your own writing experiences. Which was more pleasant for you: (1) the time spent writing a sentence or (2) the time spent between sentences? Because the time spent between sentences can be unproductive or frustrating, that time should be reduced or eliminated. For most people, writing rapidly with the intent to rewrite certain portions if necessary is the better approach by far.

Experienced writers believe that there is no such thing as good writing, but there is such a thing as good rewriting. Author Dorothy Parker once said, "I can't write five words that I change seven."[7] If you are composing at the computer, you can quickly and easily revise your first draft on the computer screen. Electronic spell checks and writing analysis software available with word processing software aid in locating spelling, typographical, and grammatical errors. Systematic revision procedures (to be covered in Chapter 4) will help you produce error-free documents that reflect positively on your company and yourself. The accompanying Strategic Forces box explores the use of technology to enhance collaborative writing.

In groups, discuss which of these writing methods works most effectively for each of you. What habits hinder your success or enjoyment of writing? Brainstorm to identify ways to overcome them.

Write Powerful Sentences

Well-written sentences will help the receiver understand the message clearly and react favorably to the writer or speaker. The following principles affect the clarity and human relations of your message: (1) use correct sentence structure, (2) rely on active voice, and (3) emphasize important points.

Use Correct Sentence Structure. The following discussion identifies problems and techniques business writers encounter frequently. For a complete review of sentences, study Appendix C or consult an English handbook.

Strategic Forces: Team Environment

Groupware Software: Enhancing the Effectiveness of Work Teams

New systems and workgroup software are easing the burden of bringing team members together and allowing them to share data on a timely basis no matter where they are located. *Workgroup computing* or *collaborative computing* are other terms used to describe this cooperative computing environment.

The most well-known software to address collaborative workgroup needs is Lotus® Notes™ from Lotus Development Corporation. Notes is a client-server package that allows workers to track, share, and organize information. An entire industry has developed to provide products that run with Notes. The TeamWARE division of International Computers, Ltd. has developed TeamWARE Office® to challenge Notes. Microsoft Corporation offers Workgroup Templates, a workgroup software product that integrates Microsoft® Mail and desktop applications at a price that even small companies can afford. Although most groupware programs have required a local area network (LAN), software is now available that runs on the World Wide Web.[10]

Groupware enhances the productivity of work teams in three areas: communication, collaboration, and coordination. The following major types of groupware functions illustrate how these three benefits are gained:[11]

- **Knowledge sharing.** Stores information in many different forms (text, diagrams, blueprints) in one place so that it is instantly accessible to everyone. The knowledge base enables companies to respond quickly to customer needs and to new market opportunities. Jim Chapman, head of Triangle, an IBM reseller says, "Everything that happens in our company is recorded in our groupware databases and everybody in the company has access to it. Our people never say 'I didn't know' or 'Nobody told me.'"[12]

- **Bulletin boards.** Stores and organizes comments submitted over long periods of time. For example, instead of calling a meeting for less important ideas, team leaders post a message that others can read and to which they can append comments. All related comments are organized together so they can be accessed and reviewed quickly when a decision must be made.

- **Real-time meetings.** Participants can be linked together to read and respond to information on their computer screens, to participate in brainstorming sessions, and to vote on issues anonymously. By adding videoconferencing software and attaching a camera to the computer, team members can hold a face-to-face meeting, or what is known as an *electronic meeting*. The visual element is an effective aid to teamwork as is the electronic white board, which allows drawings or information written on it to be displayed simultaneously on a computer screen. This information can be saved and used like any other computer file.

- **Document conferencing.** Team members in different locations can work simultaneously on the same document on their screens. The information is first placed on an electronic white board where each member can input edits and sketch drawings that are displayed simultaneously. Members can also chat about the document if videoconferencing software and a camera are available.

- **Group calendaring and scheduling.** Allows users to check schedules and set up meetings with other people.

- **Work flow.** Helps track the status of documents—who has them, who is behind schedule, who gets the document next.

Millions have taken advantage of real-time meetings and document conferencing by simply downloading CoolTalk™ from the Netscape Navigator® web browser or NetMeeting from the Microsoft® Internet Explorer web browser and adding a sound card and a microphone (and a camera if video is desired). The following screen captures illustrate the simple process of placing a call and inputting data on the electronic white board.

Electronic collaboration tools are an aid to effective communication, not a replacement for personal contact. Face-to-face meetings are the

continued

way members really get to know each other—the crucial part of teambuilding. Typically, electronic communication increases and improves after face-to-face team meetings, according to Kirby Hicks of Motorola.[13] Case studies in business and industry show that most of the benefit derived from using workgroup technology is from improvements in intragroup communications rather than from acceleration of individual work.[14] Working with four other colleagues to prepare a written document will not cut your time and energy investment to one-fifth of your solo effort. The resulting document, however, may be significantly better because of the real-time collaboration that occurred during its development.

Application

From library research or your own networking activities, identify an organization that uses work-group software for authoring and editing documents. Conduct an interview with a member of a collaborative team within the organization that includes the following information: (1) software product used for collaborative writing, (2) number and expertise of colleagues who typically collaborate on a single document, (3) reactions to the use of collaborative software in terms of advantages and disadvantages. Present the results of your interview in written or oral form, as directed by your instructor.

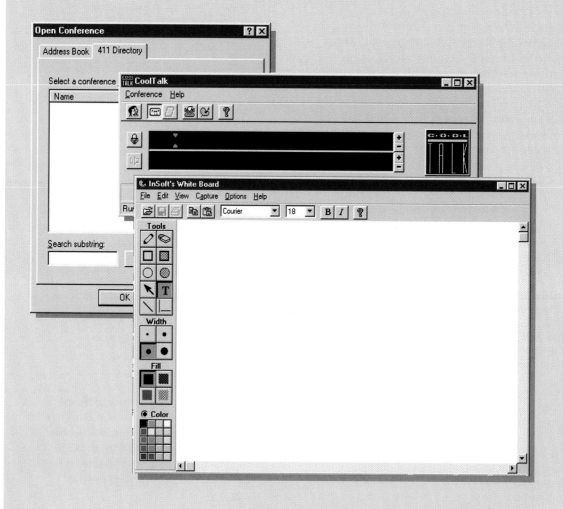

Best-selling novelist John Grisham acknowledges learning a valuable lesson about outlining when an editor deleted numerous pages of an early book that he wrote without an outline. To his credit, only a few pages were cut from his next book that he outlined completely. Today, when writing legal thrillers such as *The Street Lawyer*, Grisham says, "I work from a fairly extensive outline that sometimes runs about 50 pages. When you're writing suspense or mystery, you've got to know where you are going."[8]

All sentences have at least two parts: *subject* and *verb*. In addition to a subject and a verb, a sentence may have additional words to complete the meaning. These words are called **complements**.

Subject	*Verb*	*Complement*
Sid	transferred	overseas.
Chien	transferred	to our Hong Kong office.

A group of words that is not a complete sentence is called a **phrase** or a **clause**. A phrase does not include a subject and a verb; a clause does. The phrases are underlined in the example on the left. In the clauses on the right, the subject is underlined once and the verb is underlined twice:

Phrases	*Clauses*
One <u>of the workers</u> was absent.	As the <u>president</u> <u>reported</u> this morning . . .
The people <u>in that room</u> have voted.	If <u>construction</u> <u>is begun</u> soon . . .
The electrician fell <u>while replacing the socket</u>.	Although the production <u>schedule</u> <u>is</u> incomplete . . .

Clauses are divided into two categories: dependent and independent. A **dependent clause** does not convey a complete thought. The preceding illustrations are dependent. An **independent clause** conveys a complete thought; it could be a complete sentence if presented alone.

Dependent Clause

As the president reported this morning,

Independent Clause

sales increased in May.

Dependent Clause

If construction is begun soon,

Independent Clause

the job can be completed by the end of the year.

Could a dependent clause serve as a complete sentence?

The independent clause "sales increased in May" can be stated as a separate sentence. The dependent clause "As the president reported this morning" does not convey a complete thought and should not be presented without the remainder of the sentence. When a **sentence fragment** (a portion of a sentence) is presented as a separate sentence, receivers become confused and distracted.

Sentences fall into four categories: simple, compound, complex, and compound-complex.

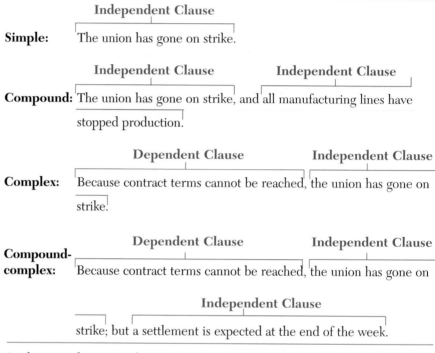

	Independent Clause	
Simple:	The union has gone on strike.	

	Independent Clause	Independent Clause
Compound:	The union has gone on strike, and	all manufacturing lines have stopped production.

	Dependent Clause	Independent Clause
Complex:	Because contract terms cannot be reached,	the union has gone on strike.

	Dependent Clause	Independent Clause
Compound-complex:	Because contract terms cannot be reached,	the union has gone on

Independent Clause

strike; but a settlement is expected at the end of the week.

What grammatical rules give you the most problems?

In the preceding examples, note the use of punctuation to separate one clause from another. When no punctuation or coordinate conjunction appears between the clauses, the result is a **run-on sentence** or **fused sentence**. Another problem is the **comma splice**, in which the clauses are joined only with a comma instead of a comma and coordinating conjunction or a semicolon.

Run-On or Fused Sentence	*Corrected Sentence*
New forms have been ordered they should be delivered next Friday.	New forms have been ordered. They should be delivered next Friday.
	New forms have been ordered; and they should be delivered next Friday.
	New forms have been ordered; they should be delivered next Friday.
	The new forms, which were ordered last week, should be delivered next Friday.

Comma Splice	*Corrected Sentence*
The number of questions has been reduced from 15 to 5, the task will require 25 percent less time.	Because the number of questions has been reduced from 15 to 5, the task will require 25 percent less time.

Rely On Active Voice.　Writers normally use active voice more heavily than passive voice because active voice conveys ideas more vividly. In sentences in which the subject is the *doer* of action, the verbs are called **active**. In sentences in which the subject is the *receiver* of action, the verbs are called **passive**. In the following example, the sentence in the left column uses passive voice; the right, active voice:

Passive Voice	*Active Voice*
Reports are transferred electronically from remote locations to the home office.	Our *sales reps* transfer reports electronically from remote locations to the home office.

The active sentence invites the receiver to see the sales reps using a computer to complete a report. The passive sentence draws attention to a report. Using active voice makes the subject the actor, which makes the idea easier to understand. Sentences written using passive voice give receivers a less-distinct picture. In the passive sentence, the receiver becomes aware that something was done to the reports, but it does not reveal who did it.

Even when a passive sentence contains additional words to reveal the doer, the imagery is less distinct than it would be if the sentence were active: *Reports compiled by our sales representatives are transferred electronically from remote locations to the home office.* "Reports" gets the most attention because it is the subject. The sentence seems to let a receiver know the *result* of action before revealing the doer; therefore, the sentence is less emphatic.

Although active voice conveys ideas more vividly, passive voice is useful

- In concealing the doer ("The reports have been compiled.").

- In placing more emphasis on *what* was done and what it was *done* to than on who *did* it ("The reports have been compiled by our sales representatives.").

- In subordinating an unpleasant thought ("The Shipping Department has not been notified of this delay." rather than "You have not notified the Shipping Department of this delay.") Review the previous discussion of using passive voice to de-emphasize negative ideas in the "Project a Positive, Tactful Tone" section of this chapter.

Write several active and passive voice sentences and note the difference in the vividness of the sentences.

Emphasize Important Ideas.　A landscape artist wants some features in a picture to stand out boldly and others to get little attention. A musician sounds some notes loudly and others softly. Likewise, a writer or speaker wants some ideas to be *emphasized* and others to be *de-emphasized*. Normally, pleasant and important ideas should be emphasized; unpleasant and insignificant ideas should be de-emphasized. Emphasis techniques include sentence structure, repetition, words that label, position, punctuation, and space and format.

Sentence structure.　For emphasis, place an idea in a simple sentence. The simple sentence in the following examples has one independent clause. Because no other idea competes with it for attention, this idea is emphasized.

Simple Sentence Is More Emphatic	*Compound Sentence Is Less Emphatic*
Nicole took a job in insurance.	Nicole took a job in insurance, but she really preferred a job in accounting.

For emphasis, place an idea in an independent clause; for de-emphasis, place an idea in a dependent clause. In the following compound sentence the idea of taking a job is in an independent clause. Because an independent clause makes sense if the rest of the sentence is omitted, an independent clause is more emphatic than a dependent clause. In the complex sentence, the idea of taking a job is in a dependent clause. By itself, the clause would not make complete sense. Compared with the independent clause that follows ("Nicole really preferred . . ."), the idea in the dependent clause is de-emphasized.

Compound Sentence *Is More Emphatic*	*Complex Sentence* *Is Less Emphatic*
Nicole took a job in insurance, but she really preferred a job in accounting.	Although she took a job in insurance, Nicole really preferred a job in accounting.

Repetition. To emphasize a word, let it appear more than once in a sentence. In the following example, "success" receives more emphasis when the word is repeated.

Less Emphatic	*More Emphatic*
The project was successful because of . . .	The project was successful; this success is attributed to . . .

Words that label. For emphasis or de-emphasis, use words that label ideas as significant or insignificant. Note the labeling words used in the following examples to emphasize or de-emphasize an idea:

But most important of all . . .
A less significant aspect was . . .

Position. To emphasize a word or an idea, position it first or last in a sentence, clause, paragraph, or composition (letter, memo, report, or speech). Words that appear first compete only with words that follow; words that appear last compete only with words that precede. Note the additional emphasis placed on the words *success* and *failure* in the examples in the right column because these words appear as the *first* or the *last* words in their clauses.

Less Emphatic	*More Emphatic*
Your efforts contributed to the <u>success</u> of the project; otherwise, <u>failure</u> would have been the result.	<u>Success</u> resulted from your efforts; <u>failure</u> would have resulted without them.
The project was <u>successful</u> because of your efforts; without them, <u>failure</u> would have been the result.	The project was a <u>success</u>; without your efforts, it would have been a <u>failure</u>.

What hidden message (metacommunication) is communicated by a message in which most paragraphs begin with I?

In paragraphs, the first and last words are in particularly emphatic positions. An idea that deserves emphasis can be placed in either position, but an idea that does not deserve emphasis can be placed in the middle of a long paragraph. The word *I*, which is frequently overused in messages, is especially noticeable if it appears as the first word. *I* is more noticeable if it appears as the first word in *every* paragraph. *However* is to be avoided as the first word in a paragraph if the preceding paragraph is neutral or positive. These words imply that the next idea will be negative. Unless the purpose is to place emphasis on negatives, such words as *denied*, *rejected*, and *disappointed* should not appear as the last words in a paragraph.

Likewise, the central idea of a written or oral report appears in the introduction (the beginning) and the conclusion (the end). Good transition sentences synthesize ideas at the end of each major division.

Punctuation. Careful writers use punctuation marks for emphasis and de-emphasis, particularly when sentences contain appositives. An **appositive** is a word that purposefully repeats or explains a preceding word. For appositives, use parentheses for de-emphasis, a comma for neutral emphasis, and a dash or a colon for emphasis. Note the variation in emphasis given to the following appositive using the parentheses, a comma, a dash, and a colon.

> How can the effective writer restate without being redundant?

Appositive	Emphasis Applied Using Various Punctuation Marks
	Parentheses
Companies are seeking job applicants with a specific skill (leadership).	Label an idea as parenthetical that could be omitted. An idea that could be omitted is not thought of as particularly important. Use of parentheses is like saying "The skill is not especially important, but just in case it is of interest, here it is."
	Comma
Companies are seeking job applicants with a specific skill, leadership.	Implies neither emphasis nor de-emphasis. "Specific skill" and "leadership" are of about equal importance.
	Dash
Companies are seeking job applicants with a specific skill—leadership.	Attaches special emphasis to an appositive. It is a strong mark of punctuation that is longer and stronger than a comma. Using a dash is similar to the long pause used in a presentation for special emphasis.
	Colon
Companies are seeking job applicants with a specific skill: leadership.	Attaches special emphasis to an appositive because it is a strong mark of punctuation.

Space and format. The various divisions of a report or speech are not expected to be of equal length, but an extraordinary amount of space devoted to a topic attaches special significance to that topic. Similarly, a topic that gets an exceedingly small amount of space is de-emphasized. The manner in which information is physically arranged affects the emphasis it receives, as presented in the related Strategic Forces Feature Box.

Develop Coherent Paragraphs

Well-constructed sentences are combined into paragraphs that discuss a portion of the topic being discussed. To write effective paragraphs, you must learn to (a) develop deductive or inductive paragraphs consistently, (b) link ideas to achieve coherence, (c) keep paragraphs unified, and (d) vary sentence and paragraph length.

Strategic Forces: Changing Technology

Visual Enhancements Facilitate Comprehension

The vast amount of information created in today's competitive global market poses a challenge to you as a business writer. You must learn to create visually appealing documents that entice a receiver to read rather than discard your message. Additionally, an effective design will enable you to highlight important information for maximum attention and to transition a receiver smoothly through sections of a long, complex document. These design techniques can be performed easily using word processing software. However, be certain to add visual enhancements *only* when they aid in comprehension; otherwise, your document will appear cluttered and will defeat your purpose to create an appealing, easy-to-read document.

Enumerations

To emphasize units in a series, place a number, letter, or bullet before each element. Words preceded by numbers, bullets, or letters, attract the receiver's special attention and are easier to locate when the page is reviewed.

Original
The personnel problems have been narrowed into three categories: absenteeism, tardiness, and pilferage.

Highlighted
The personnel problems have been narrowed into three categories: (1) absenteeism, (2) tardiness, and (3) pilferage.

Enumerated or Bulleted Lists

Many times writers want to save space; however, cluttered text is unappealing and difficult to read. *Chunking*—a desktop publishing term—is an answer to the problem. **Chunking** involves breaking down information into easily digestible pieces. It's the communication equivalent of Butterfinger® BBs, rather than the whole candy bar. The added white space divides the information into blocks, makes the page look more organized, and increases

retention by 50 percent.[9] Specific techniques include enumerated or bulleted lists.

Enumerated or bulleted lists can be used to add even greater visual impact to items in a series. Items appear on separate lines with numerals, letters, or various types of bullets (•, ❑, ✓, ◆, and so on) at the beginning. Multiple line items often are separated by a blank line. This design creates more white space that isolates the items from other text and demands attention. Bullets are typically preferred over numerals unless the sequence of the items in the series is critical (e.g., steps in a procedure that must be completed in the correct order). In the following excerpt from a long analytical report, the four supporting reasons for a conclusion are highlighted in a bulleted list:

Original
For our needs, then, the most appropriate in-service training method is computerized instruction. This training is least expensive, allows employees to remain at their own workstations while improving their skills, affords constant awareness of progress, and lets employees progress at their own rates.

Highlighted
Computerized instruction is the most appropriate in-service training method because it
- Is least expensive.
- Allows employees to remain at their own workstations while improving their skills.
- Affords constant awareness of progress.
- Lets employees progress at their own rates.

Headings

Headings are signposts that direct the receiver from one section of the document to another. They are arranged in a hierarchy with the major headings receiving more attention than minor headings or paragraph headings. The placement of headings and the choice of typestyles and print enhancements create a hierarchy of different levels of headings. For example, a centered major heading printed in a prominent boldfaced typeface would be more emphatic than a minor heading printed at the left margin with a slightly smaller size type.

continued

Headings are especially useful in organizing the content of a long report; however, they are also helpful in organizing resumes and complex letters and memorandums. Note the position and spacing of three levels of headings shown in Figure 11-4.

Brief headings tend to be more emphatic than long headings. Talking headings (headings that reveal the conclusions reached in the following discussion) are more emphatic than general topic headings. For example, "Costs Are Prohibitive" is more emphatic than "Cost Factors."

Tables and Graphs

Tables and graphs are used to simplify and clarify information and to add an appealing variety to long sections of dense text. The clearly labeled rows and columns in a table organize large amounts of specific numeric data and facilitate analysis. Graphics such as pie charts, line charts, and bar charts visually depict relationships within the data; they provide quick estimates rather than specific information. You will gain proficiency in selecting an appropriate graphic format for data and in designing effective and accurate tables and graphs in Chapter 10.

Lines and Borders

Horizontal and vertical lines can be added to partition text or to focus attention on a specific line(s). For example, a thin line followed by a thick line effectively separates the identification section of a resume from the qualifications. Placing a border around a paragraph or section of text sets that text apart; adding shading inside the box adds greater impact. For example, a shaded border might spotlight a testimonial from a satisfied customer in a sales letter, important dates to remember in a memorandum, or a section of a document that must be completed and returned.

Drawing Tools and Clip Art

A variety of interesting shapes and lines highlight information and add appeal. Examples include creating a rectangular callout box with a key idea inside with an arrow pointing to a specific number in a table, surrounding a title with a shaded oval for added impact, and using various shapes to illustrate the steps in a process. The applications are limited only by the writer's creativity. Clip art can also be added to reinforce an idea and add visual appeal. Note the variety of drawing tools (ovals, arrows, rectangles, lines, and clip art) used to depict visually the three-step process in Figure 3-1.

Application

Evaluate the visual impact of a document that you have received or one that your instructor provides. Summarize any changes you would make and explain how the changes would improve the impact of the document. Then, as you prepare documents in this course, evaluate the need for visual enhancements that will make your document say, "Read me."

Position the Topic Sentence Appropriately. Typically, paragraphs contain one sentence that identifies the portion of the topic being discussed and presents the central idea. That sentence is commonly called a **topic sentence**. For example, consider a pamphlet written to a company that has purchased a Zip drive. The overall topic is how to get satisfactory performance from the machine. One portion of that topic is installation; another portion (paragraph) discusses operation; and so forth. Within each paragraph, one sentence serves a special function. Sentences that list the steps can appear as one paragraph, perhaps with steps numbered as follows:

"To install a new Zip drive, take the following steps:
1.   Insert . . .
2.   Click . . . .

In this illustration, the paragraphs are **deductive**; that is, the topic sentence *precedes* details. When topic sentences *follow* details, the paragraphs are called **inductive paragraphs**. As discussed previously, the receiver's likely reaction

Musicians, like writers, can project what they want their audiences to hear through a number of techniques. For example, the conductor can urge the musicians to play loudly through a portion of a symphony that he or she would like to emphasize while directing them to play softly throughout a lesser part. In a similar manner, writers can employ several techniques to call attention to ideas they believe are important while de-emphasizing unpleasant or insignificant ideas.

(pleased, displeased, interested, not interested) to the main idea aids in selecting the appropriate sequence.

When the subject matter is complicated and the details are numerous, paragraphs sometimes begin with a main idea, follow with details, and end with a summarizing sentence. But the main idea may not be in the first sentence; the idea may need a preliminary statement. Receivers appreciate consistency in the placement of topic sentences. Once they catch on to the writer's pattern, they know where to look for main ideas.

These suggestions seldom apply to the first and last sentences of letters. Such sentences frequently appear as single-sentence paragraphs. But for reports and long paragraphs of letters, strive for paragraphs that are consistently deductive or consistently inductive. Regardless of which is selected, topic sentences are clearly linked with details that precede or follow.

Link Ideas to Achieve Coherence. Careful writers use coherence techniques to keep receivers from experiencing abrupt changes in thought. Although the word **coherence** is used sometimes to mean "clarity" or "understandability," it is used throughout this text to mean "cohesion." If writing or speaking is coherent, the sentences stick together; and each sentence is in some way linked to the preceding sentences. Avoid abrupt changes in thought, and link each sentence to a preceding sentence.

The following techniques for linking sentences are common:

1. ***Repeat a word that was used in the preceding sentence.*** The second sentence in the following example is an obvious continuation of the idea presented in the preceding sentence.

   . . . to take responsibility for the decision. This responsibility can be shared . . . .

2. ***Use a pronoun that represents a noun used in the preceding sentence.***
   Because "it" means "responsibility," the second sentence is linked directly with
   the first.

. . . to take this responsibility. It can be shared. . . .

---

3. ***Use connecting words.*** Examples are *however, therefore, yet, nevertheless,*
   consequently, also, in addition, and so on. "However" implies "We're continuing with the same topic, just moving into a different phase." Remember,
   though, that good techniques can be *over*used. Unnecessary connectors are
   space consuming and distracting. Usually they can be spotted (and crossed
   out) in proofreading.

. . . to take this responsibility. However, few are willing to . . .

Just as sentences within a paragraph must link, paragraphs within a document
must also link. Unless a writer (or speaker) is careful, the move from one major topic
to the next will seem abrupt. A good transition sentence can bridge the gap between
the two topics by summing up the preceding topic and leading a receiver to expect
the next topic:

Cost factors, then, seemed prohibitive until efficiency factors were investigated.

This sentence could serve as a transition between the "Cost" division heading and
the "Efficiency" division heading. Because a transition sentence comes at the end of
one segment and before the next, it emphasizes the central idea of the preceding
segment and confirms the relationship of the two segments.

Transition sentences are very helpful if properly used, but they can be
overused. For most reports, transition sentences before major headings are sufficient. Normally, transition sentences before subheadings are unnecessary. Having
encountered the previous subheading only a few lines back, a receiver should readily see its relationship to the upcoming subheading. In addition, transition sentences typically summarize, and the discussion under a subheading of a report is
seldom long enough to merit summarization. Place transition sentences before
major headings.

Keep Paragraphs Unified. Receivers expect the first paragraph of a message to
introduce a topic, additional paragraphs to discuss it, and a final paragraph to tie
them together. The in-between paragraphs should be arranged in a systematic
sequence, and the end must be linked easily to some word or idea presented in the
beginning. The effect of a message that is *not* unified is like that of an incomplete
circle or a picture with one element obviously missing.

A letter or report with unity covers its topic adequately but will not include extra-
neous material. The letter or report will have a beginning sentence appropriate for
the expected receiver reaction, paragraphs that present the bulk of the message, and
an ending sentence that is an appropriate closing for the message presented. If the
sequence is logical, coherence is easy to achieve.

A report with unity begins with an introduction that identifies the topic,
reveals the thesis, and previews upcoming points. The introduction may also
include some background, sources of information, and the method of treating
data. Between the beginning and the ending, a unified report will have paragraphs
arranged in a systematic sequence. A summary or conclusion brings all major
points together.

How are unity and coher-
ence related concepts?

Vary Sentence and Paragraph Length. Short, average-length sentences are easy to read and preferred for communicating clearly. However, keeping *all* sentences short is undesirable because the message may sound monotonous, unrealistic, or elementary. A two-word sentence is acceptable; so is a 60-word sentence—if it is clear. Just as sentences should vary in length, they should also vary in structure. Some complex or compound sentences should be included with simple sentences. You will learn more about the relationship between sentence length and readability in Chapter 4.

Variety is just as desirable in paragraph length as it is in sentence length. A paragraph can be from one line in length to a dozen lines or more. However, just as average sentence length should be kept fairly short, average paragraph length also should be kept short.

Paragraphs in business letters or memos are typically shorter than paragraphs in business reports. First and last paragraphs are normally short (one to four lines), and other paragraphs are normally no longer than *six lines*. A short first paragraph makes a letter or memo look more inviting to read than a long first paragraph. A short last paragraph enables a writer to emphasize parting thoughts.

In business reports, the space between paragraphs is a welcome resting spot. Long paragraphs are difficult to read and make a page appear unattractive. Paragraph length will vary depending on the complexity of the subject matter. However, as a general rule paragraphs should be no longer than *eight to ten* lines. This length usually allows enough space to include a topic sentence and three or four supporting statements. If the topic cannot be discussed in this space, divide the topic into additional paragraphs.

To illustrate the effect large sections of unbroken text has on the overall appeal of a document, examine the memos in Figure 3-2 that contain identical information. Without question, the memo with the short, easy-to-read paragraphs is more inviting to read than the memo with the one bulky paragraph.

Although variety is a desirable quality, it should not be achieved at the expense of consistency. Using *I* in one part of a message and then without explanation switching to *we* is inadvisable. Using the past tense in one sentence and the present tense in another sentence creates variety at the expense of consistency—unless the shift is required to indicate actual changes in time. Unnecessary changes from active to passive voice (or vice versa) and from third to second person (or vice versa) are also discouraged.

Why are paragraphs in a business letter typically shorter than those in a literary essay?

Bulky Text

R C
Rossan Corporation
480 Woodson Ridge Road
Canton, OH 44711-0480
(206) 555-8763

TO: All Employees
FROM: Victor Miranda, Manager *V.M.*
DATE: December 15, 1999
SUBJECT: EXTRA VACATION DAY

The board of directors has approved one additional vacation day for every employee. This decision is our way of expressing gratitude for the most productive and profitable year in the history of Rossan Corporation. With the approval of your department head, you may select any day between January 2 and June 30. This day of vacation is in addition to year-end bonuses you will receive soon. Thank you for all you have done to make the year successful, and best wishes for a healthy and happy new year.

Broken Text

R C
Rossan Corporation
480 Woodson Ridge Road
Canton, OH 44711-0480
(206) 555-8763

TO: All Employees
FROM: Victor Miranda, Manager *V.M.*
DATE: December 15, 1999
SUBJECT: EXTRA VACATION DAY

The board of directors has approved one additional vacation day for every employee.

This decision is our way of expressing gratitude for the most productive and profitable year in the history of Rossan Corporation. With the approval of your department head, you may select any day between January 2 and June 30. This day of vacation is in addition to year-end bonuses you will receive soon.

Thank you for all you have done to make the year successful, and best wishes for a healthy and happy new year.

FIGURE 3-2 Bulky vs. broken text. What hidden message is conveyed?

Receiver's Point of View

- Present ideas from the receiver's point of view; this "you attitude" conveys a feeling that the message is specifically for the receiver.

Bias-Free Language

- Do not use the pronoun *he* when referring to a group of people that may include women or *she* when a group may include men.
- Avoid referring to men and women in stereotyped roles and occupations.
- Avoid expressions that reflect stereotypical characteristics.
- Avoid using gender-biased occupational titles or differentiating genders in an occupation.
- Avoid referring to groups (based on race and ethnicity, age, religion, and disability) in stereotypical and insensitive ways.
- Do not emphasize race and ethnicity, age, religion, or disability when these factors are not relevant.

Goodwill

- Avoid using condescending words.
- Use euphemisms to present unpleasant thoughts politely and positively.
- Avoid using euphemisms when they will be taken as excessive or sarcastic.
- Give sincere compliments.
- Avoid using flattery.
- Avoid using demeaning expressions.
- Rely mainly on denotative words or connotative words that will elicit a favorable reaction.
- Avoid expressing surprise, doubt, and judgment when they would be interpreted as insults.
- Avoid expressing certainty when certainty is hardly possible.

Positive, Tactful Tone

- Rely mainly on positive words that speak of what can be done instead of what cannot be done, of the pleasant instead of the unpleasant. Use negative words when the purpose is to sharpen contrast or when positive words have not evoked the desired reaction.
- Use second person and active voice to emphasize a pleasant idea. For better human relations, avoid using second person for presenting negative ideas. Instead, use third person and passive voice to de-emphasize the unpleasant thought.
- Consider stating an unpleasant thought in the subjunctive mood.

Powerful Sentences

- Use correct structure when writing simple, compound, complex, and compound-complex sentences. Avoid run-on sentences and comma splices.
- Use active voice to present important points or to present pleasant ideas and passive verbs to present less significant points or unpleasant ideas.
- Emphasize important ideas:
  - Place an idea in a simple sentence.
  - Place an idea in an independent clause; for de-emphasis, place an idea in a dependent clause.
  - Use an important word more than once in a sentence.
  - Place an important idea first or last in a sentence, paragraph, or document.
  - Precede each unit in a series by a number or a letter; or a bullet; for stronger emphasis, place in an enumerated or bulleted list.
  - Use parentheses for de-emphasis, a comma for neutral emphasis, and a dash or colon for emphasizing appositives.
  - Use words that label ideas as significant or insignificant.
  - Use headings, graphics, and additional space to emphasize important ideas.

Coherent Paragraphs

- Write deductively if a message will likely please or at least not displease. If a message will likely displease or if understanding the major idea is dependent on prior explanations, write inductively.
- Strive for paragraphs that are consistently deductive or consistently inductive.
- Make sure compositions form a unit with an obvious beginning, middle, and ending and that in-between paragraphs are arranged in a systematic sequence.
- Avoid abrupt changes in thought, and link each sentence to a preceding sentence. Place transition sentences before major headings.
- Vary sentence and paragraph length to emphasize important ideas.
- Limit paragraphs in letters to six lines and paragraphs in reports to eight to ten lines to maximize comprehension.

SUMMARY

1. **Identify the purpose of the message and the appropriate channel.** Writing is a systematic process that begins by determining the purpose of the message (central idea) and identifying how the central idea will affect the receiver. In view of its effect on the receiver, you can determine the appropriate channel for sending a particular message (e.g., face-to-face, telephone, letter/memo, e-mail, voice mail, or fax).

2. **Envision the audience so you can adapt messages to the audience.** Before you compose the first draft, consider all you know about the receiver, including age, economic level, educational/occupational background, culture, existing relationship, expectations, and his/her needs.

3. **Apply techniques for adapting messages to the audience.** The insights you gain from seeking to understand your receiver will allow you to adapt the message to fit the receiver's needs. You will assume an empathetic attitude, focus on the receiver's point of view rather than your own, use bias-free language, avoid statements that destroy goodwill, and project a positive, tactful tone.

4. **Apply the guidelines for communicating ethically and responsibly.** Knowing how to analyze ethical dilemmas and to express ideas clearly and tactfully will increase your chances for success in the business world. Guidelines for communicating responsibly and ethically include stating information truthfully, expressing ideas clearly, stating unpleasant ideas tactfully, eliminating any embellishments or exaggerations, supporting viewpoints with objective facts from credible sources, and designing graphics that do not distort facts.

5. **Recognize the importance of organizing a message before writing the first draft.** Outlining involves identifying the appropriate sequence of pertinent ideas. Outlining encourages brevity and accuracy, permits concentration on one phase at a time, saves writing time, increases confidence to complete the task, and facilitates appropriate emphasis of ideas. From a receiver's point of view, well-organized messages are easier to understand and promote a more positive attitude toward the writer.

6. **Select the appropriate outline (deductive or inductive) for developing messages by identifying the central idea and the likely receiver reaction.** A part of the outlining process is deciding whether the message should be deductive (main idea first) or inductive (explanations and details first). The main idea is presented first and details follow when (1) the receiver is expected to be pleased by the message and (2) the message is routine and not likely to arouse a feeling of pleasure or displeasure. When the receiver can be expected to be displeased or not initially interested, explanations and details precede the main idea.

7. **Apply techniques for developing effective sentences and for developing unified and coherent paragraphs.** Well-written sentences and unified and coherent paragraphs will help the receiver understand the message clearly and respond favorably. To write powerful sentences, use correct sentence structure, rely on active voice, and emphasize important points. To write effective paragraphs, develop deductive or inductive paragraphs consistently, link ideas to achieve coherence, keep paragraphs unified, and vary sentence and paragraph length.

   Refer to the "Check Your Writing" checklist to review the guidelines for writing a first draft of the message that can be easily understood and received positively .

REFERENCES

[1]Dennett, J. T. (1988). Not to say is better than to say: How rhetorical structure reflects cultural context in Japanese-English technical writing. *IEEE Trans. Professional Communication, 31*(3), 116-1998. In Subbiah, M. (1992). Adding a new dimension to the teaching of audience analysis: Cultural awareness. *IEEE, 35*(1), 14–17.

[2]Amemiya, H., & Aizu, I. (1985, October 7). Defining a good Japanese user manual. *Intercom* (Society for Technical Communication newsletter), *33*, p. 7. In Subbiah, M.

(1992). Adding a new dimension to the teaching of audience analysis: Cultural awareness. *IEEE, 35*(1), 14–17.

[3]Moody, P. G. (1987). *Skills for the electronic world—reach a little higher*. Cincinnati: South-Western. [p. 155].

[4]Lawlor, J. (1994, April 21). More firms offer services for employees. *USA Today*, p. B1–2.

[5]Tyler, L. (1990). Communicating about people with disabilities: Does the language we use make a difference? *Bulletin of the Association for Business Communication, 53*(3), 65–67.

[6]Reinemund, S. S. (1992). Today's ethics and tomorrow's work place. *Business Forum, 17*(2), 6–9.

[7]Charlton, J. (Ed.) (1985). *The writer's quotation book.* Stamford, CT: Ray Freeman and Company.

[8]Willett, M. (1997, April 6). The author: Grisham still gets a kick out of writing.

[9]Dyrud, M. A. (1996). Teaching by example: Suggestions for assignment design. *Business Communication Quarterly, 59*(3), 67–70.

[10]Craft, V. (1995, May). Searching for tools to ease collaboration in cross-functional workgroups: Tapping team power. *Electronic Business Buyer,* 45.

[11]Field, A. (1996). *Group think. Inc. 18*(13), 38–44

[12]Newing, R. (1997, January). Benefits of groupware. *Management Accounting,* 56–57.

[13]Craft, V. (1995, may). Searching for tools to ease collaboration in cross-functional workgroups: Tapping team power. *Electronic Business Buyer,* 45.

[14]Newing, R. (1997, January). Benefits of groupware. *Management Accounting,* 56–57.

[15]Bredin, J. (1991, July 15). Say it simple. *Industry Week,* 19–20.

REVIEW QUESTIONS

1. What is the central idea of a message? What two purposes do most business messages serve? (Obj. 1)

2. Why is selecting an appropriate communication channel important to the overall effectiveness of the message? Provide two examples. (Obj. 1)

3. How does envisioning the audience affect the message? What factors about the audience should you consider? (Obj. 2)

4. What is empathy and how does it affect business writing? (Obj. 3)

5. List four guidelines for avoiding gender-biased language. (Obj. 3)

6. When is use of a euphemism appropriate? Detrimental? (Obj. 3)

7. Under what conditions are connotative words acceptable? (Obj. 3)

8. What are the disadvantages of using expressions such as *"I know you will want to . . ."* and *"I am sure you have . . ."*? (Obj. 3)

9. How does the expression "with power comes responsibility" relate to business writing? (Obj. 4)

10. List six guidelines for communicating responsibly and ethically. (Obj. 4)

11. What primary benefits does the writer gain from outlining before writing? How does the receiver benefit? (Obj. 5)

12. What three questions should be answered before a writer decides whether to write deductively or inductively? (Obj. 6)

13. Is writing rapidly with intent to revise or writing slowly and deliberately more effective? Explain. (Obj. 5)

14. When is active voice preferred? When is passive voice preferred? (Obj. 7)

15. Which provides more emphasis for an idea in each of the following categories: (a) a simple sentence or a complex sentence, (b) an independent clause or a dependent clause, (c) parentheses or dashes, (d) bulleted/enumerated list or paragraph arrangement? (Obj. 7)

EXERCISES

1. **Audience Analysis (Obj. 2)**
   Write a brief analysis of the audience for each of the situations presented in Exercise 7.

2. **Empathetic Attitude (Obj. 2-3)**
   In small groups, identify the communication problems created because of a manager's lack of empathy when communicating to employees.

a. A manager for a U.S. firm, who has been transferred to the company's office in Japan, provides the following message to launch the marketing/production team's work on a new product.

   We really need to put our noses to the grindstone to get this new product out and onto the shelves. I've been burning the midnight oil with my people in R&D, and I have some new ideas that need to be implemented before the competition catches on and the cat's out of the bag. So everybody get to work and hit the ground running. Keep me posted on your progress, and remember, my door is always open. Everybody got it?

b. After months of uncertainty at Ramsey, Inc., a corporate official visits an office of the national corporation with the following response to concerned questions by mostly lower-wage technical and support staff regarding layoffs and office closures:

We are realigning our resources company-wide to be more competitive in the marketplace. Our stock has been declining at an unpromising rate, but we are taking steps to ensure future market viability. Restructuring has begun at several levels. Corporate is aware of your concerns and will continue having these meetings to provide a forum for dialogue.

3. **Receiver-Centered Messages (Obj. 3)**
Revise the following sentences to emphasize the reader's viewpoint and the "you" attitude.

a. We're requesting that all customers complete the enclosed client satisfaction questionnaire to allow us to improve our services.

b. I think you should focus on developing your public speaking skills to become a better marketing professional.

c. We will be updating our records and request that new information be submitted as soon as possible.

d. To enable us to better serve the community, we ask that you help us understand your opinions on the parks project.

e. I give you permission to take an extra vacation day because of your performance on the Johnson account.

f. We want all employees to be familiar with OSHA requirements as they pertain to their job.

g. Lasky Enterprises needs employees with a variety of skills to be competitive.

h. As we expand our operations to include a more diverse work force, participation in a two-hour diversity awareness seminar is required.

i. Human Resources requires all employees who work with dangerous goods or hazardous materials to have a complete physical every year.

j. Due to our heavy backlog, we need all personnel in shipping and receiving to work overtime for the next week.

4. **Bias-Free Language (Obj. 3)**
Revise the following sentences to eliminate insensitivity toward gender, race or ethnicity, age, or disability.

a. Each project director must complete the appropriate performance evaluation forms before being awarded his raise.

b. Perkins and Hopkins welshed on the deal with Jackson.

c. The girls in the word processing department deserve a raise.

d. Reiko Harada, our new Japanese sales rep, completed her management training in Austin.

e. Only disabled customers may use the motorized shopping carts.

f. Jim, the older gentleman in receiving, is responsible for verifying purchase orders.

g. Megan Cornwall, a lady lawyer, handled the case for the city.

h. That contractor has jewed many homebuilders by skimping on insulation and using substandard materials.

i. In relation to the new policies, many people saw management as an Indian giver.

j. Each accountant must submit his time and expense report by the 15th of each month.

5. **Statements that Destroy Goodwill (Obj. 3)**
Revise the following sentences to eliminate a tone that will damage human relations. Identify the specific weakness in each sentence.

a. The grunts must submit to a drug test.

b. An ambulance chaser arrived at the scene moments after the crash.

c. Since I took a leadership role on this project, the group's performance has improved.

d. Management has the utmost appreciation for all the maintenance engineers.

e. Ms. Jacobs, the CEO, will be taking time out of her busy schedule to visit our Quality Control Department.

f. It has been quite some time since I did this type of work, but I can help you for a while.

g. The senator's vote for the bill containing revenue enhancements does not violate her campaign pledge.

h. The computer hackers completed the network system conversion several days ahead of schedule.

i. The corporate watchdogs are planning a visit next week.

j. I am sure you will understand our reasons for refusal.

k. We realize that you are upset, but the fee is due on September 15.

6. **Positive, Tactful Tone (Obj. 3)**
   Revise the following sentences to reduce the negative tone.

   a. The policyholder failed to submit his forms for adding new dependents within the 30-day time period.

   b The purchase order cannot be authorized until June 21.

   c. You did not revise the report to include the results of the most recent testing.

   d. You neglected to sign the document in all three signature blocks.

   e. Kristy forgot to include shipping and receiving personnel in this survey.

   f. Jonathan went over budget on his project.

   g. Do not leave without notifying the receptionist on your way out.

   h. Do not forget the staff meeting at noon tomorrow.

   i. I cannot authorize moving expenses for your transfer.

   j. You cannot receive benefits until after you have been with our company for three months.

7. **Appropriate Outline and Channel (Obj. 1, 2, 5)**
   Complete the following analysis to determine whether a deductive or an inductive outline is appropriate for the following situations. Identify the channel you believe would be most appropriate for conveying this message; be prepared to justify your answer. Use the format shown in the following example.

   - *Situation* The annual merit raise has increased to 5 percent.

   - *Recommended channel* Mailed memo or e-mail message; pleasant information that should reach all employees in a timely manner.

   - *Central idea* Inform employees of an increase in annual merit raise.

   - *Likely receiver reaction* Pleased.

   - *Appropriate outline (deductive or inductive)* Deductive.

   a. We cannot offer a refund on your laptop; however, we can repair it at our cost.

   b. The cost of our services has increased 3 percent.

   c. All merit raises have been delayed for six months.

   d. Performance evaluation forms must be completed before an employee may be considered for a raise.

   e. Clients are asked to complete a survey instrument about the quality and type of services rendered.

   f. Employees may participate in a new stock option plan.

   g. Refunds are being distributed to customers who purchased the Model DX laptop, which had a faulty board.

   h. Computer World is now offering a special warranty plan to its customers who recently purchased a home computer system.

   i. Discounts are available to customers who qualify.

8. **Active and Passive Voice (Obj. 3, 6, 7)**
   Revise the following sentences using active and passive voice appropriately. Justify your decision.

   a. An exemplary job was done by the design team.

   b. Elizabeth polled only the clients in the Southeast, thereby producing an inaccurate marketing report.

   c. The projections will be released tomorrow by the financial team.

   d. This innovative advertisement was designed by J. D. Mackay.

   e. Distribution of the market survey is to be no later than May 8.

   f. A proposal for consulting work for the Department of Public Works was written by Alicia.

9. **Sentence Structure (Obj. 7)**
   Analyze the structure of the following sentences: indicate the type of sentence (i.e., simple, compound, complex, or compound-complex), mark the dependent and independent clauses, and punctuate correctly.

   a. The Information Systems Department has implemented new e-mail security procedures.

   b. The consultant recommended a new marketing strategy it works much better than the strategy we formerly used.

   c. We need new marketing brochures, the ones we use now are out of date.

   d. We can generate very attractive brochures in-house the new computer software makes it easy.

   e. Because of the expansion of our overseas operation our current brochures no longer accurately portray our capabilities however the publications department is developing new materials.

10. **Emphasis Techniques (Obj. 7)**
    Decide for each pair of sentences *whic*h one is preferred? *Why* is it preferred?

    a. (1) Our petition for promotion was denied, but we were commended for our performance.

      (2) Although the petition for promotion was denied, we were commended for our performance.

    b. (1) The Lawlor account was won.

      (2) Jennifer is responsible for our winning the Lawlor account.

c. (1) Congratulations on your recent honor.

   (2) Congratulations on your receipt of the "employee of the month student" award.

d. (1) We appreciate your letting us know about your concerns.

   (2) We appreciate your letting us know about the broken equipment, the outdated materials, and the poor employee morale at your branch.

e. (1) We will not be able to fund your Internet training.

   (2) We wish we could pay for your Internet training, but funds are unavailable.

11. **Emphasis and Ordering Techniques (Obj. 6, 7)**

    Revise the following sentences, adding emphasis to the lists.

    a. Our department needs two more engineers. The workload is such that the three engineers currently on staff are out of town on site at least three days a week. Although their work is satisfactory, at this pace, it could suffer soon. Morale is also starting to become a concern. Additionally, because of the increasing work load, it has become difficult for them to attend to routine administrative tasks in a timely fashion.

    b. Our company should offer employees a choice between overtime pay or compensatory time off. Many of our employees are parents and would appreciate having more time to spend with their children. Others are more interested in earning extra money. Therefore, offering a choice would improve morale and reduce employee absenteeism, leading to a more efficient, dedicated work force.

12. **Coherence Techniques (Obj. 7)**

    Link each sentence to the preceding sentence to improve coherence (avoid abrupt changes in thought).

    a.. The design group meets every Monday at 9 a.m. They go over plans and goals for the upcoming week. Other departments have similar meetings.

    b. Diversity awareness training seems important to some employees. It is very effective in improving communication and understanding. Employees should participate in this training.

    c. Our company has initiated a new overtime policy. Employees can choose between overtime pay or compensatory time off. This policy could improve morale and productivity.

    d. The publications department is working on new marketing materials. Our current brochures and materials are out of date. The materials do not reflect the major corporate changes that have occurred in the past six months.

    e. New computer software is being loaded onto our local area network (LAN). Personnel will be able to generate expense statements from their workstations. This will make the old carbon forms obsolete.

E-MAIL APPLICATION

The guidelines for adapting your message to convey sensitivity for the receiver presented in this chapter are an excellent means for building relationships and strong interpersonal skills needed in today's highly competitive global market and in diverse work teams. Identify a specific situation in your work or educational experience, or school or community organizations that illustrates the negative effects of an individual who obviously did not consider the impact of his/her message on the receiver. Your example might include lack of empathy for the receiver's viewpoint (writer-centered), blatant use of biased language, demeaning expressions, condescending tone, misuse of euphemisms, and use of connotative meanings that cause negative reactions, and negative, tactless statements. Send your example to your instructor in an e-mail message. Be prepared to discuss your idea with the class or in small groups.

REAL-TIME INTERNET CASE

Understanding the Plain English Campaign

Effective communication is a major part of a manager's job. Yet many managers continue to bury what they want to say in pompous jargon or polysyllabic babble. Such communication fails miserably because the people to whom it is aimed either do not understand it or regard it as garbage and ignore it.[5] A Plain English movement is gaining momentum in Great Britain and the United States. Plain English Campaign, founded in 1979, is an independent U.K.-based organization that fights to stamp out all forms of gobbledygook, legalese, small print, and bureaucratic language. The campaign is funded by its professional services, which include editing, writing, design, and training in Plain English for a variety of companies as well as government and local authorities. The Plain English Campaign-USA, a subsidiary of the England-based campaign, is based in Miami, Florida.

Documents that achieve a good standard of clarity may qualify for endorsement with the Campaign's Crystal Mark, a widely recognized and respected symbol of clarity. The Mark can be found on over 2,500 documents around the world. It is a powerful marketing tool because customers can see the Crystal mark on documents and know they can be confident that the information is clear.

Misconceptions exist concerning Plain English writing. Writing in Plain English does not mean deleting complex information to make the document easier to understand. Using Plain English assures the orderly and clear presentation of complex information so that the audience has the best possible chance of understanding; it presents information to meet its audience's needs. A Plain English document uses words economically and at a level the audience can understand. Its sentence structure is tight. Its tone is approachable and direct, and its design is visually appealing. A Plain English document is easy to read and looks like it is meant to be read.

Visit the following Internet sites and complete the following activities, as directed by your instructor:

Internet Sites

http://www/plainenglish.co.uk/
http://www.plainenglishusa.com/
http://www.sec.gov/consumer/plaine.htm#A6

Activities

1. Compile a chart that lists companies, agencies, and other organizations that have benefitted from Plain English assistance and the stated results that have been realized. Arrange a telephone interview with a person representing one of the organizations to obtain first-hand information about the impact of Plain English in that organization.

2. Using links provided in the previous Internet sites, familiarize yourself with a recent news story that points out the need for Plain English. Summarize the reported incident in a one-page abstract that includes the following parts: (1) bibliographic citation, (2) brief overview of the article, (3) discussion of the major points covered in the article, and (4) application section that tells who might benefit from reading the article and why.

3. In groups of three or four, select an organization of your choice that could benefit from Plain English assistance; you may consult the "List of Shame" organizations or identify one on your own. Prepare a recommended plan for implementing Plain English that includes the following: (1) reasons for implementing Plain English, (2) training courses that are available, (3) other services that can be accessed through the Plain English Campaign, and (4) the advantages of corporate membership in the Plain English Campaign. Present your plan in an oral report.

CHAPTER FOUR

Revising and Proofreading Messages

LEARNING OBJECTIVES

When you have completed Chapter 4, you will be able to:

1 *Edit and rewrite messages for vividness, clarity, and conciseness.*

2 *Identify factors affecting readability and revise messages to improve the readability.*

3 *Revise and proofread a message for content; organization; style; mechanics; format and layout.*

When we think of proofreaders, we may picture a sour-faced, antisocial person armed with a red pen and lots of self-righteousness. But the truth is, proofreading *is* important, and you don't have to be grumpy or annoying to do it. First of all, let's consider what could happen if you don't learn to proofread carefully (and just use the spell check on your computer).

You don't have to go too far to see silly typos or obvious instances of writers relying only on the computer spell check. The classifieds in a small-town newspaper recently advertised "fully fascinated and spade damnation puppies." The advertisement was for fully vaccinated and spayed Dalmatian puppies. This error clearly illustrates how spell check can fail. But goofs like that are not limited to small-town newspapers. When Brett Favre was honored as the NFL Player of the Year by *The Sporting News*, a lovely crystal trophy was ordered from Tiffany's and not unpacked until time for the presentation at the awards ceremony. *Sporting News* contributing editor Dennis Dillon realized with horror that the recipient's name had been misspelled right on the trophy— "Brett Farve." The ceremony went on as planned, however, and the trophy was shipped to Tiffany's for correction before being sent to Favre. Simply double-checking the spelling could have prevented this embarrassing incident.[1]

Similar cases of error or failure to conduct proper research include incidents involving Reebok and Nike. Over a year ago, Reebok designers searched for a new name for a woman's athletic shoe. In-house marketers came up with the name *incubus*. After a brief search indicated that the name was not patented by any other company, Reebok adopted it. However, they should have checked the meaning of the word in the dictionary, which defines an incubus as a predatory demon who preys on women in their sleep. While Reebok's shoes did not actually sport the incubus name, it was on the boxes, and Reebok is determined to wipe out the incubus name and line.[2] Similarly, Nike developed a men's shoe carrying an abstract logo that very closely resembled words from the *Koran*, the holy book of Islam. Because those words are sacred to Islam, their appearance, intentional or not, on *anything* is an affront. Nike is in the process of smoothing over this problem.[3]

Nike and Reebok are not alone, either. Toyota named one of their automobiles after Cressida, a woman in Greek mythology noted for being unfaithful to her husband, Troilus, while he was off fighting in the Trojan War.[4] Simple misspelling occurred in naming the Millenium Hilton in Manhattan, New York (it should be spelled *millennium*), and the new Mazda vehicle, the Millenia (also an incorrect use of the word *millennium*).[5] Additionally, language differences can cause humorous examples, as in the case of the Chevrolet Nova. In Spanish, "no va" means "it doesn't go."[6]

So roll up your sleeves and take a good hard look at whatever you write (you can even smile while you do it). It just may save you from being red-faced later! In this chapter you will focus on revising your message for vividness, clarity, conciseness, and readability and on following systematic proofreading procedures.

1 *Edit and rewrite messages for vividness, clarity, and conciseness.*

Creating Vivid Images

To help the receiver understand your message easily, carefully select words that paint intense, colorful word pictures. Creating clear mental images adds energy and imagination to your message, thus increasing its overall impact. To create vivid images, use specific words, avoid camouflaged verbs, eliminate clichés, and choose descriptive adjectives and adverbs.

Use Specific Words

Typically, specific words serve business writers better than general words because *specific words are more vivid*.

General	Specific
Congratulations on your <u>recent honor</u>.	Congratulations on being named <u>employee of the month</u>.
Please submit the completed report <u>as soon as possible</u>.	Please submit the completed report by <u>March 15</u>.
Sales <u>skyrocketed</u> this month.	Sales <u>increased 10 percent</u> this month.

What are some ways that the writer can paint vivid mental images that receivers will find exciting and will remember?

Sometimes, however, general words serve better than specific words. In getting along with others, general statements can be useful; they can keep negative ideas from getting more emphasis than they deserve. In addition, writers who don't have specific information or for some reason don't want to divulge it use general words.

General	Specific
Thank you for the explanation of your <u>financial status</u>.	Thank you for writing me about your <u>problems with creditors and the possibility of filing for bankruptcy</u>.
Frank told me about <u>what happened last week</u>.	Frank told me about the <u>tragedy in your family</u>.

Avoid Camouflaged Verbs

A **camouflaged verb** is a verb that has been needlessly transformed to a noun. Words with endings such as *-ion*, *-tion*, *-ing*, *-ment*, *-ant*, *-ent*, *-ence*, *-ance*, and *-ency* often change verbs into nouns. Camouflaged verbs increase the sentence length and slow comprehension because they are abstract and thus difficult for the receiver to envision. Notice how vivid, clear, and efficient the sentences in the right column are compared to the ones in the left column.

How would you eliminate the camouflaged verb in "The success of a team is dependent on team members who are willing to accept opinions"?

Camouflaged Verb	Strong Verbs
<u>Confirmation</u> of the date will be received from the president.	The president will <u>confirm</u> the date.
<u>Cancellation</u> of the flight to Los Angeles was necessary because of icing conditions.	The <u>*flight*</u> to Los Angeles <u>was canceled</u> because of icing conditions.
The management team has been directed to identify a plan to <u>create a reduction in</u> shipping costs by 20 percent.	The management team has been directed to identify a plan to <u>reduce</u> shipping costs by 20 percent.

Writers and speakers convey clearer messages if *they avoid camouflaged verbs*.

Eliminate Clichés

Phrases that have become overused are called **clichés**. Clichés can make reading monotonous and can make the writer or speaker seem unoriginal. Less frequently used words capture the reader's attention because they are original, fresh, and interesting.

At what point does a phrase become a cliché?

Cliché	Improvement
<u>Pursuant to your request</u>, the physical inventory was scheduled for May 3.	<u>As you requested</u>, the physical inventory has been scheduled for June 30.
Please send your answer at <u>your earliest convenience</u>.	Please send your answer by <u>Friday, March 5</u>.
<u>Enclosed please find</u> a copy of my transcript.	<u>The enclosed transcript should answer your questions</u>.

Clichés present a more serious problem. Consider the following scenario: Lee is standing in line at a discount store. As the two shoppers in front of Lee prepare to leave, the cashier says, *Thanks for shopping with us today; please come again.* After Lee pays for his merchandise, the cashier uses the same line. Because Lee knows the line has been used before, he may not consider the statement genuine. The cashier has used an expression that can be stated without thinking and possibly without meaning. A worn expression can convey messages such as "You are not special" or "For you, I won't bother to think; the phrases I use in talking with others are surely good enough for you."

Clichés are common in business communications, as the following examples show. From a writer's or speaker's point of view, some of the preceding phrases are convenient; they can be used easily and quickly. However, to avoid monotony, to keep from seeming to have no originality, and to avoid possible human relations problems, *avoid clichés*.

> In groups, generate a list of clichés used by friends, instructors, or coworkers. Discuss how you feel when these expressions are used frequently.

Cliché	Improvement
at an early date, in the near future	soon; specify a date
at this time, at this writing, at this point in time	now
I have your letter, we are in receipt of your letter, this letter is for the purpose of, this will acknowledge receipt, I am writing to	Omit and get to the point. Use an indirect reference to a letter if needed (The information you requested in your recent letter. . . .")
Please contact me if you have further questions; do not hesitate to call.	Please call
in accordance with your wishes	as you wish
please be advised that	Omit and get to the point.
in regard to/relative to	about
meet with your approval	is satisfactory
thanking you in advance	thank you; I would appreciate
if the above is	if the (specify) is

Choose Descriptive Modifiers

Compared with nouns and verbs, adjectives play a less significant role in a sentence and present fewer problems in usage. However, adjectives and adverbs can arouse skepticism or resentment if they are used without care.

Overly Strong Adjectives and Adverbs. One common problem is the use of adjectives that are too strong or used too frequently:

Adjective	*Adverb*
Sales have been <u>fantastic</u>.	Our prices are <u>ridiculously</u> low.
Mr. Jones presented a <u>ridiculous</u> plan.	Our forecasts have been <u>fantastically</u> accurate.

Use of such adjectives and adverbs can cause a receiver to wonder about a sender's objectivity. A person who wants to report a highly satisfactory sales program should avoid "fantastic" and, instead, give details. Even though a plan may be worthy of ridicule, a person who comments on it is better off to point out areas needing improvement. By labeling a plan "ridiculous," a writer or speaker might risk being considered biased or overly negative. Communication is normally more effective if writers and speakers *avoid using adjectives and adverbs that are used too frequently by others, are overly strong, or are overly negative.*

Superlatives. Messages are sometimes influenced negatively by another form of adjective or adverb—the superlative. The **superlative** is the form of the adjective or adverb that compares the thing modified with two or more other things. Note the following superlatives:

Adjective	*Adverb*
This Internet provider is the <u>best</u> one on the market.	Yuan runs <u>fastest</u>.
The factory has the <u>worst</u> odor imaginable.	This item sells <u>best</u>.

Superlatives are very useful words. Frequently, the extreme unit in a series needs to be identified—the *highest* or *lowest* score, the *latest* news, the *most* qualified applicant. When superlatives are totally unsupported or unsupportable, however, their use is questionable. Furnishing proof that no other Internet provider is up to the standards of this one would be extremely difficult. Proving that one odor is the worst imaginable is practically impossible. Knowing that such statements are exaggerations, the receiver may not believe them at all. In fact, someone who has used a superlative to transmit an *unbelievable* idea may not be believed when offering support for a believable idea. For the sake of credibility, *use only supported or supportable superlatives.*

> Give an example of a television or radio commercial that overuses superlatives.

Writing Clearly

Effective messages provide the receiver clear, specific information that can be understood easily. Read each sentence carefully to identify any sentence you believe could be misinterpreted or interpreted more than one way depending on the receiver's point of reference. Clarifying unclear sentences saves time and money for the receiver and writer and leads to strong relationships.

Choose Simple, Informal Words

The degree of formality in writing is dictated by the nature of the message and the backgrounds of the receivers. The writing in dissertations, theses, legal documents, and high-level government documents is expected to be formal. Business memorandums, e-mail messages, letters, and reports are expected to be informal. Business

All industries, whether mature or emerging, have a lingo which can easily confuse those individuals on the outside or those new to the industry. As a business communicator, I am constantly looking for ways to adapt my message to the recipient's level of understanding.

One particular personal experience illustrates the importance of this valuable lesson to keep things simple. My key role at a client's annual board meeting was to present an update on the managed portfolio. The most challenging part of the presentation involved describing the holdings of a biotechnology company in the most basic language possible. After I turned the meeting over to the next presenter, one board member interrupted the meeting, "Excuse me for interrupting, but I want to thank Mrs. Plager for simplifying that description of the company. I actually think I understand our investment in Biotech." If you don't deliver a message in a way your audience can understand, you have missed an opportunity.

Pamela M. Plager, Vice President & Director
Allen & Company, Incorporated

writers prefer the informal words from the right column rather than the formal words from the left column:

Formal Words	Informal Words
terminate	end
procure	get
remunerate	pay
corroborate	support
utilize	use
elucidate	explain

Simplify this message: "Management has become cognizant of the necessity of the elimination of undesirable vegetation surrounding the periphery of our facility."[7]

Simple, informal words, compared to formal words, are readily understood, easier to spell, require less time in keyboarding and less space on a page, and are less likely to draw attention away from the idea being expressed. If a receiver stops to question the writer's motive for using formal words similar to those in the left column, the impact of the message may be seriously diminished. Likewise, the impact would be diminished if the receiver stopped to question a writer's use of simple, informal words. That distraction is unlikely, however, if the message contains good ideas that are well organized and well supported. Under these conditions, simple words enable a receiver to understand the message clearly and quickly.

Using words that have more than two or three syllables when they are the most appropriate is acceptable. However, you should avoid regular use of a long, infrequently used word when a simpler, more common word has the same meaning. Professionals in some fields often use specialized terminology, often referred to as **jargon**, when communicating with colleagues in the same field. In this case, the audience is likely to understand the words, and using the jargon saves time. However, when communicating with people outside the field, professionals should select simple, common words to convey messages.

You should build your vocabulary so that you can use just the right word for expressing an idea and can understand what others have written. Just remember the purpose of business messages is not to advertise a knowledge of infrequently used words but to transmit a clear and tactful message. For the informal writing practiced in business, *use simple words instead of more complicated words that have the same meaning.*

What are some ways that you can build your vocabulary?

Eliminate Misplaced Elements

Placing words, phrases, or clauses in the wrong position can confuse the receiver, as you can see in the following example: *We have taken the check to the bank, which was unsigned.* The sentence is confusing (or amusing) because it seems to imply that the bank was unsigned. That impression is given because the "which" clause is placed closer to "bank" than to "check." Similarly, the following sentences have very different meanings:

Confusing	*Clear*
The three-year budgets are being returned to the strategic planning committee, which have some serious defects. (*Does the committee have serious defects?*)	The three-year budgets, which have some serious defects, are being returned to the committee.
Michele displayed the financial ratios to upper-level managers on the screen. (*Are the managers displayed on the screen?*)	Michele explained to upper-level managers the financial ratios displayed on the screen.

Eliminate Dangling Modifiers

A particular type of misplaced element is the **dangling modifier**. The term is applied to incoherent verbal phrases and elliptical clauses. Consider this example: *After completing a preliminary interview, an employment test was given to each applicant.* The sentence begins with a modifying verbal phrase that precedes the independent (main) clause in the sentence. The subject of the main clause ("employment test") is presumed to be the doer of the action described by the modifier ("completing an interview"). Saying that an employment test completed an interview is certainly not the intended meaning. Likely the writer intended *After completing a preliminary interview, each applicant completed an employment test* or *After each applicant completed a preliminary interview, Human Resources administered an employment test.*

Sentences with dangling modifiers can be corrected in two ways, as shown in the following examples:

1. Change the subject of the independent (main) clause to a word the modifier properly defines or describes.
2. Recast the misplaced or dangling modifier as a dependent clause.

With either arrangement, the intended meaning is much easier to understand. Because the subject of each independent clause is placed close to the action described in each modifier, the receiver is certain who is performing the action.

Dangling	*Change subject of main clause*	*Recast phrase as a clause*
While making a presentation, a surge of electricity caused the projector bulb to blow. (*Modifier describes a speaker—not surge.*)	While making a presentation, <u>Seth</u> was interrupted when a surge of electricity caused the projector bulb to blow.	<u>While Seth was making a presentation</u>, a surge of electricity caused the projector bulb to blow.
To create that bar chart, the information must be keyed into a spreadsheet file. (*Modifier describes a person—not information.*)	To create that bar chart, <u>you</u> must key the information into a spreadsheet file.	<u>If you want to create a bar chart from this information</u>, you must key it into a spreadsheet file.
Although tired, the feasibility report had to be completed. (*Modifier describes a person—not a report.*)	Although tired, <u>Dianne</u> completed the feasibility report.	<u>Although she was tired,</u> Dianne completed the feasibility report.

Recast Expletive Beginnings

By definition, an **expletive** is a meaningless word. Expletive beginnings are not considered grammatical errors but are seldom advisable. Usually any sentence that begins with *there is*, *there are*, or *it is* can be improved.

Poor	*Improved*
<u>There</u> is a major problem with next year's budget.	Next year's budget has a major problem.
<u>There</u> are many complicated provisions within the new tax law.	The new tax law has many complicated provisions.
<u>It</u> is encouraging to note that sales have increased this month.	This month's increased sales are encouraging.

Although each of the preceding original sentences does have a subject ("there" or "it") that precedes the verb ("is" or "are"), the subject is vague. Only after having read the entire sentence do you become aware of what "it" or "there" means. The revisions use fewer words in the more conventional subject-verb-complement pattern.

Avoid Expletive Beginnings. Certain situations may, however, justify the use of an expletive beginning.

1. **The sender may not want to reveal the source of the information.** Consider the following sentence: *It has been brought to my attention that backups are not being made of all computer files.* In this instance, the sender chooses a grammatical arrangement that will not make the sender obvious.

2. ***It* can serve as a first word when the antecedent is in a preceding sentence.** An **antecedent** is a noun or pronoun to which another pronoun (it) refers. In the following sentence, "it" refers to "document"—its antecedent. *Mr. Jamison indicated needed corrections in the document. It is being revised. . . .*

Reword to eliminate the expletive in "It is important to evaluate your effectiveness each time you communicate."

This manager is aware that her writing skills, like appearance, clothing, and speech, are a reflection of her proficiency as a professional. Your writing skills can prove that you are intelligent, careful, and resourceful; or they can portray you as inconsistent, insensitive, or ignorant.

Used in this manner, the pronoun "it" can serve well as a coherence technique to link ideas.

Express Ideas in Parallel Form

When two or more ideas appear together for a similar purpose, they should have common grammatical construction, which is referred to as **parallel construction**. For example, the series "to increase production," "expand our market," and "recruit skilled workers," is parallel because all are verbs that complete the infinitive "to." If one of the ideas were presented in a different way grammatically (e.g., *recruiting skilled workers*), it would appear to be out of place or be considered unparallel. The variation in construction weakens the emphasis given to each item in the series, and the inconsistency may also distract the receiver's attention from the message.

Note the parallel construction in the following examples:

Type	*Nonparallel*	*Parallel*	
Words	The components of multimedia are text, images, sound, and adding animation.	The components of multimedia are and	‖ text, ‖ images, ‖ sound, ‖ animation.
Phrases	Animation engages the audience, highlights key points, and is used to demonstrate the progression of a process.	Animation and	‖ engages the audience, ‖ highlights key points, ‖ demonstrates the ‖ progression ‖ of a process.
Clauses	They invested in stocks and bonds, and considered mutual funds.	and	‖ <u>They</u> invested in stocks and bonds, ‖ <u>they</u> considered mutual funds.

How is parallel construction in word use and phrases similar to the concept of parallel construction in outlining?

The principle of parallel construction applies not only to elements in a series that appear in a sentence but also to major units in an outline, to subunits that appear under a major unit, to headings that appear in documents, and bulleted lists in documents and presentation visuals. If one major heading is a complete sentence, all other major headings should be complete sentences. If one subheading is a question, all other subheadings under that division should be questions.

Writing Concisely

What is the difference between conciseness and brevity?

Concise messages are essential if today's information workers are to continue to process volumes of information. Some executives have reported that they read memos that are two paragraphs long but may only skim or discard longer ones. Of course, this survival technique has serious drawbacks: A vital message may be misinterpreted or never read. Learning to write concisely—to use three words rather than ten—will mark you as a highly effective communicator. Abraham Lincoln's two-minute Gettysburg Address is a premier example. Mark Twain alluded to the *skill* needed to write concisely when he said, "I would have written a shorter book if I had had time."

Concise messages save time and money for both the writer and the receiver. The receiver's attention is directed toward the important details and is not distracted by excessive words and details. To prepare a concise message, *include only those details that the receiver needs; and state these details in the fewest possible words.*

The following techniques will help you learn to write in the fewest words possible:

In groups, generate a list of wordy phrases you have heard used. Describe ways to simplify ideas in writing and speaking.

- *Eliminate redundancies.* A **redundancy** is a phrase in which one word unnecessarily repeats an idea contained in an accompanying word. "Exactly identical" and "past history" are redundant because both words have the same meaning; only "identical" and "history" are needed. To correct "3 p.m. in the afternoon," say "3 p.m." or "three o'clock in the afternoon." A few of the many redundancies in business writing are shown in the following list. Additionally, be conscious of redundancies in your speech and writing patterns.

Redundancies to Avoid

basic fundamentals	necessary requirement
consensus of opinion	other alternative
dollar amount	personal opinion
each and every	past history
end result	refer back
exact same	serious danger
full and complete	severe crisis
honest truth	true facts
important essentials	two twins
looking forward to the future	whether or not

Redundancy is not to be confused with repetition. In a sentence or paragraph, you may need to use a certain word again. When repetition serves a specific purpose, it is not an error. Redundancy serves no purpose and *is* an error. *Avoid redundancies;* they waste words and risk distracting from the idea presented.

- *Use active voice to reduce the number of words.* Passive voice typically adds unnecessary words, such as prepositional phrases. Compare the sentence length in each of these examples:

Passive Voice	*Active Voice*
The user documentation was written by the systems analyst.	The systems analyst wrote the user documentation.
The loan approval procedures for new business ventures were revised by the commercial loan officer.	The commercial loan officer revised the loan approval procedures for new business ventures.

- *Review the main purpose of your writing and identify the details that the reader needs to understand the message and to take necessary action.* More information is not necessarily better information. You may be so involved and perhaps so enthusiastic about your message that you believe the receiver needs to know everything that you know. Or perhaps you just do not take the time to empathize with your receiver by identifying the relevant details.

Non-concise letters sometimes begin with an "empty acknowledgment." Give some examples of such openings.

- *Eliminate clichés that are often wordy and not necessary to understand the message.* For example, "Thank you for your letter," "I am writing to," "May I take this opportunity," "It has come to my attention," and "We wish to inform you" only delay the major purpose of the message.

- *Do not restate ideas that are sufficiently implied.* Notice how the following sentences are improved when implied ideas are eliminated. The revised sentences are concise yet the meaning was not affected.

Wordy	*Concise*
She <u>took</u> the Web design course and passed it.	She passed the Web design course.
The auditor <u>reviewed the figures</u> and concluded that they are accurate.	The auditor concluded that the figures are accurate.
The editor <u>checked the manuscript</u> and found three grammatical errors.	The editor found three grammatical errors in the manuscript.
<u>This is in response to your letter of March 25.</u>	Yes, I will be delighted to speak at the May meeting of the Boardtown Civic Club.

- *Shorten sentences by using suffixes or prefixes, making changes in word form, or substituting precise words for phrases.* In the following examples, the expressions on the right provide useful techniques for saving space and being concise. However, the examples in the left column are not grammatically incorrect or forbidden from use. In fact, sometimes their use provides just the right *emphasis*.

Wordy	*Concise*
She was a manager <u>who was courteous to others</u>.	She was a <u>courteous</u> manager.
He waited <u>in an impatient manner</u>.	He waited <u>impatiently</u>.
. . . the financial analysis <u>that they had not finished</u>	. . . the <u>unfinished</u> financial analysis

Too many writers go to great lengths to "write right." In their attempts to sound learned, they muddy the message beyond comprehension. The best writing closely imitates speech. It is to the point.

It uses familiar words and is interesting, and its sentences are short enough to follow. In other words, the message communicates.

Cynthia Pharr, President
C. Pharr & Company, Inc.

Wordy	**Concise**
. . . the solution <u>that we could debate about the longest</u>.	. . . the most <u>debatable</u> solution.
The production manager disregards methods considered <u>to be of no use</u>.	The production manager disregards methods considered <u>useless</u>.
. . . sales representatives with <u>high energy levels</u>.	. . . <u>energetic</u> sales representatives.
. . . <u>arranged according to the alphabet</u>.	. . . <u>alphabetically</u>.

- **Use a compound adjectives.** By using the compound adjective, you can reduce the number of words required to express your ideas and thus save the reader a little time.

Wordy	**Concise**
She wrote a report that was <u>up-to-date</u>.	She wrote an <u>up-to-date</u> report.
Duane Lollar, <u>who holds the highest rank</u> at Gosette Enterprises, is . . .	Duane Lollar, <u>the highest-ranking official</u> at Gosette Enterprises, is . . .
His policy of <u>going slowly</u> was well received.	His <u>go-slow</u> policy was well received.

**② ** *Identify factors affecting readability and revise messages to improve the readability.*

How frequently should you check the Fog Index of your business correspondence?

What is the desirable readability index for business writing?

Improving Readability

Even though sentences are arranged in a logical sequence and are written coherently, the receiver may find reading the sentences difficult. In an effort to determine the school grade level at which a passage is written, Robert Gunning (1968) developed a readability formula. This formula yields the approximate grade level a person would need to understand the material.[8] For example, a grade level of 10 means a person needs to be able to read at the tenth-grade level to understand the material. Gunning referred to this formula as the *Fog Index*.

The Strategic Forces Box shows how readability is measured using the Gunning Fog Index. Study the formula carefully and you will see that two factors affect readability: (1) length of the sentences and (2) difficulty of the words. Understanding that short sentences and short words are easier to read, you can input necessary revisions, recalculate the readability index, and repeat the process until the reading level is appropriate for the intended audience.

Strategic Forces: Changing Technology

Computing Readability by Applying the Gunning Fog Index

The Gunning Fox Index is one measure of readability. Many computer software programs calculate readability measures automatically. However, understanding the formula used to make the calculation will help you understand the two factors that affect readability: (1) length of the sentences and (2) difficulty of the words. Understanding that short sentences and short words are easier to read, you can keep these factors in mind as you write the first draft and as you revise, recalculate the readability index, and repeat the process until the reading level is appropriate for the intended audience.

1. Select a passage of 100 words or more.

Sample business letter shown in the next column.

2. Count the exact number of words.

136 words

3. Count the number of sentences. *Count compound sentences as two sentences.*

8 sentences (none of the sentences are compound). Sentences are marked with superscript numbers.

4. Find the <u>average sentence length</u>. *Divide the number of words by the number of sentences.*

136 (total words) ÷ 8 (sentences) = 17.0

5. Count the number of <u>difficult</u> words. *A <u>difficult</u> word is a word with three or more syllables. Do not include (a) compound words formed from smaller words (<u>however</u> or <u>understand</u>), (b) proper nouns, or (c) verbs formed into three syllables by the addition of <u>-ed</u> or <u>-es</u> (<u>imposes</u> or <u>defended</u>).*

26 difficult words. Difficult words are underscored. "Explained" and "enclosed" are not difficult words because they became three syllables by adding <u>ed</u>. "Davenport" is not a difficult word because it is a proper noun.

6. Find the percentage of difficult words. *Divide the number of difficult words by the total number of words.*

27 (difficult words) ÷ 136 (total words) = .198 or 19.8%

7. Add the average sentence length and the percentage of difficult words.

17.0 (average sentence length) + 19.8 (percentage of difficult words = 36.8

8. Multiply the resulting figure by 0.4.

36.1 x 0.4 (constant) = 14.72 (readability level)

Dear Mr. and Mrs. Simpson:

[1] <u>Ensuring</u> that your home <u>furnishings</u> were <u>delivered</u> to your new home in Davenport in <u>excellent</u> <u>condition</u> was a top <u>priority</u> to our <u>dependable</u>, highly trained workers. [2] <u>Providing</u> this <u>quality</u> service at an <u>affordable</u> price is also <u>important</u> to both of us.

[3] One way of keeping <u>insurance</u> <u>affordable</u> is to use a standard <u>policy</u> that insures <u>personal</u> <u>property</u> for its <u>replacement</u> cost. [4] <u>Separate</u> <u>policies</u> are <u>available</u> to insure heirlooms, such as your <u>family</u> painting, for their <u>sentimental</u> values. [5] Our <u>representative</u> explained these options before you signed our standard <u>policy</u>. [6] The enclosed check for $250 is based on our <u>estimate</u> of the cost to purchase a <u>similar</u> painting.

[7] Best of luck to you and your children as you settle into your new home in Davenport. [8] If we can assist you in future moves, please call us at 555-MOVE.

Sincerely

The reading level of this short letter is 14.72, meaning that approximately 14 to 15 years of education are needed to understand this letter. The letter should be revised to lower the readability index to 8–11, the desired level for business writing. To lower the readability index and to make this letter easier to read, you would need to write shorter sentences and reduce the number of difficult words.

Application

Compute a readability index for the letter in Exercise 11 or 12 by making the calculations manually, or for a document provided by your instructor. Note the average sentence length and the percentage of difficult words. How do these calculations affect the resulting readability index? What general suggestions could you offer to alter the readability index of this document?

Written communication is an author's and a company's introduction to you or your introduction to them. Finding simple mistakes or inconsistencies can leave an impression of shoddy work and a lack of confidence that the information has been properly researched. If your first introduction to a potential client or colleague is in the form of writing, be certain the document is error free. The absence of mistakes will help you gain the respect of the reader and open the door for a good working relationship.

Pamela M. Plager
Vice President & Director
Allen & Company, Incorporated

Jargon, slang, and figurative expressions peculiar to the United States or a specific region may be confusing to those who are from another region or who speak English as a second language. Examples include "fudge on the figures," "cue me in so I'll understand," "bite the bullet," "pick up the tab," "piddle around," "two bits of advice," "wearing two hats," and so on. Add at least two expressions that you believe are peculiar to the United States and two expressions that you believe are peculiar to your region of the country.

3　*Revise and proofread a message for content; organization; style; mechanics; format; and layout.*

The desirable Fog Index for most business writing is in the eighth-to-eleventh-grade range. A writer need not be overly concerned if the index is a little over 11 or under 8. Trying to write at the exact grade level of the receiver is inadvisable. The writer may not know the exact grade level, and even those who have earned advanced degrees appreciate writing they can read and understand quickly and easily.

A major word of caution is needed. Writing a passage with a readability index appropriate for the audience does not guarantee that the message will be understood. Numerous factors affect whether a message is communicated effectively. Chapter 1 explained how breakdowns in communication occur at all stages in the communication process. For example, the readability may be appropriate for the audience. However, the words used may not convey the precise meaning needed for understanding; gender-biased words may create barriers to understanding; jargon and other unique expressions may not be understood by a reader in a different field or from a different background. Translation problems further compound communication when different languages are involved, as discussed in the Internet case at the end of the chapter. Calculating the readability index, however, provides the writer valuable feedback about the average length of the sentences and the difficulty of the words. *For quick, easy reading (and listening), use small words and short sentences.*

Revising and Proofreading

Although errors in writing and mechanics may seem isolated and trivial to you, these mistakes can damage your credibility. Receivers of messages that contain mistakes are much less likely to take you and your ideas seriously than if you had taken special care to proofread. An owner of a successful public relations firm reported that clients seldom return work for revisions. The staff revises the document as many as five or six times to be certain that the material is written effectively and is grammatically correct before it is submitted to the client. Thus business executives and countless others have learned the invaluable lesson that errors reduce the effectiveness of the document and reflect negatively on the person who writes it. The writer is responsible for checking each document for accuracy before sending it.

Systematic Procedures for Revising and Proofreading

Following systematic revision procedures will help you produce error-free documents that reflect positively on the company and you. Using the procedures that follow, you will see that effective proofreading must be done several times each time for a specific purpose. Also, using standard proofreading marks will simplify your proofreading method and will allow others who know these marks to understand your corrections easily. Study the standard proofreaders' marks shown in Appendix A. Follow these simple procedures to produce a finished product free of errors in (1) content, organization, and style; (2) mechanics; and (3) format and layout:

1. **Use the spell check to locate simple keying errors and repeated words.** The accompanying Strategic Forces Box provides techniques for enhancing your writing using a spell check, a thesaurus, and writing analysis software.

2. **Print a draft copy of the document.** Errors on a computer screen are difficult to locate; therefore, print a draft copy on plain paper and proofread carefully. Proofreading solely from the screen may be adequate for brief routine documents.

3. **Proofread *once* concentrating on errors in content, organization, and style.** To locate errors, ask the following questions:

Content:	Is the information complete? Have I included all the details the receiver needs to understand the message and to take necessary action? Is the information accurate? Have I checked the accuracy of any calculations, dates, names, addresses, and numbers? Have words been omitted?
Organization:	Is the main idea presented appropriately, based on the receiver's likely reaction (deductive or inductive organization)? Are supporting ideas presented in a logical order?
Style:	Is the message clear? Will the receiver interpret the information correctly? Is the message concise and written at an appropriate level for the receiver? Does the message reflect a considerate, caring attitude? Is the message primarily focused on the receiver's needs? Does the message treat the receiver honestly and ethically?

4. **Proofread a *second* time concentrating on mechanical errors.** You are searching for potentially damaging errors that a spell check cannot detect. These problem areas include

   - *Grammar, capitalization, punctuation, number usage, abbreviations.* Review the grammatical principles presented in Appendix C if necessary.

   - *Word substitutions.* Check the proper use of words such as *your* and *you* and words that sound alike (*there, they're,* or *their*; *affect* or *effect*).

   - *Parts of the document other than the body.* Proofread the entire letter, including the date line, letter address, salutation, subject line, and closing lines. Errors often appear in the opening sections of letters because writers typically begin proofreading at the first paragraph.

5. **Proofread a *third* time if the document is nonroutine and complex.** *Read from right to left* to reduce your reading speed and to enable you to concentrate deliberately on each word. If a document is extremely important, you may read the document aloud, spelling names and noting capitalization and punctuation, while another person verifies the copy.

6. **Edit for format and layout.** Follow these steps to be certain the document adheres to appropriate business formats:

Using a spell check is only the *first* step in locating all errors in a document. What types of errors is a spell check incapable of locating?

- *Format according to a conventional format.* Compare your document to the conventional business formats shown in Appendix A and make any revisions. Are all standard parts of the document included and presented in an acceptable format? Are all necessary special letter parts (mailing notation, attention line, subject line, enclosure, and copy notations, second-page heading, and the writer's address for a personal business letter) included? Does the message begin on the correct line? Should the right margin be justified or jagged?

- *Be sure numbered items are in correct order.* Inserting and deleting text may have changed the order of these items.

- *Evaluate the visual impact of the document.* Could you increase the readability of long, uninterrupted blocks of texts by using enumerated or indented lists, headings, or different type styles (boldface, underlines, italics, or shadow type)? Could you increase the overall appeal by including graphics or using different fonts of various sizes and styles? Could you partition the text into logical, easy-to-read sections by using graphic lines, boxes, and borders?

- *Be certain the document is signed or initialed (depending on the document).*

7. **Print the document on high-quality paper.** The envelope and second-page paper (if needed) should match the letterhead. The printing should read in the same direction as the watermark (the design imprinted on high-quality paper). Refer to Appendix A for paper specifications and other areas related to the overall appearance of a document on the page.

The letter in Figure 4-1 has been revised for (1) content, organization, and style; (2) mechanics; and (3) format and layout. Changes are noted using proofreaders' marks, a standard, simplified way to show where changes or corrections need to be made. The detailed explanation will help you understand how the revisions improve the quality of the final draft.

A Mind-Set for Effective Revising and Proofreading

The following suggestions will be helpful as you work to develop business documents that achieve the purpose for which they are intended.

- **Attempt to see things from your audience's perspective rather than from your own.** That is, have empathy for your audience. Being empathetic isn't as simple as it seems, particularly when dealing with today's diverse work force. Erase the mind-set, "I know what *I* need to say and how *I* want to say it." Instead, ask, "How would my audience react to this message? Is this message worded so that my audience can easily understand it?"

- **Revise your documents until you cannot see any additional ways to improve them.** Resist the temptation to think of your first draft as your last draft. Instead, look for ways to improve and be willing to incorporate valid suggestions once you have completed a draft. Remember that skilled speech writers might rewrite a script 15 or 20 times. Writers in public relations firms revise brochures and advertising copy until perhaps only a comma in the final draft is recognizable from the first draft. Your diligent revising will yield outstanding dividends. Specifically, the audience (your instructor, supervisor, employees, or clients/customers, for example) is more likely to understand and accept your message.

Considering that revision is costly in terms of time invested, what is the potential cost of *not* revising documents?

September 14, 1999

FACSIMILE

Mr. Brent M. Weinberg, President
Worldwide Enterprises, Inc.
1635 Taylor Road
Baltimore, Maryland 21225-1635

Do not justify right margin

Dear Mr. Wienberg:

Welcome to the Worldwide family. With your proven ability to produce precision-quality electronic parts, our entrance into the video-cassette recorder market is certain to be successful. *We, at Worldwide, are also enthusiastic about other ways we both can benefit through sharing our expertise.*

One of the objectives of our recent merger are to update your IS to increase your competitiveness. The first step of this process is to form a steering committee whose rudimentary function is too direct the development of the new system and to ensure that it incorporates the information needs of the user and the organization. To accomplish this goal, committee members must represent inventory control, shipping, purchasing, accounting, and marketing. *Include* Further, the group must consist of members from a variety of organizational levels--hourly employees to salaried managers--and members should possess varying degrees of computer competence. *The committee's primary* *is*

Because of your knowledge of company operations, we need your input. You serving on this committee will be clear, tangible evidence of management's full and complete support of this significant transformation. In addition, would you please recommend five individuals who you believe are genuinely interested in developing an effective information system and who meet the preceding criteria. *is essential* *d* *change*

Please advise me whether or not you will serve on the Information Systems Steering Committee. Just as soon as the other members have been selected, we will schedule a meeting. *let know by September 30 that*

FORMAT AND LAYOUT

Begin all lines at the left margin in block letter style.

Insert mailing notation: "FACSIMILE."

Use two-letter state abbreviation.

Format criteria in a bulleted list for emphasis.

Use jagged right margin for improved appearance.

Center letter vertically on high-quality letterhead.

FIGURE 4-1
Rough draft of a letter (excerpts).

ORGANIZATION, CONTENT, AND STYLE

Eliminate clichés: "Welcome to Worldwide" and "Please advise me."

Insert a smooth transition from the opening paragraph into ¶2.

Spell out "IS" to ensure understanding.

Break long sentence in ¶2 into two shorter sentences to increase readability.

Use simple words for "rudimentary" and "transformation."

Eliminate redundancies: "full and complete" and "whether or not."

Write from the receiver's viewpoint: "Your input is essential."

Write a specific, action-oriented ending: "by September 30."

ERRORS UNDETECTABLE BY SPELL CHECK

Verify spelling of receiver's name, "Weinberg."

Correct word substitutions: "too" for "to."

MECHANICS

Spell "knowledge" correctly.

Use a singular verb when "one" is the subject.

Use a possessive pronoun before gerund: "your serving."

Place comma between coordinate adjectives: "clear, tangible."

Use an apostrophe to show possession: "management's."

Omit apostrophe after plural noun: "members."

- **Be willing to allow others to make suggestions for improving your writing.** Most people consider their writing very personal. That is, they are reluctant to share what they have written with others and are easily offended if others suggest changes. This syndrome, called *writer's pride of ownership*, can needlessly prevent you from seeking assistance from experienced writers—a proven method of improving communication skills. On the job, you will share your writing with the recipient (your supervisor, your employees, or clients/customers). Because a great deal of what is written in business today is written collaboratively, you will be required to subject your writing to review by others. You have nothing to lose but much to gain. Remember that the mistake hardest to detect is your own.

Refer to the "Check Your Writing" checklist to review the guidelines for revising and proofreading a rough draft.

Why are your own errors more difficult to detect than the errors of others?

Strategic Forces: Changing Technology

Using the Computer to Enhance Writing

Spell checks, thesauruses, and grammar and style checkers aid in producing an effective message.

Spell check

Using the spell check feature of a word processing program, you can automatically check the spelling of every word in a document against the program's dictionary. The words misspelled or not included in the dictionary are highlighted. You simply select the correct spelling from a list provided by the computer or input the correct spelling if it does not appear in the list. Some programs allow you to add words to the dictionary.

It is important to understand that you cannot rely solely on the spell check. To locate all errors, you must proofread the document yourself from the screen and a printed copy. Spell check cannot locate errors such as confusing words (*affect* or *effect*), homophones (*principle*, *principal*), omitted words, miskeying that results in incorrect words (*than* for *then*), enumerated items missing or out of order, and content errors.

Thesaurus

The thesaurus feature automatically generates a list of synonyms and antonyms for any word. You may choose one word from the list to substitute for the original. This feature can help you find words with very precise meanings and add freshness and variety to your writing.

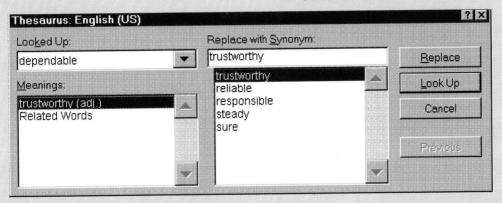

Writing Analysis Software

Leading word processing programs such as COREL© WordPerfect and Microsoft Word® have built-in grammar and style checkers that can help you locate grammatical errors and improve your writing style—the way you express ideas. These built-in grammar and style checkers compare the text created in a word-processed program against the grammar and style principles stored in the program, highlight any text that violates the principles, and may suggest a revision. Grammar and style checkers generally highlight sentence fragments, passive verbs, jargon, wordy constructions, clichés, subject-verb disagreement, pronoun usage, language, word usage, and misspelled words. Various checking styles, (quick check, formal or informal letter and memo, technical writing, speech, and fiction) give you control over the strictness of the critique.

Note Grammatik's critique of the sentence, "The projections will be released by the financial team," using the "very strict" checking style. Because this suggestion is valid, the writer can easily click "replace" to input the recommended active-voice sentence and thus improve the style. However, the writer may overrule a suggestion that is inappropriate for a particular message. In this case, for example, using active voice to achieve clear, vivid images is effective. However, the writer would retain the passive-voice construction if the intention is to de-emphasize negative information by clicking "Skip Once."

continued

Spell Checker | **Grammatik** | **Thesaurus**

Replacements: `This financial team` / `These financial teams`

[Replace] [QuickCorrect]
[Skip Once] [Undo]
[Skip Always] [Analysis]
[Turn Off] [Customize]

New sentence: `This financial team will release the projection.`

Noun Phrase: `After These you need a plural noun, not the singular noun team.`

Add to: `wt61us.uwl`
Check: `Document`

Checking style: `Very Strict`

[Close] [Help]

After reviewing the entire document, grammar and style checkers display several analyses that are helpful in pinpointing needed revisions and writing areas that require additional attention. You can review (a) basic counts such as average sentence length, (b) several readability measures based on the document's comparison to a specified document such as the Gettysburg Address or a Hemingway story, and (c) a list of flagged errors. Basic counts and readability measures are shown in the following screens.

Those who are familiar with the principles of writing will benefit most from writing-analysis programs. For example, how helpful would the preceding suggestion be if the writer does not understand what an abstract noun or passive voice is? Obviously, a writer with an effective writing style will spend less time revising and be more likely to understand and benefit from the software's suggestions.

Application

Complete Exercise 12, which requires you to use a grammar and style checker to revise a document. Based on your experience, describe the value and the limitations of this computer writing aid. Support your statement with specific information related to the suggestions you accepted and rejected when you were revising this document.

Readability - A:\simpson.wpd [unmodified]

Comparison document: `Gettysburg Address` [Add Document...]
 (dropdown: Hemingway short story / Gettysburg Address / 1040EZ Instructions)

Flesch-Kincaid grade level
- simpson.wpd: 13.28
- Gettysburg: 12.90

Passive voice (% of finite verb phrases)
- simpson.wpd: 8
- Gettysburg: 9

Sentence complexity (100 = very complex)
- simpson.wpd: 27
- Gettysburg: 75

Vocabulary complexity (100 = very complex)
- simpson.wpd: 58
- Gettysburg: 15

[Flagged...] [Basic Counts...] [Close] [Help]

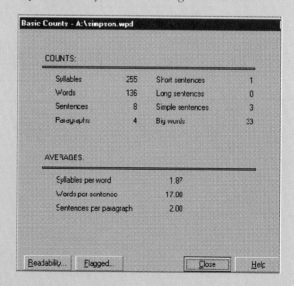

Basic Counts - A:\simpson.wpd

COUNTS:

Syllables	255	Short sentences	1
Words	136	Long sentences	0
Sentences	8	Simple sentences	3
Paragraphs	4	Big words	33

AVERAGES:

Syllables per word	1.87
Words per sentence	17.00
Sentences per paragraph	2.00

[Readability...] [Flagged...] [Close] [Help]

COMMUNICATION IN ACTION

R. D. Saenz, Chief Financial Officer
Snider Communications Corporation

According to the Department of Labor, proficiency in verbal and written business communication skills is considered a new "key basic" in the workplace today. According to R. D. Saenz, the accounting profession is no exception. A consultant with a degree in accounting, Saenz spent nearly 11 years at Price Waterhouse, one of the top six accounting firms in the United States. Having also been employed 9 years in private industry, he knows that a college degree or advanced professional certification alone no longer meets basic required skills in the workplace. While working as audit senior manager at Price Waterhouse, Saenz was directly involved in employee professional development. His duties involved more than developing employees technically in accounting. He worked with all facets of form evaluation, which involved written and oral communication. He took note of strengths and weaknesses of supervisory employees. He worked with the "cream-of-the-crop" employees who had degrees from prestigious universities. Based on the employees' backgrounds, levels of intelligence, and levels of achievement, he was sometimes appalled at their inability to communicate through writing skills. He notes, "Grammatical errors quickly detract from the credibility of the writer. Errors cast a cloud over that individual's ability or competence."

One way Saenz developed employees professionally was by focusing intently on clear writing. He responded to those who needed help with writing skills. When employees explained an exception to a policy, drafted a memo about procedures, or explained a resolution, Saenz responded to their writing. If a written report were done incorrectly, he provided positive comments that were lighthearted but professional. He set high standards for his employees and tried to communicate his knowledge of clear, concise, correct writing to them.

Saenz acquired his interest in using words effectively at an early age. By the time he was four years old, he read material advanced for his age. As a youth, he liked the precision of how words can be used and naturally gravitated toward their appropriate use. He said, "I'm a fanatic about parallel construction. From how many people have you heard that statement?"

Still an avid reader, Saenz finds many common connecting chords between communication and his work. Saenz believes that effective word use is fundamental to the workplace. He knows that oral and written skills of preciseness, simplicity, parallelism, and tone must be "second nature" to an accountant. Without these skills, employees simply will not succeed. The workplace of today has changed, he notes. "Employees must have more than the technical aptitude of accounting. They must also have proficiency in oral and written communication skills."

Applying What You Have Learned

1. Why does Saenz consider proficiency in oral and written communication skills basic to the accounting profession today?

2. Saenz commented that "grammatical errors quickly detract from the credibility of the writer." How might the credibility of a writer be "detracted from" by grammatical errors?

3. Assume that you are an employee for a large accounting firm. Your duties include careful consideration of any employee's written work that leaves your office. Following Saenz's example, discuss some considerations to keep in mind when commenting about another employee's writing.

Vivid Writing

- Use specific words.
- Avoid camouflaged verbs to achieve clear, emphatic writing.
- Avoid using clichés.
- Avoid using adjectives and adverbs that are used too frequently, are overly strong, or are overly negative.
- Use only supported or supportable superlatives to maintain credibility.

Clarity

- Use simple words for informal business writing instead of using more complicated words that have the same meaning.
- Place a word, a phrase, or a clause near the word it describes.
- Avoid dangling modifiers. When the introductory phrase identifies action without revealing the doer, present the doer immediately after the phrase.
- Avoid using expletive beginnings.
- Present multiple units in the same way grammatically—parallel construction.

Conciseness

- Do not use redundancies—unnecessary repetition of an idea.
- Use active voice to shorten sentences.
- Avoid unnecessary details; omit ideas that can be implied.
- Shorten wordy sentences by using suffixes or prefixes, making changes in word form, or substituting precise words for phrases.

Readability

- Use simple words and short sentences for quick, easy reading (and listening).
- Strive for short paragraphs but vary their lengths.
- Emphasize a sentence by placing it first or last within a paragraph or by assigning it a number in a tabulated series.

Systematic Proofreading

- Proofread for content, organization, and style; mechanics; and format and layout.

SUMMARY

1. **Edit and rewrite messages for vividness, clarity, and conciseness.** Errors in word usage and style (the way ideas are expressed) can result in lost meaning, lost time, distraction, and concern about the writer's or speaker's background. Use these techniques for vivid, interesting writing: use specific words, avoid camouflaged verbs, clichés, and overly strong or negative adjectives and adverbs, and use only supported or supportable superlatives. To ensure clarity, use simple words, position modifiers correctly, avoid expletive beginnings, and use parallel construction when presenting items in a series. To write concisely, avoid redundancies, use active voice, include only pertinent details, and use tighter word forms for long phrases and clauses.

2. **Identify factors affecting readability and revise sentences to improve readability.** The readability of a message is affected by the length of the sentences and the difficulty of the words. For quick, easy reading, use simple words and short sentences. A readability index (grade level for reader to understand the material) in the eighth-to-eleventh grade range is appropriate for most business writing. Writing a message with a readability index appropriate for an audience does not guarantee understanding but does provide feedback on the average length of the sentences and the difficulty of the words.

3. **Revise and proofread a message for content, organization, and style; mechanics; and format and layout.** Be willing to revise a document as many times as necessary to be certain that it conveys the message effectively and is error free. Use the spell check to locate keying errors, then follow systematic procedures for proofreading a printed copy of the document; proofread for content, organization, and style; mechanics; and format and layout. Refer to the "Check Your Writing" checklist to review the guidelines for revising and proofreading a rough draft.

REFERENCES

[1]Armstrong again proves strong. (1996, May 7). *The Fresno Bee*, p. C3.

[2]McKeen, S. (1997, May 25). Hooray for Reebok's gaffe! We need a chance to gloat. *Sunday Telegram*, p. C4.

[3]Muslims seek Nike's apology. (1997, April 10). *The New York Times*, p. B14.

[4]McKeen, S. (1997, May 25). Hooray for Reebok's gaffe! We need a chance to gloat. *Sunday Telegram*, p. C4.

[5]Pauly, B. (1995, December). Grammar police set up patrols. *The Cincinnati Enquirer*, p. D11.

[6]McKeen, S. (1997, May 25). Hooray for Reebok's gaffe! We need a chance to gloat. *Sunday Telegram*, p. C4.

[7]McKenna, J. F. (1990, March 19). Tales from the circular file. *Industry Week*, 38.

[8]Gunning, R. (1968). *The technique of clear writing*. New York: McGraw Hill.

[9]Schmit, J. (1993, May 25). Continental's $4 million typo. *USA Today*, p. 1B.

[10]Corbitt, T. (1994, December). A leap over the language barrier. *Accountancy*, 62

[11]Reynolds, A. (1990, September). Training that travels well. *Training & Development Journal*, 73–78..

REVIEW QUESTIONS

1. Why are specific words preferred in business writing? In what situations would general words be preferred? (Obj. 1)

2. What is a camouflaged verb? Give an example. Why should camouflaged verbs be avoided? (Obj. 1)

3. When is the use of superlatives not recommended? Why? Give an example. (Obj. 1)

4. Why are clichés such as *enclosed please find*, *would like to say*, and *at this point in time* not recommended? (Obj. 1)

5. Explain what is meant by *writing to express and not to impress*. (Obj. 1)

6. List two reasons sentences should not begin with expletives such as *There is* or *It is*. (Obj. 1)

7. Revise to provide parallel construction: *Super stores combine the convenience of one-stop shopping, quality merchandise, and the prices are low.* (Obj. 1)

8. What is a redundancy? Give two examples. Why should redundancies be avoided? (Obj. 1)

9. Why should a letter not begin with the expression *This letter is in reply to your recent letter*? (Obj. 1)

10. What shorter forms could be substituted for the expressions (a) *The customer was treated in a rude manner*, (b) *Complete the analysis in as short a time as possible*, and (c) *The design that was creative . . .* (Obj. 1)

11. What two factors should be evaluated for possible revision in an effort to reduce the readability index of a report? (Obj. 2)

12. What value does knowing the readability level of a document serve? (Obj. 2)

13. What are the seven steps for proofreading a document systematically to locate all errors? (Obj. 3)

14. Why is writer's pride of ownership an obstacle to good proofreading? (Obj. 3)

15. What are the benefits and limitations of an electronic spell check and writing-analysis software? (Obj. 3)

EXERCISES

1. **Vivid Images (Obj. 1)**
   Write specific words for each of the following general phrases. Mark "Correct" if the use of general words is preferable in any sentence.

   a. Sometime this quarter, we need to list goals for the next fiscal year.

   b. The client stated that we had performed excellent work.

   c. A large number attended our recent Client Appreciation Dinner.

   d. John Batson was honored for his efforts.

   e. Sales have slumped this quarter.

   f. I understand that you need some time off following the death of your mother.

   g. Libby's artwork for the campaign is amazing.

h. The best computers we can lease through corporate channels are horribly outdated.

i. André is the best manager in the corporation.

j. Losing this account was the worst thing that could happen to our firm.

2. **Camouflaged Verbs (Obj. 1)**
Eliminate the camouflaged verbs in each sentence.

a. Parker Communications has a commitment to its employees.

b. An assessment of the promotional campaign for our new product must be conducted.

c. A recommendation on the location of the new distribution center will be presented at the next staff meeting by the management/marketing team.

d. The employees voiced complaints about the freeze in wages during the staff meeting.

e. Implementation of a comprehensive, progressive training program at Montague, Inc., ensures the professional development of its employees.

3. **Clichés (Obj. 1)**
Substitute fresh, original expressions for each cliché.

a. We need to burn the midnight oil to get this out on time.

b. Please find attached a copy of my résumé and references.

c. In the event that sales do not improve this quarter, layoffs may be necessary.

d. We regret to inform you that we have filled the position with an internal candidate.

e. I am writing in response to your recent claim letter.

f. Pete's graphics can't hold a candle to Mary Beth's.

g. I have often thought about leaving the rat race.

h. The job market is a jungle.

i. After the recent downsizing, most employees are beginning to feel like rats on a sinking ship.

j. At this point in time, the project is at 75 percent completion.

k. Morgan said that he would let me work with him on the next big project—as if . . .

l. We don't need to reinvent the wheel on this project.

m. In conclusion, we would like to say that we appreciate your confidence in choosing Newton & Associates to represent you in this matter.

n. Since Keller transferred here from Florida, she has seemed like a fish out of water.

4. **Simple Words (Obj. 1)**
Revise the following sentences using shorter, simpler words:

a. The voluminous tome occupied the upmost shelf in the library.

b. Through strategic alliances and by internal expansion of programs, Jefferson & Co. is seeking to develop a substantial market presence as the leading provider of management consulting services in Georgia and its neighboring states.

c. The attendees of the convocation concurred that it should terminate at the appointed hour.

d. We utilized an innovative device to restore the computer's video display terminal.

e. Management as well as technical and administrative personnel will be remunerated for time exceeding forty hours per week.

f. We conclusively consolidated our endeavors to revoke the capitulation in earnings.

5. **Misplaced and Dangling Modifiers (Obj. 1)**
Revise the following sentences positioning the modifiers appropriately.

a. An informal meal was served to all attendees on paper plates.

b. Your report is being read by the department manager, which was received this morning.

c. While demonstrating the new software, a system fault occurred.

d. Until unanimously convinced, a verdict was not reached.

e. While lunch was served, we had a strategy meeting, which was delicious.

f. Taking our seats, the training session started.

6. **Expletive Beginnings (Obj. 1)**

a. There are many factors to consider before starting your own business.

b. It is advisable to meet with the client before sending them a proposal.

c. It has come to my attention that the sales forecast for next quarter has been issued.

d. There is a need for a more administrative personnel in this office.

e. There is a meeting scheduled on March 3.

7. **Parallel Construction (Obj. 1)**
Present the following ideas in parallel form.

a. Our corporation is committed to excellence in performance, responsiveness to the client, and offering cost effective services to industry.

b. As conference chairperson, Margaret reviews the papers, contacts the authors, and did not hesitate to offer her assistance.

c. After college, I set three major goals: to get a good job, to buy a new car, and paying off my student loan in three years.

d. Despite his nervousness, Rafael gave an inspirational speech, and presents to the client a strong image of our company.

e. Our main personnel problems are absenteeism, apathy, and the lowering of employee morale.

8. **Conciseness (Obj. 1)**

Revise the following sentences to eliminate redundancies and other wordy construction.

a. We will follow the exact same agenda as the last meeting and will conclude at 4 p.m. this afternoon.

b. At Westenhoeffer Incorporated, we are certain that we will overcome this serious crisis and are looking forward to coming out ahead of the competition in the future.

c. Although some damage to the building was visible to the eye, we were directed by our attorneys not to repair or change anything until the adjuster made a damage assessment.

d. The supervisor asked Jerry to go back and make revisions to the final draft of the report so the data will be completely accurate.

e. Ellen's past work history includes working as a bartender, waiting tables in a restaurant, and stocking shelves in a bookstore.

f. The basic fundamentals are outlined in the operations manual.

g. My tax forms were completed and mailed before March 15.

h. This is in response to your recent letter.

9. **Improving Readability (Obj. 2)**

Improve readability by dividing each of the following sentences into shorter sentences.

a. People from such different backgrounds as today's workers invariably bring different values, attitudes, and perceptions to the workplace, which can lead to misunderstandings, miscommunications, and missed opportunities to improve both the workers and the organizations.

b. Matters of ethics are seldom clear-cut issues of right vs. wrong and often contain many ambiguous elements, and the pressure to compromise on ethics appears to be felt most strongly by lower-level managers who are least experienced at doing their jobs.

c. As world markets expand, U.S. employees at home and abroad will be doing business with more people from other countries, so you may find yourself working abroad for a large American company, an international company with a plant in the United States, or a company with an ethnically diverse workplace.

d. Business managers have studied, completed internships, and made many sacrifices to get closer to their ultimate goals, but unless they can use electronic tools to access, assemble, and communicate information in a timely manner, however, they may find themselves lagging behind.

e. At the corporate level, the Corporate Quality Improvement Department provides guidance and recommends resources for quality improvement activities and assesses organization-wide activities, while at the branch office level, the Department assists in the collection of data, facilitates quality improvement activities, and provides education for implementing the quality improvement process.

Now suggest short, simple words to replace each of the following words that the Fog Index would highlight as difficult and thus raise the Fog index.

f. The current work load is oppressive.

g. As a consequence of submitting a flawed report, the client has refused to pay us.

h. Assembling the proposal required perusing voluminous stacks of files for the pertinent information.

i. Utilization of the new procedures by all personnel will contribute to the efficiency of this office.

j. We anticipate that the recently acquired computer applications will facilitate a reduction in the time currently required to generate large documents.

10. **Proofreading (Obj. 3)**

Use proofreading marks to mark spelling, grammar, punctuation, capitalization, and other errors in the following sentences.

a. His advise was to listen to the clients comments.

b. The project was understaffed, the schedule was not met, has gone over budget and we apologize for any inconvenience this has caused you.

c. Robert Seabrook, a Project Director, will speak at the next Staff Meeting, he will address next quarters sales fourcast.

d. Our trip included a conference in San Fanciso California before the beaver state business council meeting in Portland OR.

e. 12 persons form our office were their to here president Clinton speak at the civic center his speech was about litteracy

11. **Proofreading Application (Obj. 3)**

Use proofreaders' marks to correct errors in spelling, grammar, punctuation, numbers, and abbreviations in the following letter sent to Phelps Enterprise. Do not revise a sentence and state its idea in an entirely different way.

Congradulations on being selected to attend the two day seminar on effective listening. The seminar will be held in Los Angeles, California on January 3. These five guidelines for effective listening should be helpful as you begin to analyze you own listening skills.

1. Learn to block out distractions that interfere with effective listening.

2. Take notes on the material to reinforce you memory.

3. Become sincrely interested in what the speaker is saying, this procedure will help you retain information.

3. Listen to the entire message before responding to be certain that you here everything.

4. Listen with an open mind, otherwise, you may miss key points.

5. Identify your weaknesses in listening and work to improve them.

We are eager for you to this professional development seminar. When you return please be sure to share this valuable information with others at Philps Enterprises.

12. **Document for Analysis (Obj. 1–3)**
Complete the following tasks individually or as a group assigned by your instructor.

a.   Key the following document into your word processing program.

Armadillos, 'R Us is preparing to initiate a program whereby employees may participate in telecommuting. We anticipate that implementation of the program will begin sometime next quarter. To qualify for this program, an employee must secure the approval of his superior and also meet specific criteria. It has been learned that companys can realize substantial savings through the implementation of telecommuting, such as savings from reduced use of energy and other office resources, reduced need for office space and employees have less absenteeism. In order to qualify for the telecommuting program, employees must meet the following criteria: must own or be able to lease a computer compatible with those currently used in the office, complete with modem, must purchase or lease a fax machine if it is not included in computer package, must agree to work in the office a minimum of three days per week, must submit time and expense reports daily instead of weekly, and personnel must be within job grades 6 or above. Technical and administrative personnel obviously cannot participate due to the nature of their employment. Please see your supervisor if you are interested in this program. He will assist you in assessing whether telecommuting is a good option for you. Armadillos, Inc. is pleased to offer this new program to it's employees who qualify and will continue to be supportive of innovation in the workplace.

b.   Complete a readability analysis using the grammar checker available to you or compute the Fog Index using the formula shown in this chapter. Note the readability index, average length of sentences, number of difficult words, number of sentences in paragraphs, average number of syllables, and other statistics provided.

c.   Revise the document: (a) incorporate relevant suggestions generated by the grammar checker and (2) improve the readability by applying the principles presented in the Chapters 3–4.

d.   Complete a readability analysis for your revision and compare with the original readability analysis and note the areas where improvements were made.

E-MAIL APPLICATION

Your instructor will send you an e-mail message containing the document in Exercise 12. Import the document into the word processing software you are using. Revise the document as directed in Exercise 12. Use the redline feature to mark insertions and the strikeout feature to mark any deletions. Your instructor will direct you to submit your revision in one of the following ways: (1) Send your instructor an e-mail message explaining that a file containing the revised document is attached to the e-mail message. (2) Print a copy so that you can quickly verify the accuracy of your work when your instructor reviews the corrections during class.

REAL-TIME INTERNET CASE

It's All in the Translation

Business people frequently communicate by exchanging documents, either printed on paper or transmitted electronically. Those with overseas clients, customers, and contacts can improve their communications dramatically by using software to automatically translate these documents. The *Washington Post* and the *Los Angeles Times* use translation software to produce Spanish editions of their newspapers in short order. Such software is used by other organizations to produce documents ranging from international correspondence and invoices to complex financial and legal documents.[10]

Two commonly used translation programs are Power Translator, by Globalink Translation Software, and Translation Manager, by IBM. Versions are available to translate documents in such languages as French, German, or Spanish to English, or from English to the other languages. Some software products support in excess of 20 languages. Packages are typically based on two types of bilingual dictionaries, one for word-for-word translations and another for semantic and idiomatic phrases. Speed of translation is about 20,000 words per hour with a 90 percent or higher degree of accuracy.

Optical Character Recognition (OCR) software can be used to scan documents into the computer, where they can be automatically translated. The newest development in language translation, however, is in voice recognition. Such software allows the sender to speak into the computer and have the spoken word automatically translated into the required language. It is also possible in some countries, including the United States, to use commercial computer-based translation facilities via the telephone, using modems and fax. Messages can be translated using Globalink message translation service for a cost of five cents a word, with a minimum charge of $5. Although such services may appear costly, imagine the benefit that an organization may derive from conveying an appropriately translated message to a potential client or customer.

In a technological environment that greatly simplifies language translation, some challenges still exist. The problem is often not to translate the words, but to convey ideas across cultures. A writer from the other culture may be employed to take translated material and write the ideas in the local language. Experienced practitioners understand the need to consider cultural as well as linguistic differences.[11]

Visit the following Internet sites and complete the following activities, as directed by your instructor:

Internet Sites

http://www.tao.ca/earth/nyfreemedia/old/0148.htm
http://www.altrans.com/
http://www.tranexp.com/

Activities

1. Write a one-page summary explaining the difference between word translation and culture translation. Give examples of interpretation problems that result when word translation alone is used.

2. Assume that you work for a company that has just entered the Japanese market. Your company wishes to translate correspondence, promotional materials, and invoices into the Japanese language. Using the sites listed above as starting points, visit four sites of organizations that offer translation and interpretation services. Prepare a two-page written report that (1) compares the services offered by each organization and the accompanying costs, and (2) recommends the one your company should use for its translation services.

3. Research the two software translation programs mentioned in this case. Prepare a chart that summarizes the capabilities and features available with each.

In the Forming stage of effective team development, group members get to know one another and their purpose for being together. They make preliminary plans and identify roles of each member. Typical characteristics of the Forming stage include the lack of conflict, or even avoidance of such situations. Goal-setting and task-orientation are present, along with confusion and uncertainty.

Typical feelings of team members during the Forming stage include:

- anxiety and fear of the challenges to come.
- excitement and confusion.
- pride in being part of the team.

Typical behaviors during the Forming stage include:

- asking a lot of questions.
- expressing doubt about ability to meet the challenges.
- making attempts to get to know other team members.
- expressing anxiousness to get on with the task.
- sharing of acceptable, non-controversial things.

Team selection can have a major influence on overall performance. Several factors relate to the success of multi-talented work groups:

- Among team members, there is a range of the skills and know-how needed to deal effectively with the team's tasks.
- A range of personal skills is present; team members have different aptitudes for the various team roles required for effective team working.
- Team members respect one another, both as individuals and for the contribution each makes to the team's performance.

Team experts have agreed that people have different psychological characteristics that lead them to adopt a variety of roles at work, and it is the combination of the different roles that makes for a well-balanced, high-performance team. Team roles, however, are not personality traits, but rather they reflect patterns of behavior characteristic of the way in which one team member interacts with another so as to facilitate the progress of the team as a whole. The roles played by each member may change from one project to another, and roles may even be exchanged during the same project. During the Forming stage, the group typically discusses roles that each member might play. You may want to review the negative and positive group roles discussed in Chapter 2 of the text before proceeding with the following activities.

Exploration

Team roles have been explored by numerous authors. Read the following article that provides expanded information on team roles:

Team building and development: The analytical framework. (1994, July). *Industrial Relations Review and Report, 564.*, SSSS2-SSSS11

Compare and contrast the team roles identified by R. Meredith Belbin and those identified by Charles Margerison and Dick McCann.

Application

Visit the following web sites to obtain helpful information about responsibilities of team roles:

http://rowlf.cc.wwu.edu.8080/~techecon/teamrole.htm

http://www.dsport.com/MOWW/HSPrep/2tab1.html

http://www.cbdcom.apgea.army.mil/Staff/quality/integration/funbook/page23.html

http://www.cbdcom.apgea.army.mil/Staff/quality/integration/funbook/page24.html

With your team members, complete the following activities:

- Identify which team member will serve in each of the following roles: facilitator, harmonizer, recordkeeper, reporter, and leader. Will your roles remain constant, or will they rotate? How will you, as a group, deal with the emergence of any negative roles?
- Discuss the purpose and preparation of effective meeting minutes. Use the form you located through visiting the suggested web sites to record the activities of your meeting.
- Discuss the need for meeting evaluation. Use the form you located through visiting the suggested web sites to evaluate your meeting.
- Send an e-mail message to your instructor identifying the role(s) that each member is playing. Explain how the roles were determined.
- Submit minutes to your instructor for all team meetings held thus far. Continue to submit minutes on a weekly basis, as meetings are held.

Source: Fowler, A. (1995, February 23). How to build effective teams. *Personnel Management, 1*(4), 40–41.

VIDEO CONNECTION

Amatulli & Associates, Inc.

Developing effective training programs for organizations (skill development and employee awareness programs) involves thorough planning, articulate writing and editing, and meticulous proofreading.

The planning process involves (1) identifying the audience, the purpose, and the outcome expected by the client; (2) selecting the appropriate media (written, video, computer interactive) for presenting the message; and (3) identifying and *understanding* the message to be communicated.

After considering the crucial issues, the writer(s) develop(s) a first draft using the style, language, tone, and approach that is appropriate for the audience and the specific content to be communicated. Finally, the writer(s) and others edit for accuracy, consistency in style among collaborative writers, format, and mechanics.

Discussion Questions

1. According to Jim Amatulli, what information must a writer identify before writing the first draft of a document?

2. Describe the process involved in identifying the content of the message and organizing its effectiveness.

3. What process is used to control for consistency, accuracy, and effectiveness of the message when several writers work collaboratively on a project?

4. Describe the (a) editing process and (b) the two proofreading methods used at Amatulli.

5. How have electronic spell checks affected the writing of Jim Amatulli? What *two* cautions

does he offer about the reliability of electronic spell check?

6. Study carefully the writing project Jo Huntington described. (1) Identify the audience, the purpose and intended outcome, and the media combination selected; (2) describe the content of the message and the specific approach used to present the message, and (3) discuss how collaborative writing enhanced this project.

7. What does Jim Amatulli mean when he describes the objective and subjective nature of communication?

Applications

As a senior writer in a business communication consulting firm, your task is to *plan* a message that will increase the membership of a student organization of your choice or increase involvement in a community organization such as the United Way, Scouts, and so forth. Your preliminary planning involves providing answers to the following questions:

1. Who is the audience? What is the purpose and intended outcome of the message?

2. What medium or media combination (written document, video, interactive computer program) is appropriate for communicating the message?

3. What steps will you take to identify the content of the message and ensure that you understand the exact message to be communicated?

4. What approach (e.g., language and style) is appropriate for communicating this message effectively?

PART THREE

Communicating Through Letters, Memorandums, and E-Mail Messages

CHAPTER FIVE

Writing Good-News, Routine, and Special Letters

LEARNING OBJECTIVES

When you have completed Chapter 5, you will be able to:

1 List the steps in the deductive outline and identify the advantages of using it to convey good news or routine information.

2 Write letters presenting claims and making adjustments.

3 Write routine requests and favorable responses to routine requests.

4 Compose letters providing credit information and extending credit.

5 Write letters acknowledging customer orders.

6 Write the following special messages: thank-you, appreciation, and apologies.

7 Adapt letters to international receivers.

*D*espite its obvious benefits, many companies do not communicate good news often enough, especially within the corporation; and the result can be low employee morale and a high turnover rate. That is not the case at Southwest Airlines, where CEO Herb Kelleher never passes up an opportunity to share good news. In one case in particular he managed to transform bad news into a "win-win" situation that most people could hardly have imagined.

Southwest Airlines, founded in 1971 and based in Dallas, Texas, is now the fifth largest airline in America and the only major U.S. carrier that has shown a profit consistently since 1973.[1] Southwest has developed a reputation for its laid-back yet highly motivated corporate culture, and Herb Kelleher attributes at least a part of Southwest's success to communication. He exhorts managers to "spend a lot of time with your people and . . . communicate with them in a variety of ways. And a large part of it is demeanor. Sometimes we tend to lose sight of the fact that demeanor—the way you appear and the way you act—is a form of communication."[2] And Kelleher never misses an opportunity to praise employees, whether it is in a letter to shareholders, a news release, or an announcement for one of the fun parties or silly promotions for which Southwest is so famous. This constant communication of good news has led to Southwest's commercial success and an annual employee turnover rate of only 4.5 percent.[3]

In *Nuts! Southwest Airlines' Crazy Recipe for Business and Personal Success*, a particular incident is related that has since become legend in Texas. It seems that Southwest Airlines began using what it thought was a new slogan—"Just Plane Smart"—when the company was notified that Stevens Aviation, a company located in Greenville, South Carolina, had been using "Plane Smart" as its slogan for at least a year. Stevens proposed that the companies choose champions to arm-wrestle for the slogan, thereby saving thousands of dollars in legal fees. The winner would keep the rights to the slogan, and the loser would contribute to a charity chosen by the winner. Of course, Kelleher embraced the idea and settled the score before the press, employees from both companies, and network television cameras. Kelleher lost the arm-wrestling match to Stevens' Kurt Herwald, but soon after the event, the Stevens chairman announced that he would allow Southwest to keep its slogan. This dilemma had turned into a win-win situation: Southwest kept the slogan; the media had a circus; both companies received great press; their employees participated in a fun, morale-boosting event; and charities received approximately $15,000. And on March 23, 1992, Herb Kelleher received a good-news letter himself—from President George Bush—congratulating him on his "loss!"[4]

Communicating good news—whether it is in the form of letters, memos, speeches, or meetings—is an important task for managers. Be sure that your positive communication reaches the intended audience, is written or organized to achieve the best effect and level of understanding, and, of course, is grammatically correct.

1 *List the steps in the deductive outline and identify the advantages of using it to convey good news or routine information.*

Deductive Organizational Pattern

You can organize business messages either deductively or inductively depending on your prediction of the receiver's reaction to your main idea. Learning to organize business messages according to the appropriate outline will improve your chances of writing a document that elicits the response or action you desire.

In this chapter, you will learn to write letters that convey ideas that a receiver likely will find either *pleasing* or *routine*. Messages that convey pleasant information are referred to as **good-news messages**. Messages that are of interest to the reader but are not likely to generate an emotional reaction are referred to as **routine** messages. You will also learn to write several types of special letters that also require a deductive outline.

Good-news or routine messages follow a **deductive sequence**—the message begins with the main idea. To present good news and routine information deductively, begin with the major idea, followed by supporting details as depicted in Figure 5-1. In both outlines, the third point (closing thought) may be omitted without seriously impairing effectiveness; however, including it unifies the message and avoids abruptness.

What are other words that can be substituted for deductive and inductive?

GOOD-NEWS MESSAGES	*ROUTINE MESSAGES*
• States the pleasant idea.	• States the main idea.
• Provides details or explanations.	• Provides details or explanation.
• Reminds receiver of the good news or includes a future-oriented closing thought.	• Reminds receiver of the main idea or includes a future-oriented closing thought.

FIGURE 5-1
Deductive pattern used in good-news and routine messages.

The deductive pattern has several advantages:

- The first sentence is easy to write. After writing it, the details follow easily.
- The first sentence gets the attention it deserves in this emphatic position.
- Encountering good news in the first sentence puts receivers in a pleasant frame of mind, and they are receptive to the details that follow.
- The arrangement may save receivers some time. Once they understand the important idea, they can move rapidly through the supporting details.

According to the outline, will all deductive messages have at least three paragraphs? Explain.

Ineffective and effective applications of the deductive outline are illustrated in the sample letters in this chapter. An *avoid* symbol (see right) appears beside examples of poor writing for easy identification. Detailed comments highlight important writing strategies that have been applied or violated. To assist you in recognizing standard business formats, many letters are fully formatted with all appropriate parts and are printed correctly on letterhead. As you study these examples, refer to Appendix A for detailed explanations and illustrations of the standard formats and layout of business letters.

Routine Claims

2 *Write letters presenting claims and making adjustments.*

A **claim letter** is a request for an adjustment. When writers ask for something to which they think they are entitled (such as a refund, replacement, exchange, or payment for damages), the letter is called a *claim letter*.

Claim Letters

Requests for adjustments can be divided into two groups: **routine claims** and **persuasive claims**. Persuasive claims, which are discussed in Chapter 8, assume that a request will be granted only after explanations and persuasive arguments have been presented. Routine claims (possibly because of guarantees, warranties, or other contractual conditions) assume that a request will be granted quickly and willingly, without persuasion. Because you expect routine claims to be granted willingly, a forceful, accusatory tone is inappropriate.

Forceful, accusatory tone inappropriate for routine claims

When the claim is routine, the deductive pattern shown in Figure 5-1 will be followed. Let's consider an MIS manager who seeks an adjustment for inadequate documentation for a computer program written by an outside consulting firm. Surely the programmer intended to write the in-program documentation; otherwise, a contract would not have been signed. Because a mistake is obvious, the programmer can be expected to correct the problem without persuasion. Thus, the MIS manager can ask for the adjustment *before* providing an explanation. Note, however, that the letter in Figure 5-2 is written *inductively*—the details are presented before the main idea, and the tone is unnecessarily forceful.

The writer is confident that her routine request for an adjustment will be granted. Therefore, in the revision (Figure 5-3) she simply states the request in the first sentence and follows with the details without showing anger, disgust, suspicion, or disappointment. Beginning with the request for an adjustment gives it the emphasis it deserves.

In small groups, complete the following: (1) Identify the main idea and the details in Figure 5-2. Jot them down in the correct, deductive sequence. Compare your outline with Figure 5-3. (2) Identify words/phrases that contribute to the negative, forceful tone of this letter. (Turn back to "Adapting the Message to the Audience" in Chapter 3 if necessary.)

❶ Uses a writer-centered, forceful tone to convey details the receiver already knows. **❷** Continues with more details about the problem but shows no empathy for the receiver. **❸** Uses second person and negative language, that emphasize the receiver is at fault. **❹** Presents a reason for making the upcoming request. **❺** States the main point (claim) that should have appeared in the first paragraph; continues forceful tone that will damage human relations.

❶ We at Meta Tech contracted with you to write the new marketing analysis program for our chemical engineering subsidiary, ChemiCo, Inc. The contract required you to create the source code and write user *and* operator documentation.

❷ However, once we looked at the program, we realized you had not provided us with in-program documentation that would enable us to maintain the program efficiently. **❸** No other company has failed to supply us with this information.

❹ We would like for our people to be able to maintain the program instead of calling you repeatedly to do routine maintenance work. **❺** Please modify the program to the agreed upon specifications and fulfill your contract with us.

FIGURE 5-2 Poor example of a routine claim letter.

Deductive Outline for Routine Claim Letters

1. Request action (refund, replacement, credit on your account, free repairs, etc.).

2. Explain the details supporting the request objectively.

3. Remind of the action requested with an expression of appreciation for taking the action.

FIGURE 5-3
Good example of a routine claim letter.

META TECH 2905 West Morris Road / El Paso, TX 75510-2905 / (915) 555-5430 Fax: (915) 555-1585

June 5, 1999

Mr. Greg Whitford
Sales Manager
Quality Computer Services
492 Harding Court
Abilene, TX 79604-0492

Dear Mr. Whitford:

❶ Please include in-program documentation with the marketing analysis software you created for us.

❷ Our data processing personnel regularly modify application programs to meet the constantly changing information needs of our business. The application programmers will need in-program documentation to understand how the program code relates to the system documentation you have provided to us. Other application programs we have purchased from you were equipped with this information.

❸ The user and operator documentation appear to be well done; thus, we plan to begin training our staff immediately.

Sincerely,

Bonnie R. Foster

Bonnie R. Foster
MIS Manager

mle

❶ Emphasizes the main idea (request for adjustment) by placing it in the first sentence.
❷ Provides the explanation.
❸ Ends on a positive note, reminding writer that the company can begin using the software and the user documentation.

Format Pointers

● *Illustrates modified block format*—the date and closing lines (complimentary close and signature block begin at the horizontal center).

● *Uses mixed punctuation*—a colon follows the salutation and, a comma follows the complimentary close.

● Includes reference initials to indicate someone other than the writer keyed this document.

Favorable Response to a Claim Letter

Businesses *want* their customers to write when merchandise or service is not satisfactory. They want to learn of ways in which goods and services can be improved, and they want their customers to receive value for the money they spend. With considerable confidence, they can assume that writers of claim letters think their claims are valid. By responding fairly to legitimate requests in **adjustment letters**, businesses can gain a reputation for standing behind their goods and services. A loyal customer may become even more loyal after a business has demonstrated its integrity.

Because the subject of an adjustment letter is related to the goods or services provided, the letter can include a brief sales message. With only a little extra space, the letter can include resale or sales promotional material. **Resale** refers to a discussion of goods or services already bought. It reminds customers and clients that they made a good choice in selecting a firm with which to do business, or it reminds them of the good qualities of their purchase. **Sales promotional material** refers to statements made about related merchandise or service. For example, a letter about a company's office furniture might also mention its work-space design team. Mentioning the design team is using sales promotional material. Subtle sales messages that are included in adjustment letters have a good chance of being read, but direct sales letters may not be read at all.

Although the word *grant* is acceptable when talking about claims, its use in adjustment letters is discouraged. An expression such as "Your claim is being granted" unnecessarily implies that the writer is in a position of power.

Ordinarily, a response to a written message is also a written message. Sometimes, people write letters to confirm ideas they have already discussed on the telephone. When the response to a claim letter is favorable, present ideas in the deductive sequence.

Let's evaluate the reply Bonnie Foster received to her claim letter reporting the missing in-program documentation. How would the letter in Figure 5-4 affect MetaTech's impression of the computer company's commitment to stand behind its application programs?

Eager to learn if (and when) she will receive the in-program documentation, the MIS manager will resent having to read through the obvious facts in the first three sentences. The vague explanation with no specific assurance that the documentation has been shipped may anger the MIS manager further. Finally the last paragraph sheds considerable doubt on the integrity of the entire program.

Notice the deductive outline and the explanation in the revision in Figure 5-5. The writer knows that the MIS manager will be pleased the in-program documentation will be sent with only a brief delay. Therefore, he gives the receiver this good news in the first sentence. The details and closing sentence follow naturally and easily showing no reluctance for correcting the problem.

What is meant by resale and sales promotional material? How are they different from sales letter messages?

What wording would you suggest in order to avoid "granting" a customer's request?

AVOID

FIGURE 5-4
Poor example of a favorable response to a routine claim letter.

Thank you for your letter of June 5. It has been referred to me for reply.

We have studied your contract and talked to the programmers about your complaint. We just don't know how it could have happened, but the in-program documentation was not shipped with the rest of the program.

Thank you for calling this matter to our attention, and we certainly hope the new program and documentation meet your needs.

Deductive Outline for a Favorable Response to a Routine Claim Letter

1. Approve the customer's claim in the first sentence (good news).
2. Explain the circumstances without placing blame. Include resale to assure customer of a wise choice.
3. Close on a pleasant, forward-looking note that attempts to regain the customer's confidence in the product/service and the company.

FIGURE 5-5

Good example of a favorable response to a routine claim letter.

QualityComputerServices
492 Harding Court | Abilene, TX 79604-0492 | (915) 555-0800 | Fax (915) 555-2300

June 10, 1999

Ms. Bonnie R. Foster
MIS Manager
Meta Tech, Inc.
2905 West Morris Road
El Paso, TX 75510-2905

Dear Ms. Foster

❶ The revised source code with the proper in-program documentation should be shipped to you within three weeks.

❷ Thank you for bringing this situation to our attention so quickly while the programmers are still able to remember the program logic and write the documentation easily. **❸** Although your program was subjected to our normal operating quality control review, a separate review of program documentation was omitted inadvertently.

❹ Our programmers enjoy the opportunity of sharing new coding techniques with other computer professionals. Please call us at 555-0800 if your application programmers would like to spend a few hours touring our facilities and talking shop with our programmers.

Sincerely

Greg Whitford

Greg Whitford

❶ Begins with the good news (main idea) for deserved emphasis; assures receiver that action is being taken already.

❷ Expresses appreciation for being informed about the omission.

❸ Presents explanation and assures the manager the in-program documentation meets company's rigorous standards.

❹ Attempts to regain possible lost goodwill by offering specialized training.

Format Pointers

- *Illustrates block format*—All lines begin at the left margin.
- *Uses open punctuation*—The colon is omitted after the salutation, and the comma is omitted after the complimentary close.

Diversity Issues

- Would likely omit "talking shop" if this letter were being sent to an international audience.

Write routine requests and favorable responses to routine requests.

Routine Request Letters

Like claims, requests are divided into two groups: **routine requests** and **persuasive requests**. Persuasive claims, which are discussed in Chapter 8, assume that action will be taken after persuasive arguments are presented. Routine requests and favorable responses to them follow the deductive sequence.

Routine Requests

Most businesspeople write letters requesting information about people, prices, products, and services. Because the request is a door opener for future business, receivers accept it optimistically. At the same time, they arrive at an opinion about the writer based on the quality of the letter. Follow the points in the deductive outline for preparing effective requests that are expected to be fulfilled. Because the request in Figure 5-6 is vague, the writer is unlikely to receive information that will prove useful for his preparation to transfer overseas.

Note that the revision in Figure 5-7 starts with a direct request for specific information. Then as much detail as necessary is presented to enable the receiver to answer specifically. The revision ends confidently with appreciation for the action requested. The letter is short; but because it conveys enough information and has a tone of politeness, it is effective.

Favorable Responses to Routine Requests

The letter in Figure 5-8 responds favorably to Lance's request about international work assignments. However, it conveys the decision without much enthusiasm.

With a little planning and consideration for the executive transferring overseas, the letter in Figure 5-9 could have been written just as quickly. Note the specific answers to Lance's questions and the helpful, sincere tone.

In groups, complete the following activities: (1) Identify the main idea and the details in Figure 5-6. Jot them down in the correct, deductive sequence. Compare your outline with Figure 5-7. (2) Comment on the value of "I am writing" in Sentence 3. (3) What could you say other than "know the ropes" that an international audience would understand? (4) What genuine, original idea could you develop in the last paragraph?

❶ Delays request (the main idea of the letter).
❷ Presents the request vaguely.
❸ Contains an expression, *know the ropes*, that may be difficult to interpret if the receiver is from a culture other than the United States.
❹ Closes with a superficial statement.

❶ For the past five years, I have worked as a staff engineer in the Environmental Group at Stewart. Yesterday, I received news of my impending transfer to Paris, France, to work in our plant location there.

❷ I am writing you to ask if you have any advice to help me make my transition to the Paris operation—my first overseas assignment.
❸ Because you have been working in the Paris office for the past ten years, I felt you would already know the ropes and could be a great help.

❹ Any advice you can provide would be greatly appreciated.

FIGURE 5-6 Poor example of a routine request.

Deductive Outline for a Routine Request

1. State the major request in the first sentence.

2. Follow with the details that will make the request clear. Use a numbered or bulleted list for added emphasis, if possible.

3. Close with a forward look to the receiver's next step.

FIGURE 5-7

Good example of a routine request.

STEWART ENGINEERING CONSULTANTS

7640 North Jefferson Road | Hershey, PA 17033-7640

Telephone: (717) 555-5042 | Fax: (717) 555-3811

December 30, 1999

Ms. Tonya Peterson, Project Manager
Stewart Engineering Consultants
85, rue de Penthievre
75008 Paris
FRANCE

Dear Ms. Peterson:

❶ Would you please assist me as I begin plans to transfer to the Environmental Group in the Paris operation—my first overseas assignment? Because you have been working in this overseas location for several years, you may be able to give me some ideas on the following items:

❷ • Can you suggest a strategy to help me maximize my purchase of francs, especially during the transition period?

• What degree of proficiency should I have in the French language? If I must speak French fluently, how can I manage until I learn the language?

• Can you suggest any books or other resources that will prepare my family and me for living abroad?

❸ I will arrive on June 5 to begin work on June 10. Even though my transfer is six months away, my family and I wish to make our transition as smooth as possible. Consequently, receiving this information from you will help us achieve that goal.

Sincerely,

Lance Garrett

Lance Garrett
Staff Engineer

❶ States request plainly.

❷ Asks specific questions; uses a bulleted list for emphasis.

❸ Expresses appreciation and alludes to action.

Diversity Issues

● Illustrates the format of a French address; *rue* is the French word for street.

● Uses a traditional U.S. salutation because the recipient is North American. *Monsieur* or *Madame* is an appropriate courtesy title when addressing a French man or woman respectively. In French, *Dear* is used only when the recipient is known well.

● Omits "know the ropes," used in the poor example because this cliché could have been difficult to interpret if the receiver is from a culture other than the United States.

FIGURE 5-8 Poor example of a favorable response to a routine request.

❶ Focuses on the writer; tone suggests lack of interest in helping; is vague; uses overly complex word.

❷ Includes details that are not specific nor directly related to the questions asked.

❸ Uses too many words; is unconvincing because the rest of the letter is negative.

❶ I read your request hurriedly and hopefully my response will provide the logistics for your transition to the Paris operation.

❷ The exchange rate fluctuates rapidly; I'd say you will need at least $5,000 for starting expenses. Your other questions are difficult to answer; you'll just have to work them out when you get here. I will introduce you to some of the staff here and help you find your way around on the first day, but after that you're on your own.

❸ May we in the Paris office take this opportunity to welcome you to the overseas operation. We look forward to your arrival on June 5.

Favorable Response to a Favor

Occasionally, as a business professional, you will be asked special favors. You may receive invitations to speak at various civic or education groups, spearhead fund-raising and other service projects, or offer your expertise in other sundry ways. If you say, "Yes," you might as well say it enthusiastically. Sending an unplanned, stereotyped acceptance suggests that the contribution will be similar.

In the letter in Figure 5-10, the TV production manager of a local public relations firm graciously accepts an invitation to emcee an awards banquet for the Chamber of Commerce. His polite request for specific information assures the Chamber director that this busy manager is committed to doing an outstanding job as emcee. His closing remarks reinforce the enthusiasm evident throughout the letter.

If responses to invitations were frequent, the preceding letter could be stored in a computer file to be opened and revised when responding to the next invitation. Individualized form letters produced using computer-based technology enable businesses to communicate quickly and efficiently with clients or customers.

Form Letters for Routine Responses

Why do form letters have such a bad image? How can the weaknesses of a form letter be overcome?

Form letters are a fast and efficient way of transmitting frequently recurring messages to which receiver reaction is likely favorable or neutral. Inputting the customer's name and address and other variables (information that differs for each receiver) personalizes each letter to meet the needs of its receiver. Refer to the related Strategic Forces Box to understand how the mail-merge feature of word processing software automates the production of form letters.

To personalize letters even further, companies may use form paragraphs that have been stored in separate word processing files. Perhaps as many as five versions of a paragraph related to a typical request are available for use in a routine request letter. The originator selects the appropriate paragraph according to the receiver's request. After assembling the selected files on the computer screen, the originator inputs any variables (e.g., name and address). A copy of the personalized letter is printed on letterhead and sent to the receiver.

Deductive Outline for a Favorable Reply to a Routine Request

1. State the positive response to the receiver's request.
2. Continue with details or explanation.
3. Close with a forward look to build strong human relations with the receiver.

FIGURE 5-9
Good example of a favorable response to a routine request.

STEWART ENGINEERING CONSULTANTS
85, Rue De Penthievre I 75008 Paris, FRANCE
Tel: 14 555-08-33 I Fax: 14 555-78-56

January 4, 1999

FACSIMILE

Mr. Lance Garrett, Staff Engineer
Stewart Engineering Consultants
7640 North Jefferson Road
Hershey, PA 17033-7640

Dear Mr. Garrett:

1 Congratulations on your transfer to the Paris office. I am pleased we will be working together and am pleased to answer your questions.

2
- The franc has been declining against the U.S. dollar steadily for several weeks, and economists are predicting that this trend will continue. Therefore, I suggest you immediately purchase the francs you will need for the first several months. You can easily keep in touch with the fluctuating exchange rates by reviewing the "Money Rates" section of *The Wall Street Journal* each day.
- English is used most often in the office. However, becoming familiar with the French culture, customs, and economy will be beneficial. Several guidebooks are available from the director of International Operations at the home office. I recommend that you read these books thoroughly and share them with your spouse and children, too.
- Jason O'Lenick has just left the Paris office to work in the Houston office. He would be able to answer many of your questions. You can reach him at (403) 555-1353.

3 Please fax me your travel plans, and I will make arrangements to meet you at the airport and help you get settled in your new home.

Sincerely,

Tonya Peterson

Tonya Peterson
Project Manager

---

1 Shows sincere interest in the request and the person.

2 Provides specific answers and guidelines; uses a bulleted list to highlight answers.

3 Includes a specific offer that helps communicate genuine interest in the person and his transition.

Diversity Issues
Knowing that international mail is slow and that Lance needs a quick response, Tonya faxes the letter. The mailing notation (FACSIMILE) appears after the date.

FIGURE 5-10
Good example of a favorable response to a request for favor (invitation).

Deductive Outline for a Favorable Response to an Invitation

1. Accept the invitation; confirm the date, time, and place.
2. Provide necessary details.
3. Close with a forward look to the receiver's next step.

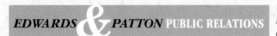
EDWARDS & PATTON PUBLIC RELATIONS

135 Copeland Street
Atlanta, GA 30304-0135
(404) 555-3000 Fax: (404) 555-1450

May 1, 1999

Ms. Colleen McGrath, President
Chamber of Commerce
980 East Wesley Street
Atlanta, GA 30304-0908

Dear Colleen:

1 Yes, I will be honored to emcee the annual Chamber of Commerce banquet beginning at 6 p.m. on July 25 in the City Auditorium.

2 The format you described with a brief motivational speech followed by the service award presentations is an excellent change for this year's program.

3 As soon as you have secured the speaker, please send me a detailed profile so that I can prepare an appropriate introduction. A brief description of each award and the person presenting it would help me plan smooth transitions between each award. Please send a tentative copy of the program when it is complete.

4 Colleen, I am eager to help the Chamber of Commerce celebrate another banner year on July 25. Let me know if I can help in any other way as plans develop.

Sincerely,

Kenya

Kenya Mason, Director

1 Accepts immediately; therefore, the receiver is relieved no one else will have to be asked. Confirms the time, date, and place.

2 Uses a *you* attitude to confirm the change in the format.

3 Outlines specific requests to ensure a highly organized, professional affair.

4 Uses the receiver's name to personalize the letter and involve the reader; closes by restating enthusiasm and commitment for the project.

Format Pointers

- Signs first name only because she knows the reader well.

- Avoids right margin justification to improve comprehension and to convey the idea the letter was not methodically generated by a computer.

Organizations with a mission of providing economical service (governmental agencies, public utilities) that serve a multitude of people use forms similar to the form in the following example. To communicate a routine message, a support staff member simply places a check mark beside the message that applies. The company's letterhead usually appears at the top of the form and a general salutation such as "Dear Customer" is used.

☐ The late charge has been waived because it resulted from circumstances beyond your control.

☐ The late charge appears to be valid; please add the amount to your next monthly payment.

☑ A late charge of $ _25_ has been waived; however, an unpaid late charge of $ _25_ remains on your account. Please add the amount to your next monthly payment.

Routine Letters About Credit and Orders

4 *Compose letters providing credit information and extending credit.*

Normally, credit information is requested and transmitted electronically from the national credit reporting agencies to companies requesting credit references. However, when companies choose to request information directly from other businesses, individual credit requests and responses must be written. Additionally, routine letters, such as customer order acknowledgments are written deductively.

Providing Credit Information

Replies to requests for credit information usually are simple—just fill in the blanks and return the letter. If the request does not include a form, follow a deductive plan in writing the reply: the major idea followed by supporting details.

When providing credit information, you have an ethical and legal obligation to yourself, the credit applicant, and the business from whom credit is requested. You must be able to document any statement you make to defend yourself against a defamation charge. Thus, good advice is to stick with facts; omit any opinions. "I'm sure he will pay promptly" is an opinion that should be omitted, but include the documentable fact that "His payments are always prompt." Can you safely say a customer is a good credit risk when all you know is that he/she had a good credit record when he/she purchased from you?

What are the legal implications of credit information letters?

Extending Credit

A timely response is preferable for any business document, but it is especially important when communicating about credit. The Equal Credit Opportunity Act (ECOA) requires that a credit applicant be notified of the credit decision within 30 days of receipt of the request or application. The party granting the credit must also disclose the terms of the credit agreement, such as the address for sending or

What legal requirements apply to letters extending credit?

Strategic Forces: Changing Technology

Creating Personalized Form Letters

The mail-merge feature of word processing software facilitates large-scale mailings of form letters. The text of a form letter is basically the same for all recipients, but the letter is personalized by adding variables—information that is different for each recipient. For example, the variables shown in parentheses in the standard text on the following page are the client's name, address, salutation, and conference attended. The personalized letter is prepared by combining the standard text with a list of variables for each letter. Special codes instruct the software to insert the variables in the appropriate location in the standard text. With this feature, each client receives an original letter instead of a photocopy of the standard text with his or her name individually keyed in—a laborious task that creates a less-than-favorable impression.

Additionally, the sort feature automatically arranges the addresses in numeric order according to ZIP Code. Printing the letters and envelopes or mailing labels in this order eliminates the time-consuming task of sorting mass mailings according to U.S. Postal Service regulations.

The most frequent complaint about the mail-merge feature is that form letters are impersonal. Many people simply refuse to read such letters for that reason. Constructing a good standard letter that does not sound like a form letter can circumvent this problem. To make a form letter more personal,

1. Add more variables to the standard text to tailor it to the individual.

2. Use personalized envelopes instead of mass-produced mailing labels.

3. Be sure to spell names correctly.

4. Produce a higher-quality document by using a better grade of paper and better-quality printers.

Application

Locate an example of a form letter you have received or have generated on the job. In small groups, discuss the appropriateness of each letter (or select one from the group's contributions). Does the form letter accurately address the recipient's problem? Does the form letter generically address numerous situations, or is it tailored to fit the specific needs of the recipients, or was the letter generic for numerous situations? What changes would you suggest for personalizing the form letter?

---

making payments, due dates for payments, and the interest rate charged. You will learn more about other legal implications related to credit when you study credit denials in Chapter 6.

When extending credit, follow the deductive outline as shown in Figure 5-11. The letter opens by extending credit and acknowledging shipment of an order. Because of its importance, the credit aspect is emphasized more than the acknowledgment of the order. In other cases (in which the order is for cash or the credit terms are already clearly understood), the primary purpose of writing may be to acknowledge an order.

The body of the letter includes the basis for the decision to extend credit in an effort to prevent collection problems that may arise later. Indicating that you are extending credit on the basis of an applicant's prompt-paying habits with present creditors may encourage this new customer to continue these habits with you. Continue by explaining your credit policies (e.g., credit terms, authorized discounts,

Why should you discuss the basis for extending credit and the credit terms?

continued

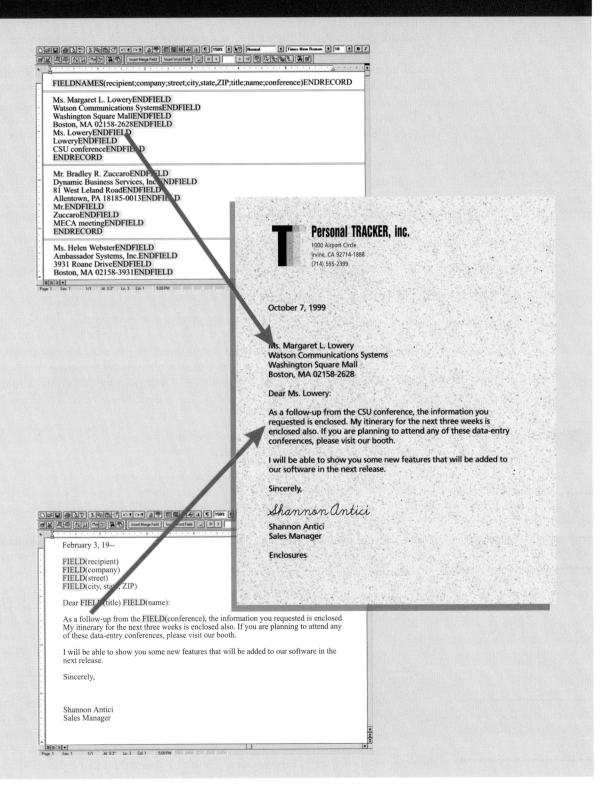

FIELDNAMES(recipient;company;street;city,state,ZIP;title;name;conference)ENDRECORD

Ms. Margaret L. LoweryENDFIELD
Watson Communications SystemsENDFIELD
Washington Square MallENDFIELD
Boston, MA 02158-2628ENDFIELD
Ms. LoweryENDFIELD
LoweryENDFIELD
CSU conferenceENDFIELD
ENDRECORD

Mr. Bradley R. ZuccaroENDFIELD
Dynamic Business Services, Inc.ENDFIELD
81 West Leland RoadENDFIELD
Allentown, PA 18185-0013ENDFIELD
Mr.ENDFIELD
ZuccaroENDFIELD
MECA meetingENDFIELD
ENDRECORD

Ms. Helen WebsterENDFIELD
Ambassador Systems, Inc.ENDFIELD
3931 Roane DriveENDFIELD
Boston, MA 02158-3931ENDFIELD

T **Personal TRACKER, inc.**

1000 Airport Circle
Irvine, CA 92714-1888
(714) 555-2399

October 7, 1999

Ms. Margaret L. Lowery
Watson Communications Systems
Washington Square Mall
Boston, MA 02158-2628

Dear Ms. Lowery:

As a follow-up from the CSU conference, the information you requested is enclosed. My itinerary for the next three weeks is enclosed also. If you are planning to attend any of these data-entry conferences, please visit our booth.

I will be able to show you some new features that will be added to our software in the next release.

Sincerely,

Shannon Antici

Shannon Antici
Sales Manager

Enclosures

February 3, 19--

FIELD(recipient)
FIELD(company)
FIELD(street)
FIELD(city, state, ZIP)

Dear FIELD(title) FIELD(name):

As a follow-up from the FIELD(conference), the information you requested is enclosed. My itinerary for the next three weeks is enclosed also. If you are planning to attend any of these data-entry conferences, please visit our booth.

I will be able to show you some new features that will be added to our software in the next release.

Sincerely,

Shannon Antici
Sales Manager

payment dates). Include any legally required disclosure documents. The final section of the letter includes resale, sales promotional material, and comments that remind the customer of the benefits of doing business with you and encourage additional future orders.

Although the letter in Figure 5-11 was written to a dealer, the same principles apply when writing to a consumer. Each one should be addressed in terms of individual interests. Dealers are concerned about markup, marketability, and display; consumers are concerned about price, appearance, and durability. Consumers may require a more detailed explanation of credit terms.

Companies receive so many requests for credit that the costs of individualized letters are prohibitive; therefore, most favorable replies to credit requests are form letters. To personalize the letter, however, the writer merges the loan applicant's name, address, amount of loan, and terms into the computer file containing the form letter information. Typically, form messages read something like this:

> Dear **[TITLE] [LAST NAME]**
>
> We are pleased to extend credit privileges to you. Temporarily, you may purchase up to **[CREDIT LIMIT]** worth of merchandise on time. Our credit terms are **[TERMS]**. We welcome you as a credit customer of our expanding organization.

Although such form messages are effective for informing the customer that credit is being extended, they do little to promote sales and goodwill. Whether to say "yes" by form letter or by individualized letter is an issue that each credit manager must settle. If the list of credit customers is relatively short and few names are being added, individualized letters may be practical. A credit manager may choose to use individualized letters if the workload in the department is such that letters can be sent without overworking personnel.

Acknowledging Customer Orders

5 *Write letters acknowledging customer orders.*

How can a company encourage future orders by sending customer order acknowledgments?

When customers place an order for merchandise, they expect to get exactly what they ordered as quickly as possible. Most orders can be acknowledged by shipping the order; no letter is necessary. For an initial order and for an order that cannot be filled quickly and precisely, companies send an **acknowledgment letter**, a document that indicates the order has been received and is being processed. Typically, acknowledgment letters are preprinted letters or copies of the sales order because individualized letters are not cost effective and will not reach the customer in a timely manner. The acknowledgment shown in Figure 5-12 was generated using a template in a major word processing software. The writer simply inputs the data into the preformatted columns and rows in the "invoice template"; preset formulas automatically calculate the amounts (extended price, subtotal, tax, and invoice total). This billing department will send an edited version of the invoice when the order is shipped. Although the form is impersonal, customers appreciate the company's acknowledging the order and giving them an idea of when the order will arrive.

What purposes does an individualized acknowledgment serve?

Nonroutine orders, such as initial orders, custom orders, and delayed orders, require individualized acknowledgment letters. Although initial orders can be acknowledged through form letters, the letters are more effective if individually written. When well-written, these letters not only acknowledge the order but also create customer goodwill and encourage the customer to place additional orders. Because

Advanced Electronics Corporation　　626 Monmouth Rd　Newport, KY 45023-0309　Phone: (517) 555-1941　Fax: (517) 555-195

October 15, 1999

Attention Order Department
Lincoln Technologies
MC2357 Succ. A
Montreal, Que.
H3C 2J7 CANADA

Ladies and Gentlemen:

1 Ten VISIONZ video cameras were shipped by Fastgo Air Express and should arrive in time for your Winter Fest.

2 Because of your favorable current credit rating, we are sending the shipment subject to the usual credit terms, 2/10, n/30. **3** By paying this invoice within ten days, you save $150. Other aspects of your credit privilege are discussed in the Credit Customer Welcome packet that you will receive separately.

4 The VISIONZ camera is known for its 8:1, fl .4 power zoom lens and 2-lux light sensitivity—features that will allow your customers to take high-quality pictures with a minimum of light. The display inside the viewer will give your customers additional helpful information.

5 Because many of your customers may be interested in a higher zoom, we strongly suggest that at least one of your display models be equipped with the telephoto adapter for the VISIONZ. Please refer to the enclosed folder for the brochure explaining this economical enhancement to a quality video camera.

Sincerely,

Martha Zumwalt

Martha Zumwalt
Credit Manager

Enclosure

Diversity Issue
- Illustrates a correct Canadian address.

Ethics Issue
- Sends letter extending credit within the required time frame (within 30 days of receipt of request) and mentions the terms of credit information that will be provided, as required by law.

Format Pointers
- Uses an attention line in letter addressed to a company to assure efficient delivery.
- Uses "Ladies and Gentlemen," the appropriate salutation for a letter sent to a company. The simplified block format could have been used to avoid using "Ladies and Gentlemen" as the salutation.
- Uses an enclosure notation to alert the receiver that something other than the letter is included.

FIGURE 5-11
Good example of a letter extending credit.

Deductive Outline for Extending Credit

1. Begin by saying credit terms have been arranged. If an order has been placed, say the order has been shipped, implying the credit has been extended.
2. Indicate the foundation upon which the credit extension is based.
3. Present and explain the credit policies (e.g., credit terms, authorized discounts, payment dates).
4. Include resale or sales promotional material and encourage future business.

1 Acknowledges shipment of the order and implies the credit extension.

2 Recognizes the dealer for earning the credit privilege and gives a reason for the credit extension. Introduces the credit terms but does not explain "2/10, n/30" because the receiver is a dealer.

3 Encourages taking advantage of the discount in terms of profits for the dealer.

4 Presents resale to remind the reader of product benefits and to encourage future business.

5 Looks confidently for future orders.

FIGURE 5-12
Good example of a computer-generated customer acknowledgment.

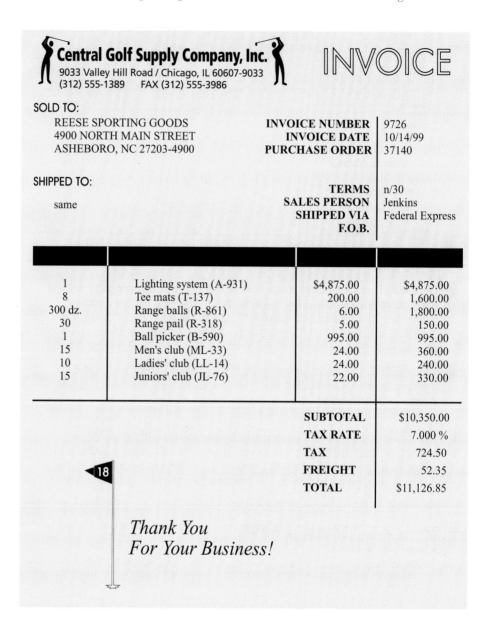

saying "Yes" is easy, writers may develop the habit of using clichés and selecting words that make letters sound cold and mechanical. The acknowledgment letter in Figure 5-13 confirms shipment of goods in the first sentence, includes concrete resale on the product and company, and is sincere and original.

6 *Write the following special messages: thank-you, appreciation, and apologies.*

Special Letters

Messages that recognize positive qualities or performances are especially effective. People usually are not reluctant to say, "Thank you," "What a great performance," "You have certainly helped me," and so on. Such letters are easy to write, and they require little time. Yet, because people seldom bother to *write* them, such messages

FIGURE 5-13
Good example of a
customer order
acknowledgment.

Deductive Outline for a Customer Order Acknowledgment Letter

1. Confirm shipment of order and verifies specific items ordered.
2. Include resale on the merchandise ordered and sales promotional material on related items.
3. Close with a positive remark that indicates future business.

Innovative Solutions
3015 Milam Road
Lansing, MI 48505-3015
Telephone: (517) 555-1085 Fax: (517) 555-1123

January 3, 1999

Attention Order Department
Blanchard Enterprises
DX3526 Succ. B
Toronto, Ont.
M5E 157 CANADA

PURCHASE ORDER NO. 37450

1 Seventy-five MMX computer systems were shipped to your store by Federal Express today.

2 Each unit has been customized according to your specifications. These modifications include 200 MHZ, minitower chassis, 6.5GB hard drive, 45MB memory, and 16x CD-ROM.

3 With these distinctive features, these computers will provide your customers with leading-edge technology. The flexibility of this system will allow your customers to take advantage of software innovations quickly and efficiently.

4 With the custom features of the MMX, your customers can work optimally at the office. The EXEC-4 is available now. This notebook computer has the power your customers will need for work they take home or to other remote locations. Its easy-to-use touch pad and backlit liquid crystal display have made the EXEC-4 a popular portable.

5 To make this preferred portable technology available to your customers, review the enclosed specifications and complete the enclosed order form. Your order will be shipped immediately.

Jason D. Merrett

Jason D. Merrett
Sales Manager

Enclosures

1 Implies sufficiently that the order has been received and filled. Refers to specific merchandise shipped and reveals method of shipment.

2 Confirms the specific modifications for this customer order.

3 Points out specific qualities of the merchandise (uses resale).

4 Mentions related merchandise (uses sales promotional material).

5 Refers to enclosures without using an entire sentence. Implies additional orders are expected.

Format Pointers

- Uses simplified block format to avoid an impersonal salutation ("Ladies and Gentlemen"). A subject line replaces the salutation, and the complimentary close is omitted.
- Uses attention line in a letter addressed to a company to ensure efficient delivery.
- Uses an enclosure notation to alert reader that other information is included.

COMMUNICATION IN ACTION

Barbara Barrett, Jackson Zoo

When Barbara Barrett's letter for support from the state legislator went all the way to the Mississippi governor's desk, little did she realize the high-profile status her routine request would receive. She was pleased to have the publicity for the Jackson Zoo, but she didn't anticipate the governor's readership.

As zoo director, Barrett corresponds regularly with legislators, media personnel, and friends of the zoo. Much of her correspondence is in the form of routine letters, which are designed to cultivate friendships. These letters reach various audiences all through the state. Each year, for instance, she writes all Mississippi television stations and legislators to thank them for their support of the zoo. With each letter, she includes free passes to the zoo for the station's staff and the legislators.

Before corresponding with legislators, Barrett asks, "What would this person want out of his or her relationship with the zoo?" She attempts to assess what legislators want from the sponsorship and how they would benefit by contributing to the zoo. If a senator or representative visits the zoo, Barrett wants "the stage to be set" so the experience will be a good one. Her letters help her to reach this goal. She knows that the easiest legislators to contact are those who have brought their children or grandchildren to the zoo. She believes no one can remember the zoo without relating it to his or her own experiences.

Attempting to assess readers' needs and prepare them for a visit to the zoo is no easy task. Through her experience, however, Barrett has learned how to write in a fresh way that communicates clearly. First and foremost, she believes her message must be clear, precise, and easily understood by the reader. In a busy legislator's office, her letter may be read only once or simply scanned. To receive the attention it needs, the letter must be clear and short. She says, "Three short letters that are read are better than one long letter that is not read."

Next, she starts every letter with a simple thank you. If she addresses a legislator, she begins with "Thank you for your involvement this past weekend." By saying thanks at first, she believes her letter makes a positive impact on the reader. Because a letter from the zoo can be less formal than similar correspondence from other nonprofit organizations, she occasionally uses humor to gain interest. Barrett tells of a sponsor who donated $10,000 for a Koala exhibit. When thanking the sponsor for the contribution, she stated, "Many visitors have related to us that this was perhaps their first and only opportunity to meet Koala bears face-to-face." This humorous statement helped stimulate the sponsor to feel positive about the zoo and about the contribution that was made.

Barrett's routine letters pave the way with visitors by cultivating goodwill and personal contact. Visitors to the Jackson Zoo are prepared to have a good time. Many visitors come with families, sharing precious leisure time together. Barrett's business communication skills are evidently working. The Jackson Zoo has succeeded in its goal of offering excellent family interactive experiences that are fun.

Applying What You Have Learned

1. Discuss how Barrett's letters prepare legislators and other visitors for a fun visit to the zoo.

2. What questions did Barrett mentally answer before writing her letter to legislators?

3. Assume that you work as the assistant director for the Jackson Zoo and will correspond with the Honorable Mary L. Jackson, State Senator, Capitol Building, Jackson, MS 35205. Senator Jackson visited the zoo last weekend with her family, having used free family passes you sent her in previous correspondence. Compose a routine letter of support to Senator Jackson, acknowledging her visit to the zoo with her family. Realizing you will have only a few moments to communicate your message, be brief.

are especially meaningful—even treasured. Compared with those who merely *say* nice things, people who take time to *write* them are more likely to be perceived as sincere. Empathetic managers take advantage of occasions to write goodwill messages that build strong, lasting relationships among employees, clients, customers, and various other groups. Additionally, sometimes regrettable situations require that a sincere written apology be sent.

Thank-You Messages

A simple handwritten note is sufficient for some social situations. However, when written in a business office to respond to a business situation, the message may be keyed on letterhead or sent electronically. After receiving a gift, being a guest, or attending an interview, or after any of the great variety of circumstances in which a follow-up letter of thanks might be desirable, a thoughtful person will take the time to send a written message. Your message should be written deductively and reflect your sincere feelings of gratitude.

> Why are *written* compliments often more effective than verbal ones?

The following thank-you note identifies the gift, tells why the recipient liked it, and describes how the gift would be used: *After conducting an in-service seminar for you, I was pleasantly surprised to receive the desk calendar. The convenience of being able to plan my week at a glance is an unexpected by-product of my work with your company. Thanks for your kindness and for this useful gift.*

An employee sent the thank-you message in Figure 5-14 electronically to a coworker. Although the format of this e-mail message differs from a letter, the message follows the same deductive sequence and conveys a specific, genuine tone.

FIGURE 5-14
Good example of a thank-you memo sent electronically.

Deductive Outline for a Favorable Response to an Invitation

1. Begin with a statement of thanks.
2. Include specific remarks about what is appreciated to reflect sincere gratitude.
3. Close with a warm statement.

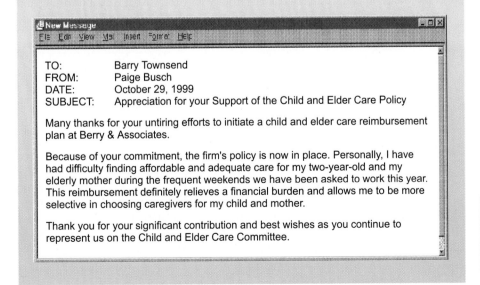

TO: Barry Townsend
FROM: Paige Busch
DATE: October 29, 1999
SUBJECT: Appreciation for your Support of the Child and Elder Care Policy

Many thanks for your untiring efforts to initiate a child and elder care reimbursement plan at Berry & Associates.

Because of your commitment, the firm's policy is now in place. Personally, I have had difficulty finding affordable and adequate care for my two-year-old and my elderly mother during the frequent weekends we have been asked to work this year. This reimbursement definitely relieves a financial burden and allows me to be more selective in choosing caregivers for my child and mother.

Thank you for your significant contribution and best wishes as you continue to represent us on the Child and Elder Care Committee.

Format Pointers
- Specific guidelines for preparing e-mail messages are provided in Chapter 7.

Appreciation Messages

How does an appreciation message benefit both the sender and the receiver?

An appreciation message is intended to recognize, reward, and encourage the receiver; however, it also benefits the sender. Contributing to another's happiness, paying tribute to one who deserves it, encouraging that which is commendable—such feelings can contribute to the sender's own sense of well-being and worth. Such positive thinking can be a favorable influence on the sender's own attitude and performance.

Some of the potential value to the sender and the receiver is lost if a letter is mechanical, such as the following example: *Your speech to the Lincoln Jaycees was very much appreciated. You are an excellent speaker, and you have good ideas. Thank you.* To a speaker who has worked hard preparing and who has not been paid, such a letter may have *some* value. After all, the sender cared enough to write. Yet such a letter could have been sent to any speaker, even if its writer had slept through the entire speech. A note closed with *sincerely* does not necessarily make the ideas seem sincere. The following revision doesn't sound like a generic form letter that could be used in numerous situations. Its specific remarks about the writer's understanding and application of the speaker's main points make the message meaningful and sincere.

> This past week I have found myself applying some of the time management principles discussed at the seminar you conducted last week for the Association of Business Professionals.
>
> Prioritizing my tasks really helped me keep my perspective. When I performed the time analysis, I easily identified some areas I can manage more effectively. Thank you for an informative and useful seminar.

In groups, discuss verbal and written appreciation messages you have sent or received. How did the action affect the sender and receiver? What changes would you recommend after reading this chapter?

In appropriate situations you may wish to address an appreciation message to an individual's supervisor and send a copy of the document to the individual to ensure that he or she is aware of your positive comments. These documents are then placed in an employee's personnel file and can serve to boost an employee's chances of promotion. Letters, such as the one that follows, should be written to commend deserving people; they should not be written for possible self-gain.

> John Melby, human resources manager for your firm, gave a very interesting and useful seminar at last week's meeting of the Society of Business Professionals.
>
> In a well-organized and interesting presentation, he offered several time management techniques that have worked very well for me. I observed the intense interest of the other members of the audience and the willingness of many of them to voice their positive reactions to his comments on how disorganization causes stress. His seminar was very well received by this group.
>
> Possibly, Mr. Melby told you that he led a seminar for our group; I wanted you know that he gave an outstanding presentation—totally consistent with the competence one sees in your employees.

Sometimes, however, those who take time to write such messages receive some unexpected benefits. For example, as an undergraduate student, Henry Kissinger, a former Secretary of State, wrote a letter of appreciation to a Prussian general who had spoken at his university. Touched by such thoughtfulness, the general invited Mr. Kissinger to dinner. Concluding that the young man had unusually keen insights into international affairs, the general was instrumental in getting Kissinger admitted to graduate study.

COMMUNICATION MENTOR

We strongly believe that our Russian staff must know that we care about them and are aware of their accomplishments. This knowledge builds teamwork and boosts confidence. However, communicating praise is quite a departure from the Soviet way and must be handled delicately, especially when commendations are distributed widely. We must always be fair without showing favoritism. Commendation letters should be brief and extremely upbeat.

Lawrence E. Wilson, Partner
Arthur Andersen, Moscow

Although generous praise is seldom objectionable, a letter or memo of appreciation may not fully achieve its purpose if it reaches the point of exaggeration or uses language that is hardly believable. The writer of the following message may believe these statements are true, but the reader may find them unbelievable. Because the language is strong and the statements are not supported, the letter could arouse thoughts about how bad other consultants were or questions about the writer's motives.

> The marketing consultants the New York office sent to us here in Texas were by far the best and most informed marketing executives we have ever worked with.
>
> Because they helped us identify our primary weakness, we are confident that the Dallas office should exceed our sales quotas during the coming fiscal period. Unlike many other consultants sent to us from the home office, this team was eager to learn to think like Texans.
>
> Once again, thank you for sending us this brilliant team.

The vice president would probably be more impressed with the revision in Figure 5-15. Although the message does not use strong language, it conveys a more sincere compliment than the previous message. Without the words "best" and "brilliant," it reveals *why* the staff's reaction was favorable. The net effects of this letter are positive: (1) The writer feels good for having passed on a deserved compliment; (2) management gains some assurance that the consulting team's efforts are effective; (3) the team about whom the letter was written is encouraged to continue an effective technique; and (4) other divisions may have an increased likelihood of exposure to similar high-quality consulting.

Apologies

The best way to handle an apology is to avoid the need for it. Sometimes, though, events do not turn out as planned, and it is your fault. Looking back, your conduct is regrettable, or some circumstance has prevented you from doing your best. In such cases, apologies are in order—for your own peace of mind and for good future relationships with an offended person.

Whether to apologize face to face, over the telephone, or in writing is a personal matter. The nature of the business, custom, seriousness of the infraction, personalities,

How would you feel about a message that begins with "I owe you somewhat of an apology . . ."?

FIGURE 5-15
Good example of an appreciation letter.

Deductive Outline for an Appreciation Letter

1. Begin with a statement of praise or appreciation.

2. Include specific comments about the outstanding qualities or performance being highlighted to convey a sincere tone. Avoid strong language and exaggerations that the receiver will not believe.

3. Close with a warm statement that looks to the future.

HUDSON STEEL CORPORATION

2500 Lincoln Green Road
Austin, TX 78710-9083
(515)555-9000
Fax: (512)555-6573

January 25, 1999

Mr. Michael Al-Wadan
Vice President of Marketing
Wallace-Taite Industries
1900 Hathorn Avenue
New York, NY 10002-1590

Dear Mr. Al-Wadan

Recently the New York office sent an outstanding team of marketing consultants to assist us in identifying methods of increasing our market share in the Southwest sales region.

The consultants listened intently as our managers helped them understand the peculiarities of the Southwest market. All members of the team functioned like professionals, asking probing questions and quietly observing our methods without placing undue pressure on our staff. Their courteous and helpful manner created an open line of communication that led to a successful two weeks of work. They left us with an accurate knowledge of our strengths and weaknesses and several new strategies for promoting our products.

After incorporating these new strategies, the Austin office should be able to meet its sales quotas during the coming fiscal period. Thank you for sending this capable team.

Sincerely

David Hollis

David Hollis
Vice President of Sales

The best way to handle apologies is to avoid getting into situations in which you will need to make them. "Dateline" on NBC made a serious mistake when a truck was rigged with an explosive material to demonstrate a defect in the manufacture of the trucks that made them prone to explode on impact. Angry reactions from the automaker forced an investigation and an embarrassing apology from the show and the network. When you must apologize, remember to be sincere, brief, and direct; avoid justifications and overly strong descriptions.

and other factors are considerations. Regardless of the channel selected, the principles are the same: Be sincere, direct, and brief.

When apologizing, people who have made mistakes are inclined to condemn themselves too severely or describe the mistake too vividly, as illustrated in the following apology: *I would like to apologize for two inexcusable errors I made in introducing you at yesterday's luncheon. Looking at the tape this morning, I watched in horror as I pronounced your name as "Newsom" instead of "Newman" and stated your alma mater as "Northwest" instead of "Northwestern." Please forgive me for making these terrible blunders.*

Mr. Newman probably had noticed the errors in pronunciation but quickly dismissed them as rather common human errors, but suppose he *had* been irritated by them. Labeling them as inexcusable and using "horror" in talking about them (along with actual restatement of the incorrect words) would reinforce his irritation. That reinforcement would work against the purpose of the apology. The revision is more effective because the writer apologizes directly and uses general terms to avoid reinforcing the unpleasantness of the mispronunciations.

> Please accept my apology for the way I pronounced two words when introducing you at yesterday's luncheon, your name and your alma mater's name!
>
> You deserved—and I wanted you to have—a memorable introduction. My tongue could have cooperated better, but it always has positive things to say when your name is mentioned.

Of course, an apology without appropriate action is of little value. Meeting Mr. Newman again and saying, "Hello, Mr. Newsom" would be fatal. Again, empathy is the key: People who have the right attitude have the best chance of finding the right words.

Sometimes, an unsolicited letter of apology removes a barrier or even preserves a business relationship. For example, at the home office of a major firm, a client's representative parked in a space designated for officers only. Before reaching the entrance, the representative was stopped by a security officer who asked that the car be moved to the visitor's lot. The vice president of finance learned that the security

Should general or specific words be used in an apology? Why?

Using an on-line database or the Internet, locate articles discussing at least two examples of public apologies made by companies or individuals (e.g., McDonald's® printing sacred *Koran* scriptures on Happy Meal® bags, Milli Vanilli's lip syncing an award-winning album). Be prepared to discuss how each apology was handled. What improvements do you recommend?

officer was obviously angry and used vulgar language in asking that the car be moved. The representative returned to the car and drove away (perhaps with the intent of terminating the business relationship).

Immediately, the VP wrote an apology to the representative. By apologizing quickly, the VP may have avoided the necessity of responding to a strongly worded letter reporting the incident. Unfortunately, a letter that focuses on the negatives and repeats the standard words of apology but provides no logical explanation or reassurance that the situation will not occur again could make the matter worse. The revision in Figure 5-16 is direct, positive, and detailed.

7 *Adapt letters to international receivers.*

Letters Written for an International Audience

The strategies discussed thus far for structuring good-news and neutral-news messages can be generally applied to North American audiences. Because message expectations and social conventions differ from culture to culture, the effective writer will adapt as necessary when writing for various audiences. When writing for intercultural audiences, keep these suggestions in mind:

- ***Write naturally but avoid abbreviations, slang, acronyms, technical jargon, sports and military analogies, and other devices.*** Many of these expressions help you clarify an idea and personalize your messages; however, they may be confusing to those unfamiliar with North American usage. Those speaking English as a second language learn English from a textbook; therefore, they may have difficulty understanding directions to complete a project "ASAP" (as soon as possible) or to convert to "WYSIWYG" (what you see is what you get) software. They may be mystified when you reject bid proposals that are "out of the ball park" or "way off target," recruit job applicants who are "sharp as brass tacks," or refer to the supervisor as "the top gun."

What are other examples of "red flag" words to avoid with intercultural audiences?

- ***Avoid words that trigger emotional responses such as anger, fear, or suspicion.*** Such words are often referred to as *red flag* words because they elicit the same response as a red flag waved in front of a raging bull. *Hot buttons*, the term used in a popular training film, *Communicating Across Cultures*, conveys a similar connotation.[5] Regardless of the term, using words such as "gal," "boy," "handicapped," and "foreigner" is a sure way to shut a reader's mind to your message, to make understanding practically impossible, and to destroy any chance of trust and cooperation.

- ***Use simple terms but attempt to be specific as well.*** Some of the simplest words might be interpreted within the context of each situation in which they are used (e.g., *fast* has several meanings). Likewise, avoid use of superlatives such as *fantastic* and *terrific* because they may be misinterpreted as overly dramatic or insincere. Also avoid overly formal and difficult expressions that may be confusing or considered pompous; for example, *pursuant to your request, ostentatious,* or *nebulous.*

- ***Follow the same techniques for increasing readability you would use in writing to someone fluent in English:*** (a) Write short, simple sentences containing only one idea, and (b) construct short paragraphs that focus on developing one major idea.

- ***Consider the subtle differences in the ways specific cultures organize messages.*** Asians, for example, typically use indirect patterns of writing, even

Deductive Outline for an Apology

1. State the apology briefly and sincerely. Avoid specific descriptions of the error and condemning statements that may reinforce the receiver's memory of the error.
2. Include measures being taken to avoid the error occurring again, if possible.
3. End on a positive note without restating the apology.

FIGURE 5-16
Good example of an apology.

905 South Nottingham Road
Knoxville, TN 37901-0905
(423) 555-8760   Fax: (423) 555-1207

December 5, 1999

Mr. Edward Davidson
North-Central Electronics
895 South Ferry Road
Knoxville, TN 37939-3109

Dear Mr. Davidson:

1 Please accept my apology for the manner in which our security officer spoke to you this morning. **2** He had been instructed to keep certain parking spaces open for company officers, but he should have remembered his obligation to be courteous and helpful.

3 The chief of security has already assigned the officer to restudy the security manual and to attend the human relations seminars now required of all newly hired employees. **4** When you call at our offices again, you can expect efficiency and courtesy, which have been our goals for the past ten years.

Sincerely,

Nancy Chen

Nancy Chen
Vice President of Finance

1 Begins with the apology. "Manner of speaking" is more positive than saying "vulgar language."

2 Confirms the officer's right to ask that the car be moved and disapproves of the officer's methods (through the subjunctive mood and positive words).

3 Reports measures taken to avoid repetition of such incidents, which strengthens credibility of the apology.

4 Closes with a positive look to future transactions.

COMMUNICATION MENTOR

The Russian language is extremely formal, and often a number of different words can be used to convey a general meaning. To ensure that the exact meaning is conveyed to the reader, a professional staff member proficient in both

Russian and English reviews much of our Russian correspondence. Detailed and significant messages and documents such as proposals and reports translated from English are reviewed carefully for possible language barriers.

Lawrence E. Wilson, Partner
Arthur Andersen, Moscow

when writing about good news; they avoid negative messages or camouflage them so expertly that the reader might not recognize them. Germans tend to be more direct than North Americans, even with bad news. The accompanying Strategic Forces Box provides additional information related to the concept that values influence communication style.

- *Use graphics, visual aids, and forms whenever possible because they simplify the message.*

- *Use figures for expressing numbers to avoid confusion with an international audience.*

- *Be aware of differences in the way numbers and dates are written.* As a general rule, use figures for numbers, and keep in mind that most people in the world use the metric system Note the following example:

U. S.	*Other Countries*
$2,400.00	2400,00
January 29, 1999	29 January 1999

- *Write out the name of the month in international correspondence to avoid misunderstandings.* When using a number to represent the month, many countries state the date before the month as shown in the following examples:

U. S.	*Other Countries*
2/10/99	2.10 1999 or 2.10.99
March 26, 1999	26th of March 1999

Investigate typical letter formats for a country you select. How do they differ from U.S. formats?

- *Become familiar with the traditional format of letters in the country of the person to whom you are writing and adapt your format as much as possible.* Note the differences in the formality of the salutation and complimentary close. The Germans, who prefer a formal salutation such as "Very Honored Mr. Professor Jones," might be offended by your choice of an informal "Dear Jim," a salutation you believed was appropriate because you had met and done prior business with Professor Jones. You will also want to check the position of various letter parts such as the letter address and the writer's name and title. For example, in German letters the company name follows the

Strategic Forces: Diversity Challenges

Basic Values Influence Communication Styles

Message patterns vary from culture to culture and are largely the product of the values held by each society. As an increasing number of U.S. businesses become international or global organizations, a need for awareness and understanding of the commonly held values of different cultures exists. Differences in societal values influence social behavior, etiquette, and communication styles. Differences in corporate cultural-value systems influence business transactions in and between members of different cultures. U.S. businesspeople are typically aware of differences in the business behaviors and practices of popular trade partners, but they may fail to recognize and understand the underlying values that shape behavior. Values accepted in Japanese culture that differ from those held in U.S. culture include the following:

- U.S. corporations value independence in the workplace, whereas Japanese corporations value dependence.

- U.S. corporations value honesty in business practices; if someone says he or she can do something it means just that. Japanese corporations, on the other hand, value "saving face," and to admit that they can't produce what you are asking for is an embarrassment. Japanese business writers would sooner tell you they can do something while knowing that they cannot than bear the shame of admitting they can't do it. [7]

- The Japanese value building business partnerships for life, while Americans are more interested in short-term profits than long-term sustained business. The Japanese prefer to develop a business relationship through a business courtship—building a relationship over time rather than establishing one immediately. They typically begin the business relationship by seeking out the contact and placing a small trial order, to see "how things go." If the customer is satisfied, more orders follow and continue to grow with the relationship. This action offers the customer a reliable supply of the desired good, and the producer can depend on the customer's business. [8]

- In negotiating situations, the Japanese are likely more comfortable when in the buyer position than the seller position, since buyers have higher status than do sellers in the Japanese culture .

- The fact that Japanese businesspeople tend to make decisions much more slowly than do their U.S. counterparts has at least two explanations that stem from culture. First, time is valued differently in Japan than in the United States. Secondly, group decision, that is not known for its expediency, is valued over individual decisions that can be made more quickly.

Understanding such value differences can aid the business communicator in understanding variations in message patterns.

Application

While the Japanese tend to write in a more indirect manner, even when conveying good news, Germans tend to prefer the direct message pattern for both positive and negative messages. Research the German culture to determine value differences that might account for the directness in communication. Write a one-page summary of your explanation.

---

complimentary close and the typed signature block is omitted, leaving the reader responsible for deciphering the writer's signature.[6]

Before writing a pleasant or routine message, study carefully the overall suggestions in the "General Writing Guidelines." After you have written a rough draft, compare your work with the "Check Your Writing" checklist and make any revisions. These checklists precede the chapter summary.

Employers cite weakness in writing skills as a major shortcoming of college graduates they hire. How will you address this issue?

Content

- Identify clearly the principal idea (pleasant or routine idea).
- Present sufficient supporting detail in a logical sequence.
- Assure accuracy of facts or figures.
- Assure message is ethical and abides by any legal requirements.

Organization

- Place major idea in the first sentence.
- Present supporting details in a logical sequence.
- Include a final paragraph that is courteous and indicates a continuing relationship with the receiver; may include sales promotional material.

Style

- Assure that message is clear and concise (e.g., words will be readily understood).
- Use active voice predominately.
- Use first person sparingly or not at all.
- Make ideas cohere (changes in thought are not abrupt).
- Use relatively short sentences that vary in length and structure.
- Emphasize significant thoughts (e.g., position, stated in simple sentences or in independent clauses).
- Keep paragraphs relatively short.
- Use original expression (sentences are not copied directly from the definition of the problem or from sample letters in text; clichés are avoided).

Mechanics

- Assure that keyboarding, spelling, grammar, and punctuation are perfect.

Format

- Use a correct letter format (block, modified block, or simplified) and punctuation style (open or mixed).
- Assure letter is balanced on page.

- Include standard letter parts in appropriate position.
- Include special parts if necessary (subject line, enclosure, copy, etc.)

International Adaptations

- Avoid abbreviations, slang, acronyms, technical jargon, sports and military analogies, and other devices peculiar to the United States.
- Avoid words that trigger emotional responses.
- Use simple terms but attempt to be specific.
- Consider the communication style of the culture when selecting an organizational pattern.
- Use graphics, visual aids, and forms when possible to simplify the message.
- Use figures for expressing numbers to avoid confusion.
- Be aware of differences in the way numbers and dates are written.
- Write out the name of the month to avoid confusion.
- Adapt the letter format to the traditional format of the recipient's country.

Thank-You Letters

- Begin with a statement of thanks.
- Be specific about that which is appreciated.
- Reflect a sincere feeling of gratitude.

Appreciation Messages

- Write for the right purpose (intent).
- Follow a deductive outline.
- Reflect a sincere tone by presenting specific facts and avoiding overly strong language.

Apologies

- Include the apology only once in the message.
- Avoid being overly critical.
- Avoid describing a mistake too vividly.
- Include a possible solution to the situation, if possible.

General Writing Guidelines

When composing letters, memorandums, and e-mail messages for the exercises, applications, and cases in this and all remaining chapters, proceed in the following manner:

1. **Study the related chapter (7–8) before composing letters, memorandums, and e-mail messages.** Look for principles that can be applied, not for expressions or sentences to paraphrase or use in your message.

2. **Study the writing problem until you understand the facts.**

3. **Assume that you are the person facing the writing problem.**

4. **Anticipate receiver reaction, and prepare an outline for your message.**

5. **Compose rapidly without looking at the definition of the problem and without looking at sample letters from the text.** A sentence written to *define* a letter-writing problem may not be appropriate in a letter designed to *solve* the problem. Concentrate on planning and expressing ideas to achieve clarity and to promote good human relations.

6. **Refer to the definition of the problem for names, addresses, and amounts before keying the message.** The receiver's name and address appear at the end of each exercise and applications. Unless otherwise instructed, key your name as the sender.

7. Consider the implications of the strategic forces influencing your message.

   - **Legal and ethical constraints.** Consider the following guidelines:

     - Investigate the problem to identify possible legal requirements and consider any ethical implications related to the message you are writing.

     - Be certain that you have expressed ideas clearly, stated unpleasant ideas tactfully and positively, included complete, accurate information, supported your ideas with objective fact, avoided embellishing or exaggerating facts, and designed graphs to depict information honestly.

     - Exercise discretion by identifying information the receiver actually needs to respond to your message. Consider the confidentiality of the information you reveal

   - **Diversity Challenges.** Adapt your messages so that they can be understood and received positively by receivers regardless of their ethnicity, age, and gender.

   - **Changing Technology.** Use appropriate technological tools to collect and analyze data, write and present information in a highly professional manner, and to transmit the message to the receiver efficiently and effectively.

   - **Team Environment.** Work collectively to compose a dynamic message that reflects the synergistic influence of an effective team.

8. **Review carefully the placement of the standard parts of the letter, the acceptable business formats, the two punctuation types, and the special letter parts required in particular situations.** Unless otherwise instructed, key the letter or memo according to the formatting instructions provided in Appendix A. Study two-letter postal abbreviations, word-division rules, abbreviation rules, keyboarding rules (e.g., number of spaces after punctuation), and proofreaders' marks in Appendix A.

9. **Refer to the "Check Your Writing" checklist (positioned before the summary in each chapter) before submitting an assignment.** By comparing your message with the list, you will (1) gain confidence that your message meets high standards and (2) identify any changes that need to be made.

Thoughtful use of the checklist can improve your grade on an assignment as well as indelibly stamp in your mind the four qualities that your writing should have:

- **Content:** The *right* ideas with sufficient support.
- **Organization:** The best *sequence* of ideas for clear understanding and human relations.
- **Style:** The most appropriate ways to *express* ideas in words and sentences.
- **Mechanics:** High *standards* in putting words on paper—keyboarding, spelling, and punctuating

SUMMARY

1. **List the steps in the deductive outline and identify the advantages of using it to convey good news and routine information.** When the receiver can be expected to be *pleased* by the message, the main idea is presented first and details follow. Likewise, when the message is *routine* and not likely to arouse a feeling of pleasure or displeasure, the main idea is presented first (as illustrated in the messages in this chapter). The deductive approach is appropriate for routine claim letters, routine requests and responses to routine requests, routine letters and responses about credit and orders, and special messages (thank-you, appreciation, and apologies).

2. **Write letters presenting claims and making adjustments.** A routine claim requests the adjustment in the first sentence because you assume the company will make the adjustment without persuasion. Continue with an explanation of the problem to support the request and an expression of appreciation for taking the action. An adjustment letter extends the adjustment in the first sentence and explains the circumstances related to correcting the problem. The closing may include sales promotional material or other futuristic comments indicating your confidence that the customer will continue doing business with a company that has a reputation for fairness.

3. **Write routine requests and favorable responses to routine requests.** A routine request begins with the major request, includes details that will clarify the request, and alludes to the receiver's response. A response to a routine request provides the information requested, provides necessary details, and closes with a personal, courteous ending.

4. **Compose letters providing credit information and extending credit.** When providing credit information, provide only verifiable facts to avoid possible litigation. A letter extending credit begins by extending credit, indicates the basis for the decision, and explains credit terms, The closing may include sales promotional material or other futuristic comments. Credit extension letters must adhere to legal guidelines related to credit.

5. **Write letters acknowledging customer orders.** Form or computer-generated acknowledgment letters assure customers that orders will be filled quickly. An individualized acknowledgment that confirms shipment and includes resale on the product and the company generates goodwill and future business.

6. **Write the following special messages: thank-you, appreciation, and apologies.** Thank-you letters express appreciation for a kindness or special assistance and should reflect sincere feelings of gratitude. Express appreciation for a specific item to create a sincere, warm tone. A thank-you message for a gift identifies the gift, tells why you like it, and describes how you will use it. Appreciation letters highlight exceptional performance and are written deductively; they avoid exaggerations and strong, unsupported statements that the reader may not believe. Apologies should be written when you believe you have not done your best. State the apology *once* at the beginning of the message; avoid making excuses and overly strong descriptions of the mistake, and be brief.

7. **Adapt letters sent to international receivers.** Avoid the use of terms peculiar to a language or terms open to several interpretations; write figures as numbers and write out the name of months to avoid confusion; and become familiar with the traditional formats of letters in the country of the person to whom you are writing.

REFERENCES

[1]Corporate culture. (1996). *Asylum West,* [On-line]. http://www.auxillium.com/culture.htm [1997, June 10].

[2]Corporate culture. (1996). *Asylum West,* [On-line]. http://www.auxillium.com/culture.htm [1997, June 10].

[3]"Those nuts at Southwest Airlines." *Houston Business Journal,* (1996, October 28). 1.

[4]Freiberg, J., & Freiberg, J. (1996). *Those nuts at Southwest Airlines.* Austin, TX: Bard.

[5]*Valuing diversity part III: Communicating across cultures.* (1987). [Film]. San Francisco: Copeland Griggs.

[6]Varner, I. I. (1987). Internationalizing business communication courses. *Bulletin of the Association for Business Communication,* 50(4), 11.

[7]Hugenberg, L.W., LaCivita, R,M., Lubanovic, A.M. (1996). International business and training: Preparing for the global economy. *Journal of Business Communication,* 33(2), 205–222.

[8]Oblander, P., & Daniels, E. (1997). International communication and the U.S.-Japan lumber trade: An exploratory study. *Forest Products Journal,* 47(3), 38-44.

[9]Cohen, S. (1997, May). On becoming virtual. *Training and Development,* 30–32.

REVIEW QUESTIONS

1. List the steps in the deductive outline recommended for good-news and routine messages. Is this outline recommended for written messages applicable to oral messages? (Obj. 1)

2. What is a claim letter? Distinguish between the two major types of claim letters and specify the outline preferable for each type. (Obj. 2)

3. Explain how claim letters and responses to requests both use the deductive message pattern. (Obj. 2, 3)

4. What is the difference between resale and sales-promotional material? Provide an example of each. Why should resale and sales-promotional material be included in an adjustment letter? (Obj. 3)

5. When is the word *grant* appropriate when communicating about claim letters? Suggest an appropriate substitution. (Obj. 2)

6. Distinguish between the two major types of request letters and specify the outline preferable for each type. (Obj. 3)

7. What technique can be used to ensure that details within a routine request are clear and easy to read? (Obj. 3)

8. Discuss several ways form letters can be used to respond to routine requests effectively. (Obj. 3)

9. Provide suggestions for writing a legally defensible credit information letter. (Obj. 4)

10. What information should be included in a letter extending credit? (Obj. 4).

11. Describe the procedure typically used by companies to acknowledge orders. (Obj. 5)

12. Provide three situations when sending an individualized letter of acknowledgment would be appropriate and explain why. (Obj. 5)

13. Provide suggestions for writing an effective thank-you or appreciation message. (Obj. 6)

14. Provide suggestions for writing an effective apology. (Obj. 6)

15. Discuss nine guidelines for writing to an international audience. (Obj. 7)

EXERCISES

1. **Critique of Good-News Letters Produced by Real Companies (Obj. 1-7)**
   Find an example of both a well-written and a poorly written good-news or routine letter. Analyze the strengths and weaknesses of each document. Be prepared to discuss them in class.

2. **International Business Letters (Obj. 7)**
   Obtain a copy of a business letter written by someone from another culture. Identify the major differences between this letter and a traditional U.S. letter. Share your letter with the class or small groups as directed by your instructor.

3. **Deductive Openings (Obj. 1-7)**
   Revise the following openings so that they are deductive.

   a. As you know, recommendations for promotions are evaluated and voted upon by the management committee semiannually. Your promotion to department manager was approved in the last meeting.

   b. In last week's budget meeting, the controller underscored that budgets are lean this quarter. However, she has approved your request for computer upgrades for personnel in your department.

   c. The Crown Club is a service organization that has always been held in high esteem within the

   automobile industry. Our membership is honored to extend an invitation for you to join us as we help the industry move forward.

   d. As you are already aware, Meerkat Software is the leading manufacturer of file compression software in the West. However, we would be happy to ship software to your office in Key West and provide the technical support you may require.

   e. It is rare that we receive a claim regarding a defect in our high-quality facsimile machines, especially in one that has only been in use for seven months. However, because of our belief in our product, we will ship you a replacement machine upon receipt of your current model.

   f. This letter is in response to your application for credit dated June 30; your application has now been received.

4. **Deductive Outline (Obj. 3)**
   Prepare a deductive outline to accept the following invitation. You need to know the exact time the dinner will begin. Does a reception precede the dinner as it did two years ago? The earliest you can arrive is 6:30 p.m. The title of your speech will be "Total Quality Management: Empowering People to Succeed."

Dear Ms. Kerr:

You can be extremely helpful to the members of the Lakeland Civic Club. Our annual interchapter meeting with three chapters in nearby cities will be held on October 17 at 6 p.m.

We are excited at the prospect of having you speak on a current topic of your choice as you did two years ago. You can enjoy good fellowship, a great audience, an excellent dinner, and a $200 honorarium.

Please let me know that you will accept the invitation by October 1. Please let us have a title for your speech to use in the program and in our correspondence to the guest chapters.

Sincerely,

5. **Document for Analysis: Claim Request (Obj. 2)**
Analyze the following letter. Pinpoint its strengths and weaknesses, and then revise the letter as directed by your instructor.

Dear Mr. Peck:

When I ordered my Golden Hamster treadmill last month, you assured me that it was the best product for cardiovascular fitness. After viewing the videotape you sent, I believed in your product and your company and soon placed my order. I received the treadmill on January 12.

The product was easy to set up, and after watching the instructional video and reading the manual, I was ready to work out on the Golden Hamster. However, I cannot seem to use the unit as shown on the instructional tape, and believe my machine may be defective.

I have read and followed all the instructions, yet the machine's spin-wheel system produces resistance, which propels me off the front.

I would like this problem solved, either through a new machine being sent to me free of charge, or a refund after I return this machine.

Please contact me at 706-555-3800 and advise me of how I should proceed in this matter.

6. **Document for Analysis: Routine Request (Obj. 3)**
Analyze the following letter. Pinpoint its strengths and weaknesses, and then revise the letter as directed by your instructor.

Dear Ms. Morgan:

I am the Vice President of Operations for Jemison Corporation, a manufacturer of golf ball components. We have operated plants across the Midwest for thirty years, and we are contemplating opening a facility in the South within the next two years.

As we evaluate our operational needs and requirements, we are collecting data from various locations we think may provide a site that will generate the maximum benefit for both Jemison and the locale under consideration. Therefore, I would appreciate it if you could send me some information about Paradise and its surrounding area, including information on population demographics and major employers, as well as geographic description of the area. I'd also like to know about the weather, education and cultural opportunities in the area, and, of course, the cost of living.

Thank you for your assistance, and I look forward to your response.

7. **Document for Analysis: Favorable Response to a Routine Request (Obj. 3)**
Analyze the following letter. Pinpoint its strengths and weaknesses, and then revise the letter as directed by your instructor.

Dear Mr. Holland:

This letter is in reply to your questions concerning the deductibility of your educational expenses. We have researched this tax question carefully.

According to Section 162 of the Internal Revenue Code, educational expenses (college tuition, books, supplies, etc.) are not deductible for a person who is acquiring skills to begin a new career. However, you explained that your employer is requiring you to take international business and computer applications courses to enhance your ability to work in your present field. Consequently, your educational expenses are deductible.

We look forward to working with you in the future.

Sincerely,

8. **Document for Analysis: Thank-You (Obj. 6)**
Analyze the following letter. Pinpoint its strengths and weaknesses, and then revise the letter as directed by your instructor.

Dear Mr. Borris:

Thank you for taking the time from your busy schedule to talk to our class. Your talk was outstanding. Without your help, I would not have known how to even start writing a resume.

Again, I really appreciate your coming to talk to us about this important topic.

9. **Document for Analysis: Apology (Obj. 6)**
Analyze the following letter. Pinpoint its strengths and weaknesses, and then revise the letter as directed by your instructor.

I missed yesterday's meeting of the Planning Committee. I am terribly sorry. I was scheduled to give my report on tax consideration, and I wanted to hear the other scheduled reports and participate in a discussion of them.

If I had known before boarding the plane in Denver that the plane would not be departing for 45 minutes, I would have called. Again, I am very sorry for any inconvenience caused by my absence.

E-MAIL APPLICATION

Create an address macro (distribution list) containing the e-mail addresses of five classmates and the instructor. Then compose a message explaining how to study effectively for a business communication exam. Send the message to the macro address recipients.

APPLICATIONS

1. **Claim Letter: Value Lost on Delayed Investment (Obj. 2)**

   During a recent telephone conversation with his investment manager, Ernie McGilberry authorized the purchase of $5,000 of Waverly Equity Fund (200 shares @ $25.00). Funds were to be transferred directly from his checking account. When Ernie received his monthly investment portfolio statement a week later, he noticed that no Waverly mutual funds had been purchased. Because the market has risen to $25.40 per share in this one-week period, he believes the investment company should compensate him for this error.

   Required: Write your investment manager, Cynthia Oliver, explaining the error and requesting an adjustment. Her address is Financial and Investment Management, 2200 South Washington Avenue, Katy, TX 77450-2200. Include your account number (97347) in a reference line to facilitate your request.

2. **Claim Letter: No Swim, No Payment (Obj. 2)**

   When he joined the Wellness Connection, a brand-new, state-of-the-art fitness center, Jim Whiteside explained to the fitness manager he was only interested in swimming laps in the center's lap pool and would not be using the treadmills, stair steppers, and weight machines or attending any special training classes. He had hoped to negotiate a reduced rate for use of the swimming pool only, but his request was refused. He was eager to begin the intense training that he experienced when he competed on a college swim team, and the Wellness Connection had the only indoor pool in the community. Therefore, he reluctantly joined at the regular membership fee of $40 a month.

   Now Jim is upset. The pool has been closed for three weeks because of a problem with the filter system. When he sees the bank draft for his past month's membership on his bank statement, he decides to write a letter to the Wellness Connection requesting an adjustment for the three weeks he was unable to swim. He thinks at least a $20 credit would be fair.

   Required: As Jim Whiteside, write a letter requesting an adjustment in your last statement. Write to the Wellness Connection, 400 Hospital Boulevard, Marion, NC 28752-2703. Include a reference line with your membership number (059) to facilitate your request.

3. **Claim Letter: Customized Drinking Cups Are Wrong Size (Obj. 2)**

   Athletic concessions at Cullman College placed an order for 50,000 twenty-ounce plastic cups at 15 cents each from Custom Plastics Products. Each cup was to be imprinted with the college's mascot and this year's basketball slogan, "Soaring to New Heights." The concessions manager noticed, when inspecting the order, that the vendor had sent 16-ounce cups and not the 20-ounce cups that were ordered. Because concession items must be priced in 50-cent intervals to expedite service time, the regular drink price of $1.50 cannot be adjusted to reflect the reduced quantity. After serious consideration, the manager decided that selling the 16-ounce drink for the same price would be inadvisable. Basketball season starts in only two weeks; therefore, the manager must act quickly.

   Required: As the concessions manager, write the vendor explaining the error in the shipment and asking that the order be filled correctly and quickly. Address the letter to Custom Plastics Products, 1200 Ridgewood Road, Springfield, MO 65808-1200.

4. **Adjustment Letter: Delayed Investment (Obj. 2)**

   Assume you are Cynthia Oliver, investment manager of Financial and Investment Management, and you received the adjustment request from Ernie McGilberry (see Application 1). Because of an unusually busy week, you inadvertently overlooked purchasing the mutual funds Ernie authorized by telephone. Explain to him that you can purchase the mutual funds (you'll pay the charges associated with this transaction) or you can purchase additional mutual funds equal to the lost market gain.

Recommend that he purchase additional shares of this mutual fund because of its excellent performance (you could refer to its $.40 increase over a one-week period). Enclose a reprint of an article highlighting Waverly Equity Fund's performance over the last quarter.

Required: Write an adjustment letter to Ernie McGilberry, 32 Anchorage Street, Katy, TX 77450-2200.

5. **Adjustment Letter: Correct-Size Cups Are Being Sent (Obj. 2)**

The claims manager at Custom Plastic Products was concerned about the error made in the plastic cups for Cullman College (see Application 3). Working at peak levels for the past three weeks, the workers made a simple but rather costly mistake. However, the immediate problem is to give this order a priority rating and get it out to Cullman College, a long-standing customer, in time for the first basketball game.

Required: Write the concessions manager at Cullman College explaining the mistake and apologizing for the inconvenience. Assure the manager that the correct order will arrive on time and ask the manager to return the 16-ounce cups at the company's expense. Address the letter to Russell Hollister, Cullman College, Athletic Department, P. O. Drawer 2153, Topeka, KS 66601-2153.

6. **Routine Request: Information Needed (Obj. 3)**

A recent publication contains a picture of a product or information about a service in which you have a special interest. If you had appropriate answers to certain questions, you might order the product or secure the service.

Required: Write a letter to the manufacturer. Ask at least three questions. Consider using enumerations or a bulleted list to emphasize the questions. For example, number the questions or precede them with bullets (✓, ❑, ❖, ◆, etc.). Indent the questions five spaces from both margins if you format the letter in modified block format.

7. **Routine Request: ISO 9000 Certification Required (Obj. 3)**

As the sales manager for Patton Manufacturing, you are interested in negotiating an agreement with West Industries to provide the electrical switches for its stereo components. Information obtained from Westinghouse's web site states clearly that all suppliers must have ISO 9000 certification and provides an address for

additional information. You know vaguely that ISO 9000 certification establishes international manufacturing standards, thereby giving buyers assurance that products meet certain quality standards. You need more detailed information about what ISO 9000 certification is and the benefits it provides to suppliers and purchasers. You know that an independent agency provides the certification but you don't know who that agency is or how long the process of being certified requires. You also need to know what actions you must take to begin the certification process.

Required: Write the letter to the attention of the Certification Department, Westinghouse, Inc., 9310 Gardner Street, Denver, CO 80202-9310.

8. **Routine Request: Surviving the Year 2000 (Obj. 3)**

Assume you are the head of a Year 2000 task force for Bristol Enterprises, a major manufacturer who has on-line connections with numerous suppliers of its component parts. Your job is to ensure that your computer systems are "Year 2000 Ready," that is, they can handle the "00" digits when the clock ticks over to the year 2000.

Many computer programs use an MM/DD/YY date format that can be embedded in millions of lines of computer code (a format was initiated decades ago as a space-saving programming trick.) In the year 2000, these programs may simply freeze up or revert to 1900. If computers process date-sensitive data incorrectly for a month, a week, or a year (who knows how long), businesses will incur significant financial losses and experts predict as many as 5 percent of businesses to fail. If the program reads the date as 1900, a computerized inventory program would sort items with a 00 date as the oldest rather than the newest items and would cause products with a shelf life based on an expiration date to be discarded prematurely. The problem will affect expiration dates on credit cards and warranties; recall dates on foods and drugs; age calculations in employee benefits or for insurance eligibility; interest and annuity calculations in financial institutions; aging of receivables, and so on. Then consider the disasters that could occur when the "Millennium Bug" hits computers that control toll bridges, traffic lights, prisoner releases, welfare checks, handling of toxic chemicals, and many more potentially dangerous actions.

You have set up a Y2K division of programmers working in shifts, 24 hours a day, seven days a week, to ensure that your company will stay in business when the new century arrives. Now you are concerned whether your suppliers are addressing the Year 2000 Problem. After all, you don't want your suppliers to have a problem and be part of the 5 percent of businesses who are predicted to fail. You decide to write each of your suppliers for the following purposes: (1) to be certain they are aware of the Year 2000 Problem and are initiating a plan for addressing it and (2) to offer the services of your task force to assess their computer systems. (Your task force will not complete the work for these suppliers, only provide an assessment.) You will include a copy of an article or provide the address of a web site that summarizes the problem and possible consequences.

Required: Write a form letter that can be sent to all your suppliers. Address a sample letter to R. P. Bethea, Purchasing Manager, 953 Four Corners Parkway, Suite 300, San Diego, CA 92199-9533. Your instructor may direct you to provide a printout of pertinent pages from the web site you recommended.

9. **Routine Request: Grand Opening of The Store (Obj. 3)**

Assume you recently opened The Store, a home design store, conveniently located in a small shopping center near a major mall; a popular bagel shop and a ladies' fitness center are next door. The Store carries an exclusive line of antique reproduction furniture—lavish plantation and sleigh beds, beautifully hand-carved shelves and tables, wall sconces, and much more. You are particularly interested in establishing a market with local interior designers who you hope will be delighted with the wide selection of accessories that include extraordinary, one-of-a-kind items at prices as low as $20. These incredible items, which often require hours for interior designers to locate at a large furniture market, can be easily purchased in your store. You have finally settled in enough to plan the grand opening for Saturday, May 5, 10-3 p.m. The grand opening will be an excellent opportunity to introduce the designers to your offerings so that they begin their search for unique furnishings for their customers at your store.

To promote the grand opening, you're working on an ad for the interior design section of the daily newspaper. Having experienced excellent results from a 30-second radio spot on WLEM radio, you have arranged for WLEM to do a remote broadcast during the grand opening. In addition to the complimentary coffee and hot tea offered to customers daily, you're planning a nice array of petit fours and other exquisite finger goods for the grand opening. A drawing for an assortment of exclusive gifts will make the grand opening as spectacular as its merchandise.

Required: Write a form letter to be sent to the interior designers on your mailing list. Provide other details that you believe would ensure a successful grand opening. Address a sample letter to Kristen Antici, 398 Codman Park Avenue, Lakeland, FL 33802-0398.

10. **Routine Request: Accommodations During an Annual Audit (Obj. 3)**

Haney and Webb, CPAs, is preparing for its annual financial audit of Nelson Processors, Inc. The staff will work in the client's office for three weeks beginning March 1. To facilitate an efficient and cost-effective audit, you as the audit manager plan to write to the controller at Nelson requesting specific arrangements. The four accountants will need adequate work space during the three-week audit. A guided tour of the production facilities should be planned for the first day of the visit. For the first time, you are recommending that the client arrange to have bills for the accountants' hotel accommodations sent directly to Nelson. This procedure will save the client the 10 percent added to the audit fee to cover the cost of processing these charges.

Required: As the audit manager, write a letter to Calvin Blette, the controller, outlining these specific arrangements. His address is Nelson Processors, Inc., 5334 Tower Building, Wichita, KS 67202-5334.

11. **Favorable Response Letter: Addressing the Year 2000 Problem (Obj. 3)**

Assume you are R. P. Bethea, computer director of Advanced Castings, and you have just received an inquiry letter from Jim Lockley, at Bristol Enterprises, to whom you supply parts (see Application 8). Mr. Lockley's letter provided background information on the seriousness of the Year 2000 Problem and inquired about your plan for addressing the problem. Like Mr. Lockley, you are convinced the Year 2000 Problem could be detrimental and have already hired consultants to assess the impact of the problem on your computer system. To date, the only problem detected is in your payroll system, which doesn't affect Bristol. Your consultants are continuing their assessment, but you would be willing for Bristol's task force to come in and see what they can find.

Required: Write a response letter to Jim Lockley, Y2K Division, Bristol Enterprises, 1285 Millersville Road, Dayton, OH 45401-1285.

12. **Favorable Response Letter: Accepting an Invitation to Perform a Civic Duty (Obj. 3)**

You have been employed for several years in your career field. Today you were asked to assist in an activity sponsored by a civic organization in your area. Depending on your interest and expertise, provide the exact nature of this activity. For example, a financial planner might have been asked to discuss mutual funds at a monthly meeting; an accountant, to prepare tax returns as a service project for seniors; and a computer programmer, to assist an organization in automating its membership records.

Required: Accept the request and include any details needed to make arrangements for your participation in this activity.

13. **Favorable Response Letter: Time to Diversify Stock Portfolio (Obj. 3)**

In your position as a financial planner, you were asked to develop a long-term investment strategy for Randall

Myers. This strategy called for 50 percent of Mr. Myers' account to be invested in New York Stock Exchange securities. As a result of increases in stock prices, the client's stock holdings now comprise 60 percent of his account. Thus, you must recommend that he sell stock amounting to at least 10 percent of his account. Using your knowledge of the stock market, identify the stocks you believe Mr. Myers should sell and justify your decision. He owns $20,000 of IBM, $10,000 of Wal-Mart, and $20,000 of Microsoft. You may obtain current stock information and forecasts by visiting each company's web site. (You may assume the client owns other stock if you wish.)

Required: As the financial planner, communicate your recommendation to Mr. Myers. You might encourage him to call for an appointment if he wishes further consultation about his investment portfolio. Your instructor may require you to provide a printout of the information you downloaded from the Internet.

14. **Credit Approval: Construction Engineer (Obj. 4)**

A construction engineer's credit application at Home Building & Supply has been approved. Initially, the engineer's credit limit is $100,000. As her construction projects expand, the limit can be raised if necessary. Home Building & Supply has prepared a pamphlet that gives details of the credit terms.

Required: As an official of the firm, write a letter conveying the good news. Call the engineer's attention to the enclosed credit-terms pamphlet. (Assume the pamphlet has been prepared already.) Ms. Celeste Berry, Room 347 Irish Hall, Southstate University, Woodland, NE 68451-5731.

15. **Customer Order Acknowledgment: Staff/Alumni Reception (Obj. 5)**

Melissa Sherman, administrative assistant to the partner in charge, is responsible for planning the annual staff/alumni reception for Brooks and Lincoln, a regional accounting firm. Arrangements already have been made to hold this annual event at the Epley Resort, one of the city's preferred hotels, on Saturday, June 27, from 7 to 5 p.m. During Melissa's initial tour of the facility, the restaurant manager gave her a complete menu including prices and asked that she place her order by May 30. He also reminded Melissa to add to the order 7 percent sales tax and 17 percent service charges on all food and beverages.

After reviewing the menu and consulting several others at the office, Melissa decided to place an order for the following items: 1 assorted international cheese tray with fruits and crackers at $125, 1 display of fresh garden vegetables served with assorted dips at $75, 1 iced jumbo gulf shrimp tray with cocktail sauce at $160, 1 baked Virginia ham tray with rolls and condiments (approximately 80 portions) at $150, 1 assorted gourmet cookie and candy tray at $50, 6 pounds of fancy mixed nuts at $14 per pound, 8 gallons of fruit punch at $18 per gallon, 1 gallon of regular coffee at $22.50, and 1 gallon of decaffeinated coffee at $22.50.

Required: Prepare a customer order acknowledgment using a template in your word processing or spreadsheet software. Send the acknowledgment to Melissa Sherman, Brooks & Lincoln, 1083 Central Avenue, Winter Haven, FL 32785-1003.

16. **Customer Order Acknowledgment: Decorative Fragrances on the Way (Obj. 5)**

As the marketing manager for Aromatique, you have just set up an account with The Store, an exclusive home design store that recently opened in Lakeland, Florida (see Application 9). Send Dan Anderson, the owner, a letter that you are shipping the starter display and his first order by UPS, with delivery expected in approximately five days. Explain that the starter display includes an attractive display unit, 12 cases of the latest 6 decorator fragrances, 6 cases of fragrance oil for refurbishing the fragrance, and an assortment of scented candles. Because this is a first-time order, you want to recommend that he display several different fragrances in attractive containers throughout the store. Your experience indicates that customers enjoy the aroma of the various fragrances, some delicate, some sweet, and some quite robust, and appreciate the beautiful textures (e.g., seashells and seaweed of various sizes and shapes in your new Bath Splendor) that separates your decorative fragrances from typical potpourri. Remind him that a case of the new fragrance introduced each month will be shipped to him automatically as a stipulation in his account. Tell Mr. Smith about your new line of luxurious bath oils and body fragrances for men and women. A speciality item such as this line would be ideal for his clientele and would make excellent gifts, especially with the holiday season approaching.

Required: Write the order acknowledgment letter to Dan Anderson, The Store, 190 Promenade Center, Lakeland, FL 33802-0398

17. **Thank-You Letter: Business Referrals (Obj. 4)**

You own a photography studio and serve a small clientele, taking class pictures for area schools and ad pictures for small businesses. Leonard Tomlinson, a photographer who worked for you several months ago, recommended you to a couple to take pictures for their wedding. The couple, Angela and Michael Upton, were so impressed with your work that they have recommended you enthusiastically to several other couples seeking a photographer for their weddings.

Required: Write Leonard a letter of appreciation for his original referral. His address is 12 Main Boulevard, Dowingtown, PA 19335-8100.

18. **Appreciation Letter: Excellent Performance in Internship (Obj. 6)**

Ferdenez Public Relations participates in an internship program with Mesa State University. Typically, the company accepts three students majoring in public relations, advertising, and commercial art to complete a one-semester internship. Depending on the student's major, an account executive is assigned to coordinate and to evaluate the intern's work. After the student has completed the internship, the account executive writes an evaluation letter, which serves as one criterion for assigning a grade for the internship. This semester you worked closely with Amanda Sorrell, a commercial art major. Her workplace demeanor was excellent; she was always eager to begin one challenging assignment after another. Unlike interns you have supervised in the past, she never used her inexperience as an excuse for mistakes (which were few). She was eager to learn, asked intelligent questions, and had a creative sense of layout and design. Janine's, an upscale clothing store and a major account, sent a letter complimenting the firm for the newspaper advertisements it prepared for Janine's spring fashion show. Amanda was responsible for a number of the creative ideas developed in this ad campaign and completed a significant portion of the work.

Required: As the account executive supervising Amanda's internship, write a letter evaluating Amanda's performance. Send the letter to Tara Warren, Associate Professor, Communications Department, Mesa State University, P.O. Drawer CO, Flagstaff, AZ 86001-2801.

19. **Apology: Error in Planning (Obj. 6)**

Allen Melton, the account executive for your ad agency, was scheduled to present a prototype of the new advertising campaign to your company's sales representatives. At his request, you arranged for a computer projector and laptop computer to be available for his presentation. Apparently, when you scheduled the equipment from Computer Resources, you inadvertently reserved the equipment for the wrong date. When you discovered the error the morning of the presentation, you attempted to obtain the equipment, but all the computer projectors were being used in remote locations. Fortunately, Mr. Melton had prepared transparencies of his presentation as a precautionary measure in the event of technical problems. You regret the inconvenience your error caused.

Required: Write an apology to Allen Melton, Melton Public Relations, 7800 Carmel Street, Suite 3300, Indianapolis, IN 46206-7900.

20. **International Letter: An Apology to Promote International Understanding (Obj. 7)**

Newman Oil is an offshore drilling company that has extensive dealings with oil concerns in Mexico. One afternoon the senior partner received a disturbing call from Leon Lopez, a business associate. Lopez was very upset and puzzled by the behavior of Charles Dixon, one of Newman's production supervisors in Mexico City. Lopez had scheduled an appointment with Dixon at 11:30 a.m. When Lopez arrived at 12:10, Dixon had already gone to lunch. Very frustrated, Lopez returned to Dixon's office at 2 p.m. (normal afternoon reopening in Mexico), but Dixon didn't have time to discuss the matter and referred Lopez to the secretary to schedule another appointment.

The partner called Charles Dixon for his side of the story. Dixon said, "I assumed that Lopez was not planning to keep his appointment; otherwise, he would have called to explain that he had been detained but was on his way." Dixon did not perceive his treatment of Lopez later that day as cold and unconcerned. The partner realizes that Dixon has not been in Mexico long enough to appreciate the importance Mexicans place on personal relationships and the relative casualness with which Mexicans regard time. However, because Dixon's behavior has created ill will for Newman, an apology must be written.

Required: As the partner, write a letter of apology to Lopez. Address the letter to Leon Lopez, Paseo Kulkulkan, 77500 Cancun, Q.R., Mexico. Be prepared to explain to your instructor changes that were necessary to adapt this message to this international reader.

21. **International Inquiry Letter: What Taxes Must Be Paid? (Obj. 7)**

Assume you have been hired by a Japanese company that is opening its first sales office in the United States. The financial vice president outlined your salary and other benefits in detail at your last meeting. However, something important just occurred to you. Because you are working for a Japanese company, you wonder whether you and the company will pay United States' social security (FICA) taxes.

Required: Write an inquiry letter to Mr. Danjiro Saga, Akita Industries, 28-43 Mita 7-chome (street, house number), Minato-ku (city), Tokyo 108 (prefecture, postal district), Japan. Because international mail is slow, Mr. Matsumi instructed you to send all mail to him by facsimile (refer to Appendix A for an appropriate mailing notation for facsimile transmissions). Be prepared to explain to your instructor changes that were necessary to adapt this message to this international reader.

22. **International Thank-You Letter: Help from Overseas (Obj. 7)**

Sheila Wagner lost her luggage in flight to a two-week international marketing seminar in Germany. To make matters worse, as she was leaving the airport to go to the hotel, she left her traveler's checks in the taxi. Immediately, Sheila called her German liaison contact,

Anna Herpfer, who offered to handle the red tape. By the first day of the seminar, Anna had given Sheila replacement traveler's checks and had assured Sheila that the airline would deliver the luggage in two days. During the overseas stay, Anna was unfailingly courteous and polite.

Required: Write the thank-you letter to Anna Herpfer, Bahnhofstr. 9, 7000 Weinstadt 2, Germany. Be prepared to explain to your instructor changes that were necessary to adapt this message to this international reader.

REAL-TIME INTERNET CASE

Telecommuting Poses New Communication Challenges

An alternative to physical commuting, telecommuting allows employees to work from home via computer/modem/fax and telephone. Also called "teleworking" or "cyberworking," this option is not suitable for all types of businesses, but can be successful for those with a high percentage of employees who spend the majority of their time in the office using the computer and telephone on a regular basis.

Telecommuting can aid the employer by saving on physical space and overhead associated with providing office facilities for workers. Employers also gain from increased productivity since studies show that employees who telecommute are more likely to fulfill their workday time commitments and take fewer sick days. Offering such flexibility can also increase employee retention and serve to attract new employees.

Telecommuting employees benefit from the flexibility provided by work at home. Child or elder care can be coordinated with work activities, and the worker can set his or her own schedule. Money is saved on automobile and commuting expenses, as well as on wardrobe and outside meals. Considering the various advantages offered by telecommuting, it is no wonder that the number of U.S. telecommuters rose by more than 30 percent from 1995 to 1997 to 11.1 million workers.

Despite its many advantages, a major challenge to telecommuting success is communication. Organizations must find successful ways to maintain adequate communication between supervisors and the virtual workforce; lack of information is frequently the source of performance problems. In addition, workers outside the traditional office environment may feel isolated and out of touch. Instead of walking down the hall to chat with a coworker,

employees will need other ways to stay in touch. That situation means new skills such as the ability to write effective e-mail, use groupware, and work on virtual teams. A careful look at the company's culture will be an important step in assuring that telecommuting is effective. Virtual communication is enhanced if a strong rapport exists among employees. Maintaining professional contacts and friends is important. Technology is not meant to replace human contact but rather to enhance it.[9]

Visit the following web sites and complete the activities, as directed by your instructor.

Internet Sites

http://www.att.com/press/1097/971024.chb.html
http://www.homeworker.com/
http://www.libertynet.org/~dctma/regional/map-telecommuting.html
http://www.acd.ccac.edu/hr/telecomx.htm

Activities

1. Research the issue of how telecommuters can keep a proper balance between work life and home life. Prepare transparencies or slides listing dos and don'ts for maintaining that division. Present your lists to the class, using your transparencies or slides as visuals.

2. Take either the pro or the con position in terms of the advisability of telecommuting. Prepare a two-page essay that summarizes the reasons for your position on the issue. Then prepare a second paper, taking the opposing position.

3. Make a comprehensive list of suggestions for organizations and individuals to help assure the success of telecommuting. Combine your list with that of a class partner, and e-mail your instructor with your suggestions.

CHAPTER SIX

Writing Bad-News Letters

When you have completed Chapter 6, you will be able to:

1 List the steps in the inductive outline and identify the advantages of using it to convey bad news.

2 Write letters refusing a request.

3 Write letters denying a claim.

4 Write letters refusing to complete an order.

5 Write letters denying credit.

6 Write letters providing constructive criticism.

7 Discuss ways to handle special problems about the unpleasant.

*O*n most days in most companies, "business as usual" is the rule. However, despite excellent quality control, customer service, and communications, sometimes bad things just happen. The point to remember when such a crisis occurs, whether it is large or small, is to keep the channels of communication open. Your company's reputation—possibly even its future—depends on it.

In recent years, we have seen how some companies have handled crisis situations, from the oily mess in the *Exxon Valdez* spill, to the racist views held by some Texaco executives that were made embarrassingly public, to America OnLine's ill-planned new member drive that caused a major traffic jam on the information superhighway. Experience has shown that companies who own up to the mishap or error, communicate openly within the corporation and with the public, and make haste to resolve the crisis fare well in the long run. That was the case with the Tylenol scare in the early 1980s, and, more recently, with Odwalla, Inc.

Odwalla, a company based in Half Moon Bay, California, could have been doomed after the crisis of 1996, when outbreaks of life-threatening E. coli infection in Washington state were blamed on tainted juice products bottled by Odwalla. Within mere hours after the first reported incident, corporate headquarters ordered all distributors in several western states and British Columbia to pull the juice off the shelves. The company had already developed a set of protocols that would serve as guidance in such a crisis, so when Chairman Greg Steltenpohl met with the CEO and communications director, they already knew they had to ensure that the company's integrity stayed intact. Steltenpohl answered the media's questions honestly and in a straightforward manner.

Despite the fact that the product had been pulled off most store shelves, the worst case scenario soon became reality. More E. coli infections were reported, this time in Colorado, and a toddler died after drinking some tainted Odwalla. Steltenpohl had contacted the family before the child's death; and when he returned to Denver for a press conference, he met discreetly with the child's family and later went to the funeral. Press releases issued after the child's death show the concern the company felt, and the fact that Steltenpohl's visits were not publicized indicated genuine sensitivity, not public relations. Shel Holtz, a communications consultant, says, "You have to show you care," even though extenuating factors may exist and your company may not be entirely at fault. Odwalla showed its concern from day one and followed through with its "Do the right thing" philosophy by offering to pay the medical bills of individuals whose illnesses resulted from drinking Odwalla juice products.

Odwalla's main strength—other than its commitment to integrity and honesty—was that it did not depend on the public media to communicate the crisis and what the company was doing about it. Within hours after the bad news broke, Odwalla launched a Web site that listed all their actions and was linked to the Centers for Disease Control. The site address was included in subsequent news releases. Also, additional 800 phone lines were opened. Their crisis plan emphasized unceasing communications, so the Web site, the 800 lines, news releases, and press conferences all worked to ensure that the public as well as company officials were constantly aware of what was happening.

Odwalla survived this crisis and is thriving today. Sydney Fisher, Odwalla's communications director, stated that the "swift action and communication with the public saved us." However, the company also had developed good relations with the media, shareholders, employees, and consumers, and during the downturn of the months following the crisis, no one was laid off. [1]

Everyone hopes he or she never has to face such a horrific scenario. And most people probably won't. But the Odwalla case proves that you can't wait until a crisis occurs to develop a plan. How would you communicate bad news so that your company does not lose in the long run?

Inductive Organizational Pattern

As illustrated in the Odwalla example, knowing how to communicate bad news as delicately and clearly as possible is an essential business skill. A skillful manager will attempt to say, "No," in such a way that the reader or listener supports the decision and is willing to continue a positive relationship with the company. To do this successfully, the manager must first have *empathy*; she or he must try to understand how the recipient of the unpleasant news will feel. If you are sending the information in a letter, you must first think how you would approach the news if the recipient were there to receive it in person. A letter is much less likely to be "cold" if you use empathy in addition to tact and effective writing skills.

Perhaps your personal response to a claim or a request, for example, would be much different from the tactful response needed to soothe negative feelings and ensure a harmonious relationship with the customer. Your response may be especially different when you doubt whether the request is legitimate or when you do not have the time required to write an effective bad-news letter. When this conflict exists, keep in mind that you are writing the letter on behalf of your company and that your response is a direct reflection on the company's image.

The importance of effective bad-news communication is illustrated by the story of a man who carried in his coat pocket a job-refusal letter he had received from a company some time past. Frequently he would show this superbly written letter to others and comment, "I'd accept a job from this company any day because this letter made me feel *good* about myself even though the company couldn't hire me." Obviously, this letter was not an impersonal form letter, nor was it written in haste without genuine empathy for the receiver's feelings.

Sequence of Ideas

Just as good news is accompanied with details, bad news is accompanied with supporting details (reasons, explanations). If the bad news is presented in the first sentence, the reaction is likely to be negative: "They never gave me a fair chance"; "That's unfair"; "This just can't be." Having made a value judgment on reading the first sentence, receivers are naturally reluctant to change their minds before the last sentence—even though the intervening sentences present a valid basis for doing so. Having been disappointed by the idea contained in the first sentence, receivers are tempted to concentrate on *refuting* (instead of *understanding*) supporting details.

From the writer's point of view, details that support a refusal are very important. If the supporting details are understood and believed, the message may be readily accepted and good business relationships preserved. Because the reasons behind the bad news are so important, the writer needs to organize the message in such a way as to emphasize the reasons.

The chances of getting the receiver to understand the reasons are much better *before* the bad news is presented than *after* the bad news is presented. If the bad news precedes the reasons, (1) the message might be discarded before this important

1 *List the steps in the inductive outline and identify the advantages of using it to convey bad news.*

How does empathy assist in conveying bad news?

Can you relay similar incidents when you had either a positive or a negative feeling for a person or company who gave you unpleasant news? Contrast the approaches used in the situations.

COMMUNICATION MENTOR

Communicating "with disagreement" is one of the most difficult tasks you will face. A few "dos and "don'ts" you will find helpful follow:

- *Do* maintain an open mind—even on points of disagreement.

- *Do* demonstrate respect for the opposition. You dislike the ideas, not the person presenting them.

- *Do* listen to your opposition.

- *Do* read body language.

- *Don't* become emotional.

- *Don't* prepare your response when you should be listening.

- *Don't* become focused on your choice of words.

- *Don't* engage in cross-talk; cross-listening is the key.

Remember you are looking for a *positive outcome*, not a body count.

Choose your words carefully when you are refusing a request in writing. You and your company often will be judged only on the basis of your letter because the recipient may never see you. A poorly written letter can be worse than an unsatisfactory oral response because the receiver has the "document on file."

Shirley F. Olson, President
J. J. Ferguson Prestress-Precast Co., Inc.

What negative consequences might occur if a proper bad-news sequence is not used?

portion is even read, or (2) the disappointment experienced when reading the bad news might interfere with the receiver's ability to comprehend or accept the supporting explanation.

The writer can simplify the process by using the four-step outline shown in Figure 6-1. These four steps are applied in letters (and later in memorandums) illustrated in this chapter.

Step 1: Introductory Paragraph. The introductory paragraph in the bad-news or refusal letter should (1) let the receiver know what the letter is about (without stating the obvious) and (2) serve as a transition into the discussion of reasons (without revealing the bad news or leading the receiver to expect good news). If these objectives can be accomplished in one sentence, that sentence can be the first paragraph.

Step 2: Facts, Analysis, and Reasons. People who are refused want to know why. To them (and to the person doing the refusing) the reasons are vital; they must be transmitted and received. A well-written first paragraph should transition the receiver smoothly into a logical, but concise, discussion of the reason for the refusal. By the time a receiver has finished reading the explanation, the upcoming statement of refusal may be foreseen and accepted as valid.

FIGURE 6-1
Inductive sequence used in bad-news messages.

BAD-NEWS MESSAGE

- Begins with the neutral idea that leads to the reason for the refusal.
- Presents the facts, analysis, and reasons for the refusal.
- States the refusal using positive tone and de-emphasis techniques.
- Closes with an idea that shifts emphasis away from the refusal.

Step 3: Refusal Statement. The refusal statement should be in the same paragraph as the reasons. It should not be placed in a paragraph by itself; this arrangement would place too much emphasis on the bad news. Because the preceding explanation is tactful and seems valid, the sentence that states the bad news may arouse little or no resentment. If the writing were strictly inductive, the refusal statement would be last. Placing a statement of refusal (or bad news) in the last sentence or paragraph, however, would have the effect of placing too much emphasis on it. Preferably, *reasons* (instead of bad news) should remain uppermost in the receiver's mind. Placing bad news last would make the ending seem cold and abrupt.

Offering a **counterproposal**—alternative to the action requested—will assist in preserving future relationships with the receiver. Because it states what you *can* do, including a counterproposal may eliminate the need to state the refusal directly. The counterproposal can follow a refusal stated in a tactful, sensitive manner.

Step 4: Closing Paragraph. A closing paragraph that is about some aspect of the topic other than the bad news itself helps in several ways. It assists in (1) de-emphasizing the unpleasant part of the message, (2) conveying some useful information that should logically follow (instead of precede) bad news, (3) showing that the writer has a positive attitude, and (4) adding a unifying quality to the message.

Although the preceding outline has four points, a bad-news letter may or may not have four paragraphs. More than one paragraph may be necessary for conveying supporting reasons. In the illustrations in this chapter (as well as examples in Appendix A), note that first and final paragraphs are seldom longer than two sentences. In fact, one-sentence paragraphs (as beginnings) look inviting to read.

The inductive sequence of ideas has the following advantages:

- It sufficiently identifies the subject of the letter without first turning the receiver off.
- It presents the reasons *before* the refusal, where they are more likely to be understood.
- It emphasizes the reasons by letting them precede the refusal.
- It avoids a negative reaction. By the time the reasons are read, they seem sensible, and the refusal is foreseen. Because it is expected, the statement of refusal does not come as a shock.
- It de-emphasizes the refusal by closing on a neutral or pleasant note. By showing a willingness to cooperate in some other way, the writer conveys a desire to be helpful.

You may speculate that receivers may become impatient when a letter is inductive. Concise, well-written explanations are not likely to make receivers impatient. They relate to the receiver's problem, present information not already known, and help the receiver understand. However, if receivers become impatient while reading well-written explanations, that impatience is less damaging to understanding than would be the anger or disgust that often results from encountering bad news in the first sentence.

Normally, the writer's purpose is to convey a clear message and retain the recipient's goodwill; thus, the inductive outline is appropriate. In the rare circumstances in which a choice must be made between the two, clarity is the better choice. When the deductive approach will serve a writer's purpose better, it should be used. For example, if you submit a clear and tactful refusal and the receiver resubmits the request, a deductive presentation may be justified in the second

What are the consequences if bad news is shared too early? Too late?

Which is less desirable: an angry or an impatient reader? What can you do to minimize the delay in presenting the bad news?

When would a deductive approach be appropriate for presenting bad news? Provide examples of your own.

refusal. Apparently, the refusal needs the emphasis provided by a deductive outline. Placing a refusal in the first sentence can be justified when one or more of the following circumstances exist:

1. The letter is the second response to a repeated request.
2. A very small, insignificant matter is involved.
3. A request is obviously ridiculous, immoral, unethical, illegal, or dangerous.
4. A writer's intent is to "shake" the receiver.
5. A writer-reader relationship is so close and long-standing that satisfactory human relations can be taken for granted.
6. The writer *wants* to demonstrate authority.

In most writing situations, the preceding circumstances do not exist. When they do, a writer's goals may be accomplished by stating bad news in the first sentence.

Style

Although a refusal (bad news) needs to be clear, subordinating it allows the reasoning for the refusal to get deserved emphasis. The following three stylistic techniques will help you achieve this goal: emphasis techniques, positive language, and implication. You may want to review the *emphasis techniques* you studied in Chapter 3 as you consider methods for presenting bad news with human relations in mind.

1. **Emphasize the positive, and de-emphasize the negative.** Keep in mind the inductive outline recommended for bad-news messages de-emphasizes the statement of bad news. In other words, it subordinates the bad news by putting it in a less important position (sandwiched between an opening buffer statement and a positive closing. Other ways to de-emphasize the refusal include (a) subordinating bad news by placing it in the dependent clause of a complex sentence, (b) using passive voice, (c) expressing it in general terms, and (d) using abstract nouns or things (instead of the person written to) as the subject of a sentence.

2. **Use positive language to accentuate the positive and de-emphasize the negative.** Simply focus on the good instead of the bad, the pleasant instead of the unpleasant, what can be done instead of what cannot be done. Compared with a negative idea presented in negative terms, a negative idea presented in positive terms is more likely to be accepted. When you are tempted to use the following terms, search instead for words or ideas that sound more positive:

chagrined	failure	lied	overlooked
complaint	ignorant	misinformed	regrettable
disappointed	ignored	mistake	ridiculous
disgusted	inexcusable	neglect	underhanded
disregard	insinuation	nonsense	upset
error	irresponsible	obnoxious	wrong

To businesspeople who conscientiously practice empathy, such terms may not even come to mind when communicating the unpleasant. Words in the preceding list evoke negative feelings that contrast sharply with the positive feelings evoked by words such as

---

You are responding to a third request from the same customer for a product you no longer carry. Would the inductive approach be appropriate?

Think of other words that could be added to the list of negative words and the list of positive words that follow.

When you must give unpleasant news or reject an employee's ideas, offering an alternative instead of a flat "no" keeps communication open and avoids damage to egos.

accurate	cordial	freedom	pretty
approval	correct	generous	productive
assist	durable	gratitude	prosper
cheerful	energetic	happy	recommendation
commend	enthusiasm	health	respect
concise	fragrance	peace	true

To increase the number of pleasant-sounding words in your writing, practice thinking positively. Strive to see the good in situations and in others. Will Rogers professed to being able to see *some* good in every person he met.

3. **Imply the refusal when the receiver can understand the message without a definite statement of the bad news.** For example, during the noon hour one employee says to another, "Will you go with me to see this afternoon's baseball game?" "No, I won't" communicates a negative response, but it seems unnecessarily direct and harsh. The same message (invitation is rejected) can be clearly stated in an *indirect* way (by implication):

I wish I could.	Other responsibilities forbid, but the recipient would like to accept.
I must get my work done.	By revealing the necessity of working instead, the worker conveys the "no" answer.
If I watched baseball this afternoon, I'd be transferred tomorrow.	By stating an unacceptable consequence of acceptance, the worker conveys the idea of nonacceptance.
I'm a football fan.	By indicating a preference for another sport, the worker conveys nonacceptance.

In groups, write a sentence that implies management's refusal to adopt a company casual dress policy. Contrast that sentence to a direct statement of refusal.

By *implying* the "no" answer, the preceding responses (1) use positive language, (2) convey reasons or at least a positive attitude, and (3) seem more respectful. These implication techniques (as well as emphasis/deemphasis, positive language, and inductive sequence) are illustrated in the letters that follow. The Strategic Forces box on page 206 addresses the feasability of the use of template letters available with major word processing software.

2 *Write letters refusing a request.*

Refusing a Request

When a request for a favor must be denied, the same reasons-before-refusal pattern is recommended. To ensure positive relationships, the recipient of a request for a favor may offer a counterproposal—an alternative to the action requested. In the letter in Figure 6-2, the writer explains why the company cannot lend an executive to direct a major community effort and recommends a member of the company's senior executive corps as a counterproposal.

The letter in Figure 6-2—which is a *response* to prior correspondence—uses the same principles of sequence and style that are recommended for letters that *initiate* communication about unpleasant topics. The same principles apply whether the communication is a letter or a memorandum sent to an employee within a company.

How does including a counterproposal improve the effectiveness of a bad-news letter?

Form letters have earned a negative connotation because of their tendency to be insensitive and impersonal. However, you can effectively personalize a form letter to keep your reader from feeling like just another "address."

Inductive Outline for Refusing a Favor

1. Begin with a neutral or factual sentence that leads to the reasons behind the refusal.
2. Present the reasons and explanations.
3. Present the refusal in an unemphatic manner.
4. Close with a thought related to the letter or to the business relationship but which addresses the refusal.

FIGURE 6-2
Good example of a refusal for a favor.

INDUSTRIES

2700 Ridgeway ▲ Cambridge, MA 02139-2700 ▲ Phone: (617) 555-8700 Fax: (617) 555-7961

March 18, 1999

Mr. Robert Duncan
Neeley Foundation
9835 Franklin Building
Cambridge, MA 02140-9835

Dear Bob

❶ You are to be commended for your commitment to create an endowment for the Kirkland Homeless Shelter. This much-needed project will aid the hundreds of homeless and increase the community's awareness of the needs of this sector of our population.

❷ The success of this project depends on a good project director. The organizational, leadership, and public relations activities you described demand an individual with upper-level managerial experience.

During the last year, Nemitz has decentralized its organization, reducing the number of upper-level managers to the minimal level needed. **❸** Although our current personnel shortage prevents us from lending you an executive, we do want to support your worthy project.

❹ Amy Murray in our senior executive corps directed a similar short-term project, Homes for Humanity. She organized the campaign, solicited area coordinators, and managed publicity. If you can benefit from her services, call her at 555-8700, extension 791.

Sincerely

Angela

Angela Larche
Director

❶ Introduces the subject without revealing whether the answer will be "yes" or "no."

❷ Gives reasons.

❸ Subordinates the refusal by placing it in the dependent clause of a complex sentence. Alludes to help in another form.

❹ Closes on a positive note by offering a counterproposal. Summarizing the executive's responsibilities and providing her telephone number increase the genuineness of the offer.

Format Pointers

Signs first name only because the writer knows the receiver well.

Strategic Forces: Changing Technology

Assessing Template Letters Available with Word Processing Software

Template letters are a common feature among leading word processing programs. To use such standard templates, the writer selects a type of letter from the menu, such as "Request." The screen then displays a form letter for request situations which the writer can modify to fit the situation at hand. This feature appears, at first, to be a great time saver for the busy writer. Unfortunately, however, such template examples frequently do not reflect the elements indicated for effective inductive, deductive, or persuasive letters. The careful writer will recognize such shortcomings of the templates and use them cautiously.

Application

Select a word processing program that includes template letters. Select a letter type that should reflect the deductive (good-news or neutral-news) pattern. Using the checklist at the end of Chapter 5, evaluate how well the template letter follows the recommended development pattern for deductive messages. Note in what areas the template deviates from the recommendations. Then choose a template letter type that should reflect the inductive (bad-news) pattern. Using the checklist at the end of this chapter, evaluate how well the template letter follows the recommended development pattern for inductive messages. Note how the template deviates from recommendations.

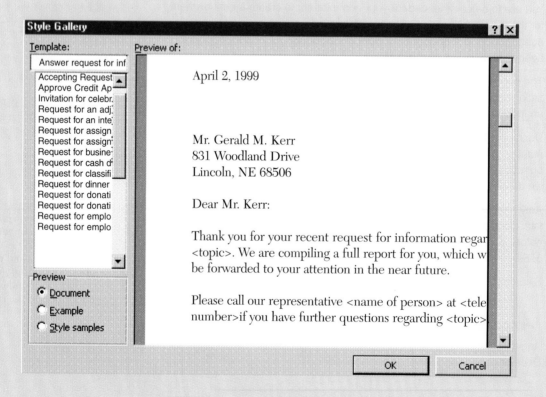

Denying a Claim

Assume a financial planner receives the following query from a client about a statement.

> Please correct my statement that explains my stock holdings with the Wynne Fund. On the day I purchased the shares, you used the per share amount in the second column of the financial section of the paper. The statement now shows my shares valued using the amount in the first column. Because I could find no explanation for the discrepancy, I assume an error has been made.

The client recently purchased 100 shares of a front-end mutual fund at $50.00 per share. The fund immediately deducted $2.50 per share as its front-end fee. Thus, the client's investment is worth only $47.50 per share. The client's inquiry shows a lack of understanding of the concept of front-end mutual funds or the buy and sell share prices reported in the newspaper. Despite the financial planner's exasperation at the client's lack of knowledge, the response must be more tactful than that illustrated in Figure 6-3.

In the revised letter in Figure 6-4, note that the first sentence reveals the subject matter of the letter and leads into a presentation of reasons. Reasons precede the refusal; the statement of refusal is de-emphasized; and the final sentence is about something other than the refusal.

3 *Write letters denying a claim.*

Are the main idea and the details in Figure 6-3 presented in the appropriate sequence? What words/phrases contribute to the negative tone? Refer to "Adapting the Message to the Audience" in Chapter 3 if necessary.

❶ Begins with an idea that is not needed (receipt of the request could be implied).

❷ Includes an unnecessary apology for a justified decision and provides the refusal before the reasons.

❸ Presents an explanation too brief and too technical to be understood. The patronizing tone may intimidate the receiver.

❹ Uses clichés that may undermine the decision and may lead to unnecessary correspondence.

AVOID

❶ Your letter questioning your investment statement has been received. **❷** I am sorry but we cannot adjust your statement as you requested. Clearly, the statement is correct.

❸ In our discussions prior to the stock purchase, I clearly explained that you would be required to pay us a front-end fee to manage your account.

❹ I am sure you can understand my position in this matter. Thank you for doing business with us; and if you have any further questions, do not hesitate to call or write.

FIGURE 6-3 Poor example of a claim denial.

FIGURE 6-4
Good example of a claim denial.

Inductive Outline for Denying an Adustment

1. Begin with a neutral or factual sentence that leads to the reasons behind the refusal.
2. Present the reasons and explanations.
3. Present the refusal in an unemphatic manner.
4. Close with a thought related to the letter or to the business relationship that does not address the refusal.

GILMER & ASSOCIATES INVESTORS

742 NORTH MAIN STREET / LAUREL, MS 39440-0742 / (606) 555-7910 FAX (601) 555-9087

January 21, 1999

Mr. Edward Kangarajah
896-D Kemp Avenue
Laurel, MS 39440-8976

Dear Ed

1 Thank you for taking such a keen interest in your investment. We appreciate your allowing us to help you clarify your recent investment statement.

2 Mutual funds use a variety of methods to offset the fund's administrative costs. The Wynne Fund is a front-end load fund, meaning that investors pay a fee only at the time they invest funds. Other mutual funds deduct administrative costs from the annual investment income credited to the account; others are rear-end load funds, deducting a percentage when funds are withdrawn. We believe that front-end mutual funds will provide you with the best return on your investment.

3 The amount columns in the newspaper report the sell and buy prices for the mutual fund. You purchased your shares for the $50.00 buy price reported in the second column. The amount in the first column, the sell amount, will be used when your shares are ultimately sold. The Wynne Fund uses this sell price on its statements to report the *current* value of your investment.

4 Ed, I'm planning a luncheon meeting on January 30 for anyone interested in learning more about mutual funds and other investment strategies for beginning investors. Please plan to come.

Sincerely

Bert R. Turnage

Bert R. Turange
Certified Financial Planner

1 Reveals the subject matter of the letter and leads to the explanation.
2 Presents a clear explanation of the fees charged for managing the investment. Explains technical terms so the reader can understand.

3 Continues to help the reader understand how to interpret the statement without sounding demeaning. Implies the refusal because the explanation indicates that the stock value is correct as shown on the statement.
4 Shifts emphasis away from the refusal and looks confidently to future business.

Legal and Ethical Constraints
Avoids corrective language that might insult, belittle, or offend. [legal/ethical]

Refusing an Order

4 *Write letters refusing to complete an order.*

For various reasons, a company may not be able to send merchandise that people have ordered. The company

- May only be able to send it following a waiting period. (At such times, you would acknowledge the order and write a letter saying "Yes, you will receive the . . . by . . .")
- May not sell directly to consumers. (You would tell the customer where to buy the merchandise.)
- May not have what the customer ordered but may have something that will serve his or her needs better. (You would wait to fill the order until you have made the customer understand that you have something better.)

Why might a company refuse to fill an order? Give some examples.

For orders that cannot be filled, the inductive approach recommended for all negative letters is preferred. A manufacturer who does not sell directly to consumers may prepare a form letter to reply to repeated requests to fill orders. However, form letters do not have to be as cold and indifferent as the following letter. Note the letter is writer oriented, presents distribution through dealers as unfortunate rather than advantageous, and closes with a cliché.

> We have your recent request that we ship you a **[ITEM]**. Unfortunately, we do not sell directly to consumers.
> Your nearest dealer is **[DEALER]** whose address is **[ADDRESS]**. May we suggest that you place you order there.
> Thank you for your interest in our merchandise.

The general plan of the revised letter in Figure 6-5 is to make customers' desire for the merchandise so strong that they will be willing to wait for it and to purchase it through conventional merchandising outlets.

If the merchandise involved in the letter in Figure 6-5 was expensive or if orders sent directly to the manufacturer were rare, sending a form letter would not be appropriate. Sometimes, customers order one item when they can more profitably use another. Consider the contractor who has ordered lights that are inappropriate for the intended use. Filling the order as submitted would be a mistake, and the customer would likely be dissatisfied.

Although the form letter in Figure 6-6 may achieve the desired results (convince the recipient that the type of light bulb ordered is not the type needed), the revised letter in Figure 6-7 is more effective. Form letters and individual letters should follow the general guidelines provided in Figure 6-7.

Assuming the letter in Figure 6-5 was directed to the attention of the Purchasing Agent, how would the letter address and salutation be presented? Turn to Appendix A ("Special Letter Parts") if necessary.

The resale and the sales promotional material in the good example did not cost anything as far as supplies and postage are concerned—the company had to write anyway. The receiver is almost sure to read this material—something that cannot be said of the many sales messages that are instantly discarded.

When people say "no" in a letter, they usually do so because they think "no" is the better answer for all concerned. They can see how recipients will ultimately benefit from the refusal. If a letter is based on a sound decision, and if it has been well written, recipients will probably recognize that the senders did them a favor by refusing.

Why should resale and sales promotional material be included in an order refusal?

FIGURE 6-5
Good example of an order refusal—company does not sell directly to customers.

Inductive Outline for an Order Refusal

1. Imply receipt of the order and confirm the customer's good choice of merchandise.
2. Use resale—favorable statements about the product ordered—to make the customer willing to reorder through the proper channel.
3. Give reasons why sales are through dealers. Suggest or spell out how advantageously customers can buy through a dealer.
4. Use positive language to explain that the order is not being filled.

❶ Introduces the subject and leads to an explanation.
❷ Provides resale on the item ordered.
❸ Begins the explanation. Reveals—in positive language—that sales are not made directly to consumers. Lets the reader see an advantage in the manufacturer's not selling to consumers directly.
❹ Closes by providing needed information.

Dear Mr. Rosinski:

❶ When we first began marketing the OpticScan II laser printer, we wanted to provide laser printer capabilities suitable for businesses of all sizes.

❷ Now available with ten scalable fonts, the OpticScan II will allow you to choose exactly the right style for any layout. ❸ As manufacturers, we devote all our time to enhancing our current products and to developing innovative new products. Because we concentrate solely on these efforts (and leave selling and advertising to retailers), we have been able to develop products that meet the ever-changing technological needs of today's businesses.

❹ To see our new OpticScan II printer in operation, visit your nearest OpticScan retailer—Moore Suppliers, 1000 Forest Hill, Wausau, WI 54401-0400.

FIGURE 6-6
Poor example of an order refusal—merchandise does not meet customer's needs.

❶ Presents information that could have been implied; focuses on writer.
❷ Reveals the refusal before an explanation. "However" reveals that negatives follow.
❸ Provides no reasons; repetitive and vague. Implies lack of expertise on part of customer.
❹ Provides a major disadvantage but does not provide any benefits for making the substitution; uses "in the long run," a cliché.
❺ Presents needed information, but the idea of "holding" the order seems a little negative. "Hear from you" is worn and implies oral communication.

SUBJECT: Purchase Order No. 430-9831-7

❶ We received your order for 400 incandescent light bulbs (Stock No. 71731).

❷ However, we need to explain why this particular bulb is inappropriate.

❸ The incandescent bulb is not appropriate for your intended use. We have another product better suited to your purposes. May we have your permission to substitute halogen bulbs? ❹ Although these bulbs are more expensive, we feel the benefits will far outweigh the costs in the long run.

❺ Your order will be held until we hear from you.

380 South Pass Road
Casper, WY 82602-0380
Phone: 307/555-0038
Fax: 307/555-9875

FIGURE 6-7
Good example of an order refusal—merchandise ordered does not meet customer's needs.

November 9, 1999

Ms. Angela Fuller
Fuller Construction Co.
1900 Water Valley Road
Lincoln, NE 68501-1900

Re: Purchase Order No. 47061

Dear Ms. Fuller:

❶ The incandescent bulb you ordered has been proven to be 10 percent brighter than others of its type and is ideal for occasional use for short intervals.

❷ According to our sales rep, Joseph Rigdon, you plan to install the bulbs in the parking lot lights of the new Clover Mall. Because these bulbs will burn all night for security reasons, the halogen bulb designed for heavy-duty, long-term use is better suited for your needs.

❸ The longer life of the halogen will more than compensate for the larger initial investment required. You will also benefit from the convenience and cost efficiency of replacing bulbs less frequently. **❹** Refer to the enclosed pamphlet for additional details about the performance of the halogen bulb (Stock No. S9-13).

❺ To authorize us to ship the long-lasting halogen bulb, simply check the appropriate square on the enclosed card and return in the enclosed envelope with your payment for the additional cost.

Sincerely,

Donald Kwasney

Donald Kwasney
Sales Manager

Enclosures

❶ Acknowledges order but is noncommittal about shipment. Includes resale on the contractor's choice, which leads to the explanation.

❷ Continues with explanation by providing specific details about the receiver's needs.

❸ Reveals a disadvantage of the alternative, but de-emphasizes it by putting it in a sentence that states primary advantages (sales promotional material).

❹ Includes an enclosure to present more details and to reinforce ideas in the letter.

❺ Seeks permission to ship a more appropriate bulb. Makes response easy. The card might include a line for canceling the order, but the letter does not discuss this option.

Format Pointers
- Uses a reference line to direct reader to source documents.
- Includes enclosure notation to alert reader that other information is enclosed.

COMMUNICATION MENTOR

Working in the business world and upholding your values and standards can prove to be challenging. You can protect yourself from obvious scrupulous characters, shady dealers, or even activities that fall in the "grey" area. But unfortunately, no matter how careful you are eventually, you will find yourself in a predicament that challenges your values. These issues that face you may tempt you to act in a manner that is against your nature. Do not jeopardize your reputation, job, or character by changing your values, even if the change could benefit your title, salary, or prestige in the working environment. All could be short-lived if the truth of an unethical practice is uncovered. My advice is to always take the high road or find another job.

Pamela M. Plager, Vice President & Director
Allen & Company, Incorporated

5 *Write letters denying credit.*

What motivation does a business have for maintaining goodwill when writing a credit refusal?

What is a good counterproposal in a credit refusal?

Why is a poorly *written* refusal worse than an unsatisfactory *oral* one?

Denying Credit

Once you have evaluated a request for credit and have decided "No" is the better answer, your primary writing problem is to refuse credit so tactfully that you keep the business relationship on a cash basis. When requests for credit are accompanied with an order, your credit refusals may serve as acknowledgment letters. Of course, every business letter is directly or indirectly a sales letter. Prospective customers will be disappointed when they cannot buy on a credit basis. However, if you keep them sold on your goods and services, they may prefer to buy from you on a cash basis instead of seeking credit privileges elsewhere.

When the credit investigation shows that applicants are poor credit risks, too many credit writers no longer regard them as possible customers. They write to them in a cold, matter-of-fact manner. They do not consider that such applicants may still be interested in doing business on a cash basis and may qualify for credit later.

In credit refusals, as in other types of refusals, the major portion of the message should be an explanation for the refusal. You cannot expect your receiver to agree that your "No" answer is the right answer unless you give the reasons behind it. Naturally, those who send you credit information will expect you to keep it confidential. If you give the reasons without using the names of those from whom you obtained your information, you are not violating confidence. You are passing along the truth as a justification for your business decision.

Both writers and readers benefit from the explanation of the reasons behind the refusal. For writers, the explanation helps to establish fair-mindedness; it shows that the decision was not arbitrary. For receivers, the explanation not only presents the truth to which they are entitled, it also has guidance value. From it they learn to adjust habits and, as a result, qualify for credit purchases later.

Because of the legal implications involved in refusing credit, a legal counsel should review your credit refusal letters to ensure that they comply with laws related to fair credit practices. For example, the Equal Credit Opportunity Act (ECOA) requires that the credit applicant be notified of the credit decision within 30 calendar days. Applicants who are denied credit must be informed of the reasons for the refusal. If the decision was based on information obtained from a consumer reporting agency (as opposed to financial statements or other information provided by the applicant), the credit denial may include the name, address, and telephone number of the

Strategic Forces: Legal and Ethical Constraints

The Fair Credit Reporting Act

If you have ever applied for a charge account, a personal loan, insurance, or a job, someone is probably keeping a file on you. This file might contain information on how you pay your bills, or whether you have been sued, arrested, or have filed for bankruptcy in the past seven years. The companies that gather and sell this information are called credit reporting agencies, of which the most common type is the credit bureau. The three main credit bureaus, Equifax, Experian (formerly TRW), and Trans Union, sell information to employers, insurers, and other businesses in the form of consumer reports (also called credit reports). In 1970, Congress passed the Fair Credit Reporting Act to give consumers specific rights in dealing with credit reporting agencies. Amendments to the act that were passed in 1996, and went into effect in September of 1997, extended the protection to the consumer. The federal Fair Credit Reporting Act (FCRA) gives consumers specific protections when they apply for and are denied credit.

- When credit is denied based on information in a credit report, the credit grantor must tell the consumer the name and address of the credit bureau used to secure the information.
- The credit bureau must supply the consumer with a free copy of his or her credit report if the consumer asks for it within 30 days of being denied credit. (Credit bureaus voluntarily extend this time to within 60 days of applying for credit.)
- If the consumer believes that information on the credit report is inaccurate, the credit bureau must investigate the item within a "reasonable time," generally defined as 30 days, and remove the item if it is inaccurate or cannot be verified as accurate.
- Consumers may request that the credit bureau not distribute their names and contact information for unsolicited credit and insurance offers.
- Complaints against credit reporting agencies may be filed with the Federal Trade Commission, Washington, DC.

Responsible consumers should check their credit reports periodically, since information in them could affect their ability to get jobs, mortgages, loans, credit cards, or insurance. The individual may request a copy of his or her credit report by contacting the credit reporting agency, who may not charge more than $8 for the report.

Application

Visit the following Internet site to obtain further information about the Fair Credit Reporting Act:

http://www.social-security-number.com/fcra-reform-act.htm#CONTENT

After reviewing the information, enumerate other specific consumer safeguards provided by the law.

agency. It may also remind applicants that the Fair Credit Reporting Act provides them the right to know the nature of the information in their credit file. In addition, credit denials may include a standard statement that the ECOA prohibits creditors from discriminating against credit applicants on the basis of a number of protected characteristics (race, color, religion, national origin, sex, marital status, age). Additional information related to this legislation is included in the Strategic Forces box above.

> Why discuss reasons for a credit refusal?

To avoid litigation, some companies choose to omit the explanation from the credit denial and invite the applicant to call or come in to discuss the reasons. Alternately, they may suggest that the receiver obtain further information from the credit reporting agency whose name, address, and telephone number are provided.

Assume that a retailer of electronic devices has placed an initial order and requested credit privileges. After examining financial statements that were enclosed, the wholesaler decides the request should be denied. Review the letter in Figure 6-8 to identify techniques used to refuse credit while preserving relations with this customer—who may very well have money in the near future.

FIGURE 6-8
Good example of credit denial.

❶ Implies receipt of the order and uses resale to confirm applicant's good choice of product. Leads to explanation by implying approval of one of the applicant's practices (supplying most recently developed items).
❷ Leads to a discussion of the basis for the refusal and continues with the explanation.
❸ Uses positive language to express the refusal. Conveys "No" to credit purchases by recommending a counterproposal to the refusal.
❹ Looks confidently to the future and reminds the applicant of the commendable practice discussed earlier.
❺ Encourages subsequent application and thus implies continued business is expected.
❻ Reminds the merchant of the desired action on the counterproposal.
❼ Closes with sales promotional material. Uses "timely" to remind the applicant of the commendable business practice and to develop unity.

LONESTAR ELECTRONICS

1800 Tally Ho Street ★ Reno, NV 89510-1800 ★ Telephone: (702) 555-3200 Fax: (702) 555-1039

May 16, 1999

Mr. Samuel Montgomery
Purchasing Agent
Pearson Office Supply
1600 Main Street
Lorain, OH 44052-1600

Dear Mr. Montgomery:

❶ The items listed in your order of May 6 have been selling very rapidly in recent weeks. Supplying customers' demands for the latest in electronic technology is sound business practice.

❷ Another sound practice is careful control of indebtedness, according to specialists in accounting and finance. Their formula for control is to maintain at least a 2-to-1 ratio of current assets to current liabilities. Experience has taught us that, for the benefit of all concerned, credit should be available only to purchasers who meet that ratio. **❸** Because your ratio is approximately $1\frac{1}{4}$ to 1, you are encouraged to make cash purchases and take advantage of a 1 percent discount.

❹ By continuing to supply your customers with timely merchandise, you should be able to improve the ratio. **❺** Then, we would welcome an opportunity to review your credit application. **❻** Use the enclosed envelope to send us your check for $1,487.53 to cover your current order, and your order will be shipped promptly.

❼ Other timely items (such as the most recent in video games) are shown in the enclosed folder.

Sincerely

Ivy Koch

Ivy Koch
Credit Manager

Legal and Ethical Constraints

- Be certain the message complies with laws related to fair credit practices.
- You may omit reasons for the refusal to avoid litigation. Identify the company's policy or seek legal advice.

COMMUNICATION IN ACTION

J. J. Ferguson Prestress-Precast Co., Inc.

Establishing empathy and goodwill with customers helps managers and employees build long-term interpersonal relationships in the workplace. For those who handle credit requests, empathy and goodwill become more important when saying "No" to a credit request. Nowhere is this fact more evident than in the residential and commercial construction industry.

J. J. Ferguson, a prestress-precast concrete company, has been in operation 12 years and is one of only four such companies in the state. To keep J. J. Ferguson successful, Shirley Olson, president, must at times say "No" to credit requests for residential or commercial development. Olson and her father have developed a unique father and daughter business in economically unstable times.

Whether the credit request involves large, state government contracts or small orders of merchandise, Olson is very careful about how she delivers bad news. She explains that a customer who is a poor credit risk today may be a good credit risk six to twelve months from now. "The construction business is very volatile," she says, "and an individual who does $5,000 a month in business today may do $50,000 a month in two years." The future of her company depends on maintaining goodwill with those customers.

To illustrate her point, she cites a recent example. One long-term customer, who at one time had been a good credit risk, had extended his credit beyond the company's limits. When the customer requested additional credit, Olson had to refuse. In doing so, she explains, "I wanted to keep his business but just not extend him credit." However, she manages to maintain empathy and goodwill when facing this difficult challenge of saying "No" to an established customer.

When first facing this challenge, Olson explained to the customer how much she appreciated his business over the years. Olson recognized the fact that he had stayed with J. J. Ferguson Prestress-Precast and with his own company during some tough times. She stated she had extended his credit 90 days further than with other customers.

Because of the volume of his business, she had extended his credit several times. She explained she wanted to keep his business but could not extend it any further. She stated, "As soon as you can reduce terms to 60 days, let's talk again. We'll get back on a credit basis. Until then, stay with us." Finally, Olson communicated that as soon as she received money from him, she would extend credit again. "Extending credit for 60 days in the construction industry is typical," she says, "since most people do not get money for 60 days to pay against their own credit."

Olson's empathy and goodwill with this customer show the importance of building strong relationships. Those relationships have helped provide the long-term business for J. J. Ferguson Prestress-Precast to grow into a successful company.

Applying What You Have Learned

1. What impact did empathy have on the organization and style of Olson's message when denying credit?

2. Assume that you work for J. J. Ferguson Prestress-Precast Co., Inc., and must correspond with Mr. Jim Read, Read Construction Co.; 203 Woolbright Road; Whitehall, OH 43213- 2987. A long-standing customer of six years with an excellent credit rating. Mr. Read has requested additional credit of $30,000 for July. Assume further that Mr. Read had extended his credit beyond the company limit of 60 days and was given an additional 30 days' extension. Write a letter refusing his credit request.

The credit refusal in Figure 6-8 provides an explanation for the refusal and offers a 1 percent discount for goods purchased on a cash basis. No information about a credit reporting agency is necessary because the applicant provided all the information on which the decision was based. It makes no apology for action taken that would only cause the applicant to speculate that the decision was arbitrary.

Including resale is helpful in a credit refusal letter because it

- Might cause credit applicants to prefer your brand and perhaps be willing to buy it on a cash basis.

- Suggests that the writer is trying to be helpful.

- Makes the writing easier—negative thoughts are easier to de-emphasize when cushioned with resale material and when you seem confident of future cash purchases.

- Can confirm the credit applicant's judgment. (Suggesting the applicant made a good choice of merchandise is an indirect compliment.)

6 *Write a letter providing constructive criticism.*

What can be gained from writing a letter that points out another person's mistakes? What are the risks?

Writing a Constructive Criticism

A person who has had a bad experience as a result of another person's conduct may be reluctant to write about that experience. However, because one person took the time to write a letter, many could benefit. Although not always easy or pleasant, writing about negatives can be thought of as a civic responsibility. For example, a person who returns from a long stay at a major hotel might, upon returning home, write a letter to the management commending certain employees. If the stay had not been pleasant and weaknesses in hotel operation had been detected, a tactful letter pointing out the negatives would probably be appreciated. Future guests could benefit from the effort of that one person. Whether negative evaluations are presented in writing or in conversation, the same principles apply: Have a positive intent; be factual; use positive language; and leave judgment to the recipient.

Suppose, for example, consultants sent to identify marketing weaknesses in a regional office had been ineffective. Before writing about the problem, an individual should recognize the following risks: (1) being stereotyped as a complainer, (2) being associated with negative thoughts and perceived in negative terms, or (3) appearing to challenge one of management's prior decisions (choice of the consultants). Yet such risks may be worth taking because of the benefits: (1) The writer gets a feeling of having exercised a responsibility; (2) management learns of changes that need to be made; (3) the team about whom the letter is written modifies techniques and is thus more successful; and (4) other divisions may be exposed to consultants who are more effective.

How can the successful writer distinguish between assessing the person and assessing the person's performance?

In the decision to write about negatives, the primary consideration is intent. If the intent is to hurt or to get even, the message should not be written. Including false information would be *unethical* and *illegal*. To avoid litigation charges and to respond ethically, include only specific facts you can verify and avoid opinions about the person's character or ability. The guidelines for writing legally defensible employee recommendations apply to this letter (see "Negative Recommendations" in Chapter 14.)

In a written message that contains negative information about a person's performance, evaluative words (your opinion) are discouraged. Instead of presenting facts, the following message judges.

Coping with bad news is never fun. When the Buffalo Bills earned the dubious title as the team to suffer the most Super Bowl defeats, team managers rushed in to shore up morale through communication. The management of the team goes into the record books as an example of a well-organized, motivated group that refuses to give up. Instead of despairing over their losses, they bounce back by taking responsibility, acknowledging their strengths, recognizing their losses, determining where they failed, and then acting on what they learned.[2]

Our recent sessions with the home office marketing consultants here in Texas were a complete waste of time.

The consultants knew nothing about our problems in the Southwest and refused to listen to us explain the specific needs of our markets. For these reasons, the consulting effort yielded no useful information.

In the writer's mind, the first sentence may be fair and accurate; but in the mind of the reader, "complete waste of time" may seem overly harsh. The phrase may convey the tone of a habitual fault-finder. Without details, the charges made in the second sentence lack force. If "complete waste of time" strikes the receiver as an exaggeration, the whole message loses impact. Overall, the letter is short, general, and negative. By comparison, the revision in Figure 6-9 is long, specific, and positive.

Handling Special Problems About the Unpleasant

7 *Discuss ways to handle special problems about the unpleasant.*

You will likely find writing the first paragraph, the statement of bad news, and the last paragraph of inductive messages challenging.

First Paragraph

The introductory paragraph of a bad-news letter should let the receiver know the topic of the letter without saying the obvious. It should build a transition into the discussion of reasons without revealing the bad news or leading a receiver to expect good news. The following introductory sentences reveal the subject of the letter, but they have weaknesses:

- *"I am writing in response to your letter requesting. . . ."* The letter is obviously a response; omission of this idea would shorten the message. Beginning with *I* signals the letter may be writer centered.

- *"Your letter of the 14th has been given to me for reply."* The fact the original writer is not responding is obvious and not important.

- *"I can understand how you felt when you were asked to pay an extra $54."* Having requested a refund, a receiver may be led to expect it. In the receiver's

Critique the first paragraph of the letter in Exercise 8 (end-of-chapter activities). Suggest an idea that would be a natural transition to the discussion of the reasons. Repeat for Exercises 9 and 10.

FIGURE 6-9
Good example of a constructive criticism letter.

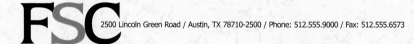

FSC
FREEMAN STEEL CORPORATION

2500 Lincoln Green Road / Austin, TX 78710-2500 / Phone: 512.555.9000 / Fax: 512.555.6573

January 25, 1999

Mr. Jeremy B. Moore
Vice President of Marketing
Clayborne-Taylor Industries
590 Avenue of the Patriots
New York, NY 10002-1590

Dear Mr. Moore:

① Introduces a discussion of the consulting project at the Austin office.

② Tries to convey fair-mindedness and establish credibility by acknowledging good points in a letter that discusses bad points.

③ Presents a statement of fact without labeling it in negative terms. Judgment is left to the reader.

④ Includes a verifiable statement. If such conduct is deplorable, outrageous, or insulting, the reader will be aware of it without the writer's use of such terms.

⑤ Ends on a pleasant note that seeks to add credibility to the preceding negatives. Uses "confidential" as a safeguard; the information is intended for professional use only, not designed to hurt and not to be thought of as gossip.

① A team of New York-based marketing consultants has just left our office. They spent two weeks attempting to pinpoint weaknesses in our marketing strategies.

② Gaining insights from successful approaches used in other divisions of the company is an excellent idea; however, several aspects of this team's performance need to be called to your attention:

③ 1. During their stay, the consultants seemed less interested in analyzing our problems and more concerned with instructing us in the strategies they have used in the Northeast. Although excellent in theory, many of these ideas are not applicable to our particular target market. When we attempted to provide essential information about our market, the team refused to listen.

④ 2. From the day they arrived, the team members clearly communicated their status as the experts. On one occasion, our marketing manager intervened to explain his perspective of a specific problem. The head consultant immediately reminded him that if we could have done the job ourselves, we wouldn't have asked for this team's help. Other similar situations occurred. Consequently, their attitude of superiority soon created a formidable barrier to communication, which obviously restricted the effectiveness of their efforts.

⑤ The marketing department appreciates your efforts to help us identify ways to improve our marketing efforts. In the spirit of helpfulness, I am passing this confidential information to you.

Sincerely,

Kirk Langford

Kirk Langford

Legal and Ethical Constraints

- Is written with the positive intent to help—not to hurt someone or to get even.
- Avoids potential litigation charges by including specific, verifiable facts and avoiding evaluative, judgmental statements.

mind, the empathy displayed in the first sentence would be sufficiently strong to reveal the disappointment of subsequent denial; surely the request is to be extended. When a preceding statement has implied that an affirmative decision will follow, a negative decision is all the more disappointing.

- *"Although the refund requested in your letter of May 1 cannot be approved, . . ."* Immediate emotional reaction may cause the letter to be put aside at this point, or it may interfere with understanding the explanations that follow.

- *"Your request for an adjustment has been considered. However, . . ."* The statement is neutral; it does not reveal whether the answer is "Yes" or "No." Such a beginning has about the same effect as an outright "No" beginning.

The following introductory paragraphs (1) identify the subject of the message and (2) serve as a transition into the discussion of reasons for a denial. (To illustrate transition/cohesion, the first words of the second paragraph are also presented.)

Subject and Transition	Explanation
The double-indemnity feature of your policy has two provisions. In each, the words are "natural causes" and "accidental." "Natural causes" are defined as . . .	*To a policyholder who has submitted a double-indemnity claim, the topic of the letter is recognized immediately. "In each" relates the second sentence to the first; "natural causes" provides the transition from the introductory paragraph to the second paragraph, which begins the explanations.*
Your application was reviewed separately by two loan officers. Each officer considered . . .	*To a potential borrower who has applied for a loan, the subject of the letter is quickly established. The use of "officer" in the second paragraph is a coherence technique—an idea introduced in the first sentence is continued in the second. In the second paragraph, discussion of the officers' reviews will satisfy an expectation aroused in the first sentence.*
After your request for permission to pick up leftover potatoes, we reviewed our experiences of recent years. Last year, two incidents . . .	*An officer of a food-for-the-hungry mission would immediately recognize the letter as a response to a request that the mission be allowed to enter a grower's field and harvest potatoes left by the mechanical pickers. The repetition of "year" ties the second paragraph to the first and indicates that the second paragraph intends to present details of the "experiences" mentioned in the introductory paragraph.*

The preceding effective introductory paragraphs initiate a discussion without stating bad news or leading the receiver to expect good news. Additional ideas can be incorporated into effective beginning paragraphs:

- ***Compliment.*** A letter denying a customer's request could begin by recognizing that customer's promptness in making payments.

- **Point of agreement.** If the letter being answered makes a statement with which you can agree, a sentence that reveals agreement could get the letter off to a positive discussion of other points.

- **Good news.** When a letter contains a request that must be refused and another that is being answered favorably, beginning with the favorable answer can be effective.

- **Resale.** If the subject of correspondence is a product that was purchased, a refusal could begin with some favorable statement about the product.

- **A review.** Refusal of a current request could be introduced by referring to the initial transaction or by reviewing certain circumstances that preceded the transaction.

- **Gratitude.** Although an unjustified request may have been made, the receiver may have done or said something for which you are grateful. An expression of gratitude could be used as a positive beginning.

Bad-News Sentence

In a sense, a paragraph that presents the reasoning behind a refusal at least partially conveys the refusal before it is stated directly or indirectly. Yet one sentence needs to convey (directly or by implication) the conclusion to which the preceding details have been leading. The most important considerations are *positive language* and *emphasis*. The following sentences illustrate contrasting treatment of the bad news:

<table>
<tr><td>

Could approving the $1,500 credit suffice without stating directly that the $3,000 has been denied?

</td></tr>
</table>

- *"Your request is therefore being denied"* or *"We are therefore denying your request."* Being negative, the idea is not pleasant. Stated in negative terms, the idea is still less pleasant. Both sentences seem to heighten abrasiveness through the use of emphasis techniques. The simple sentences are emphatic. "Denied" stands out vividly in the first sentence because it is the last word. The second sentence is in first person and active voice, which are emphatic.

- *"The preceding figures do not justify raising your credit limit to $3,000 as you requested, but they do justify raising the limit to $1,500."* The sentence uses negative language, but places the negative idea in a long, two-clause sentence that includes a positive idea.

Implication is a helpful technique to use to soften the impact of a negative idea. The following sentences illustrate commendable techniques for *implying* a refusal:

Refusal Statement	Explanation
Although the Bynum Road property was selected as the building site, nearness to the railroad was considered a plus for the Hampton property. (Statement made to the owner of Hampton.)	*Reveals what was* not *done by stating what was* done. *Note also the passive construction and the complex sentence, both of which de-emphasize. "Bynum Road property was selected"—the bad news—appears in the dependent clause, which is less emphatic than an independent clause. Inclusion of a positive (nearness to the railroad) assists in de-emphasizing the negative.*
If the price were $15,000, the contract would have been accepted.	*States a condition under which the answer would have been "Yes" instead of "No." Note use of the subjunctive words "if" and "would."*

Can you relate to the value of balancing negative feedback with a few positives when your performance on the job or in class is being critiqued? How does the balanced approach affect your feeling toward the sender and the task at hand? Give examples.

By accepting the arrangement, the ABC Company would have tripled its insurance costs.	*States the obviously unacceptable results of complying with a request.*

Last Paragraph

After presenting valid reasons and a tactful refusal, the closing paragraph should include useful information and demonstrate empathy. It cannot do so by including statements such as these:

- *"We trust this explanation is satisfactory."* This statement could be taken as a confession of doubt about the validity of the decision.

- *"We hope you will understand our position."* This statement may imply doubt about the receiver's ability to understand. Use of "position" seems to heighten controversy; positions are expected to be defended.

- *"We are sorry to disappoint you."* This statement risks a negative retort: "If it made you feel so bad, why did you do it?" It can also be interpreted as an apology for the action taken. If a decision merits an apology, its validity is questionable.

- *"Thank you for your interest."* This well-worn statement is often used thoughtlessly. Some refusals are addressed to people who have apparently *not* been interested enough to listen, read, or remember; otherwise, they would not have made the requests. For them, the sentence is inappropriate. For others, it may seem shallow and superficial.

- *"When we can be of further help, please do not hesitate to call or write."* This sentence is well worn and negative. *Further* help may seem especially inappropriate to someone who has just read a denial. The writer may see the *explanations* as helpful, but the receiver may think the *denial* is being labeled as "helpful."

The final paragraph is usually shorter than the preceding explanatory paragraphs. Sometimes, a one-sentence closing is enough; other messages may require two or three sentences. The final sentence should seem like an *appropriate* closing; that is, it should bring a unifying quality to the whole message. Repetition of a word (or reference to some positive idea) that appears early in the letter serves this purpose well. Restatement of the refusal (or direct reference to it) would only serve to emphasize it. Possibilities for the final sentence include reference to some pleasant aspect of the preceding discussion, resale, sales promotional material, an alternative solution to the receiver's problem, some future aspect of the business relationship, or an expression of willingness to assist in some *other* way. Consider the following closures that use the preceding suggestions:

> Why should a reference to the refusal not be included in the final paragraph?

Closing Statement	Explanation
Your addition of the home mortgage rider to your policy last year was certainly a wise decision.	*Refers to something pleasant from the preceding discussion. "Home mortgage" and other provisions had been mentioned in the early part of a letter to a client who was refused a double-indemnity settlement.*
According to a recent survey, a four-headed VCR produces sound qualities that are far superior; it was an ideal choice.	*Uses resale, a reminder that his four-headed VCR has a superior feature. His request for free repair had been denied.*

Mini-sized compacts and adapters are now available; see the enclosed folder.

Our representative will show you some samples during next week's sales call.

If you would like to see the orientation film we show to management trainees, you would be most welcome.

Includes sales promotional material. Request for free repair had been denied.

Looks to a future event. The samples had been proposed as a possible solution to the receiver's problem.

Seeks to show a good attitude by offering to do something else. The receiver had been refused permission to interview certain employees on the job.

Recall an incident where you received or communicated a disappointing message. Did the sender apply the principles presented in this chapter? Can you suggest ways the message could have been improved?

The principles that apply to writing bad-news letters also apply to oral messages that convey bad news. Before constructing a bad-news message, study carefully the overall suggestions in the "General Writing Guidelines" placed before the chapter exercises in Chapter 5. Then, study the specific suggestions in the following "Check Your Writing" checklist. Compare your work with this checklist again after you have written a rough draft and make any revisions.

SUMMARY

1. **List the steps in the inductive outline and identify the advantages of using it to convey bad news.** When the reader can be expected to be *displeased* by the message, the reasons for the refusal are presented before the main idea. The inductive approach is appropriate for letters denying an adjustment, refusing an order for merchandise, denying a favor, refusing credit, and sending a constructive criticism.

   The steps in the inductive outline include (1) introducing the topic with a neutral idea that sets the stage for the explanation; (2) presenting a concise, logical explanation for the refusal; (3) implying or stating the refusal using positive language; and (4) closing with a positive, courteous ending that shifts the focus away from the bad news.

2. **Write letters refusing a request.** A letter refusing a request begins with a neutral idea and presents the reasons before the refusal. The close may offer a counterproposal—an alternative to the action requested.

3. **Write letters denying a claim.** A letter denying a claim begins with a neutral or factual sentence that leads to the reason for the refusal. In the opening sentence you might include resale to reaffirm the reader's confidence in the merchandise or services. Next, present the explanation for the refusal and then the refusal in a positive, nonemphatic manner. Close with a positive thought such as sales promotional material that indicates you expect to do business with the customer again.

4. **Write letters refusing to complete an order.** A letter refusing an order implies receipt of the order and uses resale to reaffirm the customer's confidence in the merchandise. Continue with reasons for selling the merchandise through dealers and benefits to the customer. Close with information needed for the customer to reorder through the proper channel.

5. **Write letters denying credit.** Credit refusal letters must comply with laws related to fair credit practices and should be reviewed carefully by legal counsel. Begin the letter by implying receipt of an order and using resale that could convince the applicant to buy your merchandise on a cash basis when he or she learns later that credit has been denied. You may provide an explanation for the refusal and encourage the customer to apply for credit later or offer a discount on cash purchases. Your legal counsel may advise that you omit the explanation and invite the applicant to call or come in to discuss the reasons or to obtain more information from the credit reporting agency whose name, address, and telephone number you provide in the letter.

6. **Write letters providing constructive criticism.** The motive for writing letters providing constructive criticism should be to help—not to get even. The letter includes verifiable facts and omits evaluative words, allowing the reader to make logical judgments based on facts.

7. **Discuss ways to handle special problems about the unpleasant.** Writing the first paragraph, the bad-news sentence, and the last paragraph of a bad-news letter present special problems.

   First Sentence. The first sentence of a bad-news letter should identify the subject of the message without

UNPLEASANT MESSAGES

Content

- Be sure the principal idea (the unpleasant idea or the refusal) is sufficiently clear.
- Use sufficient supporting details and present them in a logical sequence.
- Verify accuracy of acts or figures.
- Structure the message to meet ethical legal requirements.

Organization

- Structure the first sentence to introduce the general subject
  - without stating the bad news.
  - without leading a receiver to expect good news.
  - without making such an obvious statement as "I am replying to your letter" or "Your letter has been received."
- Place details or explanations before bad news.
- Precede the main idea (unpleasant idea) with meaningful discussion.
- Use a closing sentence that is positive (an alternative, resale, or sales promotion).

Style

- Write clearly and concisely (e.g., words are easily understood).

- Use techniques of subordination to keep the bad news from emerging with unnecessary vividness. For example, bad news
  - appears in a dependent clause.
  - is stated in passive voice.
  - is revealed through indirect statement.
  - is revealed through the use of subjunctive mood.
- Use first person sparingly or not at all.
- Make ideas cohere (changes in thought are not abrupt).
- Use sentences that are relatively short and vary in length and structure.
- Keep paragraphs relatively short.
- Use original expression (sentences are not copied directly from the definition of the problem or from sample letters in the text); omit clichés.

Mechanics

- Ensure that keyboarding, spelling, grammar, and punctuation are perfect.

Letters

- Use correct letter format (block, modified block, or simplified) and punctuation style (open or mixed).
- Balance letter on the page.
- Include standard letter parts in appropriate position.
- Include special parts if necessary (subject line, enclosure, copy, etc.)

stating the obvious and serve as a transition into the explanation. Effective beginning paragraphs might include a compliment, a point of agreement, good news, resale, a review of the circumstances related to the message, or an expression of gratitude.

Bad-News Sentence Preceded with Reasons. When writing the bad-news sentence, avoid overly negative words and statements that automatically set up barriers to your message. Instead, use positive techniques such as stating what you can do rather than what you cannot do, including a positive fact in the same sentence with the negative idea, or offering a counterproposal to minimize the receiver's disappointment.

Use the subjunctive mood or imply the bad news if you believe the reader will understand your refusal

clearly. If you must state the bad news directly, avoid using a simple sentence for the refusal unless your intention is to emphasize the "no." Place the negative message in the dependent clause of a complex sentence to de-emphasize the negative.

Last Paragraph. The closing paragraph should demonstrate empathy but should not include statements that may cause the reader to question the fairness of your decision. Do not mention the refusal in the final paragraph. Instead, end with an idea that brings a positive, unifying quality to the letter; e.g., referring to a pleasant idea mentioned earlier in the letter, or use resale, sales promotional material, or a counterproposal.

REFERENCES

[1]Dimond, K. (1997, March). Antidote for a crisis. *Oregon Business*, 28.

[2]Schroer, J. (1994, February 3). Bowled-over Bills tackle morale issue. *USA Today*. p. 5B.

[3]Levy, S., & Hafner, K. (1997). The day the world shuts down. *Newsweek*, 52.

REVIEW QUESTIONS

1. Explain the appropriate outline for a letter that conveys bad news. (Obj. 1)

2. What two functions does the first paragraph serve? Does "I am responding to your letter of the 25th" accomplish both of these functions? Explain. (Obj. 1, 7)

3. Discuss two reactions the reader might have toward a message if the refusal precedes the explanation. (Obj. 1)

4. What would be the disadvantage of waiting until the last sentence to convey bad news? (Obj. 1)

5. How can writers reduce the risk that readers will become impatient while reading explanations that precede bad news? (Obj. 1)

6. What objectives should the final paragraph accomplish? Is placing the refusal statement in a paragraph by itself acceptable? (Obj. 1, 7)

7. List conditions under which a writer would be justified in stating bad news in the first sentence. (Obj. 1)

8. In which part of a refusal letter would resale and sales promotional material be most appropriate? (Obj. 1–7)

9. List three reasons businesses might refuse to send merchandise customers have ordered. (Obj. 4)

10. What is a counterproposal? How does it assist it achieving the human relations goal of business communication? (Obj. 1–7)

11 Discuss the legal implications involved in writing credit refusals. (Obj. 5)

12. Why should judgmental terms be avoided when writing about someone's failure to do a job well? What other advice would you offer for writing this sensitive letter? (Obj. 6)

13. List six recommended ideas for introducing the bad news in the first paragraph. Which of these ideas is used for each of the good examples in this chapter? (Obj. 7)

14 Should the closing sentence apologize for action taken? Explain. (Obj. 7)

15. Should a writer strive to achieve unity by referring to the statement of refusal in the last paragraph? Explain. (Obj. 7)

EXERCISES

1. **Appropriateness of the Inductive Outline (Obj. 1)**
Team up with a classmate to defend the use of the inductive or the deductive outline for bad-news messages. Consider whether your argument would vary if you were communicating with people of other cultures or other specific audiences. Consult the business literature to provide realistic examples and viewpoints that may strengthen your position.

2. **Critique of Bad-News Letters Produced by Real Companies (Obj. 1–7)**
Locate an example of both a well-written and a poorly written bad-news letter. Analyze the strengths and weaknesses of each document. Be prepared to discuss in class.

3. **Effective Opening and Closing Paragraphs (Obj. 1–7)**
Study each of the good examples in the chapter and compile a list of the approaches used to open and to close the letter in a positive way.

4. **De-emphasizing Bad News (Obj. 1, 7)**
Prepare a list of techniques for de-emphasizing a refusal. List each technique for projecting a positive tone and de-emphasizing negative ideas discussed in Chapter 3 ("Project a Positive, Tactful Tone" and "Emphasize Important Ideas" sections). Provide an example of your own for each technique.

5. **Determining Sequence of Ideas: Deductive or Inductive (Obj. 1)**
   Identify whether each of the following letters should be written deductively or inductively based on the reader's likely reaction to the message.

   a. A letter to the manufacturer of a national treadmill company explaining dissatisfaction with the unit and requesting a refund. A television advertisement shows an exerciser running on the unit, but the customer cannot run on the unit without being pushed off the front.

   b. A letter from the manufacturer of a national-brand treadmill refusing to extend an adjustment to a customer who cannot run on the unit.

   c. A letter to an investment manager requesting information about the benefits of front-load or back-load mutual funds.

   d. A letter refusing a customer's request to reduce his monthly payment for Internet services. He contends busy signals prevented him from connecting a majority of the time.

   e. A letter from an automobile dealer informing a customer that the delivery of a custom-order vehicle will be delayed two months.

   f. A letter from an appliance manufacturer authorizing the replacement of an under-counter ice machine that is still under warranty.

   g. A letter from a financial planner apologizing for her failure to place an order to buy mutual funds for a customer.

   h. A letter from the chief financial officer of a local business agreeing to serve on a fund-raising committee for a community service organization.

   i. A letter extending appreciation for the outstanding work of an assessment team that recently reviewed a company's computer system for potential problems with the arrival of the 21st century. (Refer to the "Real Time Case Using the WWW" at the end of the chapter for additional information about the Year 2000 problem.)

   j. A letter acknowledging shipment of an order and extending credit to a first-time customer.

6. **Inductive Openings (Obj. 1–7)**
   Revise the following openings so that they are inductive.

   a. Because your facsimile machine did not show any defects in workmanship until three months after the warranty expired, we cannot honor your claim.

   b. Although we received many applications for this position, we have chosen an internal candidate.

   c. Winterson Associates, Inc. cannot participate in the Crown Club Charity Benefit this year.

   d. This letter is in response to your complaint of April 9.

   e. Company policy does not allow me to approve the proposed transaction.

   f. Our departmental award went to Charles Henning; you were our first runner-up.

   g. We cannot grant you a refund. However, if you will agree to pay the shipping costs, we will send replacements for your defective spinning reels.

7. **Positive Tone (Obj. 1–7)**
   Revise the following sentences to ensure positive tone.

   a. We cannot accept an application sent after May 9.

   b. Employees cannot smoke in the main office.

   c. I am sorry, but we cannot be responsible for the service charges on your car; the damage occurred at the dealership, not our factory.

   d. Your request for transfer to Kyoto, Japan, has been denied.

   e. We cannot accept this poorly organized report.

8. **Document for Analysis: Denying a Request (Obj. 2)**
   Analyze the following letter. Pinpoint its strengths and weaknesses and then revise the letter as directed by your instructor.

   Dear Donna:

   I am pleased and honored to have been asked to serve as president of the Flint Jaycees for the coming year.

   However, I regret to inform you that I cannot serve in this important position. Last year, obligations kept me from attending seven of the twenty-five meetings. Unfortunately, commitments for the coming year are even greater than last year. The position of president requires a tremendous amount of attention—much more than I can give at this particular time.

   Once again, I appreciate the confidence you have placed in me but am sorry that my plans preclude my serving as president this year. I look forward to participating in this year's activities and am especially eager to chair the Goodwill Marathon project again this year.

   Sincerely,

   Grant S. Hutchins

9. **Document for Analysis: Denying an Adjustment (Obj. 3)**
   Analyze the following letter. Pinpoint its strengths and weaknesses and then revise the letter as directed by your instructor.

Dear Mr. and Mrs. Bailey:

We are sorry to hear about your painting being damaged during your recent move. We at Bartlett Movers strive to maintain the highest quality service, so this kind of thing rarely happens.

Unfortunately, we cannot reimburse you for the complete value of the painting. As you may recall, our insurance policy, which you signed before the move, clearly states that only the material cost of any damages are covered. You may wish to review the policy. I have attached a copy.

Enclosed is a check for $250, the maximum amount for which we can insure this particular item.

If you have any questions, please do not hesitate to call me. Thank you for using Bartlett Movers, and I wish you the best in your new home.

10. **Document for Analysis: Constructive Criticism (Obj. 6)**

Analyze the following letter. Pinpoint its strengths and weaknesses and then revise the letter as directed by your instructor.

Dear Pierre:

Rebecca Fuquay, a junior accountant in your firm, has been working with us on-site for about three weeks, and her conduct is deplorable. Her demeanor is absolutely unprofessional; her "no-problem" attitude has generated so much friction that a valued employee refuses to work in the same room with her.

Although extensive knowledge of auditing is important, Fuquay's personal shortcomings far outweigh her technical expertise. I seriously hope Fuquay is able to take steps to correct the situation.

E-MAIL APPLICATION

As an account manager of Patriot, a manufacturer of limited-edition furniture, you recently shipped six highback, distressed-wood chairs to Nina Hughes, an interior designer who is one of your premier accounts. Because these chairs were an introductory item, Nina's customer had waited for over a year for delivery. You received a voice-mail message from Nina explaining that the chairs will not stay together. The customer has tried gluing them, but the supports still come apart. You reported the problem to product development, who uncovered a flaw in the design of this chair—the supports are too short for the chair. Because you want to answer Nina's question as quickly as possible, you prepare to telephone her with an explanation and a promise to rush delivery of the replacement chairs produced with the modified design, along with a $300 credit for the inconvenience this error has caused. E-mail your instructor explaining how you intend to deliver this negative news with your long-standing customer (you're replacing the chairs but they must wait approximately three months for delivery). Follow the same principles for oral communication as you would for a written message. You instructor may direct you to send a letter as a written follow-up to the telephone call.

APPLICATIONS

1. **Request Refusal: Borrowers Cannot Open Up a Locked-in Interest Rate (Obj. 2)**

When they completed a mortgage application on June 7, Will and Jennifer Lee "locked in" on an 8 percent mortgage loan. When they closed on the house on June 27 (legally bought the house), the prevailing rates were lower than the 8 percent they locked in. Thus, they have requested that the bank lower the interest rate; that is, to open up the locked-in interest rate. The bank must refuse to lower the rate. The lock-in protects the borrower from rising interest rates while the mortgage application is processed. A lock-in is *not* a guarantee that a borrower will get lower rates should interest rates drop.

Required: As the loan officer, write the Lees explaining that the bank cannot lower their interest rate. The address is 103 Pinebrook Lane, Bowling Green, KY 42101-0876.

2. **Request Refusal: Restocking Fee to Be Paid on Returned Merchandise (Obj. 2)**

Snowcap Limited, a tourist shop located near a popular ski resort, purchased its stock of skis from Downhill Manufacturing. At the end of the season, Snowcap's owner, Lee Wheeler, returned the unsold skis and requested a full refund of $2,435. Downhill Manufacturing charges a 15 percent restocking fee for returned merchandise; this policy is printed clearly on the inside cover of its catalog and in bold print at the bottom of the order form. Operators explain this charge to customers placing orders on the company's 800 number.

Required: As the credit manager at Downhill Manufacturing, write Lee Wheeler, enclosing the refund check and explaining the deduction for the 15 percent restocking fee. The address is 905 Southhaven Street, Boise, ID 83707-7313.

3. **Request Refusal: Parent Company Refuses to Continue Support of Not-for-Profit Program (Obj. 2)**
ChemCon Engineering, a family-owned business, has underwritten an adult literacy program on public television for the past five years. The owners and the public relations director believe that the financial support of this worthwhile project has been a favorable public relations tool. Recently, ChemCon was bought out by Petrol Corp. When approached by the television program director to renew financial commitment to the literacy program, the new president refused. The president is not opposed to efforts to increase adult literacy; however, top management at Petrol sees little, if any, merit in sponsoring public television programs. Therefore, no advertising dollars are channeled into projects such as this one.

Required: As the public relations director, write the letter to the television station refusing to contribute to the program. Address it to Lisa Aultman, Program Director, WRMW Television, P.O. Drawer 93001, Salem, OR 97301-8461.

4. **Bad News to Community: Decision to Relocate Corporate Headquarters Is Final (Obj. 2)**
Recently the board of directors of Regal Discount Stores decided to relocate its corporate headquarters from New York City to one of the city's suburbs. The mayor of New York City, James Flynn, has written the board urging it to reconsider its decision to relocate. Despite the individual members' personal preference to keep the headquarters in the city, the board agreed that the decision to relocate was in the best interest of the company. The following factors led to the decision: (1) The lower tax rates in the suburbs would provide an economic advantage; (2) the company's salary structure is affected by the direct and indirect costs of commuting required of employees who live in the suburbs; (3) during the past few years, the company has had difficulty recruiting managerial talent, who prefer living in the suburbs; and (4) several major competitors are already located in the suburbs.

Required: As chairman of the board, write a letter to the mayor refusing his request. Address it to James Flynn, Mayor of New York City, New York, NY 10001-7600. Consult a reference manual to identify the appropriate courtesy title and salutation for this public official.

5. **Refusal: Unable to Speak at Seminar (Obj. 2)**
For several years, you as a civic-minded accountant have conducted seminars on investments for various organizations. This year, the Beta Alpha Psi chapter at the local university has asked you to assist with the annual VITA (Voluntary Income Tax Assistance) program. Specifically,

the group wishes you to devote two evenings to assist the accounting students as they complete income tax returns. The dates selected are during the last two weeks in March—a particularly inconvenient time for you. You need every moment that month if you are to satisfy the needs of your clients.

Required: Write a letter refusing the request to Dr. Marion Collier, Accounting Department, Central State College, P.O. Drawer 419, Oakwood, IA 63981-0532.

6. **Client Bad News: Interim Audit Must Be Rescheduled (Obj. 1, 7)**
The auditors from Lindsay & Associates are due to arrive Monday to begin the interim audit of FTE Enterprises. As FTE's controller, you just learned today (Wednesday) that a group of business executives from Moscow will arrive on Monday to examine your accounting information systems. Previously you had agreed to assist this group in implementing similar accounting strategies in their country whenever they could arrange to be in Milwaukee. Because the visitation involves not only you but the entire MIS Department and several employees in the Accounting Department, you must arrange for the interim audit to be rescheduled.

As you plan your message, consider the following issues:

1. What method would be most effective for transmitting this timely message? The postponement is more than a mere inconvenience because staff assignments are made several months in advance.

2. How can you organize your reasons for the postponement? Could a deductive outline be used effectively in this situation?

3. What could you do to make the rescheduling process easier in order to generate goodwill in the closing words?

Required: Depending on your answers to these questions, complete one of the following: (a) Write a letter to Paul Weseli, Lindsay & Associates, 411 McDowell Road, Charleston, IN 47111-0411 (include any necessary mailing notations), or (b) outline what you will say if you telephone Paul personally to explain the situation.

7. **Community Service Bad News: Sorry, But You Did Not Make the Team (Obj. 1, 7)**
Your job as loan manager of a local bank requires a great deal of writing, but today's project could prove to be one of your most challenging yet. For the first time, you are coaching a Little League baseball team for 12-year-old boys. Last night you completed tryouts and promised the players they would be notified of the results within a couple of days. As you left the field, one of the veteran coaches handed you the following form letter most coaches mail to players who do not make the team.

April 25, 1999

Dear Player:

Thank you for trying out for the 12-year-old competitive baseball team. However, I am sorry to inform you that you did not make it this year.

I hope your plans are to continue with baseball whether it is Little League or some other team.

Sincerely,

Glenn Brister and Phil Landrum

You appreciate the coach's willingness to help, but you believe this insensitive letter may damage these young boys' self-esteem and squelch their enthusiasm for baseball.

Required: Revise the form letter to the youths who did not make your team. You may want to customize the letter to provide specific reasons for a player's not making the team and suggest ways to improve his game. Address a sample letter to a fictitious player.

8. **Adjustment Refusal: Must Pay for an Appearance by a Substitute Celebrity (Obj. 3)**
Assume you are a sport agent and must refuse a claim from John Kelly, a hospital administrator who refuses to pay for a speaking engagement. The hospital had arranged for (specify an Olympic athlete) to deliver the keynote address at the grand opening of the community's new Healthplex. As a result of an injury to (specify an Olympian) the day before the appearance, a teammate was sent as a substitute. Mr. Kelly insists that the hospital chose the original athlete because he/she is an Olympic gold medalist, was born and reared in a nearby city, and is known and supported by the community; the substitute is not an Olympian and is known by few in the community. You must deny the adjustment because you believe you acted in good faith. Even though the accident was beyond your control and occurred at the last minute, you quickly arranged for a substitute athlete who is an exceptional speaker. The substitute told you that the speech went really well; he/she connected well with the audience, signed many autographs, and had interesting conversations with fitness enthusiasts of all ages and many community leaders.

Required: Write to John Kelly, Hospital Administrator, Woodlake Memorial Hospital, 1800 Hospital Road, Arkadelphia, AR 71923-1800.

9. **Adjustment Refusal: Caterer Must Charge for Additional Guests (Obj. 3)**
PartyTime Limited recently catered an annual staff/alumni banquet for SPL Industries. Unfortunately, when reporting the number of attendees, SPL's function organizer did not consider the number of alumni who would bring guests. Soon after the guests began to arrive, PartyTime's staff recognized the

problem and began improvising to accommodate 25 additional guests. Only a few people were aware of the confusion, and the food was served just a few minutes late. The head of accounting at SPL has refused to pay the charges for the additional guests. She insists that SPL agreed to pay the contracted rate provided in writing prior to the banquet.

Required: As manager of PartyTime Limited, write the head of accounting, refusing to allow her to deduct the charges for the additional service. Remind her that the additional charge includes only the cost of providing the food for the extra guests and not the labor involved in these last-minute preparations. Address your letter to Dena Marcum, Accounting and Budget, SPL Industries, 7821 South Third Street, Conway, AR 72032-7839.

10. **Adjustment Refusal: Price Reductions in Computer Industry Are Inevitable (Obj. 3)**
As a sales rep for Halbert Computer Systems, you recently sold Franklin Savings and Loan a local area network to replace its current obsolete system. A week later, the client asked you to delay installation of the system to allow the MIS Department ample time to finalize preparations for the system. Since the sale, the price of this system has dropped 15 percent. Jon Whiteside, the MIS manager at Franklin, learned of the price reduction and has requested a similar reduction in the cost of its system. Unfortunately, you had already purchased the hardware when the client asked for the delay and did not benefit from a manufacturer's price reduction.

Required: Write the refusal to Jon Whiteside, Franklin Savings and Loan, 8324 Randall Street, Cheyenne, WY 82009-8324.

11. **Order Refusal: Receiver's and Speakers' Capabilities Don't Match (Obj. 4)**
You have received a large order of a custom sound system from First National Bank. The bank plans to offer the system as a gift to customers purchasing a $25,000, five-year certificate of deposit. You have a problem with the order. The frequency response of the receiver is 20 to 20,000 Hz, but the frequency response for the speakers is only 35 to 18,000 Hz. Thus, the stereo receiver has the capacity to produce sound with deep, rich bass and high treble, but the speakers will not be capable of projecting these sounds. Suggest to the bank that they consider a system having components with matching frequency responses. The price for this new system will be slightly more than the system the bank ordered.

Required: Write the letter explaining the need to alter the component choices. Use an electronics catalog (printed or on-line) to specify the model numbers for the receiver and the speakers you are recommending; cite the frequency response of each model. Provide your telephone number and e-mail address so that the bank can call for additional information and authorize the order. Address the letter to Daniel Rogers, Vice President of Marketing, First National Bank, 54 Cloverleaf Mall, Harrisburg, PA 17105-0054.

12. **Order Refusal: Dry Sprinkler System Is More Appropriate for Cold Climates (Obj. 4)**
As the owner of Harrison Plumbing Contractors, you have reviewed the specifications for a new clubhouse at the Edgewood Golf Club. You are concerned that the plans include a traditional wet sprinkler system that carries water in the pipes to be used in case of fire. If exposed to subfreezing temperatures over extended periods, the water in the pipes will freeze and then break, causing water damage to the structure. This freezing problem has caused unnecessary damages to several of your previous contracts; therefore, you now recommend installation of a dry sprinkler system. In this system, the pipes contain pressurized air that opens a valve for sprinkler action when the fire is detected. Because the dry system is less conventional and more expensive than the wet system, few architects are including the dry systems in their blueprints.

The client has three options: (1) authorize the architect to redesign the blueprint to include the dry system, (2) instruct you to install the wet system with a heat source in the attic to be used during subfreezing temperatures, or (3) arrange for another contractor to install the wet system (without the heat source). You are convinced that any dissatisfaction resulting from the unnecessary damages caused by broken pipes will more adversely affect your company than sacrificing the contract.

Required: Write the letter explaining the need for the dry system and presenting the three options. Mention a brochure that you are including that explains and illustrates the dry system. Address the letter to Mr. Keith Gaskin, Manager, Edgewood Golf Club, 957 Edgewood Boulevard, Springfield, IL 62701-3498.

13. **Credit Refusal: New Credit Policies Affect Real Estate Loans Adversely (Obj. 5)**
Walley Construction Corp. has requested $14 million from Colonial National Bank to build a 200,000-square-foot shopping center. Three major chains (department store, discount store, and electronics/video outlet)—adequate anchors for this size center—have already signed leases, and 80 percent of the remaining space has been leased. Walley has presented budgets showing how the income from this center can service the loan, and the development itself is offered as collateral for the loan.

Under previous lending guidelines, the bank could approve a real estate loan if it had reasonable assurance that the borrower could repay the loan from either the income from operations or the sale of the development. Because of the current decline in the economy, however, lending guidelines for real estate loans have become stricter. The borrower must now provide assurance that the loan can be repaid from sources other than the development itself, typically the income or assets of other businesses or personal investments. Thus, these new guidelines are designed to ensure payment of the loan regardless of the success or failure of the proposed development.

Required: As the loan manager, write a letter to Julian Walley refusing to approve the loan. Be certain to adhere to the legal requirements for credit letters presented in the chapter. Address the letter to P.O. Box 9408, Eau Claire, WI 54703-9408.

14. **Credit Refusal: Loan Denied for Poor Credit Customer (Obj. 5)**
Having decided to build an addition to their home, Larry and Alice Sherman made an application for a $15,000 loan from a personal finance company. A report from a consumer reporting agency revealed a consistent record of slow payment. On more than one occasion, they paid only after forceful attempts at collection.

Required: As manager of the local branch of the finance company, write a refusal letter. Provide the name, address, and telephone number of the consumer reporting agency and invite the Shermans to come in to discuss the refusal. Write to Larry and Alice Sherman, P.O. Box 432, Baxter, WI 54321-5590.

15. **Constructive Criticism: Surly Manager Turns Off Potential Buyers (Obj. 6)**
Windham Construction is developing a new residential subdivision in an attractive location near the city park and the elementary school. Jackson has sold a number of lots and is building custom homes for these customers. For the most part, however, he is building "spec" homes to be sold by Lakeland Realty. As a realtor of Lakeland Realty, you are showing these spec homes at various stages of construction to prospective buyers. A couple you were sure would buy one of the most desirable homes in the subdivision just called to say they are not interested. When questioned about their decision, they were not reluctant to admit they were turned off by Gene Stuart, the manager of the construction crew. You understand them exactly, for you also disapprove of Stuart's behavior and are certain you have lost other sales for the same reason. On several occasions, you have observed Stuart raising his voice at workers and using profanity and vulgar comments. The tone of his voice and his belittling comments are embarrassing to you, the prospective buyers, and the workers. Stuart refuses to offer common courtesies such as speaking to you or even acknowledging your presence when you enter a construction site. He refuses to answer simple questions about construction materials, design, or construction methods, saying he's

too busy to talk with potential owners. His uncontrolled temper and aloofness are inappropriate for a manager who is representing the quality of the company's work.

Required: Write a letter to Windham Construction.

Your intent is to alert the owner of Stuart's shortcomings so that steps can be taken to help Stuart modify his actions. Address the letter to David Windham, Owner, Windham Construction, 7315 South Bradford Street, Burlington, KS 66413-7315.

REAL-TIME INTERNET CASE

Are We Ready for Year 2000?

Will power plants shut down and your telephone go out? Will your Social Security checks disappear into cyberspace? Will your bank account vanish? Could these catastrophes, and more, really happen? Incredibly, according to computer experts, corporate information officers, and congressional leaders, the answer is "Yes, yes, 2000 times yes."[3] Countless billions of dollars are being spent by business, industry, and the government to prevent the certain disaster that will occur if computer systems are left as they are.

The year 2000 looms ominously for several reasons. First of all, the year 2000 will require four digits for dates in computers that can accommodate only two digits. Computers have traditionally dropped the first two digits of a year to save precious storage space; thus, 1951 would become "51." When the clocks turn to the year 2000, the "00" will be interpreted to mean 1900. Correcting the two-digit problem is much more complex than it first appears. In most mainframe programs, the date appears about once every 50 lines of code. Typically, finding those particular lines is difficult because the original programs, often written in ancient COBOL computer language, are quirky and undocumented. Few of today's programmers are skilled in COBOL.

A second problem with the year 2000 is that it is a leap year. By convention, the first year of any century is not a leap year, except for every fourth century—2000 is it. Many software programs were written by people who didn't know this. For instance, the date functions in the first releases of Lotus, Excel, and Quattro Pro did not handle February 29, 2000, correctly, and many applications still do not. Networked systems will be a real nightmare; all you need is one node in an application system on the network to reject Leap Year Day, and the whole network is useless for that day and for probably several days to follow.

A third problem is often called the millennium factor. Computer programs have been doing arithmetic and comparisons based on the year-in-century and not on the year. For instance a 30-year mortgage taken out in 1992 will be paid out in the year 2022; but when you subtract the two year-in-centuries, you get $22 - 92 = -70$ years. It's not likely that the mortgage could be paid off in a negative time period! Product-warranty time calculations are also affected, and some warranties are already being dishonored because the service schedule dates and manufacturing dates cannot be resolved correctly. Geriatrics patients will also be assigned to children's wards in hospitals because of the two-digit birth/year problem. The real question is whether we will correct the problems in time

Hindsight is 20/20. The year 2000 problem could have been completely prevented had early computer developers envisioned the degree to which the microprocessor would change their lives. Surely no one in the early 1950s could have imagined that everything from your alarm clock to your car would be computerized. The short-term space-saving goal justified the use of only two digits for dates. How many of today's business decisions will be seen in retrospect as monumental disasters?

Visit the following Web sites and complete the activities as directed by your instructor.

Internet Sites

http://www.nyx.net/~smanley/cs3113/millenium.html
http://www.datamation.com/PlugIn/issues/1996/jan1/StartFixingYear.html
http://csn.uneb.edu/year2000AreYouReady.htm

Activities

1. Prepare an oral presentation that presents information on projected costs to business and government to solve, and not solve, Year 2000 problems.

2. In the panic that ensues as the fixed deadline approaches for correcting Year 2000 problems, computer consultants are emerging to offer solutions to distressed companies and agencies. Some fear that exploitation will likely occur in the form of price gouging. Discuss the ethical implications of charging "whatever the traffic will bear" for solutions to this critical problem.

3. Select a technological issue that has the potential to heavily affect society during the coming century. Suggested issues include Internet privacy, security of electronic payments, or on-line pornography. Write a paper that parallels the decision to use the two-digit date format in the 1950s to current response to the technological issue you have selected. Project how decisions made today could have serious consequences 40 years from now.

CHAPTER SEVEN

Writing Memos and E-Mail Messages

LEARNING OBJECTIVES

When you have completed Chapter 7, you will be able to:

1 Explain effective writing and formatting principles that apply to memos and e-mail messages.

2 Identify the benefits of e-mail.

3 Identify guidelines for preparing effective memorandums and e-mail messages.

4 Identify acceptable practices for writing effective e-mail messages and using electronic communication appropriately.

5 Identify ethical and legal implications associated with technology.

6 Write memos and e-mail messages that convey good news, routine information, or negative news.

*O*ne tactic that writers of comedy scripts can count on to get a reaction is the convention of using elements in an inappropriate setting, or the old "fish out of water" plot. Examples of this tactic in use include recent television shows like *Boston Common*, which features a small-town bumpkin who has moved to Boston, and *Fired Up* in which an executive has been downsized and now must share an apartment with a former employee while hunting for another job. And the film that launched Julia Roberts to fame, *Pretty Woman*, is another example. In this film, a wealthy man meets and falls in love with a prostitute, who must learn how to behave among the social elite. While we all appreciate the humor these situations provoke, we also know that there are definite rules for behavior in certain settings. The same is true of writing. There are times when communicating calls for writing a memorandum or sending e-mail, and there are times when either of these avenues is inappropriate. Before drafting an e-mail message or a memorandum, ask yourself the following questions:

How can the use of memos and e-mail be abused?

- *What is the purpose of this communication?* If it is just a straightforward, informative note, chances are an e-mail message or memo would be appropriate, especially if no response is required.

- *Is the information personal or confidential?* If it is, sending a memo or e-mail could have embarrassing consequences as they could become public record rather easily. Memos offer little privacy since they typically are distributed flat and not within an envelope. Remember also that your company technically "owns" your electronic communications, so keep personal correspondence off-line if you don't want it to come back and haunt you. Stick to face-to-face meetings for confidential information, or for things such as performance reviews or evaluations.

- *Could you communicate this information by telephone, in person, or through a letter?* Use e-mail when none of those options are preferred, making it your last choice.

- *Is the use of this communication tool an avoidance mechanism?* Memos (and especially e-mail messages) are inappropriate for communicating ideas to others that you would not say face-to-face. If a person can't deal with the issue in person, chances are it isn't a good idea on paper (or on the computer screen) either.

And, as always, once you have decided to write your memo or e-mail message, remember that the standard rules of written communication apply. Always check your grammar, punctuation, and spelling before signing your name or clicking "Send."

1 *Explain effective writing and formatting principles that apply to memos and e-mail messages.*

Memorandums and E-Mail Messages as Informal Communications

Memorandums and e-mail messages are two common ways that businesspeople share information of a more informal nature. Memorandums are internal communications that can be used to transfer information between superior and subordinate or between peers in the organization. E-mail has become a popular channel for sharing information both within the organization and with outside parties.

Memorandums

Because letters go to people outside a business and memorandums (commonly referred to as *memos*) go to people within a business, the formats are different. A memo needs no return address, inside address, salutation, or complimentary closing. Instead, a typical memo presents (on separate lines) (1) the name of the person *to* whom the message is addressed, (2) the name of the person *from* whom the message comes, (3) the *date*, and (4) the *subject*. When a memo is addressed to more than one person, all their names appear on the "TO" line. If the list is long, a common practice is to write "Distribution" on the "TO" line. Then, beneath the last line of the memo, write "Distribution" and follow it with an alphabetized list of the names. In addition to simplifying interoffice mailing and reference, alphabetizing eliminates the risk of having someone on the list wonder whether names appear in order of importance.

Graphics are appropriate whenever they strengthen your efforts to communicate, regardless of the medium—letter, report, or memo. Tables, graphs, charts, and pictures may be either integrated into the content of the memo or attached as supporting material. For example, the stacked bar chart integrated within the memo in Figure 7-1 clarifies the relationship between the data. You will learn techniques for preparing effective graphics in Chapter 10.

Tabulation and enumeration are also useful in memos as you will see in the examples that follow. Lengthy memos may be divided into logical sections. Additionally, using headings to denote the divisions will alert the receiver of information that is ahead and make the information easier to comprehend. A memo containing headings is illustrated in Figure A-8 in Appendix A.

Electronic Mail

Electronic mail, known as *e-mail*, is the latest corporate communication tool. Nearly 50 million users have e-mail capability.[1] One company official enthusiastically states, "Because the top tier of our management is so widely dispersed, it used to take weeks to distribute the paperwork for a meeting. Now we can turn that around in a day via e-mail."[2]

The electronic message in Figure 7-2 is the partner's response to e-mail received on the previous day (shown in Figure 7-1). The partner sent his reactions to the human resources manager's projections electronically for three reasons: (1) The electronic message will reach the manager more quickly than a printed memo and thus will expedite the completion of the revenue projections; (2) because the response is relatively brief and simple, the manager will not need a printed copy of the message and the electronic message can be read and immediately discarded; (3) the electronic message relieves the partner from playing "telephone tag" to deliver a message that is unlikely to require a verbal response.

When a single message is sent to several recipients, the savings are even greater compared to the cost of traditional communication methods. For example, suppose the vice president of production must inform six regional sales managers, located in offices across the country, that they must postpone sales of a particular model immediately because of complaints of defective workmanship. Obviously, timely delivery is a critical factor because the purpose of the message is to prevent the shipment of any more orders. Mail service is too slow, and the telephone system is inconvenient because the regional offices are located within several time zones. In fact, East Coast offices have already closed for the day. E-mail is the appropriate medium for this

> Why do communications within a business take a different form from communications to parties outside the business?

> **2** *Identify the benefits of e-mail.*

FIGURE 7-1
Memo includes a stacked
bar graph for added
clarity.

Memorandum

To: Jose Perez, Managing Partner

From: Bethanie Kinsey, Human Resources Manager ßk

Date: January 15, 1999

Re: PROJECTION OF 2000 REVENUE

The projected revenue for 2000 has been calculated as shown in the following graph. To review the spreadsheet containing these calculations, you may access BILLING.XLS.

The following factors were considered in preparing these projections:

• The business downturn has developed into a prolonged recession, thus reducing our clients' willingness to entertain consulting engagements.

• Our typical staff turnover is declining primarily because of reductions in hirings at competing companies.

• Increased client expectations are demanding the use of staff with extensive business experience.

The amount of work is expected to be about the same as in 1999. Fewer professional hours will be required because more experienced accountants will perform a larger portion of the work. Staff hours will decline as we hire fewer college graduates. Increased billing rates and a different mix of hours among the levels will result in a 12.8 percent increase in total revenues.

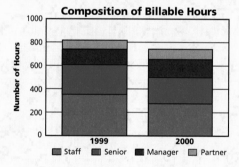

Please inform me of any changes you wish to incorporate in this projection. With your approval, I will prepare a final projection of 2000 revenue.

What are some negative
aspects of using e-mail.

message. With only a few keystrokes, the vice president sends one electronic message that reaches all managers instantly at a low cost.

Thus, e-mail provides a fast, convenient way to communicate, reduces telephone tag and telephone interruptions, facilitates sending a single message to multiple recipients, and fosters open communication among users in various locations. E-mail reduces telephone bills and eliminates time barriers by enabling users to communicate 24 hours a day, 365 days a year.

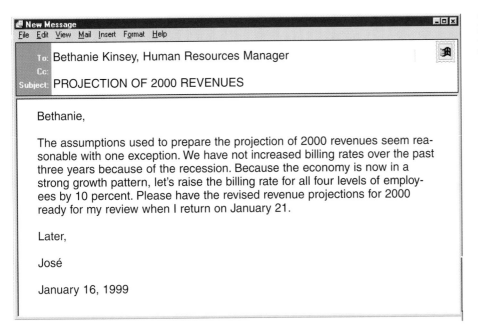

FIGURE 7-2
Instant feedback expedites
decision making.

Guidelines for Preparing Memos and E-Mail Messages

3 *Identify guidelines for preparing effective memorandums and e-mail messages.*

Principles of writing and organization (see Chapters 3 and 4) that apply to business letters generally apply to memos and e-mail messages.

Use of Jargon

An exception to the guidelines for business letters is the use of technical jargon, which is more likely to be useful in memos and e-mail messages. Because people doing similar work are almost sure to know the technical terms associated with it, jargon will be understood, will not be taken as an attempt to impress, and will save time. For the

Generate a list of technical jargon, acronyms, and abbreviations that people in your field will readily understand but that may be confusing to those outside the field.

COMMUNICATION MENTOR

Along with one-on-one contact with supervisors and peers, and skill in group presentations and meetings, the content of your memos will influence the way others view your leadership skills, judgment, and discretion.

The first mistake to avoid is writing too many memos. Avoid documenting events, for example, solely to call attention to your own contribution. (Remind your supervisor infor-

mally that you were "pleased to have a role" in the project.) Ask yourself if the information in the memo you are about to write can be communicated just as effectively with a telephone call or a brief meeting.

Too many unnecessary memos is a signal to others that you are overreaching and underachieving.

James F. Hurley, Principal
Hurley Advisors

same reasons, acronyms, abbreviations, and shortened forms, such as *info, rep, demo, pro,* and *stat,* are more useful in memos and e-mail messages than in letters.

Use of Subject Line

The **subject line** is a standard component of memorandums and e-mail messages. It expedites the understanding of the message by (1) telling the receiver what the following message is about, and (2) setting the stage for the receiver to understand the message. The following suggestions should be helpful in preparing subject lines:

- *Make the subject line as long as necessary.* If, for example, your subject is the report of a meeting, "Report of Meeting" is a poor subject line. "Report of June 10 Meeting on Relocation of Dublin Plant" is a better subject line. In addition to aiding understanding, subject lines provide information helpful to records clerks.
- *Think of the five Ws to give you some clues for good subject lines:* **Who, What, When, Where,** *and* **Why.** Key words help in the development of good subject lines.
- *Repeat the subject in the body of the memorandum.* Opening sentences should not include wording such as "This is . . ." and "The above-mentioned subject . . ." The body of the memorandum should be a complete thought and should not rely on the subject line for elaboration. A good opening sentence might be a repetition of most of the subject line. Even if the subject line were omitted, the memorandum would still be clear, logical, and complete.
- *Keyboard the subject line in all capital letters if additional emphasis is desired.*

Inductive and Deductive Ordering

Principles of organizing that apply to letters also apply to memos and e-mail messages. In both, empathy is the basis for deciding whether to proceed deductively or inductively. In addition, memos may use other bases for determining the sequence of ideas, for example, time (reporting events in the order in which they happened), order of importance, and geography. Write deductively when the memo contains good news or neutral information, and write inductively when it contains bad news or is intended to persuade. (Persuasive memos are discussed in greater detail in Chapter 8.)

Special Guidelines for E-Mail Preparation and Appropriate Protocol

Problems arise if the system is used inappropriately or if messages are too long or poorly organized. The following guidelines will direct you in preparing e-mail messages properly. The accompanying Strategic Forces box will acquaint you with acceptable protocol for electronic communication.

- *Check with receivers to see how they prefer to communicate.* Many feel that communicating through e-mail is more efficient than leaving voice-mail messages. Some may not check their e-mail frequently or at all and perhaps do not know how to check it. Some may have unreliable systems that are slow or prone to lose messages.

Write an effective subject line for a memo announcing software training classes for the upcoming month.

Turn to Appendix A and discuss the differences between the formatting of letters and memos.

What place do inductive and deductive ordering have in the composition of memos and e-mail messages?

---

4 *Identify acceptable practices for writing effective e-mail messages and using electronic communication appropriately.*

- *Limit each message to one idea.* Avoid the temptation of addressing several issues in one message.

- *Provide a useful subject line that has meaning for you and the receiver.* Write a subject line that is useful in these ways: (1) will help a receiver sort through an overloaded e-mail box, (2) describes the content in an understandable way, and (3) will be meaningful in the future. Consider these examples:

Why do memos and e-mail have a subject line in their standard format while letters have optional subject lines?

"Product Launch Snafu"	*Pinpoints a problem and will provoke a more immediate response than a message titled, "Hi, How Are You Doing?"[3]*
"Possible PC Magazine/ CNN Meeting, May 26"	*Identifies both you and the receiver and provides a specific date for the meeting.[4]*
"Strategic Planning Meeting Wednesday, 2 p.m."	*Is more useful than "Meeting."[5]*

- *Organize your message carefully just as you would a letter or memo.* Present information in the order it is likely to be needed. For example, describe the nature and purpose of an upcoming meeting before giving the specifics (date, place, time). Otherwise, the reader or listener may have to reread portions of an electronic memo or review an entire voice-mail message to extract the details. Busy managers will appreciate your using empathy (putting yourself in the receiver's position) to determine a logical, efficient sequence of information. Write deductively when writing good-news and routine e-mail and inductively when writing negative news in an e-mail.

- *Be certain the message is clear and concise.* Some experts recommend limiting your message to one screen. If you need more space, consider a short e-mail message and attach a lengthier message in a word processing file. Be certain the person at the other end can receive and read the attachment before you send it. When replying to a message, cut and paste pertinent sections with the reply (sections you believe will help the recipient understand your reply). Returning the entire message with the reply is time-consuming for the receiver to download and to sort the reply from the original message.

- *Include an appropriate salutation and closing.* For example, you might write "Dear" and the person's name or simply the person's first name when messaging someone for the first time. Casual greetings such as "Hi" are appropriate for personal messages but not business e-mail. "Sincerely yours" is too formal for e-mail messages; a simple one-word closing such as "thank you" or "later" provides a courteous close.

- *Include a signature file at the end of the message.* The signature file (known as a *.sig*) contains a few lines of text that include your full name and title, e-mail address, and any other information you want people to know about you. You might include a clever quote that you update frequently. Note the .sig in Figure 7-5 on page 248.

- *Proofread your message for correct spelling, grammar, and punctuation.* Sending e-mail from work is the same as sending out an official letter on company letterhead; the message is a reflection of the company and the writer. An error in an e-mailed sales message is just as detrimental as an error in a printed letter.

In addition to basic e-mail etiquette presented in the related Strategic Forces box, the following style guidelines make e-mail easier to read:

- ***Keep the line length short.*** Limit the line to no more than 60 characters so that an entire line will display on the monitor.

- ***Use short paragraphs that are not indented and are separated by a double space.*** This format makes the message easy to read.

- ***Use mixed case (capitals and lowercase letters).*** Mixed case is easier to read than all capitals or all lowercase. A message written in all capitals is known as "shouting" in Internet parlance and is considered rude. To emphasize a word or phrase, surround it with quotation marks or key it in uppercase letters.

- ***Avoid sending formatted documents.*** Messages with varying fonts, special print features (e.g., bold, italics, etc.), and clip art take longer to download, require more disk space, and may be unreadable by some monitors. In addition, enhancing routine e-mail messages does not support the goals of competitive organizations, and employees and clients/customers may resent such frivolous use of time.

- ***Use emoticons or e-mail abbreviations in moderation when you believe the receiver will understand and approve.*** Emoticons are a shorthand way of lightening the mood and adding emotion to e-mail messages (i.e., they help communicate the writer's tone of voice and other nuances lost from face-to-face exchanges). For example, a writer might write, "That was pure genius ;-)." Adding the wink alerts the receiver that the writer is being facetious. Emoticons are created by keying combination of symbols to produce "sideways" faces. Some examples follow:

:-)   smiling, indicates humor or sarcasm

:-(frowning, indicates sadness or anger

;-)   wink

:-/   wry face

%-(confused

Alternately, you might put a "g" for (grin) or "smile" in parentheses after something that is obviously meant as tongue-in-check to help carry the intended message to the receiver.[6]

Some e-mail users feel strongly that emoticons are inappropriate for serious e-mail and decrease productivity when the receiver must take several minutes to decipher the emoticon. Another opinion is that although emoticons can show that you are net-savvy, they are more likely to remind clients of students who dotted their i's with little circles in elementary school.[7] Before using emoticons, be certain the receiver will understand them and that the formality of the message and the receiver lends itself to this type of informal exchange. Then, use emoticons only in moderation to *punctuate* your message. If you are uncertain, do not use emoticons until a particular person uses them first.

Abbreviations are used for commonly used phrases to save space and avoid unnecessary keying. Commonly used ones are BCNU (be seeing you), BTW (by the way), FYI (for your information), FWIW (for what it's worth), HTH (hope this helps), and IMHO (in my humble opinion). Virginia Shea,

---

How do you add emphasis to a word or phrase in an e-mail message?

What role do emoticons play in e-mail messages? What are some of your favorite emoticons?

author of *Netiquette*, the industry standard for e-mail etiquette, contends that abbreviations do not save enough space to justify their use in business e-mail but says they are widely used in discussion groups and personal messages.[8]

- ***Consider ethical and legal implications of e-mail.*** First, remember you are responsible for the content of an e-mail message. Because e-mail moves so quickly between people and often becomes very informal, more like a conversation, individuals may not realize (or may forget) their responsibility. If a person denies commitments made via e-mail, someone involved may produce a printed copy of the e-mail message in question as verification. Second, abide by copyright laws. Don't use a quote and pretend it's yours. If you publish an entire written document in an e-mail, you must seek the publisher's permission and possibly pay royalties for its use. The accompanying Strategic Forces box explores in detail the legal and ethical implications of e-mail.

5 *Identify ethical and legal implications associated with technology.*

Types of Memos and E-Mail Messages

The following examples of memorandums and e-mail messages illustrate the principles of content, organization, and format previously discussed. The memos are formatted according to standard memo format. You may wish to review the illustrations of memorandum formats and layout in Appendix A before studying these examples.

6 *Write memos and e-mail messages that convey good news, routine information, or negative news.*

Deductive Messages

The memorandum in Figure 7-3 conveys good news. As a good-news message, this memo presents the main idea in the first sentence.

Routine Messages

Memos or e-mail messages are the most frequently used methods of communicating standard operating procedures and other instructions, changes related to personnel, and other matters for which a written record is needed.

Procedures or Instructions Instructions to employees must be conveyed clearly and accurately to facilitate the day-to-day operations of business and to prevent negative feelings that occur when mistakes are made and work must be redone. Managers must take special care in writing standard operating procedures to ensure that all employees complete the procedures accurately and consistently.

Before writing instructions, walk through each step to understand it and to locate potential trouble spots. Then attempt to determine how much employees already know about the process and to anticipate any questions or problems. Then, as you write instructions that require more than a few simple steps, follow these guidelines:

1. **Begin each step with an action statement to create a vivid picture of the employee completing the task.** Using an action verb and the understood subject *you* is more vivid than a sentence written in passive voice. For example, a loan officer attempting to learn new procedures for evaluating new venture loans can understand "*identify* assets available to collateralize the loan" more easily than "assets available to collateralize the loan should be identified."

FIGURE 7-3
Good example of a good-
news memo.

Deductive Outline for Good-News Memos:

1. Begin with the good news.
2. Include necessary details.
3. May omit a goodwill ending when communicating a positive idea to a receiver in the company when a statement is not necessary to build unity at the end.

IVY Industrial
105 Union Drive
Dothan, AL 36301-0105

TO: All Full-Time Employees
FROM: Everett Carlisle, President & CEO   *E. C.*
DATE: April 5, 1999
❶ **SUBJECT:** MATCHING FUNDS PROGRAM APPROVED

❷ The stockholders have approved the union's petition for the corporation to implement a matching funds program for contributions you make to institutions of higher learning.

❸ We are pleased the stockholders have expressed such strong support for your commitment to higher education. You may recall the original petition limited annual contributions to $100 a person. However, the plan approved by the stockholders raised the annual contributions limit to $250 a person.

❹ Beginning May 1 you may submit requests for Ivy Industrial to match your contributions to any institution of higher learning you choose. Simply obtain the appropriate form from the Human Resources Department. Then complete the form and return it with your canceled check written to the educational institution.

❺ Thank you for your keen interest in this program. With your generous giving and the matching funds, we at Ivy Industrial can make a significant contribution to providing quality education. ❻

❶ Gets attention by placing good news in the subject line.
❷ Includes good news in emphatic first-sentence position.
❸ Follows with an explanation.

❹ Continues with details for submitting request.

❺ Closes on a pleasant note.
❻ Emphasizes social responsibility (Legal/ Ethical).

Format Pointers

Is created without a template and includes traditional memo headings (To, From, Date, Subject) that transmits the memo. See Figure A-8 in the Appendix to review the format.

Strategic Forces: Legal and Ethical Constraints

Netiquette: Proper Behavior for On-Line Communication

E-mail is fast and convenient. A single message can be sent to several people without having to copy and distribute a memo. Messages can be read, deleted, forwarded, and printed with the touch of a button any time of day, night, or weekend. On the other hand, if used inappropriately, this time-saving device can be rude and can rob managers of valuable work time. Established standards of behavior for communicating on-line have been developed to help on-line communicators send and receive e-mail messages that are courteous of others and enhance communication effectiveness *and* productivity. Learning fundamental **netiquette**, the buzzword for proper behavior on the Internet, will cinch your on-line success.

- *Check mail promptly.* Be conscientious in checking and responding to electronic messages to avoid missing important information needed to complete an assignment. Generally, a response to e-mail is expected within 24 hours. Ignoring electronic messages from coworkers can erode efforts to create an open, honest work environment. On the other hand, don't respond so quickly (every five or ten minutes) that you appear to be paying more attention to your e-mail than your job.[9]

- *Do not contribute to e-mail overload.* To avoid clogging the system with unnecessary messages that the receiver feels compelled to answer, send business-related messages only when necessary and only to necessary people. Follow these simple guidelines:

  1. Before sending a copy of an e-mail message to another person or to a distribution list, be certain that these individuals need a copy of the e-mail.
  2. Do not forward an e-mail from one person to another without the original writer's permission.

  3. Never address an e-mail containing action items to more than one person at a time. This practice violates the old adage "Share a task between two people, and each takes 1% responsibility."[10]
  4. Follow company policy for incidental personal use, and obtain a private e-mail account if you are job hunting or sending many private messages to friends and relatives.

- *Send short, direct messages that typically would be sent through printed memos.* These messages usually are routine matters that need not be handled immediately and thus will reduce telephone interruptions (scheduling meetings, giving your supervisor quick updates, or other uncomplicated issues). Bill Howard of *PC Magazine* says the worst e-mail message he ever received was a news release he didn't need that required five minutes to download and caused him to nearly miss his plane.[11] This e-mail message did not generate a strong relationship with the receiver.

- *Do not alter messages that you are forwarding or re-posting.* Be careful what you quote, indicate attribution, and be sure to ask permission if you are forwarding a private message.

- *Keep in mind that text or graphics you find on the Internet are covered by U.S. Copyright Law.* Be careful when distributing them without permission.

- *Do not send messages that provoke a strong emotional response from the receiver.* Face-to-face communication is the most effective channel for performance appraisals, disciplinary action, or other sensitive, highly emotional situations or those subject to misinterpretation. Because e-mail messages are stripped of nonverbal communication (facial expressions, tones of voice, and body language), the message may be misinterpreted, and the tone may appear more harsh than intended.

continued

Actually, choosing an appropriate channel is an important aspect of communicating ethically. After all, if the recipient loses dignity as a result of the channel used to convey the message, you have acted unethically. Bhasin, author of *Mastering Management—A Guide for Technical Professionals*, states that supervisors who are too timid to provide unpleasant feedback in person or over the telephone will send it via e-mail. Likewise, employees often use e-mail to send critical messages to their supervisors. A heated, sarcastic, sometimes abusive message or posting to a discussion group is known as a **flame** in on-line jargon.[12]

Consider how humiliated Bo Schembechler must have felt when he was notified by fax that he had been dismissed from his position as president of the Detroit Tigers. Including this detail as part of a major sports story must have increased the embarrassment.[13] Remember, flaming may prompt the receiver to send a retaliatory response; this type of communication exchange damages relationships.

- *Do not allow e-mail to substitute for personal interaction.* Communicating on-line cannot replace the personal interaction so essential in today's work teams.[14] For example, two people sitting side-by-side or on the same floor should not have to communicate solely by e-mail; however, employees floors apart or in different offices can communicate effectively by e-mail.

- *Read each message carefully before you send it to avoid flaming.* Often writers hold a particularly sensitive letter or one written in anger and mail it the next day if they still deem the message appropriate. Unless a response is urgent, store a draft message for an hour and reread before sending it.[15] Clicking the "Send" button is simple; so keep in mind you cannot get the flaming message back, and the recipient may forward your message to someone else without your knowledge.

- *Avoid sending confidential information because the security of e-mail is low compared to other media.* Undeliverable messages are delivered to a mail administrator, and

many networks routinely store backups of all e-mail messages that pass through them. Even deleted messages can be "resurrected" with little effort as Oliver North discovered when investigators confronted him with e-mail be had written related to the Iran-Contra Affair.[16] A simple guideline: Do not send anything you wouldn't want in the public domain.[17]

- *Develop an efficient way for handling e-mail.* For example, (1) set up separate accounts for receiving mass memos and messages that require your direct attention, (2) keep your mailbox clean by deleting messages that you are no longer using, and (3) set up folders that organize messages you need to keep. If you receive a large number of messages, investigate the purchase of an e-mail handler to help you sort and prioritize messages. Programs such as Eudora® automatically send form letters you created as replies to messages received with a particular subject line, forward certain e-mail to another person, and sound an alarm when you receive a message from a particular person.[18]

- *Exercise caution against e-mail viruses.* Keep backups of important files and be wary of e-mail messages from people you don't know who promise something, such as free software or a screen saver, for running an attachment (particularly ones with an ".exe" extension). E-mail text is usually safe to open, but the attachment may contain an executable macro that can affect your files.[19]

Application

In small groups discuss incidents of inappropriate e-mail behavior you have experienced in a work or academic setting. Explain how each incident affected the individuals involved and the company. Discuss other netiquette rules you may have been required to follow that you believe are critical for courteous, productive e-mail use. Are some netiquette rules appropriate for business settings but not academic settings or vice versa? Are these rules adequate for posting to an on-line discussion group? Be prepared to share your ideas with the class.

COMMUNICATION IN ACTION

Steve Wolff, JCPenney Company, Inc.

The increasing popularity of the Internet is impacting the way JCPenney communicates and does business—both with customers and associates. Whether offering merchandise and information to customers via the Internet's World Wide Web or providing business-related information to our associates via the company's intranet, the multimedia capabilities of the medium are proving both efficient and cost-saving for JCPenney.

The Intranet

The jWeb, the Company's intranet that is accessible only to JCPenney associates, is designed to help improve the flow of information between associates. "Already the jWeb has grown beyond its original purpose," says Steve Wolff, Electronic Communications Manager. "Our challenge is to have the Company communicate with itself"; in other words, to move important internal information, quickly. News bulletins, organizational procedures, charts, forms, and manuals are on-line. The jWeb is tailor-made for manuals, as a great deal of information can be stored and easily updated without incurring printing costs. Company publications, such as *JCPenney Today* and *Management Report*, are already on jWeb and appear on-line in advance of their print counterparts.

Access to financial calendars and store and telephone directories is available with a few keystrokes. jWeb also allows for easy collaboration between teams working on the same project but in different locations, whether it's a writer/editor/pgraphic artist trio or a group of store merchandise managers within the same district.

Besides its usefulness as a workplace tool, jWeb offers some intangible benefits as well. "From a broader perspective, we're looking at increasing the feeling of community among the Company, so different stores and associates around the country feel more connected to one another," says Wolff. On a broader scale, JCPenney associates can also access the Internet, which provides instant access to research sites, news, and technical support. Internet mail allows quick communication to suppliers, support organizations, and customers.

The Internet

Just as the Company uses the intranet to deliver information to and communicate with associates, JCPenney uses its new Internet presence to serve and communicate with customers. JCPenney currently has two Internet sites.

The overall, customer-oriented side, found at **www.jcpenney.com**, provides an opportunity for customers to shop on-line and learn more about the Company's merchandise, services, and history. On-line shoppers can take advantage of daily sales, coupons, and discounts; shop for others using the store's gift registry; find the nearest store location; and read about JCPenney's salon and photography centers. Customers can also read the JCPenney annual report. "We're using this site both as a communication medium and as a way of polishing our Company image," says Wolff. The www.jcpenney.com site was recently chosen as one of the "Top 100 Web Sites" by *PC Magazine*. In choosing JCPenney, the article referred to the extensive nature of the site and the effective links where customers can purchase gift certificates and baskets, clothes, housewares, or anything else found in the store.

JCPenney maintains another site, dedicated solely to suppliers. Password protected, the site contains various manuals, policies, calendars, and addresses to aid suppliers in business dealings with JCPenney.

As both the Internet and jWeb grow with the demands of PC users, JCPenney will keep associates and customers informed using the most up-to-date technology. [25]

Application

Visit the customer-oriented JCPenney web site. Write a short report summarizing ways that JCPenney is utilizing technology in its operations.

Strategic Forces: Legal and Ethical Constraints

Ethical and Legal Implications of Technology

Technology threatens our privacy, our right to be left alone, free from surveillance, or interference from other individuals or organizations. Common invasions of privacy caused by technology include collecting excessive amounts of information for decision making and maintaining too many files, monitoring the exact time employees' spend on a specific task and between tasks and the exact number and length of employee breaks, and supervisors' or coworkers' reading another employee's electronic mail and computer files. Additionally, integrating computer files containing information collected from more than one agency without permission is a major threat to privacy. Although an individual may have authorized the collection of the individual information, merging the information may reveal things the individual may want to remain private.[20]

Our right to privacy is protected primarily by the First Amendment (which guarantees freedom of speech and association), and the Fourth Amendment (which protects against unreasonable search and seizure of one's person, documents, or home, and assures due process). However, the Fair Information Practices (FIP) form the basis of 13 federal statutes that ensure the security and integrity of personal information collected by governmental and private agencies. Set forth in the FIP are conditions for handling information about individuals in such areas as credit reporting, education, financial records, newspaper records, cable communications, electronic communications, and video rentals. Study carefully the FIP principles that follow.[21]

Principles of Fair Information Practices

1. There should be no personal record systems whose existence is secret.

2. Individuals have rights of access, inspection, review, and amendment to systems that contain information about them.

3. There must be no use of personal information, without prior consent, for purposes other than those for which it was gathered.

4. Managers of systems are responsible and can be held accountable and liable for the damage done by systems and for their reliability and security.

5. Governments have the right to intervene in the information relationships among private parties.

Despite this federal legislation and state laws passed to enhance and strengthen it, most Americans feel they have less privacy today than ever. According to a recent Harris poll, 60 percent of Americans believe they have lost all control over personal information.[22] Such statistics are not surprising, for many of us have experienced an invasion of privacy over personal information in today's highly computerized society.

As one example, consider the privacy of e-mail messages. The courts have established the right of firms to monitor the electronic mail of their employees because they own the facilities and intend them to be used for job-related communication only. On the other hand, employees expect that their e-mail messages should be kept private. To protect themselves against liability imposed by the Electronic Communications Privacy Act (ECPA), employers simply provide a legitimate business reason for the monitoring (preventing computer crime, retrieving lost messages, regulating employee morale) and obtain written consent to e-mail interception or at least notify employees. Employees who use the system after the notification may have given implied consent to the monitoring. Federal and state laws related to employee privacy are being introduced. Although litigation related to present privacy issues is underway, the development of law is lagging far behind technology; nevertheless, employers can expect changes in the laws as technology continues to develop. The Privacy for Consumers and Workers Act has been introduced into Congress and would cover most forms of electronic surveillance, requiring employers to notify present and prospective employees of any monitoring policies and forbidding secret monitoring.[23]

continued

In the present climate of controversy over privacy and ownership of information, the following ethical practices are appropriate for the collection and access of information:

- *Collect only information that is* **needed as opposed to what you would** *like to know.* Resist the urge to add a few additional questions to a survey instrument with the idea you might use that information later.

- *Develop (and use) safeguards for the security of information and instill in data handlers the values of privacy and the importance of confidentiality:*

    1. **Require employees to use passwords to gain access to the system and enforce routine changes of passwords on a periodic basis.** Also, provide guidance in assigning a password that cannot be easily broken; for instance, never use birth dates or names. Krol summarizes the criteria for selecting a good password:[24]

        - Is at least six characters long.
        - Has a mixture of uppercase, lowercase, and numbers.
        - Is not a word or a set of adjacent keys (e.g., QWERTY).

        An easy way to meet all of these criteria is to pick the first letters of a favorite phrase, like *MtFbwyYS* (May the Force be with you, Young Skywalker).

    2. **Require users to "sign off" or "logout" of e-mail when they leave their terminals.** This procedure would prevent a person from sending a harassing message or committing a computer crime with no fear of being caught since the offender's name and e-mail identification would not be displayed on an unattended terminal.

    3. **Assign user identification passwords and levels of access that limit information a person can observe and change.** Consider access to information stored on

your college's computer. A user identification number and password limit the types of information various personnel at the university (e.g., registrar, faculty, administrators, and students) can access about students and university employees.

    4. **Consider the use of encryption facilities if you are sending extremely confidential information.** Through encryption, users can encode their messages so that only the intended recipients can read them. Reading or changing encrypted messages is very difficult, a fact which, of course, limits the employer's ability to monitor e-mail for business purposes.

- *Develop a clear privacy policy that complies with the law and does not unnecessarily compromise the interests of employees or employers.* Be certain employees understand whether e-mail is considered private or corporate property. Explain exactly how employees will be monitored and the limits. For example, "we will canvass all e-mail if we suspect criminal activity, such as drug trafficking." Open communication will circumvent litigation but more importantly build trust and thus improve employee relations.

Application

Stage a classroom debate with two teams of four; one team represents the right of the employer to monitor computer activities and the other team represents the right of the employee to maintain privacy in communication. Each team will study the issue and prepare its arguments. During the debate, each team will have five minutes to present its side of the issue, followed by a two-minute cross examination by the opposing team. Class members who are not participating on the debate teams will act as judges to determine which team presents the strongest case.

2. **Itemize each step on a separate line to add emphasis and to simplify reading.** Number each step to indicate that the procedures should be completed in a particular order. If the order is not important, use bullets (●, ✦, ■, ✓) to draw attention to each step.

3. **Consider preparing a flow chart depicting the procedures.** The cost and effort involved in creating a sophisticated flow chart may be merited for extremely important and complex procedures. For example, see Figure 12-13, which simplifies the steps involved in processing a telephone order in an effort to minimize errors.

4. **Complete the procedure by following your instructions step-by-step.** Correct any errors you locate.

5. **Ask a colleague or employee to walk through the procedures.** This walk-through will allow you to identify ambiguous statements, omissions of relevant information, and other sources of potential problems.

Consider the seemingly simple task of telling employees what to do if a newly installed badge reader will not record their time when they report to work. The human resources director might quickly respond, "No need for written instructions; just tell the employees to get to work and then get them a new badge." The process of writing step-by-step procedures might alert the manager to the potential abuses that could result from issuing a new badge without obtaining the supposedly damaged card. In addition, ambiguous and inconsistent verbal instructions (developed in the midst of the chaos) could result in an inaccurate payroll. A chaotic environment and suspicion about whether management is giving them proper credit for hours worked could cause employees to mistrust management and lower morale. Having anticipated these potential problems and worked through the procedures carefully, the discerning manager wrote the instructions in Figure 7-4.

> Write a set of instructions for walking from your classroom to the campus library. Assume that the person who will attempt to follow your instructions has no familiarity with the campus.

Personnel Changes. An introductory memo or e-mail distributed on or before a newly hired person's first day on the job assists in getting the new relationship off to a good start. Before the grapevine could generate rumors, a prudent human resources manager quickly sent all employees the e-mail message in Figure 7-5 confirming an employee's resignation and at the same time soliciting support in the interim.

"To the File" or Confirmations. "To the file" or **confirmation memos** are written records of oral decisions or discussions. When information needs to be recorded in written form and filed for future reference, the record may be made in a "to the file" format as shown in Figure 7-6. Writing the information in the memo will assist the writer in remembering and using the information at a future date. Alternately, the writer may send a memo to the person involved; this confirmation memo serves as a written record of an oral agreement and assures the receiver that an oral decision was understood and will be remembered.

Summaries of disciplinary actions taken can also be written as a "to the file" memo and placed in an employee's personnel file, as shown in Figure 7-7. These memos serve as important documentation in the event of litigation—legally defensible evidence of action taken. More importantly, these confidential records can remind the supervisor of specific weaknesses in performance that employees may need help in overcoming.

FIGURE 7-4
Good example of a procedures memo.

INTEROFFICE MEMORANDUM

TO: Line Supervisors

FROM: Jack Holcombe, Human Resources Manager *J.H.*

SUBJECT: Procedures for Replacing Damaged Badge Readers

DATE: JANUARY 3, 1999

① Our recent transition from a punch clock to badge readers to record employees' time has run smoothly. However, we anticipate the possibility of defective badge readers, especially as they become worn over time.

② To ensure the accuracy of the payroll, please instruct your employees to follow these procedures in the event the reader does not read their badges:

③ 1. Complete a copy of Form PR-17 (copy attached).

2. Attach the damaged badge to the completed Form PR-17.

3. Give the card to Gena Kaminski in the Payroll Office by 10 a.m. She will prepare a new badge and send it to you with Form PR-17 by the end of the day.

4. Distribute the new badge to the employee. Instruct the employees *not* to use the new badge today but to report his/her departing time directly to you.

5. Record the employee's departing time on Form PR-17 and return it to Gena in the Payroll Office.

Attachment

① Introduces the main idea.

② Introduces the upcoming list of steps.

③ Begins each sequential step with an action verb (subject "you" understood) to help supervisors visualize themselves completing the procedures.

Format Pointers

● Uses "Memorandum Expert," a word processing template that increases the efficiency of creating a memo. Several formats are available (traditional, contemporary, cosmopolitan, elegant, etc.)

● Enumerates to direct attention to each step. Uses numbers rather than bullets (●, ◆, ♥, ✓) to emphasize that each step must be completed in sequence.

● Adds an attachment notation to alert reader that something other than the memo is included.

FIGURE 7-5
Good example of an e-mail message about personnel changes.

Organization and Content of E-Mail

1. Write a short, concise message that fits on one screen. A longer message would be included in an attachment.
2. Use the deductive outline for conveying a routine message.
3. Include a salutation and a closing to personalize the message to the audience.
4. Provide a subject line that is meaningful to the writer and the receiver.

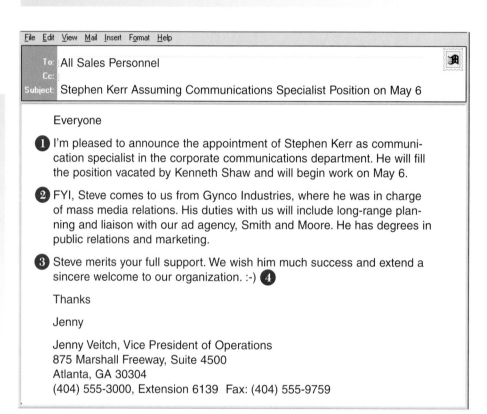

① Begins with major idea. Refers to the one being replaced and gives a general idea of the new employee's duties. Includes starting date.

② Provides relative background and duties. Uses "Steve" to suggest his preference. Reveals previous duties and education to add to the new employee's initial credibility.

③ Encourages present employees to be cooperative and seeks to make Steve feel welcome.

④ Promotes team interaction.

Format Pointers

- Keeps the lines short so an entire line will display on the monitor.
- Single-spaces paragraphs with no indention.
- Uses mixed case for easy reading. Would have used all capitals or asterisks to emphasize word(s).
- Omits any special formatting such as fonts, print features (boldface, italics), and clip art that might be unreadable by the receiver's monitor or time-consuming to download.
- Includes a signature file (.sig) that identifies the writer.
- Uses an emoticon and an e-mail abbreviation (FYI) appropriately in an informal message to a group of employees who use this shorthand regularly.

TO: File

From: Cecil Echols, Transportation Manager ⎧. Ɛ.

DATE: April 1, 1999

Subject: ROD SPECIFICATIONS FOR SHIPPING DOCK, ROSSON WAREHOUSE

❶ By telephone today, I confirmed with A. J. Anderson and Son's chief engineer, Leigh Dubois, that nothing less than 1 3/4-inch reinforcing rods be used in the support wall of the Wiggins Warehouse shipping dock.**❷** An on-site inspection will be made to substantiate this agreement.

FIGURE 7-6
Good example of a "to the file" memo—documenting actions.

❶ Records details that may be needed when the subject is discussed later.
❷ Includes additional information that affects future plans.

Format Pointers

• Uses "File" as the recipient of a "to the file" memo.

MEMO

To: File

From:

Date: June 3, 1999

Re: FORMAL DISCIPLINARY CONFERENCE WITH KELLY HUBBARD ABOUT EMBEZZLEMENT

I met with Kelly Hubbard on Monday, June 3, to discuss the disciplinary actions to be taken as a result of his embezzlement of $20,590 from the company.

During the past year, Kelly has periodically taken and cashed checks received by mail. The thefts were discovered when the accounting department investigated a complaint from a customer who alleged she had not received an order even though the check had been returned with her bank statement. When Kelly was confronted with the allegation, he confessed he had stolen the money to pay for gambling losses. Kelly has provided copies of the customer orders that accompanied these checks.

After discussing various options with Jill Ainsworth, I decided to transfer Kelly to a nonmanagerial position in the Maintenance Department. We also agreed on a repayment plan that authorizes us to withhold 5 percent of his gross salary each month until the stolen money is repaid. Kelly will also be required to attend counseling sessions approved by Human Resources.

No criminal or civil charges will be filed so long as Kelly complies with this plan. This plan should make Kelly accountable for his actions, minimize any negative publicity to the company, help ensure repayment of the stolen funds, and give Kelly a chance to redeem himself and continue supporting his family.

During the disciplinary conference, I discussed the full nature of these actions, and Kelly stated that he understood why these actions were being taken. Kelly Hubbard's transfer is effective immediately.

FIGURE 7-7
Good example of a "to the file" memorandum—summarizing disciplinary actions.

Format Pointers

• Uses "File" as the recipient of a "to the file" memo.

• Uses a memorandum template to expedite document production.

Legal and Ethical Constraints

• Provides a written record of legally defensible evidence of action taken in the event of litigation.

Managers who can communicate negative information in a sensitive, honest, and timely way are successful in calming employees' fears and doubts and in building positive employee relations. Effective managers recognize that morale, like customer goodwill, is fragile—easily damaged and difficult to repair.

Bad-News Messages

Being able to initiate messages that convey bad news is as important as responding "No" to messages from customers/clients and others outside the company. Employees are seeking *honest* answers from management about slumping profits, massive layoffs as a result of downsizing, and major changes in their organizations. Companies are reengineering to improve quality, job performance, and advancement prospects and to overcome scandals by management and other issues. For example, Northwest Airlines carried company news on-line every day and published a newsletter twice a month to calm company anxiety during a crisis. Managers who can communicate negative information in a sensitive, honest, and timely way are successful in calming employees' fears and doubts and in building positive employee relations. Effective managers recognize that morale, like customer goodwill, is fragile—easily damaged and difficult to repair.

Consider the company president who wrote the message in (Figure 7-8) to communicate to employees a relocation of the company's manufacturing facility. After sending this e-mail message, the president should not be surprised to learn that employees are resisting the relocation. In fact, many perceive the company to be an enemy uprooting defenseless families from their homes simply for financial gain.

How could the president change the message in Figure 7-8 to better gain employees' support for the relocation?

In the revision (Figure 7-9), the president anticipates the employees' natural resistance to this stunning announcement; therefore, he presents the explanations *before* the bad news. The revision focuses on the benefits employees can gain from the move. This approach should generate more support for the move and trust in management than the original blunt statement that a decision had been made for the benefit of the company. Care was used in writing a subject line that introduced the subject of the message without revealing the bad news. Retaining the original subject line "Company Will Relocate March 5" would defeat the purpose of the inductive outline developed in the revision. Sending a printed memorandum is a more effective channel for communicating such sensitive information than the efficient e-mail message.

COMMUNICATION MENTOR

Early in my career, I avoided learning to use computers, but now I understand that technology is a necessity for conducting business efficiently. Technology allows businesses to communicate information quickly anywhere in the world, is a valuable research tool, and eliminates unnecessary paper processes. For example, I find technology invaluable when generating reports my coworkers also must use. Because each of us has the capability of editing a common database, we all have access to relevant, up-to-date information without duplicating our efforts.

Take advantage of all the available technological resources your company has to offer; however, exercise good judgment in selecting the appropriate communication channel. For example,

1. Do not communicate confidential information by electronic mail.

2. Be considerate of the length of the messages you send via computer or voice mail. Because I receive as many as 80 voice mail messages daily, I am grateful for those individuals who leave concise messages.

3. Do not allow your communication to become impersonal. In some situations, an e-mail or a printed message would be more efficient, but a handwritten note or a face-to-face discussion is more effective.

Marquette L. Wilson
Manager, Human Resources
GE Capital Commercial Finance

FIGURE 7-8
Poor example of a bad-news e-mail message.

AVOID

Msg #9
E-mail from Eric Pearson   sent 09/14/99   at 8:45 a.m.

TO: All Employees

FROM: Eric Pearson, President

DATE: September 14, 1998

SUBJECT: COMPANY WILL RELOCATE MARCH 5

Effective March 5, 1999, we will relocate our plant facility to Fairfax, Virginia. Approved by the Board of Directors at its last meeting, this relocation will enable the company to reduce its operating expenses by 15 percent.

All employees wishing to relocate should notify their supervisors by the end of next week. If you have any questions, please do not hesitate to call.

<Enter> next msg   <F2> save in mailbox   <F5> save to disk   <Esc> stop reading

FIGURE 7-9
Good example of a bad-news memo.

Inductive Outline for Bad-News Memorandums

1. Begin with a neutral idea that leads to the reasons for the refusal.
2. Present the facts, analysis, and reasons for the refusal.
3. Present the refusal using positive tone and de-emphasis techniques.
4. Close with an idea that shifts the emphasis away from the refusal.

INTEROFFICE MEMORANDUM

TO: All Employees   *Ε. Ρ.*
FROM: Eric Pearson, President
DATE: September 14, 1998
SUBJECT: PROPOSED PLAN FOR INCREASING MANUFACTURING
             CAPACITY

① Uses buffer to introduce the topic and lead into reasons.

② Presents benefits the company and employees will gain from relocating.

③ Presents the bad news while reminding receiver of the benefits.

④ Assures employees that no one's job is in jeopardy.

⑤ Anticipates questions about the logistics of the move and ends with a positive appeal for unity.

① As we have projected, our present production facilities will soon be unable to meet the increased demand for our product. Therefore, for several years we have been studying whether to expand our current manufacturing facility or relocate to another site.

② High property taxes and transportation cost increases every year are compelling reasons to consider alternative sites. Likewise, attracting new talent into this high-cost metro area has become more difficult each year. In fact, both of our newly hired unit supervisors are commuting over one hour just to obtain affordable housing.

While relocating could provide a long-term economic benefit to the company, moving out of New York City could enhance the quality of life for us all. In a suburban city, we could enjoy day-to-day living in a relaxed, small-town environment with all the benefits of a large city only a short drive away. **③** These two factors alone have convinced us that moving the manufacturing facility to Fairfax, Virginia, a thriving suburb located ten miles west of Washington, D.C., would benefit the company and its employees.

④ All employees wishing to relocate may resume their duties at the same salary structure. **⑤** Your supervisor will explain the logistics of the move at your unit's next meeting. Now let us all work together for a smooth transition to many challenging opportunities awaiting in Fairfax.

Use an on-line database to locate an article about another company's success or failure in handling a similar crisis (e.g., illness and death caused by E. coli bacteria contamination, shootings at McDonald's, unethical and illegal actions of executives of major companies, etc.). Share with the class or in groups.

Legal and Ethical Constraints and Changing Technology Issue

Uses memorandum as channel for conveying a sensitive message, rather than the informal e-mail message.

Format Pointers

Uses a subject line to introduce the topic but not does not reveal the bad news.

MEMORANDUMS AND E-MAIL MESSAGES

Memorandums

Organization and Content

- Use an appropriate organization pattern (e.g., deductive for good-news and routine messages; inductive for bad-news messages).
- Write a descriptive subject line.
- Identify clearly the major idea.
- Present sufficient supporting details in a logical sequence.
- Verify accuracy of facts or figures.
- Assure that the message is ethical and abides by any legal requirements.
- Include a final paragraph that is courteous and indicates a continuing relationship with the receiver.

Style

- Structure the message to be clear and concise. Include jargon and acronyms only if the receiver will understand them.
- Use active voice predominately.
- Use first person sparingly or not at all.
- Make ideas cohere (changes in thought are not abrupt).
- Keep sentences relatively short and vary them in length and structure.
- Emphasize significant thoughts (e.g., position, stated in simple sentences or in independent clauses).
- Keep paragraphs relatively short.
- Use original expression (sentences are not copied directly from the definition of the problem or from sample letters in text); avoid cliches.

Mechanics

- Be sure keyboarding, spelling, grammar, and punctuation are perfect.

Format

- Include *TO, FROM, DATE,* and *SUBJECT* information.
- Omit courtesy titles on *TO* and *FROM* lines.
- Single space lines; leave blank space between paragraphs; paragraphs do not indent.
- Highlight text for emphasis and easy reading (e.g., bulleted or numbered list, headings, or graphics).
- Place handwritten initials by the name on the *FROM* line.
- Include special parts if necessary (reference initials, enclosure, copy, etc.).

E-Mail Messages

Organization, Content, Style, and Mechanics

- Include only one main message idea.
- Provide a useful subject line (has meaning for the writer and receiver; will help the receiver sort through numerous e-mail messages).
- Follow all other related checkpoints listed for memorandums (shown above).

Format

- Include an appropriate salutation and ending.
- Include a signature file (including writer's name, address, e-mail address, and other useful information).
- Keep message length to no longer than one screen. Use an attachment if the message must be longer.
- Keep line length the width of the screen.
- Single space lines; leave a blank space between paragraphs; do not indent paragraphs.
- Key message using mixed-case letters. Use capital letters or quotation marks to emphasize a word or phrase.
- Omit specialized formatting (bold, italics, font changes, clip art).
- Use emoticons and abbreviations in moderation only if the receiver understands them and the message is informal.

1. ***Explain effective writing and formatting principles that apply to memos and e-mail messages.*** Memos are sent to receivers inside the organization; e-mail may be sent to receivers inside the organization or outside the organization. Acceptable memo and e-mail formats are less formal than business letter formats. The writing principles that apply to letters also apply to memos and e-mail messages. Headings and graphics can be included to facilitate comprehension. Despite the perceived informality of memos and e-mail messages, writers should give the same meticulous attention to accuracy and grammatical correctness of these documents as they do to other business documents.

2. ***Identify the benefits of e-mail.*** E-mail provides a fast, convenient way to communicate by reducing telephone tag and telephone interruptions, facilitating the transmission of a single message to multiple recipients, reducing telephone bills, eliminating time barriers by enabling users to communicate 24 hours a day, 365 days a year, and fostering open communication among users in various locations.

3. ***Explain guidelines for preparing effective memorandums and e-mail messages.*** Memos and e-mail messages are written informally and normally make extensive use of jargon, abbreviations, and acronyms. An effective subject line should be long enough to fully describe the gist of the message and to prepare the receiver for understanding the message. The first line of the message should repeat the subject line for clarity. The deductive outline is used for memos and e-mail messages that convey positive or routine ideas; the inductive outline is used for negative ideas.

4. ***Identify acceptable practices for writing effective e-mail messages and using electronic communication appropriately.*** Send an e-mail message only if the receiver wishes to communicate electronically and include only one idea in a message. Provide a descriptive subject line for an e-mail message so that a receiver can sort through an overloaded e-mail box to locate important messages efficiently. Formatting guidelines for e-mail messages include the following: Limit the message to one screen and keep the lines short to display an entire line; use mixed-case (upper- and lowercase letters); and omit special print commands and other special formatting that may be unreadable and time-consuming to download. Use emoticons and e-mail abbreviations only if the receiver

will understand them and the formality of the message is appropriate for such casual shorthand.

   Appropriate netiquette includes the following: Check your e-mail promptly and minimize e-mail overload by sending concise, business-related messages only to the people who need the message. Allow negative messages to cool off before sending them. Do not send highly emotional, sensitive messages that may be misinterpreted without important nonverbal elements present in face-to-face communication. Do not send confidential messages because the security of e-mail is low compared to other media. Develop an efficient way for handling excessive amounts of e-mail and be cautious of downloading e-mail viruses that could damage computer files.

5. ***Identify ethical and legal implications associated with technology.*** As you handle information, keep these legal and ethical responsibilities in mind: (a) Be certain that information technology does not violate basic rights of individuals and that you abide by all laws related to the use of technology; (b) understand that e-mail is not private and can be monitored by a company; (c) develop and use procedures that protect the security of information (e.g., require employees to use passwords that are difficult to decipher, to change them periodically, and to sign off when away from terminal; and limit information access); and (d) develop a clear and fair privacy policy.

6. ***Write memos and e-mail messages that convey good news, routine information, and negative news.*** Use the deductive approach for memos and e-mail messages that contain good news as the central idea, for example, good-news messages, noncontroversial changes in policies and procedures, instructions, personnel changes, and written records of information included in a "to the file" memo. Use the inductive approach for messages that convey bad news. When writing memos or e-mail messages that outline procedures or give instructions, highlight the steps in a bulleted or numbered list or a flow chart and begin each step with an action statement. To check the accuracy and completeness of the document, complete the procedures by following your instructions step-by-step; then ask another person to do likewise and revise incorporating this input. "To the file" or confirmation memos are written records of oral decisions or discussions that aid a writer in remembering information for future use and in documenting actions in case of litigation.

REFERENCES

[1]McCune, J. C. (1997). E-mail etiquette. *Management Review*, 4(86), 14.

[2]Class, A. (1995, September 14). Pandora's mailbox: How to make e-mail systems more secure, cost-effective and easier to manage. *Computer Weekly*, 40.

[3]McCune, J. C. (1997). E-mail etiquette. *Management Review*, 4(86), 14.

[4]McCune, J. C. (1997). E-mail etiquette. *Management Review*, 4(86), 14.

[5]Ruiz, F. (1997, July 7.) Heed these tips to learn proper e-mail etiquette. *The Tampa Tribune*.

[6]Ruiz, F. (1997, July 7.) Heed these tips to learn proper e-mail etiquette. *The Tampa Tribune*.

[7]Pruner, M. (1996, February 12). The dangers of e-mail: How to use, not use this "killer app." *Lawyers & The Internet*, S7.

[8]Cavanaugh, J. P. (1997, June 17). Corresponding etiquette: E-mail. *The Baltimore Sun*, IE.

[9]Callaway, C. (1997, May 27). "PC" Magazine executive director talks about e-mail etiquette. *CNN Today*.

[10]Letters: E-mail etiquette (1996, July 26). *Information Week* 6.

[11]Callaway, C. (1997, May 27). "PC" Magazine executive director talks about e-mail etiquette. *CNN Today*.

[12]Bhasin, R. (1997, June). The do's and don'ts of e-mail. *Pulp & Paper*, 55.

[13]Sports News, (1992, August 7). *Los Angeles Times*, p. C5.

[14]Federico. R. F., & Bowley, J. M. (1996). The great e-mail debate. *HRMagazine*, 41(l), 67.

[15]Ruiz, F. 1997, July 7. Heed these tips to learn proper e-mail etiquette. *The Tampa Tribune*.

[16]Brown, E. (1997, February 3). The myth of e-mail privacy. *Fortune*, 66.

[17]Western, K. (1996, November 8). E-mail etiquette. *The Arizona Republic*, p. E2.

[18]Cooper, B. (1997, June 8). E-mail organizer Eudora 3.0 is good sort. *Pittsburgh Post-Gazette*, p. C-3.

[19]Pruner, M. (1996, February 12). The dangers of e-mail: How to use, not use this "killer app." *Lawyers & the Internet*, S7.

[20]Mason, R. O. (1986). Four ethical issues of the information age. In Dejoie, R., Fowler, G., & Paradice, D. (1991). *Ethical issues in information systems* (pp. 46–55). Boston: Boyd & Fraser.

[21]Laudon, K. C., & Laudon, J. P. (1994). *Management information systems: Organization and technology* 3rd ed., New York: Macmillan.

[22]The Social Security Administration and Online Privacy. Electronic Privacy Information Center, [On-line]. Available at: www.epic.org/privacy/database/ssa/ [1997, October 16].

[23]Greenlaw, P. S. (1997). The impact of federal legislation to limit electronic monitoring. *Public Personnel Management*, 26(2), 227–244.

[24]Krol, E. (1992). *The whole INTERNET*, Sebastopol, CA: O'Reilly & Associates.

[25]JCPenney Company, Inc. (1997, Spring). *Inreview*, [Newsletter]. Dallas, TX: Author.

[26]Makeever, J. J. (1996, October 3). Privacy and anonymity in cyberspace. *A law of cybcerspace?* [On-line]. Available at http://host1.jmlx.edu/cyber/1996/r-priv.html [1997, November 25].

REVIEW QUESTIONS

1. Who is the audience to whom memos and e-mail messages are addressed? Do organization principles applied in the writing of letters also apply in the writing of memos and e-mail messages? Explain. (Obj. 1)

2. Are business jargon, acronyms, shortened words, headings, and graphics useful in memos and e-mail messages? Why? (Obj. 1, 3)

3. What purpose does the subject line of a memo serve? Provide suggestions for writing an effective subject line for a memo. (Obj. 1)

4. What are the advantages of sending e-mail? (Obj. 2)

5. List two reasons a useful subject line is important in an e-mail message. Provide general suggestions for writing one. (Obj. 3)

6. What guidelines should be followed when formatting an e-mail message? (Obj. 3, 4)

7. List three types of messages that should not be sent by e-mail. Explain. (Obj. 4, 5)

8. What can you do to limit the excessive amount of e-mail that lowers a manager's productivity? (Obj. 4)

9. What practice should be followed to avoid sending a "flame"? (Obj. 4, 5)

10. What are emoticons and e-mail abbreviations? Describe their usefulness in e-mail messages. (Obj. 4)

11. List and briefly discuss two legal or ethical issues related to the use of e-mail. (Obj. 5)

12. Provide guidelines for writing instructions that can be understood and followed consistently. (Obj. 6)

13. How do enumerations (bulleted or numbered lists) affect the effectiveness of a message explaining a procedure or giving instructions? When should numbers versus bullets be used to mark each step? (Obj. 6)

14. What is a "to the file" memo? Provide circumstances when it should be used. (Obj. 6)

15. Must memos and e-mail messages be formatted as a continuous group of single-spaced paragraphs or can they contain headings to denote logical divisions in the content? Explain. (Obj. 6)

EXERCISES

1. **Critique of Memos and E-Mail Messages Produced by Real Companies (Obj. 1-6)**
   Locate an example of both a well-written and a poorly written memo or e-mail message. Analyze the strengths and weaknesses of each document. Be prepared to discuss in class.

2. **Selection of an Appropriate Communication Channel (Obj. 1, 6)**
   Indicate whether you believe e-mail would be an appropriate medium for sending the following messages. Justify your answer. Suggest an appropriate channel for messages you identify as inappropriate for e-mail.

   a. The company is expecting a visit from members of a committee evaluating your bid for this year's Malcolm Baldrige National Quality Award. All employees must be notified of the visit.

   b. After careful deliberation, the management of a midsized pharmaceutical company is convinced the only way to continue its current level of research is to sell the company to a larger company. The employees must be informed of this decision.

   c. Lincoln Enterprises is eager to receive the results of a drug test on a certain employee. The drug testing company has been asked to send the results as quickly as possible.

   d. An employee in the Atlanta office is preparing to assume an overseas assignment in the Moscow office and is seeking information from a colleague currently working there.

   e. José Perez, the recipient of the memo in Figure 7-1, requested a revised analysis of the projections. He has asked you to send the spreadsheet so that he can manipulate the data himself.

   f. A manager must alert an employee to complaints received about the employee's interactions with prospective customers.

   g. The credit manager extends credit to a new account and provides general marketing suggestions and sales promotion on a related line.

   h. The shipping department has located the common carrier currently holding a customer's shipment that should have been delivered yesterday. Inform the customer that the carrier has promised delivery by tomorrow morning.

   i. A company refuses to make an adjustment on a claim to repair an appliance that is no longer under warranty.

   j. The Director of Learning and Development announces software training sessions to be held during the upcoming quarter in two company locations.

3. **Useful Subject Lines (Obj. 1, 3, 4)**
   Write effective subject lines for the following situations.

   a. You must inform employees of the specific dates for repaving the company parking lot. Half of the normal parking spaces will be available on any given day during this process.

   b. You are part of a committee planning a reception/banquet for the company's annual alumni(ae) event. You want to give the committee a report on the menu choices available in the price range agreed on at the initial planning meeting.

   c. Notify all employees that the youth sports team (soccer, baseball, basketball) your company sponsors is playing for the league championship game. Provide a list of the players and encourage the employees to support the team (whatever you believe is appropriate).

   d. As a sales representative, send the production scheduler an e-mail message suggesting an alternative for managing overtime. Explain that hiring and training students to fill rush orders would be less expensive than paying the excessive overtime and would avoid the sensitive issue of overtime for regular employees.

   e. Encourage employees to take part in the statewide "Trash Bash" scheduled for later this month. Announce you have issued a friendly challenge to one of the company's local competitors in an effort to promote active participation in this worthy community effort.

f. Explain that a customary end-of-year employee bonus will not be possible because of declining sales. You must justify your decision without alarming the recipients.

g. Ask the human resources director if you will be able to retain your U.S. citizenship when you assume a permanent position in an international office.

h. Write a subject line for each scenario in Exercise 2 that you identified as appropriate for e-mail.

4. **Document for Analysis: Procedures Memo (Obj. 1, 3, 4, 6)**
Analyze the following section of a procedures memo intended to communicate a company's earthquake preparedness plan to all employees. Pinpoint its strengths and weaknesses, and then revise the memo as directed by your instructor.

Because earthquake tremors have been jarring Evansville and we are located in a high-rise building, we need to be sure that we are prepared for an earthquake. Therefore, the following actions should be taken in the event of an earthquake:

(1) Elevators should not be used.

(2) Fire alarms or sprinkler systems may activate and startle people.

(3) Earthquakes do not kill; buildings do.

(4) If outside, open areas are safer than areas near wires, signs, buildings, or trees.

(5) People in offices should drop to the floor, take cover under desks, and ride out the tremor.

(6) If no desks or tables are near, people should seek cover against an interior wall.

(7) Windows, glass doors, tall furniture, and hanging objects should be avoided.

If you have any questions, please let me know.

5. **Document for Analysis: Commendation E-Mail Message (Obj. 1, 3, 4, 6)**
Analyze the following e-mail message. Pinpoint its strengths and weaknesses, and then revise the e-mail message as directed by your instructor.

Msg #14

E-mail from Claire Jones-Bateman sent 12/2/1999 at 1:45 p.m.

TO: Mr. Charles Wright, Supervisor, High-Cotton Pants Section

SUBJECT: QUALITY PERFORMANCE AT BAXTER ENTERPRISES

DEAR CHARLES

BEING A SEWING-MACHINE OPERATOR IN OUR PLANT IS A VERY DEMANDING JOB. BOREDOM AND FATIGUE OFTEN CAUSES ERRORS AND CUT-RATE PRODUCTS. : - (

HOWEVER, LAST MONTH IN YOUR SECTION, ALL THE HIGH-COTTON PANTS MET OUR QUALITY STANDARDS. WE COMMEND YOUR ON THIS ACHIEVEMENT. THANK YOU FOR MAKING BAXTER PRODUCTS BETTER THAN EVER!

BCNU,

CLAIRE

| <Enter> next msg | <F2> save in mailbox |
| <F5> save to disk | <Esc> stop reading |

APPLICATIONS

1. **E-Mail Message: Select a Scenario (Obj. 1, 3–6)**
Compose an e-mail message for the scenarios described in Exercise 3 as directed by your instructor.

2. **Good News Memo or E-mail: Reaping Benefits of Total Quality Management Program (Obj. 1, 3–6)**
Several years ago Maxwell Corporation initiated a Total Quality Management program to improve the quality of the recliners it manufactures. Finally, the company is reaping the payoffs of this program: increased market share, sales, and profits. Because of employee satisfaction, the workforce is stable; absenteeism is no longer a problem; and employee turnover is almost nonexistent. To express appreciation for the employees' sustained effort, the board of directors has approved an extra day of vacation. The vacation day may be taken between January 2 and June 30 of the next year.

Required: Write a memo or e-mail message to the employees as director of human resources.

3. **Good-News Memo or E-Mail: Controlling Health Care Costs (Obj. 1, 3–6)**

Remotique Industries reduces its health care benefit costs by using a self-insured medical plan. The company pays the health care bills of each employee directly to the health care provider rather than paying an insurance premium to an insurance company. In an effort to control these costs, Remotique undertook a plan to increase the level of preventive health care. The plan included classes in smoking cessation, drug and alcohol rehabilitation, and physical fitness. The company constructed a walking track and began paying employees' membership in one of the city's exercise clubs. Now, two years after the program was initiated, the company is seeing a decline of 8 percent in the monthly medical costs.

Required: Write a memo or e-mail message to all employees informing them of the program's success and praising them for their commitment to the various programs.

4. **Routine Request E-Mail: Tax-Deferred Investment Opportunities (Obj. 1, 3–6)**

Several of the latest issues of your company newsletter have mentioned the opportunities employees of your organization have to shelter a portion of their earnings in a tax-deferred, self-directed retirement account. The account, permitted by section 403(b) of the Internal Revenue Code, is referred to as a 403(b) account. Several of your colleagues have told you they have had a 403(b) account for some time. Frankly, you don't know much about investments and income taxes; thus, all your savings are in a savings account and certificates of deposits. You are interested in receiving information about 403(b) accounts. You need to know whether these investments will be taxed and what kind of administration or brokerage fees you will have to pay, if any. You are concerned about where the money will be invested and the risk involved. Finally, you have no idea how to get started. Assume you are a computer operator.

Required: E-mail Darryl Robbins, Director of Benefits/Compensation, to get answers to your questions.

5. **Routine Request Memo or E-Mail: Intern Approved (Obj. 1, 3–6)**

Sheila Leiter, a senior account executive in a public relations firm, sent the following e-mail to the firm's chief executive officer:

The University of Springfield public relations program has asked us to participate in its internship program. The program is designed to provide its juniors at least 150 hours of on-the-job experience over a 10-week period.

The upcoming Hallman's campaign would provide a meaningful experience to an intern. In addition, the intern's contributions would help us meet the hopelessly tight deadlines inherent in a national ad campaign.

Let me have your answer by July 5 so I can initiate the interview process and have the intern on board when we begin preliminary planning for the Hallman campaign.

Required: As the chief executive officer, write a memo or e-mail message to Sheila Leiter (or substitute your instructor's name) approving the firm's participation in the internship program and authorizing her to coordinate the selection of the intern and work assignments. Provide instructions related to compensation (salary/fringe benefits) and any other information you believe is pertinent.

6. **Information Memo or E-Mail: Casual Dress Policy Announced (Obj. 1, 3–6)**

As director of human resources, you have been authorized to develop an appropriate casual dress policy for your company (you specify the type of company). Conduct the research needed to develop the policy; use your own work experience and information obtained from an on-line search to develop a policy that meets your objectives. Provide a detailed explanation of acceptable casual dress that employees can follow consistently.

Required: Compose a memo or e-mail message announcing the company's new casual dress policy that will go into effect July 1.

7. **Information Memo or E-Mail: Let's Play Ball! (Obj. 1, 3–6)**

The company president has directed you (director of human resources) to explore the feasibility of starting a company-sponsored softball team. You obtained a packet of information from the city's Parks and Recreation department that provided information related to the registration fee, costs of uniforms, and starting dates for practices/games. An e-mail survey of employees revealed significant interest in starting a team. Several potential players who have played city league softball previously commented that "we would need some serious practice" to be competitive. They suggested the possibility of converting a field behind the main building to a practice field so that players could practice during lunch and after work. A local construction company gave you a $5,000 bid for completing the work.

Required: Send a memo or e-mail to Ray Petre, president, communicating the employees' support of a team and administration costs. Recommend that the practice field be built on company property and provide cost of the conversion.

8. **Information Memo or E-Mail: New Insurance Carrier Announced (Obj. 1, 3–6)**

   You are the director of human resources for Computech, a computer manufacturer employing 1,300 people. You have changed insurance carriers recently (from Sharp & Rankin to Jaynes Insurance Company) to take advantage of lower premiums without reducing coverage. Jaynes Insurance Co. will bill Computech for its portion of the insurance premium on a quarterly rather than a monthly basis. In return for the reduced premium, Computech will assume responsibility of verifying the validity of the policyholders and dependents. Unlike the previous carrier, Jaynes requires pre-approval for nonemergency hospitalization; a brochure explaining detailed procedures will be distributed to each policyholder. With the new plan, the annual deductible is reduced from $500 to $250 annually (for the policyholder and each dependent).

   Required: Compose a memo or e-mail message to all employees. Consider what information should be included in the memo informing employees of the change of insurance carrier and whether an e-mail or memo would be the appropriate channel for this message.

9. **Information Memo: Announcing Major Change in Operations (Obj. 1, 3, 6)**

   On March 1999, the board of directors approved the expenditure of resources to convert to optical scanners to track the flow of production through the plant. After extensive research (including information from quality circles of employees directly involved in the work flow), the vice president of information systems ordered the appropriate hardware. All equipment needed for the conversion has arrived. The vice president of information systems anticipates that approximately one month will be needed to install and test the equipment. To facilitate a smooth transition, the supervisors must begin to prepare the employees for the conversion.

   Required: Conduct an on-line search to locate information related to dealing with employee resistance to change and identify an appropriate strategy (procedures) for informing employees of a major change in day-to-day operations. Write the memo to the supervisors.

10. **Information Memo: To Fire or Not to Fire (Obj. 1, 3, 6)**

    You are the controller for a regional mail-order catalog company with outlets in the Northeast. You have received a call from a customer, Penny Benjamin, who has not received her merchandise although the $564 check has been returned with her bank statement. Upon investigating this situation, you learn that similar complaints have been received over the past year. Using a variety of auditing procedures, you suspect that Kelly Hubbard, the mailroom clerk, has cashed the checks. When you call Kelly in to discuss the matter, he confesses to the thefts, explaining that he spent the money to support a gambling habit. Over the past year, he had stolen a total of $20,590.

    As the controller, you must write a memo to your supervisor telling her about the embezzlement and recommending appropriate action. You are honestly confused about which of the following options you should recommend: (a) Terminate Kelly's employment and write off the loss, (b) terminate Kelly's employment and initiate a civil lawsuit in an attempt to recover the money, (c) terminate Kelly's employment and file criminal charges of embezzlement, (d) retain Kelly in his current position with the agreement he will pay back the embezzled funds in installments, or (e) retain Kelly but transfer him to a position with no access to cash and require him to pay back the embezzled funds in installments.

    As you think about these options, consider the following issues: (a) Kelly has fully cooperated with your investigation, providing documentation and aiding you in pinpointing the exact amount embezzled. He seems repentant not because he has been caught but because he has hurt the company and understands he has broken the law. He insists that he intended to pay the money back as soon as his investment luck changed. Should his attitude influence your decision? (b) Many mail-order companies have recently been in the media for various fraud cases; this negative coverage has damaged your company's image. Could this fact affect your decision? (c) Is recovering the money critical? Is ensuring that Kelly faces the consequences of his actions critical?

    Required: Write a memo to your supervisor, Jill Ainsworth, explaining the embezzlement and presenting your recommended action with logical justification.

11. **Procedures Memo or E-Mail: Instructions for Completing a Computer Task (Obj. 1, 3–6)**

    As the director of computer resources, you want to expand employees' use of computer technology. Write a memo to all employees including instructions for completing a new computer task. For example, provide instructions for attaching a word processing file to an e-mail message; creating a distribution list for e-mail; scanning an image using a scanner; recording a sound clip and inserting it into an electronic presentation; locating and copying clip art, sounds, and video from the Internet and inserting them into an electronic presentation; linking spreadsheets and graphics so the graphics are updated automatically when the spreadsheet is revised; and so forth. To ensure its accuracy, complete the procedure following the steps you wrote and ask another person (preferably unfamiliar with the procedure) to follow your instructions. Incorporate any changes in a revised draft.

Required: Send the memo or e-mail to your instructor. Your instructor may ask you to submit a rough draft and final copy. Be prepared to discuss the types of changes required as a result of "walking through" your procedures.

12. **Procedures Memo or E-Mail: Company Donation to Community Service Organization (Obj. 1, 3–6)**
As president of Wadsworth Industries, compose a memo to all employees explaining that the company will donate $100 per quarter to a community service for any employee who donates at least 15 hours in a quarter to a community service. Provide procedures for submitting a request to the company (e.g., obtain a form from Eve Ward, human resources manager, to be submitted by the end of the quarter; provide name, address, telephone number, executive director, and not-for-profit number for community service, etc.).

Required: Send the memo or e-mail to your instructor.

13. **"To File" Memo: Confirm Reimbursement (Obj. 1, 3, 6)**
Marsha Rhodes, one of the internal auditors you supervise as director of internal audit, attended an executive education seminar where she learned of a certification program for contingency planning. She convinced you the training she would receive in preparing to take the Certified Contingency Planner examination would benefit the company by preparing it to continue operations in the event of a natural disaster. Therefore, you committed the company to reimburse her for expenses incurred in earning the certification—tuition for a preparation course and the exam registration fee. The reimbursement is contingent on her passing the exam within a two-year period. Because of the lengthy time frame involved and the unique nature of this agreement, you need a written record for your files and decide to send Marsha a confirmation for her records.

Required: Write a memo to Marsha confirming the details of this agreement.

14. **"To File" Memo: Disciplinary Conference with Surly Construction Manager (Obj. 1, 3, 6)**
Assume you are David Windham, owner of Windham Construction, and have received a letter from the realty company who is showing your "spec" homes to prospective buyers (see Application 15, Chapter 6). The realtor alerted you to the actions of your construction manager, Gene Stuart, who she believes is turning buyers away. You have talked with Gene already about these same actions, and he had agreed to adjust his behavior; you have documentation of previous conferences in his personnel file. Today you conducted a formal disciplinary conference with Gene to discuss the situation and to inform him he will be demoted to a crew member if another incident occurs.

Required: Write a memo to Gene's file confirming the details of the disciplinary conference.

15. **Bad-News E-Mail: Back to the Road for Sales Reps (Obj. 1, 3–6)**
You are the sales manager for a national pharmaceutical company. Several years ago, in an effort to cut costs, your company required sales reps to make sales contacts primarily by telephone and fax machine rather than one-to-one sales calls with doctors, who were often too busy to meet with the rep. Using communication technology allowed the company to reduce the sales staff and excessive travel costs. Morale of the sales force has increased because reps prefer working in the office. You believe, however, the company's recent decline in sales is a result of this policy. Research shows that the success rate of telephone/fax contacts is 50 percent compared to an 85 percent success rate with personal contacts. An informal survey of the company's current customers indicated that they prefer talking with the sales rep in person, especially when considering a new drug. Thus, management has accepted your recommendation that the sales force begin making personal sales calls three days a week to maintain relations with existing clients and to acquire new customers.

Required: Write an e-mail message to the sales force informing them of this change. (Your instructor may ask you to submit a printed copy of your e-mail message.)

16. **Bad-News Memo: Plant Will Close for Two Weeks (Obj. 1, 3, 6)**
Economic troubles have hit the Janata Forge Machinists Plant. Many employees have been laid off, and the grapevine has begun to promote rumors that additional employees will be laid off and the company is going bankrupt. Communication related to the initial layoffs was poor and reactive. Top management is convinced that communication between employer and employees must be improved if the company is to survive this economic downturn. As plant manager, you must announce to employees that the plant will close for two weeks at Christmas. Workers will be paid only 50 percent of their salaries for the two weeks the plant is closed.

Required: Conduct an on-line search to identify ways to communicate this negative information in an effort to minimize employee fear and inaccurate rumors. Review the research related to communication crises, specifically employer-employee relations (e.g., public relations textbooks and academic journals in the communication field); read articles from practitioners' journals to learn what approaches other companies have taken to improve communication with employees when the company is facing financial difficulty. As the plant manager, use your research to write a memo informing employees of their reduced work schedule during Christmas.

17. **Collaborative Memo: Communicating Concern for Employees (Obj. 1, 3, 6)**
At this week's staff meeting, several of the managers commented that employee morale was quite low and that employees were producing at suboptimal rates. The controller quickly interjected that the financial condition of the company would not permit raises or additional fringe benefits.

At this point you jumped in: "The answer to this situation is clearly not wages and fringe benefits. I am convinced that these employees need to feel as if the company cares about them as individuals, as members of a team. Other companies have been very successful in developing methods to communicate their concern for employees, and they have reaped the benefits in terms of increased employee morale and productivity." Because of your interest in and apparent knowledge of employee motivation, you were asked to research the situation and recommend action.

Required: Conduct an on-line search to identify managerial strategies for showing concern for a particular group of employees you have identified (select a particular business with a specific employee group and environment). Attempt to locate accounts of ideas other companies have implemented successfully. For your supervisor's signature, write a memo to the employees telling them about the idea.

18. **Collaborative Memo: An Ethical Dilemma: An Accountant's Knowledge of a Fraudulent Tax Return (Obj. 1, 3, 6)**
As a tax accountant in a large accounting firm, you prepared Dennis Gair's tax return last year. The return indicated that Mr. Gair was due a small tax refund; his business reported less net income than in the prior year. Now, more than a year later, Mr. Gair has asked your assistance in preparing a business plan to secure a loan. Immediately you notice that last year's income statement shows twice the net income of the income statement you used to prepare the tax return. When you question Mr. Gair about the discrepancy, his evasive response assures you that the understatement of net income for tax purposes was intentional.

You wrote a letter to Mr. Gair asking him to authorize you to file an amended tax return and explaining that the amended return would require him to pay additional taxes, interest, and penalties. The client refused.

Required:

1. Conduct research to answer the following questions: (1) What action does the IRS require of tax preparers when they learn that a filed tax return was fraudulent? Consult tax references such as the circulars published by the Internal Revenue Service. (2) What action does the Code of Ethics of the American Institute of Certified Public Accountants (AICPA) indicate is appropriate for a certified public accountant to take in this circumstance? For this information, refer to tax references such as the *Statements on Responsibilities in Tax Practice*.

2. Write a memo to the tax partner communicating your analysis of the situation and the action you propose that the firm take. List sources of information to increase the credibility of your position.

3. Assume the tax partner was impressed with your meticulous research and documentation and has authorized you to prepare a letter to the client communicating the firm's action. Prepare the letter for the partner's signature; include your reference initials in all capital letters to identify the originator of the message in the event clarification is needed. Address the letter to Dennis Gair, 3300 Parkway Drive, Fresno, CA 91316-3300.

E-MAIL APPLICATION

More people are gaining access to e-mail as a communication avenue. As with other new communication channels, technology often advances faster than the organization's ability to develop adequate procedures for using it. Write a company policy that applies to acceptable use of e-mail. Address such issues as message security, company monitoring of messages, appropriate message content, etc. Send your policy over e-mail to the instructor. Word it as though it is going out to all company personnel.

REAL-TIME INTERNET CASE

Anonymity in Cyberspace

Is there a right to anonymity in cyberspace? Should there be a right to anonymity in cyberspace? Two current views prevail about the right of anonymity. One view sees anonymity as limiting; by having a wealth of information available, people can communicate, shop, and conduct business with ease. Access to information allows you to find a friend's e-mail address that you had forgotten or to track down an old friend in another city. The opposing view sees the right to anonymity as a protection of individual privacy; without anonymity, unidentified parties can track where you go in cyberspace, how often you go there, and with whom you communicate. At the present time, you are typically required to reveal your identity when engaging in a wide range of activities. Every time you use a credit card, e-mail a friend, or subscribe to an on-line magazine, an identifiable record of each transaction is created and linked to you. But must this always be the case? Are there situations where transactions may be conducted anonymously, yet securely? Several methods currently exist for surfers to protect their anonymity in cyberspace: [26]

- Anonymous remailers: A completely anonymous remailer, or chain remailer, sends mail through remailing locations. Each location takes the header information off the mail and sends it to the next location. When the mail gets to its final destination, the recipient has no idea where the mail originated. What makes the system truly anonymous is that the remailing locations that the message goes through typically keep no records of the mail that comes in or goes out. This procedure makes the mail impossible to track.

- Pseudo-anonymous remailers: These single remailers work similarly to the chain remailer. The mail is sent to a remailing location, the header information is stripped at this sight, and the mail is forwarded to its final destination. As with the chain remailer, the recipient has no idea where the mail originated. What makes the single remailer pseudo-anonymous is the fact that single remailers typically keep records of the mail that comes into and goes out of their systems. This procedure makes the mail traceable.

- Pseudonymity: This process consists of sending mail through cyberspace under a false name. Like the single

remailer, the recipient will not immediately know who the mail came from, but the mail is completely traceable.

- Anonymizer web site: By using the address http://www/anonymizer.com:8080WEBSITENAME you can stop that web site from gathering any information on you. When you send your "web-site request," the anonymizer goes to that web site for you, grabs the information, and sends you the information from the site. As far as the web site knows, they have been contacted only by the anonymizer web site. This secures your transactions and keeps "nosey" web sites from gathering information on you.

In spite of consumer interest in protecting anonymity, the federal government opposes total anonymity due to legitimate interests that are at stake. If total anonymity existed, the government would be unable to track down people who use cyberspace to violate the laws of libel, defamation, and copyrights. Visit the following Internet sites and complete the activities as directed by your instructor.

Internet Sites

http://host1.jmls.edu/cyber/1996/r-priv.html
http://www.replay.com/mirror/privacy/p1.1.0.html
http://www.hallucinet.com/wednesday/thenet.html

Activities

1. Linking from the Internet sites listed for this case, locate an additional article on the issue of on-line anonymity. Print out the article and prepare a two-page abstract that includes the following sections: (1) reference citation, (2) overview, (3) major point, and (4) application.

2. Prepare a chart that summarizes the advantages and the disadvantages of on-line anonymity.

3. Take a position on the anonymity issue, either to support the right to anonymity or to defend the need for identification. In writing, present a defense of your position, giving reasons and/or evidence.

CHAPTER EIGHT

Writing Persuasive Messages

LEARNING OBJECTIVES

When you have completed Chapter 8, you will be able to:

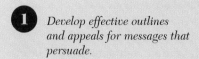 Develop effective outlines and appeals for messages that persuade.

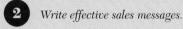 Write effective sales messages.

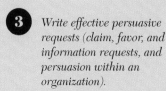 Write effective persuasive requests (claim, favor, and information requests, and persuasion within an organization).

*E*very day, we are targets of persuasion from advertisers on the radio, on television, in newspapers and magazines, on billboards, and even in movies. We are bombarded with messages designed to convince us to buy the newest sports drink, see the latest Hollywood blockbuster, and support the best cause. In an election year, we are targets of the persuasive techniques of politicians. Persuasion is an effective sales technique—but it is also a strategy businesspeople must master to gain the support of others in important decisions. Persuasion involves the ability to win others to your point of view.

For example, Steak and Ale restaurant faced the challenge of communicating to its employees a significant change in service and style, accompanied by new uniforms. Rather than coercing or demanding that employees accept the change, a letter from Bob Mande, President of Steak and Ale, emphasized reasons the changes were being made (benefits to guests, the company, and the employees) and the employee's important role in implementing the changes. An excerpt from a minimagazine developed for employees shown in Figure 8-1 includes Mande's open and honest explanation of the changes.

Using a lighthearted, entertaining approach, the magazine provides (a) a visual model of the fresh, crisp, and professional look the company expected with the uniform change, and (b) helpful information on ways to achieve this look. Note the "you" orientation in the "style flashes" that are interwoven throughout the magazine:

> Out of control hair is the biggest turnoff to Guests in restaurants—they don't want it wandering into their food. So pull your hair back and pull in a better tip.
>
> If you wear a lot of jewelry, Guests may think you don't need as large a tip.
>
> Your smile is the most important part of your appearance and it's the first signal to Guests that their Steak and Ale experience will be a memorable one. Your smile tells Guests, "I'm happy you're here!" But hey, don't take our word for it. Check out the recent study by Boston College which found that smiling suggests an awareness of the needs of others. Maybe that's the reason behind the phrase "winning smile."[1]

The detailed pages leave no doubt in an employee's mind as to what management considers clean, crisp, and professional. However, by continually emphasizing the benefits employees gain from the change, management gathers support for the high standards being imposed.

In small groups, generate a list of persuasive messages you have received or written recently. In thinking about persuasive messages you have written previously, did you feel prepared to write them effectively? Why or why not?

1 *Develop effective outlines and appeals for messages that persuade.*

Persuasion Strategies

The Steak and Ale example illustrates persuasion at work. **Persuasion** is the ability to influence others to accept your point of view. It is not an attempt to trap someone into taking action favorable to the writer. Instead, it is an honest, organized presentation of information on which a person may choose to act. In all occupations and professions, rich rewards await those who can use well-informed and well-prepared presentations to persuade others to accept their ideas or buy their products, services, or ideas.

How do you learn to persuade others through written communication? Have you ever written a cover letter, completed an application for a job, or written an essay for college entry or a scholarship? If so, you already have experience with this type of writing.

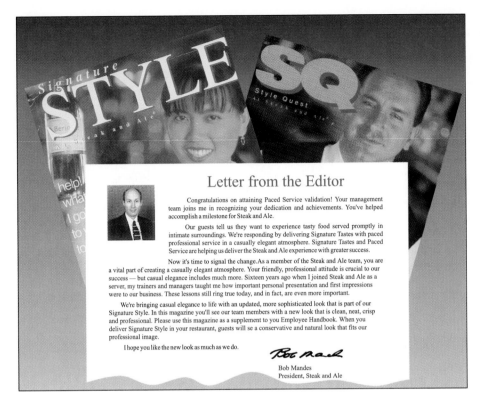

FIGURE 8-1
The persuasive message to
Steak and Ale employees
garners support for a
change in service style and
new uniforms.

For persuasion to be effective, you must understand your product, service, or idea; know your audience; anticipate the arguments that may come from the audience; and have a rational and logical response to those arguments. Remember, persuasion need not be a hard sell; it can simply be a way of getting a client or your supervisor to say, "Yes." Although many of the examples and discussions in this chapter concentrate on selling *products and services,* similar principles apply to selling an *idea, your organization,* and *your own abilities.*

What is the difference
between motivation and
manipulation?

Plan Before You Write

Success in *writing* is directly related to success in preliminary *thinking.* If the right questions have been asked and answered, the writing will be easier and the message will be more persuasive. Specifically, you need information about (1) your product, service, or idea, (2) your audience, and (3) the desired action.

Know the Product, Service, or Idea. You cannot be satisfied with knowing the product, service, or idea in a general way; you need details. Get your information by (1) reading all available literature, (2) using the product and watching others use it, (3) comparing the product, service, or idea with others, (4) conducting tests and experiments, and (5) soliciting reports from users.

Before you write, you need concrete answers to such questions as these:

- What will the product, service, or idea do for the receiver(s)?

- What are its superior features (e.g., design and workmanship or receiver benefit)?

COMMUNICATION MENTOR

When writing to persuade, your commitment to what you believe can turn your words into blunt instruments. Because no one likes being hit over the head, even figuratively, edit your work mercilessly to avoid that self-defeating trap. When done well, persuasive writing is akin to a properly used scalpel—the surgeon's knowledge combined with the precision of the instrument's edge do the work, not the pressure of the blade.

R. D. Saenz, Chief Financial Officer
Snider Communications Corporation

- How is the product or service different from its competition? How is the proposed idea superior to other viable alternatives?
- What is the cost to the receiver?

> **Consider a product you currently use. What is the major difference that makes it distinct from competing brands?**

Similar questions must be answered about other viable alternatives or competing products. Of particular importance is the question, "What is the major difference?" People are inclined to choose an item (or alternative) that has some distinct advantage. For example, some people may choose a brand of bread because it is high in fiber and contains no cholesterol; still others may choose bread because it is wrapped in two-layer paper.

Know the Receiver. Who are the people to whom the persuasive message is directed? What are their wants and needs? Is a persuasive message to be written and addressed to an individual or to a group? If it is addressed to a group, what characteristics do the members have in common? What are their common goals, their occupational levels, their educational status? To what extent have their needs and wants been satisfied? (See the discussion of Maslow's needs hierarchy in Chapter 2.)

> **Consider a decision to telecommute. What appeals would be appropriate to persuade supervisors and employees?**

Some people may respond favorably to appeals to physiological, security, and safety needs (to save time and money, to be comfortable, to be healthy, or to avoid danger). People with such needs would be impressed with a discussion of such benefits as convenience, durability, efficiency, or serviceability. Others may respond favorably to appeals to their social, ego, and self-actualizing needs (to be loved, entertained, remembered, popular, praised, appreciated, or respected). Consider the varying appeals used in a memo to employees and to supervisors seeking support of telecommuting. The memo to employees would appeal to the need for greater flexibility and reduced stress. Appeals directed at supervisors would focus on increased productivity and morale, reduced costs (office space), and compliance with the Clean Air Act (federal law requiring companies to find ways to get employees off the road to reduce air pollution and traffic congestion).

Identify the Desired Action. What do you want the receiver to do? Complete an order form and enclose a personal check? Receive a demonstration copy/model for trial examination? Return a card requesting a representative to call? Write for more information? Approve a request to allow you to telecommute two days a week? Accept a significant change in service, style, and uniforms as Steak and Ale's employees were asked to do? Whatever the desired action, you need to have a clear definition of it before beginning to compose the letter.

Apply Sound Writing Principles

The principles of unity, coherence, and emphasis are just as important in persuasive messages as in other messages. In addition, some other principles seem to be especially helpful in persuasive messages:

- **Keep paragraphs short.** The spaces between paragraphs show the dividing place between ideas, improve appearance, and provide convenient resting places for the eyes. Hold the first and last paragraph to three or fewer lines; a one-line paragraph (even a very short line) is acceptable. You can even use paragraphs less than one sentence long! Put four or five words on the first line and complete the sentence in a new paragraph. Be careful to include key attention-getting words that either introduce the product, service, or idea or lead to its introduction.

- **Use concrete nouns and active verbs.** Concrete nouns and active verbs help receivers see the product, service, or idea and its benefits more vividly than do abstract nouns and passive verbs.

- **Use specific language.** General words seem to imply subjectivity unless they are well supported with specifics. Specific language is space consuming (saying that something is "great" is less space consuming than telling what makes it so); therefore, persuasive messages are usually longer than other messages. Still, persuasive messages need to be concise; they should say what needs to be said without wasting words.

- **Let receivers have the spotlight.** If receivers are made the subject of some of the sentences, if they can visualize themselves with the product in their hands, if they can get the feel of using it for enjoyment or to solve problems, the chances of creating a desire are increased.

- **Stress a central selling point or appeal.** A thorough analysis will ordinarily reveal some feature that is different from the features of competing products or some benefit not provided by other viable alternatives. This point of difference can be developed into a theme that is woven throughout the entire letter. Or, instead of using a point of difference as a central selling point, a writer may choose to stress one of the major satisfactions derived from using the item or doing as asked (approving a claim or responding favorably to a request). A central selling point (*theme*) should be introduced early in the message and should be reinforced throughout the remainder of the message.

In small groups, brainstorm the possible central selling points for a particular automobile of your choice. With what type of audience would each selling point be most appropriate?

- **Use an inductive outline.** Well over eighty years ago, Sherwin Cody summarized the persuasive process into four basic steps called *AIDA*.[2] The steps have been varied somewhat and have had different labels, but the fundamentals remain relatively unchanged. The AIDA steps for selling are

  A Get the receiver's *attention*.
  I Introduce the product, service, or idea and arouse *interest* in it.
  D Create *desire* by presenting convincing evidence of the value of the product, service, or idea.
  A Encourage *action*.

A persuasive message written following these steps is inductive. The main idea, which is the request for action, appears in the *last* paragraph after presenting the details—convincing reasons for the receiver to comply with the request.

Each step is essential, but the steps do not necessarily require equal amounts of space. Good persuasive writing does not require separate sentences and paragraphs

Strategic Forces: Legal and Ethical Constraints

Ethical Persuasion Is Good Business

Businesses have learned that unethical behavior, such as overstating the capabilities of a product or service (promising more than can be delivered), is not good for business in the long run. Developing effective persuasion skills will be important throughout your profession as you apply for a job, seek promotion or advancement, or seek to persuade your employer to adopt your ideas. Use the effective persuasion techniques you are learning to present your argument ethically—not to exploit the receiver. The following rules will assist you in presenting facts honestly, truthfully, and objectively:

- ***Use concrete evidence and objective language to create an accurate representation of your product, service, or idea (and the competition if mentioned).*** Be certain you can substantiate all claims made about your product or service. Overzealous sales representatives or imaginative writers can use language skillfully to create less-than-accurate perceptions in the minds of receivers. However, legal guidelines related to truth in advertising provide clear guidance for misrepresentation of products or services. If you exaggerate or mislead in a letter and use the U.S. Postal Service to deliver the letter, you can be charged with

the federal offense of mail fraud. Penalties can include significant fines and imprisonment.

- ***Do not deliberately omit, distort, or hide important information that does not support your argument so that the receiver completely misses it.*** Consider the truthfulness of a president disclosing the financial benefits of a plant closing but omitting the fact that 3,000 employees were laid off in a town where the plant is the primary employer. The investor may miss this important comparison as the manager intended and may lose faith in the manager's credibility.

Application

Consider a message, such as a letter or television advertisement, that promotes a product or service that you have used or experienced (e.g., a new fast-food restaurant). How accurate was the message's representation of the product or service? Did the message embellish or exaggerate the quality of the product or service? Do you feel that you were misled in any way? Did your perception of the company change as a result of your experience? Write a memo to your instructor or be prepared to discuss your first-hand experience in class.

---

for each phase of a letter—getting attention; introducing the product, service, or idea; giving evidence; and stimulating action. Points (a) and (b) *could* appear in the same sentence, and point (c) *could* require many paragraphs. Blend the steps in the four-step outline to prepare effective and persuasive (1) sales letters, (2) claims, favors, and information requests, and (3) requests within organizations.

2   *Write effective sales messages.*

Why are unsolicited sales letters often referred to as "junk mail"? What can the writer do to dispel this attitude?

Sales Letters

The four-point outline is appropriate for an **unsolicited sales letter**, a letter written to someone who has not requested it. A **solicited sales letter** has been requested by a potential buyer or supporter, that is, the letter is written to answer this interested person's question. Someone who has invited a persuasive message has given some attention to the product, service, or idea already; an attention-getting sentence is hardly essential. However, such a sentence is essential when the receiver is not known to have expressed an interest previously. The very first sentence, then, is deliberately designed to make a receiver put aside other thoughts and concentrate on the rest of the message.

Gaining Attention

Various techniques have been successful in convincing receivers to consider an unsolicited sales letter. Some commonly used attention-getting devices include

- *A **personal experience:*** *When a doctor gives you instructions, how often have you thought, "I wish you had time to explain" or "I wish I knew more about medical matters."*

- *A **solution to a problem (outstanding feature/benefit):*** *Imagine creating a customized multimedia presentation that . . .*

- *A **startling announcement:*** *More teens die as a result of suicide each month than die in auto accidents in the same time period.*

- *A **what-if opening:*** *What if I told you there is a savings plan that will enable you to retire three years earlier?*

- *A **question:*** *Why should you invest in a company that has lost money for six straight years?*

- *A **story:*** *Here's a typical day of a manager who uses Wilson Enterprises Pager.*

- *A **proverb or quote from a famous person:*** *P. T. Barnum supposedly said, "There's a sucker born every minute." At Northland Candy Factory, we make the saying come true.*

- *A **split sentence:*** *Picture . . .*
  your audience's enthusiastic response to eye-catching graphics and colorful visuals to support your major points.

- *An **analogy:*** *With Wentman's inner sole inserts, you'll be walking in the clouds.*

Other attention-getters include a gift, an offer or a bargain, or a comment on an enclosed product sample. Regardless of the technique used, the attention-getter should achieve several important objectives:

- ***Introduce a relationship between the receiver and the product, service, or idea.*** Remaining sentences grow naturally from this beginning sentence. If receivers do not see the relationship between the first sentence and the sales appeal, they may react negatively to the whole message—they may think they have been tricked into reading. For example, consider the following attention-getter: *Would you like to be the chief executive officer of one of America's largest companies? As CEO of Barkley Enterprises, you can launch new products, invest in third-world countries, or arrange billion-dollar buyouts. Barkley Enterprises is one of several companies at your command in the new computer software game developed by Creative Diversions Software.*

  The beginning sentence is emphatic because it is a short question. However, it suggests the letter will be about obtaining a top management position, which it is not. All three sentences combined suggest that the writer is using high-pressure techniques. The computer software game has relevant virtues; one of them could have been emphasized by placing it in the first sentence.

Visit an Internet site for quotations and locate a quote that might be used to promote a product or service.

As a group, use one of the techniques presented to write a creative attention-getter for a product, service, or idea of your choice.

How can your opening sentence backfire and not achieve the desired result?

- *Focus on a central selling feature.* Almost every product, service, or idea will in some respects be superior to its competition. If it is not, such factors as favorable price, fast delivery, or superior service may be used as the primary appeal. This primary appeal (central selling point) must be emphasized, and one of the most effective ways to emphasize a point is by position in the letter. An outstanding feature mentioned in the middle of a letter may go unnoticed, but it will stand out if mentioned in the first sentence. Note how the following opening sentences introduce the central selling feature and lead naturally into the sentences that follow:

  > A complete collection of Salvador Dali prints—only at the PosterShop!
  >
  > You can select complete sets of prints by Doré and Monet, as well as Dali, at the PosterShop, the only fine arts poster dealer with this comprehensive selection of works of art by the "masters." PosterShop will also frame these prints professionally so you can display them in your home as proudly as you would the originals.

- *Use an original approach.* To get the reader's attention and interest, you must offer something new and fresh. Thus, choose an anecdote likely unfamiliar to your receiver or use a peculiar combination of words to describe how a product, service, or idea can solve a receiver's problem. The following personal story grabs the receiver's attention and leads into a presentation of the new features available with *WordPerfect*.[3]

  > I step into my favorite restaurant, and the waiters all dive for cover. Only the restaurant owner has the guts to take my order—as if she really needs to ask. "I'll have the usual," I say. "Give me . . . the *All You Can Eat Buffet*." For the next two hours, I stuff myself. I indulge at the salad bar and I gorge at the taco bar. As much as I consume, though, I haven't tried everything—I just don't have room.
  >
  > In many ways, WordPerfect is like that gigantic buffet. The new WP is packed with powerful, useful features. . . .

Introducing the Product, Service, or Idea

A persuasive message is certainly off to a good start if the first sentences cause the receiver to think, "Here's a solution to one of my problems," "Here's something I need," or "Here's something I want." You may lead the receiver to such a thought by introducing the product, service, or idea in the very first sentence. If you do, you have succeeded in both getting attention and arousing interest in one sentence. An effective introduction of the product, service, or idea is cohesive and action centered, and continues to stress a central selling point.

- *Be cohesive.* If the attention-getter does not introduce the product, service, or idea, it should lead naturally to the introduction. Note the abrupt change in thought and the unrelatedness of the attention-getter to the second paragraph in the following example: *Employees appreciate a company that provides a safe work environment. The Markham Human Resources Association has been conducting a survey for the last six months. Their primary aim is to improve the safety of office work environments.*

  The last words of the first sentence, "safe work environment," are related to "safety of office work environments"—the last words of the last sentence. No word or phrase in the first sentence connects the words of the second sentence, which creates an abrupt, confusing change in thought. In the following revision, the second sentence is tied to the first by the word "that's." "Safety" in the second sentence refers to "protection" in the third. The LogicTech low-radiation monitor is introduced as a means of providing a safe work environment. Additionally, notice that the attention-getter leads smoothly to the discussion of the survey results.

> Employees appreciate a company that provides a safe work environment.
>
> That's one thing the Markham Human Resources Association learned from its six-month survey of the safety of the office work environment. For added protection from radiation emissions, more companies are purchasing LogicTech's low-radiation computer monitors. . . .

- **Be action oriented.** To introduce a product, service, or idea in an interesting way, you must place the product, service, or idea in your receivers' hands and talk about their using it or benefitting from accepting your idea. They will get a clearer picture when reading about something happening than when reading a product description. Also, the picture becomes all the more vivid when the receiver is the hero of the story—the person taking the action. In a sense, you do not sell products, services, or ideas—you sell the pleasure people derive from their use. Logically, then, you have to write more about that use than about the product, service, or idea. If you put receivers to work using your product, service, or idea to solve problems, they will be the subject of most of your sentences.

  Some product description is necessary and natural. In the following example, the writer focuses on the product and creates an uninteresting, still picture: *The ClassicForm treadmill is powered by a five horsepower motor. The patented electronic control system features a digital display screen with variable speed and pause controls.* In the revision, a *person* is the subject of many of the sentences and is enjoying the benefits of the treadmill.

  > As you step on the ClassicForm treadmill to begin your workout, you will immediately enjoy the smooth, even movement. No more jarring starts and stops of other treadmills. That's because our unique electronic control center puts *you* in total control of your workout. All you have to do is press the ON button to start accelerating to your desired speed, which you can easily monitor on the clear digital display. Getting tired? Just press COAST to reduce the speed. Need to stop for a moment? Press the PAUSE button to bring your treadmill to a gradual stop. The strength of the three-horsepower motor will provide you this smooth, even movement for years to come.

- **Stress a central selling point.** If the attention-getter does not introduce a distinctive feature, it should lead to it. You can stress important points by position in the letter and by space allocated to the point. As soon as receivers visualize the product, service, or idea, they need to have attention called to its outstanding features; the features are therefore emphasized because they are mentioned first. If you want to devote much space to the outstanding features, introduce them early. Note how the attention-getter introduces the distinctive selling feature (ease of operation) and how the following sentences keep the receivers' eyes focused on that feature:

Turn to Figures 8-2 and 8-3. Is the receiver or product or idea the subject of most of the sentences? What benefits will the receiver receive from buying the pager and sponsoring the swim team?

Where should the central selling point be mentioned in a persuasive letter?

If you know how to write a check and record it in your checkbook, then you can operate Easy Accounting. It's that *easy to use*. Just click the check icon to display a blank check. Use the number keys to enter the amount of the check and Easy Accounting fills in the word version of the amount. Doesn't that sound *easy*?

Now click at the category box and *conveniently* view a complete listing of your accounts. Move the arrow to the account of your choice and click. The account is written on the check and posted to your records *automatically*.

By stressing one point, you do not limit the message to that point. For example, while *ease of operation* is being stressed, other features are mentioned. A good film presents a star who is seen throughout most of the film; a good term paper presents a central idea that is supported throughout; a school yearbook develops a theme—a sales letter should stress a central selling point.

Providing Convincing Evidence

After you have made an interesting introduction to your product, service, or idea, present enough supporting evidence to satisfy your receivers' needs. Keep one or two main features uppermost in the receivers' minds, and include evidence that supports these features. For example, using appearance as an outstanding selling feature of compact cars while presenting abundant evidence to show economy of operation would be inconsistent.

Present and Interpret Factual Evidence. Few people will believe general statements without supporting factual evidence. Saying a certain machine or method is efficient is not enough. You must say *how you know* it is efficient and present some data to illustrate *how* efficient. Saying a piece of furniture is durable is not enough. Durability exists in varying degrees. You must present information that shows what makes it durable and also define *how* durable. You can establish durability, for example, by presenting information about the manufacturing process, the quality of the raw materials, or the skill of the workers:

> KCC Publishing's Garnet Classics will last your child a lifetime—pages bound in durable gold-embossed hardback, treated with special protectants to retard paper aging, and machine-sewn (not glued) for long-lasting quality. The 100-percent cotton fiber paper can withstand years of turning the pages. The joy of reading can last for years as your children explore the world of classic literature with KCC's Garnet Classics.

How can the writer establish credibility in the mind of the reader?

Presenting research evidence (hard facts and figures) to support your statements is another way to increase your chances of convincing receivers to buy. Presenting results of a research study takes space but makes the letter much more convincing than general remarks about superior durability and appearance.

Evidence presented must not only *be* authentic; it must *sound* authentic, too. Talking about pages treated with special protectants to retard aging and machine-sewn pages suggests the writer is well informed, which increases receiver confidence. Facts and figures are even more impressive if the receiver can get some kind of internal verification of their accuracy. For example, the following paragraph presents figures and gives their derivation:

We insulated 30 houses in Buffalo last year. Before installing the insulation, we asked each homeowner to tell us the total fuel bill for the four coldest months—November, December, January, and February. The average cost was $408, or $102 a month. After installation, we discovered the fuel bill for the same four-month period was $296, or $74 a month—a saving of $28 a month, or 25 percent.

Naturally, your receivers will be less familiar with the product, service, or idea and its uses than you will be. Not only do you have an obligation to give information, you should interpret it if necessary and point out how the information will benefit the receiver. Be prepared to interpret technical concepts in your field to a potential customer/client (e.g., finance majors might interpret tax-deferred annuities in terms of the needs of a specific target audience). Alternatively, you could interpret a feature of a product. Notice how the following examples interpret the capacity of the compact disk in terms of receiver benefit and clearly interprets *why* a conventional foundation is superior to a traditional slab foundation before introducing the economic factors. The interpretation makes the evidence understandable and thus convincing.

Cold Statement without Interpretation	***Specific, Interpreted Fact***	
This compact disc (CD-ROM) can store 600 megabytes of information.	This compact disc (CD-ROM) can store 600 megabytes of information. With this capacity, you have enough space to store a complete set of encyclopedias and 15 minutes of informative videos.	Think of examples of concepts in your career field that might need interpretation.
Although more expensive to construct, conventional foundations virtually eliminate soil-movement problems and the resulting structural damage.	Traditional slab foundations are *one* solid 8-inch thick piece of concrete poured on the soil surface. In contrast, the walls of a conventional foundation are several feet thick, and the floor of the structure is supported by a series of columns connected to the exterior walls with steel-reinforced concrete. If soil movement results in less support under any section of the foundation, the thick walls of the conventional foundation - evenly distribute the weight throughout the wall, preventing any structural damage.	

The previous example about the CD-ROM also uses a valuable interpretative technique—the comparison. You can often make a point more convincing by comparing something unfamiliar with something familiar. Most people are familiar with the amount of information contained in an encyclopedia, so they can now visualize the storage capacity of the CD-ROM. Comparison can also be used to interpret prices. Advertisers frequently compare the cost of sponsoring a child in a third-world country to the price of a fast-food lunch. An insurance representative might write this sentence: *The annual premium for this 20-year, limited-payment policy is $219, or 60 cents a day—about the cost of a cup of coffee.*

Do not go overboard and inundate your receivers with an abundance of facts or technical data that will bore, frustrate, or alienate them. Never make your receivers feel ignorant by trying to impress them with facts and figures they may not understand.

Be Objective. Use language people will believe. Specific, concrete language makes letters sound authentic. Unsupported superlatives, exaggerations, flowery statements, unsupported claims, incomplete comparisons, and remarks suggesting certainty all make letters sound like high-pressure sales talk. Just one such sentence can destroy confidence in the whole letter. Examine the following statements to see whether they give convincing evidence. Would they make a receiver want to buy? Or do they merely remind the receiver of someone's desire to sell? *This antibiotic is the best on the market today. It represents the very latest in biochemical research.*

Identifying the best-selling antibiotic requires gathering information about all antibiotics marketed and then choosing the one with superior characteristics. You know the writer is likely to have a bias in favor of the particular drug being sold. However, you do not know whether the writer actually spent time researching other antibiotics or whether the writer would know how to evaluate this information. You certainly do not know whether the writer knows enough about biochemical research to say truthfully what the very latest is.

Similarly, avoid preposterous statements (*Gardeners are turning handsprings in their excitement over our new weed killer!*) or subjective statements (*Stretch those tired limbs out on one of our luscious water beds. It's like floating on a gentle dream cloud on a warm, sunny afternoon. Ah, what soothing relaxation!*). Even though some people may be persuaded by such writing, many will see it as an attempt to trick them. Note the incomplete comparison in the following example: *SunBlock provides you better protection from the sun's dangerous ultraviolet rays.* Is Sun-Block being compared with *all* other sun screens, *most* other sun screens, *one* unnamed brand, or others? Unless an additional sentence identifies the other elements in the comparison, you do not know. Too often, the writer of such a sentence hopes the receiver will assume the comparison is with *all* others. Written with that intent, the incomplete comparison is *unethical*. Likewise, statements of certainty are often inaccurate or misleading.

What are some other ways that the reader can be unethically misled?

Include Testimonials, Guarantees, and Enclosures. One way to convince prospective customers that they will like the product, service, or idea is to give them concrete evidence that other people like it. Tell what others have said (with permission, of course) about the usefulness of your product, service, or idea. Guarantees and free trials convey both negative and positive connotations. By revealing willingness to refund money or exchange an unsatisfactory unit if necessary, a writer confesses a negative: the purchase could be regretted or refused. However, the positive connotations are stronger than the negatives: the seller has a definite plan for ensuring that buyers get value for money spent. In addition, the seller exhibits willingness for the buyer to check a product, service, or idea personally and compare it with others. The seller also implies confidence that a free trial will result in a purchase and that the product will meet standards set in the guarantee. If terms of a guarantee are long or complex, they can be included in an enclosure.

Ordinarily, a letter should persuade the receiver to read an enclosure that includes more detailed information. Thus, refer to the enclosure late in the letter

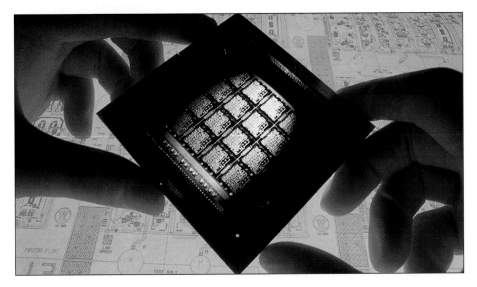

Before you can write an effective sales letter, you must know as much as possible about the product you are trying to sell. You must also be aware of the receivers' needs and any doubts or questions they may have about your product.

after the major portion of the evidence has been given. An enclosure is easily referred to in a sentence that is not a cliché ("Enclosed you will find," or "We have enclosed a brochure") and says something else: *The enclosed annual report will help you understand the types of information provided to small- and medium-sized companies by Lincoln Business Data, Inc.*

Subordinate the Price. Logically, price should be introduced late in the letter—after most of the advantages have been discussed. Use the following techniques to overcome people's natural resistance to price:

- Introduce price only after creating a desire for the product, service, or idea and its virtues. Let receivers see the relationship of features and benefits to the price.

- Use figures to illustrate that the price is reasonable or that the receiver can save money. (*Purigard saves the average pool owner about $10 in chemicals each month; thus, the $150 unit completely pays for itself in 15 months.*).

- State price in terms of small units. (Twelve dollars a month seems like less than $144 a year.)

- Invite comparison of like products, services, or ideas with similar features.

- Consider mentioning price in a complex or compound sentence that relates or summarizes the virtues of the product, service, or idea. (*For a $48 yearly subscription fee, Medisearch brings you a monthly digest of recent medical research that is written in nontechnical language.*)

What does the buyer hope to pay for a product? What does the seller hope to charge? What is the ethical dilemma in justifying an appropriate price?

How can sentence position affect the reader's acceptance of the price?

Motivating Action

For proper clarity and emphasis, the last paragraph should be relatively short. Yet the last paragraph must accomplish three important tasks: specify the specific action wanted and present it as easy to take, encourage quick action, and ask confidently.

How can the writer overcome readers' potential objections so that they will take the desired action?

- ***Make the action clear and simple to complete.*** Define the desired action in specific terms that are easy to complete. For example, you might ask the receiver to complete an order blank and return it with a check, place a telephone call, or return an enclosed card. General instructions such as "Let us hear from you," "Take action on the matter," and "Make a response" are ineffective. Make action simple to encourage receivers to act immediately. Instead of asking receivers to fill in their names and addresses on order forms or return cards and envelopes, do that work for them. Otherwise, they may see the task as difficult or time consuming and decide to procrastinate.

- ***Restate the reward for taking action (central selling point).*** The central selling point should be introduced early in the letter, interwoven throughout the evidence section, and included in the last paragraph as an emphatic, final reminder of the reason for taking action.

Why is procrastination such a common reaction to a persuasive appeal? What are some ways to reduce the likelihood of reader procrastination?

- ***Provide an incentive for quick action.*** If the receiver waits to take action on your proposal, the persuasive evidence will be harder to remember, and the receiver will be less likely to act. Therefore, you prefer for the receiver to act quickly. Reference to the central selling point (assuming it has been well received) helps to stimulate action. Commonly used appeals for getting quick action are to encourage customers to buy while prices are in effect, while supplies last, when a rebate is being offered, when it is a particular holiday, or when they will receive benefits.

- ***Ask confidently for action.*** If you have a good product, service, or idea and have presented evidence effectively, you have a right to feel confident. Demonstrate your confidence when requesting action: "To save time in cleaning, complete and return . . . ." Avoid statements suggesting lack of confidence, such as "If you want to save time in cleaning, complete and return . . . ," "If you agree . . ." and "I *hope* you will . . ."

Observe how the following closing paragraph accomplishes the three important tasks: refers to the central selling point, makes a specific action easy, and provides an incentive for quick action.

> From a Touch-Tone telephone, simply dial 1-800-555-8341. Then input the five-digit number printed in the top right corner of the attached card. Your name and address will be entered automatically into our system, an expedient way to get your productivity software to you within five working days along with a bill for payment. When you order by August 12, you will also receive 10 high-density memory disks free with your order. TMC's new productivity software is as easy to use as it is to order!

Figures 8-2 and 8-3 illustrate the principles discussed in the preceding pages. These letters illustrate *unsolicited sales letters*, one for a product and the other for an idea. The same principles apply in writing a *solicited sales letter*, with one exception: Because the solicited sales letter is a response to a request for information, an attention-getter is not essential. Typically, sales letters are longer than letters that present routine information or convey good news. Specific details (essential in getting action) require space.

Inductive Outline for Sales Letters

1. Gain the receiver's attention.
2. Introduce the product, service, or idea and arouse interest in it.
3. Present convincing evidence of the merits of the item being promoted and overcome any resistance.
4. Encourage the receiver to take the desired action (e.g., buy the product).

FIGURE 8-2
Good example of a letter promoting a product.

WORLDWIDE ELECTRONICS, INC.

55 North Park Road ◆ San Antonio, TX 78207-2963
(903) 555-6731 ◆ Fax: (905) 555-1305

April 30, 1999

Dr. Wesley Toche
875 Medical Plaza, Suite 100
Wichita Falls, TX 76307-2900

Dear Dr. Toche:

1 If you need an afternoon swinging a golf club, but you are worried you will miss an important call, you need the ProCall pager.

2 To make sure you will be able to catch that important call wherever you are, ProSystems is introducing the ProCall pager. **3** Wherever you go, you carry it with you. When people need to reach you, they simply call ProCall's 800 number and key in your code. Within seconds, our nationwide satellite system relays the message to your ProCall pager—and you never miss a call.

The ProCall system reaches you almost anywhere in the United States and weighs less (2.5 ounces) than a golf ball driving down the fairway. **4** The ProCall pager keeps you on top of your game and in touch with your important calls for only $30 a month (about a dollar a day).

5 To receive your ProCall pager, just initial the enclosed card. Mail the card before June 1 and receive your first month of service free.

Sincerely,

Alex R. Valentine

Alex R. Valentine
Sales Manager

Enclosure

1 Seeks to gain attention by introducing an experience the receiver has probably had. Presents "important call" as central selling point.

2 Introduces the product as a solution to a problem. Uses "important call" to achieve transition from the preceding sentence and to reinforce the central selling point.

3 Begins presentation of evidence. Uses receiver as subject of an active-voice sentence. Shows how easy it is to solve the problem—the reason to buy.

4 Presents price in a sentence that reinforces the primary reward for paying that price.

5 Associates action with reward for taking action, identifies specific action desired, makes action easy, and rewards quick action.

FIGURE 8-3
Good example of a letter promoting an idea.

Starkville Swim Association

763 North Wiggins Street
Starkville, MS 39759-3417
October 25, 1999

Ms. Julia Cox
Stewart Office Supply Company
89 Chadwick Lane
Starkville, MS 39759-9543

Dear Ms. Cox:

1 Begins with a sincere compliment.

❶ You are to be commended for sponsoring a Starkville Little League baseball team each year. Your investment keeps registration fees in reach of each family in our community and helps develop character in our community's youth.

2 Introduces competitive swimming as a worthwhile community effort similar to baseball—something the receiver already supports.

❷ Many youth in our community do not participate in baseball. However, some of these youth have special talents that lend themselves to different sports. Specifically, many youth who have difficulty competing in the traditional sports of football, basketball, and baseball often find they can excel in swimming.

3 Continues to build interest by showing benefits youth gain from competitive swimming, still using baseball as a parallel.

❸ Of the nearly 1,000 youth who have joined the Starkville Swim Association (SSA) during the past ten years, 50 of these athletes have received college athletic scholarships. More important, all of these youth have learned the important lessons of hard work, teamwork, and personal commitment, the same lessons learned through participation in our baseball program.

4 Summarizes problems that hinder youth participation in swimming.

❹ Unlike other sports that rely on volunteer coaches, national association guidelines mandate that swim coaches have competitive swimming experience and special safety training. Swimming associations rarely find these qualifications in parent volunteers. The increasing cost of a full-time coach and pool rental fees are making the annual registration fee prohibitive to many families.

5 Includes the request with an appeal to the receiver's known commitment to supporting the community's youth.

❺ The Starkville Swim Association invites you to become one of ten corporate sponsors of the swim team. Your sponsorship of $500 would help offset these rising costs and maintain the current annual registration fee of $100 so that more youth could take advantage of the abundant benefits of swimming.

6 Discusses the direct benefits the company can gain.

❻ Sponsoring the Starkville Fins (our team name) would also benefit your company. Your sponsorship will entitle you to display your company logo on all SSA publications. In addition, your logo would be displayed on the back of T-shirts worn by each swimmer.

7 States the specific action to be taken and again alludes to the benefit to the youth.

❼ Can we count on you to help our city's youth enjoy the experience of competitive swimming? Call me at 555-1345 to reserve your place as one of the team's sponsors.

Sincerely,

David M. Hilton

David M. Hilton
President

Format Pointers

- Includes writer's return address with letterhead because this organization does not have a company office with an address and telephone number.

Strategic Forces: Changing Technology

Desktop Publishing: Making Messages Look As Good As They Sound

Type, design, and graphics introduce new considerations that were once the concern of only graphic artists or typesetters. Desktop publishing puts a very useful tool in the hands of the untrained user; unfortunately, the results often show the lack of training. By using desktop publishing, you can create a company image at a fraction of the cost once required. This software can be used to create business cards, letterheads, forms, in-house newsletters, direct-mail advertising, catalogs, manuals, sales reports, and countless other publications. Some of these documents can be created through the use of top-of-the-line word processing programs.

In the typical flow of desktop publishing, a document (or a number of documents) is created, edited, and proofread in a word processing program. The document is then brought into a page-layout or desktop-publishing program such as PageMaker® or Ventura Publisher®, where the text can be styled with different typefaces, sizes, and other enhancements, such as rules, boxes, and other graphic images. Graphic images might include graphs to depict numerical relationships, clip art, drawings, or photographs. Many high-quality images can be imported from commercial CD-ROMs scanned with a digital scanner. Original photos can be taken with a digital camera and converted into a digital file read by computer without the expense and time of processing film.

Having the tools to design, however, does not make you a designer. Newcomers to desktop publishing, enchanted with the effects that can be created with type, rules, shadows, and boxes, clutter documents with too many type styles or with too many lines. The result is not an effective presentation but a jumble of words and graphic elements that confuse and alienate the reader.

By following some simple principles of design, however, the budding desktop publishers can effectively use the tools at their disposal:

- **Keep it simple.** The more variety included on a page, the more difficulty the reader will have in following the message. Restricting the document to no more than two or three typefaces and just a few special effects is often the best approach.

- **Keep it consistent.** Treat comparable elements in the same way. All the headlines in a newsletter with five articles should be in the same typeface and style. Save special treatments for material that is special.

- **Design graphics to avoid distorting or obscuring facts and relationships.** The Strategic Forces box in Chapter 10 will present guidelines for creating honest, accurate graphics.

- **Let form follow function.** A document should be styled in such a way that it looks like what it is. A purchase order need not be elegant; the menu of an expensive restaurant should look more dignified than the price list of a dry-cleaning service.

Application

After revising the letter in Exercise 5, use desktop publishing capabilities available to you to design a creative, attention-getting layout, including a letterhead, for this document. Provide a fictitious name and address for the civic club. Use the page-design layout principles presented in this box as a guide.

Persuasive Requests

3 *Write effective persuasive requests (claim, favor, and information requests, and persuasion within an organization).*

The preceding discussion of sales letters assumed the product, service, or cause was sufficiently worthy to reward the receiver for taking action. The discussion of persuasive requests assumes requests are reasonable—that compliance is justified when the request is for an adjustment and that compliance will (in some way) be rewarded when the request is for a favor.

Common types of persuasive requests are claim letters and letters that request special favors and information. Although their purpose is to get favorable action, the letters invite action only after attempting to arouse a desire to take action and providing a logical argument to overcome any resistance anticipated from the receiver.

Making a Claim

What is the difference between a persuasive claim and the routine claim letters discussed in Chapter 5? How can the writer decide which writing approach to use?

Claim letters are often routine because the basis for the claim is a guarantee or some other assurance that an adjustment will be made without need of persuasion. However, when an immediate remedy is doubtful, persuasion is necessary. In a typical large business, the claim letter is passed on to the claims adjuster for response.

Often, any reasonable claim will be adjusted to the customer's satisfaction. Therefore, venting strong displeasure in the claim letter is of little value. It can alienate the claims adjuster—the one person from whom cooperation is sought. Remember, adjusters may have had little or nothing to do with the manufacture and sale of the product or direct delivery of the service. They did not create the need for the claim letter.

Companies should welcome claims. First, research indicates two important facts: (1) Complainers are more likely to continue to do business with a company than those who do not complain, and (2) businesses that know how to resolve claims effectively will retain 95 percent of the complainers as repeat customers.[4] Second, only a small percentage of claims are from unethical individuals; the great bulk is from people who believe they have a legitimate complaint. Thus, the way an adjuster handles the claim determines, to a large extent, the goodwill of the company.

For the adjuster, granting a claim is much easier than refusing it. Because saying "No" is one of the most difficult writing tasks, the writer of a persuasive claim letter has an advantage over the adjuster.

Like sales letters, persuasive claim letters should use an inductive sequence. Unlike routine claim letters, persuasive claims do not begin by asking for an adjustment. The poor example in Figure 8-4 uses a deductive sequence.

Two major changes would improve this letter: (1) writing inductively (to reduce the chance of a negative reaction in the first sentence) and (2) stressing an appeal throughout the letter (to emphasize an incentive for taking favorable action). In a persuasive claim letter, an appeal serves the same purpose that a central selling feature does in a sales letter. Both serve as a theme; both remind the receiver of a benefit that accrues from doing as asked. Note the application of these techniques in the revision in Figure 8-5.

FIGURE 8-4
Poor example of a persuasive claim.

AVOID

Please reimburse us $1,250 for services not rendered at our recent meeting at your resort.

We paid $5 more per room than the rates at a comparable hotel so our guests could work out in the exercise room shown in your brochure. However, our members were unable to use the equipment because the exercise room was actually located four blocks from the hotel at a local health club.

We hope you will see fit to refund $5 for each of the 250 rooms we rented because we were not told of the location and chose the hotel on the basis of the incorrect information.

Inductive Outline for Persuasive Claims

1. Gain attention by appealing to a mutual need.
2. Present reasoning (details and evidence) that leads to the request in context of the central appeal presented in the first paragraph.
3. Present the request in context of the central appeal.

FIGURE 8-5
Good example of a persuasive claim.

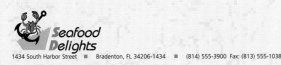

Seafood Delights

1434 South Harbor Street ■ Bradenton, FL 34206-1434 ■ (814) 555-3900 Fax: (813) 555-1038

June 5, 1999

Mr. Benjamin Lewis
Seaside Regency Resort
1465 Beachfront Vista
Sarasota, FL 34230-1465

Dear Mr. Lewis:

1 Seaside Regency and our company, Seafood Delights, are much alike: We both give customers a taste of life on the seashore and emphasize total customer well-being. **2** Both of us are providing aesthetic pleasure and physical fitness; Seafood Delights with healthy menu choices, Seaside Regency with an exercise room for resort guests.

3 This compatibility with our values is one of the reasons we chose your resort for our Annual Beach Get-Away, a meeting of our franchisees and corporate leaders, on May 15. **4** Eager for our franchisees (our guests) to use the exercise room pictured in your brochure to unwind after a full day of meetings and other events, we selected your resort over other comparable ones even though we would be charged an additional fee for the exercise room.

5 Obviously, our guests were disappointed when they learned that the exercise room was not in the resort but actually located at a health club four blocks away. A tight schedule of meetings and frequent dinner events limited the time our guests had available for commuting to the health club for a workout. Many did not feel safe leaving the resort late in the evening, the only block of time long enough for a workout.

6 Because your resort advertised the availability of a fully equipped exercise room without explaining it was located in a health club outside the resort, our guests were deprived of physical fitness opportunities available at comparable hotels. In addition, Seafood Delights was billed an additional $5 per room for this *unused* service.

7 For these reasons, please refund us $5 for each of the 250 rooms we rented, confirming your commitment to customer service—aesthetic pleasure and physical fitness.

Sincerely,

Anne Marie Lowery

Anne Marie Lowery
Human Resources Manager

1 Seeks attention by discussing goals common to receiver.
2 Reveals the subject of the letter (the exercise room) and continues the central appeal—commitment to guests' physical fitness needs.
3 Includes a further reminder of the central appeal.
4 Provides needed details.
5 Justifies the request as reasonable.

6 Presents reasoning that leads to the request for a refund and a subtle reminder of the central appeal.
7 Connects the request with the resort's commitment to serve customer's physical fitness needs.

Knowledge of effective claim writing should never be used as a means of taking advantage of someone. Hiding an unjustifiable claim under a cloak of untrue statements is difficult and strictly unethical. Adjusters are fair-minded people who will give the benefit of the doubt, but they will not satisfy an unhappy customer simply to avoid a problem.

Asking a Favor

How might the receiver react to a persuasive letter written in deductive style?

Occasionally, everyone has to ask someone else for a special favor—action for which there is not much reward, time, or inclination. For example, suppose a professional association wants to host its annual fund-raiser dinner at an exclusive country club. The program chair of the association must write a letter to the club's general manager requesting permission to use the club. Will a deductive letter be successful?

When a deductive approach is used in a persuasive situation, chances of getting cooperation are minimal. For example, what might be a probable reaction to the following beginning sentence? *Please send me, without charge, your $350 interactive CD-ROM on office safety.*

If the first sentence gets a negative reaction, a decision to refuse may be made instantly. Having thought "No," the receiver may not read the rest of the letter or may hold stubbornly to that decision in spite of a well-written persuasive argument that follows the opening sentence. Note that the letter in Figure 8-6 asks the favor before presenting any benefit for doing so.

The letter illustrated in Figure 8-7 uses an inductive approach. Note the extent to which it applies principles discussed earlier. As this letter shows, if the preceding paragraphs adequately emphasize a receiver's reward for complying, the final paragraph need not shout loudly for action.

Requesting Information

Requests for information are common in business. Information for research reports frequently is obtained by questionnaire. Validity and reliability of results are strongly influenced by the percentage of return. If a letter inviting respondents to complete

① Begins with an announcement that may be of little interest to the receiver.
② Asks the favor before letting the person see any reason for accepting.
③ Does not include important information such as the type of dance, food, and number involved; overuse of the first person pronoun *we* throughout letter.
④ Sounds somewhat doubtful.

① The Long Beach Medical Association (LBMA) will hold its annual dinner/dance on Saturday, November 5.

② We would very much like to have this event at Crystal Stream from 7 p.m. on that evening. ③ We expect several hundred guests to attend.

④ Will you let me know as soon as possible if we may hold the dance at Crystal Stream?

FIGURE 8-6 Poor example of a persuasive request (asking a favor).

Inductive Outline for Persuasive Requests

1. Gain the receiver's attention.
2. Introduce the request and emphasize benefits the receiver can gain from complying with the request.
3. Address any major resistance to the request.
4. Request specific action.

FIGURE 8-7
Good example of a persuasive request (asking a favor).

Long Beach Medical Association
7800 North Wasco Avenue   Long Beach, CA 90801-7800   Phone: (714) 555-8900   Fax: (714) 555-7619

March 23, 1999

Mr. Pedro Sanchez
General Manager
Crystal Stream
P.O. Box 2383
Long Beach, CA 90810-2393

Dear Mr. Sanchez

1 The opening of Crystal Stream was a landmark event. People all over the city are applauding your signature golf course designed to challenge golfers of all skill levels. The beautiful Williamsburg-style clubhouse and exquisite homes complement our upscale, growing community.

2 Because of the intense community interest in your facility, the Long Beach Medical Association (LBMA) believes Crystal Stream is the perfect location for its annual charity dinner/dance for the Kids for Life Foundation. Last year this foundation defrayed medical expenses for five children from our community who suffer from muscular dystrophy. We are confident that holding this event at Crystal Stream would increase participation in this worthy community event by at least 25 percent.

3 Many LBMA members are interested in memberships in Crystal Stream. While participating in this community event, these members would have an ideal chance to learn more about the recreational and social opportunities of the exclusive Crystal Stream.

4 This black-tie dinner/dance is scheduled for November 5, from 7 p.m. to 1 a.m. Typically 400 guests have attended; however, at least 500 members are expected if the event were held at Crystal Stream. A definite number can be confirmed two weeks prior to the event.

5 Please send a confirmation by May 1 that Crystal Stream will be the site for this year's dinner/dance. Then we can finalize the details and promote this sure-to-be spectacular event at Crystal Stream.

Sincerely,

Colleen B. Plier

Colleen B. Plier, M.D.
Program Chair

1 Begins on a point that is related and of interest to the receiver.

2 Reveals membership's enthusiasm for holding the dinner/dance at the club and presents benefits that help to increase the receiver's enthusiasm for the proposal. Provides additional benefits for saying "Yes."

3 Provides additional benefits for saying "Yes."

4 Provides details that will be useful if the receiver accepts.

5 Seeks specific action by tactfully assuming acceptance.

COMMUNICATION MENTOR

Let's say you are preparing a memo to your supervisor; you're hoping for approval of a cost-saving project you want to spearhead. Something fairly similar to it had been tried years ago; it failed miserably, embarrassing your supervisor and the department manager. You know that seeking approval is an uphill battle, but you believe in yourself and the project. What tone should this sensitive memo take?

The temptation may be to position your project point-for-point in contrast to the old one, pounding on the relative merits of yours in an effort to convey its superiority.

Resist this temptation as you would a term paper over spring break. Never directly mention the other project in your memo. Memories of its failure may be keen, and direct comparisons will be counterproductive to the objectivity you want to elicit in your receivers. Rather, emphasize the strength of your plan by stressing features that are designed to avoid known pitfalls.

Your supervisor and the department manager will get the message, and you will get your project. The moral to take away from all of this: don't stand on the grave of a bad idea to sell a new one.

James F Hurley, Principal
Hurley Advisors

a questionnaire is written carelessly, responses may be insufficient. Analyze the effectiveness of the request in the example in Figure 8-8.

The most serious weaknesses of the letter in Figure 8-8 are asking too quickly for action and providing no incentive for action. Sometimes the reward for taking action is small and indirect, but the letter needs to make these benefits evident. Note the reward in the revision of the letter in Figure 8-9 (it appeals to Maslow's higher order of needs as discussed in Chapter 2).

❶ Invites action without having first given any incentive.
❷ Puts writer and receiver on different levels by suggesting humility. Use of "impose" could serve as a reminder that the request is an imposition and therefore should be denied.
❸ Reveals the nature of the research—a point that should have been introduced earlier. Risks alienation by introducing doubts about the receiver's knowledge.
❹ Lets the receiver know what to expect but needs to include some incentive for responding. Uses an action ending, but it seems a little demanding, especially when no incentive has been introduced.

 AVOID

❶ Please complete the enclosed questionnaire and return it to me in the envelope provided. **❷** I dislike having to impose on the valuable time of a busy executive such as you, but in order for me to complete the research for my thesis at the university, I must seek first-hand information from business leaders.

❸ The study deals with the attitudes of purchasing agents toward vendor gratuities. As I believe you know, gifts from sellers to executives who do the buying for companies pose a problem of great concern. The questionnaire seeks information about practices in your firm and about your own opinions.

❹ Responses will be kept confidential, of course. Please return the questionnaire to me by April 18.

FIGURE 8-8 Poor example of a persuasive request for information.

Inductive Outline for Persuasive Request for Information

1. Gain receiver's attention.
2. Introduce the request and emphasize benefits the receiver can gain from complying with the request.
3. Address any major resistance to the request such as assuring that the information will remain confidential.
4. Request specific action by a specified date.

FIGURE 8-9
Good example of a request for information.

132 Cedar Court
Augusta, GA 31902-1910
February 1, 1999

Mr. Stephen Fyodorovich
Purchasing Agent
City National Bank
2500 Center Street
Augusta, GA 31902-2500

Dear Mr. Fyodorovich:

1 What if vendors continue making more and larger gifts to purchasing agents? For ethical and economic reasons, this question is of vital importance to purchasing agents. **2** Yet it has not been answered in the literature, and recent purchasing journals have emphatically called for answers based on research.

3 For my master's thesis on purchasing behavior, I am seeking opinions from selected purchasing managers. Results will be shared with participants soon after the data are interpreted.

4 To ensure that the study is complete and authoritative, please participate by completing the enclosed questionnaire and returning it to me in the envelope provided. **5** Your answers, which can be indicated quickly by making check marks, will be confidential and reported only as part of group data.

6 To send a report of the findings to you and other participating managers before school ends in early June, I need to receive the enclosed forms by May 1.

7 I would appreciate your help and am eager to share with you a summary of what I learn about vendors and gratuities.

Sincerely,

Carmen L. Rankin

Carmen L. Rankin

Enclosures

1 Seeks attention by establishing the letter as a document related to the receiver's work.

2 Leads to an introduction of the questionnaire as one step toward finding answers.

3 Introduces the questionnaire and reminds of the reward for taking action. Professional managers who now have (or already had) an interest in the problem would see the sharing of results as a positive.

4 Makes the request for action in a complex sentence that contains an additional idea that is positive.

5 Presents some needed assurance. With "quick marks," the effort is pictured as consuming little time.

6 Mentions a deadline in a sentence that reminds managers of the reward for complying.

7 Expresses gratitude, alludes to the reward for participating, and adds unity by using the words "vendors" and "gratuities," words that tie in with the first paragraph.

Format Pointers

- Provides the writer's address above the date because the letter is printed on plain paper.
- Uses enclosures notation to alert the reader that something is included.

Persuading Within an Organization

Why are routine requests shorter than persuasive requests?

The majority of memos are of a routine nature and essential for the day-to-day operation of the business, for example, instructions for performing work assignments, scheduling meetings, providing progress reports on projects, and so on. These routine memos as well as memos conveying good news are written deductively. However, some circumstances require that a supervisor write a persuasive memo that motivates employees to accept a change in their jobs that might have a negative effect on the employee or generate employee resistance in some form (e.g., being transferred to another position or office, automating a processing that has been performed manually, changing computer software programs, changing the style of service and new uniforms at Steak and Ale, etc.).

Often employees must make persuasive requests of their supervisors. For example, they may recommend a change in procedure, acquisition of equipment or a particular software, or attendance of a training program to improve their ability to complete a job function. They may justify a promotion or job reclassification or recommendation. Persuasive memos are longer because of the extra space needed for developing an appeal and providing convincing evidence.

When preparing to write the memo in Figure 8-10, the store manager recalled a past attempt to computerize perpetual inventory that failed miserably. At that time, most employees could be easily categorized as computer illiterate; they required extensive training and were resistant to any effort to computerize. The company finally abandoned the computerization effort when the computer system could not be upgraded to handle higher inventory levels.

Anticipating the managing partner's resistance, the store manager decided to write the memo inductively. Thus, the subject line does not reveal how the manager proposes to improve the efficiency of maintaining inventory counts. To increase his chances of gaining approval, the store manager, Jay Griffith, heeded the previous advice from your mentor, James F. Hurley. Griffith stressed the features designed to avoid known pitfalls (computer literacy of employees and obsolescence of computer systems) but did not mention the past failure.

Laura Nobles, the writer of the persuasive memo in Figure 8-11, may have been one more burnout statistic had it not been for her initiative and, most important, her excellent writing skills. Laura is a manager for a large national firm who enjoys her career and thrives on the challenge of performing at her peak while rearing her two children. However, last year she began showing signs of burnout. Managing her career and finding time to care for the children without feeling exhausted most of the time had become increasingly difficult. While skimming a business publication one day, she noticed an article about telecommuting—a plan that enables employees to work from home on certain days with the assistance of a computer with a modem and facsimile machine. Intrigued, Laura discovered that telecommuting offers several advantages for both employees and companies, and she concluded this work plan was a perfect solution for her.

Of course, she needed to obtain permission from her supervisor to begin telecommuting, so she developed a plan. First, Laura made a list of her job duties that could be performed at home and those that must be completed at the office. Then, she made a list of the benefits of telecommuting, emphasizing in particular how the company would benefit. She anticipated possible objections to her plan and developed responses for those protests. Finally, she drafted a proposal in the form of a letter to her supervisor, including the information she had organized. She even included copies of her research materials for support.

Inductive Outline for Persuasive Memos

1. Gain the receiver's attention.
2. Build interest in the idea by presenting objective evidence, including benefits the company and the writer can gain.
3. Address any major resistance to the idea.
4. Request specific action to be taken.

FIGURE 8-10
Good example of a persuasive memo.

CRAFTS GALORE

397 Peachway Drive ● Knoxville, TN 37901-0397 ● (615) 555-9200 ● Fax: (615) 555-3909

TO: Yang Lin, Managing Partner
FROM: Jay Griffith, Store Manager J. G.
DATE: September 20, 1999
❶ SUBJECT: Proposal to Improve the Efficiency of Maintaining Inventory Counts

❷ One of our competitive advantages is the wide variety of materials we offer crafts enthusiasts in our city. However, our manual system has become inadequate for maintaining this large inventory.

❸ A computerized perpetual inventory would eliminate the need to close the store two days in each major season to count stock and update our records. This system would also provide management with timely and accurate information about inventory levels.

❹ Our employees have been using computers for other applications (word processing and general ledger) for several months; therefore, I would anticipate little resistance to this type of change in daily operations. In fact, several inventory clerks have suggested getting perpetual inventory on the computer already. This prior computer training would likely reduce the cost of implementing this computerized system significantly.

❺ Unlike older computer equipment, today's hardware is designed to be flexible. No longer must new computers be purchased to take advantage of new technologies. For example, more powerful microprocessors can be inserted directly into this system. Thus, as our business grows and technology changes, we would be able to upgrade this system to meet our changing demands.

❻ Take a look at the attached brochure describing the exact specifications and the cost of a perpetual inventory system. After you have considered this change, please call so we can discuss this critical enhancement to our efficient delivery of products to our customers.

Attachment

❶ Gives the purpose of the memo without revealing the specific request.
❷ Links a company strength that leads logically to the problem; does not reveal the actual request.
❸ Builds interest by providing specific benefits of the computerized system.
❹ Reduces resistance by discussing changes that will alleviate prior problems experienced with a computerized system; does not refer to past failures directly.
❺ Expands discussion of advantages of the proposed system.
❻ Refers to attachment after presenting evidence. Alludes to benefits and closes with a specific action to be taken.

Because compliance with the Clean Air Act was the subject of a staff meeting, Laura opens her request (Figure 8-11) with a straightforward statement about the problem and her telecommuting proposal. She presented a thorough analysis of duties that could be efficiently completed away from the office, thus reducing her commuting time. This analysis provided convincing evidence that telecommuting is a feasible recommendation. The specific changes she suggests in scheduling required meetings and the progress report on equipping a home office aid her in counteracting any resistance to her proposal. Her call to discuss the proposal at the next meeting is clear and specific and reminds the supervisor of the benefits of the proposal. After some minor negotiating, Laura was allowed to begin telecommuting on a temporary basis while management evaluated its efficiency. Now she is a permanent telecommuter and plans to maintain this schedule until her children are older. She is more productive because of reduced stress and fewer interruptions, and the company is benefitting from this increased productivity.[5]

Before writing a persuasive message, study carefully the overall suggestions in the "General Writing Guidelines" placed before the summary in Chapter 5. Then, study the specific suggestions in the following "Check Your Writing" checklist. Compare your work with this checklist again after you have written a rough draft and then make necessary revisions.

INTEROFFICE MEMORANDUM

TO: Nathan Landrum, Gifts Marketing Director
FROM: Laura Nobles, Buyer, Gift Department *L. N.*
DATE: November 16, 1999
SUBJECT: Enhancing Productivity Through Telecommuting

❶ Since the announcement in last week's meeting that we must identify ways to reduce the number of daily commuters, I've considered several possible options. I believe telecommuting could not only reduce my number of commutes but increase my productivity as well.

❷ One component of my job is conducting research and compiling marketing reports; e.g., weekly product line sales and inventory reports, competitors' new catalog analyses, and suppliers' new product reports. Preparing these reports efficiently requires a day of uninterrupted time. With my current work schedule, with sales representatives randomly calling for marketing advice throughout each day, I am pressured to get these reports prepared in time for Friday's marketing managers' meeting.

❸ Telecommuting on Wednesdays would allow me to concentrate on preparing these reports and coordinate product ordering and marketing strategies without distractions. On Thursday morning, we could discuss the sales reports and marketing plans before Friday's meeting. This plan still allows sales representatives to contact me four days each week.

❹ Can we meet to discuss the benefits of my telecommuting during our Monday meeting? By then I should know how soon I could get the equipment and software needed to equip a home office to process information and to communicate with appropriate personnel effectively.

❶ Opens with discussion of a company problem and the telecommuting proposal.

❷ Outlines duties that can be completed more efficiently away from the office. Recommends specific changes in meetings in an effort to address resistance to the proposal.

❸ Alludes to the benefits of telecommuting.

❹ Closes with specific action to be taken next.

FIGURE 8-11 Good example of a persuasive memo.

COMMUNICATION IN ACTION

Mike Mills, American Woodmark

Persuading company executives to accept new ways of doing business presents a challenge for many senior managers. As a transportation manager for American Woodmark Corporation, Mike Mills is responsible for moving his company from the "dark ages" of transportation to new technologies in distribution. He serves as a change agent in American Woodmark, scanning the business environment and recommending improvements in the distribution of their products, including kitchen cabinets for residential homes. Implementing changes through persuasive communication is an important part of Mills's work at American Woodmark.

Working in a company that employs 2,500 personnel and recorded sales of $171 million in 1993, Mills manages one of three regional assembly distribution facilities, directly supervising about 30 personnel. Persuasive communication commonly occurs in a company this size in proposals, reports, and internal memos. When submitting persuasive proposals, Mills follows a persuasive process of defining the problem, outlining objectives, selecting alternatives, and choosing a solution. He also includes cost estimates, time for implementation, and schedule of payback for the company. He once proposed a new computer system and projected it would result in $120,000 annualized savings. After the system was installed, American Woodmark conducted a 28-workday analysis of the system's effectiveness and found that it actually saved $130,000, a very accurate prediction indeed.

Such successful change comes about as a result of persuasive communication and hard work. Recently, Mills developed a transportation change and submitted it through a written proposal. At the time, American Woodmark's trucks were delivering products directly to builders in the Baltimore-Washington area. Mills proposed instead that a third party or outside carrier deliver the products to builders. However, some company executives, including his supervisor, were uncomfortable with this proposed change. They raised quality control issues and discussed customer service problems. Mills knew he faced a tough sell. In his proposal, he asserted, "We may lose some control, but from a cost standpoint and improved service standpoint, it is an overall good move for the company."

Mills based his presentation to his supervisor on statistics and numbers. "My supervisor is a numbers person, so I adapt to his style," Mills remarked. "I support my cost analysis with as many facts and figures as I can." The persuasion worked. Mills' supervisor approved the outside carrier. In an analysis conducted several months later, the change proved cost effective for the company. Mills commented, "When you're asked to be a change agent and suggest a major change, you hope the change proves beneficial." The third-party carrier saved the company money, and quality customer service was maintained. To Mills's credit, persuasion and business communication go hand-in-hand, creating success for him at American Woodmark.

Applying What You Have Learned

1. Mills used facts and figures as evidence in the outside carrier proposal. Give an example of a different proposal in which using evidence other than numbers or statistics would be appropriate.

2. Assume that you are a transportation manager at American Woodmark. After preliminary research and analysis, you develop a plan for a Home Delivery Program in which products are delivered directly to residential homes. Normally, American Woodmark uses commercial stores such as Home Depot to reach its customers. This new program is innovative and will begin on a trial basis in Milwaukee, Wisconsin. Write a memo to your supervisor, Cyndi Johnson, convincing her to approve a pilot test of this new distribution system.

SALES LETTERS

Content

- Convince the writer that the product or service is worthy of consideration.
- Include sufficient evidence of usefulness to the purchaser.
- Reveal price (in the letter or an enclosure).
- Make the central selling point apparent.
- Identify the specific action that is desired.
- Assure that the message is ethical and abides by legal requirements.

Organization

- Use inductive sequence of ideas.
- Assure that the first sentence is a good attention-getter.
- Introduce the central selling point in the first two or three sentences and reinforce it through the rest of the letter.
- Introduce price only after receiver benefits have been presented.
- Associate price (what the receiver gives) directly with reward (what the receiver gets).
- Introduce a final paragraph that mentions (a) the specific action desired, (b) the receiver's reward for taking the action, and (c) an inducement for taking action quickly. It also presents the action as easy to take.

Style

- Use objective language.
- Use active verbs predominately.
- Use concrete nouns predominately.
- Keep sentences relatively short but vary in length and structure.
- Place significant words in emphatic positions.
- Make ideas cohere; avoid abrupt changes in thought.
- Frequently call the central selling point to the receiver's attention through synonyms or direct repetition.
- Use original expression (sentences are not copied directly from the definition of the problem or from sample letters in the text). Omit clichés.
- Achieve unity by including in the final paragraph a key word or idea (central selling point) that was introduced in the first paragraph.

Mechanics

- Place letter parts in appropriate positions; use acceptable format.

- Include an enclosure notation if a document other than the letter is to be enclosed.
- Keep first and last paragraphs short (no more than two or three lines).
- Keep all paragraphs relatively short.
- Assume that keyboarding, spelling, and punctuation are perfect.

PERSUASIVE REQUESTS

Content

- Convince the writer that the idea is valid, that the proposal has merit.
- Point out the way(s) in which the receiver will benefit.
- Incorporate primary appeal (central selling feature).
- Identify specific action desired.

Organization

- Use inductive sequence of ideas.
- Use a first sentence that gets attention and reveals the subject of the message.
- Introduce a major appeal in the first two or three sentences and reinforce it throughout the rest of the message.
- Point out receiver benefits.
- Associate desired action with the receiver's reward for taking action.
- Include a final paragraph that makes reference to the specific action desired and the primary appeal. Emphasize the ease of taking action and (if appropriate) include a stimulus for quick action.

Style

- Use language that is objective and positive.
- Assure that active verbs and concrete nouns predominate.
- Keep sentences relatively short but vary them in length and structure.
- Place significant words in emphatic positions.
- Make ideas cohere; changes in thought are not abrupt.
- Call primary appeal to the receiver's attention frequently through synonyms or repetition of a word.
- Use original expression (sentences are not copied directly from the definition of the problem or from sample letters in the text). Omit clichés.
- Achieve unity by including in the final paragraph a key word or idea (the primary appeal) that was used in the first paragraph.

Mechanics

- Place letter parts in appropriate position; use acceptable format. In memos, properly complete the TO, FROM, DATE, and SUBJECT lines.

- Omit courtesy titles in the TO and FROM lines for memos.

- Keep paragraphs relatively short but vary them in length.

- Include an enclosure notation if a document other than the letter/memo is to be enclosed.

- Assure that keyboarding, spelling, and punctuation are perfect.

SUMMARY

1. **Develop effective outlines and appeals for messages that persuade.** The purpose of a persuasive message is to influence others to take a particular action or to accept your point of view. Effective persuasion involves understanding the product, service, or idea you are promoting; knowing your audience; presenting convincing evidence; and having a rational response to anticipated resistance to your arguments.

   Effective persuasive letters build on a central selling point interwoven throughout the message. The receivers, rather than the product, serve as the subject of many of the sentences. Therefore, receivers can envision themselves using the product, contracting for the service, or complying with a request. Persuasive messages are written inductively.

2. **Write effective sales messages.** A sales letter is written inductively following the four-point AIDA steps for selling:

   - **Gain attention.** Use an original approach that addresses one primary receiver's benefit (the central selling point) in the first paragraph.

   - **Introduce the product, service, or idea.** Provide a logical transition to move the receiver from the attention-getter to information about the product, service, or idea. Hold the receiver's attention by using action-oriented sentences to stress the central selling point.

   - **Provide convincing evidence.** Provide specific facts and interpretations that clarify the nature and quality of a feature, nonexaggerated evidence people will believe, and research and testimonials that provide independent support. De-emphasize the

   price by presenting convincing evidence first but not in the last paragraph, showing how money can be saved, stating price in small units, illustrating that the price is reasonable, and placing the price in a sentence that summarizes the benefits.

   - **Motivate action.** State confidently the specific action to be taken and the benefits for complying. Present the action as easy to take, and provide a stimulus for acting quickly.

3. **Write effective persuasive requests (claim, favor, and information requests, and persuasion within an organization).** A persuasive request is written inductively, is organized around a primary appeal, and is longer than a typical routine message because you must provide convincing evidence of receiver benefit.

   - **Persuasive claim**—When an adjuster must be convinced that a claim is justified, gain the receiver's attention, develop a central appeal that emphasizes an incentive for making the adjustment, and end with the request for an adjustment you consider fair.

   - **Request for a favor or information**—Gain the receiver's attention, build interest by emphasizing the reward for taking action, and, encourage the receiver to grant the favor or send the information.

   - **Persuasion within an organization**—When persuading supervisors to take specific actions (e.g., change a procedure or purchase new equipment, etc.), gain the supervisor's attention, introduce and build interest and support for the proposed idea, address any major resistance, and encourage the supervisor to take a specific action.

REFERENCES

[1]Steak and Ale. (1997). *Signature style at Steak and Ale*. Dallas, TX: Author.

[2]Cody, S. (1906). *Success in letter writing: Business and social*. Chicago: A. C. McClurg. [pp. 122–126].

[3]Nelson, E. (1993). WordPerfect 6.0: 10 new things it does for you. *WordPerfect Magazine*, 5(7), 36–38, 40, 42–43. [p. 37].

[4]Bell, J. D. (1994). Motivate, educate, and add realism to business communication using the claim letter. *Business Education Forum*, 48(2), 42–43.

[5]Dumas, L. S. (1994, June). Home work: The telecommuting option. *Working Mother*, 22–26.

REVIEW QUESTIONS

1. Summarize the types of information you should gather as you plan a persuasive message. (Obj. 1)

2. List the writing principles that are important in writing an effective persuasive message. (Obj. 1)

3. What are the legal and ethical implications of persuasive messages? (Obj. 1)

4. Define "central selling feature." When should it be introduced and included in a persuasive message? (Obj. 1)

5. List the four steps in the outline recommended for persuasive messages. (Obj. 1)

6. What are the characteristics of a good attention-getter? List five techniques for getting receivers' attention. (Obj. 2)

7. Why are sales letters normally longer than routine letters? Should the first and last paragraph be shortest or longest? (Obj. 2)

8. Under what condition would the use of superlatives be acceptable in persuasive messages? (Obj. 2)

9. In persuasive messages, why are incomplete comparisons to be avoided? Compose a sentence that includes an incomplete comparison; rewrite, completing the comparison. (Obj. 2)

10. Summarize the effective techniques for convincing the receiver that your product, service, or idea has value. (Obj. 2)

11. Describe effective techniques for presenting the price. (Obj. 2)

12. Describe the characteristics of an effective action ending. (Obj. 2)

13. What is the principal difference between a persuasive claim and a routine claim? (Obj. 3)

14. What is meant by an "appeal" in a persuasive letter? (Obj. 3)

15. Should a persuasive memo to a supervisor address any known or anticipated resistance to a proposed idea? Explain. (Obj. 3)

EXERCISES

1. **Critique of Sales Letters Produced by Real Companies (Obj. 1)**
   Select an unsolicited sales letter you (or a friend) received. List (a) the principles it applies and (b) the principles it violates. Rewrite the letter retaining its strengths and correcting its weaknesses.

2. **Effective Opening Paragraphs (Obj. 1–3)**
   Analyze the effectiveness of each sentence as the opening for a persuasive message.

   a. Don't you want to make the world a better place? Instead of worrying about the starving in Africa, let's take care of our own—donate canned food to the local Homeless Haven in time for the holidays!

   b. John F. Kennedy said, "Ask not what your country can do for you; ask what you can do for your country." One of the best ways to support American capitalism is to let Carville Consultants make your business better.

   c. You haven't lived until you've owned a Multi-Sound Compact Disc Storage Chest!

   d. For an investment of $550, you can own the best high-pressure washer on the market from Sims, Inc.

   e. The enclosed folder shows our latest prices on lead glass windows.

   f. This new policy I am proposing will revolutionize our sales figures within three months. (request)

g. I am requesting to be promoted to regional sales manager because I have a proven track record of turning around sales revenues within two months. (request)

h. The merchandise you sent Maxwell Corporation on September 3 is defective, and we refuse to pay for it. (claim)

3. **Convincing Evidence (Obj. 1–3)**
Analyze the effectiveness of the convincing evidence included in the following sentences in a persuasive request.

a. Reorganizing the loan department will help us serve our clients better and cut costs.

b. I know you are extremely busy, but we would really like to have you come speak to us on effective investing.

c. Southside Recycling has four regional offices in each county in Texas, with headquarters in Dallas. Our professional staff consists of 15 members at each location.

d. You wonder if you can get quality education at our school and still save money? Dollar for dollar, tuition and fees at Carlton State give you the best education value for your money.

4. **Document for Analysis: Sales Letter (Obj. 1–2)**
Analyze the following letter. Pinpoint its strengths and weaknesses, and then revise the letter if directed by your instructor.

November 5th, 1999

Chris L. Graham
86 Campus View Road
Lake City, FL 32055-9019

Dear Sir,

I thank you for your inquiry regarding our schooner, The Mary Ann. Please find the enclosed information which I hope you will find interesting.

The Mary Ann is a 103 year-old gaffed rugged wooden schooner currently able to accomodate 32 passengers. Early next season we will be increasing our capacity to 49 passengers. The Mary Ann is 89 feet long and weighs approximately 60 gross tons.

Our rates for the 1999 season were $300 per hour for a minimum of three hours. There will be a price increase next year but it will be minimal.

Although the 1999 season is over, we are currently taking reservations for next season, which will commence during April 1999. Please consider advance booking with us if you are at all interested in that special day as each year we have to turn away so many people who request a particular time and day. We do offer discounts to customers who are able to make reservations and pay in full before March 31st, 1999.

Should you have any questions or like to view our unique, historic sailing vessel then please do not hesitate to contact me.

Yours sincerely,

Cynthia Sprecher
Office Manager

5. **Document for Analysis: Persuasive Request (Obj. 1, 3)**
Analyze the following letter. Pinpoint its strengths and weaknesses, and then revise the letter if directed by your instructor.

The Thirteenth Annual Holiday Store will be held in the lobby of the Main Street Fire Station on Dec. 6, 7, and 8 from 3:00 to 6:00 p.m. New toys will be given to the parents of approximately 400 underprivileged children at this time.

If you can HELP any or all of the following afternoons, we will need YOU to help set up and operate the store. We need volunteers on the afternoon of Dec. 6, 7, and 8 to set up the store and work as clerks and gift wrappers. We need you to please sign your name below, indicating the date you will be able to help.

Name _____

Phone _____

Date & Time Available _____

Also, contributions to The Holiday Store are needed and will be greatly appreciated.

Please return this form to either Mari Cooper, 3771 Abilene Street, Cambridge, MA 02140-3771 (555-1043) or Frances Kuhnle, 101 Mangrove Drive, Boston, MA 02184-0101 (555-9031). THANK YOU!

E-MAIL APPLICATION

Identify a situation in your work, educational experience, or school and community organizations that requires persuasion. How are you uniquely qualified for a scholarship, award, internship, admission into graduate school or honorary organization, or election to an officer position in a student or community organization? How could a change in a procedure improve the quality and efficiency of your work? How could a particular software product, training program, or piece of equipment improve your ability to complete a job function? Why should you be promoted or your present job reclassified to a level of higher responsibility?

Send your instructor an e-mail message describing the exact nature of your persuasive situation and asking approval for this topic. After receiving your instructor's approval, write the persuasive message to the appropriate person, convincing him or her to accept your idea or take the action you have recommended. Obtain the facts and figures necessary to present your argument, identify the benefits the receiver will derive from complying, anticipate the arguments that may come from the receiver, and have a rational and logical response to those arguments. Indicate the exact action you wish to be taken.

APPLICATIONS

1. **Promoting a Product of Your Choice (Obj. 1, 2)**
Select a product that you own, assume that you are its distributor, and write a sales letter addressed to customers who are your age. Regardless of whether you select an item as expensive as a car or as inexpensive as a small pocket calculator, choose a product on which you are sold. You have pride in it; you have benefitted greatly from its use; you are well informed about it; and you could heartily recommend it to others. You may assume an accompanying picture, folder, or pamphlet is included with the letter.

   Required: Write a sales letter providing an inside address for a fictitious customer.

2. **Sales Letter: Promoting a Home Security System (Obj. 1, 2)**
As the local sales manager for Southern Alarm Systems, you are preparing a sales letter to send to prospective customers; you plan to target the letter primarily to families with small children. Your system, Security Plus, can identify as many as 16 different protected zones—doors, windows, smoke and motion detectors and others—allowing flexibility in the protection customers desire. For example, customers can engage all protected zones when away from home. However, when in the house, customers can secure the doors and windows but disengage the motion detectors for free movement around the house. A variety of sensors put in selected places in the home send a clear signal whenever there is a problem, pinpointing the exact location of the problem (e.g., a motion sensor reports the exact hallway or protects silverware cases or other valuable items). In the event of intrusion or fire, the alarm sounds (it has a special sound if a fire has been detected), and the system's computer dials the police dispatcher with a report. To facilitate entering the protected house, a delay can be programmed on one door, allowing customers 30 seconds to disarm the system before the alarm goes off; the system beeps to remind the customer to turn off the system when he or she enters this door. At night when everyone has entered the house, the customer can disengage the delay so that the alarm would sound immediately if a problem were detected at any door or window.

   One-touch commands are used to control the system from a command panel mounted on the wall or free standing on a desk; the back-lighted keypad makes it easy to give commands in a dim room. One-touch keys can be programmed for special uses (e.g., to instruct the system to sound a signal when a certain door is opened to alert parents that a toddler has left the house). The command panel displays important information about the status of the home's protection. Levels of protection include perimeter instant (doors and windows; alarm sounds instantly), perimeter delay (doors and windows; 30-second delay on one door), and all instant (doors and windows, interior motion detectors, and other zones; instant alarm). The user's guide contains complete operating instructions. Available in bright brass or stainless steel, the command center compliments any decor. As an incentive to purchase, you plan to offer the first six months' service contract ($20 a month) for free. Customers should call your toll-free number to arrange for a personal sales call.

   Required: Write a sales letter providing a letter address for a fictitious customer.

3. **Sales Letter: Securing a Radio Advertisement to Promote a Grand Opening (Obj. 1, 2)**
You are the sales manager for WLOX, a radio station that specializes in classic rock—the music of the 60s to now—the favorite tunes of the 25–40 age group. Your

research shows that your regular broadcast audience consists of 9,900 households in suburban Seattle. The average household in this area consists of 3.7 people.

A deli-style restaurant is scheduled to open within your broadcast area during the next month. You feel that your audience demographics fit well into the deli's marketing niche. A well-placed spot aired during "drive time" (7:30 to 8:30 a.m. and 4:00 to 6:00 p.m.) could attract customers to the deli for lunch and dinner. You plan to recommend that the owner purchase forty 30-second spots to be run during the week of the deli's grand opening. You sell 30-second spots for $150 each.

Required: Write a letter to Carmen Costello, Ole Tyme Deli, 1405 McKee Boulevard, Tacoma, WA 98413-1405.

4. **Sales Letter: Earning a Finder's Fee for Exceptional British Stamps (Obj. 1, 2)**
A client who wishes to start a collection of high-quality European stamps for his son has asked you, a dealer in European stamps, to locate them. You have located a solid page of 100 stamps issued ten years ago to commemorate British statesman Winston Churchill. This page is intact; no rows have been removed. Your own investigation has authenticated the dyes and inks on the stamps; you have also inspected the glue on the back and found no flaws. In short, the stamps are in mint condition. The owner paid 50 British pounds for the entire sheet and wishes to sell it for 200 pounds. You feel that the stamps are a very good buy for a beginning collector.

Required:
1. Locate the currency exchange rate so that you can give your client the price in U.S. dollars. Add 10 percent to the price for a finder's fee.

2. Write a sales letter to Glenn Marshall, 1103 Commerce Street, Denton, TX 76205-2955.

5. **Sales Letter: Exposing Potential Members to Resort Property and Privileges (Obj. 1, 2)**
As the public relations director of Crystal Stream, an upscale residential/recreational development in Sacramento, California, one of your major responsibilities is to secure memberships. You believe people must be given an opportunity to experience Crystal Stream firsthand; that is, to see your signature golf course and to dine in your luxurious Williamsburg-style clubhouse. You intend to write a letter to prospects and include a certificate to be redeemed for 18 free holes of golf and a delicious appetizer and beverage in your dining room. Prospects will be instructed to call the pro shop to schedule a tee time. Accompanying the letter and certificate will be a four-color brochure that tells the history of the 712-acre development and includes pictures of the clubhouse, dining and meeting rooms, pool, and fitness rooms. The brochure also includes a detailed map of the course.

Required: Write a persuasive letter to Mr. and Mrs. David R. Denson, 373 Joline Avenue, Sacramento, CA 95813-0373.

6. **Persuasive Claim: Your Dilemma (Obj. 1, 3)**
Identify a situation in which you believe an adjustment is warranted but you doubt the company will comply without persuasion. Perhaps a retailer has already refused to make an adjustment, but you believe the manufacturer should be informed of your dissatisfaction.

Required: Write the claim letter to the appropriate recipient.

7. **Persuasive Claim: Substitute Celebrity Did Not Fit the Bill (Obj. 1, 3)**
Assume you are Jim Kelly, the Hospital Administrator at Woodlake Memorial Hospital. The hospital had arranged for (specify Olympic athlete) to deliver the keynote address at the grand opening of the community's new Healthplex. The athlete was chosen because he/she is an Olympic gold medalist, was born and reared in a nearby city, and is known and supported by the community. As a result of an injury to (specify an Olympian) the day before the appearance, a teammate was sent as a substitute. You are certain that the sports agent believes his arrangement for a substitute athlete to address the group at the last minute was a fair, professional way to handle this uncontrollable situation. You believe the hospital deserves an adjustment because the substitute is not an Olympian, not a native of your state, and is known by few in the community; he/she did not fit the criteria you had set for the speaker at this important community event.

Required: Write the sports agent persuading him to reimburse the hospital for a significant portion of the speaker's fee (e.g., one-half). Send the letter to Lance Woodard, 385-A Jarnagin Street, Los Angeles, CA 90052.

8. **Persuasive Claim: Music Video Missing Creative Symbolism (Obj. 1, 3)**
After negotiating with a number of video producers, the rock group Thunderbolt contracted with Harrelson Producers to direct and produce the band's first music video. Thunderbolt was extremely impressed with the clips from other music videos that Harrelson presented as examples of its work. All these videos were heavy with graphic symbolism and creative shots of the musicians. The producer assured the band members they would be allowed to critique the first draft of the video; the $100,000 fee would be payable when the final video was delivered. When the first draft arrived, Thunderbolt and its general manager eagerly began to critique the tape. Their almost uncontrollable excitement quickly vanished. Unlike the clips they had reviewed, at least half of this videotape depicted the band singing in a live-concert format. The video

included little symbolism, dancing, or any shots of the band in any format other than live concert.

Required: Write a persuasive letter outlining the specific changes you, as Thunderbolt's general manager, believe are necessary for the video to meet the specifications upon which you agreed. Address the letter to Harrelson Producers, 3674 Elmhurst Avenue, Los Angeles, CA 90052-3674.

9. **Persuasive Claim: Equipment Malfunction Justifies an Exchange (Obj. 1, 3)**
Six months ago you bought what was considered a top-of-the-line VCR from an electronics franchise in your town. After one week of use, it malfunctioned. Because it had a two-year warranty, you returned it to the dealer for repair. One week later you took it home, and it broke again. After six months of continually returning the malfunctioning VCR for repair, you feel you deserve a new VCR. The local dealer will not give you a new machine, so you decide to write to the manufacturer.

Required: Write a persuasive letter explaining that you feel justified in asking for a new VCR because yours has been in the repair shop more than it has been available for use. Address the letter to Televideo, 580 West Lakes Blvd., Milwaukee, WI 53202-0580. (You may adapt this case to an actual problem you have experienced for which you would have written a persuasive claim.)

10. **Persuasive Request: Beauty Lies in the Eyes of the Beholder (Obj. 1, 3)**
Down-Home Barbeque, a restaurant chain in the Southeast, routinely seeks weathered wood and antique pieces to create a rustic decor in its family restaurants. While driving his son's friend home from a scout meeting, the manager of the Mena store noticed a large, run-down building several yards to one side of a small, immaculate farmhouse. When he inquired about the building, the owner, Mrs. Hilton, reported that she and her husband had used it for storing canned goods and farm tools over the nearly fifty years they had owned the farm. She commented, "I know it doesn't look like much, but I've never had the heart to tear it down. It's full of so many memories. But that's not all—the legend is it was once a general store, a real hub of activity in its time."

Immediately the manager reports to the owner that this lucky find could provide a majority of the items the company will need to build the new restaurant planned for Mountain View and to refurbish the Jackson store (weathered lumber, cross-cut saws, corn shellers, pump handles, washboards, various old dishes and much more). However, convincing Mrs. Hilton to sell this building—this family landmark and perhaps county legend—would require an empathetic appeal.

Required: Write a letter persuading Mrs. Hilton to allow you to purchase the building and its contents for use in your restaurants. Write to Louise Hilton, 976 Thompson Road, Mena, AR 71953-0976.

11. **Persuasive Request: Volunteer Must Complete Commitment (Obj. 1, 3)**
HomeBuilders, a not-for-profit organization that builds low-mortgage houses for needy families, recently initiated its annual fund-raising drive. Tom McHann, the manager of McHann Electronic Service, was among numerous business executives who volunteered to solicit pledges from 50 area businesses. These volunteers agreed to submit pledges weekly and to complete the drive by May 15. With the deadline only two weeks away, Tom has turned in only five pledge cards. Most of the other volunteers have completed at least 80 percent of their solicitations.

Required: Write a letter to Tom persuading him to call on the remaining 45 businesses and to submit the pledges by the deadline. Tom's address is 1239 McDowell Road, Indianapolis, IN 46206-1239.

12. **Persuasive Request: Advertising Inconsistent with Company Philosophy (Obj. 1, 3)**
Since the turn of the century, Williams Department Store has been the most influential business in your home town. The Williams family have been pillars of the community, taking leadership roles in religion, civic, and economic development activities. The current company president, Patrick Williams, is especially active in an agency that works with drug rehabilitation. Having returned home as the company's new data processing manager, you are puzzled that the company is advertising during a weekly television program that regularly displays parental discretion notices. The show frequently shows drug use (or specify some other action) in a way that would be enticing to children. You believe advertising on this show is inconsistent with the company's long-standing corporate culture and may hurt the company's reputation.

Required: Write a memo to the company president that will persuade the president to discontinue the advertisements on the television show (specify program) that carries parental discretion notices.

13. **Persuasive Request: Using Effective Persuasion Techniques to Prevent a Hostile Takeover (Obj. 1, 3)**
Winton-Pearson, Inc., is attempting a hostile takeover of Carroll Industry by offering to buy stock at $55 when the current level is $40. As the chief executive officer of Carroll, you hope to prevent this takeover by communicating to the stockholders the benefits of not selling at the higher price. Two years ago, Carroll Industry renegotiated its contract with union workers. That action positioned the company at a cost disadvantage to its

competitors, thus reducing corporate profits. You have learned through reliable sources that your major competitors will renegotiate their union contracts within the year. Consequently, they will face the same increases in employee wages, and their current advantage will be dissipated. Management is confident that Carroll will quickly reap the benefits of taking the initiative and renegotiating the labor contracts of two years ago.

Required: Write a letter to the stockholders persuading them not to sell their stock; you are the chief executive officer of Carroll. Address the letter to Mrs. Helen Munson, 8311 Desert Lane, Tucson, AZ 85702-8311.

14. **Persuasive Request: Seeking Support for a Proposed Tax Hike (Obj. 1, 3)**
A special election has been scheduled for a referendum on a 2 percent tax on prepared food and beverages. The tax has been proposed by the Tucson City Planning Board (the municipal government) as a means of providing public funding for the newly formed Tucson Development Council (TDC). Officials estimate the tax will produce approximately $900,000 in revenues. According to the bill, half the funds would be used to fund the TDC, which will handle all local economic developmental projects. Twenty-five percent would be used by the Visitors and Convention Council for the development of tourism within the county, and 25 percent would be used to construct a welcome center. As president of the Tucson Chamber of Commerce, you are convinced that economic development, especially increased tourism, will benefit the entire community. Bringing more people to Tucson will create jobs and income for the people here. You have obtained current membership lists of the area civic clubs.

Required: Compose a form letter to be sent to members of the other civic clubs persuading them to support the tax. Address the letter to Alex Davies, 104 Duggar Acres, Tucson, AZ 85702-0104.

15. **Persuasive Request: Securing Volunteer Services for Service Organization (Obj. 1, 3)**
You are responsible for finding a suitable person to perform a special activity for a service organization to which you belong. Using your own interests and creativity, specify the exact nature of this activity. For example, you might ask a financial planner to discuss mutual funds at a monthly meeting; an accountant to prepare tax returns for senior citizens; or a computer programmer to assist in automating membership records. Assume that the individual must be convinced to respond favorably because of circumstances that you specify (e.g., too busy, not a member of your organization, no previous experience in such civic activities, etc.).

Required: Write a letter to the person of your choice inviting him/her to assist in the activity you specified. Include any details needed to make arrangements for his/her participation in this activity.

16. **Persuasive Memo: Persuading Employees to Enhance Financial Planning (Obj. 1, 3)**
Several years ago your company ran a campaign to enroll employees in 403(b) plans. Section 403(b) of the Internal Revenue Code allows employees to invest up to 15 percent of their gross wages in tax-deferred annuities. Contributions to the annuities are not taxed until funds are withdrawn upon retirement. Unfortunately, a recent report from your human resources department indicates that only 22 percent of your employees have taken advantage of this plan. Based on your conversations with several employees, you believe that many employees do not understand the benefits of the plan.

Required: As director of human resources, write a memo to all employees persuading them to attend a meeting to gain additional information about this financial planning strategy.

17. **Persuasive Memo: Convincing Employees to Follow Computer Security Policy. (Obj. 1, 3)**
When you read about the most recent incident of computer abuse (a student used a friend's e-mail address and password to send a threatening e-mail message to the President of the United States), you knew you had to do a better job of enforcing the company's computer security policy. You are especially concerned that few employees seem to understand that e-mail is not confidential and that they must write secure passwords, change them often, and follow logout procedures when leaving a terminal, and other security precautions.

Required: Write a memo, as MIS manager, to all employees persuading them to adhere to these computer security measures. Review the Strategic Forces box in Chapter 7 on pages 244-245 and obtain any other facts needed to help employees recognize the benefits they can gain from complying.

18. **Persuasive Memo: Investigating On-line Connections Important for Company Productivity. (Obj. 1, 3)**
You have read extensively about the information superhighway and the benefits small companies are gaining from on-line services and Internet connections. You are convinced that your company could operate more productively and perhaps do more business if you were on-line. Although most of the managers you have talked with about the feasibility of going on-line seem interested, none has the expertise needed to initiate the startup. You noticed an ad for a three-day seminar entitled "Making On-line Services Work for You," and decide that this intensive training would provide the

knowledge needed to develop a strategic plan for the company to take advantage of this new technology.

Required: Write a persuasive memo to the president requesting approval for you, as the assistant accountant, to attend the seminar at company expense. Attach a copy of an article or a printout from a web site that outlines the value of being wired and provides specific examples of companies' innovative use of on-line technology.

19. **Persuasive Memo: Persuading a Manager to Start a FaxFood Line (Obj. 1, 3)**
Gordon's Deli is filled to capacity during the lunch hour because of its convenient location in the center of the downtown business district and its reputation for delicious specialty foods. As a summer employee, daily you watch small groups of office workers stand impatiently checking their watches as they wait for a table; other groups leave as soon as they see the long lines. While waiting for a table, numerous customers have told you they prefer your wide selection of healthy food choices over the other fast-food restaurants in the area. Often they cannot leave the office for lunch because of pressing deadlines and are forced to skip lunch or eat snacks from a vending machine. No space is available for expanding the dining room to shorten the waiting line. However, you believe customers who are eating on the run would react favorably to what you are calling a FaxFood Line: Customers would fax their orders, with delivery to their office guaranteed within a half hour. You realize that not all your menu items can be delivered effectively, and you cannot afford to deliver small orders. Other resistance includes the logistics of receiving and confirming orders, especially for those ordering as a group from the same office but wanting individual totals.

Required:

1. Write a memo to persuade the manager to introduce the FaxFood Line. Mention you are attaching a draft of a sales letter promoting the new service to downtown office workers and the forms (see Step 3) needed to expedite your plan. (You do not have to design the forms unless directed by your instructor.)

2. Write a sales letter promoting this new service to downtown office workers. (Provide your own name for the service if you wish.)

3. Design an order form for the FaxFood Line and the confirmation form you will send after the order is received. Use your own creativity to generate a list of menu items or select them from the menu of your favorite deli.

REAL-TIME INTERNET CASE

Using the Internet to Bridge the Cultural Gap

The Internet has the potential to become the primary tool for helping people of the world understand each other and view citizens of other cultures as real individuals living similar lives, while in different ways. Exploring the cultures of the world via the Internet is one step toward tolerance and acceptance of all people, regardless of race, ethnicity, religion, or national heritage.

You can use the Internet to obtain information on virtually any country in the world. The W3 Servers site is a listing of national information servers. These are the official or semiofficial servers from each country that provide information about the country and include links to related sites. Another helpful site is the Central Intelligence Agency's on-line World Factbook, which contains a vast amount of information on every country in the World, as collected by the agency. Chat sites for cultural discussion are widely available, such as the Yahoo! Net Events: Cultures site. When planning travel outside the country, you might want to consult the U.S. State Department site's area for "Crisis Abroad." The site also includes the latest travel warnings, consular information, entry requirements, crime information, and embassy locations.

If you need to know at least a little of the language of the culture you plan to visit, be sure to check the Foreign Language for Travelers site. Here you can select any one of 57 different languages for translating. The site not only displays the words, but actually recites them for you via short audio files. And of course you will want to know what your U.S. Dollars will convert to in your visited country. The Currency Convertor on the Net lets you input the number of dollars and obtain the exchanged amount for another currency.

Armed with accurate information about a given country, you are able to understand and appreciate cultural variety. As globalization of business results in a world that grows progressively smaller, it becomes imperative for professionals to possess broad-based cultural awareness. Visit the following sites and complete the activities as directed by your instructor.

VIDEO CONNECTION

Tracy-Locke/ Pharr Public Relations

Preparing effective persuasive communication requires a carefully tuned set of skills. First, the writer must understand the needs and motivations of the intended audience and how to make the product, service, or idea appealing. Second, the writer must be able to predict and overcome any reason the receiver may have for rejecting the message, so as to assure the desired outcome. Third, the writer must be convincing, yet courteous; persuasive, yet polite.

Whether selling products, services, or ideas, a business's success or failure often rests on its employees' strengths of persuasion.

Discussion Questions

1. Cynthia Pharr likens the sales letter to a personal sales call. Explain how the two activities are similar.

2. Michael Fleming puts forth the idea that practicing conciseness shows concern for your receiver/audience. Explain this concept.

3. What constitutes an effective opening for a sales letter? Give examples of techniques that may attract the receiver's attention. What should the writer guard against in structuring the opening?

4. Explain the concept of being receiver oriented. How is this idea applied in sales messages?

5. How do surface characteristics, such as the envelope and stationery, affect the receiver's response to a sales letter?

Application

You must construct an effective persuasive message to persuade your audience to support a product, service, or idea of your choice (e.g., the idea your instructor approved in the e-mail application in the end-of-chapter activities). Remember to include (1) an effective opening; (2) a concise, on-target discussion of your product, service, or idea; (3) convincing evidence that your product, service, or idea will meet the receiver's needs, including a logical argument to overcome any resistance you anticipate; and (4) a courteous, effective call for action.

Internet Sites

http://vlib.stanford.edu/Servers.html
http://www.odci.gov/cia/publications/factbook/index.html
http://www.yahoo.com/Society_and_Culture/Cultures/
http://travel.state.gov/
http://www.travlang.com/languages/

Activities

1. Select a country for study. Visit the sites listed and gather the following information: location and size, official language(s), religion(s), customs, currency, major products, and crime statistics. Learn three phrases in the predominant language of the country. Share your information in a short oral report.

2. Locate other Internet sites that provide information about your selected country. Prepare a list of dos and don'ts for the traveler visiting that country.

3. Prepare a one-page essay that uses the metaphor of a bridge to describe the role of the Internet in linking cultures.

*I*n the Storming stage of team development, conflict occurs in interpersonal relationships. Although frustrations may be suppressed or masked, open hostility sometimes occurs. Members experience a growing awareness of others' hidden agendas, and cliques may form.. When goals are not in harmony, conflict is inevitable. In spite of the turmoil of the Storming stage, organization does typically advance in task functions and roles.

Some conflicts within teams are due to disagreements about how the work should be done. These are task-oriented conflicts, and they focus on the process the team will use to achieve its goals or its mission. The other type of conflicts are people-oriented conflicts that arise out of personality differences, struggles for leadership or turf, and rudeness by one member to another.

Typical feelings of team members during the Storming stage include anxiety, doubt, and frustration. Typical behaviors during the Storming stage include:

- expressing anger when it is realized the task ahead is more complicated than originally perceived.
- questioning leadership.
- resisting working together and asserting of individual opinions.
- showing impatience because of slow progress.

Conflict is a natural part of life and, therefore, of team development. Conflict can involve two or more individuals, or the whole team. It can be either constructive or destructive, depending on how we handle it and choose to react. Conflict can be considered constructive if:

- people change and grow personally from the conflict.
- it results in a solution to the problem.
- it increases the involvement of everyone affected by the conflict.
- it builds cohesiveness among members of the team.

Conflict is destructive when:

- no decision is reached and the problem still exists.
- it diverts energy from more important activities or issues.
- it destroys the morale of the team or individual team members.
- it polarizes or divides the team.

Most conflicts can be resolved or managed so that the team can work together. Successful team members learn that they don't have to like everyone they work with or always agree completely; but they do have to work courteously and effectively with team members. Negotiation and mediation are two methods of getting two or more members to reach an agreement based upon their satisfying a mutually held goal. When negotiating, you are a participant in the process and represent your own interests. When mediating, you help others negotiate successfully. For critical team issues, it is important to reach consensus, a condition that is achieved when everyone in the team can fully support a decision. Discussion and negotiation proceed until all members can say they "are comfortable with" or "can live with" a position. When they achieve this level of agreement, they must ALL commit to completely supporting the decision.

Some teams are unable to overcome the problems that occur during this stage and may dissolve. If the members elect to stay together, they will typically decide if they are to function as a team or a mere group. In work groups, individuals are assigned pieces of the project which are brought together in pieces at a later date; very little collaborative work actually occurs. Work groups are, in essence, a collage of single works. In teams, however, face-to-face interaction is usually required to create high performance. Teams have four other main characteristics:

- Positive interdependence. Members of the team have to rely on each other in order to complete the project.
- Individual accountability. Each member is held responsible for his or her contribution to the completion of the project.
- Group processing/Interaction. Group members feel quite comfortable working with each other. They feel free to express their feelings.
- Social and role definition. The required roles are being performed by team members.

Teams provide a favorable environment to foster open communication, interaction, and insight. This makes them far superior to working groups and individuals in generating new ideas.

Exploration

Read the following two articles that provide helpful suggestions for resolving team conflicts:

> How to cope with conflicts within the team (1996, April). *Getting Results . . . For the Hands-On Manager, 41*(4), 1.

> Capozzoli, T. K. (1995, December). Conflict resolution: A key ingredient in successful team. *Supervision, 56*(12), 3–5.

Compile a list of the suggestions for conflict resolution as given in the two articles. Brainstorm in your team to come up with additional strategies that can be added to the list. Share how you as individuals have resolved conflicts that occurred in other groups or teams of which you were a part.

Application

Visit the following web site that provides some simple tips for resolving conflict

http://www/cyfc.umn.edu/Other/conflictresolution.html.

Individually, send an e-mail message to your instructor describing any problems or conflicts that have occurred thus far in your team. Explain how you individually and your team as a whole have responded to the issues. Ask for your instructor's help, if necessary, in reaching resolution.

With your team members, complete the following activities:

- Prepare an outline of your project, giving major topics and subtopics to be covered.

- Prepare a progress report memo addressed to your instructor that includes:

  1. The steps you have taken thus far in progress on your project; include dates, names of participants, and major activities.

  2. The major activities that you have identified as remaining to be completed on your project; include projected dates and names of persons responsible for each activity.

  3. A request for any needed assistance or suggestions from your instructor.

PART FOUR

Communicating Through Reports and Business Presentations

CHAPTER NINE

Understanding the Report Process and Research Methods

When you have completed Chapter 9, you will be able to:

1 Identify the characteristics of a report and the various classifications of business reports.

2 Identify the four steps in the problem-solving process.

3 Select appropriate secondary and primary methods for solving a problem.

4 Locate both printed and electronic sources of information.

5 Explain three common methods of primary research.

6 Explain the purpose of sampling and four sampling techniques.

7 Apply techniques for developing effective questionnaires.

8 Discuss the common problems encountered in collecting and interpreting data.

*I*n a typical U.S. supermarket, Campbell's soup consumes nearly half an aisle with its wide assortment of red and white labels. In a Tokyo supermarket, however, Campbell's has a mere token presence. With slow sales and market saturation at home, Campbell Soup Company is seeking to build new business overseas. As consumers in emerging economies become busier with factory and office jobs, they have less time to make homemade soup and begin to see condensed soup as an attractive option. Outside the United States, the market for commercial soup is about $5.2 billion a year, of which Campbell has only a 10 percent share.

Campbell is finding, however, that marketing their product in other countries requires different strategies. "For a long time, international marketing was more a hobby than an area of strategic imperative for us," said Dale Morrison, Campbell's president of International and Specialty Foods. "We thought we could just put it out on the shelf, and they would come." By applying the results of its marketing research, Campbell hopes to appeal more successfully to consumer demand in targeted countries. Japan, where most commercially sold soup is dry, is a prime battleground. The first obstacle for Campbell is the can itself. In Japan, most food is sold fresh, or in clear packaging. Cans are considered dirty. So when Campbell began its latest push into Japan in the mid 90s, it decided to go with a cleaner, more expensive pop-top opener. Then it created a character called Mr. Campbell, a talking soup can with a winning smile, who stars in Japanese television commercials. Campbell's desire is that the strategy will build brand-name recognition and cause Japanese consumers to feel affection for a can.

Campbell plans to double advertising spending in Japan to help build its market, which has recently grown from a 2 percent market share to a 9 percent share. Ongoing consumer research will enable Campbell to target its marketing activities effectively and maximize its sales opportunities.[1] As a manager, you will be faced with the challenge of maximizing results for your organization, division, or department. Unless you can successfully conduct research, you will be a part of the problem instead of the solution.

① *Identify the characteristics of a report and the various classifications of business reports.*

The Characteristics of Reports

> Hello, Laura. This is Ganesh in customer services. The boss wants to know how things are going with the 400-case Sleepwell order. Are we going to make the 4 p.m. shipping deadline?
>
> Oh hi, Ganesh. We are going to make the deadline, with time to spare. We have about 250 cases on the loading dock, 100 on the box line, and 50 going through the labeling process. They'll all be ready for the loader at two o'clock.

This brief exchange illustrates a simple reporting task. A question has been posed; the answer given (along with supporting information) satisfies the reporting requirement. Although Laura may never have studied report preparation, she did an excellent job; so Ganesh, in turn, can report to his supervisor. Laura's oral report is a simple illustration of four main characteristics of reports:

- ***Reports typically travel upward in an organization because they usually are requested by a higher authority.*** In most cases, people would not generate reports unless requested to do so.

- ***Reports are logically organized.*** In Laura's case, she answered Ganesh's question first and then supported the answer with evidence to justify it.

Through your study of the organization of letters, you learned the difference between deductive and inductive organization. Laura's report was deductively organized. If Laura had given the supporting evidence first and followed that with the answer that she would meet the deadline, the organization of her reply would have been inductive and would still have been logical.

- **Reports are objective.** Because reports contribute to decision making and problem solving, they should be as objective as possible; when nonobjective (subjective) material is included, the report writer should make that known.

- **Reports are generally prepared for a limited audience.** This characteristic is particularly true of reports traveling within an organization and means that reports, like letters, can be prepared with the receivers' needs in mind.

Types of Reports

Based on the four characteristics, a workable definition of a **report** is an orderly, objective message used to convey information from one organizational area to another or from one organization to another to assist in decision making or problem solving. Reports have been classified in numerous ways by management and by report-preparation authorities. The form, direction, functional use, and content of the report are used as bases for classification. However, a single report might be included in several classifications. The following brief review of classification helps explain the scope of reporting and establishes a departure point for studying reports and reporting.

- **Formal or informal reports.** The formal/informal classification is particularly helpful because it applies to all reports. A **formal report** is carefully structured; it is logically organized and objective, contains much detail, and is written in a style that tends to eliminate such elements as personal pronouns. An **informal report** is usually a short message written in natural or personal language. The internal memo generally can be described as an informal report. All reports can be placed on a continuum of formality, as shown in Figure 9-1. The distinction among the degrees of formality of various reports is explained more fully in Chapters 10 and 11.

- **Short or long reports.** Reports can be classified generally as short or long. A one-page memo is obviously short, and a report of twenty pages is obviously

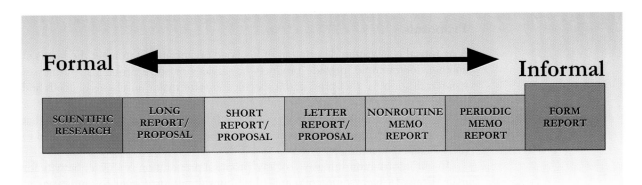

FIGURE 9-1 Report formality continuum.

long. What about in-between lengths? One important distinction generally holds true: as it becomes longer, a report takes on more characteristics of formal reports. Thus, the formal/informal and short/long classifications are closely related.

Why do organizations need information generated from both informational and analytical reports?

- *Informational or analytical reports.* An **informational report** carries objective information from one area of an organization to another. An **analytical report** presents suggested solutions to problems. Company annual reports, monthly financial statements, reports of sales volume, and reports of employee or personnel absenteeism and turnover are informational reports. Reports of scientific research, real-estate appraisal reports, and feasibility reports by consulting firms are analytical reports.

- *Vertical or lateral reports.* The vertical/lateral classification refers to the directions reports travel. Although most reports travel upward in organizations, many travel downward. Both represent vertical reports and are often referred to as *upward-directed* and *downward-directed* reports. The main function of vertical reports is to contribute to management *control*, as shown in Figure 9-2. Lateral reports, on the other hand, assist in *coordination* in the organization. A report traveling between units on the same organizational level, as between the production department and the finance department, is lateral.

- *Internal or external reports.* An **internal report** such as a production and a sales report travels within an organization. An **external report**, such as a company's annual report to stockholders, is prepared for distribution outside an organization.

- *Periodic reports.* A **periodic report** is issued on regularly scheduled dates. They are generally directed upward and serve management-control purposes. Daily, weekly, monthly, quarterly, semiannual, and annual time periods are typical for periodic reports. Preprinted forms and computer-generated data contribute to uniformity of periodic reports.

- *Functional reports.* A **functional report** serves a specified purpose within a company. The functional classification includes accounting reports, marketing reports, financial reports, personnel reports, and a variety of other reports that take their functional designation from their ultimate use. For example, a justification of the need for additional personnel or for new equipment is described as a *justification report* in the functional classification.

Proposals

A **proposal** is a written description of how one organization can meet the needs of another, for example, provide products or services or solve problems. Businesses issue "calls for bids" that present the specifications for major purchases of goods and certain services. Most governmental agencies issue "requests for proposals," or RFPs. Potential suppliers prepare proposal reports telling how they can meet that need. Those preparing the proposal create a convincing document that will lead to their obtaining a contract.

In our information-intensive society, proposal preparation is a major activity for many firms. In fact, some companies hire consultants or designate employees to specialize in proposal writing. Chapter 11 presents proposal preparation in considerable detail.

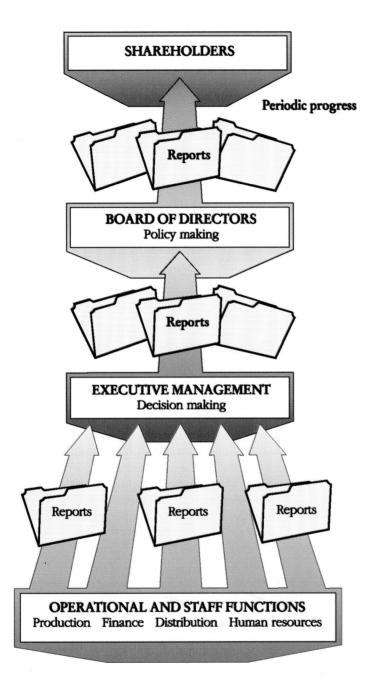

FIGURE 9-2
The general upward flow
of reports.

As you review these report classifications, you will very likely decide—correctly—that almost all reports could be included in these categories. A report may be formal or informal, short or long, informational or analytical, vertically or laterally directed, internal or external, periodic or nonperiodic, functionally labeled, a proposal, or some other combination of these classifications. These report categories are in common use and provide necessary terminology for the study and production of reports.

Basis for Reports: The Problem-Solving Process

The upward flow of reports provides management with data that someone may use to make a decision. The purpose is to use the data to solve a problem. Some problems are recurring and call for a steady flow of information; other problems may be unique and call for information on a one-time basis. A problem is the basis for a report. The following steps are used for finding a solution:

1. Recognize and define the problem.
2. Select a method of solution.
3. Collect and organize the data.
4. Arrive at an answer.

Only after all four steps have been completed is a report written for presentation. Reports represent an attempt to communicate how a problem was solved. These problem-solving steps are completed *before* the report is written in final form.

Recognizing and Defining the Problem

Problem-solving research cannot begin until the researchers define the problem. Frequently, those requesting a report will attempt to provide a suitable definition. Nevertheless, researchers should attempt to paraphrase to ensure they will be on the right track.

Using Problem Statements, Statements of Purpose, and Hypotheses. The **problem statement**, or statement of the problem, is the particular problem that is to be solved by the research. The **statement of purpose** is the reason for which the report is being prepared. Research studies often have both a problem statement and a statement of purpose. For example, a real estate appraiser accepts a client's request to appraise a building to determine its market value. The problem is to arrive at a fair market value for the property. The purpose of the appraisal, however, might be to establish a value for a mortgage loan, to determine the feasibility of adding to the structure, or to assess the financial possibility of demolishing the structure and erecting something else. Thus, the purpose may have much to do with determining what elements to consider in arriving at an answer.

In other words, unless you know why something is wanted, you might have difficulty knowing what is wanted. Once you arrive at the answers to the *what* and *why* questions, write them down. You will be on your way to solving the problem.

A **hypothesis** is a statement to be proved or disproved through research. For example, a study of skilled manufacturing employees under varying conditions might be made to determine whether production would increase if each employee were part of a team, as opposed to being a single unit in a production line. For this problem, the hypothesis could be formulated in this way:

Of what value is a research study in which the hypotheses are disproven?

Hypothesis: Productivity will increase when skilled manufacturing employees are members of production teams rather than single units in a production line.

Because the hypothesis tends to be stated in a way that favors one possibility or is prejudiced toward a particular answer, many researchers prefer to state hypotheses in the null form. The **null hypothesis** states that no relationship or difference will be found in the factors being studied, which tends to remove the element of prejudice toward an answer. The null hypothesis for the previous example could be written as follows:

Null hypothesis:	No significant difference will be found in productivity between workers as team members and workers as individual production line units.

Using the problem/purpose approach and/or the hypothesis approach is optional. In many ways, the purpose of a study is determined by the intended use of its results.

Write a statement of purpose for this study of teams.

Limiting the Scope of the Problem.　A major shortcoming that often occurs in research planning is the failure to establish or to recognize desirable limits. The **scope** of the report helps to establish boundaries in which the report will be researched and prepared. Assume, for instance, that you want to study salaries of office support staff. Imagine the enormity of such a task. Millions of people are employed in office support jobs. Perhaps a thousand or so different types of jobs fall into this classification. To reduce such a problem to reasonable proportions, use the *what, why, when, where,* and *who* questions to limit the problem. Here are the limits you might derive as the human resources manager at a metropolitan bank:

How does the scope of a report serve a similar purpose as a scope on a rifle?

What:	A study of salaries of office support staff.
Why:	To determine whether salaries in our firm are competitive and consistent.
When:	Current.
Where:	Our metropolitan area.
Who:	Office support staff employees in banks.

Now you can phrase the problem this way:

Statement of Purpose:	The purpose of this study is to survey salaries of office support staff in local banks to determine whether our salaries are competitive and consistent.

Note that this process of reducing the problem to a workable size has also established some firm limits to the research. You have limited the problem to current salaries, to the local area, and to a particular type of business. Note, too, how important the *why* was in helping establish the limits. Limiting the problem is "zeroing in on the problem."

In some reports, it is desirable to differentiate between the boundaries that were placed on the project outside the control of the researcher(s) and those that were chosen by the researcher(s). Boundaries imposed outside the control of the researchers are called **limitations**; they may include the selection of the topic, assigned budget, and time for completion of the report. These boundaries affect what and how the topic can be researched. Boundaries chosen by the researcher(s) to make the project more manageable are called **delimitations**; they may include the sources and methods chosen for both primary and secondary research.

Defining Terms Clearly.　Vague terms contribute greatly to faulty communication. Words often have more than one meaning; thus a definition of the specific terms in the current study would be necessary. Additionally, technical or special-use words

COMMUNICATION MENTOR

An effective report begins with understanding the objectives and expectations of a client. This understanding should be confirmed and reconfirmed as a finding early in the process might change the entire thrust of the project. For example, a client was interested in acquiring a Russian legal entity. Throughout our initial discussions of the project scope, the client continually referred to necessary "due diligence" and "purchase investiga-

tion" procedures. After we presented the report, the client clarified a need for an audit of the financial statements in accordance with generally accepted auditing standards—an entirely different report than the one we prepared. Ultimately, we solved the client's problem while learning a valuable lesson about the importance of effective communication in preparing a report that meets a client's needs.

Lawrence E. Wilson, Partner
Arthur Andersen, Moscow

may occur in the report that are not widely used or understood. These terms would also require a definition for the reader's understanding of the information presented. In the previously used example concerning the study of office support staff salaries, a comparison of one bank's salaries with those paid by others would be meaningful only if the information gathered from other banks relates to identical jobs. A job description defining the duties performed by an administrative assistant, for example, would help ensure that all firms would be talking about the same job tasks regardless of the job title. In addition, the term *salary* requires definition. Is it hourly, weekly, monthly, or yearly? Are benefits included?

Documenting Procedures. The procedures or steps a writer takes in preparing a report are often recorded as a part of the written report. This **procedures** section, or **methodology**, adds credibility to the research process and also enables subsequent researchers to repeat, or replicate, the study in another setting or at a later time if desired. Reports that study the same factors in different time frames are called **longitudinal studies**.

The procedures section of a report records the major steps taken in the research, and possibly the reasons for their inclusion. It may, for instance, tell the types of printed sources that were consulted and the groups of people interviewed and how they were selected. Steps in the procedures section are typically listed in chronological order, so that the reader has an overall understanding of when the research steps took place and the timetable that existed for the project.

Selecting a Method of Solution

After defining the problem, the researcher will plan how to arrive at a solution. You may use secondary and/or primary research methods to collect necessary information.

Secondary Research. Secondary research provides information that has already been created by others. Researchers save time and effort by not duplicating research that has already been undertaken. They can access this information

3 *Select appropriate secondary and primary methods for solving a problem.*

4 *Locate both printed and electronic sources of information.*

easily through the aid of electronic databases, bibliographic indexes, and catalogs. Suppose that a marketing manager has been authorized to investigate the feasibility of implementing a strategic information system. The manager knows other companies are using this technology. By engaging in library research, the manager can determine the boundaries of knowledge before proceeding into the unknown.

Certain truths have been established within the confines of a field of knowledge. These truths are treated as principles and reported in textbooks and other publications. However, because knowledge is constantly expanding, the researcher knows that new information is available. The job, then, is to become familiar with the library, canvass the literature of the field, and attempt to redefine the boundaries of knowledge. This redefinition is the function of secondary research. Researchers then explore the unknown. Through redefinition of boundaries, library research accomplishes the following objectives: (1) establishes a point of departure for further research, (2) avoids needless duplication of costly research efforts, (3) reveals areas of needed research, and (4) makes a real contribution to a body of knowledge. Secondary research can be gathered by means of more traditional published sources or by using electronic tools.

> Describe the proper balance between secondary research and primary research.

Published sources. Major categories of published sources are books, periodicals, and government documents. Books are typically cataloged in libraries by call number, with most larger libraries using the Library of Congress classification system. The card catalog in most libraries has been replaced by an "on-line catalog," which allows the user to locate desired books by author, title, subject, or key word. A wide assortment of reference books is typically available for use within the library; these include dictionaries, encyclopedias, yearbooks, and almanacs. Some of these volumes contain general information on a wide array of topics, while others are designed for a specific field of study.

Periodicals, referred to as *serials* by librarians, include various types of publications that are released on a regular, periodic basis. Thus, newspapers, magazines, and journals are all types of periodicals. Newspapers, which are usually published daily, are a good initial source for investigation, since they give condensed coverage of timely topics. Magazines may be published weekly, monthly, bimonthly, or in some other interval. They are typically written for a general readership, providing expanded coverage in an easy-to-read format. Journals, on the other hand, are written for more specialized audiences, and are more research oriented. Journal articles share the results of research studies and provide interpretive data that supports their findings. They also provide bibliographies or citation lists that can be very useful for locating related materials. Articles on specific topics can be located using both published and on-line indexes. A non-inclusive list of these sources is shown in Figure 9-3.

Electronic sources. The availability of computer-assisted data searches has simplified the time-consuming task of searching through indexes, card catalogs, and other sources. Weekly and monthly updates keep electronic databases current, and they are easy to use. Databases such as Lexis-Nexis and the Internet have full-text retrieval capability, meaning you can retrieve the entire reference into your word processing program so that you can review and/or print a copy. A research process that may have taken several hours can be completed in a matter of minutes. Note the list of electronic databases for business users listed in Figure 9-3.

> How have computer-assisted data searches revolutionized the research process?

FIGURE 9-3
Useful reference and
source books.

Printed Indexes
Business Periodicals Index
Education Index
New York Times Index
Readers' Guide to Periodical Literature
Social Science and Humanities Index
The Wall Street Journal Index

Electronic Sources
ProQuest
Business Dateline
DIALOG Information Services
ERIC (educational)
Internet
Lexis/Nexis (news and business)
Moody's International Company Data
Westlaw (legal)

General Facts and Statistics
Statistical Abstract of the United States and other Bureau of the Census publica-
    tions (available on statistical databases)
Dictionary (general and discipline specific)
Encyclopedia (*Americana* or *Britannica*)
Fortune Directories of U.S. Corporations
World Atlas
Almanacs

Biography
Who's Who in America (and a variety of similar directories for specific geographic
    areas, industries, and professions)

Report Style and Format
American Psychological Association. (1994). *Publication manual of the American
    Psychological Association.* (4th ed.). Washington, DC: Author.
Gibaldi, J. (1995). *MLA handbook for writers of research papers,* (4th revised ed.).
    New York: Modern Language Association.
University of Chicago Press. (1993), *The Chicago manual of style.* (14th ed.).
    Chicago: Author.

The Internet, and its subset, the World Wide Web, have made thousands of reference sources available in a matter of minutes. However, the vastness of this resource can be overwhelming to the novice researcher. Cautions related to the use of the Internet are discussed in the accompanying Strategic Forces box. The following tips will help to make your Internet search more productive:

- **Choose your search engine appropriately.** A search engine is a cataloged database of web sites that allow you to search on specific topics. Several popular search engines exist, including Yahoo!, Alta Vista, InfoSeek, and Excite. While Yahoo! contains about 300,000 entries, Alta Vista and InfoSeek hold 30 to 50 million each.[2] You want to obtain a sufficient number of "hits," but not thousands. (A hit is a located web site that contains the word or words specified in the search.) Although the variety of these larger engines is greater, they pose

Strategic Forces: Legal and Ethical Constraints

Internet Sources Vary: Caution Advised

The Internet has been likened to a wild, untamed frontier, open to all who desire to exercise their right to free speech. In its decision to declare the Communications Decency Act unconstitutional, the Supreme Court said, "The interest in encouraging freedom of expression in a democratic society outweighs any theoretical but unproven benefit of censorship."[3] Because of the uncensored status of the Internet, the serious researcher has several reasons for exercising caution in using information found there.

- *Internet resources are not always accurate.* Because the Internet is not patrolled or edited, postings come from a wide variety of sources. Some of these sources are reliable and credible; some are not.

- *Certain uses of Internet sources may be illegal.* Some material available on the Internet is copyright protected and therefore not available for some uses by those who download the files. For instance, photograph files that are copyrighted may be viewed by Internet users but not incorporated into documents that have commercial use, unless permission is granted by the copyright holder. Such permission often involves a royalty fee.

- *Internet resources are not always complete.* Selected text of articles and documents are often available via the Internet, while full text may be available only in published form.

- *Electronic periodicals are not always subjected to a rigorous review process.* Because most traditional magazines and journal articles are reviewed by an editorial board or peer reviewers, they are considered to be of more value than an article prepared by one or a few individuals that is not critiqued by other experts before its publication. Articles available over the Internet may not have benefitted from such a review process.

Because of these limitations, the Internet should not be seen as a substitute for traditional library research, but rather as a complementary search tool.

Application

Select a business topic, if one is not assigned to you by your instructor, and search for resources related to that topic using the Internet. Locate at least one article you feel is a reliable source of valuable information for use in a business report on the assigned topic. Locate at least one article you feel would not be a good choice for use as a reference in a business report. Compose a brief explanation of the reasons for your selections; attach printouts of the selected articles and submit the assignment to your instructor.

---

more difficulty in narrowing a search. Start with a small search engine and then move to a larger one if necessary.

- *Structure searches from broad to specific.* Use words for your topic that are descriptive and do not have multiple meanings. Once sites have been located for your general topic, you can use **Boolean logic** to narrow the selection. Boolean operands (and, or, not) serve to limit the identified sites. The following example shows how these delimiters can assist you in locating precisely what you want:

  - Using the key phrase "workplace productivity" will produce all sites that have either of the key words in the title or descriptors.
  - Placing "and" between the key words will produce only those hits that have both words.
  - Keying "workplace productivity not United States" will eliminate hits that refer to the United States.

- *Use quotation marks when literal topics are desired.* Putting quotation marks around your topic words can drastically affect the number of hits. The quotation marks cause the search engine to look for the designated words as a phrase, thus producing only those sites that have the phrase present. Without the quotation marks, the search engine will treat the words individually and produce many more hits, most of which may not be useful. For instance, if you are looking for sites related to international communication, placing quotation marks around the desired phrase would eliminate the sites that deal with international topics that are not communication oriented.

- *Look for web pages that have collections of links to the other related topics.* Clicking on these **hyperlinks** will allow you to maximize your time investment in the data-gathering phase of your research.

- *Be adaptable to the various access format requirements.* Each search engine and database has its own particular format and instructions for use. Some require keyboard input and do not respond to your mouse. The method for specifying and narrowing your search will vary.

5 *Explain three common methods of primary research.*

Primary Research. After reviewing the secondary data, you may need to collect primary data to solve your problem. **Primary research** relies on firsthand data, for example, responses from pertinent individuals or observations of people or phenomena related to your study. Recognized methods to obtain original information are observational studies, experimental research, and normative surveys.

Observational research. In **observational research**, the researcher observes and statistically analyzes certain phenomena in order to assist in establishing new principles or discoveries. For example, market analysts observe buying habits of certain income groups to determine the most desirable markets. An information systems manager tabulates the number of input-operator errors made to assess the effectiveness of a computer-training program. Executives analyze the frequency of ethical misconduct to determine the effectiveness of a comprehensive ethics program. Developing an objective system for quantifying observations is necessary to collect valid data. For example, to gain insight on the effect of a comprehensive ethics program, a researcher might record the number of incidents of ethical misconduct reported or the number of calls made to an ethics help-line to seek advice about proper conduct.

Experimental research. **Experimental research** involves the study of two samples that have exactly the same components before a variable is added to one of the samples. The differences observed are due to the variable. Like scientists, businesses use experimental research. As a simple example, assume that a company has a large number of machinists doing the same routine job. Management decides to research the effects of work groups on productivity (hypotheses discussed earlier in this chapter). The study involves the machinists in two plants with similar previous productivity rates. The machinists in one plant are organized into work groups; each machinist in the other plant continues to work as a single unit in the production line. During the period of the study, the difference in the two study groups is noted. Because the workgroup organization is assumed to be the only variable, any difference is attributed to its influence.

Normative survey research. **Normative survey research** is undertaken to determine the status of something at a specific time. Survey instruments such as

COMMUNICATION MENTOR

Technology provides valuable tools for improving the efficiency of a business, relationships with clients, and personal lives. Keep in mind, however, that technology often reduces the human element that is critically important in some circumstances and for particular individuals. As an example, take a look at the number of people who wait to be serviced in the bank lobby or in the drive-through line closest to the bank teller. The following examples of our use of technology supports our goal of providing personal service to our clients:

- Technology allows us to access and communicate information quickly, inexpensively, and professionally:
  - Monitor the current position of stocks and analyze in-depth stock performance data using the Internet. My computer regularly autodials and downloads the most up-to-date information related to the financial market and any other area that I believe will impact my clients and their assets (weather, political issues, current developments reported in major business publications such as *The Wall Street Journal*, *Fortune*, etc.).
  - Use computers with the latest software to organize and manage time efficiently (instant access to telephone numbers, a calendar, and appointments) and to produce documents that portray the reputable image

we desire (e.g., word processing software, laser printers, scanners, and color copiers).
- Submit orders and transfer funds electronically using a dedicated Internet connection to the brokerage house.
- Send and receive client information via fax and e-mail. However, these technological tools are reserved for routine information that facilitates a specific investment decision. Face-to-face meetings are necessary to develop relationships and gain the understanding needed to provide expert financial advice to individual clients.

- Our telephones have intercom and conferencing capability, and we stand by our commitment to answer our telephone by the fourth ring. Messages left on our answering machine are returned the same day. We chose not to install voice-mail because we believe people want to talk with a live person—especially during regular office hours.

Be committed to staying abreast of fast-changing technology that is certain to increase your company's efficiency and will enhance your professional image in a competitive business environment. At the same time, be certain that the efficiency gained does not reduce your effectiveness in other ways that are inherent to the success of the product or service you provide.

Ernest T. George, III
Certified Financial Planner and Registered Principal
Investment Management & Research, Inc.

questionnaires, opinion surveys, checklists, and interviews are used to obtain information. Election opinion polls represent one type of normative survey research. The term *normative* is used to qualify surveys because surveys reveal "norms" or "standards" existing at the time of the survey. An election poll taken two months before an election might have little similarity to one taken the week before the election.

Surveys can help verify the accuracy of existing norms. The U.S. Census is conducted every decade to establish an actual population figure, and each person is supposedly counted. In effect, the census tests the accuracy of prediction techniques used to estimate population during the years between censuses. A survey of what employees consider a fair benefits package would be effective only for the date of the survey. People retire, move, and change their minds often; these human traits make survey research of human opinion somewhat tentative. Yet surveys remain a valuable tool for gathering information on which to base policy making and decision making.

> Why is the U.S. census conducted in 10-year intervals rather than longer or shorter ones?

6 *Explain the purpose of sampling and four sampling techniques.*

Can a sample be too small? Too large? Why?

Researchers normally cannot survey everyone, particularly if the population is large and the research budget is limited. **Sampling** is a survey technique that eliminates the need for questioning 100 percent of the population. Sampling is based on the principle that a sufficiently large number drawn at random from a population will be representative of the total population; that is, the sample will possess the same characteristics in the same proportions as the total population. For example, a company collecting market research data before introducing a new low-fat food product would survey only a few people. The data are considered *valid* if the sample of people surveyed has the same percentage of ages, genders, purchasing power, and so on as the anticipated target market. A number of sampling methods are available that you will study in research and statistics courses. Some common methods include the following:

- *Simple random sampling.* Selecting a random sample using a random number generator program is the easiest sampling technique. To determine the career plans of a college student body, a researcher could generate a list of random numbers, using a number of computer software programs, and then select the students to be included in the survey. Because the entire student body is included in the computer system, each student would have an equal opportunity to be selected.

- *Stratified random sampling.* Stratified random sampling involves dividing the population into subgroups. In surveying the student body using this method, you would divide the population into student classifications: for example, seniors, juniors, sophomores, and freshmen. Suppose the total student body of 10,000 is composed of 30 percent freshmen, 27 percent sophomores, 23 percent juniors, and 20 percent seniors. If you want to survey 1,000 students, you would randomly select students from each classification until you have 300 freshmen, 270 sophomores, 230 juniors, and 200 seniors. Stratified samples are useful for comparing responses between subgroups.

- *Systematic random sampling.* Systematic random sampling is useful when the researcher has access to a listing of elements or persons within the population to be studied. For instance, a membership list of all members of an organization could give rise to a systematic random sample. The process involves selecting every *nth* element, or name, for inclusion in the study. For instance, if the total membership of an organization is 1,000, and a sample of 100 is desired, the value of *n* would be 10. Thus, every tenth name would be selected for inclusion in the study. In this way, the sample will be drawn from throughout the entire membership list.

- *Convenient sampling.* A convenient sample is one that is selected merely by the convenience of the researcher, with no assurance that it is representative of the population under study. Convenient sampling is not scientific and therefore not recommended for research gathering; it is, nevertheless, frequently used because it is easy and yields quick results. A professor, for example, might want to find out students' opinion on the adequacy of academic advising available in her university. For convenience, she might choose to survey students in her own classes. The opinions obtained would be questionable as to whether they accurately reflected the opinions of the entire student population, since no procedure was followed to select a random sample. Businesses, too, make frequent use of convenient sampling by conducting "straw polls" of employees, consumers, or other specific groups.

The researcher must be cautious about drawing conclusions from a sample and generalizing them to a population that might not be represented by the sample. For

COMMUNICATION IN ACTION

David Martin, Martin Corporation

Whether gathering information for a small research project or working with an international corporation, David Martin, president of Martin Corporation, understands the value of good research. His firsthand experience establishes that a company's investment in conducting valid research can yield literally millions of dollars in savings. He cites one specific example of an international cellular company entering an emerging South American market that saved literally millions of dollars. Martin's research expertise has helped him build two successful marketing research companies primarily involved in conducting corporate marketing research, political polling, and public opinion surveys.

Martin stresses the importance of selecting an appropriate research method. A client hired Martin to conduct focus groups to investigate a problem in the company. After gaining a clear understanding of *what* information the client wanted and *how* the client would use the information, Martin recommended another research method. "Focus groups are not an appropriate research method for obtaining the information you need for the decision you want to reach," he told the client.

Martin also believes no one research method will give a complete perspective on information gathering. "For example, focus groups are a good research tool but cannot be used in and of themselves," he states. "Nor should telephone surveys, historical sales records, customer satisfaction surveys, and other methods such as comment cards

or complaints be used alone," he adds. Martin urges the researcher to integrate many research methods to complete the information-gathering picture.

To emphasize his point, Martin relates an example of a recent political campaign. A client asked Martin to conduct a telephone survey and find out *everything* about the electorate. "First, no one will stay on the telephone long enough to tell you *everything*, and second, obtaining broad, general information is usually not necessary," he adds. To get the kinds of information the client needed, Martin suggested trying other research sources before conducting a telephone interview.

For instance, before surveying public opinion for a political campaign, Martin analyzes the results from previous political races retrieved from databases to gain a historical perspective. "Obtaining this 'precinct-by-precinct' analysis from databases is more cost effective than a telephone survey," he said. The researcher uses a number of tools to meet client needs. "Information is not limited to a one tell-all, be-all, and end-all survey," says Martin.

Applying What You Have Learned

1. Why is research so important to many of the clients with whom Martin works?

2. Why does Martin believe no one research method gives a complete perspective on information gathering?

3. Assume that Martin asked you to conduct research that describes political party affiliations in your community. What research methods would you consider using in gathering this information?

example, early-morning shoppers may differ from afternoon or evening shoppers; young ones may differ from old ones; men may differ from women. A good researcher defines the population as distinctly as possible and uses a sampling technique to ensure that the sample is representative.

Whether a survey involves personal interviewing or the distribution of items such as checklists or questionnaires, some principles of procedure and preplanning are common to both methods. These principles assure the researcher that the data gathered will be both valid and reliable.

Why are public opinion polls often inaccurate?

A major factor affecting the value of a survey is the way in which it is conducted. The results of any survey are only as valid and reliable as the methods the researchers use to select and question a representative sample of the population.

- **Validity** refers to the degree to which the data measure what you intend to measure. It generally results from careful planning of the questionnaire or interview questions or items. Cautious wording, preliminary testing of items to detect misunderstandings, and some statistical techniques are helpful in determining whether the responses to the items are valid. A **pilot** test of the instrument is often conducted prior to the full-scale survey. Through this means, a smaller number of participants can test the instrument, which can then be revised prior to wide-scale administration.

- **Reliability** refers to the level of consistency or stability over time or over independent samples; that is, reliable data are reasonably accurate or repeatable. Reliability results from asking a large enough sample of people so that the researcher is reasonably confident the results would be the same even if more people were asked to respond or if a different sample was chosen from the same population. For example, if you were to ask ten people to react to a questionnaire item, the results might vary considerably. If you were to add 90 more people to the sample, the results might tend to reach a point of stability, where more responses would not change the results. Reliability would then be assured.

What steps can you take to ensure that your data are valid and reliable?

Responses to surveys conducted by mail often represent only a small percentage of the total mailings. In some cases, a return of 3 to 5 percent is considered adequate and is planned for by researchers. In other cases, depending on the population, the sample, and the information requested, a return of considerably more than half the mailings might be a planned result. Selecting an appropriate data collection method and developing a survey instrument are crucial elements of an effective research study.

Collecting and Organizing the Data

Collecting the right data and assuring that they are recorded appropriately is paramount to the success of a business report. Various techniques can assist in this process when collecting both secondary and primary research.

Collecting Secondary Data. When beginning to collect secondary data, beware of collecting too much information—one of the major deterrents to good report writing. Although you want to be thorough, you do not want to collect and record such a large amount of information that you will hardly know where to begin your analysis. Suggestive or cue notes or a card system will help you keep the volume at a minimum.

- *Suggestive or cue note.* A suggestive or cue note is a reminder of something you want to recall. Whether you put these reminders on a single sheet of paper or on separate sheets or cards, the goal is to reduce bulky material to small, convenient-to-use data. Develop a system that satisfies your own needs.

- *Card system.* Standard 3 x 5 or 4 x 6-inch cards are useful for library research. When library information is needed, go first to catalogs, bibliographic indexes, or electronic databases to compile a basic bibliography. By preparing a complete bibliographical entry for each reference on a separate card, you may save a trip to the library or your database.

As stated earlier, the availability of computer-assisted data searches has simplified the time-consuming task of searching through indexes, card catalogs, and other sources. For example, suppose you select a search engine such as WebCrawler™ to research the topic "cross-cultural communication." By inputting the key term *cross-cultural*, you receive the screen output shown in Figure 9-4, which contains information to facilitate your research. First, you can quickly evaluate the relevance of each reference by reading the title and the brief summary that may be provided and then clicking on the hyperlink (underlined title) of each reference that appears to have merit. The full text of the selected articles, which can then be saved to disk or printed out, will be displayed. Retrieved articles can then be read and analyzed for useful information.

After you have located the relevant sources, you can begin taking notes using various methods. Because your aim is to *learn*, not to accumulate, the following technique for taking notes is effective: (1) Read an article rapidly, (2) put it aside; (3) list main and supporting points *from memory*; and (4) review the article to see whether all significant points have been included. Rapid reading forces concentration. Taking notes from memory reinforces learning and reduces the temptation to rely heavily on the words of others. If you really learn the subject matter of one source, you will (as research progresses) see the relationship between it and other sources. You will see yourself growing toward mastery of the subject.

> How does the statement, "Become an expert before becoming an author" apply to summarizing secondary research?

Traditionally, researchers have read the article and immediately written notes on note cards. With photocopiers so readily available, many researchers prefer highlighting important points on a photocopy of the article; then from the highlighted material, they write note cards or compose notes at the keyboard. In addition, some researchers use portable computers to facilitate library research. Rather than spending time and money photocopying large volumes of information, researchers compose notes at the keyboard in the library and then return the reference material to the shelf. This efficient method of gathering secondary data will grow as the price of portable computers decreases.

You can use two kinds of note-taking: direct quotation or paraphrase. The **direct quotation method** involves citing the exact words from a secondary source. This method is useful when you believe the exact words have a special effect or you want to give the impact of an expert. The **paraphrase method** involves summarizing information in your own words without changing the author's intended meaning. Put direct quotations in quotation marks as a reminder. Indicate the page numbers

FIGURE 9-4
A sample computer-
assisted data search.

from which cited material is taken. This information may save you another trip to the library.

Plagiarism is the presentation of someone else's ideas or words as your own. To safeguard your reputation against plagiarism charges, be certain to give credit where credit is due. Specifically, provide a citation (in-text parenthetical reference, footnote, or endnote) for each (1) direct quotation and (2) passage from someone else's work that you stated in your own words rather than using the original words (the words are your own, but the idea is not). After identifying the text that must be credited to someone else, develop complete, accurate citations and a reference page according to some recognized referencing method.

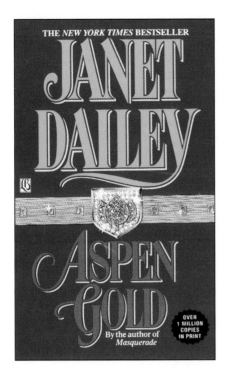

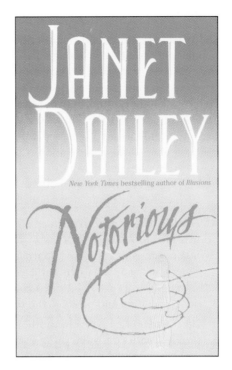

Plagiarism can diminish your professional reputation and result in costly lawsuits. Romance novelist Janet Dailey acknowledged plagiarizing the work of her rival Nora Roberts; she said two other novels, *Aspen Gold* and *Notorious*, contain ideas and passages lifted from several of Ms. Roberts's novels. The copying was discovered during on-line computer chats with readers.[4]

Documenting Referenced Material.   A crucial part of honest research writing is documenting or referencing sources fairly and accurately. Although time consuming and tedious, meticulous attention to documentation marks you as a respected, highly professional researcher. The *Publication Manual of the American Psychological Association* points out the importance of documentation with a forceful quote by K. F. Bruner: An inaccurate or incomplete reference "will stand in print as an annoyance to future investigators and a monument to the writer's carelessness."[5]

An important first step is to pledge that you will not, for any reason, present someone else's ideas as your own. Then, develop a systematic checklist for avoiding plagiarism. Carelessly forgetting to enclose someone else's words within quotation marks or failing to paraphrase another's words can cause others to question your ethical conduct. When you feel that the tedious work required to document sources fairly and accurately is not worth the time invested, remind yourself of the following reasons for documentation:

7 *Apply techniques for developing effective questionnaires.*

What incidents of plagiarism can you recall that have been reported in the media?

- *Citations give credit where it is due—to the one who created the material.* People who document demonstrate high standards of ethical conduct and responsibility in scholarship. Those exhibiting this professional behavior will gain the well-deserved trust and respect of peers and superiors.

- *Documentation protects writers against plagiarism, which occurs when someone steals material from another and claims it as his or her own writing.*

- *Documentation supports your statements.* If recognized authorities have said the same thing, your work takes on credibility; and you put yourself in good company.

- *Documentation can aid future researchers pursuing similar material.* Documentation must be complete and accurate so that the researcher can locate the source.

Many style guides are available to advise writers how to organize, document, and produce reports and manuscripts. Refer to Figure 9-3 for a list of the most popular authoritative style manuals. The *Publication Manual of the American Psychological Association* has become the most-used guide in the social and "soft" sciences and in many scholarly journals. The *MLA Handbook for Writers of Research Papers* is another authoritative source in the humanities. *The Chicago Manual of Style* is yet another popular style manual. All of these style guides and these format requirements are discussed further in Appendix B. In business reports and college papers, any of the various documentation methods is usually suitable. As you read professional literature and write business reports, you may need to become familiar with many methods.

Follow these general suggestions for preparing accurate documentation:

What are the legal and ethical consequences of failing to document the sources for quoted and paraphrased material?

- ***Decide which authoritative reference manual to follow for preparing in-text parenthetical citations or footnotes (endnotes) and the bibliography.*** Some companies and most journals require writers to prepare reports or manuscripts following a particular reference manual. Once you are certain you have selected the appropriate style manual, follow it precisely as you prepare the documentation and produce the report.

- ***Be consistent.*** If you are carefully following a format, you shouldn't have a problem with consistency. For example, one style manual may require an author's initials in place of first name in a bibliography; another reference requires the full name. The placement of commas and periods and other information varies among reference manuals. Consult the manual, apply the rules methodically, and proofread carefully to ensure accuracy and consistency. If you cannot locate a format for an unusual source in the reference manual you are using, use other entries as a guide for presenting information consistently.

- ***Follow the rule that it is better to include more than enough than too little when you are in doubt about whether to include certain information.***

Citations. Two major types of citations are used to document a report: source notes and explanatory notes. Depending on the authoritative style manual used, these notes may be positioned in parentheses within the report, at the bottom of the page, or at the end of the report.

- ***Source notes*** acknowledge the contributions of others. These citations might refer readers to sources of quotations, paraphrased portions of someone else's words or ideas, and quantitative data used in the report. Source notes must include complete and accurate information so that the reader can locate the original source if desired.

- ***Explanatory notes*** are used for several purposes: (1) to comment on a source or to provide information that does not fit easily in the text, (2) to support a statistical table, or (3) to refer the reader to another section of the report. The following sample footnote describes the mathematics involved in preparing a table:

  *The weighted opinion was arrived at by assigning responses from high to low as 5, 4, 3, 2, 1; totaling all respondents; and dividing by the number of respondents.

In this case, the asterisk (*) was used rather than a number to identify the explanatory footnote both in the text and in the citation. This method is often used when only one or two footnotes are included in the report. If two footnotes appear on the same page, two asterisks (**) or numbers or letters are used to distinguish the second from the first. An explanatory note that supports a visual or a source note that provides the reference from which data were taken appears immediately below the visual.

Referencing Methods. Several reference methods are available for the format and content of source notes: in-text parenthetical citations, footnotes, and endnotes. Note the major differences among the methods in the following discussion.

- ***In-text parenthetical citations.*** The *APA Manual, MLA Handbook, The Chicago Manual of Style* (CMS), and other documentation references eliminate separate footnotes or endnotes. Instead, an **in-text citation**, which contains abbreviated information within parentheses, directs the reader to a list of sources at the end of a report. The list of sources at the end contains all publication information on every source cited. This list is arranged alphabetically by the author's last name or, if no author is provided, by the first word of the title (excluding articles). The reader uses the information in an in-text parenthetical citation to locate the original source in the list of sources.

  The citations contain minimal information needed to locate the source in the complete list. In-text citations prepared using APA and CMS include the author's last name and the date of publication; the page number is included if referencing a direct quotation. An MLA citation includes the author's last name and the page number but not the date of publication. See Appendix B for additional information on APA, MLA, and CMS formats.

- ***Footnote method.*** Placing citations at the bottom of the page on which they are cited is the footnote citation method. It is often referred to as the traditional method because of its long use. The reader can conveniently refer to the source if the documentation is positioned at the bottom of the page. You can prepare footnotes and endnotes using MLA or CMS style; however, APA permits the use of in-text citations only.

  Footnotes and endnotes are easy to create with word processing software; you simply input the citation and the computer numbers the footnotes and paginates the report. When revisions are made, footnote numbers are automatically updated.

- ***Endnote method.*** This method places all citations in a list called "Notes" at the end of a report. A list of citations at the end of a report is obviously easier to prepare than footnotes. However, readers will be forced to turn to the end of a report rather than glance at the bottom of the page to locate a source. Endnotes are listed in the order in which citations appear in a report. You would indicate the in-text citation either by placing a superscript number above the text line as in the footnote method or by placing the citation figure in parentheses on the line of writing. Word processing software programs have also simplified the task of preparing endnotes. The process is similar to that of preparing footnotes except that you instruct the software to print the endnotes in the correct sequence on a separate page rather than at the bottom of each page.

- ***References (or Works Cited).*** This document is an alphabetized list of the sources used in preparing a report. Each entry contains publication information necessary for locating the source. In addition, the bibliographic entries give evidence of the nature of sources the author consulted. *Bibliography* (literally "description of books") is sometimes used to refer to this list. A researcher often uses sources that provide information but do not result in citations. To acknowledge that you may have consulted these works and to provide the reader with a comprehensive reading list, include these sources in the list of sources. The APA and MLA styles use different terms to distinguish between these types of lists, as shown in Appendix B.

7 *Apply techniques for developing effective questionnaires.*

What are the major advantages of mail or telephone surveys? Do personal interviews offer additional advantages or disadvantages?

Collecting Data Through Surveys. The method of distribution and the makeup of the questionnaire are critical factors in successful survey research.

Selecting a data collection method. Selecting an appropriate data collection method and developing a survey instrument are crucial elements of an effective research study. Researchers must consider many factors when selecting an appropriate method for collecting data:

- *Questionnaire surveys by mail* are inexpensive and not limited geographically. Respondents may remain anonymous, which might result in honest answers, and a mailed survey removes difference-in-status barriers. For example, a corporation president may respond readily to a mailed questionnaire whereas the researcher might never succeed in getting a response by telephone or by personal interview. At the same time, mail survey instruments must be concise; or they will be discarded. Most people who respond have strong feelings about the topic, so this group of respondents might not be representative of the intended population. The researcher must prepare persuasive transmittal messages that indicate how the respondent can benefit by answering. That persuasion often takes the form of a thank-you gift for participating.

- *Personal interviews* allow the interviewer to obtain answers in depth and perhaps to explore otherwise sensitive topics. But interviews are expensive in terms of time and money spent traveling, and more so if interviewers are paid; additionally, many people simply don't want their opinion identified.

- *Telephone interviews* are inexpensive as a rule. But like mailed questionnaires, a low percentage of total telephone calls will actually provide usable information.

- *Participant observation* is frequently used in consumer research with the observer simply noting how people seem to make selections. A problem, of course, is that observation is sight only and does not give clues about the reasons for behavior.

7 *Apply techniques for developing effective questionnaires.*

Developing an effective survey instrument. No matter which survey technique or combination of techniques is used, the way in which the survey instrument is designed and written has much to do with response validity and reliability, response rate, and quality of information received.

The construction of the survey instrument—usually a questionnaire or interview guide—is critical to obtaining reliable and valid data. Before formulating items for a questionnaire or opinion survey, a researcher should visualize the ways responses will be assembled and included in a final report. Here are some suggestions for effective questionnaires:

- *Arrange the items in a logical sequence.* If possible, the sequence should proceed from easy to difficult items. Easy, nonthreatening items involve respondents and encourage them to finish. You might group related items such as demographic data or those that use the same response options (multiple choice, rating scales, open-ended questions).

- *Ask for factual information whenever possible.* Opinions may be needed in certain studies, but opinions may change from day to day. As a general rule, too, the smaller the sample, the less reliable are conclusions based on opinions.

- *Ask for information that can be recalled readily.* Asking for information going back in time may not result in sound data.

- *Strive to write clear questions that respondents will interpret in the same way.* Follow these suggestions:

  - **Provide brief, easy-to-follow directions.** Explain the purpose of the study in the cover letter or in a brief statement at the top of the questionnaire so that the respondents understand your intent.

  - **Avoid words with imprecise meanings (e.g., *several, usually*) and specialized terms and difficult words that respondents might not understand.** Be sure you have used accurate translations for each concept presented if other cultures are involved. Provide examples for items that might be difficult to understand.

  - **Use short items that ask for a single answer to one idea.** Include only the questions needed to meet the objectives of your study; questionnaire length affects the return rate.

  - **Avoid "skip-and-jump" instructions.** Questions such as "If you answered Yes to 4, skip directly to 9; if you answered No, explain your reason under 5 and 6" are confusing.

  - **Avoid questions that may be threatening or awkward to the respondent.** The following illustrates the problem:

Have you stopped humiliating employees who question your management decisions?

- ❑ Yes
- ❑ No
- ❑ Undecided

- *Design questions that are easy to answer and to tabulate.* Suppose you want to determine the most pressing problems facing employees in a production line. You could ask them to list the problems, but the responses might be so ambiguous that tabulating them would be impossible. A rating scale such as the following one would be an improvement.

Circle the degree to which each of the following factors affects your job satisfaction.

Acceptance by others

1	2	3	4	5	6
Little effect		Moderate effect			Great effect

Note that six numbers have been used to indicate how respondents feel. When an odd number of choices, such as five, is provided, responses tend to converge toward the middle number. This tendency to converge may create a bias in the responses.

Similar information could be obtained by listing the potential problems and by asking respondents to rank the problems in order of their importance:

What does convergence toward the middle on questionnaire items reveal about human nature?

Rank the following factors in order of their importance to you. Place a 1 in the space following the most important problem, a 2 in the space following the second most important problem, and so on until all have been ranked. Two blank lines have been left for you to write in problem areas that may have been omitted.

Acceptance by others   _____
Interest in job   _____
Economic security   _____
Health   _____

_____   _____
_____   _____

To determine which factor is most critical to a production employee, a *forced answer* question can be used:

Of all the problems listed, which is the *single* most critical problem for you personally?

- **Provide all possible answer choices on multiple-choice and rating scale questions; add an "undecided" or "other" category so that respondents are not forced to choose a nonapplicable response.** Note the following examples.

Should city taxes be levied to fund a city recreational complex?
❑   Yes
❑   No
❑   Undecided

Which of the following factors is the single most critical factor for you personally? Place a check in the space provided.
a. Acceptance by others   _____
b. Interest in job   _____
c. Economic security   _____
d. Health   _____
e. Other (specify)   _____

- **Allow respondents to select among ranges if possible.** Checking a range is especially useful when the respondent may have difficulty remembering the exact information requested or if the information is sensitive, for instance, age and income. Tabulating information in ranges requires less effort from the respondent. Questions about age might be arranged in the following manner:

Indicate your age group:
❑ 20-29   ❑ 50-59
❑ 30-39   ❑ 60-69
❑ 40-49   ❑ 70 and over

In this example, respondents whose ages are between 20 and 29 years would check 20-29, and the assumed average age for everyone in that group would be the midpoint, 25.0.

- **Test the instrument by asking others to complete and/or critique the questionnaire; consider conducting a pilot study involving a small group of the population.** This process will allow you to correct problems in clarity, ease of answering, and quality of answers. A pilot study may uncover factors affecting your results, which you can incorporate into the final research design.

- *Provide enough space for respondents to answer open-ended questions.* "What effect would an additional tax on oil and natural gas have on the economy?" may require a lengthy answer.
- *Include a postage-paid envelope with a mailed questionnaire.* A higher percentage of questionnaires is returned when this courtesy is provided. Include your name and address at the bottom of the questionnaire in the event the envelope is misplaced.
- *Create an appealing, easy-to-comprehend design using word processing or desktop publishing software.* Use print enhancements such as typefaces, bold, underline, and italics to emphasize important ideas and graphic lines and boxes to partition text so that the reader can identify and move through sections of a questionnaire quickly.

Researchers must select from among the several formats available the one best suited to the situation. Criteria for selecting one alternative over the others might include the following: Which format leaves the least chance for misinterpretation? Which format provides information in the way it can best be used? Can it be tabulated easily? Can it be cross-referenced to other items in the survey instrument?

Avoiding Data-Gathering Errors. If acceptable data-gathering techniques have been used, data will measure what they are intended to measure (have validity) and will measure it accurately (have reliability). Some common errors at the data-gathering stage that seriously hamper later interpretation are

8 *Discuss the common problems encountered in collecting and interpreting data.*

- Using samples that are too small.
- Using samples that are not representative.
- Using poorly constructed data-gathering instruments.
- Using information from biased sources.
- Failing to gather enough information to cover all important aspects of a problem.
- Gathering too much information (and then attempting to use all of it even though some may be irrelevant).

Arriving at an Answer

Even the most intelligent person cannot be expected to draw sound conclusions from faulty information. Sound conclusions can be drawn only when information has been properly organized, collected, and interpreted.

Analyzing the Data. Having decided on a method, researchers must outline a step-by-step approach to the solution of a problem. The human mind is susceptible to digressions. Although these digressions may be short lived, they distract from the job at hand; if given free rein, they can lead you to demolish the real object of the study.

Therefore, *keep on the right track*. Plan the study and follow the plan. Question every step for its contribution to the objective. Keep a record of actions. In a formal research study, the researcher is expected to make a complete report. Another qualified person should be able to make the same study, use the same steps, and arrive at the same conclusion. Thus, a report serves as a guide.

Suppose you have made a survey and have collected several hundred replies to a 20- or 30-item questionnaire in addition to many cards or notes from library sources. What do you do next? Notes must be carefully considered for relevance and organized for relationships among ideas. Appropriate statistical analysis must be applied to interpret what has been found through the survey. Tabulation techniques should be used to reduce quantitative data such as numerous answers to questionnaire items. Other statistical techniques may be used. For example, **correlation analysis** might be used to determine whether a relationship existed between how respondents answered one item and how they answered another. Were males, for example, more likely to have chosen a certain answer to another item on the survey than were females?

The report process is one of reducing the information collected to a size that can be handled conveniently in a written message, as shown in Figure 9-5.

Visualize the report process as taking place in a huge funnel. At the top of the funnel, pour in all the original information. Then, through a process of compression within the funnel, take these steps:

1. Evaluate the information for its usefulness.
2. Reduce the useful information through organization of notes and data analysis.
3. Combine like information into understandable form through the use of tables, charts, graphs, and summaries. (See Chapter 10.)
4. Report in written form what remains. (See Chapter 11.)

8 *Discuss the common problems encountered in collecting and interpreting data.*

Interpreting the Data. If you avoid data collection errors, you are more likely to collect valid and reliable data and reach sound conclusions. However, if you interpret valid and reliable data incorrectly, your conclusions will *not* be sound.

Your ethical principles affect the validity of your interpretations. Through all steps in the research process, you must attempt to maintain the integrity of the research. Strive to remain objective, design and conduct an unbiased study, and resist any pressure to slant research to support a particular viewpoint (e.g., ignoring, altering, or falsifying data). Common errors that seriously hinder the interpretation of data include the following:

- *Trying, consciously or unconsciously, to make results conform to a prediction or desire.* Seeing predictions come true may be pleasing, but objectivity is much more important. Facts should determine conclusions.

- *Hoping for spectacular results.* An attempt to astonish supervisors by preparing a report with revolutionary conclusions can have only a negative effect on accuracy.

- *Attempting to compare when commonality is absent.* Results obtained from one study may not always apply to other situations.

- *Assuming a cause-effect relationship when one does not exist.* A company president may have been in office one year, and sales may have doubled. However, sales might have doubled *in spite* of the president rather than *because* of the president.

The women's basketball team has won every game since you began attending the college. Is this record a coincidence or your influence? How does this example reveal the difference between correlation and causation?

- *Failing to consider important factors.* For example, learning that McDonald's was considering closing its restaurants in Kassel, Germany, a manager of an industrial supply company recommended that his firm reconsider its plans to expand its operation into Germany. The manager failed to recognize that the adverse impact of a new tax on disposable containers, not an unfavorable German economy or government, was the reason McDonald's was considering closing its restaurants.[6] Other diversity issues that affect research are explored in the accompanying Strategic Forces box.

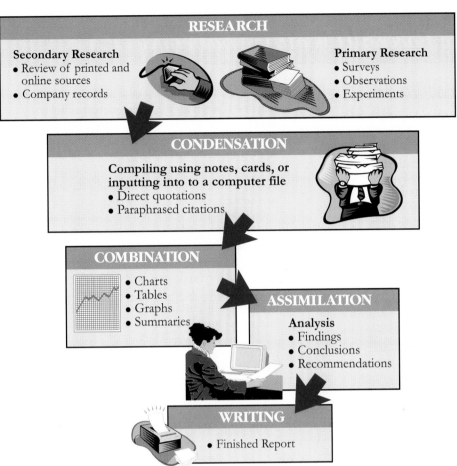

FIGURE 9-5
The report process.

- ***Basing a conclusion on lack of evidence.*** "We have had no complaints about our present policy" does not mean that the policy is appropriate. Conversely, lack of evidence that a proposed project will succeed does not necessarily mean that it will fail.

- ***Assuming constancy of human behavior.*** A survey indicating 60 percent of the public favors one political party over the other in March does not mean the same will be true in November. Because some people paid their bills late last year does not mean a company should refuse to sell to them next year. The reasons for slow payment may have been removed.

Keep in mind the differences in meaning of some research terms as you analyze your material and attempt to seek meaning from it.

- **Finding:** A specific, measurable fact from a research study
- **Conclusion:** Derived from findings
- **Recommendation:** A suggested action based on your research

Consider the following examples, conclusions, and recommendations generated by analyzing the data collected:

Do you agree with the statement that statistics can be used to prove just about anything? Why?

Strategic Forces: Diversity Challenges

International Marketing Research

Cautious interpretation should be given to the results of research conducted within particular cultural settings as to their appropriateness for other groups. For instance, concluding that a certain product would sell well in Canada or Mexico because it sold well in the United States is risky.

Disney executives presumed company policies successful in the United States would be equally as successful at their French theme park, EuroDisney. This *faulty logic* caused immediate problems. Employees resisted Disney's disregard for national customs—the unpopular dress code prohibiting facial hair and limiting makeup and jewelry. Visitors to the park were unhappy with the no-alcohol-in-the-park policy, as the French generally include wine with most meals.[7]

Cold Water Creek, a U.S. firm that began selling in Japan recently, found through research that Japanese favor clothing in brighter colors than the dark palette popular in the United States. They also found it necessary to add petite sizes to Japanese catalogs. Coca-Cola and McDonald's products sold successfully across international boundaries until they managed to offend the entire Muslim world by putting the Saudi Arabian flag on their packaging. The flag's design includes a passage from the *Koran*, and Muslims feel very strongly that their Holy Writ should never be wadded up and tossed as garbage. Hence the first rule of international marketing: Never assume what works in one country will work in another.

While information about related populations may serve as a basis for study, effort should be made to conduct research within the particular group that will be affected by the business decision. A good source for secondary research on international markets is the Columbus, Ohio-based Trade Point, USA, a nonprofit on-line and print information service that was set up in cooperation with the United Nations in 1994. However, secondhand information can take you only so far. In many cases, it will be necessary to go to the target country yourself or to hire an outside firm with solid experience in that country to do grassroots primary research in the country. Some products will be unsuitable or unattractive to certain nations because of differences in culture, lifestyle, or preferences.

Experts recommend thorough country-by-country testing before a product launch to help identify problems inherent in cross-cultural marketing. Testing provides insights into potential market sizes and responses and uncovers the extent to which language and consumer preference will be problematic. While such market research is expensive, it is justified when considering the essential information that will result.[8]

Application

Conduct an on-line search to discover an example of a company whose product(s) experienced a negative reception in another country's consumer market. What issues were involved in the poor sales performance? How could the problem have been avoided?

- **Finding:** Nearly 75 percent of the recruiters responding indicated they were more likely to hire a candidate who was involved in extracurricular activities.

- **Conclusion:** Active involvement in extracurricular activities is an important job-selection criteria.

- **Recommendation:** Students should be involved in several extracurricular activities prior to seeking a job.

- **Finding:** Only 16 percent of the consumers interviewed knew that Hanson's Toy Company sells educational computer software.

- **Conclusion:** Few consumers are knowledgeable of our line of educational software.

- **Recommendation:** An advertising campaign focusing on educational software should be launched.

SUMMARY

1. ***Identify the characteristics of a report and the various classifications of business reports.*** The basis of a report is a problem that must be solved through data collection and analysis. Reports are usually requested by a higher authority, are logically organized and highly objective, and are prepared for a limited audience. Reports can be classified as formal/informal, short/long, informational/analytical, vertical/lateral, internal/external, or proposal.

2. ***Identify the four steps in the problem-solving process.*** The four steps in the problem-solving process must be followed to arrive at a sound conclusion: (a) Recognize and define the problem; (b) select an appropriate secondary and/or primary method for solving the problem; (c) collect and organize data, using appropriate methods; (d) interpret the data to arrive at an answer.

3. ***Select appropriate secondary and primary methods for solving a problem.*** Research methods in report preparation involve locating information from appropriate secondary sources to identify research that has already been done on the topic and then collecting primary data needed to solve the problem.

4. ***Locate both printed and electronic sources of information.*** Location of secondary sources of information involves appropriate use of printed indexes and application of electronic search techniques that can lead the researcher to books, periodicals, and other documents that are needed for topic exploration.

5. ***Explain three common methods of primary research.*** Three methods are commonly used for conducting primary research:

   - **Observational research**—observing and analyzing certain phenomenon to assist in establishing new principles.

   - **Experimental study**—identifying the differences between two samples observed when a different treatment is administered to each group.

   - **Normative survey**—collecting information from a sample group to determine the status of something at a particular time.

6. ***Explain the purpose of sampling and describe four sampling techniques.*** Selecting a sample that is representative of the entire population affects the validity and reliability of the data reported. Simple random sampling, stratified random sampling, and systematic random sampling are recognized techniques used to produce a representative sample for study. Convenient sampling, while often used, does not assure representativeness.

7. ***Apply techniques for developing effective questionnaires.*** Developing an effective questionnaire is critical to obtaining valid and reliable data. Effective questionnaires are clear, ask for information the respondent can recall and is willing to answer, and are easy to complete and tabulate. A pilot test involving a small subset of the population provides feedback for improving the survey instrument and redesigning the study.

8. ***Discuss the common problems encountered in collecting and interpreting data.*** Obtaining valid and reliable data can be impossible if the researcher allows human error to affect data collection and interpretation. Common errors in collecting and interpreting data include (a) using samples that are too small or not representative, (b) using ineffective data gathering techniques, (c) attempting to compare when commonality is not present, (d) assuming a cause-effect relationship, (e) failing to consider important facts, (f) basing a conclusion on lack of evidence, and (g) assuming constancy of human behavior.

REFERENCES

[1] Warner, S. (1997, June 14). Slow simmer: Campbell's behind overseas but aims to make its soup good food outside U.S. *Dallas Morning News*, pp. 1F, 11F.

[2] Nelson, J. (1997, April 28). Finding the web site you want. *The Daily Sentinel*, p. 8A.

[3] Syllabus of Supreme Court Opinion for 96-511(1997). Reno, Attorney General of the United States, et al. v. American Civil Liberties Union et al. [On-line] Available http://supct.law.cornell.edu/supct/html/96–511.ZS.html [1998, February 27].

[4] Romance novelist Dailey apologizes for plagiarism (1997, July 30.) *The Daily Sentinel*, p. 10A. Janet Dailey is in the hot seat. (1997, August 1). [On line]. Available http://www.calweb.com/~dgass/liquid/0897/jdailey.htm [1998, April 4].

[5] Bruner, K. F. (1994). The *Publication manual of the American Psychological Association*, (4th ed.). American Psychological Association. Washington, DC: Author. [p. 175].

[6] Kinzer, S. (1994, August 22). Germany upholds tax on fast-food restaurants. *The New York Times*, p. 2.

[7]Kets de Vries, M. F. R. (1994). Toppling the cultural tower of Babel. *Chief Executive, 94,* 68.

[8]Heath, R. P. (1996, October). Think globally. *American Demographics,* 48–54.

[9]Rx for information overload (1997, September/October). *Futurist,* 53.

[10]Boles, M. (1997, September). Help!—Information overload. *Workforce,* 76(9).

[11]Alfvin, C. B. (1997, May). Information please! . . . or not. *Once a Year Magazine.* (On-line). Available. http://www.tefnet.org/oay97/overload.html (1997, December 16).

[12]Johnson, M. (1997, April/May). Battling information overload. *Communication World,* 26–27.

REVIEW QUESTIONS

1. What characteristics do all reports have in common? (Obj. 1)

2. How do informational and analytical reports differ? (Obj. 1)

3. In a bank, the internal auditing division performs semi-annual audits of each branch. Then the audit reports are sent to the bank's chief executive officer and chief financial officer and to the manager of the audited branch. The purpose of the audits is to determine whether policies and practices are properly followed. Into what report classifications might the audit report fall? Explain. (Obj. 1)

4. How do the four steps in problem solving apply when a student realizes that he or she does not have enough money to pay the upcoming tuition bill? (Obj. 2)

5. How might a null hypothesis be stated for a research study attempting to determine whether television or magazine advertising has greater influence on athletic shoe sales? (Obj. 2)

6. How does library research make a contribution to all studies? (Obj. 3)

7. What techniques can help make the Internet search process more efficient? (Obj. 4)

8. How are observational and experimental research different? (Obj. 5)

9. Distinguish between reliability and validity. (Obj. 6)

10. What is meant by simple random sampling? (Obj. 6)

11. What questions might you ask of someone who wants assistance in planning a questionnaire survey to determine automobile-owner satisfaction with certain after-the-sale services provided by dealers? (Obj. 7)

12. Why is an even number of rating scale responses supposedly better than an odd number? (Obj. 7)

13. Gathering so much information that the researcher is "snowed under" by the amount is often a barrier to good reporting. How might researchers protect themselves against this possibility? (Obj. 8)

14. Which data collection errors are directly related to construction of data-gathering instruments? (Obj. 8)

15. How does the assumption that human beings behave in consistent ways over time present a danger in data interpretation? (Obj. 8)

EXERCISES

1. **Classifying Business Reports (Obj. 1)**
   Classify each of the following reports in one or more of the ways described in this chapter.

   a. Your company's two-year study of traditional classroom training versus distance-learning instruction is to be written for publication in an industrial training journal.

   b. You have surveyed company personnel on their perceptions of the need for a company-sponsored day care facility. You are preparing a report for the president that conveys the results.

   c. You have completed your department's weekly time sheets to send to payroll.

   d. As department head, you have sent a report to the Vice President for Finance requesting additional funding for an equipment acquisition.

   e. You have prepared an article on product updates for publication in your consumer newsletter that is mailed out free of charge to customers who request it.

   f. As director of end-user computing, you have prepared a report for circulation to all departments. The report summarizes hardware, software, and training offerings available through your department.

2. **Writing a Hypothesis (Obj. 2)**
   Write a positive hypothesis and then restate it as a null hypothesis for each of the following research topics. Hypotheses for topic (a) are given as an example.

   a. A study to determine functional business areas from which chief executive officers advanced in their organizations. Functional areas are legal, financial, accounting, marketing, production, and other.

Positive Hypothesis:	Chief executives advanced primarily through the legal area.
Null Hypothesis:	No relationship exists between chief executives' advancement and the functional field backgrounds.

   b. A study to determine whether a person's career success is related to mentoring experiences.

   c. A study to determine the relationship between college students' ages and their final grades in the business communication course.

3. **Limiting the Scope of the Problem (Obj. 2)**
   What factors might limit or influence your findings in any of the studies in Exercise 2? Could you apply the findings of Exercise 2 studies to a broader population than those included in the studies? Why or why not?

4. **Selecting a Research Method (Obj. 3)**
   What research method would you use for each of the research problems identified in Exercise 2?

5. **Outlining a Search Strategy (Obj. 4)**
   Outline a secondary search strategy for one of the topics in Exercise 2. What published indexes would you use? What electronic search techniques would you use?

6. **Identifying Challenges Posed by Human Subjects (Obj. 5)**
   What challenges do researchers face when conducting experimental research with human subjects? How can they be managed?

7. **Using Sampling Techniques (Obj. 6)**
   If you were to conduct a survey of residents' attitudes toward recycling in a town of 35,000 people, describe how you might construct a sampling procedure to avoid having to survey the entire population.

8. **Developing Questionnaire Items (Obj. 7)**
   What types of items would you include on a customer satisfaction questionnaire for a fast-food restaurant?

9. **Overcoming Problems in Data Collection and Interpretation (Obj. 8)**
   How can statistics be used to "prove" just about anything? What errors in data collection and interpretation could lead to false conclusions?

E-MAIL APPLICATION

This activity will allow you to perform an electronic search of a business research topic selected by you or assigned by your instructor.

Instructions:

1. Select a business topic for investigation; for example, computer viruses.

2. Access the Internet, using Netscape, Internet Explorer, or some other browser.

3. Look up your topic, using two of the following search engines/databases:

    Yahoo! (http://www.yahoo.com)

    AltaVista (http://www.altavista.digital.com)

    Infoseek Ultra (http://ultra.infoseek.com)

    Search.Com (http://www.search.com)

4. Broaden or narrow your search as necessary to obtain appropriate hits.

5. Locate one or more appropriate articles on your topic and save them to disk.

6. Send your instructor an e-mail message, explaining how you located the article. Attach a copy of the article to your e-mail message.

APPLICATIONS

1. **Designing a Research Study (Obj. 2, 3, 4, 5, 6).**
   Prepare a one-page description of your plan to solve the problem for each of the following research studies. Use the following headings for the problem assigned: (1) Statement of the Problem, (2) Research Method and Sources of Information, (3) Nature of Data to Be Gathered and Analyzed, (4) Hypothesis or Hypotheses to Be Proved or Disproved (if feasible).

   a. Investigate a problem occurring on your campus (inadequate parking, long cafeteria lines, ineffective career services, limited number of internships, or value-added experiences available) or in a job or student organization position you hold.

   b. Pacific Electronics initiated a bulletin board service via the Internet to provide answers to frequently asked questions and product-update information. Customer response has been outstanding, freeing up the company's toll-free telephone lines for calls about more technical, nonrecurring problems—a primary goal of the service. As marketing manager, you are considering the possibility of allowing customers to order computer accessories and software packages via the Internet.

   c. Karen's Frozen Foods, Inc., is considering adding frozen breakfast pizza to its product line in an effort to overcome the flat profit line it has experienced for several years. The marketing staff intends to target the product to teenagers and working couples whose busy schedules require foods that can be heated quickly. Because all production facilities are currently operating at full capacity, introducing the frozen pizza will require adding production capacity.

   d. As research director of George-Parsons & Associates, a stock brokerage firm, you have mailed a highly professional newsletter containing tax-saving strategies to your investment clients. Although you know that these clients are in a financial position to take advantage of the strategies you are recommending, very few clients have scheduled appointments to seek additional information or to initiate these more aggressive investment plans.

   e. For the first time, Allied Pharmaceutical Company held a national conference for its entire sales force, three days filled with new product information, sales training, and numerous social activities. Eight months following the conference, sales have not increased significantly, and the time is near when you must decide whether to schedule this conference for the coming year.

2. **Developing a Survey Instrument (Obj. 7, 8)**
   Design a survey instrument for one of the research studies you analyzed in Application 1.

REAL-TIME INTERNET CASE

Coping with Information Overload

The greatest challenge of our times is to reduce information, not to increase it. Until about 50 years ago, more information was always a good thing. Now we can't see our way through the "data smog." An ever-growing universe of information translates to masses of data through which people must search to find what is useful and meaningful to them.[9] Consider the following statistics:

- The average American now receives 3,000 advertising messages a day, up sixfold since 1970.

- Office workers spend 60 percent of their days processing documents.

- A typical manager reads about a million words a week.

- The average Fortune 1000 worker sends and receives approximately 178 messages and documents each day.[10]

While the original intent of advanced communication technologies was to make communication faster and more efficient, the result has been a communications gridlock and heightened stress for many workers. "Actually, it is probably a fact of everyday life that we all suffer from some degree of information overload," says Barry Gordon, noted neurologist. "If you wonder why our memories do not work as well as we need them to, consider this: Our brains were not built for the modern world. In the Stone Age . . . there were no clocks, no papers, no news flashes. Contrast that with everything we expect to remember today."[11]

Some companies are going so far in battling information overload as hiring people whose job it is to filter and sort through the communications gridlock. These "information architects" are the translators and traffic controllers that help to bridge the communication gaps in the organization and deliver usable information in a concise way. The information architect reorganizes information for more effective communication, gives structure and order to pertinent information, and maps out the best way for the organization's people to access it.[12]

VIDEO CONNECTION

INTELECO

Effective research is vital if a business is to respond to the changing requirements of customers and other interest groups. Various methods exist for obtaining necessary information. Secondary research yields results of information that already exists; primary research reveals new information that cannot be obtained elsewhere. Primary research can be obtained in a variety of ways, each possessing advantages and limitations. Questionnaire design is critical to effective data collection. Random sampling assures that the results obtained are representative of the larger population.

The written report brings all the elements of effective research into a readable format. Careful attention to organization, conciseness, visual presentation, and objectivity is essential as the report is the basis on which the research will be judged. The report must respond to the readers' needs.

Discussion Questions

1. David Martin and Bruce Brown mention several primary research methodologies. List five and for each give a major consideration in choosing it for data collection.

2. How are the concepts of sampling and validity related?

3. What role do computers play in research report preparation?

4. List four characteristics of a well-designed questionnaire.

5. Explain the role of visual and written presentation in producing an effective research report.

Application

You are conducting marketing research on consumers of Jennas, an all-natural, low-fat yogurt. You are interested in the characteristics of typical purchasers and the reasons for their purchasing the product. Design a one-page questionnaire that might be used in a mall-intercept survey.

Whether for improved job performance, a better product, or increased productivity, more and more organizations are recognizing that good information means good business. And good information must somehow be made available in spite of increasing information overload. Visit the following web sites and complete the activities as directed by your instructor.

Internet Sites

http://www.tefnet.org/oay97/overload.html
http://www.ackisland.com/computer/article.htm
http://www.umich.edu/~fasap/stresstips/7.html

Activities

1. In teams of four, visit the listed sites and prepare an oral presentation on Information Overload (IO). The presentation should include the following elements: (1) seriousness of the problem, (2) suggestions for reducing IO in e-mail usage, (3) suggestions for reducing IO in Internet usage, and (4) suggestions for reducing stress that results from IO.

2. "The information age has brought about a reduction in the quality of life." Choose to either support or defend the statement; write a one-to-two page paper that explains your position and gives supporting evidence and/or examples.

3. Select a personal example from your academic or work life in which you have experienced information overload (IO). Prepare a written analysis that (1) describes the situation, (2) identifies the reasons for the IO that occurred, and (3) outlines strategies for reducing your IO.

CHAPTER TEN

Managing Data and Using Graphics

LEARNING OBJECTIVES

When you have completed Chapter 10, you will be able to:

1 *Manage quantities of data efficiently.*

2 *Analyze quantitative data using measures of central tendency.*

3 *Understand principles of effectiveness and ethical responsibilities in the construction of graphic aids.*

4 *Select an appropriate type of graphic for specific data interpretation.*

5 *Design and integrate graphics within reports.*

*M*TV, with its combination of music video and lifestyle shows, is enormously popular with the 18- to 34-year-olds who are early in their careers—so popular that MTV's annual ad revenues have tripled in the last five years to $600 million.[1] Judy McGrath, president of MTV, knows, however, that her job depends on pleasing kids now too young to vote, as they move up the generational ladder. Being able to keep up with the moods of the very young—a moving target—is the company's goal. "I do lots of scientific and unscientific research," says McGrath in describing how she keeps up with what 14-year-olds are thinking. In an effort to attract a stronger share of the coveted children's viewer market, MTV plans to spend $420 million over the next five years to develop a dozen or more animated programs for its cable networks Nickelodeon and MTV. The new deals will double Nickelodeon's animation production budget, adding another $350 million while increasing MTV's spending 10 percent.[2] MTV's on-air promotions department, consisting of a 25-person graphics and production department and a 100-person studio, will be busy churning out visual images and sound for their planned animated programming.

Walt Disney, recognized pioneer in the field of animation, cleverly combined the magic of visual art with the artistic power of music in numerous full-length movie productions. Realizing that many people, especially children, were missing out on classical music, he developed his film *Fantasia*. After all, classical music has had a reputation for being boring. In *Fantasia*, however, Disney showed how fascinating this music could be by setting it to clever animation. This film interpreted the music through animated graphics, thus bringing concrete images to abstract musical themes.

In much the same way that MTV and Disney harnessed the capabilities of visual appeal, you can use creative and captivating graphics to interpret complex numerical data or highlight important ideas in your business reports and presentations. In your involvement in virtually any business, you will be writing reports and planning presentations. A report's success depends largely on how well you have accessed information through research, processed the information through careful study of the data, and organized that information into a comprehensible format. What techniques can keep you and your audience from being overwhelmed by your data? How can you make sure that your information achieves the impact that you desire?

---

① *Manage quantities of data efficiently.*

Managing Quantitative Data

Before you can interpret the data, you must classify, summarize, and condense it into a manageable size. This condensed information is meaningful and can be used to answer your research questions. For example, assume that you have been given a stack of 400 completed questionnaires from a study of employee needs for financial planning. This large accumulation of data is overwhelming until you tabulate the responses for each questionnaire item by manually inputting or optically scanning the responses into a computer. Then, you can apply appropriate statistical analysis techniques to the tabulated data.

The computer generates a report of the total responses for each possible response to each item. For example, the tabulation of responses from each employee about his or her most important need in financial planning might appear like this:

Fundamentals of Money Management	104
Mutual Funds	68
Internet Stock Trading	24
IRA and Retirement Annuities	192
Effective Charitable Giving	12
	400

The breakdown reduces 400 responses to a manageable size. The tabulation shows only five items, each with a specific number of responses from the total of 400 questionnaires. Because people tend to make comparisons during analysis, the totals are helpful. People generally want to know proportions or ratios, and these are best presented as percentage parts of the total. Thus, the numbers converted to percentages are as follows:

Personal Development Need	Number	Percentage
Fundamentals of Money Management	104	26
Mutual Funds	68	17
Internet Stock Trading	24	6
IRAs and Retirement Annuities	192	48
Effective Charitable Giving	12	3
	400	100

Now analyzing the data becomes relatively easy. Of the survey participants, 17 percent selected mutual funds, and only 3 percent selected effective charitable giving. Other observations, depending on how exactly you intend to interpret percentages, could be that nearly one-half of the employees selected individual retirement accounts and retirement annuities, and approximately a quarter of the employees selected fundamentals of money management.

When tabulating research results of people's opinions, likes, preferences, and other subjective items, rounding off statistics to fractions helps paint a clear picture for readers. In actuality, if the same group of people were asked this question again a day or two later, a few probably would have changed their minds. For example, an employee who had not indicated a desire for retirement planning may have learned of the benefits of a Roth IRA during a civic club meeting. The next day, the employee might indicate a desire for training in IRAs and Retirement Annuities.

How does the description "snapshot view" apply to survey data?

Common Language

Fractions, ratios, and percentages are often examples of **common language**. In effect, common language reduces difficult figures to the "common denominators" of language and ideas. Although "104 of 400 prefer fundamentals of money management" is somewhat easy to understand, "26 percent prefer . . ." is even easier, and "approximately one out of four indicate a need for fundamental money management skills" is even more understandable.

Common language also involves the use of indicators other than actual count or quantity. The Dow Jones Industrial Averages provide a measure of stock market performance and are certainly easier to understand than the complete New York Stock Exchange figures. "Freight car loadings" are weight measurements used in railroad terminology rather than "pounds carried," and oil is counted in barrels rather than in the quart or gallon sizes purchased by consumers. Because of inflation, dollars are

Assume that you earned 112 points out of a possible 150 on an exam; present this data using the most understandable terms. How could you describe the storage capacity of a hard drive or a CD-ROM so that a computer novice could understand? In groups, generate other examples of using common language.

not very accurate items to use as comparisons from one year to another in certain areas; for example, automobile manufacturers use "automobile units" to represent production changes in the industry. The important thing for the report writer to remember is that reports are communication media, and everything possible should be done to make sure communication occurs.

Measures of Central Tendency

2 *Analyze quantitative data using measures of central tendency.*

Measures of central tendency are simple statistical treatments of distributions of quantitative data that attempt to find a single figure to describe the entire distribution. The range assists the researcher in considering the distribution of the scores; the mean, the median, and the mode are descriptions of the average value.

- *Range.* When researchers first glance at a distribution, they probably look for the **range**—the difference between the lowest and highest values. For example, test scores of 20, 30, 75, 75, 75, 80, 85, 90, and 95 would have a range of 20 to 95, or 76 points (95 – 20 + 1, to count both the 20 and the 95). The range helps a researcher determine how many classes should be used in tabulating large numbers of values. In general, a first glance at the range reveals the extremes of values and assists in data analysis.

  Some researchers use the **interquartile range**—the spread of the middle 50 percent of the values—as a form of central tendency measurement. For example, in a distribution such as 7, 19, 21, 23, 24, 25, 29, and 41, the interquartile range is 21 to 25. Because eight items are included, two are in each quarter of the distribution. The two middle quartiles, the middle half, have the figures 21, 23, 24, and 25. Even though the total range is 7 to 41, the interquartile range shows that most figures are grouped tightly. Thus, the extreme values of 7 (the low) and 41 (the high) become less important.

What does "curving grades" mean? Who benefits from a grade curve? Why?

- *Mean.* The **mean** is the figure obtained when all the values in a distribution (table of values) are totaled and divided by the number of values. If, for example, eight people score values of 60, 65, 70, 75, 80, 85, 90, and 95 on a test, the total of these values is 620. Dividing 620 by 8 gives a mean of 77.5. Most people would call 77.5 the average score, but *mean* is a more accurate term.

  It is sometimes valuable to group a set of data into classes, or subsets. When material is tabulated by classes, such as "10 people scored between 80 and 89," statisticians would take the midpoint—84.5—and multiply it by 10 to get a total score for that class. Doing the same for other classes would provide a total for all scores in the tabulation. Dividing the total scores of all classes by the number of scores would provide a group mean. Grouping scores (placing them in classes) is not much different from totaling them separately. Determining the mean is simply the process of totaling all values and dividing by the number, whether totaled by classes or by individual scores.

- *Median.* The **median** is the middle value in a distribution. For example, the median for the values 20, 65, 70, 75, 80, 85, and 100 in a distribution would be 75. Half the values are above 75 and half are below 75. In this case, the median is more descriptive than the mean because the very low score of 20 does not skew the measure of central tendency. When a distribution has an odd number of values, the median will be the value exactly in the middle of the distribution. To find the median of a distribution with an even number of values, take the two middle values and calculate their mean. When values are counted in classes, find the middle value of the distribution of class means by counting from the top down or from the bottom up to the class containing the middle value. This class is described as the *median class*.

- *Mode.* The **mode** is the value that occurs most frequently in a distribution. For example, ten test scores of 65, 65, 65, 70, 75, 75, 80, 85, 95, and 100 would have a mode of 65—the most frequent score. The mean would be the total, 775, divided by 10, or 77.5. The median would be halfway between 75 and 75—the fifth and sixth scores of the ten—or 75. In this case, either the mean or the median would be an acceptable and more desirable measure than the mode, since they better describe the central tendency of the distribution.

In general, the mean is more stable than the median or the mode and usually fluctuates less than the other two measures. The mean is extremely reliable when distributions are large. In small distributions, the median is often a good indicator, especially when some very high or very low extreme values would affect the mean.

The researcher can greatly influence the reader's perception of information by selectively using the mean, median or mode to describe an "average" condition. For example, if a researcher reports that the average annual household income in a third-world country is $40,000, the reader might logically assume that the standard of living for citizens of that country is rather high. The reader's assumption might be changed if the researcher reports that the distribution of incomes includes millions of people in the $0–$7,000 range and a few multibillionaire oil sheiks in the million-dollar ranges of annual income. In this case, the median or mode would likely yield a more accurate view of the condition of the typical citizen.

The mean, median, and mode are statistical measures that help report writers describe the content and meaning of tables and graphs. These measures are part of the common language of statistics and are especially efficient and effective in reporting to people who understand their meanings. Good judgment on the part of the report writer should determine which measure to use or whether to use one at all.

> Which measure of central tendency would you recommend for a small distribution with several extreme sources? Provide an example.

Using Graphics

Managing data effectively protects a report writer from being overwhelmed by the data. To protect readers from being overwhelmed, report writers must select appropriate means of presenting the data. Data reported in a table, picture, graph, or chart will make your written analysis clearer to the reader.

Effective and Ethical Use of Graphics

Imagine trying to put in composition style all the information available in a financial statement. Several hundred pages might be necessary to explain all material that could otherwise be contained in three or four pages of balance sheets and income statements. Even then, the reader would no doubt be thoroughly confused! Graphics go hand in hand with the written discussion to achieve clarity. As you proceed through the remainder of this chapter, ask yourself if the discussion would be effective if the accompanying graphic figures were not included.

Throughout this chapter, the term **graphics** will be used to refer to all types of illustrations. In reports, the most commonly used graphics are tables, bar charts, line charts, pie charts, pictograms, maps, flow charts, diagrams, and photographs. These graphic presentations are often used as aids during oral reports as well. In both written and oral reports, several questions can help you determine whether using a graphic presentation is appropriate and effective:

3 *Understand principles of effectiveness and ethical responsibilities in the construction of graphic aids.*

Strategic Forces: Legal and Ethical Constraints

Ethical Implications in Creating Graphs

Creators of visuals can mislead their audience just as surely as can creators of text. In fact, visuals can sometimes have more impact than their accompanying text, for three reasons: (1) Visuals have an emotional impact that words often lack; (2) skimmers of items will see visuals even when they don't read text; and (3) readers remember visuals longer. Ethical considerations become an issue in visual communication because developers of this type of communication can mislead their audiences either through lack of expertise or deliberate ambiguity. Today's professionally oriented communicators will need to defend themselves from unethical uses of visual aids and determine what choices are ethical in the design of their own visuals.

Visual distortion can occur in a number of ways. For instance, distortion can occur in bar charts when the value scale starts at some point other than "0," as illustrated in the following graph.

The left bar chart seems to indicate a much greater improvement in test scores over the covered time period than actually occurred. This distortion could lead a student, parent, taxpayer, or employee to form a false impression about the schools' performance.

Another type of distortion can occur in bar charts when increments on the Y-axis that are visually equal are used to represent varying values. For instance, if intervals are set at 100, then each additional increment must also represent an increase of

100. When graphic placement or eye appeal would be jeopardized by including all intervals, a break line can be used to show that intervals have been omitted, as shown in Figure 10-4. This technique makes accurate reader interpretation more likely.

Other visual distortions, such as the misuse of relative-size symbols in pictograms, as illustrated in Figure 10-11, can also confuse or mislead a reader. The researcher has a responsibility to report data as clearly and accurately as possible and should be able to answer the following questions in a favorable manner: [3]

- Does the visual actually do what it seems to promise to do? Does the design cause false expectations?
- Is it truthful? Does it avoid implying lies?
- Does it avoid exploiting or cheating its audience?
- Does it avoid causing pain and suffering to members of the audience?
- Where appropriate, does it clarify text? Does the story told match the data?
- Does it avoid depriving viewers of a full understanding? Does it hide or distort information?

Application:

Construct a bar chart with intervals of unequal value on the Y-axis; then construct the same chart using intervals of equal value. Describe the difference in interpretation that the reader might have in viewing the two visuals.

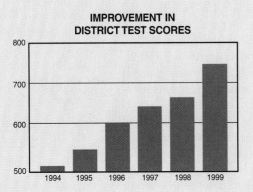

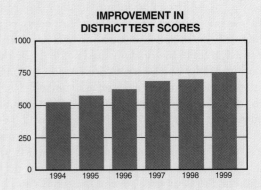

- Does the graphic presentation contribute to the overall understanding of the subject? Would a graphic assist the reader?
- Can the material be covered adequately in words rather than in visual ways? Graphics, both in written and oral reports, should be saved for data that are difficult to communicate in words alone.
- Will the written or spoken text add meaning to the graphic display?
- Is the graphic easily understood? Extreme use of color, complicated symbols, confusing art techniques, and unusual combinations of typefaces detract from the impact of the material presented.
- If the visual presentation is part of an oral report, can it be seen by the entire audience? Flip charts, white boards, overhead projector transparencies, and on-screen computer presentations are the visual means most often used to accompany oral reports.
- Is the graphic honest? Visually presented data can be distorted easily, leading the reader to form incorrect opinions about the data. The Strategic Forces box on page 344 provides directions for preparing ethical graphics.

Discuss this adage from a business perspective: "A picture is worth a thousand words."

Types of Graphic Aids

The greatest advantage of computer graphics is their value to the individual decision maker who formerly had to battle through a maze of computer-printed output. With powerful software programs available on desktop personal computers, managers can perform the data management functions discussed in this chapter to produce highly professional graphics. The information can be reproduced in a variety of ways for integrating into reports and for supporting highly effective oral presentations.

Selecting the graphic type that will depict data in the most effective manner is the first decision you must make. After identifying the primary idea you want your receiver to understand, you can choose to use a table, a bar chart, line chart, pie chart, flow chart, organization chart, photographs, models, and so on. Use Figure 10-1 to help you choose the graphic type that matches the objective you hope to achieve.

4 *Select an appropriate type of graphic for specific data interpretation.*

Graphic Type	Illustration	Objective
Table	Figure 10-2	To show exact figures
Bar chart	Figures 10-3, 10-4, 10-5, and 10-6	To compare one quantity with another
Line chart	Figure 10-7 and Figure 10-8	To illustrate changes in quantities over time
Pie chart	Figure 10-10	To show how the parts of a whole are distributed
Map	Figure 10-12	To show geographic relationships
Flow chart	Figure 10-13	To illustrate a process or procedure
Photograph	Photo, page 346	To provide a realistic view of a specific item or place

FIGURE 10-1
Choosing the appropriate graphic to fit your objective.

Above all, technology provides options to business communications. Through revolutionized graphic techniques, almost limitless production capabilities are available via computers. As recently as the 1980s, use of professional typesetters for high-quality projects was the common practice. Now advancing technology offers businesses many alternatives—internally meet all or some of their graphics needs or continue to outsource graphics production for complex projects.

Cynthia Pharr, President
C. Pharr & Company

A variety of graphics commonly used in reports is illustrated in Figures 10-2 through 10-13. These figures illustrate acceptable variations in graphic design: placement of the caption (figure number and title), inclusion or exclusion of grid lines, labeling the Y-axis at the top of the axis or turned sideways, proper referencing of the source of data, and others. When designing graphics, adhere to the requirements in your company policy manual or the style manual you are instructed to follow. Then be certain that you design all graphics consistently throughout a report. When preparing a graphic for use as a visual aid (transparency or on-screen display) in an oral presentation, you may wish to remove the figure number and include the title only.

Tables. A **table** presents data in columns and rows, which aid in clarifying large quantities of data in a small space. Clear labeling techniques make the content clear. Guidelines for preparing an effective table follow and are illustrated in Figure 10-2:

- ***Number tables and all other graphics consecutively throughout the report.*** This practice enables you to refer to "Figure 1" rather than to "the following table" or "the figure on the following page." Incidentally, the term *figure* should be used to identify all tables, graphs, pictures, and charts. Note that all illustrations in this chapter are identified as figures.

- ***Give each table a title that is complete enough to clarify what is included without forcing the reader to review the table.*** Table titles may be quite long and even extend beyond one line. A two-line title should be arranged on the page so that neither line extends into the margins. The second line should be shorter than the first and centered under it. Titles may contain sources of data, numbers included in the table, and the subject; for example, "Base Salaries of Chief Executives of the 200 Largest Financial Institutions in the United States." Titles may be written in either all capitals or upper-and-lowercase letters.

Why should a multiple-line title resemble an inverted pyramid?

- ***Label columns of data clearly enough to identify the items.*** Usually, column headings are short and easily arranged. If, however, they happen to be lengthy, use some ingenuity in planning the arrangement.

- ***Indent the second line of a label for the rows (horizontal items) two or three spaces.*** Labels that are subdivisions of more comprehensive labels should be indented, and summary labels such as *total* should also be indented.

- *Place a superscript beside a figure that requires additional explanation and include the explanation beneath the visual.*
- *Document the source of the data presented in a visual by adding a source note beneath the visuals.* If more than one source was used to prepare the visuals, use superscripts beside the figures extracted from other sources.

Bar Charts. A **bar chart** is an effective graphic for comparing quantities. The bar chart is often referred to as a *column chart* when the bars are presented vertically. The length of the bars, horizontal or vertical, indicates quantity, as shown in Figures 10-3 and 10-4. The quantitative axis should always begin at zero and be divided into equal increments. The width of the bars should be equal, or the wider bar will imply that it represents a larger number than the narrower bar. Here are further suggestions:

- *Use shadings (or cross-hatchings) or variations in color to distinguish among the bars.*
- *Consider the audience's use of the data to determine the need for labeling specifics.* Printing the specific dollar or quantity amount at the top of each bar assists in understanding the graph. Readers tend to skim the text and rely on the graphics for details. Omit actual amounts if a visual estimate is adequate for understanding the relationships presented in the chart. Excluding nonessential information such as specific amounts, grids, and explanatory notes actually increases the readability of the chart by reducing the clutter.
- *Include enough information in the scale labels and bar labels to be understandable but not so complicated that readers will skip over the graph.* The horizontal bar chart in Figure 10-3 shows unit sales for five departments in a retail store. Amounts appear in the vertical scale labels; departments, in the bar labels.

How does a grouped bar chart differ from a simple bar chart?

Should specific quantities and grids be included in graphics? Provide an example to justify your answer.

FIGURE 10-2
Effective table layout identifying captions, labels, footnote, and source.

Figure 3

Wal-Mart Stores, Inc.
Market Price of Common Stock

Fiscal Years Ended January 31				
	1997		**1996**	
Quarter	**High**	**Low**	**High**	**Low**
April 30	$24.50*	$20.88	$26.00	$23.13
July 31	26.25	22.88	27.50	23.00
October 31	28.13	24.50	26.00	21.63
January 31	27.00	24.13	24.75	19.25

*Quarterly dividend raised from $.05 to $.0525

Source: Wal-Mart Stores, Inc., *Annual Report*, 1997.

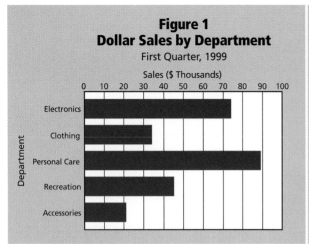

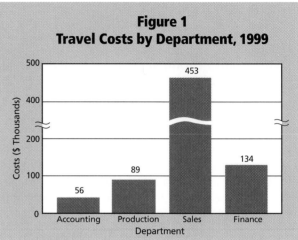

FIGURE 10-3
Horizontal bar chart.

FIGURE 10-4
Vertical (column) bar chart
indicating omission of part of the bar.

- **Break the bars to indicate omission of part of each bar if some quantities are so large that the chart would become unwieldy.** A broken-bar chart is illustrated in Figure 10-4.

Grouped bar chart. A **grouped bar chart**, also called a *clustered bar chart*, is useful for comparing more than one quantity (set of data) at each point along the x-axis. The frequency of defects in three product lines over the four quarters of a fiscal year are compared in Figure 10-5. Because the chart was printed using a color printer, each quantity appears in a specific color to facilitate comparison. Cross-hatchings differentiate the quantities if a color printer is not available.

Segmented bar chart. The **segmented bar chart**, also called a *subdivided, stacked bar chart*, or *100 percent stacked bar*, is shown in Figure 10-6. When you want to show how different facts (components) contribute to a total figure, the segmented chart is desirable. This graphic is particularly useful when components for more than one time period are being compared. Figure 10-6 shows the relative amount of sales earned from products in the various stages of the product life cycle. The actual percentage of each component is displayed in this example; however, these numbers can be omitted to reduce excessive clutter if you believe the reader's visual assessment of the proportions is adequate. Because this graph was printed using a color printer, colors distinguish the components, with a key included at the bottom of the chart.

Line Charts. A **line chart**, such as the one shown in Figure 10-7, depicts changes in quantitative data over time and illustrates trends. When constructing line charts, keep these general guidelines in mind:

- *Use the vertical axis for amount and the horizontal axis for time.*

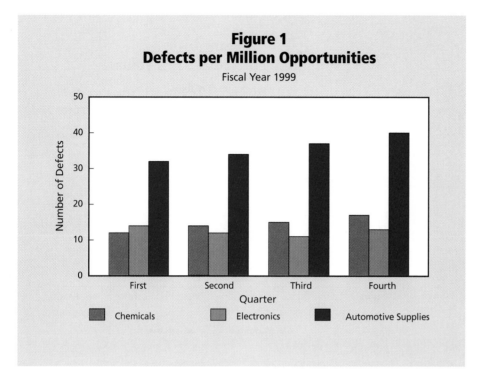

FIGURE 10-5
A grouped bar chart is useful for comparing more than one quantity over time.

Based on the data in Figure 10-5, in which of the three product lines should the Quality Control Department concentrate its efforts to reduce defects?

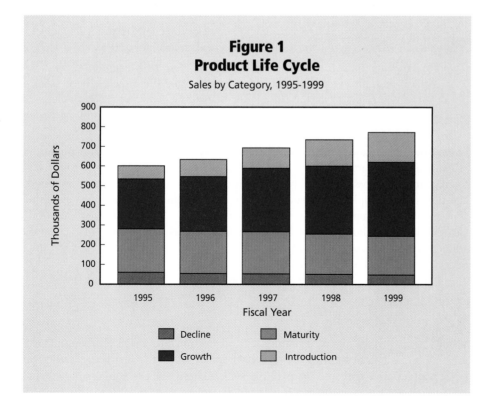

FIGURE 10-6
A segmented bar chart shows how proportional relationships change over time.

Suppose management is considering allocating fewer dollars to product research and development. Use the data in Figure 10-6 to justify your decision to support or reject this decision. Write a brief statement.

FIGURE 10-7
A line chart expresses changes in quantity over time.

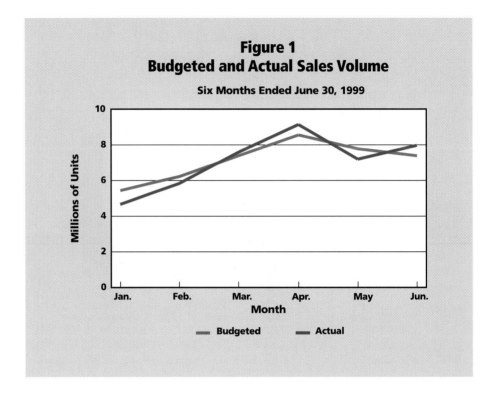

- ***Begin the vertical axis at zero.*** If the height of the chart becomes unwieldy, break it the same way the vertical scale was broken in Figure 10-4.
- ***Divide the vertical and horizontal scales into equal increments.*** The vertical or amount increments, however, need not be the same as the horizontal or time increments so that the line or lines drawn will have reasonable slopes. (Unrealistic scales might produce startling slopes that could mislead readers.)

Compare and contrast an area chart to a segmented chart.

An **area chart**, also called a *cumulative line chart* or a *surface chart*, is similar to a segmented bar chart because it shows how different factors contribute to a total. An area chart is especially useful when you want to illustrate changes in the components over time. For example, the area chart in Figure 10-8 illustrates the changes in the components of a company's retail sales over a fiscal year. The cumulative total of the five departments is illustrated by the top line on the chart. The amount of each component can be estimated by visual assessment. Color adds visual appeal and aids the reader in distinguishing the components.

Unlike bar charts, which show only the total amount for a time period, line charts show variations within each time period. In oral presentations, an area chart can be made more effective by having a separate transparency or animated graphic object created for each component. During the presentation, each transparency could be laid over the previous one or each object displayed in progression for a cumulative effect. In the example shown in Figure 10-8, for instance, the first transparency or object may show only personal care; the second, other; the third, clothing; the fourth, recreation; the fifth, electronics—the completed chart.

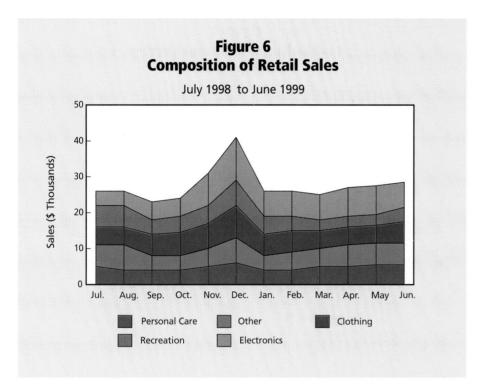

Figure 6
Composition of Retail Sales
July 1998 to June 1999

FIGURE 10-8
An area chart shows how
proportional relationships
change over time.

The chart in Figure 10-9 poses a particular challenge because the two quantities (sales and number of representatives) require scales of different intervals. The graphic is designed so that the reader can interpret the data easily, using the correct interval for each quantity. The bars use the left vertical axis to depict sales, and the line uses the right vertical axis to show the number of sales representatives. A line graph or a grouped bar chart could be used; however, this combination line and bar chart provides the contrast needed to interpret the relationship between sales and the number of sales representatives clearly.

Pie Charts. A **pie chart**, like segmented charts and area charts, shows how the parts of a whole are distributed. As the name indicates, the whole is represented as a pie, with the parts becoming slices of the pie. Pie charts are effective for showing percentages (parts of a whole), but they are ineffective in showing quantitative totals or comparisons. Bars are used for those purposes.

Here are some generally used guidelines for constructing pie charts:

- *Position the largest slice or the slice to be emphasized at the twelve o'clock position.* Working clockwise, place the other slices in descending order of size or some other logical order of presentation.

- *Label each slice and include information about the quantitative size (percentage, dollars, acres, square feet, etc.) of each slice.* If you are unable to attractively place the appropriate labeling information beside each slice, use a legend to identify color or pattern labeling for slices. Note the labeling in Figure 10-10.

Can the information in a pie chart also be represented in a bar chart? Can the information in a bar chart also be represented in a pie chart? Give an explanation for your answer.

FIGURE 10-9
A combination bar and line chart facilitates interpretation of two quantities requiring different intervals.

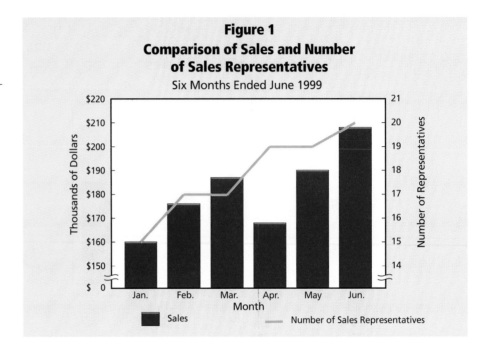

- *Draw attention to one or more slices for desired emphasis.* Special effects include (a) exploding the slice(s) to be emphasized, (that is, removing it from immediate contact with the pie) or (b) displaying or printing only the slice(s) to be emphasized.
- *Use color or patterns (cross-hatchings) to aid the reader in differentiating among the slices and to add appeal.*

FIGURE 10-10
A pie chart with exploded section and three-dimensional effect shows percentages of a whole.

Given the fact that more than 50 percent of the company's total inquiries are about database software, what conclusions might a user documentation manager draw from the pie chart in Figure 10-10?

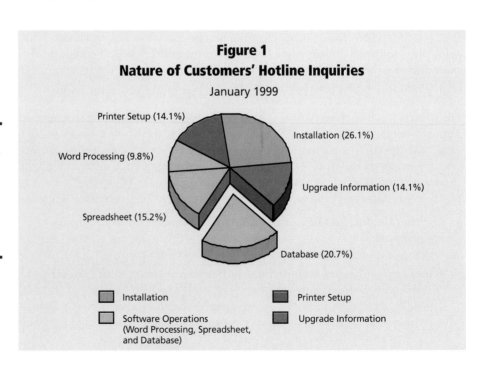

Use your own judgment in constructing a pie chart. Your software may limit your ability to follow rules explicitly. Likewise, the nature of the data or the presentation selected may require slight deviations to increase the clarity of the graphic. For example, if you intend to explode the largest slice, placing it in the twelve o'clock position may not be desirable because the slice is likely to intrude into the space occupied by a title positioned at the top of the page. If your style manual or company policy requires that titles be positioned above the graphic, starting with a slice other than the largest is acceptable. For dramatic effect, many periodicals and reports vary from these general rules. Other deviations are discussed in the accompanying Strategic Forces box.

Can you think of other situations that might warrant slight deviations from the rules presented in this chapter?

Pictograms. A **pictogram** uses pictures to illustrate numerical relationships. A pictogram can convey a more literal, visual message to the reader than can a bar chart. For example, the pictograms in Figure 10-11 use visual images of money instead of bars to depict lumber production in the United States. However, pictograms can be more dramatic than meaningful if they are not planned properly. For example, doubling the height and width of a picture increases the total area four times. Therefore, all symbols must be the same size so that true relationships are not distorted. Note that the relative sizes of the trees in the pictogram on the left in Figure 10-11 are misleading and make the actual amounts and relationships hard to understand. In the pictogram on the right, using the same-size trees makes both amounts and relationships instantly clear. Refer to the accompanying Strategic Forces box for additional discussion of the ethical implications of graphical presentation.

Clip a pictogram from *USA Today* and share with groups in class. Discuss the effectiveness of the symbols used and the ethical presentation of the data.

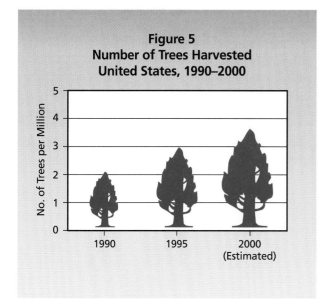

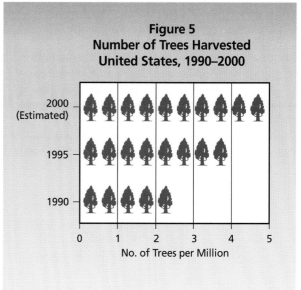

FIGURE 10-11
Relative-size symbols (left) distort data; same-size symbols
(right) depict relationships accurately.

Strategic Forces: Changing Technology

Presentation Software and Graphic Design Principles

Technological advancements in the fields of presentation software and hardware have enhanced presentation capabilities. Sadly, technology alone does not guarantee a good result. In the early days of software development, some businesspeople made the mistake of assuming that because technical capabilities existed for creating a variety of graphic materials, everyone who could type could perform the job of designer. This was not, and still isn't, the case. Fortunately, the latest generation of presentation software packages do try to guide the user away from the worst errors of taste and judgment. PowerPoint offers the chance to curb the noncreative user's worst lapses of taste by offering wizards that lead the user through the process of preparing a presentation that follows one of a series of style templates.[4] Other vendors have inserted relevant rules into their products, such as incorporating graphic design principles in presentation applications. The Quattro Pro® spreadsheet program picks the most appropriate chart type for various types of graphed data. AutoCorrect™ in Microsoft® Word® incorporates intelligent corrections by watching for the most common mistakes and correcting them for you automatically. Aldus has also been working to build graphic design rules into its desktop-publishing software.[5]

In spite of ongoing improvements in presentation software applications, developers still often do not reflect good rules for formation of graphic aids in the default settings of their products. For instance, many presentation programs automatically arrange pie slices in random-size order. For example, if the pie contains many small slices, the program may intersperse the small slices with the larger slices to increase readability and enhance appearance. Some programs also do not automatically start pie charts at the twelve o'clock position. Software applications often include an unnecessary series legend indicator for charts, even when only one value is represented.

With a little work on your part, you can usually achieve accurate graphic depictions when using presentations and graphics applications. Some software programs allow you to organize charts following acceptable guidelines by changing the format options. Many times, you can select options, optional settings, or some similar command and instruct the program to arrange the graphic according to the appropriate rules. A competent software user never assumes the software application will automatically produce the desired arrangement.

Application

Select two different presentation or graphics software products (PowerPoint®, Corel® Presentations®, Freelance®, Harvard Graphics®, etc.). Using the following data and the default settings of the application, construct a simple bar chart and a simple pie chart in both of the selected products.

Operating Budget for Administrative Support Department, XYZ Company: salaries & benefits, 62%; training & development, 11%; supplies & materials, 12%; and operating chargeback, 15%.

Print out your results. What differences did you find in the output of each product? How did the outcomes deviate from the rules in this chapter? How were they in compliance with the rules?

Maps. A map shows geographic relationships. A map is especially useful when a reader may not be familiar with the geography discussed in a report. The map shown in Figure 10-12 effectively presents sales growth by state and shows the locations of the home office, distribution centers, and retail stores within the geographic region. The map gives the information visually and thus eliminates the difficulty of explaining the information in words. In addition to being less confusing, a map is more concise and interesting than a written message would be.

COMMUNICATION MENTOR

Absorption and retention of information are unquestionably enhanced by the use of graphics, whether you have time and budget to produce video, computer-generated 35mm slides or slide show, elect to hand-draw graphics on a flip chart, or use an overhead projector. (Perhaps you are considering graphics right now to support a term paper or research project.)

Don't be afraid to use graphics to present simple information. On the contrary, be afraid *not* to use them when you are tackling a complex subject. Readers and audiences expect them and will consistently reward you for your extra work.

James F. Hurley, Principal
Hurley Advisors

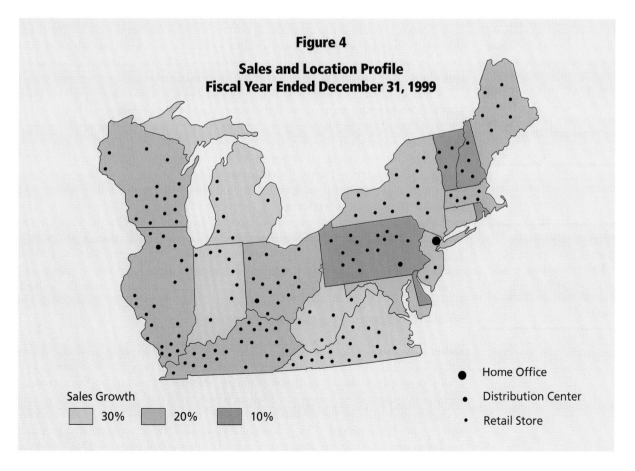

FIGURE 10-12 A map depicts geographical relationships.

Stockholders reading Wal-Mart's annual report can visualize the company's team approach as they look at this photograph of a company executive and associate interacting in a Wal-Mart retail store.

Draw a flow chart outlining the procedure that shipping dock employees should follow when shipping packages. Decisions may include priority of package, destination (in-state or out-of-state), and weight of package.

Flow charts. A **flow chart** is a step-by-step diagram of a procedure or a graphic depiction of a system or organization. A variety of problems can be resolved by using flow charts to support written analyses. For example, most companies have procedures manuals to instruct employees in certain work tasks. Including a flow chart with the written instructions minimizes the chance of errors.

A flow chart traces a unit of work as it flows from beginning to completion. Symbols with connecting lines are used to trace a step-by-step sequence of the work. A key to a flow chart's symbols may be included if the reader may not readily understand standard symbols. For example, the flow chart in Figure 10-13 illustrates the procedures for processing a telephone order. If this information had been presented only in a series of written steps, the customer service manager would have to rely not only on the input operator's reading ability but also on his or her willingness to read and study the written procedures.

Locate an organization chart of a company with a flat organizational structure. Compare it with the tall structure shown in Figure 2-2.

Organization charts, discussed in Chapter 2, are widely used to provide a picture of the authority structure and relationships within an organization. They provide employees with an idea of what their organization looks like in terms of the flow of authority and responsibility. When businesses change (because of new employees or reorganization of units and responsibilities), organization charts must be revised. Revisions are simple if the organization chart is prepared using graphics software and saved to be retrieved when changes must be made.

Other Graphics. Other graphics, such as floor plans, photographs, cartoons, blueprints, and lists of various kinds, may be included in reports. The increased availability of graphics and sophisticated drawing software is leading to the increased inclusion of these more complex visuals in reports and oral presentations. Because managers can prepare these visuals themselves less expensively and more quickly than having them prepared by professional designers, these sophisticated graphics are being used increasingly for internal reports. Photographs are used frequently in annual reports to help the general audience understand a complex concept and to make the document more appealing to read.

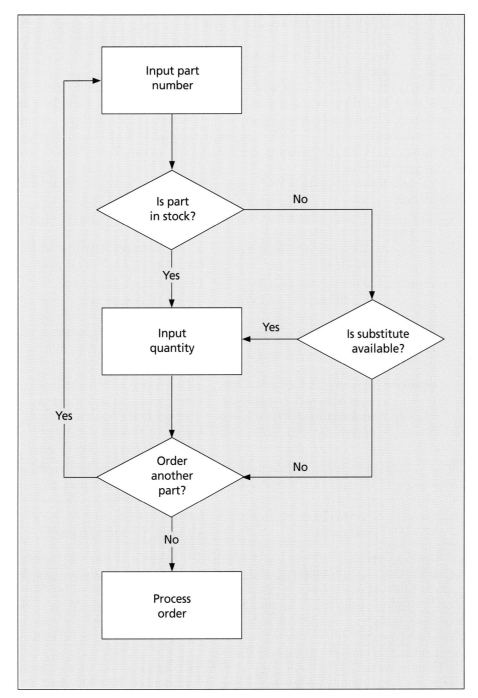

FIGURE 10-13
A flow chart simplifies understanding of work tasks.

Frequently, you must include some material in a report that would make the narrative discussion unwieldy. In this case, the material might be placed in an appendix and only referred to in the report.

5 *Design and integrate graphics within reports.*

Introducing Graphics in Text

Always introduce a graphic in the textual material immediately preceding the graphic. Text and graphics are partners in the communication process. If graphics appear in the text before readers have been informed, they will begin to study the graphics and draw their own inferences and conclusions. A graphic that follows an introduction and brief explanation will supplement what has been said in the report. Additional interpretation and analysis that may be needed should follow the graphic. The pattern, then, for incorporating graphs in text is (1) introduce, (2) show, and (3) interpret and analyze.

Note how the language in the following sentences introduces graphic or tabular material:

Poor:	Figure 1 shows reader preferences for shopping locations.	*This sentence is poor because it tells the reader nothing more than would the title of the figure.*
Acceptable:	About two-thirds of the consumers preferred to shop in suburban areas rather than in the city. (See Figure 1.)	*This sentence is acceptable because it does the job of interpreting the data, but it puts the figure reference in parentheses rather than integrating it into the sentence.*
Improved:	As shown in Figure 1, about two-thirds of the consumers preferred to shop in suburban areas rather than in the city.	*Although improved over the previous examples, this sentence puts reference to the figure at the beginning, thus detracting from the interpretation of the data.*
Best:	About two-thirds of the consumers preferred to shop in suburban areas rather than in the city, as shown in Figure 1.	*This sentence is best for introducing figures because it talks about the graphic and also includes introductory phrasing, but only after stressing the main point.*

Ideally, a graphic should be integrated within the text material immediately after its introduction. A graphic that will not fit on the page where it is introduced should appear at the top of the following page. The previous page is filled with text that would have ideally followed the graphic. In this chapter, figures are placed as closely as possible to their introductions in accordance with these suggestions. However, in some cases, several figures may be introduced on one page, making perfect placement difficult and sometimes impossible.

In interpreting and analyzing the graphic, the writer should avoid a mere restatement of what the graphic obviously shows. The analysis that follows the figure may make summary statements about the data, compare information in the figure to information obtained from other sources, or extend the shown data into reasonably supported speculative outcomes. Every attempt should be made to bridge naturally from the discussion of the graphic into the next point the writer wishes to make.

Throughout the discussion of tables and graphics, the term *graphics* has been used to include all illustrations. Although your report may include tables, graphs, maps, and even photographs, you will find organizing easier and writing about the

Assume that a graphic has been introduced on p. 8 of a report, but the graphic will not fit on the page. Where should you place the graphic? What should you do with any blank space on p. 8?

COMMUNICATION IN ACTION

Paul Lehman, Macom Corporation

When he earned his general engineering degree from the University of Illinois, Paul Lehman had learned how to work with technical concepts and jargon. Communicating these complex concepts so that non-engineers could understand, however, presented another challenge. Thus, he later earned an MBA degree. As president of Macom Corporation, he capitalizes on his technical expertise and business knowledge to develop land and to market property in the Chicago area. Lehman's company spearheaded the development of a large residential community around an Arnold Palmer Signature Golf Course near Chicago.

"Presenting data in graphic form is the key to communicating the technical information required in my business," says Lehman. "For example, putting statistical information about property values in clear, honest graphics enables prospective buyers to see and understand the perceived value of the land they wish to purchase."

"Developers market perceived value—not technical or absolute value. Using visuals to communicate perceived value has worked successfully for Macom Corporation," asserts Lehman. For example, some people desire the majestic view of living on a golf course and the exclusive privilege of observing golfers making shots, golf carts passing by, and even golf balls landing on their lawn. Other people like to be a part of a golf course community but do not want to be a member of the golf club or to own a lot adjacent to the course. A comparable lot in another residential community will sell for less. Because the perceived value of a lot adjacent to an Arnold Palmer golf course is higher, buyers are willing to pay a premium price.

The following segmented bar chart compares the cost of three lots: Lot A is located in another Macom development without a golf course; Lot B, in a golf course development but not on the course; and Lot C, adjacent to the golf course with a view of a green. The buyer can visualize the relative price difference of the three lots and, therefore, the value attached to the attributes of each lot. Thus, Macom will sell a lot on the golf course when the buyer perceives that the benefits of living on the course are worth at least $30,000.

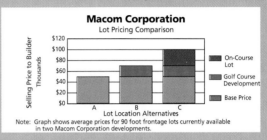

Note: Graph shows average prices for 90 foot frontage lots currently available in two Macom Corporation developments.

Lehman also uses a segmented bar chart to assess the progress of each builder. The chart contains crucial information, such as the number of homes constructed, the number of homes under construction, and the number of vacant lots. By keeping abreast of his builders' progress, Lehman stays competitive: "A segmented chart gives me the comparisons I need to make competitive decisions. Pie charts, tables of percentages, or absolute numbers will not accurately describe these comparisons."

Applying What You Have Learned

1. Prepare a segmented chart Lehman could use to explain price variations for lots along the golf course. Factors such as proximity to lakes, a green, a tee, the clubhouse, and a fairway affect the perceived value of a lot. Assume that lot prices range from $100,000 to $150,000.

2. Why is a segmented bar chart appropriate for assessing the progress of Lehman's builders?

3. Prepare a segmented bar chart using first-quarter data. In January, Lehman's top builder (provide name) had 80 completed homes, 20 homes under construction, and 50 vacant lots. In February, the builder had 95 completed homes, 15 under construction, and 40 vacant lots. In March, the builder had 105 completed homes, 20 under construction, and 25 vacant lots. Provide a descriptive title. What topics does the graph suggest Lehman should discuss with the builder at tomorrow's meeting?

Discuss the two numbering systems for report graphics. Which system would you use if you were writing a report for your supervisor?

illustrations more effective if you label all items as "Figure" followed by a number and number them consecutively. Some report writers like to label tables consecutively as "Table 1," etc., and graphs and charts consecutively in another sequence as "Graph 1," etc. When this dual numbering system is used, readers of the report may become confused if they come upon a sentence saying, "Evidence presented in Tables 3 and 4 and Graph 2 supports . . ." Both writers and readers appreciate the single numbering system, which makes the sentence read, "Evidence presented in Figures 3, 4, and 5 supports . . ."

SUMMARY

1. *Manage quantities of data efficiently.* Graphics complement written text by clarifying complex figures and helping readers visualize major points. An important aspect of writing effective reports is protecting yourself and the reader against a deluge of data. Tabulating data and analyzing data using measures of central tendency aid in summarizing or classifying large volumes of data into manageable information you can interpret. You can then communicate this meaningful data using common language—fractions, ratios, and percentages—that the reader can easily understand.

2. *Analyze quantitative data using measures of central tendency.* Measures of central tendency identify a single figure to describe the entire distribution. These measures and their purposes follow:

   - **Range:** the difference between the lowest and highest values (add one to include the high and low values).

   - **Mean:** the arithmetic average and the most stable measure of central tendency.

   - **Median:** the middle value in a distribution; especially good indicator when extremely high or low values would influence the mean.

   - **Mode:** the value that occurs most frequently.

3. *Understand principles of effectiveness and ethical responsibilities in the construction of graphic aids.* The following questions serve as a guide for determining if a graphic is appropriate for presenting a particular idea:

   - Would a graphic assist the reader in understanding the subject?

   - Can the material be covered adequately in words rather than in visual ways?

   - Will the written or spoken text add meaning to the graphic display?

   - Is the graphic design uncluttered and easily understood?

   - Is the graphic large enough to be seen by an audience if it is supporting an oral presentation?

   - Does the graphic display the information honestly?

4. *Select an appropriate type of graphic for specific data interpretation.* The type of graphic presentation should be chosen based on the ability to communicate the information most effectively. Tables present data in systematic rows and columns. Bar charts (simple, grouped, and stacked) compare quantities for a specific period. Line charts depict changes in quantities over time and illustrate trends. Pie charts, pictograms, and segmented and area charts show the proportion of components to a whole. Maps help readers visualize geographical relationships. Flow charts visually depict step-by-step procedures for completing a task; organization charts show the organizational structure of a company. Floor plans, photographs, cartoons, blueprints, and lists also enhance reports.

5. *Design and integrate graphics within reports.* The writer should always introduce a graphic before presenting it. The graphic will then reinforce your conclusions and discourage readers from drawing their own conclusions before encountering your ideas. An effective introduction for a graphic tells something meaningful about what is depicted in the graphic and refers the reader to a specific figure number. The graphic should be placed immediately after the introduction if possible. If the graphic will not fit on the page where it is introduced, it should be positioned at the top of the next page, filling the previous page with text that would ideally have followed the graphic. Analysis or interpretation follows the graphic, avoiding a mere repetition of what the graphic clearly shows.

REFERENCES

[1]Machan, D. (1997, September 8). A more tolerant generation. *Forbes*, 46–47.

[2]McConville, J. (1996, September 9). MTV earmarks $420 million for animation. *Broadcasting & Cable*, 50.

[3]Kienzler, D. S. (1997). Visual ethics. *The Journal of Business Communication*, 34(2), 171–187. [p. 17].

[4]Hewitt, M. (1997, March 13). Armed to present. *Marketing*, 33–36. [p. 3].

[5]Berst, J. (1994, May 2). The software industry is starting to wise up. *PC Week*, 134.

[6]Ross, P. E. (1995, August 14). Lies, damned lies and medical statistics. *Forbes*, 130–132+.

REVIEW QUESTIONS

1. In what ways does managing data help protect researchers and readers from being overwhelmed by the material? (Obj. 1)

2. What is meant by common language? Provide several examples. (Obj. 1)

3. Which measure of central tendency do most people describe as the average? How is it calculated? (Obj. 2)

4. Which measures of central tendency would be appropriate for the following distribution: 12, 65, 68, 72, 73, 79, 81, 85, and 85? Why? (Obj. 2)

5. Discuss the major principles involved in preparing effective tables. (Obj. 3)

6. What basic rules are used to determine whether a graphic should be used to present certain information? (Obj. 3)

7. Why should increments on the vertical axis be equal in a graphic? Is variation in the sizes of horizontal increments acceptable? (Obj. 3)

8. Describe a broken bar chart. (Obj. 4)

9. What is the difference between a segmented (component) chart and an area (cumulative line) chart? Give an example of how each might be used. (Obj. 4)

10. Why can pie charts and simple line charts not be used to depict the same type of data effectively? (Obj. 4)

11. What are some examples of distortions in graphics that can mislead the reader about the data presented? (Obj. 3)

12. Why might a writer use a pictogram instead of a bar chart to present data? (Obj. 4)

13. Where should a graphic be placed in a report in relation to the text that describes it? (Obj. 5)

14. Should every graphic be introduced in a report? Is interpreting a self-explanatory graphic necessary? Explain. (Obj. 5)

15. Discuss the appropriate way to introduce a graphic in a report. (Obj. 5)

EXERCISES

1. **Recognizing Common Language (Obj. 1)**
   Select an article from a business journal that presents the findings of a research study. Find examples of how percentages and common language are used in the reporting of the data. Describe how effective or ineffective the author(s) was/were in assuring that the data were understood by the intended audience.

2. **Computing Measures of Central Tendency (Obj. 2)**
   The following figures represent the value of stock options in thousands of dollars issued to executive management of 25 local high-tech firms.

   a. Compute the range, mean, median, and mode of the following distribution.

50	91	164	217	425
60	130	170	260	596
65	139	170	283	600
70	143	170	350	650
78	159	204	390	690

   b. Tally the scores in Exercise (2a) in eight classes beginning with 0–99, 100–199, and so on to 700–799. When you have tallied the scores, compute the mean, median, and modal class.

3. **Preparing a Table (Obj. 3)**
   Prepare a table for the data used in Exercise 2 and indicate the appropriate percentages for each class. Write a sentence to introduce the table in a report.

4. **Selecting Graphics (Obj. 4)**
   Select the most effective graphic means of presenting the following data. Justify your decision.

   a. Data showing the availability of apartments by type (studio, number of bedrooms) in a designated area.

b. Data showing the functional areas of a company from the CEO to the vice presidents to the line supervisors.

c. Figures showing the number of MBA or graduate business employees hired by Addy Industries during the past five years.

d. Predicted senior citizen population by state for 2000.

e. Company capital investments in each of five countries during the last fiscal year.

f. Figures comparing the percentage of warranty claims of a company's three product lines for the past four quarters.

g. Instructions to human resources managers for conducting team interviews.

h. Figures showing the volume of flood insurance policies by state.

5. **Improving Introductions to Graphics (Obj. 5)**
   Improve the following statements taken from reports:

   a. As can be seen in Table 3, the correlation between interest rates and credit card sales was .68.

   b. Professional salaries in the southeast have increased about 12 percent while the national average has increased 3 percent. (See Figure 10-6.)

   c. Take a look at Figure 10-5, where a steady decline in the price of writeable CD-ROMs during the year is shown.

   d. The data reveal (Figure 10-4) that only 7 out of 10 customers are satisfied with our service department.

E-MAIL APPLICATION

Use the annual report obtained for Application 8 to critique a graphic in the report. Complete the following steps:

1. Identify *one* graphic that violates one or more of the principles presented in this chapter. For example, the graphic may be an inappropriate type to present the data meaningfully, may be drawn incorrectly, may distort the true meaning of the data, have too much clutter, contain typographical or labeling errors, or contain other ineffective design elements.

2. Revise the graphic, incorporating your suggestions. Send your instructor an e-mail message, outlining the major weaknesses in the graphic and your suggestions for improving it. Attach the computer file containing your revised graphic.

3. Be prepared to present an oral report to the class. To support your report, prepare a transparency of the poor and revised graphic and a list of the weaknesses if your graphic contained several errors.

APPLICATIONS

1. **Creating a Table (Obj. 4, 5)**
   Prepare a table to show the *total* revenue Nashville Sports Connection earned from membership fees for a fiscal period. Fees were collected by type of membership: single, $25; double, $40; family (3+ members), $50; corporate, $22.50; senior, $20. Nashville Sports Connection has 1,439 single memberships, 642 double, 543 family, 3,465 corporate, and 786 senior membership.

2. **Drawing a Bar Chart (Obj. 4, 5)**
   Prepare a bar chart showing the frequency of injuries reported at each of Gardner Manufacturing's three plants (Dallas, Huntsville, and Cleveland) for each quarter in the last fiscal period. The number of injuries by quarter follow: Dallas: 1, 2, 6, 8; Huntsville: 3, 4, 3, 4; Cleveland: 6, 5, 3, 1. Write a title that clearly identifies the data depicted in the chart. Write a sentence to introduce the graphic and emphasize the most important idea(s) in the graphic.

3. **Drawing a Line Chart (Obj. 4, 5)**
   Prepare a line chart showing the total number of

injuries at Gardner Manufacturing for each of these years: 1995, 43; 1996, 51; 1997, 58; 1998, 62. Write a title that clearly identifies the data depicted in the chart. Write a sentence to introduce the graphic and emphasize the most important idea(s) in the graphic.

4. **Drawing a Segmented Chart (Obj. 4, 5)**
   The director of the Nashville Sports Connection wishes to compare the usage rate of various activities offered to its members over the past four quarters. Using the data provided in the following table, prepare a segmented chart that will make comparison of these usage rates easier to understand.

Activity	1st Q	2nd Q	3rd Q	4th Q
Aerobics classes	2,451	2,315	2,248	2,258
Aerobics machines (treadmills, steppers)	6,245	6,458	6,835	6,994
Strength machines	4,212	4,259	4,205	4,213
Free weights	945	845	758	789
Swimming pool	894	974	1,048	1,245

5. **Drawing a Pie Chart (Obj. 4, 5)**
   Prepare a pie chart showing the percentage of revenue Video Central generated from sales categories during the second quarter of the current year: video rental (42%), game rental (22%), new video sales (16%), previewed video sales (14%), and concessions (6%). Write a title that clearly identifies the data depicted in the chart. Write a sentence to introduce the graphic and emphasize the most important idea(s) in the graphic.

6. **Drawing a Map (Obj. 4.5)**
   Haley Manufacturing Company is initiating a distance education program for delivering instruction on new production methods to its 15 manufacturing plants. Use computer software such as a spreadsheet with a map option to prepare a map showing (a) Haley's home office in Kansas City, the live site where the instruction will originate, and (b) the location of the 15 remote sites: Los Angeles, Seattle, houston, New Orleans, Little Rock, Denver, Chicago, Orlando, Philadellphia, Boston, Bowling Green, Indianapolis, Cincinnati, Albuquerque, and Green Bay. Write a title that clearly identifies the data depicted in the map. Write a sentence to introduce the graphic and emphasize the most important idea(s) in the graphic.

7. **Selecting and Drawing an Appropriate Graphic (Obj. 3–5)**
   Create the graphic that would most effectively aid a human resources manager in identifying potential areas for training and development.

Hours of Computer Usage by Department
March 1999

Dept.	Word Processing	Spreadsheet	Data base	E-Mail	Internet
Acct./ Finance	2,548	3,415	488	3,154	484
Marketing	4,842	1,488	345	4,743	1,847
Production	1,548	2,458	315	842	310

8. **Evaluating Graphics in Annual Reports. (Obj. 3–5)**
   Obtain a copy of a corporate annual report. Prepare a one-page memorandum to your instructor that evaluates the appropriateness of each graphic in the report, its effectiveness in clarifying or reinforcing major points, and the ethical presentation of information.

9. **Evaluating and Revising Graphics (Obj. 3–5)**
   Evaluate the effectiveness of each of the graphics on the following page. Revise the graphic, incorporating your suggestions for improvement. Write a title and a sentence to introduce the graphic and emphasize the most important idea(s) in the graphic.

   a. Dollar sales (in thousands of dollars) over a six-year period. Graphic is being prepared for inclusion in the annual report.

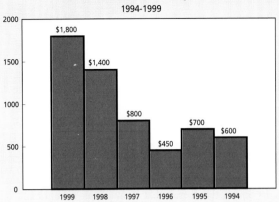

b. Unit production per plant during the third quarter of 1999.

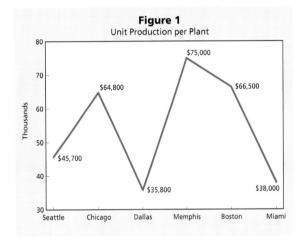

c. Number of customers by sales representatives during October 1999.

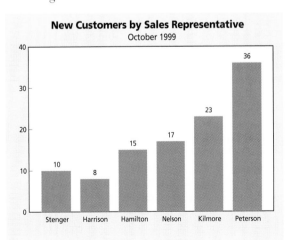

REAL-TIME INTERNET CASE

Lying Statistics

Three kinds of lies are possible, according to Benjamin Disraeli, a British prime minister in the nineteenth century—lies, damned lies, and statistics. A related notion exists that "you can prove anything with statistics." Such statements bolster the distrust that many people have for statistical analysis. On the other hand, many nonmathematicians hold quantitative data in awe, believing that numbers are, or at least should be, unquestionably correct. Consequently, it comes as a shock that different research studies can produce very different, often contradictory results. To solve this paradox, many naive observers conclude that statistics must not really provide reliable indicators of reality after all, and if statistics aren't "right," they must be "wrong." It is easy to see how even intelligent, well-educated people can become cynical if they don't understand the concepts of statistical reasoning and analysis.

Consider, for instance, the frequent reporting of a "scientific discovery" in the fields of health and nutrition. The United States has become a nation of nervous people, ready to give up eating pleasures at the drop of a medical report. Today's "bad-for-you" food was probably once good for you, and vice versa. Twenty years ago, many consumers were turned away from consuming real butter to oily margarine, only recently to learn that the synthetically solidified oils of margarine, trans-fatty acids, are worse for our arteries than any fat found in nature. In the year following the publication of this latest finding, margarine sales dropped 8.2 percent and butter sales rose 1.4 percent.[6]

Distrust also arises concerning studies that link exercise to health. Numerous studies have established statistically that people who exercise live longer. But the conclusion that exercise is good for you may put the cart before the horse. Are people healthy because they exercise? Or do they exercise because they are healthy? Correlation, once again, does not establish causation.

How do such incorrect and partial research findings become published and consequently disseminated through the media? Some of the responsibility should probably be cast upon researchers who may overstate the significance or the generalizability of their findings. The media should also shoulder some blame, as preliminary findings of small or limited studies are often reported as foregone conclusions. Consumers should also assume some responsibility in the interpretation of reported research. Questions such as the following should be asked when considering the value of reported findings.

- Is the study sample representative of the population involved?
- Were the statistical procedures used appropriate to the data?
- Has the research involved a sample of significant size and a sufficient time period of study?
- Were adequate controls applied to assure that outcomes are actually the result of the studied variable?
- Has the margin for error been taken into account in interpreting the results?
- Has any claim of causation been carefully examined using appropriate approaches?

The statement that "you can prove anything with statistics" is true only if statistics are used incorrectly. Understanding the basics of statistics is becoming increasingly important. With the prevalence of computers, vast amounts of data are available on every subject; and statistical packages allow analysis of these data with the press of a button, regardless of whether the analysis makes sense. Our professional and business lives thrive on numbers and our ability to interpret them correctly. Visit the following web sites and complete the activities as directed by your instructor.

Internet Sites

http://www.psych.qub.ac.uk/LearningResources/PitfallsofDataAnalysis
http://www.northland.ac.nz/npoly/essays/lies.htm
http://www.inman.com/news/9610/961018dr.htm

Activities

1. Compile a list of behaviors or practices that can lead to the reporting of "lying statistics." For each item on your list, indicate whether the behavior or practice is likely an intentional or unintentional attempt to distort.

2. Write a one- to two-page analysis of the researcher's ethical responsibilities in reporting statistical results of a study versus the consumer's responsibilities in reading and interpreting the results.

3. Prepare a short oral report in which you describe some of the issues that arise when reporting international economic statistics.

CHAPTER ELEVEN

Organizing and Preparing Reports and Proposals

LEARNING OBJECTIVES

When you have completed Chapter 11, you will be able to:

1 Identify the parts of a formal report and the contribution each part makes to the overall effectiveness of a report.

2 Organize report findings.

3 Prepare effective formal reports using an acceptable format and writing style.

4 Prepare effective short reports in letter and memorandum formats.

5 Prepare effective proposals for a variety of purposes.

*T*he Gap, Inc. has built a successful business on the private label concept. The chain has averaged 28 percent annual profit for the last decade and has for the last seven years sold only its own private labels. Gap's own-store market research has led them to expand into specialty stores that include Gap-Kids, babyGap, Banana Republic, and Old Navy. Successful private labeling not only cuts out the middleman and retains all the profits for the company, but it also creates a unique identity for the store, because the private label is offered only in Gap stores. Although the Gap's private labeling originally focused on staples like jeans just to increase profit margins, now the stores' perspectives have broadened about what kind of goods to private-label, and how to merchandise and price them.

Gap founder and chairman Don Fisher credits private labeling with saving his company in the late 1970s, when the Gap, as a Levi's dealer, made the significant decision to begin focusing on its own brand. By the time the Gap dropped Levi's altogether in 1991, Levi's accounted for only 2 percent of sales. Private-label stores have a huge edge over the manufacturer, because they have a clear view of the shelves and racks at all times and can gear what they make immediately to what they sell. Each of the Gap lines is carefully designed for manufacture and quick sale, using the latest equipment and computerized costing. For instance, the Gap starts a seasonal collection with a color palette drawn from consultants' recommendations and in-house designers' research into what's new in London, Paris, and Milan. The Gap's design department, like designer manufacturers, has two goals: find out what existing customers want and make more of it.[1]

Like the building of a successful private label, a business report must also be skillfully constructed. Each part must be carefully "worked" and then reviewed to make sure it is as perfect as possible. If a part is missing, the report is incomplete and will not be effective. After gathering information for your report, be sure to check the style manual approved by your company to make sure that your report has all the required components and to see how to assemble those parts into a clear, complete whole.

1 *Identify the part of a formal report and the contribution each part makes to the overall effectiveness of a report.*

Parts of a Formal Report

The differences between a formal report and an informal report lie in the format and possibly in writing style. The type of report you prepare depends on the subject matter, the purpose of the report, and the readers' needs. At the short, informal end of the report continuum described in Chapter 9, a report could look exactly like a brief memorandum. At the long, formal extreme of the continuum, the report might include most or all of the parts shown in Figure 11-1.

A business report rarely contains all of these parts. They are listed here simply to name all possible parts. The preliminary parts and addenda are mechanical items that support the body of a report. The body contains the report of the research and covers the four steps in the research process. The organization of the body of a report leads to the construction of the contents page.

Because individuals usually write to affect or influence others favorably, they often add parts as the number of pages increases. When a report exceeds one or two pages, you might add a cover or title page. When the body of a report exceeds four or five pages, you might even add a finishing touch by placing the report in a plastic cover or ring binder, or binding in a professional manner. Reports frequently take on the characteristics of the formal end of the continuum simply by reason of length.

What factors determine the parts of a report that are desirable to include?

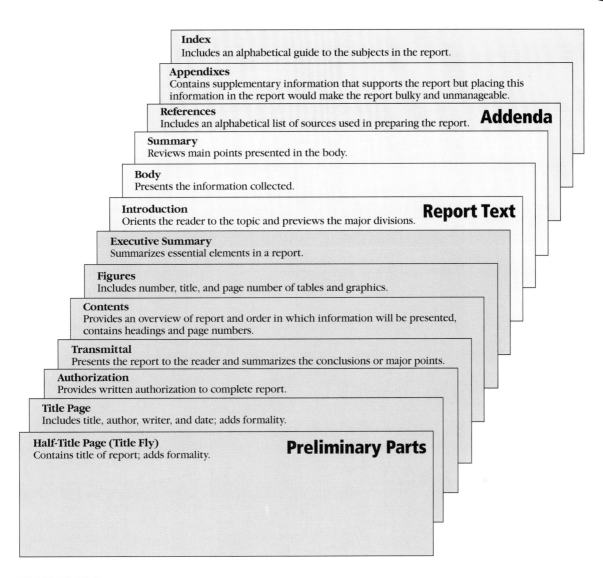

Index
Includes an alphabetical guide to the subjects in the report.

Appendixes
Contains supplementary information that supports the report but placing this information in the report would make the report bulky and unmanageable.

References
Includes an alphabetical list of sources used in preparing the report. **Addenda**

Summary
Reviews main points presented in the body.

Body
Presents the information collected.

Introduction
Orients the reader to the topic and previews the major divisions. **Report Text**

Executive Summary
Summarizes essential elements in a report.

Figures
Includes number, title, and page number of tables and graphics.

Contents
Provides an overview of report and order in which information will be presented, contains headings and page numbers.

Transmittal
Presents the report to the reader and summarizes the conclusions or major points.

Authorization
Provides written authorization to complete report.

Title Page
Includes title, author, writer, and date; adds formality.

Half-Title Page (Title Fly) **Preliminary Parts**
Contains title of report; adds formality.

FIGURE 11-1
Parts of a formal report: preliminary parts, report text, and addenda.

First, note how the preliminary parts and addenda items shown in Figure 11-2 increase in number as the report increases in length. Second, notice the order in which report parts appear in a complete report.

Memo and letter reports are seldom longer than a page or two, but they can be expanded into several pages. As depicted, long reports may include some special pages that do not appear in short reports. The format you select—long or short, formal or informal—may help determine the supporting preliminary and addenda items to include.

To understand how each part of a formal report contributes to reader comprehension and ease of access to the information in the report, study the following explanations of each part in the three basic categories: preliminary parts, report text, and

FIGURE 11-2
The number of assisting items increases as the length of a report increases.

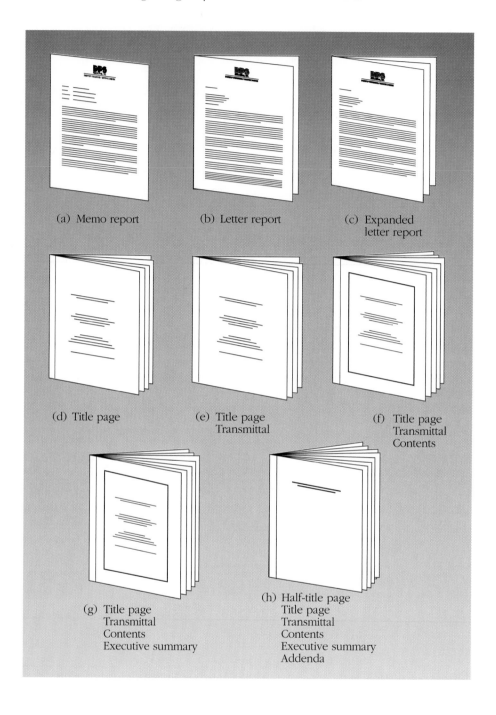

(a) Memo report

(b) Letter report

(c) Expanded letter report

(d) Title page

(e) Title page
Transmittal

(f) Title page
Transmittal
Contents

(g) Title page
Transmittal
Contents
Executive summary

(h) Half-title page
Title page
Transmittal
Contents
Executive summary
Addenda

addenda. Figure 11-1 illustrates how these three sections are combined to prepare a complete formal report.

Preliminary Parts

How would you respond to the statement that preliminary pages are mere window dressing?

Preliminary parts are included to add formality to a report, repeat report content, and aid the reader in locating information in the report quickly and in understanding the report more easily. These parts include the half-title page, title page, authorization, transmittal, contents, figures, and executive summary. Preliminary pages are numbered with small Roman numerals (i, ii, iii, and so on).

Half-Title Page. Often called a **title fly**, the **half-title page** is a single page containing only the report title. This page simply adds formality and enhances the appearance of a report. In less formal reports, including letter and memorandum reports, the half-title page is omitted.

Title Page. The **title page** includes the title, author, date, and frequently the name of the person or organization that requested the report. A title page is often added when the writer opts to use a formal report format rather than a memorandum or a letter arrangement.

> Write an effective title for a report to select an automobile type to replace company cars driven by a real estate company's sales staff.

The selected title should be descriptive and comprehensive; its words should reflect the content of the report. Avoid short, vague titles or excessively long titles. Instead, use concise wording to identify the topic adequately. For example, a title such as "Marketing Survey: Noncarbonated Beverages" leaves the reader confused when the title could have been "Noncarbonated Beverage Preferences of College Students in Boston." To give some clues for writing a descriptive title, think of the "Five Ws": *Who, What, When, Where,* and *Why.* Avoid such phrases as "A Study of . . .," "A Critical Analysis of . . .," or "A Review of. . . ."

Follow company procedures or a style manual to place the title attractively on the page. If the title is longer than one line, arrange it in the inverted pyramid format; that is, make each succeeding line shorter than the line preceding it. Arrange the title consistently on the half-title page, title page, and the first page of a report. The inverted pyramid format also should be used in titles of graphics. Note the arrangement of the following title of a graphic:

Incorrect:	AVERAGE PER CAPITA INCOME IN 1999 FOR TEN STATES
Incorrect:	AVERAGE PER CAPITA INCOME IN 1999 FOR TEN STATES
Correct:	AVERAGE PER CAPITA INCOME IN 1999 FOR TEN STATES

Authorization. An **authorization** is a letter or memorandum authorizing the researcher to conduct a specific research project. The authorization is included as a formal part of the report and follows the title page. If no written authorization is provided, authorization information may be included in the letter of transmittal or the introduction. This information might include a clear description of the problem, limitations restricting the research, resources available, and deadlines.

Transmittal. As a report becomes more formal, the writer may attach a **letter** or **memorandum of transmittal**. The transmittal serves two purposes: (1) to present the report to the one who requested it, and (2) to provide the conclusion from an analytical study or highlights from an informational report. If the writer has prepared a report for a person or a department inside the company, the writer uses the memorandum format for the transmittal. A consultant preparing a report for another company arranges the transmittal in a letter format.

The transmittal letter or memorandum is the writer's opportunity to speak directly to the reader in an informal tone. Thus, the writer may include first- and second-person pronouns in the transmittal. If the report includes an executive summary or a detailed introduction, the transmittal is short. Use the deductive approach and follow these suggested steps:

1. Let the first sentence present the report and remind the reader that he or she requested it.
2. Explain the subject of the report in the first paragraph.
3. Present brief conclusions and, if called for, the recommendations.
4. Close cordially. The closing paragraph may also express appreciation for the cooperation given by the company.

Contents. The **contents** provides the reader with an analytical overview of the report and the order in which information is presented. Thus, this preliminary part aids the reader in understanding the report and in locating a specific section of it. The list includes the name and location (beginning page number) of every report part except the half-title page, title page, and contents. Include the list of figures and the transmittal, executive summary, report headings, references, appendixes, and index. Placing spaced periods (leaders) between the report part and the page numbers helps lead the reader's eyes to the appropriate page number.

Word processing software simplifies the time-consuming, tedious task of preparing many of the preliminary and addenda report parts, including the contents. Because the software can generate these parts automatically, report writers can make last-minute changes to a report and still have time to update preliminary and addenda parts.

Figures. To aid the reader in locating a specific graphic in a report with many graphics, the writer might include a list of figures separate from the contents. The list should include a reference to each figure that appears in the report, identified by both figure number and name, along with the page number on which the figure occurs. The contents and the figures can be combined on one page if both lists are brief. Word processing software can be used to generate the list of figures automatically.

Executive Summary. The executive summary (also called the abstract, overview, or précis) summarizes the essential elements in an entire report. This overview simplifies the reader's understanding of a long report. The executive summary is positioned before the first page of the report.

Typically, an executive summary is included when the writer believes it will assist the reader in understanding a long, complex report. Because of the increased volume of information that managers must review, managers tend to require an executive summary regardless of the length and complexity of a report. The executive summary presents the report in miniature: the introduction, body, and summary as well as conclusions and recommendations, if they are included in the report. Thus, an executive summary should (1) introduce briefly the report and preview the major divisions, (2) summarize the major sections of the report, and (3) summarize the report summary and any conclusions and recommendations. Pay special attention to topic sentences and to concluding sentences in paragraphs or within sections of reports. This technique helps you write concise executive summaries based on major ideas and reduces the use of supporting details and background information.

To assist them in staying up-to-date professionally, many busy executives require assistants to prepare executive summaries of articles they do not have time to read and conferences and meetings they cannot attend. Many practitioner journals now include an executive summary of each article. Reading the executive summary provides the gist of the article and alerts the executive to pertinent articles that should be read in detail.

How does the contents page contribute to the coherence of a formal report?

How can the executive summary serve a useful purpose without being redundant?

Using your library's on-line database, locate an article about effective report writing. Write a summary of the article and be prepared to share with the class.

Report Text

The report itself contains the introduction, body, summary, and any conclusions and recommendations. Report pages are numbered with Arabic numerals (1, 2, 3, and so on).

Introduction. The introduction orients the reader to the problem. It may include the following items:

- What the topic is.
- Why it is being reported on.
- The scope and limitations of the research.
- Where the information came from.
- An explanation of special terminology.
- A preview of the major sections of the report to provide coherence and transitions:
  - How the topic is divided into parts.
  - The order in which the parts will be presented.

Body. The **body**, often called the heart of the report, presents the information collected and relates it to the problem. To increase readability and coherence, this section contains numerous headings to denote the various divisions within a report. Refer to "Organization of Formal Reports" in this chapter for an in-depth discussion of preparing the body.

Summary, Conclusions, and Recommendations. An informational report ends with a brief **summary** that serves an important function: It adds unity to a report by reviewing the main points presented in the body. A summary includes only material that is discussed in a report. Introducing a new idea in the summary may make the reader wonder why the point was not developed earlier. It may suggest that the study was not adequately completed or that the writer did not adequately plan the report before beginning to write. Finally, a summary, which is expected to be fairly short, does not provide enough space for developing a new idea.

What is the difference between an informational and an analytical report? What applications do the two types have in business settings?

An **analytical report**, designed to solve a specific problem or answer research questions, may also include a summary of the major research findings, particularly if the report is lengthy. Reviewing the major findings prepares the reader for the conclusions that follow. An analytical report also includes **conclusions**, inferences the writer draws from the findings. If required by the person/organization authorizing the report, recommendations follow the conclusions. **Recommendations** present the writer's opinion on a possible course of action based on the conclusions. Review the examples of findings, conclusions, and recommendations presented in Chapter 9 if necessary.

For a long report, the writer may place the summary, the conclusions, and the recommendations in three separate sections. For shorter reports, conclusions and recommendations can be combined into one section, or all three sections can be combined.

Addenda

What addenda parts might be added to a report on a comparison of three brands of office copiers?

The **addenda** to a report may include all materials used in the research but not appropriate to be included in the report itself. The three basic addenda parts are the references, appendixes, and index. Addenda parts continue with the same page numbering system used in the body of the report.

References. The **references** (also called *works cited*) section is an alphabetical listing of the sources used in preparing the report. Because the writer may be influenced by any information consulted, some reference manuals require all sources consulted to be included in the reference list. When the reference list includes sources not cited in the report, it is referred to as a **bibliography** or a **list of works consulted**. If a report includes endnotes rather than in-text parenthetical citations (author and date within the text), the endnotes precede the references. Using word processing software to create footnotes and endnotes alleviates much of the monotony and repetition of preparing accurate documentation. Refer to "Documenting Referenced Material" in Chapter 9, Appendix B, or a style manual for specific guidelines for preparing and citations.

When executives for Seattle-based Starbucks Coffee, now a sizable coffee shop franchise, decided to expand the business nation wide, they thought logically about the merits of each potential location. They weighed carefully the advantages and disadvantages of each location against a list of criteria. An analytical report written to justify a particular site should be organized using the same logic. The pros and cons of each alternative are presented in major sections that *emphasize the criteria* used in making the decision.

Appendix. An **appendix** contains supplementary information that supports the report but is not appropriate for inclusion in the report itself. This information may include questionnaires and accompanying transmittal letters, summary tabulations, verbatim comments from respondents, complex mathematical computations and formulas, legal documents, and a variety of items the writer presents to support the body of the report and the quality of the research. Placing supplementary material in an appendix prevents the body from becoming excessively long.

If the report contains more than one appendix, label each with a capital letter and a title. For example, the four appendixes (or appendices) in a report could be identified as follows:

Appendix A: Cover Letter Accompanying End-User Questionnaire

Appendix B: End-User Questionnaire

Appendix C: Means of 20 Technology Competencies

Appendix D: Number and Percentage of Ratings Given to 20 Technology Competencies

Each item included in the appendix must be mentioned in the report. References within the report to the four appendixes mentioned in the previous example follow:

A copy of the end-user questionnaire (Appendix A), a cover letter (Appendix B), and a stamped, preaddressed envelope were mailed to 1,156 firms on February 15, 1999.

Means were computed, and the total means were ranked to establish an order of importance for the 20 technology competencies as shown in Table 10. The means are shown in Appendix C, and the frequency distribution from which these means were computed is provided in Appendix D.

Index. The **index** is an alphabetical guide to the subject matter in a report. The subject and each page number on which the subject appears are listed. Word processing software can generate the index automatically. Each time a new draft is prepared, a new index with revised terms and correct page numbers can be generated quickly and easily.

Organization of Formal Reports

Organize report findings.

The authors of certain types of publications known as tabloids typically have no valid documentation to support their claims, so they make their own support. Hopefully, absolutely no one believes them. The purpose of such publications is to entertain, not to inform. The writer of a bona fide report must, however, do a much more convincing and thorough job of reporting.

Writing Convincing and Effective Reports

As discussed in Chapter 9, reports often require that the writer conduct research to find quotes, statistics, or ideas from others to back up the ideas presented. This support from outside sources serves to bolster the research as well as the writer's credibility. Doing research and taking notes, however, are only parts of the process of putting together a well-documented, acceptable report. Careful organization and formatting assure that the reader will be able to understand and comprehend the information presented. While many companies have their own style manuals that gives examples of acceptable formats for reports, this section presents some general organization guidelines.

Locate a brief article on a topic assigned by your instructor. Outline the article, using first, second, and third level headings.

Outlining and Sequencing. The content outline serves as a framework on which to build the report. In the development of the outline, the writer identifies the major and minor points that are to be covered in the report and organizes them into a logical sequence. Outlining of a formal report is an essential prerequisite to writing the report. The outline is a planning document and is thus subject to modification as the writer develops the report.

Development of an outline requires that the writer think about the information to be presented and how it can best be organized for the clear understanding of the reader. Assume, for instance, that you must select a personal computer from among three comparable brands from three vendors—IBM, Compaq, and Gateway. You must choose the computer that will best serve the computing needs of a small office and present your justification and recommendations in a **justification report**.

You gather all information available from suppliers of the three computers; you operate each computer personally; and you compare the three against a variety of criteria. Your final selection is the Gateway. Why did you select it? What criteria served as decision guides? When you write the report, you will have to tell the reader—the one who will pay for the equipment—how the selection was made in such a way that the reader is "sold" on your conclusion.

If you organize your report so that you tell the reader everything about the IBM, the Compaq, and then the Gateway, the reader may have trouble making comparisons. Your content outline might look like this:

> I. Introduction
>   A. The Problem
>   B. The Method Used
> II. IBM
> III. Compaq
> IV. Gateway
> V. Conclusion

Note that this outline devotes three Roman-numeral sections to the findings, one to the introduction that presents the problem and the method, and one to the conclusion. This division is appropriate because the most space must be devoted to the findings. However, the reader may have difficulty comparing the expansion capacity of the computers because the information is in three different places. Would discussing the expansion capacity of all three in the same section of the report be better? Would prices be compared more easily if they were all in the same section? Most reports should be divided into sections that reflect the criteria used rather than into sections devoted to the alternatives compared.

If you selected your computer based on cost, service/warranties, and expandability, these criteria (rather than the computers themselves) might serve as divisions of the findings. Then your content outline would appear this way:

> I. Introduction
>   A. The Problem
>   B. The Method Used
> II. Compaq Is Least Expensive
> III. Service/Warranties Favor Gateway
> IV. Expandability Is Best on Gateway
> V. Availability of Software Is Equal
> VI. Gateway Is the Best Buy

The outline now has six major sections and two subsections. Four major sections are devoted to the findings. When the report is prepared in this way, the features of each computer (the evaluation criteria) are compared in the same section, and the reader is led logically to the conclusion.

Note the headings used in Sections II–VI. These are called **talking headings** because they talk about the content of the section and even give a conclusion about the section. Adding page numbers after each outline item will convert the outline into a contents page. Interestingly, the headings justify the selection of the Gateway. As a result, a knowledgeable reader who has confidence in the researcher might be satisfied by reading only the content headings.

In addition to organizing findings by criteria, report writers can use other organizational plans. The comparison of three computers was an analytical process. When a report is informational and not analytical, you should use the most logical organization. Treat your material as a "whole" unit. A report on sales might be divided by geographic sales region, by product groups sold, by price range, or by time periods. A report on the development of a product might use chronological order. By visualizing the whole report first, you can then divide it into its major components and perhaps divide the major components into their parts. Remember, a section must divide into at least two parts, or it cannot be divided at all. Thus, in an outline you must have a "B" subsection if you have an "A" subsection following a Roman numeral, or you should not have any subsections. **Parallel language** should also be used in subdivisions of the same level. For instance, if Point A is worded as a noun phrase, Point B should be worded in the same manner. Or if Point I is a complete sentence, Points II and III should also be worded as sentences.

A final caution: Beware of overdividing the sections. Too many divisions might make the report appear disorganized and choppy. On the other hand, too few divisions might create a problem for the reader. Note how the four steps of research have been developed through headings to the Roman-numeral outline and to a contents page for a report, as shown in Figure 11-3.

> Write talking headings for a report designed to select an automobile type to replace company cars driven by a real estate company sales staff.

> Why is parallel structure necessary in outlining and also in report divisions?

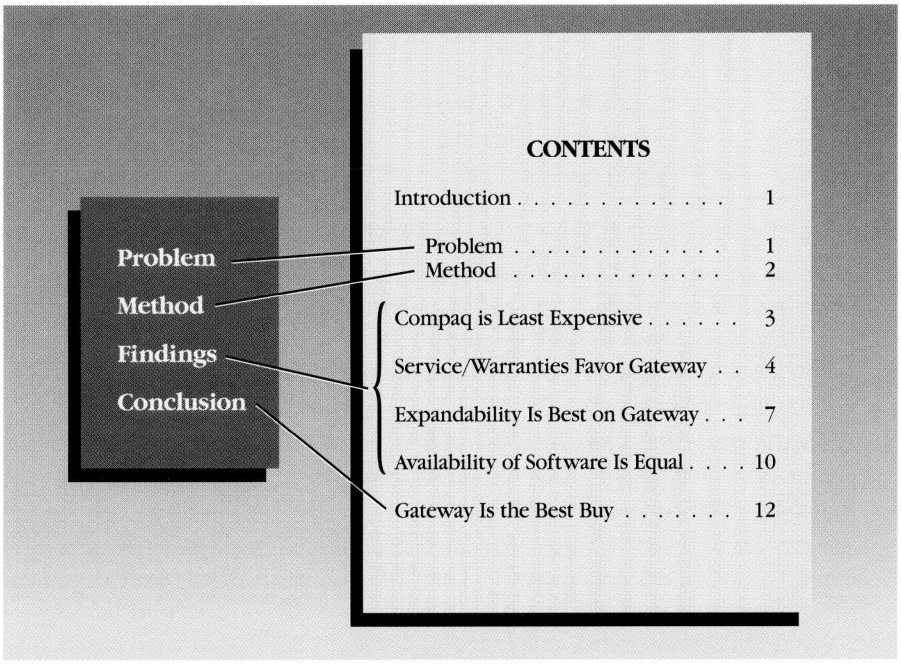

FIGURE 11-3
The basic outline expands into a contents page.

CONTENTS

Introduction   1

Problem   1
Method   2

Compaq is Least Expensive   3

Service/Warranties Favor Gateway . .   4

Expandability Is Best on Gateway . . .   7

Availability of Software Is Equal 10

Gateway Is the Best Buy 12

Problem
Method
Findings
Conclusion

When developing content outlines, some report writers believe that readers expect the beginning of the body to be an introduction, so they begin the outline with the first heading related to findings. In our example, then, Section I would be "Compaq Is Least Expensive." Additionally, when they reach the contents page, readers may eliminate the Roman numeral or other outline symbols.

The research process consists of inductively arranged steps as shown in Figure 11-3: (1) Problem, (2) Method, (3) Findings, and (4) Conclusion. When the report is organized in the same order, its users must read through the body to learn about the conclusions—generally the most important part of the report to users. To make the reader's job easier, report writers may organize the report deductively, with the conclusions at the beginning. This sequence is usually achieved by placing a synopsis or summary at the beginning:

REPORT TITLE IN DEDUCTIVE SEQUENCE REVEALS THE CONCLUSION

    I. Conclusion Reported in the Synopsis
   II. Body of the Report
        A. Problem
        B. Method
        C. Findings
  III. Conclusion

This arrangement permits the reader to get the primary message early and then to look for support in the body of the report. The deductive arrangement contributes to the repetitious nature of reports, but it also contributes to effective reporting.

Using Headings Effectively. Headings are signposts informing readers about what text is ahead. Headings take their positions from their relative importance in a complete outline. For example, in a Roman numeral outline, "I" is a first-level heading, "A" is a second-level heading, and "1" is a third-level heading:

    I. First-Level Heading
        A. Second-Level Heading
        B. Second-Level Heading
            1. Third-Level Heading
            2. Third-Level Heading
   II. First-Level Heading

Two important points about the use of headings also relate to outlines:

- ***Because second-level headings are subdivisions of first-level headings, you should have at least two subdivisions (A and B).*** Otherwise, the first-level heading cannot be divided—something divides into at least two parts or it is not divisible. The same logic applies to the use of third-level headings following second-level headings.

- ***All headings of the same level must be treated consistently.*** Consistent elements include the physical position on the page, appearance (type style, underline), and grammatical construction.

As you review Figure 11-4, note that one blank line precedes first- and second-level headings. This method is not universal; identify the format specified by the documentation style you are using and follow it consistently to aid the reader. A further suggestion, as you will observe in the sample report in Figure 11-10, is to avoid placing two headings consecutively without any intervening text. For example, always write something following a first-level heading and before the initial second-level heading.

With word processing programs, you can develop fourth- and fifth-level headings simply by using boldface, underline, and varying fonts. In short reports, however, organization rarely goes beyond third-level headings; thoughtful organization can limit excessive heading levels in formal reports.

Writing Style for Formal Reports. The writing style of long, formal reports is more formal than that used in many other routine business documents. The following suggestions should be applied when writing a formal report:

- *Avoid first-person pronouns as a rule.* In formal reports, the use of *I* is generally unacceptable. Because of the objective nature of research, the

FIGURE 11-4

Effective heading formats for reports divided into three levels.

❶ **REPORT TITLE**

xxxx xxxx xxxxxxx xxx xxxx xxxxxxx xxxxxxxx xxxxxxxxx xxx xxx xxxx xxxx xxxxxxxxx xxxxxxx xxxx xxxxxxxxx xxxxxxx. xx xxxxxxx xxxxxxxx xxxxxxxxxxxxxxx xxxxxxxx xxxxx xxxxxxxx xxxx xxxxx xxxxxxx.

xxx xxxxxx xxxxxxxx xxxxx xxxxxx xxxxx xxxxxx xxxxx xxxxx xxxx xxxx xxxxxxxxx xxxx xxxxxxx xxxxxxx xxxxxxx. xxxxxxxx xxxxxxx xxxxx xxxxxxxx xxx x xxxxxx xxxx xxxxxxxxx xxxxx xxxxx xxxxxx xxxxxxxxx xxxxx xxxxxxxxx.

❷ **First-Level Heading**

xxxx xxxxxxxx xxxx xxxx xxxxxxx xxxxxx xxxxx xxxx xxxxxxx xxxxx xxx xxxxxxxx xx xxxxxxx x xxxxxx xxxxx xxxxx xxxxx xxxxx xxxxxxxxx.

❸ <u>Second-Level Subheading</u>

xxx xxxxxxx xxxx xxx xxxxxxx xxxxx xx xxxx xxxx xxxxxxx xxx xxxx xxxx xxxxxx x xxxxxxxx xxxx x xxxxxx xxxxxxxxx xxxxxxx. xxxxxxxx xxxxxx xxxxxxx xxxx.

<u>Second-Level Subheading</u>

x xxxx xxxxxxxxx xxxx xxxx xxxx xxxx xxxx xxxx xxx xxxxxx xxxx xxxx xxx xxxxxx xxx xxxxxxx xxxxxx xxxxxxx xxxxxxxx xxxxxxxx xxxxx.

❹ <u>Third-level subheading</u>. xxxxxx xx xxxx xxxxxxxx xxxxx xxx xxx xxxxxx xxxxx xxx xxxx xxxxxx xxxx xxx xxxx xxxx xxxx.

<u>Third-level subheading</u>. x xxxxxxx xxxxxxx xxx xxxxxx xxxxx xxxxxx xxxx xxx xxxxxxxx xxxxxxx xxx xxx xxxxxxxxxx xxxxxxxxx. xxxxxxx xxxx xxxxxxx.

First-Level Heading

xxxxxxx xxxxxxxxxx xxxx xxxxxx x xxxxxx xxxxxxx xxxx xxxxxxxx xxxx xxxxxx xxxxxx xxxxxx xxxxxxxxx xxxx xxxxxx xxxxx xxxx.

❶ Centers and capitalizes all letters in the report title.

❷ Centers first-level headings and capitalizes initial letters.

❸ Places second-level subheadings at the left margin, underlines, and capitalizes initial letters.

❹ Indents third-level subheadings as a part of the paragraph, underlines, and capitalizes first letter.

fewer personal references you use the better. However, in some organizations the first person is acceptable. Certainly, writing is easier when you can use yourselves as subjects of sentences. People who can change their writing by avoiding the use of the first person will develop a genuine skill.

- ***Use active voice.*** "Authorization was received from the IRS" might not be as effective as "The IRS granted authorization." Subjects that can be visualized are advantageous, but you should also attempt to use the things most important to the report as subjects. If "authorization" were more important than "IRS," the writer should stay with the first version.

- ***Use tense consistently.*** Because you are writing about past actions, much of your report writing is in the past tense. However, when you call the reader's attention to the content of a graphic, remember that the graphic *shows* in the present tense. If you mention where the study *will take* the reader, use a future-tense verb.

- ***Use transition sentences to link sections of a report.*** Because you are writing a report in parts, show the connection between those parts by using transition sentences. "Although several advantages accrue from its use, the incentive plan also presents problems" may be a sentence written at the end of a section stressing advantages and before a section stressing problems.

- ***Use a variety of coherence techniques.*** Just as transition sentences bind portions of a report together, certain coherence techniques bind sentences together: repeating a word, using a pronoun, or using a conjunction. If such devices are used, each sentence seems to be joined smoothly to the next. These words and phrases keep you from making abrupt changes in thought.

Compose a transition sentence that could be used to move from a discussion of Brand A photocopier to Brand B as the better choice for company purchase.

Time Connectors	**Contrast Connectors**
finally	although
further	despite
furthermore	however
initially	in contrast
meanwhile	nevertheless
next	on the other hand
since	on the contrary
then	yet
thereafter	
while	
at the same time	

Similarity Connectors	**Cause-and-Effect Connectors**
for instance	but
for example	conversely
likewise	because
in the same way	consequently
just as	hence
similarly	therefore
thus	

These words and phrases keep you from making abrupt changes in thought. Refer to Chapter 3, "Link Ideas to Achieve Coherence" to review a detailed discussion of coherence techniques.

- ***Use tabulations and enumerations.*** When you have a series of items, give each a number and list them consecutively. This list of writing suggestions is easier to understand because it contains numbered or bulleted items.

- ***Define terms carefully.*** When terms might have specific meanings in the study, define them. Definitions should be written in the term-family-differentiation sequence: "A dictionary (*term*) is a reference book (*family*) that contains a list of all words in a language (*point of difference*)." "A sophomore is a college student in the second year." Refer to Chapter 9 for additional information on defining terms in a research study.

- ***Check for variety.*** While you write, most of your attention should be directed toward presenting the right ideas and support. When reviewing the rough draft, you may discover certain portions with a monotonous sameness in sentence length or construction. Changes are easy and well worth the effort. These stylistic techniques become habitual through experience; you can apply them while concentrating primarily on presenting and supporting ideas at the first-draft stage. Make necessary improvements later.

Enhancing Credibility. Readers are more likely to accept your research as valid and reliable if you have designed the research effectively and collected, interpreted, and presented the data in an objective, unbiased manner. The following writing suggestions will enhance your credibility as a researcher:

- ***Avoid emotional terms.*** "The increase was fantastic" doesn't convince anyone. However, "The increase was 88 percent—more than double that of the previous year" does convince.

- ***Identify assumptions.*** Assumptions are things or conditions taken for granted. However, when you make an assumption, state that clearly. Statements such as "Assuming all other factors remain the same, . . ." inform the reader of an important assumption.

- ***Label opinions.*** Facts are preferred over opinion, but sometimes the opinion of a recognized professional is the closest thing to fact. "In the opinion of legal counsel, . . ." lends conviction to the statement that follows and lends credence to the integrity of the writer.

How can the report writer "dignify" an included opinion?

- ***Use documentation.*** Citations and references (works cited) are evidence of the writer's scholarship and honesty. These methods acknowledge the use of secondary material in the research.

The preparation of reports is also influenced by diversity, as discussed in the Strategic Forces box.

If you have not learned to use the automatic footnoting feature of your word processing software, take the time to master that feature now.

Creating an Environment Conducive to Writing. A writing procedure that works well for one person may not work for another; however, consider the following general suggestions:

- ***Begin writing only after you have reached a conclusion and prepared a suitable outline.*** Avoid floundering.

- ***Select a good writing environment.*** Avoid distractions.

- ***Start planning early and give yourself more time than you anticipate using.*** "Burning the midnight oil" is sometimes necessary, but it does not always produce your best work.

Strategic Forces: Diversity Challenges

Disclosure in Annual Financial Reports of International Firms

The annual financial report is the basic tool used by investors to compare the performance of various companies. While U. S. firms must comply with Security and Exchange Commission (SEC) requirements for disclosure, the extent to which information is reported by companies based abroad varies. For the most part, companies in English-speaking countries do a good job with disclosure. Annual reports of American and British firms provide much more than just a balance sheet and a profit-and-loss statement; they typically provide a comprehensive set of notes giving additional information—for instance, on how a firm's pension liabilities are calculated or whether assets have been sold and leased back. Heightened requirements for disclosure in the United States represent solid progress in enhancing the user's understanding of the choices and judgments that underlie a set of financial statements. On the other hand, some information published in the annual report must be limited in detail, to prevent competitors and possible takeover bidders from gaining useful but damaging knowledge of the organization.[2]

In other countries, however, such as Germany, any information beyond the basic annual report is often nonexistent, in published form or otherwise. National requirements vary, as do the voluntary responses of individual companies within a given country. More and more international firms, however, are beginning to report their financial results according the International Accounting Standards (IAS)—a body of rules developed in the 1970s, and currently under revision by an international committee of accountants, financial executives, and equity analysts. In the United States, the SEC still

requires, however, that international firms that wish to list their shares on an American exchange must comply with the United States. Generally Accepted Accounting Principles. The IAS is, however, a step in the right direction for improving disclosure.

Currently, in the United States and some other countries, the annual financial report of a firm is recognized as communicating much more than just the accounting summary for the organization's performance. Management realizes that this single communication document is scrutinized by three vital partners to the organization's success: the customers, the owners, and the employees. In addition to projecting profitability, many U. S. firms see the annual report as a vehicle for illuminating prevailing management philosophy, projecting corporate charisma, and humanizing themselves to their publics.[3]

Application:

Using the Internet or a published source, obtain the annual financial report for a company based abroad. Write a short report that analyzes your responses to the following questions:

- Did the report contain the company's mission statement?
- Was the company's code of ethics, or credo, included?
- Was information provided about the company directors, officers, and/or executives?
- Were the major shareholders reported?
- What currency was used in the financial reporting (dollars, yen, pounds, etc.).
- Was evidence provided of company concern for the environment or charities?
- How extensive and sophisticated were the report's graphics and photos?

- ***Set aside long, uninterrupted blocks of writing time.*** It takes time to get your thought processes moving; interruptions of time require you to backtrack.

- ***Write rapidly and plan to revise later.*** Do not attempt to edit as you go—you only waste time and lose your train of creative thought.

- ***Begin with an easy section.*** The confidence gained from completing this section may help prepare you for more difficult ones.

- ***Skip difficult places when composing and return to them later.*** Usually you won't find these sections as difficult then.

- ***Set aside the first draft for a day or two. Editing and rewriting immediately may not pay off.*** A report you have just written may look great; tomorrow you may see that it needs some work.

- ***Review for possible improvement.*** Some points might need more supporting evidence. Reading your writing aloud reveals awkward grammatical construction and poor wording. Silent reading often misses these errors.

- ***Rewrite where necessary.*** Rewriting is more than editing; sometimes you may have to rewrite weak material completely without reference to the original.

Analyzing a Formal Report

A complete, long report is illustrated in Figure 11-10 beginning on page 415. The notations next to the text will help you understand how effective presentation and writing principles are applied. APA style requires that reports be double-spaced and that the first line of each paragraph be indented five spaces; however, a company's report-writing style manual may override this style and stipulate single-spacing without paragraph indents. The sample report in Figure 11-10 is single-spaced, and paragraphs are not indented to save space and give a more professional appearance. The report may be considered formal and contains the following parts:

> Title Page
> Transmittal
> Contents
> Executive Summary
> Figures
> Report Text (Introduction, Body, Summary, Conclusions, and Recommendations)
> References
> Appendix

This sample should not be considered the only way to prepare reports, but it is an acceptable model. Following the sample report, the "Check Your Writing" section provides a comprehensive checklist for use in report writing.

3 *Prepare effective formal reports using an acceptable format and writing style.*

Short Reports

Short reports incorporate many of the same organizational strategies as do long reports. However, most **short reports** include only the minimum supporting materials to achieve effective communication. Short reports focus on the body—problem, method, findings, and conclusion. In addition, short reports might incorporate any of the following features:

4 *Prepare effective short reports in letter and memorandum formats.*

- Personal writing style using first- or second-person. Contractions are appropriate when they contribute to a natural style.

- Graphics to reinforce the written text.

- Headings and subheadings to partition portions of the body and to reflect organization.

- Memorandum and letter formats when appropriate.

COMMUNICATION IN ACTION

James F. Hoobler, Inspector General
U.S. Small Business Administration

In a place as large as Washington, D.C., James Hoobler simply cannot have one-to-one meetings with all the constituencies his office serves. As a result, written reports must fill the gap. Hoobler, Inspector General in the Small Business Administration (SBA), is appointed by the President, confirmed by the Senate, and reports directly to the administration of the Executive Branch and to the Congress. The numerous reports his office produces compete with large volumes of written materials from other areas in Washington. Because of the nature of his office, his reports are distributed widely.

Hoobler stresses the importance of audience analysis. "We target senior administration officials, including the head of the SBA, deputy director, Congress, and the Office of Management and Budget. Typically, they will only read the executive summary," he said. "On the other hand, our program managers, who direct various divisions in the SBA, will 'pick the report apart.'"

"SBA's credibility is on the line every time we produce a report," Hoobler said. He understands the importance of articulating findings clearly and writing sensible recommendations. "Consider our audit reports. They must be anchored in hard research with the right amount of empirical support," he emphasizes. "In Washington, if the material you have written does not make sense, or is poorly or sloppily written, your report will go to the bottom of the heap."

Hoobler's office has three principal functions. Having responsibility for all internal and external auditing in the SBA, the office communicates results to a wide array of audiences. These audiences include "bureaucrats," U.S. citizens, program participants, and whoever benefits from the SBA. In addition to auditing, his office produces criminal investigation reports. These factual reports reach unique audiences in the Justice Department. The Inspector General's office also evaluates program performance and efficiency and develops reports within its agency.

When stressing the importance of including the right parts of a report, Hoobler tells how investigative reports differ from audit and evaluative reports: "Our 'Best Practices' report, for example, is an evaluation study. We always include an executive summary, the part most read by our program managers." While audit reports also include an executive summary, he notes that they differ by addressing a problem, finding a solution, and presenting a series of recommendations.

On the investigative side, Hoobler frequently presents evidence to the Executive Office of the U.S. Attorney. "These reports are factual and must be defensible. Again, your credibility is on the line. What you communicate must be clear," Hoobler asserts. "If someone is misled or gets the wrong impression, our office loses credibility." Depositions frequently appear in these reports and include a person's background and history. Although the investigative report is not quite as formal as an audit or an evaluative report, Hoobler includes an executive summary. If a congressional representative asks for a follow-up report of an investigation, Hoobler includes a longer summary report, which is not made public.

Applying What You Have Learned

1. How will a reader be affected by a sloppily written Small Business Administration report?

2. Explain how Hoobler adapted formal reports to various audiences.

Currently I am a participant on a "quality team" with the task to redesign the staffing process. Only two team members are human resource professionals. Thus, our team has seen that input from members from other areas of the business brings another dimension to the hiring process and allows human resources to become a strategic partner with the business.

At the beginning of each meeting, we review the day's agenda. The team abides by ground rules that each team member agreed upon when the team was established. Rules include the following: no side conversations are allowed; keep focused (no digressing); no idea is stupid; no one member can dominate the discussion; and everyone is expected to participate. Without the buy-in of each team member, any one of these issues could have become a point of contention for the team. Additionally, we, have a "parking lot" that serves as a resource bank where we "park" ideas that should be reserved for

later discussions or ideas that we, as a team, have no authority to change but can refer the issue to the appropriate individual(s) who can affect change.

The reward of teamwork is not only rolling out a final product that adds value to the company but also gaining the opportunity to build relationships, brainstorm, and share ideas with other professionals who may become future resources for other projects and a referral source for other business professionals. For example, recently I was able to identify expert speakers for an event I was planning—all as a result of networks made during previous teambuilding sessions.

Because of the vital importance of teamwork, this job skill is an important criterion for job selection. During the interviewing process, I attempt to determine an applicant's ability to play different roles, to discuss input points that lead the group toward consensus, to be flexible, and to compromise one's ideas for the success of the team.

Marquette L. Wilson, Manager, Human Resources
GE Capital Commercial Finance

Memorandum and Letter Reports

Short reports are often written in letter or memorandum format. The letter report is directed to a reader outside the organization, while the memorandum report is directed to an organizational insider. Both types of short reports are illustrated in the examples in Figures 11-5 and 11-6. The commentary in the left column will help you understand how effective writing principles are applied.

The report in Figure 11-5 communicates the activity of a company's child care services during one quarter of the fiscal period. This periodic report is formatted as a memorandum because it is prepared for personnel within the company and is a brief, informal report. Outside consultants present their audit of a company's software policy in the letter report in Figure 11-6.

The report in Figure 11-7 is written deductively. Effective nonverbal communication is presented as the key ingredient in the success of the client's expansion into the Kuwaiti market. The consultant briefly describes the procedures used to analyze the problem, presents the findings in a logical sequence, and provides specific recommendations. The letter format is appropriate because a consultant is writing to a client (external audience).

Form Reports

Form reports meet the demand for numerous, repetitive reports. College registration forms, applications for credit, airline tickets, and bank checks are examples of simple form reports. Form reports have the following benefits:

FIGURE 11-5
Short, periodic report in
memorandum format.

① Includes headings to
serve the function of the
transmittal and a title
page in a formal report.

② Includes a horizontal
line to add interest and to
separate the transmittal
from the body of the
memo.

③ Uses deductive
approach to present this
periodic report requested
by management on a
quarterly basis.

④ Uses headings to
highlight standard infor-
mation; allows for easy
update when preparing a
subsequent report.

⑤ Includes primary data
collected from a survey
completed by parents.

⑥ Attaches material to
the memorandum. The
attachment would be an
appendix item in a formal
report.

TELCO CHILDCARE SERVICES
8300 Lincoln Green
Jacksonville, FL 32203-8300
(904) 555-9340   Fax (904) 555-3087

① **TO:**   M. L. Irvin, Director, Human Resources

    FROM: Janice Simms, Coordinator, Child Care Services *J.S.*

    DATE: July 14, 1999

    SUBJECT: Quarterly Report on In-House Child Care Center, Second
                Quarter, 1999

②
———————————————————————————————

③ The in-house child care center experienced a successful second quarter.
Data related to enrollment and current staffing follow:

④   **Enrollment:** 92 children, up from 84 at end of first quarter.

    Staff: Nine full-time staff members, including five attendants,
              three teachers, and one registered nurse.

Registration for the upcoming school year is presently underway and is
exceeding projected figures. Current staff size will necessitate an enrollment cap of 98. Further increases in enrollment will be possible only if
additional personnel are hired.

The payroll deduction method of payment, instituted on January 1, has
assured that operations remain profitable. It has also eliminated the time
and expense of billing. Parents seem satisfied with the arrangement as well.

Full license renewal is expected in August as we have met and/or exceeded
all state and county requirements for facilities, staff, and programs.

⑤ Favorable results were obtained to the employee satisfaction poll, which
was administered to parents participating in the child care program.
Ninety-one percent indicated that they were very satisfied or extremely
satisfied with our in-house child care program. The most frequently
mentioned suggestion for improvement was the extension of hours until
7 p.m. This change would allow employees time to run necessary errands
after work, before picking up their children. We might consider this
addition of services on a per hour rate basis. A copy of the survey instrument is provided for your review.

Call me should you wish to discuss the extended service hours idea or
any other aspects of this report.

⑥ Attachment

FIGURE 11-6
Audit report in letter
format, page 1.

═══LARMOUR BUSINESS CONSULTANTS═══

1800 RBC Parkway, North
Seattle, WA 98109-3933
(206) 555-9087 Fax (206) 555-3872

April 3, 1999

Ms. Janice Barnett, CEO
Spectrum Analysis, Inc.
P. O. Box 993
Portland, OR 97238-0993

Dear Ms. Barnett:

❶ The personal computer software audit for Spectrum Analysis has been completed according to the procedures recommended by Software Publishers Association. These procedures and our findings are summarized below.

❷ PROCEDURES

Specific procedures involved

❸ • Reviewing the software policy of the organization and its implementation and control.

• Reviewing the organization's inventory of software resources, including a list of all personal computers by location and serial number. Using SPAudit, we obtained a list of all the software on the hard disk of each computer.

• Matching purchase documentation with the software inventory record we had established. This procedure included reviewing software purchase records, such as invoices, purchase orders, check registers, canceled checks, manuals, diskettes, license agreements, and registration cards.

FINDINGS

In the area of software policy and controls, we found that the organization owns a total of 432 copies of 11 applications from seven vendors. No record of registration with the publisher was available for 81 of the programs owned. In addition, we identified 47 copies of software programs for which no corresponding purchase records existed. These copies appear to be illegal.

Of the 113 personal computers, we found 14 machines with software that had been brought from home by employees.

❶ Introduces the overall topic and leads into procedures and findings.

❷ Uses side heading to denote the beginning of the body.

❸ Uses a bulleted list to add emphasis to this important information.

FIGURE 11-6
Audit report in letter format, page 2.

④ Summarizes major point in the table and refers the reader to it. Does not number this single figure. Formats data in four-column table to facilitate reading and uses a clear title and column headings.

⑤ Uses side heading to denote the beginning of the recommendation section.

⑥ Uses enumerations to emphasize the recommendations.

Ms. Janice Barnett, CEO
Page 2
April 3, 1999

④ A summary of the software license violations identified follows:

Software	Total Copies Found	Legal Copies	Copies in Violation
WordPerfect 8.0	56	52	4
Lotus 1-2-3	48	45	3
Windows 98	115	75	40

We have deleted all copies in excess of the number of legal copies, and you are now in full compliance with applicable software licenses. We have also ordered legal software to replace the necessary software that was deleted.

⑤ CONCLUSIONS AND RECOMMENDATIONS

While some departments had little or no illegal software, others had significant violations. Therefore, the following recommendations are made:

⑥ 1. Institute a one-hour training program on the legal use of software and require it for all employees. Repeat it weekly over the next few months to permit all employees to attend. Additionally, require all new employees to participate in the program within two weeks of their start date.

2. Implement stricter software inventory controls, including semiannual spot audits.

Thank you for the opportunity to serve your organization in this manner. Should you wish to discuss any aspects of this report, call me.

Sincerely,

Marty G. Honnoli

Marty G. Honnoli
Software Consultant

mdy

GLOBAL CONCEPTS
9000 Delaware Street
New Orleans, LA 70126-9000
(504) 555-8700   Fax (504) 555-7581

June 10, 1999

1 Mr. Lewis Manasco
Vice President of Operations
Unipro Corporation
1700 Gentilly Boulevard
New Orleans, LA 70126-1700

Dear Mr. Manasco:

RECOMMENDATIONS FOR COMMUNICATING WITH THE KUWAITIS

2 Thank you for allowing us to assist you in preparing for your expansion into the Kuwaiti market. Your concern about how your company's personnel might be received in the Middle East is certainly warranted. Effective nonverbal communication is a vital element in overall business success.

Procedures

3 In preparing this report, a variety of books, newspaper and magazine articles, and government documents were examined. Additionally, interviews were conducted with 12 businesspersons from a variety of organizations, all of whom had lived and worked in the Middle East. Nonverbal communication patterns throughout the culturally complex Middle East vary because of the huge distances and different nationalities residing there. **4** However, the following general advice related to eye contact, gestures, and proxemics applies throughout the Muslim world.

5 Differences in Eye Contact

Several important differences exist in the interpretation of nonverbal communication patterns of North Americans and those of Middle Easterners. One important difference occurs in the interpretation of eye contact and gaze, as summarized in the following table:

FIGURE 11-7
Short report in letter format, page 1.

1 Letterhead, letter address, and subject line function as a title page and transmittal.

2 Uses deductive approach to present this informational report to the vice president.

3 Provides research methods and sources used to add credibility to the report.

4 Previews the three major divisions and transitions reader smoothly into the body.

5 Uses side headings to denote the three major divisions of the body.

FIGURE 11-7
Short report in letter
format, page 2.

6 Mr. Lewis Manasco
Page 2
June 10, 1999

6 Includes second page
heading to denote contin-
uation; appears on plain
paper.

7 Uses three-column
table to make comparison
easy; table immediately
follows its introduction; is
not numbered because it
is the only figure.

7

Differences in Nonverbal Communication Between North Americans and Middle Easterners		
Gesture	**North American**	**Middle Easterner**
Stare	Rude, a threat	Contact with other's soul
Gaze (between strangers)	Sexual interest	Intimacy, sexual, and non-sexual interest
Gaze (conversational)	Speaker gazes to and from listener	Speaker and listener hold gaze
Avoiding gaze	Hiding something	Rude in conversation
Lowering gaze	Submission; expected between strangers in a crowd	Submission; expected with religious person, strangers of different genders
Hand covers eyes	Possible headache	Swearing by one's eyes

8 Source: Argyle, 1988, p. 26

Obviously, a North American could inadvertently offend or confuse a
Middle Easterner through poorly executed eye contact.

8 Provides source note
for data obtained from an
outside source. Note
other APA citations for
direct quotes and para-
phrased information.

Differences in Gestures

9 A second area of concern in nonverbal communication is that of gestures. According to Axtell (1990), "in this area of the world, the left hand
is customarily used for bodily hygiene; therefore, it should not be used
for eating, handing over gifts or business cards, or other such gestures"
(p. 52). Kissing on the cheek is a common business practice among men,
as is the taking of another's hand or walking hand in hand. When seated,
be careful that the sole of the shoe is not visible; this action is considered highly offensive to the Middle Easterner, as the foot is considered
the lowliest and dirtiest part of the body (Walker, 1981).

9 Heading and transi-
tion sentence lead reader
to second major point.

Differences in Proxemics

Middle Eastern men typically stand much closer to one another than do
North Americans. Conversational distance may shrink to 10 inches or
less (Ruch, 1989). Standing close to or touching a woman in public is
unacceptable behavior for a man unless he is part of the immediate
family (Chuck, 1993).

Mr. Lewis Manasco
Page 3
June 10, 1999

Summary

Unipro's international operations depend to a large extent on the ability to communicate effectively. The following guidelines are offered to assure better nonverbal communication in the Middle East:

10 1. Assemble a reading library containing books and articles about Kuwaiti culture and customs. Require all employees departing for Kuwaiti assignments to familiarize themselves with these materials.

2. Investigate on-line sources of information on nonverbal communication, such as the web site at Pepperdine University (1997). Encourage employees to visit such sites for up-to-the-minute information and resources.

3. Employ a native Kuwaiti in a support role to advise Unipro personnel concerning appropriate verbal and nonverbal communication in Kuwait.

4. Include elements of appropriate nonverbal communication in the language training required of all personnel assigned to Kuwait.

11 These suggestions should assist you in establishing effective verbal and nonverbal communication in the Middle Eastern culture. Please let us know how we can assist you further with this project or with other international endeavors.

Sincerely,

Arlena J. Medders

Arlena J. Medders
Consultant

ksm

Enclosure: Reading list

FIGURE 11-7
Short report in letter format, page 3.

10 Uses enumerations to highlight recommended guidelines.

11 Closes with a courteous offer to provide additional service.

Reading List

Argyle, M. (1988). *Bodily communication*. New York: Methuen & Co. Ltd.

Axtell, R. (1990). *Do's and taboo's around the world*. New York: Parker Pen Company.

Chuck, L. (1993, February 22). Converts to Islam say they gain belief system, new way of life. *Austin (Texas) American Statesman*, pp. 1A, 5A.

Leathers, D. (1997). *Successful nonverbal communication: Principles and applications*, (3rd edition). New York: Allyn &Bacon.

Pepperdine University. (1997, May 8). *Nonverbal communication sources*. [On-line]. Available http://rigel.pepperdine.edu/Guides/nonverbal.htm [August 13, 1997].

Ruch, W. V. (1989). *International handbook of corporate communications*. Jefferson, NC: McFarland & Company, Inc.

Walker, S. (1981). Business travelers handbook: *A guide to the Middle East*. New York: Wiley.

FIGURE 11-7
Short report in letter format, page 4.

- When designed properly, form reports increase clerical accuracy by providing designated places for specific items.

- Forms save time by telling the preparer where to put each item and by preprinting common elements to eliminate the need for any narrative writing.

- In addition to their advantages of accuracy and time saving, forms make tabulation of data relatively simple. The value of the form is uni*form*ity.

Most form reports, such as a bank teller's cash sheet, are informational. At the end of the teller's work period, cash is counted and totals entered in designated blanks. Cash reports from all tellers are then totaled to arrive at period totals and perhaps verified by computer records.

In addition to their informational purpose, form reports assist in analytical work. A residential appraisal report assists real-estate appraisers in analyzing real property. With this information, the appraiser is able to determine the market value of a specific piece of property.

Many form reports are computer generated. For example, the flowchart in Figure 11-8 illustrates a hospital's automation of repetitive patient reports. The admission clerk inputs the patient information using the carefully designed input screen beginning with the patient's social security number. If the patient has been admitted previously, the patient's name, address, and telephone number are displayed automatically; all the clerk must do is verify the accuracy of information. When the clerk inputs the patient's date of birth, the computer calculates the patient's age, eliminating the need to ask a potentially sensitive question and assuring accuracy when patients cannot remember their age. All data are stored in a computer file and retrieved as needed to generate numerous reports required during a patient's stay: admissions summary sheet, admissions report, pharmacy profile, and even the addressograph used to stamp each page of the patient's record and the identification arm band.

Using the computer to prepare each report in the previous example leads to higher efficiency levels and minimizes errors because recurring data are entered only once. Preparing error-free reports is a critical public relations tool because even minor clerical errors may cause patients to question the hospital's ability to deliver quality health care.

Proposals

⑤ *Prepare effective proposals for a variety of purposes.*

A **proposal** is a written description of how one organization can meet the needs of another, for example, provide products or services as defined in Chapter 9. Managers prepare **internal proposals** to justify or recommend purchases or changes in the company; for instance, installing a new computer system, introducing telecommuting or other flexible work schedules, or reorganizing the company into work groups. Written to generate business, **external proposals** are a critical part of the successful operation of many companies.

Proposals may be solicited or unsolicited. A **solicited proposal** is generated when a potential buyer submits exact specifications or needs in a **request for proposal**, commonly referred to as an **RFP**. Governmental agencies such as the Department of Defense solicit proposals and place orders and contracts based on the most desirable proposal. The RFP describes a problem to be solved and invites respondents to describe their proposed solution.

An **unsolicited proposal** is prepared by an individual or firm who sees a problem to be solved and submits a proposal. For example, a business consultant is a

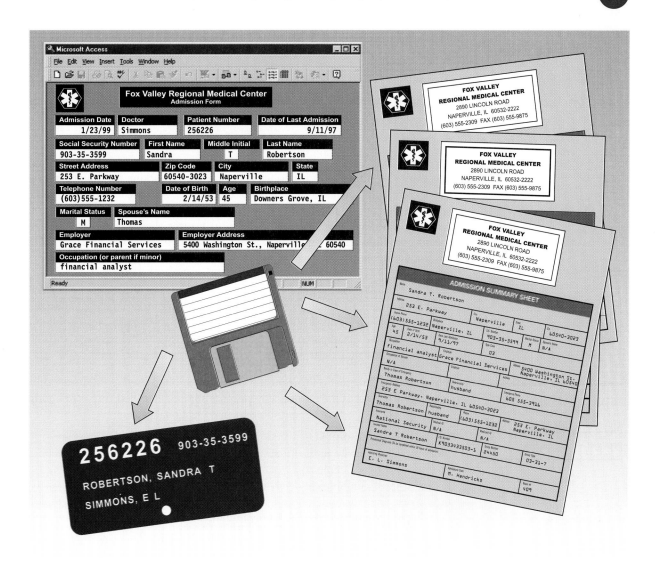

FIGURE 11-8 Computer-generated reports increase efficiency and accuracy.

regular customer of a family-owned retail store. On numerous occasions he has attempted to purchase an item that was out of stock. Recognizing that stock shortages decrease sales and profits, he prepares a proposal to assist the business in designing a computerized perpetual inventory with an automatic reordering system. For the business to accept the proposal, the consultant must convince the business that the resulting increase in sales and profits will more than offset the cost of the computer system and the consulting fee.

Structure

A proposal includes (1) details about the manner in which the problem would be solved and (2) the price to be charged. Often the proposal is a lengthy report designed to "sell" the prospective buyer on the ability of the bidder to perform. However, a simple price quotation also constitutes a proposal in response to a request for a price quotation.

> When would price be the only deciding factor for distinguishing between competing proposals?

The format of a proposal depends on the length of the proposal and the intended audience:

Format	Proposal Length and Intended Audience
Memorandum report	Short; remains within the organization
Letter report	Short; travels outside the organization
Formal report	Long; remains within the organization or travels outside the organization

Most work resulting from proposals is covered by a working agreement or contract to avoid discrepancies in the intents of the parties. In some cases, for example, users of outside consultants insist that each consultant be covered by a sizable general personal liability insurance policy that also insures the company. Many large firms and governmental organizations use highly structured procedures to assure understanding of contract terms.

The following general parts, or variations of them, may be used as headings in a proposal: (1) Problem or Purpose, (2) Scope, (3) Methods or Procedures, (4) Materials and Equipment, (5) Qualifications, (6) Follow-up and/or Evaluation, (7) Budget or Costs, (8) Summary, and (9) Addenda. In addition to these parts, a proposal may include preliminary report parts, such as the title page, transmittal message, and contents; as well as addenda parts, such as references, appendix, and index.

Problem and/or Purpose. Problem and purpose are often used as interchangeable terms in reports. Here is the introductory purpose statement, called "Project Description," in a proposal by a firm to contribute to an educational project:

> **Project Description:** Logan Community College has invited business and industry to participate in the creation of *Business Communication*, a television course and video training package. These materials will provide effective training in business communication skills to enhance the performance of individuals in business and contribute to organizational skills and profitability. In our rapidly evolving information society, skill in communication is integral to success.

Note how the heading "Project Description" has been used in place of "Purpose." In the following opening statement, "Problem" is used as the heading:

> **Problem:** The Board of Directors of Oak Brook Village Association has requested a proposal for total management and operation of its 1,620-unit permanent residential planned development. This proposal demonstrates the advantages of using Central Management Corporation in that role.

The purpose of the proposal may be listed as a separate heading (in addition to "Problem") when the proposal intends to include objectives of a measurable nature. When you list objectives such as "To reduce overall expenses for maintenance by 10 percent," attempt to list measurable and attainable objectives and list only enough to accomplish the purpose of selling your proposal. Many proposals are rejected simply because writers promise more than they can actually deliver.

Scope. When determining the scope of your proposal, you can place limits on what you propose to do or on what the material or equipment you sell can accomplish. The term *scope* need not necessarily be the only heading for this section. "Areas Served," "Limitations to the Study," and "Where (*specify topic*) Can Be Used" are examples of headings that describe the scope of a proposal. Here is a "Scope" section from a consulting firm's proposal to conduct a salary survey:

How can the writer make the proposal more successful in the competitive process?

What the Study Will Cover: To assist Sun Valley Technologies in formulating its salary and benefits program for executives, Patterson Consulting will include an analysis of compensation (salary and benefits) for no fewer than 20 of Sun Valley's competitors in the same geographic region. In addition to salaries, insurance, incentives, deferred compensation, medical, and retirement plans will be included. Additionally, Patterson Consulting will make recommendations for Sun Valley's program.

Another statement of scope might be as follows:

Scope: Leading figures in business and industry will work with respected academicians and skilled production staff to produce fifteen 30-minute television lessons that may be used in courses for college credit or as modules dealing with discrete topics for corporate executives.

Method and Procedure. The method(s) used to solve the problem or to conduct the business of the proposal should be spelled out in detail. In this section, simply think through all the steps necessary to meet the terms of the proposal and write them in sequence. When feasible, you should include a time schedule to indicate when the project will be completed.

How do the introductory sections build creditability for the proposal and the writer(s)?

Materials and Equipment. For large proposals, such as construction or research and development, indicate the nature and quantities of materials and equipment to be used. In some cases, several departments will contribute to this portion. When materials and equipment constitute a major portion of the total cost, include prices. Much litigation arises when clients are charged for "cost overruns." When contracts are made on the basis of "cost plus XX percent," the major costs of materials, equipment, and labor/personnel must be thoroughly described and documented.

Qualifications. Assuming your proposal is acceptable in terms of services to be performed or products to be supplied, your proposal must convince the potential buyer that you have the expertise to deliver what you have described and that you are a credible individual or company. Therefore, devote a section to presenting the specific qualifications and special expertise of the personnel involved in the proposal. You may include past records of the bidder and the recommendations of its past customers, and the proposed cost. Note how the brief biography of the principal member in the following excerpt from a proposal contributes to the credibility of the proposer:

Principals: Engagement Principal: Charles A. McKee, M.B.A., M.A.I. Partner in Property Appraisers, Inc., consulting appraisers since 1974. Fellow of the American Institute of Appraisers, B.A., M.B.A., Harvard University. Phi Kappa Phi and Beta Gamma Sigma honorary societies. Lecturer and speaker at many realty and appraisal conferences and at the University of Michigan.

In another related section, the proposal might mention other work performed:

Major Clients of Past Five Years: City of Tulsa, Oklahoma; Dade County, Florida; City of San Francisco, California; City of Seattle, Washington; Harbor General Corporation, Long Beach, California; Gulf and Houston, Incorporated, Houston, Texas. Personal references are available on request.

Follow-up and/or Evaluation. Although your entire proposal is devoted to convincing the reader of its merit, clients are frequently concerned about what will happen when the proposed work or service is completed. Will you return to make certain your work is satisfactory? Can you adjust your method of research as times change?

If your proposal is for a research grant, do not promise more than you can deliver. Not all funded research proves to be successful. If you propose to make a study in your firm's area of expertise, you may be more confident. A public accounting firm's proposal to audit a company's records need not be modest. The accountant follows certain audit functions that are prescribed by the profession. However, a proposal that involves providing psychological services probably warrants a thoughtful follow-up program to evaluate the service.

Budget or Costs. The budget or cost of the program should be detailed when materials, equipment, outside help, consultants, salaries, and travel are to be included. A simple proposal for service by one person might consist of a statement such as "15 hours at $200/hour, totaling $3,000, plus mileage and expenses estimated at $550." Present the budget or costs section after the main body of the proposal.

Summary. You might conclude the proposal with a summary. This summary may also be used as the initial section of the proposal if deductive sequence is desired.

Addenda. When supporting material is necessary to the proposal but would make it too bulky or detract from it, include the material as addenda items. A bibliography and an appendix are examples of addenda items. References used should appear in the bibliography or as footnotes. Maps, questionnaires, letters of recommendation, and similar materials are suitable appendix items.

What other types of items might appear in a proposal addendum?

A short, informal proposal that includes several of the parts previously discussed is shown in Figure 11-9. This proposal consists of three major divisions: "The Problem," "Proposed Course of Instruction," and "Cost." The "Proposed Course of Instruction" section is divided into five minor divisions to facilitate understanding. Wanting to increase the chances of securing the contract, the writer made sure the proposal was highly professional and had the impact needed to get the reader's attention. In other words, the writer wanted the proposal to "look" as good as it "sounds." To add to the overall effectiveness of the proposal, the writer incorporated appealing, but not distracting, page design features. Printing the proposal with a laser printer using proportional fonts of varying sizes and styles resulted in a professional appearance and an appealing document. The reader's positive impression of the high standards exhibited in this state-of-the-art proposal is likely to influence his or her confidence in the writer's ability to present the proposed communication seminar.

Preparation

Writers have much flexibility in preparing proposals. When they find a particular pattern that seems to be successful, they no doubt will adopt it as their basic plan. The ultimate test of a proposal is its effectiveness in achieving its purpose. The writer's task is to assemble the parts of a proposal in a way that persuades the reader to accept it.

To put the proposal together expeditiously, determine the parts to include, select one part that will be easy to prepare, prepare that part, and then go on to another. When you have completed the parts, you can arrange them in whatever order you like, incorporate the transitional items necessary to create coherence, and then put the proposal in finished form. As with most report writing, first prepare the pieces of

FIGURE 11-9
Short proposal in memo-
randum format, page 1.

PROPOSAL FOR STAFF DEVELOPMENT SEMINAR: INTERPERSONAL COMMUNICATION SKILLS FOR SUPERVISORY AND MIDDLE MANAGEMENT

by Miriam L. Naugles, Staff Development Coordinator

July 15, 1999

❶ The Problem

Management has perceived a need for improved communication perfor-mance on the part of supervisory and middle management personnel to strengthen relationships among them and their employees. The pro-posed training course is designed to help participants develop effective interpersonal communication skills.

❷ Proposed Course of Instruction

Based on our experience, the following concepts should be effective in improving understanding and improved performance.

❸ Teaching-Learning Method

The acquisition of interpersonal skills results from an activity-oriented training program where participants apply theory through role playing, case discussion, and feedback.

In this approach, the instructor is a learning facilitator rather than a lec-turer. Frequent use of video playback accompanied by instructor and group feedback reinforces learning.

Content

The following topics constitute the content core of the program:

❹
- Perception and self-concept
- A positive communication climate
- Sending, receiving, and nonverbal skills
- Reduction of communication barriers
- Resolving conflict
- Interviewing
- Small-group communication

❶ Describes the nature of the problem and pre-sents the proposed plan as a solution to the problem.

❷ Uses headings to aid the reader in understand-ing the organization of the proposal. Larger, boldface font adds emphasis.

❸ Divides the "Proposed Course of Instruction" section into five minor divisions for easier com-prehension. Describes the course content, instruc-tional method, and design in detail.

❹ Uses bullets to high-light components of the course content.

FIGURE 11-9
Short proposal in memo-
randum format, page 2.

5 Includes a
subsequent-page heading
to identify the second
page. Adds the horizontal
line to increase the pro-
fessional appearance.

5 Staff Development Proposal   **July 15, 1999**

Learning Materials

Because participants seem to feel more comfortable when they have a
textbook to guide them, we use the Verderber book, *Interact*. Additionally, case problem handouts are provided for role playing and discussion.

Length of Course

This course consists of 12 two-hour sessions over a six-week period.

Number of Participants

Because of the activity orientation of the program, a maximum of 12
participants is desirable.

Cost

All teaching-learning materials will be provided by us and include textbooks, handouts, and video camera and recorder. Based on a 12-session,
12-participant program, the total cost is $2,292. When two courses are
offered on the same day, the total cost is reduced to $4,400. Exact
charges:

6 Itemizes costs so the
reader understands
exactly how the total cost
was calculated. Disclos-
ing this detailed break-
down gives the reader
confidence that the cost
is accurate.

6 | | |
|---|---:|
| *Interact* (12 copies @ $35) | $ 420 |
| Case Problem Handouts (12 copies at $6) | 72 |
| Professional Fees (24 hours' instruction at $75/hr., travel, meals, and lodging) | 1,800 |
| Total | $2,292 |

Writing a report is a major project. For the report to be a success, you must begin planning early, work at a steady pace, and allow time after finishing your draft to edit and rewrite. If you underestimate the amount of effort required (or overestimate your abilities), you may share the fate of the overconfident hare in the fable, losing the race to the slow-but-steady tortoise.

information that you will assemble later as the "whole" report. Trying to write a report by beginning on line one, page one, and proceeding to the end may prove to be frustrating and time consuming. Keep in mind that you should complete the research and planning before you begin to write.

If you become part of a collaborative writing team producing a proposal of major size, you probably will be responsible for writing only a small portion of the total proposal. For example, a proposal team of sixteen executives, managers, and engineers might be required to prepare an 87-page proposal presenting a supplier's plan to supply parts to a military aircraft manufacturer. After the group brainstorms and plans the proposal, a project director delegates responsibility for the research and origination of particular sections of the proposal. Finally, one person compiles all the sections, creates many of the preliminary and addenda parts, and produces and distributes the final product.

The accompanying Strategic Forces box provides additional information about collaborative writing in teams.

Strategic Forces: Team Environment

Collaborative Skills for Team Writing

Many of the problems faced by organizations cannot be solved by a rugged individualist because no one person has all the experience, all the resources, or all the information needed to accomplish the task alone. Team writing produces a corporate document representing several points of view. Group support systems (GSSs) are interactive computer-based environments that support concerted and coordinated team effort toward completion of joint tasks. Group Support Systems alone, however, are insufficient to improve the collaborative writing process. Rather, GSS technology can be combined with an appropriate task and process structure to produce significant gains in productivity and output. Numerous GSS products have been developed, and the style of the team editing process dictates which GSS application will be most appropriate:

- **Sequential editing.** Collaborators divide the task so that the output of one stage is passed to the next writer for individual work. Editors that support this process are called markup tools. Examples of these include ForComment™, as well as recent extensions to popular word processing programs such as Microsoft® Word® and Lotus® WordPro®.

- **Parallel editing.** Collaborators divide the task so that each writer works on a different part of the document at the same time. Then the document is reassembled in an integration stage. Examples of software to assist with this style are Quilt™, SharedBook™, ShrEdit™, and Group-Systems® GroupWriter™.

- **Reciprocal editing.** Collaborators work together to create a common document, mutually adjusting their activities in real time to take into account each other's changes. One example of an editing application that accommodates this style is MULE™.

Early attempts at collaborative writing typically used an unstructured process in which participants contributed at will; the lack of structure in such situations usually proved to be dysfunctional and frustrating to participants. The more successful collaborative writing projects typically involve a multistage process:

1. **Open discussion.** Collaborators develop the objectives and general scope of the document using brainstorming or parallel-discussion software.

2. **Generation of document outline.** Collaborators develop main sections and subsections that will provide the structure for the document using a group outlining tool.

3. **Discussion of content within outline.** Collaborators interactively generate and discuss document content in each section using parallel discussions in a group outlining tool.

4. **Composing by subteams.** Subteams may consist of a few people or in some cases may be only one person. The task is to take the content entries from a section and organize, edit, and complete the section as a first draft using a collaborative writing tool.

5. **On-line feedback and discussion.** Using either a collaborative annotation tool or a parallel-discussion tool, the team reviews each section and makes suggestions in the form of annotations or comments. The section editors accept, reject, or merge the suggestions to improve their own sections.

6. **Verbal walkthrough.** Using a collaborative writing tool, the team does a verbal walkthrough of the document.

Stages 1 through 3 are sequential and are undertaken only once. Stages 4 through 6 are circular in nature, and in some cases multiple loops are carried out before the document is finalized. Minimal time and energy are spent on formatting the document. As synchronous group time may be limited and valuable, it is used as much as possible to add and refine document content. Formatting can be accomplished later by team members or by an outside editor.

The collaborative writing process is not flawless. Although disputes often do arise during collaborative writing sessions, the process described above helps to identify, focus, structure, and resolve disputes. Often, disputes arise when team members have incorrect or incomplete information.

Strategic Forces: Team Environment

Other times, disputes arise because team members have different philosophical approaches to an issue. To address these incongruencies and to avoid pulling the entire team off track, the disputing team members can be assigned to work together on a subteam. This work enables them to negotiate their differences without an audience and to compromise without losing face. When the subteam returns to the group with compromised text, the group readily accepts it, knowing that multiple points of view went into its composition.[4]

Application

In teams of four, research one of the GSS products described above, or select another of your choice. Prepare a five-minute oral report about the product that includes the following: (1) description of the product, (2) applications for which it is suited, (3) requirements and specifications for use, and (4) limitations of the product.

SUMMARY

1. **Identify the parts of a formal report and the contribution each part makes to the overall effectiveness of a report.** As reports increase in length from one page to several pages, they also grow in formality with the addition of introductory and addenda items. As a result, reports at the formal end of the continuum tend to be repetitious. These report parts and their purposes are summarized as follows:

Preliminary Parts

Half-Title Page (Title Fly)—contains title of report; adds formality.
Title Page—includes title, author, writer, and date; adds formality.
Authorization—provides written authorization to complete the report.
Transmittal—presents the report to the reader and summarizes the conclusions or major points.
Contents—provides an overview of the report and the order in which information will be presented; contains report headings and page numbers.
Figures—includes number, title, and page number of tables and graphics.
Executive Summary—summarizes essential elements in a report.

Report Text

Introduction—orients the reader to the topic and previews the major divisions.
Body—presents the information collected.
Summary—reviews main points presented in the body.
Conclusions—draws inferences based on the findings.
Recommendations—presents possible actions based on the conclusions.

Addenda

References—includes an alphabetical list of sources used in preparing the report.
Appendixes—contains supplementary information that supports the report but placing this information in the report would make the report bulky and unmanageable.
Index—includes an alphabetical guide to the subjects in the report.

The following checklist provides a concise, useful guide for your use as you prepare a report.

Transmittal Letter or Memorandum

(Use the following points for a letter-style transmittal in reports going outside the organization. For internal reports, use a memorandum transmittal.)

- Transmit a warm greeting to the reader.
- Open with a "Here is the report you requested" tone.
- Establish the subject in the first sentence.
- Follow the opening with a brief summary of the study. Expand the discussion if a separate summary is not included in the report.
- Acknowledge the assistance of those who helped with the study.
- Close the letter with a thank-you and a forward look.

Title Page

The title page includes

- Include the title of the report.
- Provide full identification of the authority for the report (the person for whom the report was prepared).
- Provide full identification of the preparer of the report.
- Provide the date of the completion of the report.
- Assure an attractive layout.

Contents Page

- Use *Contents* as the title.
- Use indentation to indicate the heading degrees used in the report.
- List numerous figures separately. (Otherwise, figures should not be listed because they are not separate sections of the outline but only supporting data within a section.)
- Center the entire contents outline horizontally; allows 1½" top margin.

Executive Summary

- Use a one-word title, such as *Executive Summary*, *Synopsis*, or *Abstract*.
- Condense of the major sections of the report.
- Use effective, generalized statements that avoid detail available in the report itself. Simply tell the reader what was done, how it was done, and what conclusions were reached.

Report Text

In writing style, observe the following guidelines:

- Avoid the personal *I* and *we* pronouns. Minimize the use of *the writer, the investigator,* and *the author*.
- Use active construction to give emphasis to the *doer* of the action; use passive voice to give emphasis to the *results* of the action.
- Use proper tense. Tell naturally about things in the order in which they happened, are happening, or will happen. Write as though the reader were reading the report at the same time it is written.
- Avoid ambiguous pronoun references. (If a sentence begins with *This is*, make sure the preceding sentence uses the specific word for which *This* stands. If the specific word is not used, insert it immediately after *This*.)
- Avoid expletive beginnings. Sentences that begin with *There is, There are,* and *It is* present the verb before presenting the subject. Compared with sentences that use the normal subject-verb-complement sequence, expletive sentences are longer and less interesting.
- Use bulleted or enumerated lists of three or more items if tabulation will make reading easier. For example, a list of three words such as *Ivan, George,* and *Diana* need not be tabulated; but a list of three long phrases, clauses, or sentences would probably warrant tabulation.
- Incorporate transition sentences to ensure coherence.

In physical layout, observe the following guidelines:

- Use headings to assist the reader by making them descriptive of the contents of the section. Talking headings are preferred.
- Maintain consistency in the mechanical placement of headings of equal degree.
- Use parallel construction in headings of equal degree in the same section of the report.
- Incorporate the statement of the problem or purpose and method of research as minor parts of the introduction unless the research method is the unique element in the study.
- Use the picture-frame layout for all pages. Recommended margins depending on the bindings are
  Unbound: 1" for all margins (top, bottom, left, and right).
  Leftbound: 1 1/2" left margin; 1" for other margins.
  Topbound: 1 1/2" top margin; 1" for other margins.
  Begin first page 1/2" lower than other pages to add appeal to the first page.

- Number all pages, with the first page of the body of the report being page 1. For page 1, omit the number or place it in the center approximately 1" from the bottom of the page. For all other pages, place the number 1" from the top of the page.

In using graphics or tabular data, observe the following guidelines:

- Number consecutively figures (tables, graphics, and other illustrations) used in the report.
- Give each graph or table a descriptive title.
- Refer to the graph or table within the text discussion that precedes its appearance.
- Place the graph or table as close to the textual reference as possible and limit the text reference to analysis. (It should not merely repeat what can be seen in the graph or table.)
- Use effective layout, appropriate captions and legends, and realistic vertical and horizontal scales that help the table or graph stand clearly by itself.

In reporting the analysis, observe the following guidelines:

- Question each statement for its contribution to the solution of the problem. Is each statement either descriptive or evaluative?
- Reduce large, unwieldy numbers to understandable ones through a common language, such as units of production, percentages, or ratios.
- Use objective reporting style rather than persuasive language; avoid emotional terms. Identify assumptions and opinions. Avoid unwarranted judgments and inferences.
- Tabulate or enumerate items when it will simplify the reading or add emphasis.

In drawing conclusions:

- State the conclusions carefully and clearly, and be sure they grow out of the findings.

- Repeat the major supporting findings for each conclusion if necessary.
- Make recommendations grow naturally from the conclusions if they are required.

Citations

If citations are used:

- Include a citation (in-text reference, footnote, or endnote) for material used from another source.
- Adhere to an acceptable, authoritative style or company policy.
- Present consistent citations, including adequate information for readers to locate the source in the reference list.

References

- Include an entry for every reference cited in the text.
- Adhere to an acceptable, authoritative style or company policy.
- Include more information than might be necessary in cases of doubt about what to include in an entry.
- Present the bibliography in alphabetic sequence by authors' surnames.
- Include separate sections (e.g., books, articles, and nonprint sources) if the references (works cited) section is lengthy and your referencing style allows it.

Appendix

- Include cover letters for survey instruments, maps, explanations of formulas used, and other items that should be included but are not important enough to be in the body of a report.
- Labels each item beginning with *Appendix A*, *Appendix B*, and so on.
- Identifies each item with a title.

2. ***Organize report findings.*** Organizing the content of a report involves seeing the report problem in its entirety and then breaking it into its parts. Because reports are written after the research or field work has been completed, writers may begin writing with any of the report parts and then complete the rough draft by putting the parts in logical order. Short reports usually are written in memorandum or letter format. They are called "short" because they simply are not long enough to require the many supporting preliminary and ending parts of longer reports. Nevertheless, short reports require the same organizing and writing skills as long reports. Although reports grow in formality as they increase in length, writers determine whether to prepare a report in formal style and format before they begin writing. As they organize and make tentative outlines, writers learn quickly the format and style best able to communicate the intended message.

3. ***Prepare effective formal reports using an acceptable format and writing style.*** In preparing effective long reports, outlining assists the writer with logical sequencing. Appropriate headings lead the reader from one division to another. The writing style should present the findings and data interpretation clearly and fairly, convincing the reader to accept the writer's point of view, but in an unemotional manner. Opinions should be clearly identified as such. The writer should lay the first draft aside long enough to get a fresh perspective, then revise the report with a genuine commitment to making all possible improvements.

4. ***Prepare effective short reports in letter and memorandum formats.*** Short reports are typically written in a personal writing style and in memorandum or letter format. Form reports provide accuracy , save time, and simplify tabulation of data when a need exists for numerous, repetitive reports.

5. ***Prepare effective proposals for a variety of purposes.*** Proposals call for thorough organization and require writing methods that will be not only informative but convincing. Proposals often are written by teams; in this way, they typify the nature of reports as having discrete parts that writers can prepare in any order and then assemble into whole reports.

REFERENCES

[1]Henricks, M. (1997, October). Convergence 2: Vertical retail. *Apparel Industry Magazine*, 38–46.

[2]Osundiya, G. (1997, March). Making the annual report more relevant. *Management Accounting— London*, p. 58.

[3]Pratt, L. (1996, December). Annual reports: In transition. *CA Magazine*, 13–14.

[4]Nunnemaker, J. F., Jr., & Briggs, R. O., Mittleman, D. D., Vogel, D. R., Balthazard, P. A. (1996/1997). Lessons from a dozen years of group support systems research: A discussion of lab and field findings. *Journal of Management Information Systems*, 13(3), 163–207.

[5]Dart, B. (1997). Internet copyright treaty: The stakes are high. Cox News Service. [On-line]. Available at

http://nytsyn.com/live/Latest/237_082597_094213_ 1037.html [1997. December 19].

[6]Wallack, T. (1997, January 20). Copyright protection now your job. *Network World*, 1, 14.

[7]Note: Spencer, B. A., & Lehman, C. M. (1990). Analyzing ethical issues: Essential ingredient in business communication, *Bulletin of the Association for Business Communication*, 53(3), 7–16. [Application extracted by permission].

[8]Lehman, C. M., & Spencer, B. A. (1991). Creative thinking: An integral part of effective business communication, *Bulletin of the Association of Business Communication*, 54(1), 21–27. [Application extracted by permission].

REVIEW QUESTIONS

1. List each of the parts of a formal report and briefly discuss the purpose of each one. (Obj. 1)

2. Provide guidelines for writing an effective report title. (Obj. 1)

3. How does a report writer determine which preliminary or addenda parts to include in a report? (Obj. 1)

4. Briefly discuss the primary principles involved in writing an executive summary. What are other names given to this preliminary report part? (Obj. 1)

5. Distinguish among findings, conclusions, and recommendations. Can the report summary, conclusions, and recommendations be presented in separate sections, or must they be combined into one section? Explain. (Obj. 1)

6. Differentiate between a references page (works cited) and a bibliography (works consulted). (Obj. 1)

7. Give two or three examples of emotional terms. Why should you avoid them in a formal report? (Obj. 2)

8. Why is the use of the pronoun *I* generally unacceptable in formal report writing? (Obj. 2)

9. Explain the relationship between the content outline of a report and the placement of headings within the body of a report. (Obj. 2)

10. Must formal reports be organized in only one way? Must they contain all the preliminary parts, report text, and addenda parts? (Obj. 3)

11. What are the differences between long and short reports? (Obj. 3, 4)

12. What factor(s) determine(s) whether memorandum or letter format should be used for short reports? (Obj. 4)

13. How do form reports increase the accuracy of information? (Obj. 4)

14. What is the primary purpose of a proposal? What is meant by RFP? (Obj. 5)

15. When a lengthy, complex proposal is prepared in industry, is the original writing typically done by one person? Explain. (Obj. 5)

E-MAIL APPLICATION

Your instructor has provided detailed instructions for completing a long or short report or proposal in groups of three or four. Send your instructor a weekly progress report via e-mail. The report should contain the following information about each meeting held during the week: date, place, and duration of meeting; members present; report of work accomplished since the last meeting; brief description of work accomplished during the current meeting; and work allocated to be completed before the next meeting.

Send your instructor an e-mail message containing your evaluation of each member of the group. Rate each member on a five-point scale or assign a percentage indicating the contribution each member made to the group. Ideally each member should contribute 100 percent. However, assume that a group consisted of four members; one person contributed more than his or her equal share, and one person contributed less. You might rank these two members 120 percent and 80 percent respectively and rank the other two members 100%. Note the total percentages awarded equal 400 percent (100 percent × 4 members). Write a brief statement justifying the rating you assigned each member; provide specific, verifiable evidence.

APPLICATIONS

Informational Reports

1. **Summarizing a Professional Meeting (Obj. 2, 4)**
   Attend a professional meeting of a campus or community organization. Take notes on the program presented, the issues discussed, and so on. Submit a report to your instructor summarizing the events of the meeting, and include a section that describes the benefits that might be derived from membership in that organization.

2. **Researching Security of Electronic Payments (Obj. 2, 4)**
   Read three articles on a method for securing electronic payments. Submit a report to your instructor that explains what it is, how it works, and its strengths and weaknesses.

3. **Evaluating a Career Field. (Obj. 2, 4)**
   Select a career field in which you have some interest. Study government handbooks, yearbooks, and other materials that project the outlook of that career. Submit a report to your instructor that includes the following sections: (1) The career you have chosen, with reasons; (2) the relative demand for that career over the next five to ten years; and (3) the pay scale and other benefits that are typical of that career.

4. **Auditing a Computer Lab (Obj. 2, 4)**
   Visit the computer lab on your campus. Through observation and interviews, prepare an audit report of the lab's offerings. Include the following items in your report: (1) The types of equipment available (e.g., IBMs and compatibles, Macs, mainframe terminals), (2) the number of each type, and (3) the operating systems and applications software available (product, version). Submit the report to your instructor.

5. **Evaluating the Performance of a Stock Portfolio (Obj. 2, 4)**
   Select ten stocks listed on the New York Stock Exchange and reported in your daily newspaper, in *The Wall Street Journal*, or on-line. Assume that you will purchase 100 shares of each of the ten stocks at the prices listed at the market close on a particular day. You are going to keep a record of changes in the stocks for a one-week period—five trading days.

   Required: Submit a memorandum to your instructor

on the purchase date reporting your ten stocks according to the following format:

Name of Stock   Price per Share   Total Cost (× 100)

At the end of the five-day period, submit another memorandum to your instructor detailing how your investments fared during the week. Record the Dow Jones Industrial Average of thirty stocks for both your purchase date and the end of the five-day period. Compare your total performance—percentage gain or loss—with that of the Dow Jones average.

6. **Promoting International Understanding (Obj. 2, 4)**
Complete Chapter 5, Application 20. Research the cultural differences between business executives in the United States and Mexico and then write a memorandum report communicating this information to U.S. managers working in Mexico. Write another memo to Jeanne Pitman, director of international assignments, persuading her to develop other ways to promote international understanding in the company. You may vary this case by selecting a country of your choice.

7. **Communicating Concern for Employees (Obj. 2, 4)**
Complete Chapter 7, Application 17. Review research related to employee motivation and current practitioners' journals to identify ways to solve a company's problems with low morale and productivity, and write an informational report. A basic scenario is provided. To make the case more meaningful to you, identify an employee group and environment with which you are familiar.

8. **Communicating during a Crisis (Obj. 2, 4)**
Review research related to crisis communication to prepare for communicating information about a financial crisis to employees, and write an informational report. You may vary this case: For example, communicate financial crisis information to stockholders; or negative information about defective products, product tampering, environmental hazards, or ethical misconduct to clients and other groups.

Analytical Reports

9. **Protecting Against Computer Viruses (Obj. 2, 4)**
Prepare a report on computer viruses and protection against their intrusion. Include the following parts in your report: (1) What are viruses and how do they function? (2) What is the risk from viruses? (3) What protective measures are available? End your report with a recommendation to your organization on how to best protect itself from damage caused by computer viruses.

10. **Comparing the Merits of Franchising Versus Starting an Independent Business (Obj. 2, 4)**
You and a silent partner plan to open a business establishment in your city. You are unsure whether to obtain a franchise for such an establishment or to start your own independent restaurant. Select a franchise opportunity of your choice, and research it. Include in your findings the initial investment cost, start-up expenses, franchise requirements and fees, and success and failure rate. Compare the franchise opportunity to the option of an independent business.

Required: Prepare a proposal for your intended silent partner that compares the options of franchising versus independent ownership. Make a recommendation as to the more desirable action to take.

11. **Assessing the Feasibility of Constructing a Recreational Complex (Obj. 2–4)**
Oakdale University has established a committee to study the feasibility of constructing a recreational center for students, faculty, and staff. To help determine the interest of faculty and staff, the committee has administered a questionnaire. The findings will be combined with other aspects of the feasibility study in a presentation to the president. The committee believes the 668-person sample is representative of the faculty and staff. The results of the survey follow:

1. On average, how often do you exercise each week?

136	0–1 day
274	2–3 days
197	4–5 days
61	6–7 days

2. During a week, in which of the following activities do you participate? Check all that apply.

171	Aerobic exercise
157	Jogging
147	Weightlifting
299	Walking
67	Tennis
42	Other

3. If you had access, in which of the following activities would you participate? Check all that apply.

196	Racquetball
361	Swimming
72	Basketball
126	Running or walking on an indoor track
165	Weight machines

4. If a recreation center were constructed for employees, what is the maximum amount you would be willing to pay per month to provide use of the center to your immediate family members?

125	$0–$10
69	$11–$20
156	$21–$30
261	$31–$40
57	$41–$50

Required: As a member of the committee, prepare a short report for the president, Michelle Karratassos. You asked respondents to estimate the amounts they would be willing to pay a month for their family to use the center as $0 to $10, $11 to $20, and so on. If you were to do mathematical computations, you would probably use midpoints such as $5, $15.50, $25.50, and so on as values for each class. In this case, however, write in generalities simply using percentages. Measures of central tendency are not necessary.

12. **Preparing an Analytical Report (Obj. 2, 4)**

    Prepare a short report on the selection of an alternative in *one* of the following cases. Make any assumptions and collect any background information needed to make an informed decision. Reviewing this list may help you identify a business-related problem you have encountered that you would like to investigate; evaluate possible alternative solutions, and make a recommendation.

    a. Recommend one of three laptop computers for use by the company's sales representatives to update accounts, process orders, prepare sales proposals, and so forth. The computer must have the ability to connect by modem to the central office for transmitting daily reports.

    b. Recommend how you would invest $2 billion of excess cash that your company will not need until the plant expands in two more years.

    c. Recommend a printer for a company installing a personal computer-based information system. The company will use the printer for both internal and external correspondence; some correspondence requires graphics.

    d. Recommend whether a bank should require its employees to wear uniforms.

    e. As director of human resources, recommend the type of network configuration that would best serve the needs of the department's 26 employees. Your computers are presently not networked, and only three can access the company mainframe. Investigate the advantages and disadvantages of the star, ring, and bus configurations. Make a recommendation to upper management.

    f. You and six other investors are considering opening a restaurant in your city. Determine the most desirable form of organization for your business: sole proprietorship, partnership, or corporation. Consider the legal, tax, and other implications of each alternative.

    g. Your government agency has always purchased the automobiles used by its social workers. The cars are typically driven approximately 30,000 miles a year and are sold for about 20 percent of their purchase value at the end of three years. Consider the cost effectiveness of the current policy and a car dealer's offer to lease the cars. Recommend whether the agency should purchase or lease the automobiles.

    h. One of your sales representatives has provided literature that claims a sales representative's productivity can increase by as much as 30 percent when a cellular telephone is used to make sales calls. Recommend whether the company should invest in the installation and use of cellular telephones.

    i. A family-owned business, having had substantial growth, is considering WATS-line service. The company currently incurs $3,000 in long-distance telephone charges a month. Evaluate the feasibility of the WATS-line service.

    j. You have noticed a substantial increase in the number of employees who spend their lunch hour exercising at one of several health clubs in your community. Furthermore, your insurance agent has reported that claims of your company are increasing at less than the national average. Attributing this positive fact to your employees' commitment to physical fitness, you are considering either (1) installing exercise equipment in underused areas of your plant or (2) subsidizing membership dues. You are also thinking about extending the lunch hour to make exercising more convenient. Weigh the alternatives and make a recommendation.

    k. As vice president of production, investigate whether introducing background music would improve productivity in a manufacturing environment.

    l. Office support staff in each department of your company make all photocopies on convenience copiers in their departments. Weigh the benefits and expenses of establishing a central copy center.

13. **Analyzing Legal and Ethical Constraints (Obj. 2, 4)**

    Use the ethical framework in Figure 1-6 to analyze the following cases involving legal and ethical constraints. For the case assigned by your instructor, consider the costs and benefits of the action on each of the company's stakeholders (persons who will be affected by the decision): Consider which of Ross's five duties are relevant and which may be violated for any of the stakeholders.[7] You may wish to review the tables in Chapter 1, Exercise 8, that will serve as a helpful guide for your analysis.

    a. *Chapter 7, Application 18.* Determine what action is appropriate when an accountant has knowledge that a client has filed a fraudulent tax return. Use a formal framework for analyzing ethical issues. You must determine the ethical and legal implications of this case: What behavior is ethical according to the standards in the Code of Professional Conduct of the American Institute of Certified Public Accountants? What action, if any, does the Internal

Revenue Service require? Communicate this analytical decision to your supervisor and the client.

b. *Is Reducing Quality to Cut Costs Ethical?* Haynes-McReynolds Industries, a major supplier of engine parts for a major airplane manufacturer, has developed a new production process. This process reduces the cost of production by 11 percent. The new product meets company, governmental, and customer safety standards; but the risk of failure is greater than using the present, more costly production method. If part failure occurs, an engine will shut down during flight.

   Required: Use the ethical framework in Figure 1-6 to analyze the situation. Based on your analysis, what decision would you make? Outline the major points of your answer to the company president. As vice president of production, you adamantly opposed implementing the new production process. However, you have been instructed to initiate the more efficient process. Should your memo to the production supervisor include the issues involved in this ethical decision? Or should you provide only the details needed for the supervisor to implement the plan? Outline the major points of your answer to the production supervisor. Compose a memorandum to the president and a memorandum to the production supervisor if your instructor requires them.

c. *Is an Ethical Issue Involved in Replacing Humans with Machines?* Lolley Corporation currently employs five workers to produce Part W-132. The engineering department has identified a robotic machine that can produce the same quantity and quality of parts and would reduce annual production costs by $15,000. The five employees would be terminated if the machine were placed in service. Last year Bradford earned $9.6 million, or $3 per share (3.2 million shares). As vice president of production, you must submit a recommendation to the company president.

d. *Is Overlooking a Vendor's Error to Your Advantage Ethical?* Douglas is responsible for checking the accuracy of invoices received from suppliers for purchases of inventory. A supplier recently shipped the company $5,000 worth of merchandise but neglected to include the merchandise on the invoice. Immediately, Douglas requested a revised invoice from the supplier. Learning of this request, Douglas's supervisor severely reprimanded him for not overlooking the vendor's error, thus costing the company $5,000.

   Functioning as plant manager, you hear nothing of this conversation from Douglas or his supervisor. However, several comments filtering through the grapevine convince you that you must take appropriate action.

   Required: Decide whether it is ethical to overlook the erroneous billing. Based on your decision, complete *one* of the following: (a) Write a memorandum (or e-mail message if your instructor requires) to Douglas commending him for his ethical behavior. State that this document will be placed in his personnel file for use in future performance appraisals. (b) Write a persuasive memorandum to Douglas explaining that overlooking similar errors in the future would be in his "best interest" and write a memorandum to Douglas's supervisor, Scott Lindsay, explaining the action that you took regarding Douglas's behavior.

e. *Charitable Contributions or Shrewd Public Relations?* As the president of a bottled water company, you have been looking constantly for a way to promote your product. The United States has just sent hundreds of troops to a foreign country to defend it against a possible military attack. Soldiers will need plenty of water in this dry climate. Military officials refused to offer your company a contract to supply bottled water to the military troops; however, your marketing/public relations department has proposed that the company donate 500,000 bottles of water to the military.

   Required: Complete *one* of the following: (a) Write a letter to the president voicing your dissenting opinion, as a stockholder, on the donation of the water. Address the letter to Michael Stevens, Sparkling Springs Water Company, 2731 North Lake Street, Chicago, IL 60607-2731. (b) Write a news release, as the public relations director, stating that your company has decided to donate 500,000 bottles of water to the military.

f. *Is Providing Possibly Faulty Swing Sets Unethical?* For the last six months, you have been responsible for inspecting and approving the quality of swing sets (Model 2353) before they are shipped to customers. One afternoon as you were reviewing past records, you noted a change in the product specifications and were curious about the reason for this change. Discussing this issue with the production manager, you learned that later product research indicated that the original metal used was not heavy enough. You are upset because you know that at least 10,000 of these swing sets are still in use. You contend that if the reinforcement bars break while a child is swinging, an accident could occur. The production manager says, "Even our new swing sets will eventually break. It's been over two years and we haven't had any complaints yet. The problem's been solved; why bring it up now? It will not only cost money to recall the product but would also damage our image." The production manager advises you not to bring the issue up again; otherwise, you may not be considered a team player.

Required: Complete *one* of the following: (a) Write a letter to the vice president of production advocating recall of these products. Include complete justification for your decision. (b) Write a memo to the production manager stating that you have reconsidered your thoughts on the swing sets and believe the sets should not be recalled. Include complete justification for your decision.

g. *Analyzing an Ethical Situation: A Sound Decision or a Clever Way Out?* In an effort to secure a large investment account, Eastman, Inc., has decided to host a weekend boating expedition for a select group of prospective clients. Today you received the following e-mail message from your supervisor.

Pat O'Hara in personnel just told me that a boat called *The Princess*, registered with Royal Charters out of Gulfport, Mississippi, will be in Tampa, Florida, around the time of the boating expedition we planned with Eastman, Inc. *The Princess* will be on a four-week layover at Cutlass Harbor between charters, from April 10 to May 7.

O'Hara says we'd be foolish not to get this gorgeous luxury boat for our upcoming boating expedition. Because so many of the prospective clients invited to attend are avid boating fans, this luxury boat could just be our ticket to secure several sizable accounts.

Meet with the captain ASAP and arrange to charter the boat for Thursday to Sunday, April 22-25. When you've worked out the details with Royal Charters, give me a call.

When you reached the captain, he explained that the owner does not usually allow unscheduled charters. After you convinced him of the importance of chartering *The Princess* for this expedition, the captain offered to let you charter the boat for $1,000 a day (normal rate is $2,000). He assured you he would submit the money to the owner and explain the situation when he returned to the home port.

Required: Decide whether it is ethical to accept the captain's offer. Based on your decision, complete *one* of the following: (a) Write to the captain accepting the offer to charter the boat, confirming the $1,000 rate, and providing details about the dates. Decide whether any other information should be included to ensure that the captain fulfills his side of this verbal contract. Address the letter to Doug Perez, 234 Sandy Beach Road, Tampa, FL 33602-2098. (b) Write a letter to the owner requesting a special charter; you consider the captain's offer unethical. Based on your ethical analysis, decide whether to mention the captain's offer. Address the letter to David Crenshaw, Royal Charters, 4029 Beach Drive, Gulfport, MS 39507-0234. Awaiting a reply from the owner or the captain (depending on your decision), write a memo to your supervisor (Martin Sinclair) informing him of your action and including your analysis of this ethical situation.

h. *Is Hiring the Homeless to Purchase Tickets Ethical?*[27] You are a junior partner in a small ticket brokerage firm in Omaha, Nebraska. The purpose of your company is to purchase tickets to popular concerts and sporting events that will be resold. Your typical market is upper-level executives and other professionals who do not have time to stand in long lines to purchase their own tickets. The concert promoter allows each individual to purchase only four tickets to a particular event. In the past, you hired students to stand in line to purchase tickets. Even paying minimum wage, you found this practice to be far too expensive to maintain adequate profits. You soon realized that some other, less-expensive method must be identified to secure the tickets.

Several weeks ago you hired a homeless person to stand in line. While he was waiting in line, you gave him two meals (pizza for lunch and chicken for dinner). In return for the four tickets, you paid him $50. Quite pleased with this experiment, you hired more homeless people to purchase tickets. They seemed to like the food and the money, and your profits rose steadily. You thought everything was going well until yesterday, when you received a telephone call from one of the record stores where tickets are sold. The store manager was upset about two things. First, loyal customers were complaining that they have stood in line for hours, only to be told that all tickets had been sold. Second, the manager complained that these individuals camping out in front of the store may damage the store's image. One particularly irate customer voiced displeasure with having to wait in line with "shabby-looking people with unwashed hair." Today the morning paper contained a very brash article questioning the ethics of your practice. With paper in hand and very disturbed, Carmen Morgan, the senior partner, rushes into your office. Having already read the article, you quickly say, "Honestly, this negative publicity came as a real surprise to me. I believed that we were not only serving our customers but were also helping the homeless—giving them two meals and money they otherwise would not have had."

Regaining her usual calm disposition, your partner asks you to analyze this practice more thoroughly, and you agree to provide a written report of your analysis. Starting your analysis, you ask yourself these questions: Are you really helping the homeless, or are you taking advantage of their predicament? Are you hurting anyone? Should you continue to hire the homeless to buy tickets? If so, should you change your procedures?

Required: Compose a memorandum to your partner.

14. **Shareware versus Commercial Software (Obj. 2, 3)**
Your company, Support, Inc., is considering the possibility of using shareware for its software needs rather than commercial software. You have been asked by the owner and president of your organization to research the issue of shareware and to conduct a business survey of the use of shareware and the satisfaction of users. You have surveyed 66 companies that have used shareware and have obtained the following results:

1. What type(s) of shareware have you used? (Check all that apply)

    __34__ Word processing

    __26__ Spreadsheet

    __20__ Database

    __24__ Graphics

    __23__ Communications

    __28__ Other

2. In general, how would you rate the quality of shareware as compared to software products sold commercially? (Check one)

    __4__ Shareware quality is very inferior to that of commercial software.

    __31__ Shareware quality is somewhat inferior to that of commercial software.

    __26__ Shareware quality is about the same as that of commercial software.

    __3__ Shareware quality is somewhat better than that of commercial software.

    __2__ Shareware quality is much better than that of commercial software.

3. What, if any, problems have you encountered with the use of shareware that you have registered with the owner? (Check all that apply)

    __26__ Inadequate documentation

    __25__ Glitch(es) in the program

    __9__ Virus in the program

    __22__ Lack of technical support

    __2__ Other problems

    __16__ No problems

4. Where have you used shareware? (Check one)

    __22__ Used only at home

    __17__ Used only at work

    __27__ Used at both home and work

5. How did you obtain your shareware? (Check all that apply)

    __34__ Obtained from a friend or acquaintance

    __21__ Obtained from a computer bulletin board

    __18__ A copy was provided on my job

    __16__ Purchased it

    __3__ Other

6. How much would you be willing to pay to register a copy of a shareware program? (Check one)

    __10__ Nothing

    __28__ Under $25

    __21__ Between $25 and $50

    __4__ Between $50 and $75

    __3__ Over $75

7. What is your opinion of a company purchasing shareware products instead of commercial software for employee use? (Circle one)

(11)	(4)	(15)	(19)	(6)	(10)
1	2	3	4	5	6

Definitely					Definitely
would not					would
recommend					recommend

Required: As director of information systems, write a report with findings, conclusions, and recommendations. Prepare any preliminary and addenda parts you believe will enable the reader to understand the report.

15. **Merits of Mentoring (Obj. 2, 3)**
Your company, Ultron Oil, is considering implementing a formal mentoring program as a means for developing managerial talent. Your supervisor, the division director, has commissioned you to prepare a report on the effectiveness of mentoring. As a part of the study, you have surveyed 70 managers representing a variety of businesses; 64 were male, and 6 were female. They ranged in age from 22 to 69, with the median age being 45. Their responses are follows:

1. In your career development, have you ever had a mentor?

    __66__ Yes. Answer all items.

    __4__ No. Skip to Item 6.

2. Which of the following describes your mentoring relationship(s)?

    __6__ Formal; my mentor(s) was/were appointed or assigned to me.

    __38__ Informal; the relationship(s) just evolved.

    __22__ One or more was formal, and one or more was informal.

3. How long did the typical mentoring relationship last?

    __12__ Less than one year

    __12__ One to two years

    __16__ Three to five years

__14__ More than five years

__14__ Varying lengths of time (answers varied from one month to life)

4. Did you perceive that you benefited from the mentoring relationship?

__60__ Yes

__0__ No

5. Did you perceive that your mentor benefited from the relationship?

__62__ Yes

__4__ No

6. Have you ever been a mentor to another person?

__54__ Yes

__16__ No

7. Does your company have a mentoring program in place?

__32__ Yes

__38__ No

Required: Prepare the report for the division director. Present your findings, draw conclusions, and make recommendations. Prepare any preliminary and addenda parts you believe will enable the reader to understand the report.

16. **Attitudes Toward Software Piracy (Obj. 2, 3)**
You are conducting a study of college seniors concerning their awareness of and attitudes toward software piracy. You have surveyed 100 students as a part of your project. The first category of questions asked to them deal with their knowledge of software piracy. The correct answer to each of these questions is "true." Their responses are as follows:

1. Purchased software is covered by copyright law and generally allows for only a backup copy to be made by the purchaser.

__84__ True

__16__ False

2. Making copies of copyrighted software for distribution to others (software piracy) is a federal crime.

__94__ True

__6__ False

3. Making a copy of a software program owned by my company for use at home, unless expressly allowed, is a violation of copyright law.

__82__ True

__18__ False

4. Software piracy is punishable by both fine and imprisonment.

__92__ True

__8__ False

The second category of questions dealt with specific situations. To each, students were instructed to give their *honest* responses. Their responses are as follows:

1. Your employer has purchased Corel WordPerfect 8.0® for use on your computer at work. You have a computer at home and would like to have a copy of the program for you and your family's personal use. You would

__38__ Make a copy of the disk for use at home and buy a manual from Walden Books.

__50__ Make a copy of the disk and photocopy the manual for home use.

__12__ Wait until you could afford to purchase a copy yourself.

2. You visit a local computer software store and see Corel WordPerfect 8.0® with a price of $195. You would

__100__ Buy it now or if money is short, come back later to buy

__0__ Shoplift the software

3. You obtain a copy of Corel WordPerfect 8.0. A friend asks you for a copy of it. You would

__58__ Give your friend a copy of the program.

__22__ Trade your friend a copy of Corel WordPerfect 8.0 for a copy of Lotus 1-2-3®.

__6__ Sell your friend a copy for $25.

__14__ Tell your friend that he/she must purchase a copy.

Required: Present your findings, conclusions, and recommendations in a formal report to your college administrators. Prepare any preliminary and addenda parts you believe will enable the reader to understand the report.

17. **Spiraling Health Costs: Do Employee Assistance Programs Help? (Obj. 2, 3)**
As director of human resources management of Soto, Inc., you receive the following voice-mail message from Pablo Soto, president of the company:

Hi. I just finished reading your quarterly analysis of benefits and compensation costs. Frankly, I'm overwhelmed with the consistent increase in health claims since last year. If this trend continues, we'll have to eliminate employee health coverage or go out of business. What are the other companies doing to curtail health care costs? Do these employee assistance programs really work? Please complete a thorough investigation so that we can make an informed decision if the situation worsens. Let's schedule a meeting to discuss this issue later this month.

Required:

1. To help you focus your research, select a particular business with which you are familiar. Then identify the major health problems that you believe employees in this type of company might have. Among the problems you might list are heart disease, high cholesterol, diabetes, poor physical fitness, substance abuse, stress and burnout, and physical problems caused by using computers or being exposed to other hazardous materials or equipment.

2. Using the problems you listed in Step 1, conduct the necessary research to answer the president's questions; provide accurate, useful, and well-documented information. Specifically, review the research related to employee assistance programs or methods of reducing health care costs. In addition, read current general business magazines and practitioners' journals to learn about employee assistance programs at other companies and other relevant issues.

3. As director of human resources, write an informational report relating your research about employee assistance programs (relevant to Soto's employee health problem profile) to the president. Include complete and accurate documentation of your sources; use in-text parenthetical citations unless your instructor requires another citation method.

4. Prepare the following preliminary and addenda parts to support the report prepared in Step 3: title page, executive summary, transmittal memorandum to President Soto (mention the attached references page), and references page. Provide complete, accurate references so that you can readily relocate the information if the president requests a copy.

18. **Cross-Cultural Misunderstandings (Obj. 2, 3)**
McClarney's, a successful fast-food restaurant in the United States, has expanded its operations to Hong Kong, Paris, and now Moscow. In almost every case, U.S. managers were transferred to open and manage restaurants in the company's international operations. These highly competent managers continually make unintentional, yet costly, mistakes because they are unfamiliar with the differences among the customs, culture, and business practices of these countries and the United States. The price being paid for these innocent mistakes is high: damaged or lost goodwill of customers, employees, and suppliers, and eventually reduced profits.

When the company decided to expand its operation to Moscow, management agreed unanimously to establish an International Assignments Division. This division is charged with preparing managers transferring to overseas operations for functioning in a new culture. Although some misunderstandings cannot be avoided, a carefully designed orientation program is sure to improve international understanding.

Required:

1. As director of the International Assignments Division, one of your first tasks is to prepare an informational report to the U.S. managers transferring to *one* of the company's three international locations: Hong Kong, Paris, or Moscow. Your purpose is to highlight the major cultural differences and business practices between the United States and the country you select. Conduct the research needed to provide these managers with accurate, useful, and well-documented information. Use in-text parenthetical citations unless your instructor requires another citation method. Use the following suggestions to help you organize your report:

   a. Consider the specific information that managers would need to know to manage a fast-food restaurant in the country you select.

   b. Consider whether the information can be classified. If it can, would headings be appropriate to subdivide this section? How would you present headings in the report?

2. Prepare the following preliminary and addenda parts to support the report prepared in Step 1: (a) title page, (b) contents page if the report is long enough to require one, (c) executive summary, (d) transmittal letter addressed to a manager (provide name and address) in the country you selected in a format acceptable to the country selected, (e) references page (provide complete, accurate references so that managers are able to locate your sources for additional study if needed).

19. **A Business Problem To Be Solved (Obj. 2, 3)**
Select one of the following problems to solve. Provide the necessary assumptions and background data. Then write a formal report of your analysis, conclusions, and recommendations. Include preliminary and ending parts you believe appropriate. You may need to design a questionnaire and administer it to an appropriate sample. Reviewing this list may help you identify a business-related problem you have encountered during your employment or cooperative education and intern experiences. If you choose to solve your own problem, provide the necessary assumptions and background data.

   a. Choose from the five research studies presented in Chapter 9, Application 1.

   b. While touring the manufacturing plant of a professional friend, you observe the use of universal product code (UPC) symbols to track the movement of inventory through the plant. Propose how UPC symbols could monitor the movement of employees within the manufacturing plant and investigate the implications of this action.

c. Your information systems department soon will begin to analyze the current manual information system used in your department. Investigate effective methods of preparing your employees for the impending investigation (people asking drilling questions about their work) and later for the conversion to a computer-automated information system—a major change in employees' primary work tasks.

d. Your department handles highly sensitive information and, as a result, requires extremely reliable user identification. You are considering ocular scanning or perhaps some other type of biometric identification. Investigate the advantages and disadvantages of such a system and recommend whether your organization should pursue it.

e. For some time you have recognized that drug abuse is present in your plant. The problem is becoming increasingly worse, and the company is paying the price in extra health care costs, lost productivity, and absenteeism. Investigate strategies for coping with this problem.

f. A committee of employees has recommended that the company establish a recycling center where employees can deposit recyclable items when entering the parking lot. The president has asked you to think the idea through and present a report of the cost, public relations implications, employee relations, and logistics of operating the recycling center.

g. Present a report on the cost and logistics of establishing a recycling procedure for computer paper used to prepare internal reports. Select a real or fictitious company.

h. You have received reports that several of your major competitors have installed electronic surveillance devices to monitor employees' performance. The president wants your immediate attention on this issue. Investigate the implications of using technology to monitor employees' performance. Will employees consider this procedure an invasion of privacy? Anticipate all possible problems and present strategies for dealing with them.

i. Although no employees have made formal complaints of sexual harassment in the workplace, information from the grapevine has convinced you that the company needs a formal policy concerning sexual harassment. To develop this company policy, research the legalities related to this issue and gather information (strategies) from other companies with sexual harassment policies.

j. The upcoming downsizing of your company will result in the displacement of approximately 10 percent of your middle- and upper-level managers. Investigate strategies for supporting these managers in their search for new employment. Many of these managers have worked for your company 15 to 20 years; therefore, they are quite apprehensive about the job search process.

k. You are in charge of recruiting accounting graduates for entry-level positions in your firm. You believe your current approach needs improvement because too many of the top-notch students interview with you on campus but do not accept office interviews. Investigate the problem and identify effective strategies for recruiting quality students. For example, consider the following questions and anticipate many others: Should you hold a formal reception or casual party to get to know the interviewees? Should you take the accounting faculty to lunch to increase your contact with them? What can you do to make your recruitment effort cost effective?

l. Investigate the possibility of hiring senior citizens to fill selected positions in your company.

m. A client has $10,000 to invest for her children's college education. Their ages are 12, 9, and 4. Investigate alternatives and prepare a proposal for her consideration.

20. **Analyzing the Effect of Cellular Telephones on Sales (Obj. 2, 4)**
Today you received the following electronic message from the president and CEO concerning the impact of cellular telephones on gross profit. Firmly convinced that cellular telephones can increase the company's financial picture, you decide to take a closer look at last quarter's sales activity. Specifically, you want to compare the sales performance of each sales representative with his/her use of the cellular telephone. Hopefully, this analysis will help explain the decrease in gross profits and give you the objective evidence you need to convince Mr. Cannon to change his mind.

E-mail from Scott Cannon sent 07/15/99 at 01:25 p.m.

SUBJECT: IMPACT OF CELLULAR TELEPHONES ON GROSS PROFIT

When we agreed to sink all that money into installing cellular telephones, we were assured we would see an increase in gross profit. All those studies clearly show that cellular telephones can increase the productivity of a company's sales staff.

But where are we three months after adding cellular? We've incurred exorbitant cellular telephone charges, $25,000 last month alone. What's more, the second quarter financial statements show a decrease in gross profit. It's clear to me we've invested in some new fad that isn't yielding the expected return. I've decided we should dump the cellular telephones before we lose any more profits. Take the necessary steps to discontinue our service with Cellular 2000 immediately.

H4: +D14*0.2-F14   READY

	A	B	C	D	E	F	G	H
1	Weston Engineering							
2	Analysis of Sales by Sales Representative							
3	For the Two Quarters Ended June 30, 1999							
4								
5	Sales Representative		Net Sales		Cellular Phone		Gross Profit	
6			First	Second	Phone		First	Second
7	Number	Name	Quarter	Quarter	Minutes	Cost	Quarter	Quarter
8								
9	14	Davis, S.	$55,200	$78,600	4,190	$2,724	$11,040	$12,997
10	5	Evans, C.	$64,100	$84,900	7,895	$5,132	$12,820	$11,848
11	12	Franks, F.	$62,300	$61,200	1,322	$ 859	$12,460	$11,381
12	16	Greco, B.	$58,600	$60,400	917	$ 596	$11,720	$11,484
13	18	Holt, J.	$64,700	$62,200	480	$ 312	$12,940	$12,128
14	8	Milliard, P.	$63,600	$82,800	3,390	$2,204	$12,720	$14,357
15	9	Peters, R.	$60,600	$77,200	7,745	$5,034	$12,120	$10,406
16	6	Reategui, V.	$52,300	$69,500	8,802	$5,721	$10,460	$ 8,179
17	10	Schwartz, W.	$58,500	$53,000	475	$ 309	$11,700	$10,291
18	21	Stephens, R.	$52,700	$58,100	800	$ 520	$10,540	$11,100
19	11	Wang, J.	$65,300	$84,900	3,922	$2,549	$13,060	$14,431

Required:

1. Study the accompanying spreadsheet carefully.

2. Compute the following calculations to help you analyze the data. To increase your efficiency, use an electronic spreadsheet. If software is not available, compute these calculations manually.

   a. Calculate the increase or decrease in gross profit from the first to second quarter without considering the effect of the cellular telephones. Multiply the difference between first- and second-quarter sales by the company's 20 percent gross profit rate.

   b. Calculate the increase or decrease in gross profit, including the cost of cellular telephones. Calculate the difference between the first- and second-quarter gross profit.

   c. Calculate the total of each column.

   d. Sort the information in the table in ascending order by each sales representative's telephone minutes.

3. Prepare a combination bar/line chart using the spreadsheet completed in Step 2 or graphics software. If spreadsheet or graphics software is *not* available, your instructor will provide you with a printed copy of the graph. Follow these instructions to prepare the graph:

x-axis	Identify each salesperson by number. Begin at the left, listing staff in ascending order according to cellular telephone use.
y-axis, left side	Plot the change in gross profit from the first to second quarter before

and after including cellular telephone costs; use comparative (multiple-range) bars.

y-axis, right side	Plot cellular telephone use in thousands of minutes using a line graph.

Input a descriptive title for the graph labels (*x*-axis and *y*-axis, left and right), and a legend (identify the data shown in the two bars and the line). Input an explanatory note denoting the installation of cellular telephone use at the beginning of the second quarter.

4. Analyze the data in the graph prepared in Step 3 to determine the impact of cellular telephones on gross profit.

5. Write a short memorandum report explaining your analysis to Mr. Cannon. Integrate the graph into the memo to support your recommendation.

21. **The Riverside Café (Obj. 2, 4)**[8]

Around eight o'clock on a warm, summer evening, you and a friend arrive at the Riverside Café and stop for a moment to watch a barge slowly make its way down the Arkansas River. You are eagerly greeted by Mr. James Becker, the owner, who has asked you to visit the restaurant and recommend some changes.

Mr. Becker explains, "I opened the restaurant two years ago with the purpose of attracting the young singles market. You know, a group who will come in around seven in the evening, have several drinks and some appetizers, and visit with their friends until about midnight. We're earning a reasonable rate of return; but I'm concerned that our earnings are falling short of projections."

As you find a table facing the river, you notice about six young couples with children ranging from tot-size to about ten years. While you are munching on your hamburger, a disc jockey starts playing music, but no one goes to the dance floor. In addition, your friend brings to your attention the provocative pictures hanging on the wall over the bar.

Around ten o'clock, the restaurant is practically empty except for a lone couple. Mr. Becker returns to see if you have any questions and says, "I'm leaving tomorrow on a camping trip in the Ozark Mountains—no phones, a great getaway. Could we meet as soon as I return? I'm eager to get some feedback."

Required:

1. What is Mr. Becker's problem? You can look at this situation in several ways. What do you think is wrong here? Write your answer in the form of a problem statement using clear, specific language.

2. What are three alternative solutions to the problem you defined in Step 1? In developing your solutions, be open-minded and consider every idea presented—even what may seem to be the most bizarre, off-the-wall idea. Does each alternative solution solve the problem as defined? Is each alternative solution different, or has the solution simply been rephrased using different language?

3. Write an analytical report to Mr. Becker including the following points: (a) State the problem as you see it; (b) describe briefly the three alternative solutions you identified; (c) state the solution you believe will best solve the problem, based on your objective analysis of each solution; (d) discuss the factors that led to your decision; and (e) list and explain several recommendations Mr. Becker should take to implement your solution. Explain each recommended change thoroughly.

4. Prepare a title page and transmittal letter. Address the letter to Mr. James Becker, Riverside Café, 151 Riverside Road, Little Rock, AR 72204-0151.

5. Congratulations! Mr. Becker was very impressed with your recommended changes and wants to get started right away. Although you may not be able to develop every aspect of your recommended solution, you can help Mr. Becker communicate these recommendations to the appropriate group(s). You may use any technology available to you; for example, word processing, spreadsheet, desktop publishing, graphics, and other software programs. Develop your solution, and write a letter of transmittal to Mr. Becker explaining how each item relates to the solution. Use your professional judgment to determine the manner in which you will physically present the letter and the documents to Mr. Becker.

6. You have arranged to present your ideas to Mr. Becker tomorrow at 8 a.m. in his office at the Riverside Café. Develop a ten-minute oral presentation to explain your recommended changes to Mr. Becker. Carefully consider these questions: Have I analyzed my audience and designed my message accordingly? Do my nonverbal communication cues agree with my worded messages? Have I prepared the visual aids needed to present my message effectively?

Proposals

22. **Bidding for a Convention Site (Obj. 5)**
The National Insurance Appraisers Association is planning an upcoming convention. This association of 500 members conducts a three-day conference during late October that includes at least one general session and as many as five breakout groups of 50–75 participants. The chair of this group's convention site committee has invited your city to submit a proposal bidding for the convention's 2002 national convention.
Required: As the executive director of the Economic Development Council, write a proposal including specific information to convince the group that your city can provide the needed meeting facilities, hotel accommodations, economical transportation from major U.S. cities, and a variety of social and recreational activities for members and guests.

23. **Applying for a Franchise to Open a Miniature Golf Course (Obj. 5)**
Interested in opening a miniature golf course, Vicente Cruz wrote Treasure Island, Inc., a franchiser of a popular miniature course, solicited franchise information. In answer to his request, Vicente received an extremely receptive letter requesting standard information designed to help Treasure Island determine the economic viability of the proposed location. After analyzing this preliminary information, Treasure Island will decide whether to accept Vicente's franchise application.
Treasure Island has requested preliminary information regarding the economic and social environment of the proposed site. Specifically, Vicente must provide valid, objective data concerning the population of the service area, the economic status of the population, the impact of the climate on the operation of an outdoor business, the nature and extent of competing entertainment businesses, the local tourist industry, and any other information that would support the economic success of the proposed franchise.
Required: As Vicente Cruz, prepare a letter report to the franchiser. Address it to Treasure Island, 9700 Gulfside Drive, Pensacola, FL 32501-9700.

24. **Proposing to Install an Office System (Obj. 5)**
As sales manager of Office Innovations, you are preparing a proposal to automate the Mortgage Department of City National Bank. The Mortgage Department consists of five office support staff, who prepare all mortgage forms and correspondence manually. Five loan officers advise customers on the implications of selecting various

options available in making the loan such as interest rate, points, fixed versus variable rates, and term.

Required: Write a proposal that includes the following information: (1) an explanation of how the system described in your proposal would increase the efficiency and effectiveness of the Mortgage Department; (2) complete specifications for the hardware and software you believe will solve the Mortgage Department's problem; (3) a description of the installation procedures, including a time line, if necessary, and the training included with the purchase; and (4) a budget for each item proposed in the system.

REAL-TIME INTERNET CASE

Cybertheft

One of the World Wide Web's most attractive features, easy access to a universe of information and data, is also one of its greatest vulnerabilities. Computer users can easily access, download, copy, cut, paste, and publish any of the text, pictures, video, sound, program code, and other data forms available on the Internet. An inherent conflict of interest prevails because of the consumer's appetite for data and the creator's right to remuneration for original work.

Copyrights provide an economic incentive for the development of creative works in literature, computer applications, and the performing arts. For instance, songwriters in the United States are paid royalties by radio stations for broadcasting their copyrighted musical works. Because of copyrights, it is illegal to make and sell an authorized audio duplicate of a commercial CD or a video copy of a movie. This assures that creators receive remuneration from sales for their investment of time, talent, and energy. The information superhighway, however, crosses borders where U.S. copyright laws do not apply. With the proper equipment, for example, millions of cyberfans can each buy a blank CD and make high-quality digital copies of downloaded music rather than purchasing CD recordings. Rapid advances in technology will allow consumers to download movies onto their home computer systems; thus, operators of foreign web sites would be able to provide U.S.-made movies to anyone with a computer and a credit card number, effectively bypassing copyright requirements.

Like software program applications that are widely pirated, web pages are another type of creative expression that is falling victim to cybertheft. Dealernet, an organization that helps car dealers sell vehicles over the Internet, was shocked recently to discover that a Southern California company had downloaded Dealernet Web pages and reproduced them on their own web site. The competing site deleted the pages when Dealernet threatened legal action.

Cybertheft deprives musicians, artists, and other creative parties from the income that would otherwise result from the sale and licensing of their artistic works. The World Intellectual Property Organization, sponsored by the United Nations, is working to assure copyright protection worldwide. Representatives of the United States and 160 other countries who are members of the group have signed treaties that extend copyrights to the Internet and strengthen copyright laws in many of the world's nations. On the home front, various representatives of the computer industry have joined entertainment groups such as the Recording Industry Association of America and the Motion Picture Association of America to form the Creative Incentive Coalition; a major activity of the group is to lobby Congress for legislation and treaties that would provide better copyright protection.[5]

Every business entity has a responsibility to avoid situations of copyright infringement and to assure that its employees do so as well. Companies are legally responsible for violations if the copyright owner can prove that they knew or should have known about the infringement. Texaco, for instance, agreed to a $1 million settlement in 1995 after a federal appellate court ruled that it was liable for copyright violations.[6] While it is rare for employees to be taken to court for copyright violation, it does occur and carries heavy penalties. Such liability makes it advisable for organizations to develop policies against copyright violation and to provide training to employees about the risks and responsibilities. Visit the following sites and complete the activities as directed by your instructor.

Internet Sites

http://www.wipo.org/
http://www.benedict.com:80/
http://www.tht.com/VUartF96copyright.htm

Activities

1. Visit the listed sites to determine current international copyright issues or cases. Provide a one-page written summary to your instructor that describes the issue and the country(ies) involved.

2. Write a short, informative report describing how a company's web site can violate the copyrights of others and giving advice to organizational web page developers for avoiding possible copyright infringement.

3. "The nature of cyberspace defies copyright enforcement." Write a one- to two-page justification for this statement, giving reasons and/or examples.

FIGURE 11-10
Good example of long report.

EXAMINATION OF THE ISSUE OF ELECTRONIC MONITORING OF EMPLOYEES

Prepared for

**Courtney Hardin-Burns
Chief Information Officer
Federated Underwriters
Dallas, Texas**

Prepared by

**Justine Houston, Research Assistant
James Barnes, Research Assistant
Amanda Keene, Research Assistant**

April 1, 1999

FIGURE 11-10
Good example of long report.

CONTENT:
- Provides specific title to give reader overview of topic covered in report. Arranges title in inverted pyramid format; will use same format on page 1 of report.
- States the name and title of reader—person who authorized report.
- Includes the name and title of person and/or organization that prepared report. Including address is a matter of preference and company requirements.
- Includes date report was submitted for later reference.

FORMAT:
- Omits page number but counts the page.

GRAPHIC DESIGN TO ENHANCE APPEARANCE AND EFFECTIVENESS:
- Uses all capital letters and boldface, large font size to emphasize title.
- Uses different font for remaining items to add interest and to distinguish them from title.
- Uses double border to add professional flair.

FIGURE 11-10
continued.

CONTENT:

- Uses informal, natural tone that involves reader. Note personal pronouns.
- Presents the report and reminds reader that she authorized it.
- Discusses the methods used (secondary and primary data) to solve the problem.
- Summarizes major conclusions; expresses willingness to discuss the results.

FORMAT:

- Uses an acceptable memorandum format for a report submitted to someone inside the company.
- Adds enclosure notation to indicate report is included.
- Center page number in small Roman numerals at bottom of page; may omit number but count as a page.

FEDERATED UNDERWRITERS
1340 JOHNSON AVENUE, NORTH / DALLAS, TX 75260-1340 / (214) 555-3193 FAX: (214) 555-9783

TO: Courtney Hardin-Burns, Chief Information Officer

FROM: Justine Houston, Research Assistant *J.H.*
            James Barnes, Research Assistant *J.B.*
            Amanda Keene, Research Assistant *AK*

DATE: April 2, 1999

SUBJECT: Report on Electronic Monitoring of Employee Activity

Here is the report on electronic monitoring of employees that you authorized on February 15.

The report presents the case both for and against electronic monitoring and makes recommendations about its use to the company. Current business literature was examined to form a conceptual basis for the study. A survey was conducted of 98 business managers representing various segments of the business community; results revealed how and why firms are using electronic monitoring.

Electronic monitoring offers advantages for objective performance appraisal but must be used with caution. Issues related to employee privacy, staff morale, and information access and dissemination must be addressed.

Thank you for allowing us the opportunity to participate in this worthwhile study. We are confident that this report will aid you in making appropriate decisions about the use of electronic monitoring, and we will be happy to discuss its findings with you.

asl

Attachment

ii

1½"

CONTENTS

DS

FIGURES

iii

FIGURE 11-10
continued.

CONTENT:

- Omits the outline numbering system (I, II, A, B) but arranges the outline to indicate the importance of the headings (main heads placed at left margin; minor ones indented).

- Presents each heading exactly as it appears in the report.

- Prepares the contents after completing the report; allows word processing software to generate contents so it can be updated quickly with each draft of the report.

- Omits the word "table" or "list," an obvious fact.

FORMAT:

- Combines contents and figures on same page to save space.

- Adds leaders (spaced periods) to guide the eyes from the heading to the page number.

- Includes the page number on which each major and minor section begins.

FIGURE 11-10
continued.

CONTENT:

- Uses Executive Summary, the term commonly used in business rather than "Abstract," the term APA recommends.

- Provides needed background and explains problems leading to need for the study. Presents purpose of study and identifies person authorizing it.

- Describes method used to solve the problem.

- Synthesizes major findings focusing on specific findings needed to support conclusions that follow.

- Highlights the conclusions and recommendations based on analysis of the findings.

FORMAT:

- Centers heading in all capital letters using a larger, boldface font for emphasis.

1½″

EXECUTIVE SUMMARY
DS

Federated Underwriters, a large, full-service insurance company, maintains offices throughout the 48 contiguous states. Courtney Hardin-Burns, chief information officer, oversees the management information systems mainframe functions as well as end-user computing. In her efforts to improve productivity and increase efficiency of information control and dissemination, electronic monitoring of employees has been considered. Current capabilities of the mainframe and network systems would allow electronic logging of user identification, file usage, file manipulation, on-line user time, and so on. In essence, the computer user leaves an "electronic fingerprint" that could be traced and analyzed in a number of ways. Hardin-Burns authorized a study to examine issues related to the electronic monitoring of employee computer activities.

Research was conducted in two ways: (1) Current business literature was examined, and (2) 98 business managers were surveyed concerning the use of electronic monitoring in their work settings.

The report addressed the following questions: (1) What is the frequency of electronic monitoring within organizations? (2) What are the advantages and disadvantages of monitoring? (3) What are the legal and ethical issues related to monitoring? (4) What factors are related to successful electronic monitoring? (5) Should Federated Underwriters institute an electronic monitoring procedure? Legal, ethical, and productivity issues were examined, and guidelines were developed for the effective use of electronic monitoring.

The study concluded that electronic monitoring does offer some advantages that justify its use by Federated Underwriters. Certain safeguards should be applied to its use, however, including the protection of employee privacy, development of policies for access and dissemination of information, and maintenance of staff morale.

iv

1½″ **EXAMINATION OF THE ISSUE OF ELECTRONIC MONITORING OF EMPLOYEES**

DS

Introduction

Monitoring of worker activities is not new. Nearly a century ago, Frederick Taylor used detailed worker monitoring through time and motion studies to find the most efficient methods of carrying out tasks. Today's technology provides employers with the means to gather information about employees' work activities in unprecedented detail (Ottensmeyer & Heroux, 1991). Mainframe and network capabilities allow electronic logging of data, such as user identification, file usage, file manipulation, and on-line user time. In essence, the computer user leaves an "electronic fingerprint" that can be traced and analyzed in a number of ways.

Purpose of the Study

The purpose of the study was to determine whether Federated Underwriters should implement electronic monitoring of employees. Answers were sought to the following questions:

1. What is the frequency of electronic monitoring within organizations?

2. What are the advantages and disadvantages of electronic monitoring?

3. What legal and ethical issues are raised by the use of computer monitoring?

4. What factors are related to successful electronic monitoring?

5. Should Federated Underwriters institute electronic monitoring?

Methods and Procedures Used

Secondary research was conducted through traditional and electronic searches of periodicals, books, and government documents. Interviews were conducted with 98 conveniently selected business managers from throughout Texas. The sample represented a cross section of business

1

FIGURE 11-10
continued.

CONTENT:

- Gives specific purpose of study. Provides methods and procedures and sources of information used to add credibility.

- Refers reader to Appendix figure listing types of businesses surveyed.

COHERENCE:

- Uses side heading to move reader from one minor division of the introduction to another.

- Uses centered heading to move reader from introduction to first major division. Follows with a lead-in paragraph that previews the information to be presented and separates a major and a minor heading (text must separate two headings).

FORMAT:

- Sinks first page to 1½ inches for added appeal.

- Centers title in all capital letters; overrides APA format (upper and lowercase) as directed in company style manual. Uses larger, boldface font for emphasis.

- Formats centered and side headings in boldface font. Note capitalization style for each level.

- Centers Arabic numeral 1 inch from bottom of page.

FIGURE 11-10
continued.

CONTENT:

- Uses in-text citations to indicate ideas paraphrased from secondary sources. Page numbers required for direct quotes only.

COHERENCE:

- Uses side heading to indicate the second minor division of the major division started on previous page.
- Uses centered heading to denote the next major division. Follows with transition sentence that introduces the information to be presented and separates a major and a minor heading.

FORMAT:

- Numbers page 2 and remaining pages with an Arabic numeral at the top right margin 1 inch from the top (or default top margin of the word processing software used).
- Uses consistent format for centered and side headings.
- Single-spaces final copy of report for space efficiency; APA style requires double-spacing.

2

types (see Appendix, Figure 4). Interviewees were asked a set of questions dealing with the application of electronic monitoring in their respective companies.

Background of Electronic Monitoring

While monitoring of employees is common, widespread disagreement exists over its scope and effectiveness.

Frequency of Monitoring

Determining the extent to which electronic monitoring is occurring is difficult because workers, in many cases, may not be aware of it. A study conducted by the National Association of Working Women examined data processing, word processing, and customer-service operations in 110 work sites and found that 98 percent used computers to track the movements of workers (*Computer monitoring*, 1988). According to an American Civil Liberties Union study of the workplace, more than 20 million workers have their e-mail computer files and/or voice mail searched by the employers (Dichter & Burkhardt, 1996). The National Institute of Occupational Safety and Health estimates that two thirds of users of visual display terminals are monitored (Bible, 1990); and in industries such telecommunications, insurance and banking, it is estimated that eighty percent of employees are subject to monitoring (Dichter & Burkhardt, 1996).

Advantages and Disadvantages of Monitoring

Electronic monitoring can count the number of keystrokes per hour and indicate how often an employee does certain activities or uses a terminal. Keeping tabs on the quality of service, enhancing productivity, and detecting dishonesty are the most common reasons employers monitor. Some workers are pleased that their work is being observed because they want to be rewarded for their efforts. When monitoring is used to evaluate work, the machine can be fairer than a person because machines are color-blind and do not recognize gender. Electronic monitoring can make data about performance available more quickly and

FIGURE 11-10
continued.

3

more frequently, thereby increasing employee awareness of personal productivity (Bible, 1990).

Monitoring may, however, be counterproductive, given the animosity and stress that it prompts in employees. Judging by complaints from employees and unions, the general feeling among workers is that monitoring threatens their privacy, intrudes on their personal work in progress, and leads to their being evaluated on criteria that they do not understand. Workers tend to feel that "Big Brother" is always watching, and the fact that everyone is subject to the same scrutiny does little to relieve that sense of exposure (Ottensmeyer & Heroux, 1991). Some companies have implemented monitoring and then stopped because they discovered how counterproductive it could be (Bible, 1990).

Employees frequently find ways to counter attempts at monitoring. When keystrokes are monitored, for example, a key can be held down continuously to make the count go up (although some software programs can detect this deception). Some employees, offended by what they perceive as a sudden lack of trust, reduce their work efforts to the bare minimum needed to get by. Middle managers foil monitoring attempts by filling in their electronic schedules with meetings because employers may tend to think managers are productive if they are in meetings (Bible, 1990).

Legal and Ethical Considerations in Monitoring

Courts and legislatures have historically allowed employers broad rights of observation and record keeping when monitoring workers. These rights are based on employer ownership of the premises at which the work is done and on the basic right of management to control the work process (U.S. Congress, 1987). Currently, no federal laws ban or restrict electronic monitoring of work performance. One law that vaguely relates to the issue of electronic monitoring is the Omnibus Crime Control and Safe Streets Act of 1968, which was designed to protect the privacy of wire and oral communications. Advances in technology have rendered the wording of the act obsolete

CONTENT:
- Uses in-text citations to indicate ideas paraphrased from secondary sources. Provides page number for direct quotation.
- Summarizes major section before moving to the next one.

COHERENCE:
- Uses centered heading to move reader from one major division to the next. Follows with transition sentence that previews the information to be presented.

FIGURE 11-10
continued.

FORMAT:

- Indents quotation from both margins for emphasis.
- Ensures the page does not end or begin with a single line of a paragraph (applies to all pages in a report).

4

and thus inapplicable to electronic monitoring (Cooney, 1991). Presently, in the absence of any policy to the contrary, users should assume that they have no privacy in workplace environments. Courts have upheld the right of the employer to monitor any and all employee communications over the employer's computer system regardless of implied or explicit statements regarding employee message privacy (*Computer Professionals*, 1996).

Congress is considering legislation that would have considerable effect on the future of monitoring. This legislation, the Privacy for Consumers and Workers Act, would limit the use of electronic devices in monitoring employees' activities. The act would require employers to provide employees with prior written notice of electronic monitoring and to signal them orally or visually when monitoring is being performed. Furthermore, it would require that employees be informed of the forms of electronic monitoring to be used, the personal data to be collected, the frequency of monitoring, and the use of the data (Smith, 1993). In addition to action pending at the federal level, many states, including Connecticut, Massachusetts, Minnesota, New Jersey, Oregon, Rhode Island, New Mexico, and New York, are developing their own comprehensive monitoring bills (Nussbaum, 1989).

In the absence of existing legislation related to electronic monitoring, the Department of Justice in Washington has ruled it legal. The Justice Department, however, strongly advises system administrators to inform users of monitoring. If keystroke monitoring is used—even for purposes of detecting intruders, they should "ensure that all system users, authorized and unauthorized, are notified that such monitoring may be undertaken" (Smith, 1993, p. 204).

Organizations that represent employees have expressed strong reservations about the use of electronic monitoring. The 1987 AFL-CIO Convention adopted the following resolution on the issue:

> Electronic surveillance invades workers' privacy, erodes their sense of dignity, and frustrates their efforts to do high-quality work, by placing a single-minded emphasis on speed and other

5

purely quantitative measurements. Numerous studies have shown that monitoring creates high levels of workplace stress that results in a variety of adverse health conditions (Lund, 1991, p. 197).

In general, opponents of monitoring argue that it undermines customer service, teamwork, and the quality of work life (Grant & Christopher, 1989).

As surely as workers need to be protected against abuses in electronic monitoring, business has the legal right to ensure that it provides a safe working environment. Proponents of monitoring point out that businesses need it to investigate criminal activity and misuse of company property; therefore, the right to unobstructed monitoring is essential to business security. Under current law, monitoring that serves a legitimate business purpose could be vigorously and probably successfully defended. However, possible new legal developments should be carefully watched.

Electronic monitoring of employees is, for at least some purposes, legal. A more difficult question is whether it is desirable; and if so, under what conditions? Impressive gains in productivity must be carefully weighed against potential damage to quality of work life.

Guidelines for the Use of Electronic Monitoring

Research into work environments where electronic monitoring is used reveals interesting information about worker acceptance of the procedure. The following guidelines help ensure cooperation:

- **Reasonable work.** Work standards must be perceived by employees as reasonable and attainable. This feature is essential to a perception of fairness in the process. Furthermore, time spans must be set for measurement performance (Angel, 1989).

- **Relevant tasks.** Only relevant tasks should be included in an electronic monitoring system. Overwhelming insignificant data does not usefully serve employees or employers. Further, excessive monitoring can increase the cost of employee performance appraisal while providing few additional benefits (Henriques, 1986).

FIGURE 11-10
continued.

COHERENCE:
- Uses centered heading to move reader from one major division to the next. Follows with a lead-in paragraph that previews the information to be presented.

FORMAT:
- Uses bullets to emphasize the guidelines; would use numbers if the sequence were important.

FIGURE 11-10
continued.

6

- **Timely intervals.** Evaluation intervals should be appropriate. Production of continuous reports is not only resource consuming but rarely necessary (Henriques, 1986).

- **Employee access.** Employers should have access to their computer-monitored records, which can be used for improving performance and eliminating errors (Henriques, 1986).

- **Specified standards.** Specific, well-defined standards should be set for each monitored task. Under such conditions, workers know exactly what is expected of them (Angel, 1989).

- **Measurable tasks.** Chosen tasks must be measurable and definitive (Angel, 1989).

- **Results-oriented output.** Output from the system should be results oriented. The important element is the measuring of output, not the means of achieving it (Angel, 1989).

- **Congruent pay.** The monitoring system should include a pay schedule congruent with different performance levels. This requirement ensures that those who consistently perform above predetermined standards are appropriately compensated (Angel, 1989).

- **Mutual goals.** Computerized monitoring is an effective aid only if benefits to employer and employees are explicitly stated. Procedures that appear to advance only the employer's best interest will not be successful (Angel, 1989).

- **Effective supervision.** Grant and Christopher (1991) found that supervisors played a critical role in determining whether monitoring would be stressful and whether data feedback would undermine or promote employee satisfaction.

Thus, when safeguards are incorporated into the electronic appraisal process, the result can be better satisfied and more efficient workers. Employees will experience less work-related anxiety, will be more gratified and content, will be objectively evaluated for work performed, and will be properly compensated for output produced. Positive impact on employers will include low-cost, effective and meaningful evaluation

7

tools; methods to identify unique, individual problems; procedures for providing direction and guidelines for employees; and improved training programs (Angel, 1989).

Survey of Businesses Concerning Electronic Monitoring

Of the 98 managers who participated in the current study, 66 (67%) indicated that their companies engaged in some type of electronic monitoring of employee activities. These respondents provided information related to the uses of monitoring and employee access to the data collected.

Reported Uses of Monitoring

When asked about the types of computer activities that were monitored in their respective organizations, respondents indicated log-on identification, files accessed and changed by users, user time on the system, electronic mail, and random checks of file accuracy, as shown in Figure 1.

Figure 1

How the Results of Electronic Monitoring Are Used

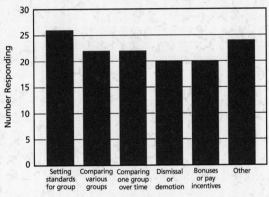

FIGURE 11-10
continued.

FORMAT:

- Uses centered heading to move reader from one major division to the next. Follows with a lead-in paragraph that previews the information to be presented and separates a major and a minor heading.

- Uses side heading to divide the major section into minor divisions.

CONTENT:

- Includes survey data not depicted in a graph or table.

- Summarizes major points in the bar chart and the table and refers the reader to the figures. Provides title specific enough to assist readers who skim the report.

FORMAT:

- Places Figure 1 immediately following its textual references.

- Labels a bar chart as figure and numbers consecutively with one numbering system.

FIGURE 11-10
continued.

CONTENT:

- Summarizes major points in the table and refers reader to figure. Provides figure number and specific title.

FORMAT:

- Places Figure 2 immediately following its textual reference. Centers figure number and title on separate lines separated by a double space. (Refer to Chapter 10 for specific guidelines for formatting tables.)
- Labels the table as a figure and numbers consecutively with one numbering system.
- Places Figure 3 at top of next page.

8

Results of electronic monitoring were used in a variety of ways, with the setting of standards and comparative data analysis being the most common uses.

Employee Access to Monitoring Data

Managers in the current study were asked to what extent employees were informed of the company's monitoring activities. In nearly one half the cases, employees were informed orally or perhaps orally as well as by one of the other means, such as in writing or with a message on the computer. In 18 percent of cases, employees were not informed of the monitoring activity, as shown in Figure 2.

Figure 2

Extent to Which Employees Are Informed of Monitoring

Method of Informing	Number Responding	Percent
Orally, as to possibility	32	48
By the system during monitoring	18	27
In writing, as to possibility	14	21
Other means	8	12
Not informed	12	18

Two thirds of the companies performed continuous monitoring; one fourth used random monitoring; and the remainder reported intermittent monitoring at set intervals. Respondents were also asked to indicate the ways in which the data acquired through monitoring was reported. More than one half said that group or department data was the method of reporting; 42 percent used individual reporting, and 18 percent used company-wide data reporting. Some businesses used a combination of the reporting methods. In a related item, managers were asked who sees the results of the electronic monitoring. Upper-level management is most likely to see the results of monitoring. In only one third of the organizations surveyed do employees see their own data, as reported in Figure 3.

9

Figure 3
Who Sees the Results of Electronic Monitoring

Party Who Views Data	Number Responding	Percent
Upper-level management	46	70
Immediate supervisor	38	58
Employee	22	33
Peers of employee	20	30
Other	14	21

While supervisors are typically the recipients of information obtained from electronic monitoring, only one third of the responding organizations indicated that employees are allowed to see information about the monitoring of their own work.

Summary, Conclusions, and Recommendations

Consideration of primary and secondary research has led to a thorough analysis of the electronic monitoring issue.

Summary

Electronic performance monitoring evokes strong and often contradictory responses among the parties concerned with its use. The potential for impressive gains in productivity must be carefully weighed against possible damage to the quality of work life. Managers who choose to use electronic monitoring must consider effective and fair system design carefully. They must demonstrate that the data generated through electronic monitoring helps them see the positive as well as the negative aspects of employee performance, and individual performance must be tied to salary incentives or performance ratings.

Issues in data reporting must be considered. The need for timely system data must be balanced against the risk that information overload will occur. Dissemination of data is an issue; low producers find the comparison of their performance to that of coworkers demoralizing,

FIGURE 11-10
continued.

CONTENT:

- Discusses major points in the table. Provides figure number and specific title.
- Combines "Summary, Conclusions, and Recommendations," an appropriate heading for a report designed to solve a problem.
- Includes a logical lead-in to a subsection to avoid stacked headings.

FORMAT:

- Places Figure 3 following its textual reference.
- Uses centered heading to indicate major division. Includes side headings to divide summary, conclusions, and recommendations into minor divisions.

FIGURE 11-10
continued.

CONTENT:

- Provides a lead-in sentence to introduce conclusions and recommendations sections.
- Includes broad generalizations drawn from the findings and does *not* repeat specific findings.

FORMAT:

- Enumerates conclusions and recommendations for emphasis and clarity.
- Ensures that page begins with at least two lines of text.

10

and even high performers can find the public display of their productivity to be undesirable.

Finally, which tasks should be monitored? Monitoring a task may confirm a belief that a task is important while failure to include a task or behavior can be interpreted as a signal that management does not consider that factor worth watching.

Conclusions

Based on the findings of this research, the following conclusions were drawn:

1. The most significant result of the study was the realization that companies need to address the issue of electronic monitoring and develop a policy for its use.
2. While the current legal structure permits the use of electronic monitoring, informing employees of its use seems advisable.
3. Each organization must examine issues of morale and productivity to determine whether electronic monitoring will be a worthwhile means of assessment.

Recommendations

Federated Underwriters should institute an electronic monitoring program that includes the following features:

1. A study should be undertaken to identify the activities that should be monitored.
2. All computer users should be notified in writing that their computer activities are subject to monitoring.
3. Individual data derived from monitoring should be available to employees.
4. Data derived from monitoring should be used as only one indicator of employee performance.

11

Electronic monitoring is a controversial and complicated issue with implications for performance appraisal, worker productivity, and employee privacy. A promising tool in the managerial process, it is not without its dangers. The challenge to Federated Underwriters is to develop acceptable procedures and guidelines for managing this electronic capability successfully.

FIGURE 11-10
continued.

CONTENT:

• Provides logical closure to convince the reader that the report is thorough and complete.

FIGURE 11-10
continued.

CONTENT:

- Presents in-text paren-
thetical citations formatted in APA style.
Italicizes titles of books
and periodicals and vol-
ume numbers because
software supports the
feature.

- Indents first line five
spaces as required by
APA.

FORMAT:

- Continues page number-
ing used in the report.

- Centers heading in all
capital letters with larger,
boldface font used for
similar headings in the
report (title, contents,
executive summary, and
appendix).

- Single-spaces references
to be consistent with the
single spacing in the
report.

1½″   12

REFERENCES
DS

Angel, F. N. (1989, November). Evaluating employees by computer. *Personnel Administrator, 34*(11), 67–72.

Bible, J. D. (1990). *Privacy in the Workplace.* New York: Quorum Books.

Computer monitoring and other dirty tricks. (1988). New York: National Association of Working Women.

Computer Professionals for Social Responsibility. (1996, September 3) *Electronic Privacy Principles.* [On-line]. Available http://cpsr.org/dox/privacy8.htm [1997, August 12].

Cooney, C. M. (1991). Who's watching the workplace? The electronic monitoring debate spreads to Capitol Hill, *Security Management, 35*(11), 26–35.

Dichter, M. S., & Burkhardt, M. S. (1996). *Electronic interaction in the workplace: Monitoring, retrieving, and storing employee communications in the Internet age.* [On-line]. American Employment Law Council, Fourth Annual Conference, Asheville, NC, October 2–5, 1996. Available http://www.mlb.com/speech1/htm#2 [1997, August 12].

Grant, R., & Christopher, H. (1989, Spring). Monitoring service workers via computer: The effect on employees, productivity, and service. *National Productivity Review,* 101–112.

Grant, R., & Christopher, H. (1991, November). Computerized performance monitors: Factors affecting acceptance. *IEEE Transactions on Engineering Management,* 306–316.

Henriques, V. E. (1986, December). In defense of computer monitoring. *Training,* 120.

Lund, J. (1991). Computerized work performance monitoring and production standards: A review of labor law issues. *Labor Law Journal, 43*(4), 195–203.

Nussbaum, K. (1989). Computer monitoring: A threat to the right to privacy? Speech delivered to the Computer Professionals for Social

FIGURE 11-10
continued.

13

Responsibility Annual Meeting, Washington, D.C., 1989. In DeJoie, R., Fowler, G., & Paradice, D. (Eds.), *Ethical issues in information systems*. Boston: Boyd and Fraser, 1991.

Ottensmeyer, E., & Heroux, M. (1991). Ethics, public policy, and managing advanced technologies: The case of electronic surveillance, *The Journal of Business Ethics*, 10(7), 519–526.

Smith, L. B. (1993, June 28). Electronic monitoring raises legal and societal questions, *PCWeek*, 204.

U.S. Congress, Office of Technology Assessment. (1987, September). *The electronic supervisor: New technology, new tensions*. (OTA-CIT-333). Washington, DC, U.S. Government Printing Office.

FIGURE 11-10
continued.

FORMAT:

- Continues page numbering used in the report.
- Centers "Appendix" and title in all capital letters; uses larger, boldface font to add emphasis and to ensure consistency with similar headings (title, contents, executive summary, and appendix).

CONTENT:

- Includes Figure 4 that was referenced on page 1.

14

APPENDIX

DEMOGRAPHIC DATA

Figure 4

Types of Businesses Surveyed

Type of Business	Number Responding	Percent of Total
Banking/Finance	20	20.4
Manufacturing/Construction	16	16.3
Wholesale/Retail Sales	14	14.3
Miscellaneous Services	14	14.3
Agriculture/Drilling/Mining	10	10.2
Communication/Transportation/Utility	10	10.2
Insurance	8	8.2
Education/Government	4	4.1
Legal	2	2.0

CHAPTER TWELVE

Designing and Delivering Business Presentations

LEARNING OBJECTIVES

When you have completed Chapter 12, you will be able to:

1 Plan a business presentation that accomplishes the speaker's goals and meets the audience's needs.

2 Organize and develop the three parts of an effective presentation.

3 Select, design, and use presentation visuals effectively.

4 Deliver speeches with increasing confidence.

5 Discuss effective strategies for adapting oral presentations to an intercultural audience.

"**T**he more things change, the more they stay the same" is a commonly heard expression. This saying is indeed true in the rapidly changing environment of business communications, particularly in the area of oral presentations.

As basic presentation tools, the flip chart and pointer may have seemed appropriate at one time, but technological advances since then have made the old standbys "go the way of the dinosaur."[1] New technology, including user-friendly software packages, increasingly powerful laptop computers, and a host of other electronic media has enabled businesspeople to rely less on corporate art departments or personal assistants to generate effective presentations. This portability allows sales personnel to incorporate client feedback quickly, which can make a more positive impression on the client, thus enhancing the potential for success.

To compete in this changing environment, businesspeople need to be knowledgeable and skilled in the use of new electronic tools. However, it is important to remember that a presentation can fall flat if it relies too heavily on graphics and multimedia teasers with little or no substance at its core. You need to keep in mind the basics of preparing an effective presentation, which have not changed with the advent of computer graphics and multimedia packages. These basics include keeping the audience in mind, making clear what the issues are, and being sincere and responsive. So, although many components of business communication are changing at a rapid pace, the foundation has remained the same: the ability to relate ideas clearly and effectively—those skills that you develop through your own critical thinking for which no amount of innovative technological tools can substitute.

Each time you communicate effectively, you gain status and earn respect. You find managing others easier, and you become promotable to increasingly higher levels. This chapter provides guidelines for refining your speaking ability; you will learn to plan and organize your presentation, develop dynamic presentation media, refine your delivery, and adapt your presentation to an intercultural audience.

1 *Plan a business presentation that accomplishes the speaker's goals and meets the audience's needs.*

Planning an Effective Business Presentation

An oral presentation is an important means of obtaining and exchanging information for decision making and policy development. Because several people receive the message at the same time, and the audience is able to provide immediate feedback for clarification, oral presentations can significantly reduce message distortion and misunderstanding. Understanding the purpose you hope to achieve through your oral presentation and a conception of your audience will enable you to organize the content for an effective presentation.

Identify Your Purpose

Determining what you want to accomplish is an important first step in planning a presentation. In his book, *Do's and Taboo's of Public Speaking*, Axtell provides two excellent mechanisms for condensing your presentation into a brief, achievable purpose that will direct you as you identify the major points to be covered and the content to support those points:[2]

- Ask yourself, "What is my message?" Then, develop a phrase, a single thought, or a conclusion you want the audience to take with them from the presentation.

A comfortable command of public speaking is one of the most empowering skills any businessperson can have. Whether they are physicians, engineers, politicians, or salespeople, the best speakers will always have a better chance of rising to a leadership position. All management hopefuls should begin training early and often for public speaking—through high school and college debate teams, speech classes, as Toastmasters, in professional and civic organizations—in fact, at any opportunity available to them.

Cynthia Pharr, President
C. Pharr & Company, Inc.

This elementary statement likely may be the final sentence in your presentation—the basic message you want the audience to remember.

- Imagine your audience is leaving the room and someone has asked these people to summarize the message they had just heard in as few words as possible. Ideally, you would want to hear the people describe your central purpose.

Know Your Audience

As a general observation, audiences *do* want to be in tune with a speaker. A well-prepared speaker can establish audience rapport easily. Your speaking goal is to have the audience react favorably to you and to your message. Keep in mind that your success will be judged by only one group: the audience. From planning your speech to practicing its delivery, focus your preparation on the audience.

How is preparation of written messages and oral presentations similar in terms of empathy for the audience?

Because all audiences are not the same, speakers must be able to identify characteristics common to each audience. A research scientist should not deliver a speech to a lay audience in highly technical terms. A speech about acid rain to a farm group should address the farmers' problems, for example, and not focus on scientific causes of acid rain. People listen to speeches about things of interest to them. "What's in it for me?" is the question most listeners ask. Here are some important facts you can obtain about most audiences: ages, genders, occupations, educational levels, attitudes, values, broad and specific interests, and needs, if any.

Your analysis of most of these factors enables you to direct your speech specifically to your audience. In addition to these factors, you should also consider certain things about the occasion and location. Patriotic speeches to a group of military veterans will differ from speeches to a group of new recruits, just as Fourth of July speeches will differ from Memorial Day speeches. Seek answers to the following questions when you discuss your speaking engagement with someone representing the group or audience:

1. *Who* is the audience and *who* requested the presentation? General characteristics of the audience to consider include gender, age, background and extent of knowledge and experience with the topic, attitude toward topic (receptive or not eager to listen), anticipated response to the use of electronic presentation technology, and required or volunteer attendance.

2. *Why* is this topic important to the audience? What will the audience do with the information presented?

3. *What* environmental factors affect the presentation?

- How many will be in the audience?
- Will I be the only speaker? If not, where does my presentation fit in the program? What time of day?
- How much time will I be permitted? Minimum? Maximum?
- What are the seating arrangements? How far will the audience be from the speaker? Will a microphone be available?

Answers to these questions reveal whether the speaking environment will be intimate or remote, whether the audience is likely to be receptive and alert or nonreceptive and tired, and whether you will have to develop additional motivational or persuasive devices.

To illustrate the planning stage of a presentation, assume that you are a promotional representative for Project COPE (Challenging Outdoor Personal Experiences), a personal development program. Through a weekend of mentally and physically challenging events, participants develop self-confidence, trust, communication, and teamwork. Participants build these valuable managerial skills as they attempt to do things they have never done before and work together to develop creative ways to overcome the various obstacles. The "trust fall" (falling backwards to be caught by a team member) and climbing a 30-foot tower and leaning out to catch a bar being held by team members are examples of these demanding events. Several of the senior executives of a large multinational company are sold on your program as a viable alternative for alleviating the company's slow response to the marketplace—a common problem with large companies. You have been invited to speak during the company's annual two-day management retreat. You are scheduled to speak at 10 a.m. and will have 30 minutes to present your message to 300 managers representing various ages, genders, and cultures. Your analysis of the purpose and your audience follow:

Purpose:	To convince managers that COPE can prepare them to deal effectively with slow response rates inherent in large companies.
Audience:	Simple message will be well received by managers desiring to improve the quality of their work and the company's competitiveness. Audience should be alert for this early morning presentation; retreat environment should minimize mental distractions. Managers will likely welcome a captivating electronic presentation with realistic images of the activities you will describe.

2 *Organize and develop the three parts of an effective presentation.*

What purpose does each main part of an oral presentation serve? How can the speaker avoid redundancy in the delivery of the three parts?

Organizing the Content

With an understanding of the purpose of your oral presentation—why you are giving it, what you hope to achieve—and a conception of the size, interest, and background of the audience, you are prepared to outline your presentation and identify appropriate content. First introduced by Dale Carnegie, a famous speaker and speech trainer, and still recommended by speech experts today, the simple but effective presentation format includes an introduction, a body, and a close:

Introduction:	Tell the audience what you are going to tell them.
Body:	Tell them.
Close:	Tell them what you have told them.

This design may sound repetitive; on the contrary, it works quite well. An audience processes information verbally and cannot slow the speaker down when information is complex or reread a confusing section. Thus, the repetition aids the listener in processing the information that supports the speaker's purpose.

Introduction

What you say at the beginning sets the stage for your entire presentation and initiates your rapport with the audience. However, inexperienced speakers settle for unoriginal and overused introductions, such as "My name is . . ., and my topic. . . ." or "It is a pleasure . . .," or negative statements, such as apologies for lack of preparation, boring delivery, or late arrival, that reduce the audience's desire to listen. An effective introduction accomplishes the following goals:

Consider an effective oral presentation or speech you have heard. What factors made it successful?

- *Captures attention and involves the audience.* Choose an attention-getter that is relevant to the subject and appropriate for the situation. Attention-getting techniques may include
  - a shocking statement or startling statistic.
  - a quotation by an expert or well-known person.
  - an appropriate joke or humor.
  - a demonstration or dramatic presentation aid.
  - a related story or anecdote.
  - a reference to the occasion of the presentation.

  To involve the audience directly, ask for a show of hands in response to a direct question, allow the audience time to think about the answer to a rhetorical question, or explain why the information is important and how it will benefit the listeners. For example,

  A speech on highway safety might begin with a startling statistic:

  "Just last year 15 young people from our community were killed in the prime of their lives by automobile crashes that could have been avoided."

  A drug awareness speech to young people might begin with a true story:

  "I live in a quiet, middle-class, comfortable neighborhood. That is, until just a few months ago—when four young people from three different families were killed in an automobile accident following a party at which drugs were used."

  A report presenting a site-selection recommendation could introduce the subject and set the stage for the findings (inductive sequence) or the recommendation (deductive sequence):

  Inductive: "When we were granted the approval to open a new distribution facility in Madison, South Carolina, we assigned a team to select the best possible suburban location."

  Deductive: "I want to inform you about why and how we selected Madison, South Carolina, as the location for the distribution facility.

- *Establishes rapport.* Initiate rapport with the listeners; convince them that you are concerned that they benefit from the presentation and that you are qualified to speak on the topic. You might share a personal story that relates to the topic but reveals something about yourself, or discuss your background or a specific experience with the topic being discussed.

- ***Presents the purpose statement and previews the points that will be developed.*** To maintain the interest you have captured, present your purpose statement directly so that the audience is certain to hear it. Use original statements and avoid clichés such as "My topic today is . . . or "I'd like to talk with you about . . ." Next, preview the major points you will discuss in the order you will discuss them. For example, you might say,

---

"First, I'll discuss . . ., then, . . ., and finally. . . ."

"The acquisition and construction cost of all three sites were comparable. The decision to locate the new distribution facility in Madison, South Carolina, is based on three criteria: (1) quality of living, (2) transportation accessibility, and (3) availability of an adequate workforce.

How can the speaker effectively guide the audience from one major section of the presentation to another?

Revealing the presentation plan will help the audience understand how the parts of the body are tied together to support the purpose statement, thus increasing the coherence of the presentation. For a long, complex presentation, you might display a presentation visual that lists the points in the order they will be covered. As you begin each major point, display a slide that contains that point and perhaps a related image. These divider slides partition your oral presentation as headings do a written report and, thus, move the listener more easily from one major point to the next.

Body

In a small group, develop a captivating introduction for the COPE presentation or a topic your instructor provides. Be prepared to discuss the techniques you used to capture the audience's attention, to involve the audience and yourself, and to preview the major points.

In a typical presentation of 20 to 30 minutes, limit your presentation to only a few major points (three to five) because of time constraints and your audience's ability to absorb only a few major points, regardless of the length of the speech. Making every statement in a presentation into a major point—something to be remembered—is impossible, unless the presentation lasts only two or three minutes.

Once you have selected your major points, locate your supporting material. You may use several techniques to ensure the audience understands your point and to reinforce it.

- ***Provide support in a form that is easy to understand.*** Two techniques will assist you in accomplishing this goal:
  1. *Use simple vocabulary and short sentences that the listener can understand easily and that sound conversational and interesting.* Oral communication is more difficult to process than written communication; therefore, complex, varied vocabulary and long sentences included in written documents are not effective in an oral presentation.
  2. *Avoid jargon or technical terms that the listeners may not understand.* Instead, use plain English that the audience can easily comprehend. Make your speech more interesting and memorable by using word pictures to make your points. Hughes provides this example: If your message is a warning of difficulties ahead, you could say: "We're climbing a hill that's getting steeper, and there are rocks and potholes in the road."[3] Drawing analogies between new ideas and familiar ones is another technique for generating understanding. For example, comparing the power supply of a computer to the horsepower of an automobile engine, floppy disks to a briefcase, and a hard drive to a filing cabinet would help a computer novice comprehend complex concepts easily.

- *Provide relevant statistics.* Provide statistics or other quantitative measures available to lend authority and believability to your points. In your presentation about COPE, you could (1) locate evidence to support your thesis that large companies are less responsive than smaller companies and (2) obtain statistics from companies that have participated in COPE (e.g., reduced turnover and absenteeism, reduced time to develop products, increased responsiveness to the customer/client, and other measures of increased managerial effectiveness).

   A word of warning: Do not overwhelm your audience with excessive statistics. Instead, use broad terms or word pictures that the listener can remember. Instead of "68.2 percent" say "over two thirds"; instead of "112 percent rise in production" say "our output more than doubled." Hearing that a CD-ROM holds "over 400 times as much as a 3½-inch floppy disk" is less confusing and more memorable than hearing the exact number of megabytes for each medium. Choose novel, interesting word pictures such as "McDonald's has sold enough burgers to feed lunch to every person in the world" rather than trite images such as the number of football fields or how many times around the world.[4]

- *Use quotes from prominent people.* Comments made by other authorities are always helpful. In the case of COPE, comments from top management of leading companies represent a credible source of quotations.

- *Use jokes and humor appropriately.* A joke or humor can create a special bond between you and the audience, ease your approach to sensitive subjects, disarm a nonreceptive audience, make your message easier to understand and remember, and make your audience more willing to listen.[5] Plan your joke carefully so that you can (1) get the point across as quickly as possible, (2) deliver it in a conversational manner with interesting inflections and effective body movements, and (3) deliver the punch line effectively. If you cannot tell a joke well, use humor instead—amusing things that happened to you or someone you know, one-liners, or humorous quotations that relate to your presentation. Refrain from any humor that may reflect negatively on race, color, religion, the opposite sex, age, and nationality.

   For the COPE presentation, you could incorporate a few amusing incidents that actually occurred during a COPE session. Each incident is relevant to your speech and appropriate to your audience. You believe these humorous accounts will make the audience more receptive to the idea of a weekend of intense activities.

- *Use interesting anecdotes.* Audiences like anecdotes or interesting stories that tie into the presentation. Like jokes, be sure you can get straight to the point of the story. You might include stories about leading companies that have participated in COPE and can relate their firsthand experiences.

- *Use presentation visuals.* Presentation visuals, such as handouts, whiteboards, flip charts, transparencies, computer presentations, and demonstrations enhance the effectiveness of the presentation. Develop presentation visuals that will enable your audience to see, hear, and even experience your presentation.

Although stories, statistics, quotations, and the like may seem trivial, they are critical to effective speaking. They retain listener interest, provide proof and evidence supporting major points, and often provide the humor and enlightenment that

Why do audiences generally respond positively to the use of statistics, human interest stories, quotes, and humor? How can these techniques produce negative results?

On-line databases and the Internet give you instant access to numerous sources of timely information to support your points. Access a database available to you and key in a subject of your choice (perhaps an issue that currently is receiving media coverage). Share with the class at least two possible sources to support your topic.

turn an otherwise dreary topic into a stimulating message. They are among the professional speaker's most important inventory items. You can begin accumulating these items from personal reading and by accessing quotations from prominent people, information about your topic, and techniques for speaking effectively from commercial CD-ROMs and the Internet. Start a file for materials you come across that seem worth remembering,

Close

The close provides unity to your presentation by "telling the audience what you have already told them." The conclusion should be "your best line, your most dramatic point, your most profound thought, your most memorable bit of information, or your best anecdote.[6] Because listeners tend to remember what they hear last, use these final words strategically. Develop a close that supports and refocuses the audience's attention on your purpose statement—something clear and memorable.

- ● ***Commit the time and energy needed to develop a creative, memorable conclusion.*** An audience is not impressed with endings such as "That's all I have" or "That's it." Because an audience tends to remember what they hear last, you must use these final words strategically to accomplish your speaking goal. Techniques that can be used effectively include summarizing the main points that have been made in the presentation and using techniques such as anecdotes, humor, and illustrations that can also be used in the introduction. When closing an analytical presentation, you would state your conclusion and support it with the highlights from your supporting evidence: *"In summary, we selected the Madison, South Carolina, location because it had. . . ."* In a persuasive presentation, the close is often an urgent plea for the members of the audience to take some action or to look on the subject from a new point of view.

- ● ***Tie the close to the introduction to strengthen the unity of the presentation.*** For example, you might answer the rhetorical question you asked in the opening, refer to and build on an anecdote included in the introduction, and so on. A unifying close to a drug awareness presentation might be *"So, my friends, make your community drug free so you and your friends can grow up to enjoy the benefits of health, education, family, and freedom."*

How can the speaker make a smooth transition from the body to the close? What type of close is most effective?

- ● ***Use transition words that clearly indicate you are moving from the body to the close.*** Attempt to develop original words rather than rely on standard statements such as "In closing," or "In conclusion."

- ● ***Practice your close until you can deliver it without stumbling.*** Use your voice and gestures to communicate this important idea clearly, emphatically, and sincerely rather than swallow your words or fade out at the end as many inexperienced speakers often do.

- ● ***Smile and stand back to accept the audience's applause.*** A solid close does not require a "thank you"; the audience should respond spontaneously with applause to thank you for a worthwhile presentation.[7]

At this point of development, a working outline of your presentation about COPE might take this form:

COPE (Challenging Outdoor Personal Experiences):
Survival Skills for Competing in Today's Dynamic Workplace

I. Introduction
    A. Attention-getter that involves the audience and establishes my credibility
    B. Purpose statement
    C. Preview of three major points

II. Body
    A. Self-confidence
    B. Communication skills
    C. Team building skills

III. Close: Restatement of primary benefits to be derived

Preparing Presentation Visuals

3 *Select, design, and use presentation visuals effectively.*

Speakers who use presentation visuals are considered better prepared and more persuasive and interesting, and win their points more often than speakers who do not use visuals. Presentation visuals support and clarify a speaker's ideas and help the audience visualize the message. A speaker using presentation visuals hits the listener (receiver) with double impact—through the eyes and the ears—and achieves the results quoted in an ancient Chinese proverb: "Tell me, I'll forget. Show me, I may remember. But involve me and I'll understand." Research studies have confirmed this commonsense idea that using visual support will enhance an oral presentation.[8] Use of presentation visuals

- Clarifies and emphasizes important points.

- Increases retention from 14 percent to 38 percent.

- Reduces the time required to present a concept.

- Results in a speaker achieving goals 34 percent more often than when presentation visuals are not used.

- Increases group consensus by 21 percent when presentation visuals are used in a meeting.

How important are visuals to the overall effectiveness of a presentation? How can visuals become a negative, rather than a positive, factor?

Types of Presentation Visuals

A speaker must select the appropriate medium or combination of media to accomplish the purpose and to meet the needs of a specific audience. The most common presentation visuals are handouts; models and physical objects, whiteboards, flip charts, overhead transparencies, electronic presentations, and video and audiotapes.

Handouts. A printed handout is a widely used presentation visual. It's important to remember that the impression made by a handout is as important as your delivery and any other presentation visuals you use. A handout includes reference information about your topic and you and, thus, serves as an advertisement long after your presentation.[9] Follow these guidelines for preparing a well-designed, highly professional handout:

- ***Keep the handout simple.*** Summarize major points, but do not provide the audience with your entire presentation.

- *Limit the amount of text you include on the page.* Even though you can include much more information on a printed page than on other visuals, generally, at least 50 percent of your handout should be white space. Arrange the information in an uncluttered format that is easy to read. Short sentences and bulleted lists are easy to scan.
- *Include clip art and other images.* These graphics create visual appeal and may convey an idea more effectively than words.
- *Include your name, telephone number, and company logo in a strategic location.* This information identifies your handout properly, will facilitate questions or interest in your topic, and creates a professional appearance.
- *Use an attractive format that supports the purpose of your presentation.* Figure 12-1 illustrates three formats that can be generated easily using your computer.

Models or Physical Objects. Looking at an object being discussed or a scale model involves the audience and helps the members visualize the idea being presented. A realistic miniature model of a new fitness center might motivate prospective members to join. An airline manager, who wanted to convince the airline to replace foil food containers with fiber containers, brought some pastry packed in one of the fiber containers to the seminar. As the participants bit into the sweet, moist pastry, they became "instant believers."[10] Passing an object among a large audience can distract the audience. Therefore, for large groups, consider adding a scanned photograph of the object in your presentation or using a computer camera that allows you to project the object so that everyone in the audience can see it at the same time. For example, a group of engineers, troubleshooting a problem in a particular valve, can study a zoomed-in view of the problem at the same time as they discuss possible solutions.

Whiteboards. A whiteboard is useful for preparing informal visuals to small groups. Some major problems presented by the whiteboard are the slickness and lack of cleanliness of some boards, poor penmanship of the user, and the failure of the user to erase items once they have been considered. If you plan to use a board, practice and make certain the board is satisfactory before your presentation. If your visual is sizable or complex, plan to place it on the board before your presentation. Many portable whiteboards have two sides, thus permitting you to keep your material from view until you need it. Electronic whiteboards display images created on one or more computer screens for viewing by an entire audience.

Flip Charts. A flip chart consists of paper attached to a pad and displayed on an easel. Thus, a speaker can prepare a series of visuals before the presentation and simply "flip" from one visual to the next as the speech progresses. Additionally, a flip chart often is used to record ideas generated during a discussion or to display material (such as an outline of the presentation) for a long time. Although it serves many of the same purposes as a whiteboard, a flip chart permits the speaker to use color to advantage and to prepare material in advance, factors not always available with a whiteboard.

List three reasons for the wide use of overhead transparencies. What do you envision in terms of use of transparencies ten years from now?

Overhead Transparencies. Overhead transparencies are a popular presentation visual because they are inexpensive and easily prepared. An overhead transparency can be made of anything from freehand drawings to sophisticated computer-generated pages by simply running the original copy through a copier or printing it directly on a

Slides printed six per page

Provides each slide to accompany the speaker during the presentation as well as useful information for later reference.

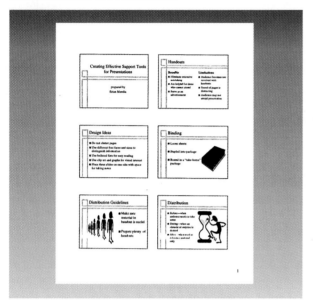

Slides printed three per page

Provides each slide follow accompany the speaker during the presentation as well as space for taking notes.

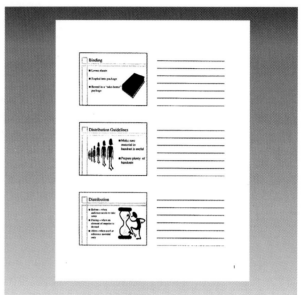

Notes pages

Used to prompt the speaker during delivery and to provide cues to a projectionist or as handouts to the audience.

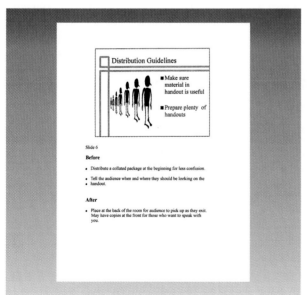

Word processed handout

Provides *selected* slides from the presentation with key points and additional information keyed beside each slide. The header/footer lines enhance the professional image and identify the speaker and company. (This example was created using the Send-to-Word feature in PowerPoint.)

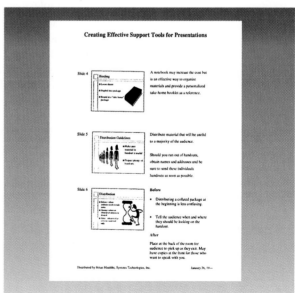

FIGURE 12-1 Typical Formats for Handouts Prepared with Presentation Software

transparency. Additionally, you can write on transparencies with specially designed pens; in this way, a blank transparency serves the same purpose as a whiteboard or a flip chart, except, of course, you are facing the audience. You can maintain eye contact with the audience because overheads can be displayed in a fully lighted room. You can easily omit or resequence overheads to adjust your presentation to the time slot or audience feedback. Transparencies are also popular because most meeting rooms and classrooms are equipped with overhead projectors. Limitations to the use of overhead transparencies include the distraction caused by placing and removing the visuals and reduced freedom of movement away from the projector to interact with the audience.

Electronic Presentations. Increasing numbers of speakers are preparing electronic presentations with computers on their own desktops. The availability of easy-to-operate, Windows-based presentation software has enabled the "average business user" to replace antiquated flip charts and boring overheads with multimedia presentations that help maintain a high level of interest during the meeting, increase two-way interaction, and allow last-minute changes to reflect information that may have become available after the beginning of the presentation.[11,12] Additional information about the use of multimedia to enliven a presentation is included in the accompanying Strategic Forces box.

Slides. Presentations built around 35-millimeter slides usually involve several visuals in a planned sequence and are displayed with a carousel or other slide projector. A major disadvantage is that the room usually must be darkened considerably. However, for presentations involving ordinary photography (depicting persons, places, and things), the slide method is the most appropriate. For example, colorful photographs of Hawaii's beautiful sandy beaches and scenes of happy tourists enjoying the entertainment and experiencing the Polynesian culture are effective means to attract tourists to Hawaii.

Videos and Audiotapes. Videos and audiotapes can be used to illustrate major points. For example, a video showing mock interviews would help illustrate effective interviewing strategies in a human resources management training seminar. In today's visual age, an audience relates well to the color and professional quality of these visuals. Many speakers, however, allow a videotape or film to become the entire presentation. This practice violates a central principle in using visuals: The visual is intended to supplement your presentation and is *not* a substitute for it.

Design of Presentation Visuals

How does the advice "more is not necessarily better" apply to the design of presentation visuals?

Mastering basic design principles will enable you to create effective presentations to support your message. Attention should be paid to basic slide design, addressed in the following guidelines.

- *Develop a standard design.* This design creates a sense of continuity and consistency (e.g., company or product logo or graphic object to appear on each slide; color scheme, text alignment, font face and size, etc.). Templates available with presentation graphics software, such as those illustrated in the Strategic Forces box on p. 445, provide ideas for standard designs. Customize the design by including your company name and other standard information that meets the specific needs of your audience.

Strategic Forces: Changing Technology

Designing an Effective Electronic Presentation

Traditional presentation visuals use only one medium, text and images, to deliver the information and to help the audience visualize an idea. Using popular software programs, such as Microsoft PowerPoint®, Aldus Persuasion®, and Lotus Freelance Graphics®, speakers can produce multimedia presentations that combine more than one medium to deliver the message. Media used in speaker-directed presentations include text, still images, sound, animation, and video.

An **electronic presentation** is a series of slides that presents information on a single topic. A **slide** is a single screen in a presentation that can be thought of as a single page in a word processing document. Preparing an electronic presentation involves the following simple steps:

1. **Organize and create content.** You can complete this time-consuming step several ways:

   a. *Design your presentation using a master presentation (or wizard) available with your software.* You simply select a master presentation that fits your subject (e.g., financial report, employee orientation, creativity, etc.), edit a suggested outline or follow simple suggestions for adding text to each slide, and select the style or look for the presentation from thumbnail images or a menu (e.g., professional or contemporary). A disadvantage of using a master presentation is that your presentation could be nearly identical to one delivered by your competitor.

   b. *Input your ideas into a built-in outliner.* This outliner will help you organize your thoughts and hone your ideas.

2. **Select a template (prepared designs).** A template is a predesigned format that lays out the basic design for the slides in a presentation and ensures consistency of placement and design throughout the presentation. (A template is automatically selected when you choose the style/look of a master presentation.) Template designs include (a) the color scheme for the background and foreground, as well as

accent colors; (b) an artistic design including graphic objects, borders, and lines to convey a specific mood; (c) typography elements such as font face and size, color for titles, text, bullets, and so on, and (d) various slide layouts (e.g., title slide, bulleted list, text and clip art, text and graph, text and organization chart, etc.). The following slides illustrate the use of a template to create a desired mood and standard layouts to ensure consistency

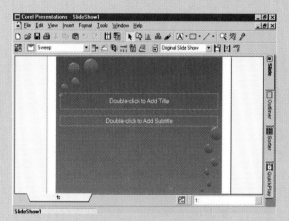

SLIDE 1: Corel Presentations Template: Bubbles; Layout: Title slide

SLIDE 2: PowerPoint Template: Twinkles; Layout: Bulleted list

3. **Embellish the presentation with images, sound, and animation.**

   a. *Add images to help the audience visualize an idea or illustrate a complex concept.*

      - **Clip art and photographs**—Hundreds of clip art images are available with presentation software. Additional clip art images and photographs can be purchased on CD-ROMs from software companies or downloaded from the Internet.

      - **Drawing tools**—Various shapes and lines that are useful for drawing diagrams and sketches provide creative, artistic avenues for presenting information. For example, a rectangular box provides a colorful and effective backdrop to a simple clip art image. A color wheel drawn with the drawing tools and colored with the primary and secondary colors communicates the primary color palette more effectively and creatively than a bulleted list simply naming the six colors. The steps in a process displayed in creative shapes and animated to appear in sequence as the speaker discusses each step adds variety to a presentation that may include several bulleted lists already. A callout box highlights the central idea that many business presentations have been rated boring and unbearable in the slide on page 449.

      - **Scanned images**—Generic clip art images and photographs from commercial collections sometimes are inappropriate for your presentation. Your presentation may require original photographs of actual people, places, or objects. You can use a scanner to scan photographs taken with a regular camera and convert the photograph to an image file that can be imported into your presentation. You can use a digital camera to capture the photograph as a computer file that can be imported into a presentation without developing the film; this process saves time and money and eliminates the use of chemicals that are not environmentally friendly.

      - **Video**—Footage from commercial videotapes, downloaded from the Internet, or recordings made from live events or television recordings can add ultimate impact to a presentation. The moving images captured by a video camera are converted to a form that can be imported into a presentation file. For example, video footage of a new plant warehouse likely would be more effective and exciting than a series of still shots.

   b. *Add animation—apparent movement that adds interest, highlights key points, and gives strong support to the speaker.* A word of caution: Overuse of animation can distract the audience from the basic objective of the presentation. Therefore, be certain that animation effects draw attention to a *central idea* and are not added solely for glitz. Common uses of animation follow:

      - **Adding transition effects between slides.** Transition effects add interest as you move from one slide to the next. This motion between slides engages the audience's attention and is an improvement over the burst of light and noise that accompanies a 35-millimeter slide advancing in a carousel. Common transitions include box in or out, wipe or uncover from various directions, dissolve, checkerboard across, and so on.

      - **Building bullet points.** Each point of a bulleted list is displayed as it is discussed to focus the audience's attention on the idea being discussed. As you move to the next point, the previous point can be dimmed or made to disappear for added control over the audience's attention.

      - **Animating the title and other multimedia objects.** Animation effects can be added to any multimedia object (text, image, graph, or drawing) on a slide giving it the impression of apparent movement. Animation effects include making the object move from a position such as top, bottom, left, or right of the page into its position on the page, uncovering or wiping in various directions, dissolving in focus, and various other effects. Consider the added effect of bringing in the various levels of an organization chart or the steps in a process one at a time as you discuss each one, or of blowing apart a diagram of a computer system and bringing in each part as you discuss its use (e.g., CPU, monitor, keyboard, printer, scanner, etc.)

   c. *Add sound to add interest and focus the audience's attention.* Brief sound effects can be added each time a multimedia object

continued

(title, image, or point in the bulleted list) is displayed or when the slide transitions to the screen. Sounds commonly included with presentation software include the typewriter, a drive-in effect with the sound of screeching brakes, a laser gun, the camera, and whoosh. Other sounds are available on CD-ROM (e.g., sparkle, drum roll, gong), or exciting sounds can be downloaded from the Internet (X-Wing straight from *Star Wars*, the twitch from *Bewitched*, and millions more). More dramatic results can be achieved by incorporating longer sound files. Possibilities include inserting prerecorded sound files available on CD-ROMs, recording short segments of a commercial CD (e.g., popular music), downloading sound files from the Internet (e.g., television theme songs, popular lines from movies,

etc.), and recording a person's voice (referred to as a *voice-over*).

Clip media collections are available that include clip art, photographs, sounds, animations, and videos. Most collections are packaged on CD-ROM to give you a wide selection, and the price is reasonable. Be sure that you are aware of limitations on the use of these copyrighted media. For instance, some media collections are royalty free; others may require you to pay a royalty if you earn money from the use of the presentation containing any of these objects.[13]

4. **Determine the exact sequence of each visual.** You can review the order of the slides in a presentation by displaying them side by side on one screen (referred to as *slide sorter view*) and easily rearrange the order or zoom in on a particular slide to make changes.

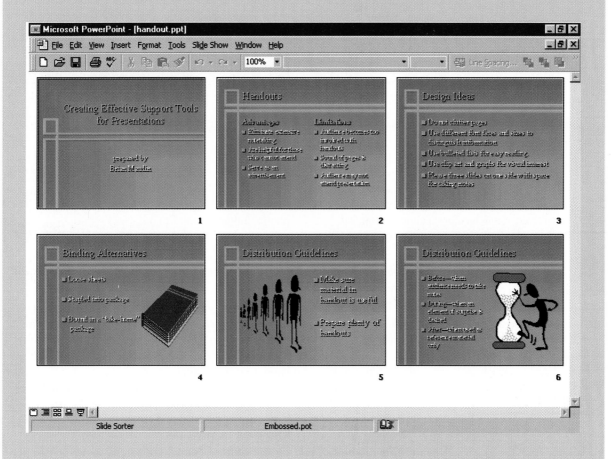

continued

5. **Generate the output from the electronic presentation file:**

- **Overhead transparencies**. The printed pages can be reproduced on transparency acetate or printed directly on acetates. Overhead transparencies printed with a color printer are more appealing than standard black-and-white overheads.
- **35-millimeter slides.** Professional slides are produced directly from the computer files.
- **Computer presentation.** The presentation is displayed on a computer monitor, a LCD projection panel or projector, or television monitor. If you are giving the presentation in a remote location, you may need to transfer the computer file from your desktop computer to a laptop computer. Because multimedia presentations including many image and sound files require large amounts of storage space, likely you will have to compress your presentation to fit on multiple floppy diskettes and then uncompress the file onto the laptop. Recent versions of presentation software include wizards that walk you through this highly technical process. Zip drives that hold 100MB (approximately 70 floppy disks) are an excellent investment when preparing multimedia presentations frequently.
- **Notes pages.** Use the presentation software to generate a notes page for each slide. The miniature image of the slide appears at the top of the page; space appears at the bottom for you to key notes. You can use this space to (a) key reminders for creating the slide later or for developing the content of the presentation, (b) input notes to be used for practicing your delivery and for use during the presentation, and (c) print a set of complete notes to give to the audience. Refer to the guidelines for constructing a useful notes page in the "Delivery Style" section that follows.
- **Audience handouts.** Handouts can be printed using three methods as illustrated in Figure 12-1:
  - Print miniature slides with or without space for the audience to take notes.
  - Print notes pages with the miniature slide at the top of the page and key points added in the space at the bottom.
  - Import slides into a word processing program and create a highly professional look. Wizards automatically import the slides into the software and set up a template where key points can be keyed beside a miniature slide. This detailed, professional format is especially useful if the audience will make decisions related to your presentation, summarize ideas for coworkers or supervisors, or use the information at a future date. Binding can be added to generate an attractive take-home packet.

Application

Critique an electronic presentation you have seen or one provided by your instructor. Write a memo to your instructor summarizing the use of the following multimedia elements: template, clip art, photos, animation, and sound.

Make sure you know how to change the page orientation setting in your presentation software. Design a simple graphic and print a copy in each orientation.

- *Select a page layout orientation appropriate for the presentation visual you are creating:*
  - Use **landscape orientation** for computer presentations and 35-millimeter slides. This horizontal placement provides a wide view that (a) creates a pleasing, soothing feeling similar to looking over the horizon, (b) provides longer lines for text and images, and (c) ensures that no text is included so low on the slide that it cannot be seen properly.
  - Use **portrait orientation** for overhead transparencies. This vertical placement positions the text to be read across the shortest side of the page, which makes additional lines available for text on an overhead transparency. Note the orientation of the slides on page 449.
- *Limit the amount of text on the slide.* Generally, do not fill more than 75 percent of the slide with text. Include no more than four words in a heading. Use the

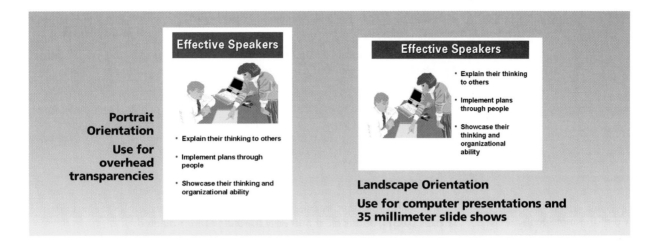

7 x 7 rule as a general rule for controlling the amount of text on the slide; in other words, include no more than *seven* lines of text on the slide and no more than *seven* words on a line.[14]

- *Use left alignment of text as a general rule.* Text is flush at the left margin and ends at various points along the line, creating an informal, personal appearance. Left alignment is neat and easy to read because it leads the viewer's eyes consistently back to the same position to read each item. Left alignment also provides consistent spacing between each word, unlike right alignment that adds extra spacing to create an even right margin. If necessary, revise the text to minimize any excessive variations in the length of the lines, but avoid hyphenation. Use centered alignment when you have only a few words on the slide or want to create a formal look. Use right alignment to format numerical data.

- *Use graphic devices—borders, boxes, shadows, lines, bullets (circles, squares, pointers of some sort) to separate items and direct attention.*

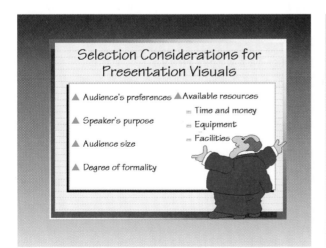

A border surrounding the bulleted list adds emphasis to the selection considerations.

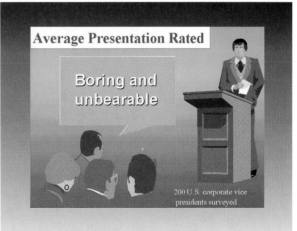

A voice balloon adds impact to this startling fact. The voice balloon is dropped from the top of the screen after the survey is introduced.

Use numbers only if the sequence is important; otherwise, bullets are easier for an audience to follow and do not clutter the visual as much as numbers.

- *Use clip art, scanned art, or cartoons to illustrate important points and break the monotony of a series of visuals containing only text.* Note the examples provided in the previous slides.

Proper presentation of text is essential in effective slide design. The use of appropriate fonts is a key ingredient to text acceptability. The following guidelines concerning fonts will help assure that your textual message supports the tone of your presentation.

- *Choose a font that conveys the mood of your presentation and can be read easily by your audience.* Use a san serif font to convey a modern tone and to ensure maximum readability. A san serif font does not have short cross strokes (serifs) and is clear and easy to read when projected.

Helvetica, Univers, *Optima*

Use a serif font to convey a traditional mood. A serif font has short cross-strokes (serifs) that project from the top and bottom of the main stroke of a letter. One common strategy is to use a bold, highly visible san serif font to emphasis the slide title and a softer serif font for the text.

Times New Roman, Times Ten, New Century Schoolbook

- *Avoid script or highly decorative fonts that are difficult to read when projected.*

Brush Script, *Kaufmann*

- *Attempt to identify interesting fonts that have not been overused to create a fresh, appealing presentation different from your competitors.*

Fonts often used in software templates: Times New Roman, Helvetica
Interesting alternatives: **INFORMAL**, Kids, Humanist

- *Limit the number of fonts to one or two.* Create special effects by using various fonts in the same family; by applying an attribute such as boldface, italics, shadow, outline; or by using color.

Font Family: Helvetica, **Helvetica Narrow Bold**, **Helvetica Black**

Attributes added to a plain font: **bold**, *italics*, underline, shadow, outline, SMALL CAPS, and embossed.

- *Use a font size large enough that the people in the back row can easily read the text.* Text size is measured in points: one point equals 1/72 of an inch; that is, a one-inch letter measured from the top of the highest part of the letter to the lowest part of the letter is 72 points. Determine the viewing distance for your presentation and select the text size to create hierarchies for the following textual elements:

  - Titles—24 to 36 points
  - Subtitles and text—18 to 24 points
  - Footnotes and source notes—one half the size of the body text

Using your word processing software, type several words in various fonts. Which font would be effective for a presentation to your board of directors? to a potential client? to your department staff?

The text component of slides should also follow accepted rules for literate business expression. Follow these capitalization and punctuation rules:

- *Use capital letters sparingly.* Uppercase was the only way to emphasize ideas in the age of the typewriter, but now numerous other methods are available—boldface, color, type size, and so on. Using all-caps for headings sets those units apart, but remember that using all capital letters creates a block of information that is difficult to read from a distance. Capitalize only the first letter of the first word of a bulleted list.

- *Omit punctuation at the end of bulleted lists.* Avoid punctuation elsewhere on the slide because punctuation is too small to be read from a distance. Consider inserting special characters when punctuation such as an exclamation point is needed.

- *Avoid abbreviations that might confuse the reader.*

Effective Use of Presentation Visuals

Many speakers will go to a great deal of effort to prepare good presentation visuals—and then not use them effectively. Inexperienced speakers often ignore the visual altogether or fall into the habit of simply nodding their heads toward the visual. Neither of these techniques is adequate for involving the audience with the visual. In fact, if the material is complex, the speaker is likely to lose the audience completely.

A multimedia presentation can be automated to move from one visual to another without speaker intervention. An automated presentation is quite effective for a booth in a trade show where you must attract the attention of passersby. Another effective use of automated presentations is a customized presentation for a potential client/customer or employees working in remote locations. The clients or employees can run the presentation on their own personal computers privately at their convenience and are able to repeat the presentation as many times as necessary (the software used to create the presentation is not needed to run it). A fully automated presentation tends to overwhelm a smaller face-to-face audience, limits the interaction important in typical meetings or presentations, and prevents the speaker from adapting a visual directly from the computer screen to accommodate an audience.

To enhance the impact of your presentations, follow these guidelines for preparing and using presentation visuals:

- *Limit the number of visual aids used in a single presentation.* Too many visuals can overwhelm, bore, and tire the audience. While the audience values being able to "see" your points, they also welcome the variety provided by listening and the break from concentrating on visuals, especially if they are being displayed in a darkened room. Take a thorough look at the entire presentation and prepare visuals needed to (a) direct the reader's attention to major points and (b) clarify or illustrate complex information.

- *Include only one major idea on each visual.* This rule requires you to keep the visual simple and allows you to make the print large enough for the audience to see. Include only the major point you want the listener to remember—not everything you intend to say about the idea. Too much detail may lead the audience to concentrate on unimportant items and results in letters and figures too small to be read from a distance. Keep the text lines short so the eye can

Strategic Forces: Changing Technology

Effective Use of Color in Presentation Design

Color is the most exciting part of presentation design. The colors you choose and the way you combine them determine the formality, readability, and overall effectiveness of your presentation and add a personal touch to your work. Choose colors to convey the formality of the presentation, to create a desired tone, or to associate your presentation with your company, a product, or the subject of the presentation.

- **Formality.** Conservative colors (blue) add formality; brighter colors (yellow) lend a less formal and perhaps trendy look.

- **Effect.** Generally, warm colors such as reds, oranges, and yellows stimulate your audience; cool colors such as blues and greens create a more relaxed and receptive environment.[15] Consider the effect colors have on people.

- **Association.** Select colors that the audience naturally associates with certain ideas: green for money or go; yellow for caution; red for stop, danger, or financial loss; blue for calm; and pink and light blue for nursery. Because of a natural association of red with financial loss, never use red in a table of numbers or a graph depicting growth or a healthy financial situation. Colors can also be used to create an

association with a company or a product (e.g., red and white and Coca-Cola). You might use a specific color scheme on slides related to a particular product and change to a different color scheme when the discussion moves to another product.

- **Differentiation.** Color helps the audience distinguish between different elements. For example, a hierarchy indicating level of importance is created for the audience when the title of every slide appears in one color and the text in another color consistently throughout the presentation. Color can be used to

  - Highlight a specific piece of information.
  - Emphasize key elements in a graph.
  - Connect a set of numbers in a table that are to be considered as a group.
  - Color code related components in a line drawing or an organizational chart.
  - Help the audience find a particular sheet in handouts by printing pages on different colors of paper. The speaker can simply say, "On the yellow sheet . . ."

  Avoid using red and green to differentiate important points because almost 10 percent of the population is color impaired and cannot distinguish between red and green (e.g., red and green bars in a graph might be seen as one large area).

  Follow these guidelines for using color effectively:

Colors	Effect	Examples
Black and red Red: anger and action black: death	Violence	Insecticide cans, suspense novel covers, horror movie posters, and heavy metal albums
White and blue or white and green create crisp, clean, pure images	Cleanliness	Bleach, toothpaste, first aid products, bathroom cleaners
Earth tones, brown, tans, and off whites	Naturalness	Conservation promotion, natural foods, promotion of Project COPE
White, black, shades of gray with splashes of bright color to add interest	High-tech	Promotion of technological themes
Purple, black, gold, rich red Black/gold/white combination	Elegance/luxury	Luxury products; prestigious companies

continued

- **Limit the number of colors.** Include no more than four colors on one slide to avoid an overwhelming, distracting design.
- **Choose the color scheme in this order:**
  1. **Choose the background color (largest area of color) first and then the foreground color (the body type).** Consider the preliminary issues of formality and mood discussed previously as well as the following issues:

     Output medium: Choose a color scheme that will be legible with the output medium you have chosen. Note the color scheme of the computer slide and the overhead transparency illustrated previously.

Output Medium	Background/ Foreground
Computer presentations and 35-millimeter slides presented in a darkened room.	Use dark-to-medium backgrounds with light text.
Overhead transparencies shown in a well-lit room.	Use light backgrounds with dark print.

Contrast: Colors that have a high contrast are easier to read. Black elements against a white background, the color scheme used traditionally in overhead transparencies, have the greatest contrast. A blue background with yellow text contrasts well, but a yellow background with white text would be difficult to read because of the low contrast.

Black text on a white background provides outstanding contrast and is easy to read.

White text on a light blue background is hard to see because of low contrast.

Yellow text on a dark blue background is easy to see because of high contrast.

After you have chosen the background and foreground colors, evaluate the readability of the font(s) you are using. Colored text tends to wash out when projected; therefore, be certain that the fonts are sturdy enough and large enough to be read easily using the color scheme you selected.

  2. **Choose the accent colors that complement the color scheme.** Accent colors are used in small doses to draw attention to key elements: bullet markers; bars in graphs, backgrounds (fills) of boxes, geometric shapes, lines, selected text; or drawings that are color coded for emphasis.

  3. **Consider using shaded colors (also called *graduated* or *variant*) that are appealing and create a sense of depth and dimension in visuals.** Audiences are attracted to this special effect, which allows one color to dissolve into another without a hard break, giving an airbrush effect. The lighter shades come forward as the darker areas recede into the background. Shading can be used in the slide background or in accent boxes, such as a bulleted list or text area. (Note the graduated color in the slides in the templates illustrated in the previous Strategic Forces box.) Use trial and error to select appealing shading effects; however, be certain the text is legible in the light sections of the shading. Choose a direction that enhances the content and the design.

Project your presentation ahead of time in the room where you are to present so you can adjust the color scheme. This process is essential because colors display differently on a computer monitor than they do on projection devices such as a computer projector or a LCD panel that fits over an overhead projector. You can also check the readability of the text and double-check for typographical errors at the same time.

continued

Application

You have been asked to design an electronic presentation for a talk you are delivering to assist managers in refining speaking skills. Develop a planning sheet that outlines important design issues for this particular presentation: standard template design, appropriate page layout orientation, amount of text on each slide and each line, appropriate fonts and font sizes, capitalization and punctuation rules, appropriate color scheme (make necessary assumptions about the type of company; 30 managers will attend). Sketch two or three slides that illustrate your presentation design decisions; use information related to speaking effectiveness that you have learned in this chapter as the content for your slides. Create the slides using presentation software if resources are available. Write brief annotations outside the slide to highlight each principle applied. Be prepared to present your analysis to the class.

A speaker has an ethical obligation to communicate information honestly and truthfully. Is it ethical for a manager to "overstate" an insignificant change in unit sales by drawing a bar chart with the vertical axis beginning above zero, giving the instant impression that the change is much greater than it actually is? Using data of your own, construct a bar chart with the vertical axis beginning at zero and one beginning at 20 and note the difference in perception.

follow them easily. Shortening the text lines has the added benefit of opening up the page with more white space, thus giving the eye a break and making the visual look more appealing.

- ***Keep the design simple and clean.*** Resist the temptation to clutter the page with too many colors, fonts (type styles), and graphics. "Less is more" is a cardinal rule when preparing an effective visual. Computer technology has raised the standards for presentation materials; however, inexperienced designers are likely to use the power of the technology to make visuals overly complex and difficult to understand. For example, squeezing too many ideas or too much data into a text chart or a graph and using every available font, color, texture, clip art (predrawn art available on disk, scanned art, or company logo), cartoon, or decorative border defeats the purpose of a visual. Your goal is to provide the audience with at-a-glance comprehension. After spending time experimenting with numerous features available on presentation software (few companies provide training in graphic design), experienced users usually learn that the most effective visuals are simple and clean, not colorfully chaotic. The Strategic Forces box on page 452 offers other suggestions for the use of color.

- ***Design the graphic to avoid distorting facts and relationships.*** Using inappropriate scales or designing confusing graphics that hide significant information are unethical ways to communicate. Chapter 10 presents the principles of designing graphics (e.g., line, bar, and pie charts) to enhance readability of information.

- ***Be sure that the visual can be read by everyone in the audience.*** Study the design strategies for text presented in the "Design of Presentation Visuals" section on page 444.

- ***Proofread the visual carefully following the same systematic proofreading procedures used for printed letters and reports.*** Misspellings in handouts or displays can be embarrassing and can adversely affect your credibility. Many presentation software programs have built-in spellcheckers to help ensure complete accuracy. When preparing visuals that are customized for a prospective client/customer, double-check to be certain that names of people, companies, and products are spelled correctly.

- ***Paraphrase the visual rather than reading it line for line.*** To increase the quality of your delivery, develop a workable method of recording what you plan to say about each graphic. For example, record your statements for each visual on a small index card. Print notes below a miniature version of each slide in an electronic slide show or transparencies created with presentation software. As you proceed from one visual to another, simply move to the next card or printed page. Sometimes you may write notes lightly in pencil directly on the back of posters or the borders framing transparencies. You can then refer to these notes without the audience seeing them. Detailed guidelines for preparing useful notes are included in the "Delivery" section of this chapter.

- ***Step to one side of the visual so the audience can see it.*** Use a pointer if necessary. Direct your remarks to the audience, so that you can maintain eye contact, and resist the temptation to look over your shoulder to read the information from the screen behind you.

Refining Your Delivery

After you have organized your message, you must identify the appropriate delivery method, develop your vocal qualities, and practice your delivery.

4 *Deliver speeches with increasing confidence.*

Delivery Method

Four presentation methods are available: memorized, written-and-read, impromptu, and extemporaneous. Impromptu and extemporaneous are useful for business presentations.

Memorized. The speaker writes out the entire speech, commits it to memory, and recites it verbatim. Memorization has the greatest limitations of the speech styles. Speakers are almost totally unable to react to feedback, and the speaker who forgets a point and develops a mental block may lose the entire speech. Memorized speeches tend to sound monotonous, restrict natural body gestures and motions, and lack conviction. For short religious or fraternal rites, however, the memorized presentation is often impressive.

What delivery methods do you think are used most often by professionals in your chosen career field?

Written-and-Read. The speaker writes out the entire speech and reads it to the audience. For complex material and technical conference presentations, written-and-read presentations ensure content coverage. Additionally, this style protects speakers against being misquoted (accuracy is absolutely critical) and also fits into exact time constraints, as in television or radio presentations. Speeches are sometimes read when time does not permit advance preparation, or several different presentations are given in one day (e.g., the speaking demands of the President of the United States and other top-level executives). Written-and-read presentations prevent speaker-audience rapport, particularly when speakers keep their eyes and heads buried in their manuscripts. Electronic devices now make it possible to project manuscripts on transparent screens on each side of the speaker. The speaker may read the rolling manuscript but appear to be speaking extemporaneously.

Impromptu. Impromptu speaking may be frightening to most people because the speaker is called on without prior notice. Experienced speakers can easily analyze the request, organize supporting points from memory, and present a simple, logical response. In many cases, businesspeople can anticipate a request and be prepared to discuss a particular idea when requested (e.g., status report on an area of control at a team meeting). Because professionals are expected to present ideas and data spontaneously on demand, businesspeople must develop the ability to deliver impromptu presentations.

Extemporaneous. Extemporaneous presentations are planned, prepared, and rehearsed but not written in detail. Brief notes prompt the speaker on the next point but the exact words are chosen spontaneously as the speaker interacts with the audience and identifies this audience's specific needs. Extemporaneous presentations allow natural body gestures, sound conversational, and can be delivered with conviction because the speaker is speaking "with" the listeners and not "to" them. The audience appreciates a warm, genuine communicator and will forgive an occasional stumble or groping for a word that occurs with an extemporaneous presentation. Learning to construct useful notes will aid you in becoming an accomplished extemporaneous speaker; guidelines are provided in the "Delivery Style" section that follows.

Vocal Qualities

The sound of your voice is a powerful instrument used to deliver your message and to project your professional image. To maximize your vocal strengths, focus on three important qualities of speech—phonation, articulation, and pronunciation.

Phonation. Phonation involves both the production and the variation of the speaker's vocal tone. You project your voice and convey feelings—even thoughts—by varying your vocal tones. Important factors of phonation are pitch, volume, and rate. These factors permit us to recognize other people's voices over the telephone. Changes in phonation occur with changes in emotional moods.

> How do the "voice of experience" and the "voice of authority" sound? Name at least two individuals who you believe exhibit these vocal qualities.

Pitch. Pitch is the highness or lowness of the voice. Good voices have medium or low pitch; however, a pleasant voice has a varied pitch pattern. The pitch of the voice rises and falls to reflect emotions; for example, fear and anger are reflected in a higher pitch; sadness, in a lower pitch. Lower pitches for both men and women are perceived more authoritative sounding; higher pitches are perceived to be less confident and sometimes pleading or whining. Techniques to be discussed can help you lower the pitch of your voice.

Volume. Volume refers to how loud the tones are. Generally, good voices are easily heard by everyone in the audience but are not too loud. Use variety to hold the audience's attention, to emphasize words or ideas, or to create a desired atmosphere (energetic, excited tone versus quiet, serious atmosphere).

Rate. Rate is the speed at which words are spoken. Never speak so quickly that the audience cannot understand your message or so slowly that they are distracted or irritated. Vary the rate to the demands of the situation. For example, speak at a slower rate when presenting a complex idea or emphasizing an important idea. Pause to add emphasis to a key point or to transition to another major section of the presentation. Speak at a faster rate when presenting less important information or when reviewing.

An inherent problem related to speaking rate is verbal fillers—also called *nonwords*. Verbal fillers, such as *uhhh, ahhh, ummm, errr* are irritating to the audience and destroy your effectiveness. Many speakers fill space with their own verbal fillers;

these include *you know, I mean, basically, like I said, okay, as a matter of fact.* Because of the conversational style of impromptu and extemporaneous presentations, a speaker will naturally grope for a word or the next idea. Become aware of verbal fillers you frequently use by critiquing a tape or video recording and then focus on replacing them with a three- to five-second pause. This brief gap between thoughts gives you an opportunity to think about what you want to say next and time for your audience to absorb your idea. Presenting an idea (sound bite) and then pausing briefly is an effective way to influence your audience positively. The listener will not notice the slight delay, and the absence of meaningless words will make you appear more confident and polished. Also avoid annoying speech habits, such as clearing your throat or uttering a soft cough constantly, that shift the audience's attention from the speech to the speaker.

Practice the following exercises to help you achieve good vocal qualities: medium to low pitch and audible, steady pace, with variations to reflect mood:

- ***Breathe properly and relax.*** Nervousness affects normal breathing patterns and is reflected in vocal tone and pitch. The better prepared you are, the better your phonation will be. Although relaxing may seem difficult to practice before a speech, a few deep breaths, just as swimmers take before diving, can help.

- ***Listen to yourself.*** A tape recording of your voice reveals much about pitch, intensity, and duration. Most people are amazed to find their voices are not quite what they had expected. "I never dreamed I sounded that bad" is a common reaction. Nasal twangs usually result from a failure to speak from the diaphragm, which involves taking in and letting out air through the larynx, where the vocal cords operate. High pitch may occur from the same cause, or it may be a product of speaking too fast.

- ***Develop flexibility.*** The good speaking voice is somewhat musical, with words and sounds similar to notes in a musical scale. Read each of the following sentences aloud and emphasize the underscored word in each. Even though the sentences are identical, emphasizing different words changes the meaning.

<u>I</u> am happy you are here.　　　　Maybe I'm the only happy one.

I <u>am</u> happy you are here.　　　　I really am.

I am <u>happy</u> you are here.　　　　Happy best describes my feeling.

I am happy <u>you</u> are here.　　　　Yes, you especially.

I am happy you <u>are</u> here.　　　　You may not be happy, but I am.

I am happy you are <u>here</u>.　　　　Here and not somewhere else

Articulation. In articulate speaker produces smooth, fluent, and pleasant speech. Articulation is the way in which a speaker produces and joins sounds. Faulty articulation is often caused by not forming individual sounds. Common examples include

- Dropping word endings—saying *workin'* for *working.*

- Running words together—saying *Snoo* for *What's new, kinda* for *kind of, gonna* for *going to.*

- Imprecise enunciation—saying *Dis* for *this, wid* for *with, dem* for *them, pen* for *pin,* or *pitcher* for *picture.*

These examples should not be confused with *dialect,* which people informally call an *accent.* A **dialect** is a variation in pronunciation, usually of vowels, from one part

Poorly articulated expressions such as *gonna, gotta,* and *how come* can diminish your acceptance as a credible speaker. Honestly evaluate your articulation; identify and eliminate words that you enunciate incorrectly.

of the country to another. Actually, everyone speaks a dialect; and speech experts can often identify, even pinpoint, the section of the country from where a speaker comes. In the United States, common dialects are New England, New York, Southern, Texan, Mid-Western, and so forth. Within each of these, minor dialects may arise regionally or from immigrant influence. The simple fact is that when people interact, they influence each other even down to speech sounds. Many prominent speakers may have developed a rather universal dialect that seems to be effective no matter who the audience is. This speech pattern, known as the General American Standard Speech Pattern, is widely used in the United States, is used by major broadcasters, and is easily understood by those learning English as a second language because they likely listened to this speech pattern as they learned the language.[16] The Real-Time Internet case at the end of the chapter provides you with the opportunity to further explore the issue of accents.

You can improve the clarity of your voice, reduce strain and voice distortion, and increase your expressiveness by following these guidelines:

- ***Stand up straight with your shoulders back and breathe from your diaphragm rather than your nose and mouth.*** If you are breathing correctly, you can then use your mouth and teeth to form sounds precisely. For example, vowels are always sounded with the mouth open and the tongue clear of the palate. Consonants are responsible primarily for the distinctness of speech and are formed by an interference with or stoppage of outgoing breath.

- ***Focus on completing the endings of all words, not running words together, and enunciating words correctly.*** To identify reoccurring enunciation errors, listen to a tape or video recording and seek feedback from peers and others.

- ***Obtain formal training to improve your speech.*** Pursue a self-study program by purchasing tapes that help you reduce your dialect and move more closely to the General American Standard Dialect. You can also enroll in a course to improve your speech patterns or arrange for private lessons from a voice coach.

Learn the vowel sound symbols used in a dictionary and work to pronounce words correctly. To get started, what is the preferred pronunciation of *status*, *often*, *economics*, and *envelope*?

Pronunciation. A dictionary provides the best source to review pronunciation. People may articulate perfectly but still mispronounce words. Perhaps the best rule is to pronounce words in the most natural way. The dictionary often gives two pronunciations for a word. The first one is the desired pronunciation and the second, an acceptable variation. For example, to adopt a pronunciation commonly used in England such as *shedule* for *schedule* or *a-gane* for *again* could be considered affected speech. In other cases, the dictionary allows some leeway. The first choice for pronouncing *data* is to pronounce the first *a* long, as in *date*; but common usage is fast making pronunciation of the short *a* sound, as in *cat*, acceptable. Likewise, the preferred pronunciation of *often* is with a silent *t*. Good speakers use proper pronunciation and refer to the dictionary frequently in both pronunciation and vocabulary development.

When your voice qualities combine to make your messages pleasingly receptive, your primary concerns revolve around developing an effective delivery style.

Delivery Style

Speaking effectively is both an art and a skill. Careful planning and practice are essential for building speaking skills.

Before the Presentation. Follow these guidelines before your presentation:

- *Prepare thoroughly.* You can expect a degree of nervousness as you anticipate speaking before a group. This natural tension is constructive because it
increases your concentration and your energy and enhances your performance. Being well prepared is the surest way to control speech anxiety.
Develop an outline for your presentation that supports your purpose and
addresses the needs of your audience. Additionally, John Davis, a successful
speech coach, warned: "Never, never, never give a speech on a subject you
don't believe in. You'll fail. On the other hand, if you prepare properly, know
your material, and *believe* in it . . . your audience will not only hear but *feel*
your message."[17]

What are the causes and
symptoms of public speak-
ing anxiety?

- *Prepare effective presentation aids.* Follow the guidelines presented in the
prior section on presentation visuals for selecting and designing presentation
visuals appropriate for your audience.

- *Prepare useful notes on small index cards or pages generated by electronic presentation software.* Study the example of a useful notes page
shown in Figure 12-1 and follow these guidelines:

  - Include brief phrases that you can scan easily and that will trigger the next
  point you are to discuss. To ensure accuracy and high impact, you might
  consider writing out completely sections you want to deliver without stumbling: segments of the introduction, a quotation, exact statistics or figures,
  the punch line of a joke, and the close.
  - Prepare legible notes that are neat and large enough to read easily.
  - Use boldface and all capitals for emphasis only. If all words were keyed with
  boldface, underline, or all capitals, the notes would be difficult to read.
  - Consider using bulleted lists and other formats that are easily read.
  - Key notes in 14-point font if the room will be darkened; 10–12 point may be
  adequate in a well-lighted room.
  - Keep notes clean and uncluttered. Highlight important points with a colored marker, but do not draw arrows during a rehearsal to indicate a
  change in of order of material; these changes will be confusing during the
  pressure of a presentation.

- *Practice, but do not rehearse.* Your goal is to become familiar with the key
phrases on your note cards so that you can deliver the presentation naturally as
if you are talking with the audience—not reciting the presentation or acting out
a role. Avoid overpracticing that may make your presentation sound mechanical
and limit your ability to respond to the audience.

  - *Practice the entire presentation.* This practice will allow you to identify
  (1) flaws in organization or unity, (2) long, complex sentences or impersonal expressions inappropriate in an oral presentation, and (3) "verbal
  potholes." Verbal potholes include word combinations that could cause
  you to stumble, a word you have trouble pronouncing ("ask" or "task"), or
  a word you perceive accentuates your dialect ("get" may sound like "git"
  regardless of the intention of a Southern speaker).

  - *Spend additional time practicing the introduction and conclusion.* Thus, you
  will be able to deliver these important parts with finesse while making a confident connection with the audience. A good closing serves to leave the audience in a good mood and may help overcome some possible mistakes made
  during the speech. Depending on the techniques used, consider memorizing

these brief statements to ensure their accuracy and impact (e.g., direct quotation, involved statistic, etc.).

- *Seek feedback on your performance that will enable you to polish your delivery and improve organization.* Critique your own performance by practicing in front of a mirror and evaluating a videotape of your presentation. If possible, present to a small audience for feedback and to minimize anxiety when presenting to the real audience.

- **Request a lectern to hold your notes and to steady a shaky hand, at least until you gain some confidence and experience.** Keep in mind, though, that weaning yourself from the lectern will eliminate a physical barrier between you and the audience. Without the lectern, you will speak more naturally. If you are using a microphone, ask for a cordless, portable microphone so that you can move freely.

- **Insist on a proper, impressive introduction if the audience knows little about you.** An effective introduction will establish your credibility as the speaker on the subject to be discussed and will make the audience eager to hear you speak. You may prepare your own introduction as professional speakers do, or you can provide concise, targeted information that answers these three questions: (1) Why is the subject relevant? (2) Who is the speaker? and (3) What credentials qualify the speaker to talk about the subject?[18] Attempt to talk with the person introducing you to verify any information, especially the pronunciation of your name, and to review the format of the presentation (time limit, question-and-answer period, etc.). Be certain to thank the person who made the introduction. "Thank you, Mr. President" or "Thank you for your kind introduction, Ms. Garcia" for a speech are adequate. Then, follow with your own introduction to your presentation.

- **Dress appropriately to create a strong professional image and to bolster your self-confidence.** An audience's initial impression of your personal appearance, your clothing and grooming, affects their ability to accept you as a credible speaker. Because first impressions are difficult to overcome, take ample time to groom yourself immaculately and to select clothing that is appropriate for the speaking occasion and consistent with the audience's expectations.

- **Arrive early to become familiar with the setup of the room and to check the equipment.** Check the location of your chair, the lectern, the projection screen, and light switches. Check the microphone and ensure that all equipment is in the appropriate place and working properly. Project an electronic presentation so you can adjust the color scheme to ensure maximum readability. Finally, identify the technician who will be responsible for resolving any technical problems that may occur during the presentation.

During the Presentation. The following are things you can do during your presentation to increase your effectiveness as a speaker:

What can you do as a speaker to build rapport with the audience? How do you know when you have succeeded?

- **Communicate confidence, warmth, and enthusiasm for the presentation and the time spent with the audience.** "Your listeners won't care how much you know until they know how much you care," is pertinent advice.[19] Follow these guidelines:

  - *Exhibit a confident appearance with alert posture.* Stand tall with your shoulders back and your stomach tucked in. Stand in the "ready position"—

COMMUNICATION MENTOR

Your appearance is a part of what you communicate about yourself and your employer. Given my background growing up in a family-owned clothing business, I felt I knew the proper dress for the New York business environment. Much to my surprise early in my career, my supervisor suggested that I make some changes in my business attire. I began to take notice of my colleagues and peers and adjusted my wardrobe to attain a needed touch of sophistication. Especially when you are one of the youngest in your business environment, appropriate dress is critical in gaining respect.

The suggestions that are made by others regarding your appearance should be critiqued. I was criticized once while traveling with a business colleague for wearing the color red to a client review. Because I was traveling on a day trip and did not have a change, I was pleasantly surprised when we arrived at the meeting to see our client in a red suit. A marketing person from the same firm had a different experience. She wore a red suit to see a religious charity client and received a letter of reprimand for her choice in colors. The point is to be smart about your appearance. Try to figure out what type of company or client you will be meeting and adjust your appearance to meet the need of the environment and your own firm's environment.

Pamela M. Plager, Vice President & Director
Allen & Company, Incorporated

---

no slouching or hunching over the lectern or leaning back on feet. Keep weight forward with knees slightly flexed so you are ready to move easily rather than rooted rigidly in one spot, hiding behind the lectern.[20]

- *Smile genuinely throughout the presentation!* Pause as you take your place behind the lectern and smile before you speak the first word. Smile as you finish your presentation and wait for the applause.

- *Maintain steady eye contact with the audience in random places throughout the room.* Stay with one person approximately three to five seconds—long enough to finish a complete thought or sentence to convince the listener you are communicating individually with him or her. If the audience is large, select a few friendly faces and concentrate on speaking to them rather than a sea of nondescript faces.

- *Refine gestures to portray a relaxed, approachable appearance.* Vary hand motions to emphasize important points; otherwise, let hands fall naturally to your side. Practice using only one hand to make points unless you specifically need two hands, such as when drawing a figure or showing dimensions or location. Eliminate any nervous gestures that can distract the audience. Names have been coined to describe the common positions people assume when they are speaking and do not have anything to grasp:

"Fig leaf"	Hands together in front of body (one hand on top of the other)
"Napoleon"	Stiff body with hand in coat
"Praying hands"	Hands held together in front of body in praying position
"Jangler"	Stuffing hands in pockets and perhaps jingling keys or change

- *Move from behind the lectern and toward the audience to reduce the barrier created between you and the audience.* You may stand to one side and casually present a relaxed pose beside the lectern. However, avoid methodically walking from place to place without a purpose.

- *Exercise strong vocal qualities.* Review the guidelines provided for using your voice to project confidence and credibility.

- *Watch your audience.* They will tell you how you are doing and whether you should shorten your speech. Be attentive to negative feedback in the form of talking, coughing, moving chairs, and other signs of discomfort.

- *Handle questions from the audience during the presentation.* Questions often disrupt carefully laid plans. At the same time, questions provide feedback, clarify points, and ensure understanding. Often people ask questions that will be answered in a later part of the presentation. In these cases, you should say, "I believe the next slide will clarify that point. If not, we will come back to it." If the question can be answered quickly, the speaker should do so while indicating that it will also be covered later in the presentation. If necessary, the speaker might also indicate that questions will be answered following a certain portion of the presentation.

  Attempt to anticipate questions that might be raised so that you can prepare. You may generate presentation visuals pertaining to certain anticipated questions and display them only if the question is posed. An audience will appreciate your thorough and complete explanation and your willingness and ability to adjust your presentation to their needs—much more professional than stumbling through an explanation or delaying the answer until the information is available. Speakers giving electronic presentations have ready access to enormous amounts of information stored in other software programs or in other presentation files that can be instantly displayed for audience discussion. For example, by clicking on a hyperlink created within a presentation file, a speaker can move instantaneously to a specific slide within the presentation, a different presentation, or even a spreadsheet file. The hyperlink can be used to play a music file embedded in a presentation, to start a CD inserted in the CD-ROM of the computer, or to connect the speaker to a specific site on the Internet.

- *Keep within the time limit.* If your presentation is part of a busy program, be prepared to complete the presentation within the allotted time. In many organizations, speakers have one or more rehearsals before making reports to groups such as a board of directors. These rehearsals, or dry runs, are made before other executives, and are critiqued, timed, revised, and rehearsed again. Presentation software makes rehearsing your timing as simple as clicking a button and advancing through the slides as you practice. By evaluating the total presentation time and the time spent on each slide, you can modify the presentation and rehearse again until the presentation fits the time slot.

After the Presentation. How you handle the time following a presentation is as important as preparing for the presentation itself:

- *Be prepared for a question-and-answer period.* Encourage the audience to ask questions, recognizing an opportunity to ensure that your presentation meets your audience's needs. Restate the question, if necessary, to ensure that everyone heard the question and ask the questioner if your answer was adequate. Be courteous even to hostile questioners so you will maintain the audience's

Considering a speaker's mannerisms, what are some nonverbal actions that could have different interpretations among cultures? How can you adapt your delivery to fit your audience?

respect. Stay in control of the time by announcing that you have time for one or two more questions and then invite individual questions at the end.

- **Distribute handouts.** Distribute the handout when it is needed rather than at the beginning of the presentation. Otherwise, the audience may read the handout while you are explaining background information needed to understand the idea presented in the handout. If you expect the audience to take notes directly on the handout (see Figure 12-1) or if the audience will need to refer to the handout immediately, distribute the handout at the beginning of the presentation or before it begins. To keep control of the audience's attention, be sure the listeners know when they should be looking at the handout or listening to you. If the handout is intended as resource material only, place the handout on a table at the back of the room and on a table at the front for those who come by to talk with you after the presentation.[21]

Adapting to an Intercultural Audience

5 *Discuss effective strategies for adapting oral presentations to an intercultural audience.*

When speaking to an intercultural audience, attempt to be natural while adjusting your message in consideration for important variations in cultures. To "see ourselves as others see us"—the gift Robert Burns asked for—is excellent advice for communicating with any audience and especially one from a different culture. [22] Thus, first and foremost, try to empathize with the audience; imagine your presentation from the audience's viewpoint rather than your own. Focus on the listener as an individual rather than a stereotype of a specific culture. Be open and willing to learn from other cultures and ready to reap the benefits of communicating effectively with people with a variety of strengths and creative abilities. Be patient and willing to devote the additional effort needed to communicate with other cultures. In addition to these general skills, follow these suggestions to communicate more clearly with an intercultural audience:

- **Use simple English and short sentences that are easy to understand.** "Write for the ear" just as you have learned to do already.

- **Avoid acronyms and expressions that may be confusing to nonnative English speakers, namely, slang, jargon, figurative expressions, and sports analogies.** Many of these expressions help you clarify an idea and personalize your message; however, they may be confusing to those unfamiliar with American usage. Those speaking English as a second language learned English from a textbook; therefore, they may have difficulty understanding expressions such as the following:

Acronyms:	ASAP, CPU, HMO, IPO, NYSE, FASB
Slang:	Referring to a dollar as a *buck*, using *cool* and *bad* to indicate approval, *flop* or *bomb* to indicate failure.
Figurative expressions:	*Break a leg, dying on the vine, hanging by a thread, went up in smoke, bent out of shape, fly off the handle, right on the money, hold down the fort, hit the nail on the head, down the tubes, worn to a frazzle, hard road to travel, sharp as brass tacks, dead ringer, brainstorm.*

COMMUNICATION IN ACTION

Watson Communications International, Inc.

Dr. Thomas Watson stands confidently before the group of manufacturing employees, conducting management training. Working easily with flip chart, easel, and markers, his relaxed manner belies the fact that he once experienced severe communication anxiety before groups. His listeners see and hear a relaxed, clear communicator. However, he has struggled with communication anxiety as most speakers do, perhaps even more than most. Can the average speaker overcome communication anxiety? Are there some practical tips for managing anxiety?

Watson believes communication anxiety can be managed and even overcome. A professional trainer and experienced speaker, he typically appears confident and relaxed when speaking before groups. As founder and president of Watson Communications International, Inc., Watson directs a management consulting and training company headquartered in Texas with offices in California and Guam. He has consulted for government and business entities internationally, including the Government of Guam, the Bank of Hawaii, and the Government of Saipan; his clients include businesses such as AT&T, Texas Instruments, North American Coal Corporation, and TRW. His successful company grew as a result of hard work, but he first had to overcome the obstacle of communication anxiety before his company would grow.

As a youth, Watson so feared speaking that he avoided any situation where he would be required to speak, especially before groups. This fear, he says, was based in a childhood stuttering disorder that lasted through his high school years. Watson's story changed, however, when he enrolled as a college freshman in a beginning speech class and delivered his first presentation. The topic was amateur radio. Watson stuttered some before the class, but he slowly gained confidence, spoke more clearly, and finished the presentation. As the speech progressed, he became more "caught up" in his topic and spoke conversationally. The subject of amateur radio was one with which he was very familiar, and he had prepared and practiced his presentation thoroughly. The hard work paid off. He received an "A" from a professor who didn't give many. This first speaking success motivated Watson to try future presentations.

To become a confident speaker, Watson believes, a person must "have something to say, and say it well." Having a sincere, well-informed, and well-prepared message builds a speaker's confidence and greatly increases his or her ability to convince or move the audience to action.

Watson believes that good public speaking does not come naturally for people but is a skill that must be cultivated. He admits some people have a "propensity" for pubic speaking—their personalities seem to "fit" the activity well. However, when comparing the so-called "born speaker" with the trained speaker, he has found that the person with training will be more successful every time.

Applying What You Have Learned

1. Why is preparation so important in handling communication anxiety?

2. Does good public speaking come naturally for you? Give examples of your personal experiences in public speaking. What technique assisted Watson in overcoming his fear of speaking?

3. Assume that you are faced with giving a presentation to your class and are experiencing communication anxiety. What are some ways you can reduce this anxiety?

Sports analogies:	*Batting a thousand, struck out, made it to first base, out of the ball park, drop back and punt, on target, way off target, right on line, par, kick off, shot down, springboard, caught off guard, pitch hit.*

To ensure that your message is understood, substitute the definitions defined in the dictionary as shown in the following examples:

Your analysis was *right on the money* [or right on target] (accurate).

A client just arrived for an initial planning meeting, and the assigned rep is out of the office. Can you pinch hit? (substitute)

The proposal was a *bomb* (a failure). The proposal *bombed* (failed). I *blew it* (failed).

He was caught *redhanded* (committing the act).

The speaker was *dying on the vine* (doing a very poor job).

The supervisor's unfair criticism *took the wind out of my sails* (was discouraging).

That doesn't *ring a bell* (I can't remember.)

Are you willing to *walk the talk*? (do what you have boasted you can do).

We need approval from the *top gun* (president or supervisor).

His actions were *out of line* (inappropriate).

Go for it. (You have approval to . . .)

Think of other figures of speech that might be difficult for someone of another culture to understand.

- *Avoid words that trigger emotional responses such as anger, fear, or suspicion.* Such words are referred to as "red flag" words because they elicit the same response as a red flag waved before a raging bull. "Hot buttons," the term used in a popular training film, *Communicating Across Cultures,* conveys a similar connotation.[23] Regardless of the term, using words such as "gal," "boy," "handicapped," and "foreigner" is a sure way to close a listener's mind to your message, to make understanding practically impossible, and to destroy any chance of trust and cooperation. Different words are red flags or hot buttons for different people; thus, before you speak, try to anticipate your audience's reaction to the words you use and choose them carefully.

- *Enunciate each word precisely and speak somewhat more slowly.* Clear, articulate speech is important in any speaking situation but even more when speaking to an audience who is not familiar with the sounds of various dialects. Avoid the temptation to speak in a loud voice to get your point across. Speaking too loudly is considered rude in any culture. Additionally, cultures such as the Japanese perceive North Americans to speak too loudly in a normal tone.

- *Be extremely cautious in the use of humor and jokes.* People in different cultures may find your humor and jokes inappropriate. Cultures that prefer more formality might perceive you are not serious about your purpose.

- *Learn the culture's preferences for a direct or indirect presentation.* Although North Americans prefer a direct approach to most messages with the main idea presented first, many cultures, such as the Japanese, Latin American, and Arabic cultures, consider this straight forward approach tactless and rude.

- *Adapt to subtle differences in nonverbal communication.* North Americans expect an attentive, respectful audience to maintain eye contact, but don't get rattled by Asian listeners who keep their eyes lowered and avoid eye contact during your presentation to show respect to the speaker or Arab audiences, who may stare into your eyes in an attempt to "see into the window of the soul." Cultures also vary on personal space and the degree of physical contact (slap on the back or arm around the other as signs of friendship) that may affect a speaker's interaction with an audience—especially a small group.

Potential frustrations can occur when presentations or meetings involve cultures who are not time conscious and who believe that personal relationships are the basis of business dealings (e.g., Asian, Latin American) or North Americans who see "time as money," which should be used efficiently. When communicating with these cultures, be patient with what you may consider time-consuming formalities and courtesies and lengthy decision-making styles when you would rather get right down to business or move to the next point. Recognize that the presentation may not begin on time or stay on a precise time schedule. Be prepared to allow additional time at the beginning of the presentation to establish rapport and credibility with the audience, and perhaps provide brief discussion periods during the presentation devoted to building relationships. Be patient and attentive during long periods of silence; in many cultures people are inclined to stay silent unless they have something significant to say or if they are considering (not necessarily rejecting) an idea. In fact, some Japanese have asked how North Americans can think and talk at the same time. Understanding this pattern can help you feel more comfortable during these seemingly endless moments of silence and less compelled to fill the gaps with unnecessary words or to make concessions before the other side has a chance to reply.

- *Adapt your presentation style and dress to fit the degree of formality of the culture.* Some cultures prefer a higher degree of formality than the casual style of North Americans. To accommodate these preferences, you likely would dress conservatively, strive to connect with the audience while maintaining a formal, reserved manner, and design highly professional formal presentation visuals rather than jot ideas on a flip chart or whiteboard. Understanding the proper way to address an individual using a surname and formal title would be extremely important.

- *Seek feedback to determine whether the audience is understanding your message.* Observe the listeners carefully for signs of misunderstanding, and restate any ideas you sense have not been understood. Restating a message is far superior to repeating the same words more loudly. If the presentation format allows, you might allot time for questions and informal interaction with the audience after completing short segments of your presentation. Avoid asking "Is that clear?" or "Do you understand?" Both of these direct statements might elicit a "Yes" answer if the person perceives saying "No" may be interpreted as incompetence or if the person's culture advocates saying "Yes" to save face.

- *Research variations in gift-giving practices in different cultures.* When you believe a gift should be presented to a speaker, investigate the appropriateness of gift giving, types of gifts considered appropriate or absolutely inappropriate, and colors of wrapping to be avoided in the speaker's culture. For example, liquor is an inappropriate gift in Arab countries.

- *Become familiar with appropriate conventions for greetings and introductions in various cultures.* For example, should you use the traditional American handshake or some other symbol of greeting? Is using the person's

How would you phrase your questions in order to solicit effective feedback?

given name acceptable? What formal titles should be used with a surname? Can you introduce yourself, or must you have someone else who knows the other person introduce you? Are business cards critical, and what rules should you follow when presenting a business card? Gaining competence in greetings and introductions will enable you to make a positive initial impression and thus to concentrate on the presentation rather than agonize over an awkward, embarrassing slip in protocol. Your audience will appreciate your willingness to learn and value their customs.

A business card printed in two languages is an efficient and effective tool. The two business cards in Figure 12-2 are the front and back sides of the same card. One side is printed in English; the other, in Russian.

Being sensitive to cultural differences and persistent in learning specific differences in customs and practices can minimize confusion and unnecessary embarrassment. Thus, you develop increased competence and self-confidence in your ability to communicate in today's diverse workplace.

Before planning a business presentation and designing effective presentation visuals, study carefully the specific suggestions in the "Check Your Presentation" checklist that precedes the chapter summary. Practice your delivery at least once, and then compare your style with the points listed in the delivery section of the checklist. Make necessary improvements as you continue to polish your presentation skills.

> Using the Internet, research the subject of business card etiquette. Be prepared to share your findings with the class.

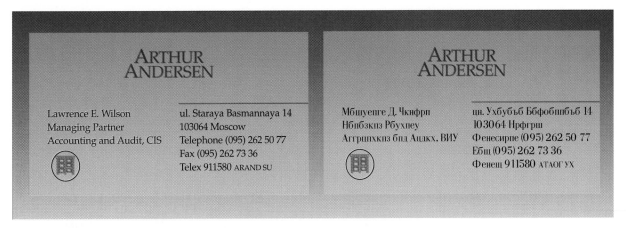

FIGURE 12-2
Proper introductions require presenting business cards in cultures such as the Chinese and Japanese with respect. Because these cultures consider the business card an extension of the self, damage to the card is damage to the individual.

Planning and Organizing a Presentation

- Identify your purpose. Be certain you understand exactly what you hope to accomplish so you can choose content that will support your purpose.

- Analyze your audience. Identify characteristics common to the audience and the speech setting (number in audience, seating arrangements, time of day).

- Develop an effective opening. The opening must capture attention, initiate rapport with the audience, and preview the main points.

- Develop the body. Select a few major points and locate support for each point: statistics, anecdotes, quotes, and appropriate humor. Use simple, nontechnical language and sentences the listener can understand, avoid excessive statistics and use word pictures when possible, and use jokes or humor appropriately.

- Develop an effective close. The close calls for the audience to accept your idea or provides a conclusion with recommendations.

Selecting an Appropriate Presentation Visual

- Select a presentation visual appropriate for the audience and the topic.

- Use whiteboards and flip charts for small audiences in an informal setting and when no special equipment is available. Prepare flip charts in advance.

- Use overhead transparencies for small, informal audiences and when it is desirable to write audience comments that can be displayed.

- Use slides for presentations requiring photography; prepare them from visuals displayed on computer; arrange in a planned sequence, and show in a darkened room.

- Use electronic presentations for large audiences and to enliven the topic and engage the audience with text, images, sound, and animation. Last-minute changes to visuals are possible.

- Use video- and audiotapes to illustrate major points in an engaging manner; use as a supplement to the presentation, not a replacement.

- Use models and physical objects to allow the audience to visualize and experience the idea being presented.

Designing and Using Presentation Visuals

- Limit the number of visual aids used in a single presentation to avoid overload.

- Create a standard design for each visual:
  - Include only the major idea the audience is to remember.
  - Make the design concise, simple, and large enough to be read by the entire audience.
  - Avoid graphics that distort facts.
  - Design horizontal (landscape) visuals for electronic presentations and vertical (portrait) visuals for overhead transparencies.
  - Proofread the visual carefully to eliminate any errors.

- Use the presentation visuals effectively. Paraphrase the visual rather than read it line for line and step to one side of the visual so the audience can see it.

Delivering a Presentation

Before the presentation

- Prepare thoroughly to minimize natural nervousness.

- Prepare easy-to-read note cards or pages to prompt your recall of the next point.

- Practice to identify any organizational flaw or verbal stumbles; do not rehearse until your delivery is mechanical.

- Request a lectern to steady your hands but not to hide behind.

- Insist on a proper, impressive introduction.

- Dress appropriately to create a professional image.

- Arrive early to acquaint yourself with the room and check last-minute details.

During the Presentation

- Use clear, articulate speech and proper pronunciation.

- Use vocal variety and adjust volume and rate to express and emphasize ideas.

- Avoid irritating verbal fillers and other annoying speech habits.

- Maintain steady eye contact with audience in random places.

- Smile genuinely and use gestures naturally to communicate confidence and warmth.

- Watch your audience for important feedback and adjust your presentation accordingly.

- Handle questions from the audience politely.

- Keep within the time limit.

After the Presentation

- Be prepared for a question-and-answer period.
- Distribute handouts.

SUMMARY

1. ***Plan a business presentation that accomplishes the speaker's goals and meets the audience's needs.*** First, determine what you want to accomplish in your presentation. Second, know your audience so you can direct your presentation to the specific needs and interests of the audience. Identify the general characteristics (age, gender, experience, etc.), size, and receptiveness of the audience.

2. ***Organize and develop the three parts of an effective presentation.*** An effective presentation has an introduction body, and close. An effective introduction captures the audience's attention, involves the audience and the speaker, presents the purpose statement, and previews major points. The body is limited to a few major points that are supported and clarified with relevant statistics, anecdotes, quotes from prominent people, appropriate humor, presentation visuals, and so forth. The close should be a memorable idea that supports and strengthens the purpose statement.

3. ***Select, design, and use presentation visuals effectively.*** Using visual aids reduces the time required to present a concept and increases retention because the audience can visualize major ideas and follow the presentation more easily. Visual aids available to speakers include handouts, models and physical objects, whiteboards, flip charts, overhead transparencies, electronic presentations, videotapes, and audiotapes. Each type provides specific advantages and should be selected carefully. Guidelines for preparing visual aids include limiting the number of visuals; including one major idea in a simple, easy-to-understand design large enough for the audience to read; and proofreading to eliminate all errors. To use a visual aid effectively, paraphrase rather than read the visual, and step to one side so the audience can see the visual.

4. ***Deliver speeches with increasing confidence.*** Business speakers use the impromptu and extemporaneous speech methods more frequently than the memorized or written-and-read methods. Enhance a presentation by developing strong, professional vocal qualities. Good voices have medium or low pitch, are easily heard, vary in tone and rate to reflect moods and add interest, and minimize distracting verbal fillers. Articulate speakers enunciate words precisely and refer to a dictionary frequently to ensure proper pronunciation.

Before your presentation, prepare thoroughly, develop any presentation visuals needed to support your presentation, prepare useful notes to aid your delivery, request a lectern to hold notes but not to hide behind, insist on a proper introduction, dress appropriately, and arrive early to check last-minute details. During the presentation communicate confidence and enthusiasm for the audience, watch your audience for feedback, answer questions from the audience politely, and stay within your time limit. After the presentation answer questions from the audience and distribute handouts.

5. ***Discuss effective strategies for adapting oral presentations to an intercultural audience.*** When communicating with other cultures, use simple English and short sentences and avoid abbreviations, slang, jargon, and figurative expressions or "red flag" words. Enunciate precisely and speak slowly. Consider the appropriateness of jokes and humor, and use a straightforward, direct approach with the main idea presented first. Be aware of differences in nonverbal communication (e.g., eye contact, personal space, value of time), preference for formality, gift-giving practices, and social protocol that may require flexibility and adjustments to your presentation style. Observe the audience carefully for signs of misunderstanding. Avoid asking directly whether an idea has been understood; instead restate ideas using different words when necessary or consider allowing a brief time for questions following short segments of your presentation.

REFERENCES

[1]Eastwood, A. (1995). Presenting: A way to boost business. *Computer Dealer's News, 11*(14), S14.

[2]Axtell, R. E. (1992). *Do's and taboos of public speaking: How to get those butterflies flying in formation.* New York: John Wiley.

[3]Hughes, M. (1990). Tricks of the speechwriter's trade. *Management Review, 9*(11), 56–58.

[4]Hughes, M. (1990). Tricks of the speechwriter's trade. *Management Review, 9*(11), 56–58.

[5]Iapoce, M. (1988). *A funny thing happened on the way to the board room: Using humor in business speaking:* New York: John Wiley.

[6]Axtell, R. E. (1992). *Do's and taboos of public speaking: How to get those butterflies flying in formation.* New York: John Wiley.

[7]Mayer, K. R. (1988). *Well spoken oral communication for business.* New York: Dryden.

[8]Decker, B. (1992). *You've got to be believed to be heard.* New York: St. Martin's Press.

[9]McGraw, J. L. (1992). *Creating desktop presentations that work.* Englewood Cliffs, NJ: Prentice Hall.

[10]Rockey, E. H. (1977). *Communicating in organizations.* Cambridge, MA: Winthrop Publishers.

[11]Jurek, K. (1995, May 29). Presentations call for top technology. *Crain's Cleveland Business,* p. 11.

[12]Eastwood, A. (1995). Presenting: A way to boost business. *Computer Dealer's News, 11*(14), S14.

[13]Haskin, D. (1994). *The complete multimedia guide for idiots.* Indianapolis: Apha Books.

[14]Strasser, D. (1996). *Tips for good electronic presentations, 20*(1), 78.

[15]Klinger, C., & Siegel, J. B. (1996). *Computer multimedia presentations, 66*(6), 46.

[16]Newcombe, P. J. (1991). *Voice and Diction,* (2s ed.) Raleigh, NC: Contemporary Publishing Company.

[17]Axtell, R. E. (1992). *Do's and taboos of public speaking: How to get those butterflies flying in formation.* New York: John Wiley.

[18]Axtell, R. E. (1992). Do's and taboos of public speaking: *How to get those butterflies flying in formation.* New York: John Wiley.

[19]Decker, B. (1992). *You've got to be believed to be heard.* New York: St. Martin's Press. [p. 137].

[20]Decker, B. (1992). *You've got to be believed to be heard.* New York: St. Martin's Press. [p. 137].

[21]Kupsh, J., Jones, C. L., & Graves, P. R. (1990). Presentation design strategies. *Business Education Forum, 45*(3), 28-31.

[22]Marcus, B. W. (1991). Cross-cultural concerns. *New Accountant, 6*(6), 21, 42.

[23]Valuing diversity part III: *Communicating Across Cultures.* (1987). [Film]. San Francisco: Copeland Griggs Productions.

[24]Stern, D. A. (1996). *Speaking without an accent.* Dialect Accent Specialists, Inc. [Online] Available at http://plainfield.bypass.com/dasinc/#sw [1997, April 30].

REVIEW QUESTIONS

1. What two techniques can you use to condense the purpose of a presentation into a brief statement? (Obj. 1)

2. What important facts should a speaker know about the audience when planning a presentation? (Obj. 1)

3. What is the basic three-part structure of an effective presentation? (Obj. 2)

4. What three goals should an effective introduction accomplish? (Obj. 2)

5. How many major points should a speaker develop? Explain. (Obj. 2)

6. What does a speaker hope to accomplish in the close? What suggestions will help a speaker accomplish this goal? (Obj. 2)

7. In what ways do presentation visuals enhance a presentation? (Obj. 3)

8. Why are electronic presentations gaining popularity as a support tool for business presentations? (Obj. 3)

9. What are three general guidelines for preparing an effective presentation visual? (Obj. 3)

10. Which delivery methods are used most often by business speakers? (Obj. 4)

11. What are verbal fillers and what can be done to minimize them in a presentation? (Obj. 4)

12. What are suggestions for preparing useful notes pages? (Obj. 4)

13. How can a speaker communicate to the audience that he/she is enthusiastic about the topic and committed to helping the audience benefit from the presentation? (Obj. 4)

14. What ethical responsibility does a speaker have when planning and delivering a presentation? (Obj. 1)

15. What can a speaker do to ensure that a presentation is understood and does not offend an audience of various cultures? (Obj. 5)

EXERCISES

1. **Evaluating a Speaker (Obj. –5)**
   Evaluate the speaking skill of a well-known television newscaster or commentator or a recognized speaker on your campus. What are the strengths? Weaknesses? Use the "Check Your Presentation Skills" (positioned before the chapter summary) to direct your attention to the various components of effective speaking. Offer suggestions for improving the person's oral communication skills. Pay special attention to vocal qualities, audience eye contact, rapport, and organization.

2. **Presenting an Impromptu Presentation (Obj. 1-2, 4–5)**
   In groups of four assigned by your instructor, select four topics related to effective business communication or some other business-related topic. A group leader may randomly assign a topic to each member or allow the members to select a topic. You may select the following questions or use them as a guide for developing similar ones:

   a. Why are communication skills a key ingredient in your career (specify a career)?

   b. Why are effective intercultural communication skills important in an increasingly competitive global economy?

   c. How has downsizing affected the need for communication skills?

   d. Why is being a team player an important element of success in today's economy?

   e. What actions reflect the values of a team player who is focused on helping an organization succeed?

   f. How has rapidly changing technology revolutionized communication in business organizations?

   g. What would business be like if legality were a company's only ethical benchmark or criterion?

   h. Are business organizations less (or more) ethical today than they were a decade ago?

   Following a brief preparation time, each member will give a one- to two-minute presentation to the group. After all presentations are given, the group will briefly discuss the strengths and weaknesses of each presentation and attempt to provide each member with a few specific suggestions for improvement.

3. **Critiquing Your Speaking Ability (Obj. 1–2, 4–5)**
   Deliver a presentation on one of the topics listed in Exercise 2 and videotape it. What was your overall impression of your performance after you completed the presentation? Use the "Check Your Presentation Skills" to direct your attention to the various components of effective speaking, and identify at least three strengths and three weaknesses that you noted as you viewed the videotape. Ask two other people in your class to view the videotape and critique your performance; they should provide at least two strengths and two suggestions for improvement. Finally, what is your overall impression of your performance after you analyzed the videotape and received feedback from class members? Does this impression different from your impression before viewing the videotape? Explain.

4. **Preparing an Outline and an Extemporaneous Presentation on Communication Effectiveness (Obj. 1–2, 4–5)**
   Read an article from a business-related magazine or practitioner journal related to the importance of oral communication or strategies for enhancing communication effectiveness in your field. Write an outline indicating the introduction, major points (body), and the summary. Give a short (two- to three-minute) oral presentation to the class.

5. **Preparing an Extemporaneous Presentation on Team Building (Obj. 1–5)**
   As the manager of a company, develop a short (three- to five-minute) presentation to be given to employers for the purpose of increasing their ability to communicate effectively as a team. Design the appropriate visuals following the guidelines presented in the chapter and use them effectively in your presentation.

6. **Designing Effective Presentation Visuals (Obj. 1–5)**
   In small groups, develop three to five presentation visuals on one of the following topics using outside sources to supplement the information presented in the chapter. Use the presentation visuals in a presentation to the class. Topics include overcoming speech anxiety, preparing an effective introduction or close, supporting the main points of a presentation, the role of humor in a presentation, importance of oral communication skills in your field, rehearsing proper vocal qualities, nonverbal communication in a presentation, handling questions, using visual aids effectively, guidelines for using various techniques in an electronic presentation (typography, color, animation, images, drawing tools, etc.), importing and exporting objects between software programs and the Internet, ethical implications of multimedia objects, and so on. If required by your instructor, prepare an extemporaneous presentation and deliver it to the class using the visuals to support your presentation.

7. **Preparing an Extemporaneous Presentation on a Chosen Topic (Obj. 1–5)**
   Select a topic from the following list of suggested topics for a five- to ten-minute oral presentation. Alternately,

you may use these suggested topics as a springboard for other appropriate topics that will provide timely, relevant information to the students in your class. Obtain your instructor's approval for your topic before beginning work.

a. What adjustments would be required for an oral presentation given to an audience from (supply a culture)?

b. How has the electronic revolution changed the way a person seeks a job?

c. How can a computer be used to perform one of the following functions: manage the calendar of a manager who holds numerous regular and periodic meetings with company staff and clients, edit a report simultaneously by two managers working in remote locations, rank potential applicants for a job, locate relevant information for decision making, ensure the mechanical accuracy of an important document, enhance the professional appearance of a document, and so on?

d. What are several business applications for multimedia? What benefits do they provide?

e. What ethical implications are involved in the use of the following technology: multimedia, property rights, software, and privacy and accessibility of information?

f. What are common examples of computer abuse in today's companies and what can be done to combat it?

g. Does an employer have the right to read an employee's e-mail (or conduct other forms of electronic surveillance)? What laws govern this issue?

h. What are the major differences in the management styles of men and women?

i. How do you prepare a résumé that will be scanned into an applicant tracking system?

j. How can you manage your time (or stress) more effectively?

k. What benefits are realized by working cooperatively in diverse work groups?

l. What are characteristics of effective and noneffective team members?

m. What can corporate leaders do to increase employees' sensitivity toward diversity (cultures, genders, ages of coworkers, and potential markets)?

n. Explain one of the values presented in Steven Covey's *Seven Habits of Highly Effective People* in terms that will be beneficial to the class.

o. Obtain a copy of *Emotional Intelligence* by Daniel Goleman and discuss his theory that emotional intelligence can be used to "Manage with Heart."

p. What are the benefits and drawbacks of videoconferencing? What hardware and software are needed? What suggestions can you provide a job applicant being interviewed by videoconference?

q. How can the Internet enhance a company's productivity?

r. Explain the difference between Internet and Intranet.

8. **Preparing an Extemporaneous Report to Stockholders (Obj. 1–5)**
As a part of a team of four, present a mock annual shareholders' meeting before the class. You should work from an annual report of a major company. One person should be the chief executive officer, one the chief operating officer, one the financial officer, and one the chief marketing officer. Each will speak for two to three minutes. The CEO should preside and introduce each of the others appropriately before each speaks. Your report should include a review of the year's activities, plans for the next year, and information about the firm's role in the community. Design effective visuals and use them effectively in your presentation.

E - M A I L   A P P L I C A T I O N

Your instructor has provided specific instructions for preparing an oral presentation. Using an on-line database, locate several resources on your topic from the campus library or an external library. Using these resources, develop an outline for your presentation. Send your instructor an e-mail message containing the outline and a list of the sources you intend to use.

REAL-TIME INTERNET CASE

Now About that Accent . . .

Most individuals "pick up" the accent spoken in the region in which they live, and those who learn English as a second language typically retain some elements of pronunciation that are indicative of their first language. When you leaves your native area, your accent may be a subject of interest, humor, or even ridicule.

The seeming lack of accent among public broadcasters is often the result of extensive retraining in vocal delivery. Corporations often also desire to enhance universal acceptance by cultivating "Standard English" among their management; corporate accent-reduction speech clients have included executives from Beech Aircraft, Mitsubishi Bank, NCR Corporation, Union Carbide, and Wells Fargo Bank.[24]

Not everyone, however, feels that accents are detrimental. A countering opinion is that an accent may at times serve as an asset to the speaker. It reflects personhood and adds dimension and interest to the individual. Furthermore, the "best English" is often dictated by audience expectation and the circumstances in which a speaker functions. Visit the following web sites for information on the issue, and respond to one or more of the following activities, as directed by your instructor.

Internet Sites

http://www.edunet.com/nec/u4-2.html#accent
http://linguistlist.org/~ask-ling/msg02649.html

Activities

- Locate at least one additional web site on the subject of accents that you found interesting. What was the URL of the site? Summarize the important aspects of the information in outline form.

- Analyze your own accent, responding to the following questions: Of what region is it typical? What distinguishes your accent from others? Is your accent stronger at certain times? If so, why? E-mail your instructor with your self-analysis.

- How are accent and dialect different yet related? Prepare a chart that illustrates the relationship.

- What are the advantages and disadvantages of a regional accent? How can accent work to enhance or worsen a businessperson's communication? Write a one- to two-page summary of your position on the issue.

Team Building Projects

The Norming stage is marked by harmonious cohesiveness. It is a pleasant time in the team's evolution, when good feelings and a free exchange of ideas, feelings, and feedback abound. Sometimes, though, there is an abandonment of task goals so that social needs of the team can be pursued. Typical feelings in the Norming stage include:

- a new ability to express criticism constructively.
- acceptance of membership in the team.
- relief that it seems everything is going to work out.

Common behaviors in the Norming stage include:

- achievement of harmony by avoiding conflict.
- greater friendliness as members demonstrate acceptance of each other.
- increased cooperation and teamwork.
- cohesion, common spirit, and common goals.
- establishment and maintenance of team rules and boundaries.
- recognition of others' contributions.
- unfocused, irrelevant, and overly friendly communications.

While enjoying the Norming stage, team members should guard against the tendency to spin wheels on small talk and discussions that do not lead to the accomplishment of the task at hand.

Another serious problem to guard against during the Norming stage is Groupthink.. Social psychologist Irving Janis described groupthink as a mode of thinking people engage in when they are involved with a cohesive group; their strivings to be unanimous override their motivation to realistically appraise alternative courses of action. Group pressure to agree leads to carelessness, poor decisions, and low quality actions. Some common symptoms of groupthink include:

- illusions of invulnerability: feeling that the group is beyond making mistakes.
- self-censorship: members censor thoughts that are opposed to group ideas.
- pressure on dissenters: members with different opinions are pressured to conform.
  - mind-guarding: outside ideas that might contradict the group decision or ideas are rejected.
  - apparent unanimity: members are in agreement on the surface but individuals may hide doubt from the group.

One protection against groupthink is the presence of team diversity. A team made up of "cookie cutter" look-alikes and act-alikes tends to produce less creative solutions than would a more diverse team. Differences can add depth, create strength, and bring balance to the team. But for diversity to bring value, those with individual differences must be respected and encouraged to utilize their talents and resources. While diversity may make teaming seem more difficult at first, it produces a more powerful unit. Ironically, the desirable quality of high group cohesion actually contributes to the formation of groupthink. As the team becomes more united, members should guard against progression into groupthink: (1) Leaders should remain impartial and encourage dissent; (2) subgroups should work on some tasks independently; (3) the team should "rethink" important decisions; and (4) outside opinions should be sought to provide feedback.

Each team member should be encouraged to present ideas with no fear of reprisal. Remember that creativity involves "hitchhiking"; one idea, no matter how ridiculous it may seem, may trigger another idea, which may be the perfect solution.

Exploration

Visit the following web site to broaden your knowledge of the groupthink. Go to the related links that discuss various settings in which groupthink has been identified.

http://oak.cats.ohiou.edu/~ef129994/efindexgroup.html

As a team, discuss situations in which you have experienced or observed groupthink at work. Identify real or hypothetical situations from the business world in which groupthink produced less than optimal team results.

Application

With your team members, complete the following activities:
- Schedule an appointment with your instructor to review the draft of your project.
- Identify someone outside your team with strong writing and grammatical skills who would be willing to read through your completed project and note needed corrections and improvements prior to finalizing.

Source: Griffin, E. (19940) *A first look at communication theory.* New York: McGraw-Hill, Inc.

Salsbury Communication, Inc.

Fear of public speaking is reported to be the number one fear of American adults. This enormous fear results primarily from the typical lack of experience in public-speaking situations. Practice is the most effective antidote for fear, and the speaker who can overcome the fear of public speaking certainly possesses a marketable skill.

An accomplished speaker gives careful attention to nonverbal dimensions, articulation of words, topic selection, and content structuring. When the verbal and nonverbal channels match, the speaker has a much greater chance of having the audience believe the message.

Discussion Questions

1. What five characteristics does Greg Salsbury mention as nonverbal dimensions of oral communication? Why are they considered nonverbal?

2. What does Salsbury say is the best way to overcome nervousness in public speaking?

How much of this technique is desirable?

3. What is the most critical part of an oral presentation? Why?

4. What role does humor play in public speaking?

5. Salsbury uses the 1984 presidential race between Reagan and Mondale as an example of the importance of having "everything in sync." Explain the concept, referring to the two candidates for examples.

Applications

You have been asked to give a brief oral presentation to a group of high school students at a career day. Your topic is on why students should consider a career in your chosen field.

1. Prepare a three-point outline for the talk that includes an introduction, body, and summary.

2. Be prepared to make your presentation to the class (maximum length of three minutes).

Communicating About Work and Jobs

CHAPTER THIRTEEN

Preparing Résumés and Application Letters

LEARNING OBJECTIVES

When you have completed Chapter 13, you will be able to:

1 Complete systematic self-, career, and job analyses.

2 Prepare an effective chronological, functional, or combination chronological/functional résumé.

3 Prepare a résumé that can be scanned and processed by an electronic applicant-tracking system.

4 Identify employment tools other than the résumé that can enhance employability.

5 Locate employment opportunities using traditional and electronic methods.

6 Identify the components of an effective on-line résumé.

7 Write an application letter that effectively introduces an accompanying résumé.

*J*ason Secosky, a computer science student at the University of Washington, knew he wanted to return to his native North Carolina after graduation. Job hunting from 3,000 miles away required more than traditional job search techniques. He accessed the web site of SAS Institute, a Raleigh-Durham-based software company and found it was hiring. He faxed his résumé, scheduled an interview to take place during a planned trip home, and landed two job offers from the company. Secosky's on-line savvy even gave him an unexpected jump on the competition. Although the company had ads in the newspaper, it had not posted listings for the jobs he was offered.

Technology is radically changing the employment market. Forrester Research estimates that while $30 million was spent in 1997 for on-line recruiting, the figure will exceed $218 million by the year 2000. Potential employees find that the job-seeking process is vastly improved. Using the Net, they can do much more than just post résumés or research companies. When Tyler Munson graduated from the University of Illinois and couldn't find the advertising job he was looking for, he put a portfolio of his designs on the Web and registered his site with Yahoo! An on-line art gallery began to feature his work; and eventually, a California web-design company saw his portfolio, flew him out for an interview, and offered him a job.[1]

In spite of the seeming success of on-line job searching, experts do not suggest that students give up on more traditional job search strategies such as careful résumé preparation, networking, career counseling, or mock interviewing. On-line employment search capabilities extend, rather than replace, the range of possibilities previously available to the job seeker. The diagram in Figure 13-1 provides an overview of the employment process you will need to follow to land a job interview—from identifying the qualifications that fit the organization's needs to preparing a powerful résumé and application letter to identifying prospective employers using traditional and electronic sources. With this overview in mind, you will move through a detailed explanation of each step in the process.

1 *Complete systematic self-, career, and job analyses.*

Have you set *your* career goals? What is your plan for reaching them?

Setting Goals and Planning

For many years, a financial counselor conducted seminars for people who had very high economic aspirations. He asked participants to ponder the question "How rich do I want to be?" He asked each person to write that figure on a small card, place it in his or her wallet, and look at it each night and morning. Two things were vital to success: setting a goal and developing a plan for reaching it. The daily reminders of the goal increased the likelihood of attaining it.

Goal setting does for individuals what management by objectives does for businesses. Setting goals forces people to consider these questions: What is to be accomplished? How is it best accomplished? How is progress measured? Are decisions congruent with goals? Important as such questions are, they sometimes do not get the attention they deserve. Many college seniors have confided to advisers, "About all I've ever done is go to school. Now I'll have to earn a living. How do I find a suitable job?"

Because the answer to that question can mean the difference between a pleasant life and an unpleasant one, it deserves careful attention. A suitable job provides satisfaction at all of Maslow's needs levels, from basic economic to self-actualizing needs. During your working lifetime, you will spend about one third of your nonsleeping time on the job (and probably much additional time thinking about your work). The

Process of Applying for a Job

Gather Essential Information

- Self-analysis
- Job analysis
- Career analysis
- Interview with career person

Prepare a Company/Job Profile

Identify specific qualifications related to the job

Construct a Résumé and an Application Letter

Consider Supplementing the Résumé

- Portfolio
- Videotape
- CD ROM

Identify Prospective Employers

Traditional Sources

- Printed sources
- Networks
- Career services
- Employer's office
- Employment agencies
- Classified ads
- Professional

Electronic Sources

- Locate career guidance information
- Identify job listings
- Post an on-line résumé on a job site or corporate home page
- Post a résumé on your personal web site

FIGURE 13-1 Process of applying for a job.

right job for you will not be drudgery; the work itself will be satisfying. It will give you a sense of well-being; you can see its positive impact on others. The satisfaction derived from work has a positive influence on enjoyment of nonworking hours.

Students often devote too little time and thought to career decisions, or they unnecessarily postpone making career decisions. Of the many courses required to achieve your degree, how much time is devoted to one course? (Think of reading assignments, doing research, preparing for tests, writing a term paper, and so on.) Are you willing to spend that much time gathering, recording, and analyzing information that will lead to a satisfying career? Would you be willing to start compiling information that would guide you to the best career?

Just as finding the right career is important for you, finding the right employees is important for the employer. Before they can offer you a job, employers need information about you—in writing. Your **résumé** is the written document that provides a basis for judgment about your capabilities on the job. In preparing this vital document, your major concerns should be (1) gathering essential information, (2) planning a résumé, and (3) constructing a résumé.

Getting Essential Information

You will want to arm yourself with as much pertinent information as possible for your job search. Having accurate information about yourself, your chosen career, and specific job positions will help you decide how to market yourself to potential employers.

Self Analysis

Knowing yourself is a prerequisite for preparing a résumé. To sell yourself in a résumé, you must first identify your qualifications, focusing primarily on your capabilities that meet the employer's needs. A self-analysis might include the following types of questions:

Take a few moments to answer the self-analysis questions. Compare your answers with those of a classmate.

- What kind of person am I? Am I dependable, energetic, a good time manager, a leader, and so on?

- What are my aptitudes? How are my quantitative, verbal, mechanical, or problem-solving skills?

- What are my achievements? Have I excelled in grades, extracurricular activities, work, and so forth?

- What are my interests? What kinds of courses, activities, reading, and leisure do I enjoy?

- What is my education preparation? What is my major, minor, special training, or skills?

- What work experience do I have? What full- or part-time jobs have I held?

After answering such questions, you will have a good chance of providing ready answers for questions asked during an employment interview.

Career Analysis

The same technique—asking and answering questions—is helpful in career analysis. In this step of career investigation, you consider the career field that interests you and answer questions about work in that field. Pertinent questions might include the following:

- What type of career is it? Is it a "pressure occupation"? Do hazards exist? Is travel expected?

- What preparation is necessary? What are the academic, training, and/or professional requirements?

- What rewards does it offer? What is the standard salary? What opportunities exist for advancement? What are the fringe benefits?

- What is the future for the field? Will it likely expand or contract? Will it be strongly influenced by technology? Will political or governmental influences be significant?

To locate answers to the career-analysis questions, refer to the following sources. These and other books are available in school or community libraries, in many college and university career service centers, and on the Internet. Additional resources for conducting an electronic job search are included in a later section of this chapter.

> What other sources for career information can you locate in your library, college bookstore, or Career Services Center?

- Bolles, R. N. (1998). *What color is your parachute? A practical manual for job hunters and career changers.* Berkeley, CA: Ten Speed Press.

- *Career opportunities.* Chicago, IL: J. G. Ferguson (published monthly).

- U.S. Department of Labor. (1996). *Dictionary of occupational titles.* New York: Rosen.

- U.S. Department of Labor. *Occupational outlook handbook.* Baton Rouge: Claitor (published yearly).

- Powell, C. R. (1996). *Career planning today.* (3rd ed.). Dubuque, IA: Kendall-Hunt.

After answering career-oriented questions about a selected career field, you almost certainly will have either an increased enthusiasm for your chosen career or a feeling that you should consider other careers. Either way, the effort has been worthwhile.

Job Analysis. Once you have selected the right field for your career, you can begin to examine a specific job in that field. Most college graduates with little or no experience expect to accept what is commonly known as an *entry-level position.* Many businesses provide training or orientation programs for newly hired employees. Before preparing a résumé, students need to ask and answer the following questions:

> Form a small group with others majoring in your field and brainstorm about answers to questions listed under "Career Analysis" and "Job Analysis." Then, conduct necessary research to complete the career and job analyses on your own.

- What are the specific duties and responsibilities?

- Do my personal characteristics seem compatible with the specified duties and responsibilities?

- Does my education satisfy requirements for the position? Would I be willing to continue my education?

- Are my experiences directly related to the job's specified duties and responsibilities?

Interview with a Career Person. Before making the decision to embark on a certain career, you can profit from interviewing someone who is already pursuing it. The interview is to your advantage, regardless of whether it increases your enthusiasm or reveals that the career is definitely not for you. For maximum benefit, prepare a set of questions such as the ones that follow:

> Interview a career person in your field, using the questions in the "Interview with a Career Person" section as a guide.

- When did you become interested in this field?
- What do you see as an ideal preparation for entry?
- What was your first job in this field?
- Do reasonable opportunities for advancement exist?
- Does the field have potential for growth?
- What tasks do you perform on a typical day?
- What do you like best about your career?
- What do you dislike?
- What is your advice to someone who is considering entry into this field?

Prepare a company/job profile for the company/job for which you expect to be interviewing.

Completing the self-, career, and job analyses has allowed you to collect a great deal of information. The next step is to compile this information in a format that will allow you to compare your qualifications with the company and job requirements—to determine whether a match between you and the potential job is possible.

A company/job profile for an entry-level audit accountant in an international public accounting firm is shown in Figure 13-2. After completing the two columns, an individual can easily identify the exact areas in which company/job requirements and qualifications and needs do not match. Basic qualifications and salary and advancement expectations seem compatible; the major differences are in work surroundings, amount of travel and overtime, and communication (oral and interpersonal) skills. By identifying the relative importance of these areas, the individual can decide whether pursuing a job in an international public accounting firm would be wise. Would he/she be willing to seek assistance in refining communication skills? Would he/she be willing to learn to work effectively in groups? How important are limited overtime and few travel requirements? Could he/she adapt to working in temporary locations without a desk of his/her own?

What reasons account for the fact that most entry-level employees are seeking a second job within six months?

You will probably never find the job and the organization that will satisfy all your needs and meet all your requirements. Some factors will be more important to you than others. The benefits gained from this analysis will far outweigh the time and energy spent in gathering valid information about a company and job requirements and in evaluating your qualifications and needs. This analysis may prevent you from becoming one of the increasing number of entry-level workers who are looking for another job after only six months because their qualifications and needs were not compatible with the company and the job requirements.

What purpose do these analyses serve?

Completing your self-, career, and job analyses should have helped you (1) identify your qualifications as they relate to an employer's needs, (2) ensure that you have selected the right career, and (3) compare your qualifications to the duties and responsibilities of the job you are seeking. This information should help you decide what should be included on your résumé.

2 *Prepare an effective chronological, functional, or combination chronological/functional résumé.*

Planning Your Résumé

A job announcement that appeared in several mid-western newspapers described a career opportunity for someone with two years' sales experience to sell medical equipment to hospitals. John W. applied. He was well qualified and had sold medical equipment before. He knew the territory, was willing to relocate, and had a proven track record of successful selling—but he was not invited to an interview. The same was true of countless others. Of the nearly 200 people who applied for the position,

COMPANY/JOB PROFILE
Entry-Level Audit Staff—International Accounting Firm

	Company/Job Requirements	My Qualifications and Needs
Education:	Master's degree in accountancy with 3.5 or higher GPA	Will receive M.P.A. degree with 3.8 GPA.
Certification:	CPA preferred; expected within three years.	Committed to earning CPA within two years.
General knowledge:	Broad understanding of all business areas (marketing, finance, management, information systems, etc.); history; world cultures; economic, political, and social systems; and ethical theories.	Curriculum provided courses in each area.
Intellectual skills:	Highly analytical; able to solve diverse and unstructured problems for many unfamiliar settings (represent clients in various businesses); meticulous attention to detail.	Excelled in quantitative courses; performed well in preparing cases requiring creative solutions to problems without clear-cut answers.
Computer skills:	Proficiency in spreadsheet, word processing, and Windows; knowledgeable of general ledger and data management programs.	Proficient in the operation of Windows, Microsoft Office 97 Suite, and familiar with leading general ledger programs.
Communication:	Secure and transfer information easily; present and defend views formally and informally in writing or orally.	Proficient in written communication; attempting to overcome fear of speaking before groups; often reluctant to defend ideas if I encounter resistance.
Interpersonal skills:	Work efficiently in groups of diverse members to accomplish a task (e.g., with other members of the audit staff assigned to each audit and with the client); must withstand and resolve conflict (with peers and clients).	Prefer working independently; have had poor experiences completing class team projects.
Management skills:	Organize and delegate tasks; motivate and develop other people.	Part-time work and leadership roles in student groups provided opportunities to refine these management skills.
Work environment:	Work primarily on location at the client's office with temporary work sites (conference table, work room); may share a desk with other staff when days spent in the office rotate.	Must feel in control of my own work space; a desk organized for my sole use is important.

FIGURE 13-2 Comparison of company and job requirements with qualifications.

	Company/Job Requirements	My Qualifications and Needs
Psychometric profile:	Able to work on numerous audits simultaneously, to shift gears from one project to another readily, to set priorities and organize work, to meet tight and often coinciding deadlines, and to meet any unexpected requirements; willing to revise work until it meets the high standards set by an international accounting firm.	Prefer to complete one project before moving to another; difficult to manage more than one major activity at once; often take criticism personally.
Ethical standards:	Must abide by the AICPA Code of Professional Conduct.	High moral standards as result of family background; willing to abide by code of ethics that upholds the high standards of the profession.
Salary range:	$30,000–$35,000 annually.	$28,000–$34,000 annually.
Travel:	Approximately 25%.	No more than 10%.
Overtime:	Average 15 hours per month; peaks between February 1 and April 1.	Limited overtime desired.
Career path:	Well-defined path; typically promoted from staff accountant to audit senior after 3 years; from audit senior to manager after 6 years; eligible for partner after 10 years.	Well-defined career path with frequent changes in responsibilities.
Prestige level:	High.	Medium to high prestige desired.

FIGURE 13-2 continued.

What *three* decisions must you make when planning a résumé?

fewer than a dozen were selected for interviews.[2] This true story occurs every day. Without a résumé that sells your qualifications in terms of the employer's needs, you will never have an opportunity to sell yourself at an interview.

Because an employer typically spends two minutes or less reading a résumé, you have very little time to explain why you are the best person for the job.[3] You must selectively choose *what to say*, *how to say it*, and *how to arrange it* on the page so that it can be read quickly but thoroughly. A concise, informative, easy-to-read summary of your relevant qualifications will not only get you an interview but also will tell the employer that you possess the straightforward communication skills demanded in today's information-intensive society.

The standard parts of a winning résumé and an overview of the content of each section is shown in Figure 13-3. Study this overview carefully before reading the more in-depth explanation that follows.

What is your reaction to "I'll just use the format and style my friend used on her résumé; she got a job with it"?

Examples of résumés are provided in this chapter (Figures 13-3 to 13-7) to illustrate these standard résumé parts and various résumé formats. No *one* universal résumé works effectively in today's job market. The format, content, and style of your résumé depend on your specific qualifications, the job field (conservative or creative), and the individual personality you wish to portray. In fact, you will

Standard Sections of a Résumé

Identification
Name and where you can be reached.

Objective
Statement that specifies the job sought.

Summary of Achievements (Optional)
Summary statement about qualifications; tells employers why applicant should be hired.

RESUME

- Identification
- Objective
- Summary of Achievements
- Qualifications
- Personal Information
- References

Qualifications

- **Education**—begins with most recent degree earned, institution, major, GPA if above 3.0, special abilities (computer or foreign language), and experiences that set you apart. Omits high school graduation.
- **Work Experience**—specifies job title and employer, describes related job duties and derived skills (interpersonal skills, time management, dependability). Ties derived skills to specific job duties to enhance credibility. Arranged with most relevant experience first.
- **Honors and Activities**—divides these activities into short readable sections. Includes only activities that enhance applicant's qualifications.

Personal Information

- Omits information that might lead to discriminatory hiring practices (gender, religion, marital status, disability, or national origin).
- Includes information related to job duties and that shows applicant as a productive, well-rounded individual.

References
Includes "Available on request" or lists the names, addresses, and telephone numbers of three persons who can support applicant's qualifications.

FIGURE 13-3
Standard sections of a résumé.

What is the best format and arrangement for a résumé?

likely develop different résumés for slightly different job objectives. The information you include on each résumé will be based on your assessment of whether the receiver will want or need the information, your personal preference, and your moral judgment.

The goal of the résumé is to get an interview, so ask yourself this question: "Does including this information increase my chances of getting an interview?" If the answer is "Yes," include the information; if the answer is "No," omit the information and use the space to develop your qualifications.

Identification

Your objective is to provide information that will allow the interviewer to reach you. Include your name, current address, and telephone number. You may also include your e-mail address and Internet address to facilitate an interviewer's communication

Strategic Forces: Legal and Ethical Constraints

Inflated Résumés: High Price of Career Lies

Corporate downsizing has created intense competition for fewer jobs, and desperate job seekers are increasingly more willing to lie or at least "enhance" their résumés. According to outplacement specialist James Challenger, as many as one third of the job applicants will lie when the job market is tight or when they think it will help on something such as salary.[4] Many applicants feel lying is necessary to get past the initial screening and "get their feet in the door." Some rationalize their actions by saying, "Nobody is checking, so who will ever know?"; "Everyone does it"; or "I deserve it."[5]

Common ways to lie on résumés include the following:

- **Fabricate or embellish academic experience.** Applicants claim they earned degrees from institutions they never attended or earned degrees they only partially completed. Applicants also fudge on their class ranks and grade-point averages and list fictitious honors and activities.
- **Fudge employment dates to hide gaps in employment.** Rather than lying, applicants should answer honestly: "Yes, I was laid off at Company X . . . and spent six months looking for the right employer, so there is a gap in my employment dates for that year."[6]

Murphy's Law No. 2

The *one* little exaggeration on your résumé is the one they check!

C86-4 The Drawing Board™ Box 660429 Dallas, Texas © Wheeler Group, Inc., 1985

- **Overinflate job title and exaggerate job duties.** For example, a job seeker might report a job title as "supervisor" rather than "senior clerk." To further embellish the résumé, he or she might write "facilitated daily production of property/casualty documentation" when "typed and processed 200 insurance forms a day" would be more truthful and useful to the recruiter.[7] A secretary might be tempted to write "prepared financial statements" when they were merely keyed.

Companies do verify information such as education, dates of employment, and other data presented on the résumé. Computerized interview programs, employee honesty tests, and countless other strategies are used to spot inconsistencies that would alert a company to a deceptive applicant. What happens when a lie is detected?

Companies cannot risk the safety of their people and resources to people they can't trust; therefore, they generally will not hire an applicant who submits false information and will terminate employment as soon as the deception is discovered. "Never hire a liar. In the team environment of today's workplace, it's important that you respect and trust your team members," one manager advised.[8] However, deceptive employees who are retained face negative consequences for their unethical action. Loss of trust may prevent advancement in the company, and job performance will eventually suffer if an employee lacks the qualifications to perform the job.

When selecting information to be included, honestly ask yourself, "Does this information present my qualifications honestly and ethically, or does it inflate my qualifications to increase my chances of getting the job?" If you have the slightest inclination that including a piece of information will inflate your qualifications, omit it. What you believe is a "career booster" could end your career. Present your accomplishments honestly and take pride in deserved advancements.

Application

Review your résumé carefully. Is it truthful? Does it promote your accomplishments in a direct, simple, and accurate way? Is it clear where you were working when you gained the experience that you describe?

with you and to entice him/her to view your home page. Including these electronic addresses will bring attention to your ability to communicate electronically—important skills in a technological age.

To ensure that the interviewer can quickly locate the identification information, center it on the page or use graphic design elements to target attention to your name (e.g., change the font face and size, add graphic lines and borders, etc.). You may also include a permanent address (parents' address) if you are interviewing when classes are not in session. If you are rarely at home during typical office hours (the time the interviewer is likely to call), provide a telephone number where messages can be left. Explain to those taking messages that prospective employers may be calling; thus, the accuracy of their messages and the impression they make while taking the message could affect your job search. Evaluate the personal message on your answering machine to be certain that it portrays you as a person serious about securing a job.

Job and/or Career Objective

Following the "Identification" section, state your job/career objective—the job you want. Interviewers can see immediately whether the job you are seeking matches the one they have to offer. A good job/career objective must be specific enough to be meaningful yet general enough to apply to a variety of jobs. The following example illustrates a general objective that has been revised to describe a specific job.

What are the characteristics of a good job/career objective?

General Objective	Specific Objective
A position that offers both a challenge and a good opportunity for growth.	To secure an entry-level position in sales leading to sales management.
A responsible position with a progressive organization that provides the opportunity for managerial development and growth commensurate with ability and attitudes.	To enter the management training program of a progressive firm that provides opportunities for advancement.

Some experts argue that a statement of your job or career objective may limit your job opportunities. Your objective should be obvious from your qualifications, they say. In general, however, making your objective clear at the beginning assures the interviewer that you have a definite career goal.

Summary of Achievements

In the "Summary of Achievements" section, summarize your major qualifications. By reading the career objective and a summary statement about your achievements, interviewers know *what* you want (whether your interests match theirs) and *why* the employer would want to hire you. A recent survey revealed that hiring officials consider summary statements an important item to include on a résumé; yet few job applicants include summary statements.[9]

To be certain that you highlight qualifications, write the "Summary of Achievements" section after you have written the entire résumé. Barnum's three methods for summarizing qualifications are illustrated in the following examples:[10]

Why might including a summary statement set your résumé apart from those of competitors?

Separate Objective and Qualifications

OBJECTIVE: To secure an entry-level position in international sales, leading to sales management.

SUMMARY OF ACHIEVEMENTS: Bachelor of Science in Marketing including three semesters of cooperative education experience with a large retail store and three international business courses (one completed abroad); proficiency in Spanish and French; effective team worker and communicator.

Combine Objective with Qualifications in One Section

OBJECTIVE: To secure a position in sales, leading to sales management. International sales/marketing executive with three years' successful experience in sales, marketing, advertising, and contract negotiation with international suppliers.

Link Objective and Summary in One Section

OBJECTIVE: Position as a sales representative where demonstrated commission selling and hard work bring rewards.

Accomplishments:
- Three years' straight-commission sales.
- Average of $35,000–$55,000 a year in commissioned earnings.
- Consistent success in development and growth of territories.

The "Summary of Achievements" section is optional. Some experts argue that this section is not beneficial unless your background is unusually varied. If you include a summary statement, be certain that the remainder of the résumé supports the statement; otherwise, you may not be considered further.[11]

Qualifications

The "Qualifications" section varies depending on the information identified in the self-, career-, and job analyses. This information is used to divide the qualifications into appropriate parts, choose appropriate labels for them, and arrange them in the best sequence. Usually, qualifications stem from your education and work experience (words that appear as headings in the résumé). Arrange these categories depending on which you perceive as more impressive to the employer, with the more impressive category appearing first. For example, education is usually the chief qualification of a recent college graduate; therefore, education appears first. However, a sales representative with related work experience might list experience first, particularly if the educational background is inadequate for the job sought.

Education.   Beginning with the most recent, list the degree, major, school, and graduation date. Include a blank line between schools so that the employer can see them at a glance. Using empathy for the interviewer's needs, determine the order for this information and follow that order consistently for each school attended. For example, the interviewer would probably want to know first whether you have the appropriate degree, then the institution, and so on. Recent or near college graduates should omit high school activities because that information is "old news." However, include high school activities if they provide a pertinent dimension to your qualifications. For example, having attended high school abroad is a definite advantage to an applicant seeking employment in an international firm. In addition, high school accomplishments may be relevant for freshmen or sophomores seeking cooperative education assignments, scholarships, or part-time jobs. Of course, this information will be replaced with college activities when the résumé is revised for subsequent jobs or other uses.

Include overall and major grade-point averages if they are B or better—but be prepared to discuss any omissions during an interview. Honors and achievements that relate directly to education can be incorporated in this section or included in a separate section. Examples include scholarships, appearance on academic lists, and initiation into honor societies. If honors and achievements are included in the "Education" section, be sure to include plenty of white space or to use bullets to highlight these points (see Figures 13-4 and 13-7).

The "Education" section could also include a list of special skills and abilities such as foreign language and computer competency. A list of courses typically required in your field is unnecessary and occupies valuable space. However, you should include any courses, workshops, or educational experiences that are not usual requirements. Examples include internships, cooperative education semesters, "shadowing," "over-the-shoulder" experiences, and study abroad.

> Write on paper any educational experiences you have had other than degrees earned.

Work Experience. The "Work Experience" section provides information about your employment history. For each job held, list the job title, company name, dates of employment, primary responsibilities, and key accomplishments. The jobs may be listed in reverse chronological order (beginning with the most recent) or in order of job relatedness. Begin with the job that most obviously relates to the job being sought if you have gaps in your work history, if the job you are seeking is very different from the job you currently hold, or if you are just entering the job market and have little if any related work experience.

> In what order should work experience be listed?

Arrange the order and format of information about each job (dates, job title, company, description, and accomplishments) so that the most important information is emphasized—but be sure all job information is formatted consistently. An applicant who has held numerous jobs in a short time should bury dates of employment within the text rather than surround them with white space. If the job relates directly to the job being sought, you might give the job title prominence by listing it first or surrounding it with white space.

Omit *obvious* job duties. The job title provides basic information about what you did. By stressing what you accomplished on the job, you will set yourself apart from other applicants who simply list a job description; and you will provide deeper insight into your ambition, capability, and personality. Recall instances when your personal involvement played a key role in the success of a project. Perhaps you uncovered a wasteful, labor-intensive procedure that was resolved through your innovation, or you bridged a gap in a communication breakdown. These instances neatly bulleted (see Figure 13-4) under the company name and job title "glitter like diamonds."[12]

Because interviewers spend such a short time reading résumés, the style must be direct and simple. Therefore, a résumé should use crisp phrases to help employers see the value of the applicant's education and experiences. To save space and to emphasize what you have accomplished, use these stylistic techniques:

1. Omit pronouns referring to yourself (*I, me, my*).
2. Use subject-understood sentences.
3. Begin sentences with action verbs as shown in the following examples:

Instead of	*Use*
I had responsibility for development of new territory.	*Developed* new territory.
My duties included designing computer systems and writing user documentation manuals.	*Developed* computer programs to monitor accounting systems including carefully written documentation manuals that enabled users to operate these sophisticated systems effectively.
I was the store manager and supervised eight employees.	*Managed* operations of store with sales volume of $1,000,000 and supervised eight employees.
My sales consistently exceeded sales quota.	*Earned* average of $35,000–$55,000 a year in commissioned earnings. *Received* service award for exceeding sales quota two of three years employed.
I was a member of the Student Council, Society for the Advancement of Management, Phi Kappa Phi, and Chi Omega Social Sorority.	*Developed* effective interpersonal skills through involvement in student organizations such as the Student Council. . . .

Because employers are looking for people who will work, action verbs are especially appropriate. Note the subject-understood sentences in the right column of the previous example: action words used as first words provide emphasis. The following list contains action verbs that are useful in résumés:

accomplished	developed	planned
achieved	drafted	prepared
administered	established	presented
analyzed	expanded	proposed
assisted	implemented	recruited
compiled	increased	researched
completed	initiated	scheduled
computed	invented	sold
controlled	maintained	studied
counseled	managed	supported
created	organized	wrote

To give the employer a vivid picture of you as a productive employee, you may find some of the following adjectives helpful as you describe your work experience:

adaptable/flexible	dependable	resourceful
analytical	efficient/productive	sensitive
conscientious	independent	sincere
consistent	objective	tactful
creative	reliable	team player

Describe the value you gained from one job experience that can be transferred to the job being sought. Use action verbs and an understood subject.

To avoid a tone of egotism, do not use too many adjectives or adverbs that seem overly strong. Plan to do some careful editing after writing your first draft.

Honors and Activities. Make a trial list of any other information that qualifies you for the job. Divide the list into appropriate divisions and then select an appropriate label. Your heading might be "Honors and Activities" unless you listed honors and achievements in the "Education" section. You might include a section for "Activities," "Leadership Activities," or "Memberships" depending on the items listed. You might also include a separate section on "Military Service," "Civic Activities," "Volunteer Work," or "Interests." If you have only a few items under each category, use a more general term and combine the lists. If your list is lengthy, divide it into more than one category; interviewers prefer "bite-size" pieces because they are easier to read and can be remembered more readily.

> The title of this section varies depending on the items listed within the section. What sections will you include on your résumé?

Resist the urge to include everything you have ever done; keep in mind that every item you add distracts from other information. Consider summarizing information that is relevant but does not merit several separate lines—for example, "Involved in art, drama, and choral groups." To decide whether to include certain information, ask these questions: How closely related is it to the job being sought? Does it provide job-related information that has not been presented elsewhere?

> Ask yourself: Does the information relate to the job being sought?

Personal Information. Because a résumé should contain primarily information that is relevant to an applicant's experience and qualifications, you must be selective when including personal information (not related to the job). The space could be used more effectively to include more about your qualifications or to add more white space. Personal information is commonly placed at the end of the résumé just above the "References" section because it is less important than qualifications (education, experience, and activities).

Under the 1964 Civil Rights Act (and subsequent amendments) and the Americans with Disabilities Act (ADA), employers cannot make hiring decisions based on gender, age, marital status, religion, national origin, or disability. Employers prefer not to receive information that provides information about gender, age, and national origin because questions could be raised about whether the information was used in the hiring decision. Thus, follow these guidelines related to personal information:

- ***Do not include personal information that could lead to discriminatory hiring.*** Exclude height, weight, and color of hair and eyes and a personal photograph on the résumé.

- ***Reveal ethnic background (and other personal information) only if it is job related.*** For example, certain businesses may be actively seeking employees in certain ethnic groups because the ethnic background is a legitimate part of the job description. For such a business, ethnic information is useful and appreciated.

- ***Include personal information (other than the information covered by employment legislation) that will strengthen your résumé.*** Select information that is related to the job you are seeking or portray you as a well-rounded, happy individual off the job. Typically, include interests, hobbies, favorite sports, avocations, and willingness to relocate. You can also include these topics if you have not covered them elsewhere in the résumé: oral and written communication skills, computer competency, foreign-language or computer skills, military service, community service, scholastic honors, job-related hobbies, and professional association memberships.

Olympic athletes know that a split second or a fraction of an inch often determines who wins. Today's job market is almost that competitive. Even a minor error can mean the difference between employment and joblessness.

- ***Consider whether personal information might be controversial.*** For example, listing a sport that an interviewer might perceive to be overly time-consuming or dangerous would be questionable. An applicant seeking a position with a religious or political organization may benefit from revealing this affiliation.

References

Providing potential employers a list of references (people who have agreed to supply information about you when requested) is an important component of your employment credentials. Listing names, addresses, and telephone numbers of people who can provide information about you adds credibility to the résumé. Employers, former employers, instructors, and former instructors are good possibilities. Friends, relatives, and neighbors are not (because of their bias in your favor).

Who could serve as a positive work reference for you?

References can be handled on the résumé in two ways: Include (1) a list of references or (2) a brief statement that references are available on request. Research related to the employers' preferences for references has been mixed; however, a recent survey of employers' preferences supports providing the "on request" statement and using the remaining space for developing qualifications.[13] However, if you know a company interviews applicants *after* references are contacted, list the references on the résumé. Otherwise, include the "on request" statement. You may also include a statement such as "For references . . . " or "For additional information . . ." and give the address of the career services center of your college or university. As a service to graduates, the career services center will mail to prospective employers a complete employment portfolio that includes recommendation letters collected from your references.

If references are not listed on a résumé, a list of references can be provided after a successful interview. By withholding references until they are requested, applicants

- ***May avoid unnecessary or untimely requests being sent to the present employer.*** The interview gives an applicant a chance to assess the desirability of the job. Until then, the applicant may not want the present employer to receive inquiries (which may be interpreted as dissatisfaction with the present job).

- ***Convey genuine courtesy to the references.*** Even the most enthusiastic references may become apathetic after providing recommendations to endless interviewers. For this same reason, applicants should communicate with references if a job search continues longer than is expected. A letter of thanks and an update on the job search will assure references that their efforts are appreciated. Refer to Chapter 14 for guidelines for communicating with references.

What are the advantages and disadvantages of including a list of references in your résumé?

On a separate list of references, place the word *References* and your name in a visible position and balance the list (name, address, and telephone number) attractively on the page. Use paper of the same size, color, weight, and texture as your résumé. When asked for references at the end of a successful interview, you can immediately provide the references page to the interviewer. If you need additional time to consider the interview, you can mail the references page within a day or so. Whether it is handed to the interviewer personally or mailed, the references page professionally complements your résumé. Furthermore, you have impressed the interviewer with your promptness in completing this task—a positive indicator that you will handle other duties similarly. An example of a references page is shown in Figure 13-5.

Your résumé will need to meet high standards of content. All parts are important, but the most important portion is the one that covers your qualifications. If they seem compatible with job requirements, you have a good message to present. Confident that you have a good message, you are now ready to put it on paper—to construct a résumé that will impress an employer favorably.

Constructing a Résumé

Instead of constructing a résumé to suit *you*, try to make one that you think will suit the person who will read it. The acceptable résumés illustrated later in this chapter are not intended to restrict your own creativity. Your goal is to produce a résumé that will emphasize the compatibility of your qualifications and the prospective employer's job requirements using effective organization, style, and mechanics.

Selecting the Organizational Plan

The general organization of all résumés is fairly standard: identification (name, address, and telephone number), job objectives, qualifications, personal information, and references. The primary organizational challenge is in dividing the qualifications section into parts, choosing labels for them, and arranging them in the best sequence. Reviewing your self-, career, and job analyses data and company/job profile, you will recognize that your qualifications stem mainly from your education and your experience. Your task is to decide how to present these two categories of qualifications. Résumés usually are organized in one of three ways: reverse chronological order (most recent activity listed first), functional order (most important activity

Résumés should be straightforward, complete, and to the point. Too often, attempts to create unique résumés backfire and do more harm than good. Including a concise recap of your course of study is important, as is listing significant work experience gained while in school. Don't underestimate the importance of referencing personal interests. Employers consider hobbies and leisure-time activities to get a sense of the individual behind the statistics.

Cynthia Pharr, President
C. Pharr & Company, Inc.

listed first), or a combination of chronological and functional orders. To determine which organizational plan to use, make trial outlines using each one.

Chronological Résumé. The **chronological résumé** is the traditional organization format for résumés. Two headings normally appear in the portion that presents qualifications: "Education" and "Experience." Which one should appear first? Decide which one you think is more impressive to the employer, and put that one first. Within each section, the most recent information is presented first (reverse chronological order). Reverse chronological order is easier to use and is more common than functional order; however, it is not always more effective.

The chronological résumé is an especially effective format for applicants who have progressed up a clearly defined career ladder and want to move up another rung. The format is less effective for applicants who have gaps in their work histories, are seeking jobs different from the job currently held, or are just entering the job market with little or no experience.[14]

If you choose the chronological format, look at the two headings from the employer's point of view, and reverse their positions if doing so is to your advantage. Under the "Experience" division, jobs are listed in reverse order. Assuming you have progressed typically, your latest job is likely to be more closely related to the job being sought than the first job held. Placing the latest or current job first will give it the emphasis it deserves. Include beginning and ending dates for each job. Listing jobs in chronological order is not a requirement. If listing jobs in order of their *relatedness* to the job sought or the *value of experience provided* is to your advantage, deviate from the time-oriented sequence. Begin with the job that will make the best impression.

Functional Résumé. In a **functional résumé**, points of primary interest to employers—transferable skills—appear in major headings. These headings highlight what an applicant can *do* for the employer—functions that can be performed well. Under each heading, an applicant could draw from educational and/or work-related experience to provide supporting evidence.

A functional résumé requires a complete analysis of self, career, and the job sought. Suppose, for example, that a person seeking a job as an assistant hospital administrator wants to emphasize qualifications by placing them in major headings. From the hospital's advertisement of the job and from accumulated job appraisal information, an applicant sees this job as both an administrative and a public relations job. The job requires skill in communicating and knowledge of accounting and finance. Thus, headings in the "Qualifications" section of the résumé could be

Five years after graduation, would education or experience likely appear first on a résumé? Why?

How do functional résumés report experience and education?

COMMUNICATION IN ACTION

Julie Thompson McCallum, Merck & Company, Inc.

Having earned a marketing degree and acquired background courses in the medical field, Julie Thompson McCallum sought employment with a large pharmaceutical company. She knew competition for positions in large corporations was intense, but she was surprised when she learned 50,000 applicants had applied for 350 positions in Merck & Company, Inc., a large pharmaceutical company. What would give her credentials a competitive edge over other applicants?

"I learned firsthand the importance of a good résumé—one that set me apart from other applicants and that was tailored to the position for which I was applying," shared McCallum. She strategically positioned her pre-med courses in a summary of achievements at the beginning of her résumé. Her science background, coupled with her marketing degree, matched a position with Merck and caught the attention of the interviewer.

McCallum is now employed as a pharmaceutical specialist for Merck & Company, Inc., successfully representing three pharmaceutical products. Calling on physicians and pharmacists at hospitals, she has wide latitude and independence in the use of her time. McCallum relates, "Merck was looking for someone who could manage time well, work independently, and maintain self-motivation. I put on my résumé that I had financed 100 percent of my college education to show a work ethic, independence, and motivation."

McCallum's approach is typical of a more general, important point in writing résumés. McCallum states, "Put things you want to talk about on the beginning of the résumé; by doing so, the

employer will focus on these things. This emphasis will help you in the interview process." Thus, the applicant can talk about important or comfortable things in the interview. When giving her educational background, McCallum also included her 3.5 grade point average. She knows many companies require at least a 3.0 grade point average, although exceptions are sometimes made. She cautions against including a low average because the applicant may draw unnecessary attention to his or her grades. "You want to emphasize your strong points; the interviewer can ask about GPA later. Besides, the 3.0 criterion is flexible with many employers."

McCallum believes other points helped give her résumé a competitive edge. She listed her involvement in numerous groups and organizations toward the end of her résumé. "By holding office in some of these organizations, I showed leadership qualities." McCallum states, "Merely attending class is easy. Show that you are willing to get involved, even if you do so during your last semester in college. Companies look for involvement. By getting involved, you show you can balance activities and manage time." By including memberships and offices held, she believes her résumé caught the interest of Merck. Her approach certainly proved successful for her.

Applying What You Have Learned

1. Select from the organizational plans discussed in Chapter 13 the one you think McCallum followed when writing her résumé. Explain your choice.

2. Assume that you were applying for a position in a large medical company. What job analysis questions would you ask yourself before you prepared your résumé?

(1) "Administration," (2) "Public Relations," (3) "Communication," and (4) "Budgeting." Under "Public Relations," for example, an applicant could reveal that a public relations course was taken at State University, from which a degree is to be conferred in June, and that a sales job at ABC Store provided abundant opportunity to apply principles learned. With other headings receiving similar treatment, the qualifications portion reveals the significant aspects of education and experience.

Order of importance is probably the best sequence for functional headings. If you have prepared an accurate self- and job analysis, the selected headings will highlight points of special interest to the employer. Glancing at headings only, an employer could see that you have the qualities needed for success on the job. By carefully selecting headings, you reveal knowledge of the requisites for success on that job.

Having done the thinking required for preparing a functional résumé, you are well prepared for a question that is commonly asked in interviews: "What can you do for us?" The answer is revealed in your major headings. They emphasize the functions you can perform and the special qualifications you have to offer.

If you consider yourself well qualified, a functional résumé is worth considering. If your education or experience is scant, a functional résumé may be best for you. Using "Education" and "Experience" as headings (as in a chronological résumé) works against your purpose if you have little to report under the headings; the format would emphasize the absence of education or experience.

Combination Chronological and Functional Résumé. The **combination chronological and functional résumé** *combines* features of chronological and functional résumés. This format can give quick assurance that educational and experience requirements are met and still use other headings that emphasize qualifications. For example, the "Qualifications" section could have headings such as these:

Education	List the degree, major, school, and graduation date.
Experience	Briefly list jobs held currently and previously.
Administration	Give details drawn from education and/or experience.
Communication	Give examples of tasks, activities, or achievements that indicate communication skills.
Budgeting	Give examples drawn from education and/or experience.
Public Relations	Give examples of tasks, activities, or achievements that indicate public relations skills.

Functional headings vary for different jobs. In fact, two people applying for the same job would likely choose different headings or list similar headings in a distinctive sequence. Select headings that are appropriate for you and that the employer will see as directly related to the job.

When planning the résumé, take note of specific job requirements. They are good possibilities for functional headings. For example, for a job that requires bonding, "Top Security Clearance" gets deserved attention as a heading. Each of the following conditions, if it applies to the job sought, could be the basis for a heading: The work is in small groups; the work requires much overtime in certain seasons; travel is frequent; overseas assignments are a possibility; adaptability to rapid changes is desirable; ability to take criticism is essential; long and detailed reports are required; or lateral transfers can be expected. Choosing appropriate headings is a critical decision in résumé preparation.

Enhancing the Layout

Because first impressions are so powerful, the arrangement of a résumé on the page is just as important as the content. If the page is arranged unattractively, is unappealing, or is in poor taste, the message may never be read. Errors in keyboarding, spelling, and punctuation may be taken as evidence of a poor academic background, lack of

What do the headings in the functional résumé emphasize? What important question do they answer?

respect for the employer, carelessness, or haste. Many interviewers believe that a résumé is an example of an applicant's best work. Hence, they believe that a person who submits a sloppily prepared résumé will probably do the same type of work if hired. With this in mind, strive for perfection; give your best effort to this important task—one that could open the door to the job you really want. Follow these guidelines for designing and producing a highly professional résumé with your own computer:

Explain how poor mechanics counteract superior content, organization, and style.

- *Print the résumé on standard size (8 1/2" by 11") high-quality, preferably 24-pound, 100-percent cotton fiber paper.* Select a neutral color— white, buff, or gray. Be certain that the watermark is positioned so that it can be read across the sheet in the same direction as the printing. Because an application letter will accompany a résumé, use the large (No. 10) envelope. You may want to consider using a mailing envelope large enough to accommodate the résumé and letter unfolded. Unfolded on the reader's desk, the résumé and letter may get favorable attention and will scan correctly if an interviewer chooses to scan it into an electronic database. (A detailed discussion of scannable résumés follows.)

- *Print with a laser printer to produce top professional quality.* Use the desktop publishing capability of high-end word processing software to enhance the style, readability, and overall impact. For example, use various styles and size. To emphasize the identification section and the headings, select a bold sans serif font (block-type font without cross strokes, e.g., **Arial** or **Univers**) slightly larger than a serif font (font with cross strokes, e.g., Times New Roman or **New Century Schoolbook**) used for the remaining text. A word of warning: Limit the number of type styles and sizes so the page is clean and simple to read. The résumé examples in this chapter illustrate graphic enhancements made using word processing software.

- *Format information for at-a-glance comprehension.* To make your résumé easy to read, (a) use headings to partition major divisions so that the interviewer can locate pertinent information easily and quickly and add graphic lines and borders to further separate sections of text; (b) use an outline format when possible to list activities and events on separate lines and include bullets (●, ◆) to emphasize multiple points; and (c) use indention, underlining, italics, boldface, capitalization, and font changes (size and appearance) to add emphasis.

- *Balance the résumé attractively on the page with approximately equal margins.* Use generous white space so the résumé looks uncluttered and easy to read.

- *Be consistent throughout the résumé.* For example, if you double-space before the first heading and key it in bold print with all capital letters, key all headings in the same way. Select the order for presenting information about education and work experience; then be consistent with each school and job. Consistently include the information listed under each school or job unless you have a specific reason for omitting it, for example, a grade-point average below B.

- *Include your name and a page number at the top of the second and successive pages of a résumé.* With each new page, the interviewer is exposed to your name once again. If the pages of the résumé are separated, they can be collated again if each page is identified.

- *Consider adding a statement of your creativity and originality.* Be certain, however, that your creativity will not be construed as gimmicky and consequently distract from the content of the résumé. For example, preparing a

Strategic Forces: Diversity Challenges

Gender Issues Affecting Employability

In addition to the legal considerations for résumé design that were discussed in the earlier Strategic Forces box, other considerations that apply especially to women should be taken into account. While gender discrimination in employment has been illegal for over 30 years, it still persists in some instances, often subtly.[15] Consider the following situations:

- *Marital status:* A man who includes marital status on the résumé may enhance his desirability as an applicant. For instance, indicating "married" may be interpreted as being stable. A woman who indicates "married" may be viewed as unreliable or temporary because she has and or may have children who could interfere with her job performance. She may also be seen as likely to leave the company if her husband is transferred or relocates. Indicating "single" is not necessarily a plus for a woman either. She may be viewed as seeking temporary work until she marries.

- *Physical appearance:* A physically attractive man who includes with his résumé a photo or video of himself may enhance his employability.

Given that qualifications among candidates are equal, physical attraction has been found to be positively correlated with job offers for men. On the contrary, physical attractiveness has been found often to work against women. While unattractive men and women are rejected by the potential employer about equally, a woman who is very attractive may be bypassed because a feeling still persists in some camps that a woman cannot be both beautiful and smart. Thus, a woman can be too attractive for employment.

Women should be aware that such subtle forms of sex discrimination do still occur and should prepare their employment documents accordingly. Both job candidates and employers should be aware that discrimination on these grounds can have legal repercussions.

Application

In small groups, brainstorm a list of other ways that gender discrimination may occur in employment. For each incidence of possible discrimination, propose an action that the applicant may take to minimize or eliminate it. Compose a class list that summarizes the discussion of each small group.

---

highly effective résumé layout including borders, lines, and graphics communicates creativity as well as proficiency in the use of computer-based technology. Demonstrating creativity is particularly useful for fields such as advertising, public relations, and graphic design and in fields in which computer competency is required.

As in writing other difficult documents, prepare a rough draft as quickly as you can and then revise as many times as needed to prepare an effective résumé that sells you. After you are confident with the résumé, ask at least two other people to check it for you. Carefully select people who are knowledgeable about résumé preparation and the job you are seeking and can suggest ways to present your qualifications more effectively. After you have incorporated those changes, ask a skillful proofreader to review the document.

What is the ideal length for a résumé?

For most students, a résumé can be arranged on one page. As students gain experience, additional pages are needed. Some employers insist that the "best" length for a résumé is one page. A one-page résumé that includes irrelevant information is too long. A two-page résumé that omits relevant information is too short.

A person with few qualifications applying for a lower-level job may be able to present all relevant information effectively on one page. A person with a great deal of experience applying for a higher-level job would struggle to include all relevant information on one page. The résumé probably would appear dense and complicated because of narrow margins and large blocks of run-on text (multiple lines with no space to break them). This crowded résumé reformatted onto two pages would have high initial impact. This easy-to-read format would simplify the interviewer's task of identifying an applicant's qualifications, and busy interviewers would appreciate the effort. As you gain significant experience, you may need two or more pages to format an informative, easy-to-read résumé.

Examples of Résumés

The résumés illustrated in Figures 13-4, 13-6, and 13-7 demonstrate the organizational, formatting, and layout principles discussed so far. Figure 13-5 is an example of a references page.

Electronic Résumés (Scannable)

In today's computer age, employers in small, medium, and large companies are using **electronic applicant-tracking systems** to increase the efficiency of processing the volumes of résumés being submitted in a competitive market. A conservative estimate is that 30 to 40 percent of mid-size and large companies use computers to read résumés, and the number is predicted to increase to 80 percent by the end of the century.[16] Knowing how an electronic applicant-tracking system works will enable you to adapt your job search to meet the demands of this technology. An automated tracking system does the following:

1. ***Scans résumés using an OCR scanner and stores them in an electronic database.*** This database contains not only the printed résumés received by mail or fax that are scanned but also résumés that applicants e-mail to companies or post to corporate home pages and job banks on the Internet. Any of these résumés is technically an **electronic résumé** because it will be read by the computer and not by a human. However, the printed résumé that is scanned into the database is often referred to as a **scannable résumé**. Additional information about preparing an on-line résumé (posted on the Internet) is provided in the "Electronic Job Searches" section that appears later in this chapter.

2. ***Compares the electronic résumés to a list of keywords identified from a job description.*** The **keywords** describe an ideal candidate and include mandatory and desired traits (would be helpful but are not required). For example, GM needs an electrical engineer to work in Mexico who has five years' experience, can speak Spanish, and is willing to relocate. Keywords describing required traits would include electrical engineering, five years' experience, Spanish speaker, and willing to relocate. Desired keywords may include professional associations, experience with certain large companies, and interpersonal traits such as team player, sensitive to diversity, innovative, and so forth. The computer scans each résumé, picking up keywords no matter where they appear on the page.

3. ***Categorizes and ranks the applicants based on the number of keyword matches found in each résumé.*** The more matches of keywords included in a résumé, the higher the ranking on the computer's short list of candidates.

3 *Prepare a résumé that can be scanned and processed by an electronic applicant-tracking system.*

What are the advantages and disadvantages of an electronic tracking system?

FIGURE 13-4
Chronological résumé.

❶ The statements of goals and qualifications reveal what type of work is sought and why the employer would want to hire Jennifer.

❷ Educational strengths include high GPA (B or better) and a list of specific computer competencies.

❸ Action verbs vividly portray work experience.

❹ Listing voluntary work indicates a service attitude and people-oriented experiences.

❺ References will be provided after a successful interview.

JENNIFER M. WHITE
53 Garrison Street
Worchester, MA 01613-0053
(508) 555-6543 e-mail jwhite@netdoor.com

❶ **CAREER OBJECTIVE**
To obtain a management position in the information systems division of a major corporation. Emphasis in developing applications.

SUMMARY OF ACHIEVEMENTS
Bachelor's degree in management information systems; proficient in operation of Windows and Unix systems and major software applications. Applied computer knowledge while completing cooperative education requirements with a leading company. Willing to relocate.

❷ **EDUCATION**
B.B.A. INFORMATION SYSTEMS, Slade University. To be conferred June, 1999. Grade-point average: 3.6 (4.0 scale). Financed 80 percent of education with scholarships and part-time work.

Environments: Windows and Unix
Languages: C, C++, COBOL, Visual Basic, Java
Application Word, Excel, Access, PowerPoint
Software:

RELATED EXPERIENCE
Management Assistant, Cooperative-Education Program, Central Computer Services, Boston, Massachusetts, January 1998 to May 1998.
* Provided technical support to end users for hardware and software.
❸ • Configured modem and Internet connections for file transfers between office and remote locations.
* Developed interpersonal skills while interacting with computer users.

❹ **VOLUNTEER WORK**
Served as unpaid assistant at Melba Hospital, 15 hours a week, Summers 1994 to 1995. Acquired valuable work habits—dependability, time management, and human relations skills.

HONORS AND ACTIVITIES
Dean's Scholar (3.6 GPA or higher)
Gamma Beta Phi Honorary Society
Data Processing Management Association
   Vice President
   Chair, Program Committee

❺ **REFERENCES**
Available on request.

Format Pointers
* The centered format and larger type size emphasize the identification section.
* Two-column format allows interviewer to locate specific sections easily. Headings are consistently displayed in bold, slightly larger typeface and all capital letters.
* Uses sans serif typeface for the identification section and the headings; serif typeface, for the text.

FIGURE 13-5
References page.

REFERENCES FOR JENNIFER M. WHITE
53 Garrison Street
Worchester, MA 01613-0053
(508) 555-6543 e-mail jwhite@netdoor.com

Mr. C. Thomas Linford, Director
Management Information Systems
Central Computer Services
P.O. Box 47399
Boston, MA 02139-1894
(617) 555-9000

Dr. Yang Shen
Associate Professor
Information Systems Department
Slade University
P.O. Box 5937
Augusta, ME 04330-8070
(207) 555-4382

Ms. Barbara Oliver, RN
Melbay Community Hospital
150 Lamar Drive
Brewer, ME 04412-4950
(207) 555-4385

Format Pointers

- Prepared at the same time as the résumé, the references page can be provided immediately following a successful interview. Paper (color, texture, and size) and print type match the résumé.

- References include two former employers and a professor. The list does not include friends, relatives, or clergy.

- Each reference includes courtesy title, full name, company affiliation, address, and telephone number (where the person can be reached during regular office hours). An e-mail address is provided if available.

- References are balanced attractively on the page.

FIGURE 13-6
Functional résumé.

Ioana M. Focsa
135 Ivy Street
Dallas, TX 75208-7310
(214) 555-6743

❶ Headings emphasize qualities the applicant offers as a solution to the employer's problem. A quick look at the headings suggests that Ioana knows important requisites for success in sales.

OBJECTIVE	To acquire a position in retail clothing sales with possible advancement to sales management.
❶ SALES-ORIENTED	Since childhood, have had a strong interest in sales and fashion; began designing and making clothes for myself and others at age 14. Have had three years' part-time experience in fast foods. Currently, a senior majoring in marketing at West State College. Subscribe to *Retail Selling.* Graduate in May 1999.
PUBLIC RELATIONS SKILLS	Learned tactfulness when taking and filling orders in the fast-food business (Marketplace Bagel, part-time from August 1996 to May 1998). Commended by manager for diplomacy with patrons and staff. Earned an A in Interpersonal Communication and will take Public Relations next year. Gained experience coping with various personality types while volunteering as a counselor at Camp Seminole for three summers.
RECORDKEEPING SKILLS	Used cash register and balanced receipts against records each day at Marketplace Bagel. Now taking two classes (accounting and computer science) that emphasize keeping records electronically.
DEPENDABILITY	Report regularly and promptly when scheduled for work. In three years, have never been late for work. Attend classes regularly. Open, close, and take cash to bank.
LEARNING CAPACITY	Commended for learning work procedures quickly. On the Dean's List for the last two semesters. Achieved 3.6 grade-point average (on a 4.0 scale) in major courses to date.
❷ REFERENCES	Dr. Rick Trice, Adviser, Marketing Department, West State College, P.O. Box 4293, Temple, TX 76501-3293, (817) 555-2746.
	Ms. Marge Sherman, Camp Director, Camp Seminole, 1493 Dunlap Drive, Kingsville, TX 78363-1493, (512) 555-8934.
	Mr. Oscar Perez, Manager, Marketplace Bagel, 151 Bark Street, Corpus Christi, TX 78469-7310, (512) 555-6789.

❷ References are listed because Ioana is confident she wants to work for this company and believes providing them will strengthen her résumé.

Format Pointers
- Centered format and larger type size emphasize the identification section.
- Horizontal line adds interest and partitions the identification section from the evidence that follows.
- Two-column format allows interviewer to locate specific sections easily. Bold typeface and all-capitals are used consistently to display headings.
- Uses sans serif typeface for identification section and headings; serif typeface for text.

Greg R. Thorne
Rockland College
P. O. Box 739
Wilmington, DE 19735-7189
❶ **(302) 555-6753   Messages: (302) 555-8312**
gthorne@aol.com

CAREER OBJECTIVE	To enter a management trainee program and later specialize in human resources management.
EDUCATION	Bachelor of Science, Rockland College, Wilmington, Delaware. To be conferred May 1, 1999.

Major: MANAGEMENT with a concentration in human resources management. Related courses: International Management, International Communication, Spanish (three semesters), and Computer Applications courses.

❸ **Grade-Point Average:** Major: 3.8; overall 3.7 (based on 4.0 scale).

❹ **Honors:** Initiated into Beta Gamma Sigma (business honorary society) and Phi Kappa Phi (top 10% of junior/senior class).
Recipient of Robert L. Parvin Academic Scholarship (ACT score above 30).
Listed on the Dean's or President's List for seven semesters (GPA 3.6 or better).

EXPERIENCE **Desk manager**, Freemont Inn, Smyrna. Part-time since May 1997.
- Promoted from desk clerk to desk manager after one year.
- Make room reservations, register guests, keep computerized records, and supervise bellhops and desk clerks.

Residence Hall Director, Rockland College, August 1996, to present.
- Supervise 72 upper-class male residents and enforce college regulations.
- Provide individual and group counseling to residents having academic and personal problems.
- Prepare work schedules and handle payroll for 5 resident assistants and 13 desk assistants.
- Designed computer-based work scheduling program that was adopted for use by all other residence hall directors.

FIGURE 13-7
Combination chronological/functional résumé.

❶ This telephone number is necessary because Greg is away from his telephone during regular office hours.

❷ "Education" and "Experience" are traditional headings on a chronological résumé.

❸ Subdividing the "Education" section emphasizes major points and increases readability (eliminates large sections of run-on text).

❹ Academic honors are integrated within the "Education" section and provide evidence of Greg's ability to succeed. Other activities could be included in a separate section following "Experience."

FIGURE 13-7
continued.

 Heading clearly identifies the second page of Greg's résumé.

❷ Other headings are commonly placed on a functional résumé. Headings that emphasize the skills vital to success in a trainee program were identified through self- and career analysis (including an interview with a successful manager who had completed a management training program).

All major divisions have one common denominator; each is a factor in managerial success.

❸ If references are needed before an interview, a call to the career services center will produce them.

---

❶ **Greg R. Thorne**   **Page 2**

COMMUNICATION SKILLS
Developed effective communication skills while counseling residents; learned the value of empathic listening and seeing ideas from the other person's perspective—skills relevant to quality employee training. Developed effective interpersonal skills through continuous interactions with hotel guests and supervision of 12 employees. Wrote memos, letters, business reports, and term papers and gave oral presentations in business courses.

❷ **ACCEPT CRITICISM**
Benefitted from criticism of written materials and from critiques of oral presentations. Sensitive at first, came to recognize criticism as intent to help. Improved oral presentations after self-criticisms of taped presentations. Appreciate the need for tact in giving constructive criticism.

COMPUTER LITERATE
Elected to take three computer courses in addition to the two required for management majors. The most recently studied software programs (*Micosoft Word* and *Access*) are especially useful in producing effective reports. Applied basic computer skills and learned software programs specific to hotel management while working for Freemont Inn. Designed computer-based work scheduling program for residence hall management.

❸ **REFERENCES**
Letters from references and a transcript are available from Career Services Center, Rockland College, P.O. Box CS, Wilmington, DE 19735-3000, (302) 555-2390.

---

4. ***Prepares letters of rejections and interview offers, stores the résumés, and accesses them for future openings.*** This automation is beneficial to job seekers who may receive no communication from companies processing applications manually.

Computerized résumé searches provide several distinct advantages to job seekers: (1) Applicants are considered for every position in the company (not just reviewed by the recruiter whose desk on which the résumé happens to land; (2) an applicant's résumé may be matched with a position he or she would not have applied for otherwise; (3) the résumé remains in the system and is accessed whenever a new position is posted; (4) an applicant can submit an updated résumé to be entered into the database every six months; and (5) the résumé is transferred from the applicant tracking system to an employee tracking system when the applicant is hired; the employee's résumé is reviewed for any job postings and internal promotions.[17]

When seeking a job with a company that scans résumés into an electronic database, you will need to submit an **electronic résumé**, one that can be read by a computer, and a traditional résumé that will be read by a human if you are among the applicants selected to be interviewed. If you are unsure whether a company scans résumés, call and ask. If still in doubt, take the safe route and submit your résumé in both formats. Guidelines for formatting and modifying the content of an electronic résumé follow:

Format Requirements of an Electronic Résumé. To ensure that the scanner can read your résumé accurately and clearly, you must prepare a plain résumé with no special formatting that career experts call a "vanilla, no-frills" résumé.[18] Your objective is to use print with distinctive edges that can still be read after it has been mushed and run together in the scanning process, and to resist the temptation to add graphic enhancements that cannot be read by a scanner. Follow these guidelines to prepare an electronic résumé that can be scanned accurately:

- *Use popular, nondecorative typefaces.* Typefaces such as Helvetica, Univers, Times New Roman, and New Century Schoolbook are clear and distinct and will not lose clarity after scanning.

- *Use 10- to 14-point font.* Computers cannot read small, tight print. With a larger font, your résumé may extend to two pages, but page length is not an issue because a computer is reading the résumé.

- *Do not include italics, underlining, open bullets, or graphic lines and boxes.* Use boldface or all capitals for emphasis. Italicized letters often touch and underlining may run into the text above; therefore, the scanned image may be garbled. Design elements, such as graphic lines, shading, and shadowing effects, confuse equipment designed to read text and not graphics. Use solid bullets (•); open bullets (○) may be reads as o's.

- *Use ample white space.* Use at least one-inch margins. Leave plenty of white space between the sections of a résumé so that the computer recognizes the partitions.

- *Print on one side of white, standard-size paper with sharp laser print.* Send an original that is smudge-free; the scanner may pick up dirty specks on a photocopy. Colored and textured paper is hard to read.

- *Use a traditional résumé format.* Complex layouts that simulate catalogs or newspaper columns are confusing to the scanner.

- *Do not fold or staple your résumé.* If you must fold, do not fold on a line of text. Staples, when removed, make the pages stick together.

If you have a résumé, convert it to electronic format by applying the guidelines provided. If you do not have a résumé, convert one of the ones on the preceding pages to electronic format.

Making an Electronic Résumé Searchable. A few significant changes must be made in a traditional résumé to make it "computer-friendly." You have two concerns: (1) You want to be certain information is presented in a manner the computer can read, and (2) you want to maximize the number of "hits" your résumé receives in a computerized résumé search. You may use more than one page if needed to present your qualifications. The more information you present the more likely you are to be selected from the database of applicants, and computers can read your résumé more quickly than humans can. Follow these guidelines for modifying the content of your traditional résumé to make it searchable:

Identify keywords from your résumé that should appear in the electronic version.

- *Position your name as the first readable item on each page.* Place your address and telephone number below your name. Include your e-mail address and a fax number. Placing an address on one line is confusing to some systems.

- *Prepare a keyword summary.* An applicant tracking system depends on finding particular keywords in your résumé. The more matches of keywords you present the higher your ranking on the computer's short list of candidates. To prepare the keyword summary, follow this advice:

1. *Using a copy of your traditional résumé, highlight only the nouns you think the computer might use as keywords in the search.* Ask yourself if these words describe your qualifications and continue looking for other words that label your qualifications. Kennedy and Morrow, leading consultants in the electronic job revolution, suggest these techniques: Ask yourself, "What achievements would I discuss with my supervisor if I were meeting to discuss a raise?" Consider a job-related problem and describe the solution and every step required to solve the problem; consider the results. Consider actions, if done poorly, that would affect goals of the job. Then state them in a positive way. For example, a negative action is "an employee not getting to work on time"; stated positively, it becomes "efficiency minded and profit conscious."[19]

2. *Insert the keyword summary after the identification section (your name, address, and telephone number) and just prior to the objective.* Note the keywords in Jeanne Fulton's résumé in Figure 13-8 based on the qualifications for an entry-level auditing position (see the company/job profile in Figure 13-2).

   Here are several important format requirements for the keyword summary:

   - **Use "Keywords" or "Keyword Summary" as the section title.** Use the same format as in all other section titles.
   - **Capitalize the first letter of each word and separate each keyword with a period.**
   - **Position the keywords describing your most important qualifications first and move to the least important ones.** Order is important because some systems stop scanning after the first 80 keywords. The usual order is (a) job title, occupation, or career field, (b) education, and (c) essential skills for a specific position. Be certain to include keywords that describe interpersonal traits important to human resource managers. Your list might include adaptable, flexible, sensitive, team player, willing to travel, ethical, industrious, innovative, open minded, and detail oriented.
   - **Maximize the use of industry jargon and abbreviations in the keyword summary and the body of the résumé.** These buzzwords will likely be matches with the computer's keywords. However, minimize the number of general abbreviations. The computer can only recognize standard, easily recognizable abbreviations such as B.A., M.S., Ph.D., and so forth.

3. *Support your keywords with specific facts in the body of the résumé.* Keep the keyword summary a reasonable length so that you have space to support your keywords. Use synonyms of your keywords in the body in the event the computer does not recognize the keyword (e.g., use M.B.A. in the keyword summary and Master of Business Administration in the body; use

presentation graphics software in the keyword summary and a specific program in the body). One unfortunate applicant reported using "computer-assisted design" consistently throughout his résumé when the computer was searching for "CAD." Also, use a specific date of graduation in the education section. Some computer programs read two dates beside an institution to mean the applicant did not earn the degree (e.g., 1996–1999). If the degree is programmed as a requirement for the job (rather than a desirable qualification), this applicant would be excluded from the search.

- ***Include enough information to market yourself effectively.*** The one-page rule is no longer applicable.
- ***Send a cover letter to reinforce your résumé.*** This letter is stored electronically with the résumé and will be read by a human if the applicant is selected by the database.

The electronic résumé Jeanne Fulton prepared when seeking an entry-level audit position in a public accounting firm appears in Figure 13-8. Note how she presents qualifications that correspond to the company/job profile shown in Figure 13-2. The electronic résumé is formatted so that it can be scanned into an electronic database and the content is searchable for an employee attempting to match applicants with an entry-level audit position.

Supplementing the Résumé

4 Identify employment tools other than the résumé that can enhance employability.

Some candidates may feel their career accomplishments are not appropriately captured in a standard résumé. Two additional tools for communicating your qualifications and abilities are the portfolio and the employment video.

Developing a Professional Portfolio

The professional portfolio can be used to illustrate past activities, projects, and accomplishments. It is a collection of artifacts that demonstrate your communication, people, and technical skills. Although portfolios were once thought of as only for writers, artists, or photographers, they are now seen as appropriate for other

High-tech firms such as Hewlett-Packard Co. prefer that candidates apply directly through the corporate job site on the Internet. "That way, the data is coming directly from the candidate to us," said Pat Wolcott, HP staffing manager at the Boise site. "There is no possibility of it getting lost or delayed in having to be scanned in. The résumé will go directly to our database."[20]

FIGURE 13-8
Electronic résumé.

1 Positions name as the first readable item on the page. Entices employer to e-mail or to visit her web site for additional qualifications; displays computer proficiency.

2 Includes "Objective" section to identify the job sought (same as a traditional résumé).

3 Includes "Keyword Summary" section listing qualifications that match the job description.

4 Supports the keywords with specific facts; uses as many nouns as possible that might match those in the job description.

Uses synonyms of the keywords in the body to ensure a match with the database (e.g., includes B.B.A. and M.P.A. and spells the degrees out; includes general references to software applications and Internet browsers as well as names of specific software).

---

1 JEANNE FULTON
89 Lincoln Street
San Antonio, TX 78285-9063
512 555–9823
jfulton@netdoor.com
www.netdoor/jfulton

2 Objective
First-year audit staff with an international accounting firm; interest in working with information systems.

3 Keywords
Entry-level audit position. Master's and bachelor's degrees in accounting. Sam Houston University. 3.5 GPA. Beta Alpha Psi. Cooperative work experience. Inventory control. Spanish fluency. Traveled Mexico. Analytical ability. Computer proficiency. Communication skills. Team player. Ethical. Creative. Adaptable. Willing to relocate. Windows. Software applications. Word, Excel, Access, PowerPoint. General ledger. Internet. Netscape. Web design.

Education
M.P.A., Accounting, Sam Houston University, August 1999. GPA 3.8.

B.B.A., Accounting, Sam Houston University, May 1998, GPA 3.6.
President's Scholar 1994–1998
Beta Alpha Psi (honorary accounting society)
Mortar Board
Lloyd Markham Academic Scholarship

4 Employment
Cooperative Education Program, Smith & Lewis, CPAs, San Antonio, Texas, June 1998–December 1999
- Assisted in modifying the inventory control system to facilitate electronic data interchange transactions with suppliers.
- Created and designed a web site to describe the type of management advisory services the firm provides. Displayed initiative by leading the firm's entry into web development.
- Developed time management skills, team building, and communication skills while completing several independent projects with teams of accounting staff at various levels.
- Demonstrated ability to accept and respond to criticism, learn job tasks quickly, and perform duties with minimal supervision.

Format Pointers
- Keeps résumé simple and readable by the computer: ample white space especially between sections; font that does not allow letters to touch; font size within the font range of 10 to 14 points; solid bullets; and no italics, underlining, or graphic lines or borders.
- Will mail the résumé with a cover letter and a traditional résumé unfolded and unstapled in a large envelope.

FIGURE 13-8
continued.

5 Jeanne Fulton   Page 2

Projectionist/cashier/usher, DeVille Cinema, Marshall, Texas,
March 1997–August 1998.
    Learned the technical skills needed to run and maintain projection
equipment; developed interpersonal skills while interacting with customers and co-workers, and trained employees to operate equipment.

Leadership Activities
Phi Beta Lambda, National Business Organization, 1995–present
- Served as state president and state treasurer and local chapter president and treasurer.
- Managed the activities of the state chapter, planned meetings/agenda
for the state board and conventions, coordinated various conferences
and leadership workshops. Prepared registration materials, informational mailings, and conference programs. Refined communication skill
by presenting speeches and conducting workshops for business students. Maintained a statewide network of business contacts and peers.

Campus Activities Board, Chair, Lectern Division, 1997–1998
    Scheduled and coordinated the CAB Lecture Series, which involved
contacting agents, reserving facilities, and publicizing events.

Student Government Association, assistant director, University Services,
Sam Houston University, 1997
    Led a committee to conduct student polls to identify ways to improve
student services; assisted in the research of the feasibility of projects
such as campus transportation and an on-campus shuttle service.

Skills
- Computer proficiency in Windows, word processing, spreadsheet,
graphics, (Microsoft Office Suite), general ledger software, Internet
browsers (Netscape, Internet Explorer), and web design.
- Speak Spanish fluently; have traveled to Mexico.

6 **References and Portfolio**
Available on request.

5 Can extend beyond one page without concern because a computer will read this résumé.

6 Emphasizes the availability of other sources of information about her qualifications—references and a portfolio.

fields of work when the applicant wants to showcase abilities. Some possible items for inclusion are

- sample speeches.
- performance appraisals.
- awards.
- certificates of completion.
- reports, proposals, or computer samples from classes.
- brochures describing workshops attended.
- records or surveys showing client or customer satisfaction with service.
- attendance records.
- thank-you letters.

Select items that demonstrate that you have the characteristics the employer is seeking. The portfolio should be continually maintained even after you are hired because it can demonstrate your eligibility for promotion, salary increase, advanced training, or even justify why you should not be laid off.[20]

Preparing an Employment Videotape

A videotape may be used to visually extend the impact of the printed résumé. A videotape can capture your stage presence and ability to speak effectively and add a human dimension to the paper process. The most current technology enables applicants to embed video segments into **multimedia résumés** created with presentation software such as PowerPoint and sent to prospective employers on a CD-ROM or posted on the applicant's personal home page. Accessing this information from a computer that is likely positioned on a recruiter's desk is much more convenient than having to move to a VCR to play a videotape.

The following guidelines apply when preparing an employment video:

- Make sure the video makes a professional appearance and is complimentary to you. A "home movie" quality taping will be a liability instead of an asset to your application.
- Avoid long "talking head" segments. Include segments that reflect you in a variety of activities; shots that include samples of your work are also desirable.
- Remember that visual media (such as photographs and videos) encourage the potential employer to focus on your physical characteristics and attributes, which may lead to undesired stereotyping and discrimination.

Employment videotapes are more commonly used to obtain employment in career fields for which verbal delivery or visual performance are key elements. These fields include broadcasting and the visual and performing arts.

Finding Prospective Employers

Organization is desirable when conducting a search of prospective employers. You would begin by recording the name, address, and telephone number of each employer who has a job in which you have an interest. Later, record the date of each job call you make and receive (along with what you learned from the call), the date of each returned call, the name of the person who called, the date you sent a résumé,

---

Would a video enhance employability in your career field? If so, what elements would you include in your video?

5 *Locate employment opportunities using traditional and electronic methods.*

and so on. Maintaining this list alphabetically will enable you to find a name quickly and respond effectively to a returned telephone call. Software, such as Winway® Resume, is now available to assist in tracking employers that have been contacted as well as developing job credentials.[22]

A student who expects to graduate in May should begin the search for prospective employers months beforehand. Waiting too long to begin and then hurrying through the job search process could be detrimental to future employment. Information about career and job opportunities is available from many traditional sources, as well as the through electronic job searches.

Using Traditional Sources

Traditional means of locating a job include printed sources, networks, career services centers, employers' offices, employment agencies and contractors, help-wanted ads, and professional organizations.

Printed Sources. The following printed sources are useful in identifying firms in need of employees. Some of these sources are now available on the Internet.

> Annual reports from major firms
> *Black Enterprise* (annual June issue)
> *Career, The Annual Guide to Business Opportunities*
> *College Placement Council (CPC) Manual*
>
> Company newsletters
> *Directory of American Firms*
> *Operating in Foreign Countries*
> Dun and Bradstreet's *Million Dollar Directory*
> *Encyclopedia of Careers and Vocational Guidance*
> *Engineering Index*
> *Forbes* (Annual Directory Issue published May 15)
> *Fortune* and Moody's *Manuals*
> *Science Research Associates' Occupational Briefs*
> Standard and Poor's *Register of Corporations, Directors,* and *Executives*
>
> Trade or professional journals
> United States Civil Service Commission job listings
> *The Wall Street Journal*
> *National Business Employment Weekly*

Networks. The majority of job openings are never advertised. Therefore, developing a network of contacts may be the most valuable source of information about jobs. Your network may include current and past employers, guest speakers in your classes or at student organization meetings, business contacts you met while interning or participating in shadowing or over-the-shoulder experiences, and so on. Let these individuals know the type of job you are seeking and ask their advice for finding employment in today's competitive market.

Make a list of network contacts that might assist you in your job search.

Career Services Centers. Be certain to register with your college's career services center at least three semesters before you graduate. Typically, the center has a browsing room loaded with career information and job announcement bulletins. Career counseling is usually available. Through the center, students can attend job fairs to meet prospective employers and schedule on-campus interviews with company recruiters who make regular visits to the campus. Additionally, the career services center provides workshops on résumé writing and interviewing skills, and other job search skills.

Visit your campus career services center. What services and materials are available? Register if your expected graduation date is within a year.

Many career services centers are using electronic tracking systems just as companies are doing. A career services director reports that her office can "quickly search its electronic database of more than 2,000 undergraduate résumés, plus those of graduates, to respond within hours to any of the more than 10,000 job postings the college receives annually."[23] Rather than submitting printed résumés, students input their résumés into a computer file following the specific requirements of the tracking system used by the college or university. An employer calls with keywords to include in a search, and the career services center conducts a search, and faxes or e-mails the résumés selected in the computer search to the company. Some colleges extend the usefulness of the electronic database beyond locating jobs for graduating seniors; the software is being used to match undergraduates to internship opportunities and link undergraduates with undecided majors with alumni with similar interests, and so forth.

Career services centers that process applications manually collect from students information about their academic major, progress toward a degree, graduation date, and career goals, as well as obtain three to five references (professors, employers, or others who could provide valid information). The center sends a student's employment packet (an application letter, résumé, and recommendation letters from references) to prospective employers when requested by the student or an employer. With this arrangement, a reference submits only one letter of recommendation; but it can be sent to many different employers. By making one call to the career services center, a prospective employer can get three or more recommendations plus additional data.

Employers' Offices. Employers who have not advertised their employment needs may respond favorably to a telephoned or personal inquiry. The receptionist may be able to provide useful information, direct you to someone with whom you can talk, or set up an appointment.

Employment Agencies and Contractors. Telephone directories list city, county, state, and federal employment agencies that provide free or inexpensive services. Some agencies offer a recorded answering service; by dialing and listening, callers can get information about job opportunities and the procedure for using the agency's services. Fees charged by private agencies are paid by either the employee or the employer. This fee usually is based on the first month's salary and must be paid within a few months. Some agencies specialize in finding high-level executives or specialists for major firms. Employment contractors specialize in providing temporary employees. Instead of helping you find a permanent job, a contractor may be able to use your services on a temporary basis until you find a full-time job.

Classified Ads. Responses to advertised positions should be made as quickly as possible after the ad is circulated. If your résumé is received early and is impressive, you could get a favorable response before other applications are received. If an ad invites response to a box number without giving a name, be cautious. The employer could be legitimate but does not want present employees to know about the ad or does not want applicants to telephone or drop by the premises. However, you have a right to be suspicious of someone who wants to remain obscure while learning everything you reveal in your résumé.

Professional Organizations. Officers of professional organizations, through their contacts with members, are sometimes good sources of information about job opportunities. Much job information is exchanged at meetings of professional associations. In response to help-wanted and position-wanted columns in journals of some professional organizations, interviews are sometimes arranged and conducted at hotels or schools in which the organization holds its annual meeting.

In addition to the professional growth that comes from membership in professional organizations, active participation is a good way to learn about job opportunities. Visiting lecturers sometimes provide job information. In addition, employers are favorably impressed when membership is listed on the résumé. They are even more impressed if the applicant is (or has been) an officer in the organization (implies leadership, community commitment, willingness to exert effort without tangible reward, social acceptance, or high level of aspiration). By joining and actively participating in professional, social, and honorary organizations for their majors, college students increase their opportunities to develop rapport with peers and professors. One of the benefits is sharing job information.

Using Electronic Job Searches

Experts predict that within five years, on-line recruiting will become the prevalent method of finding qualified job candidates, with 95 percent of all advertised jobs being advertised on the Internet.[24] Presently, employment experts agree, however, that it is too early to rely solely on the Internet for locating a job. Instead job seekers should use the Internet along with the traditional means previously discussed.

Numerous printed sources and excellent on-line assistance are available for learning to use the Internet in the job search process. Several of these outstanding references are listed below:

- Bounds, S., & Karl, A. (1996). *How to get your dream job using the Internet.* Scottsdale, AZ: The Coriolis Group.
- Kennedy, J. L., & Morrow, T. J. (1995). *Hook up, get hired.* New York: John Wiley.
- Kennedy, J. L., & Morrow, T. J. (1994). *Electronic job search revolution: Win with the new technology that's reshaping today's job market.* New York: John Wiley.
- Kennedy, J. L., & Morrow, T. J. (1994). *Electronic job search revolution. Create a winning résumé for the new world of job seeking.* New York: John Wiley.
- Riley, M. (1996). *The Riley guide: Links to job resources all over the Internet.* [On-line]. Available at http://www.dbm.com/jobguide [March 13, 1998].
- Siegel, D. (1997). *Creating killer web sites: The art of third generation site design,* (2nd ed.). Indianapolis: Hayden Books.
- Branscomb, H. E. (1998). *Casting your net: A student's guide to research on the Internet.* Boston: Allyn and Bacon.
- Bolles, R. N. (1997). *What color is your parachute: The net guide.* Berkeley, CA: Ten Speed Press.

This chapter will provide an overview of ways the Internet can be used in the job search process. These include (a) locating a wealth of career-guidance resources, (b) locating job openings, (c) posting an on-line résumé to job banks or the employment section of a prospective employee's home page, and (d) posting your résumé on your personal web site.

Locating Career Guidance Information. According to one career consultant, "Most people in the old days could go into an organization [during a job interview] and not really know about it and hope for the best. Now, people can understand the organization before they even apply."[25] The Internet places at your fingertips a wealth of information that will prepare you for the job interview, that is, if you are wise enough to use the Internet as a research tool and not just a place to post your résumé in many job banks. Examples of the type of career guidance information you can locate on the Internet follow:

- *Visit job sites for information related to various phases of the job search.* For example, Jobtrak's site (www.jobtrak.com) discusses a wide range of topics: how to conduct an effective job search, researching employers, career fairs, cover letters and related job search communication, designing your résumé, writing an electronic résumé (one to be scanned and searched by an electronic database), and others.

- *Visit corporate web sites to learn about the company.* According to *The Riley Guide* (www.dbm.com), when reading an employer's web site, begin by looking at anything that says "News" or "What's New" to learn the latest information and possible new developments that might be of interest. Next, read any mission statements or description of services to see how the organization describes itself and read the annual report and strategic plan to learn about the financial condition and predicted growth rates. Then, search for career opportunities, jobs, and postings on the human resources link. Riley also suggests that critiquing the development and professional nature of the web site will give you an impression of the organization. Keep in mind that companies likely will not post negative information on the Internet; therefore, consult other independent sources to confirm the financial health of the company. Look at job sites to learn more about the company, salary ranges of competitors, and benefits they offer. Because on-line résumés are not confidential, you can study your competitors' résumés to see how they are positioning themselves and then use this information to improve your résumé.[26]

- *Identify specific skills companies are seeking.* Study the job descriptions provided on corporate home pages and job boards to learn the latest industry buzzwords and the skills required for the job. Use these words as keywords on your résumé.

- *Network electronically with prospective employers.* Attend electronic job fairs, participate in chat sessions with career counselors, subscribe to and contribute to Usenet news groups applicable to your field, and network by e-mail with a contact at a company. These electronic networking opportunities will give you a chance to make a good impression, continue to learn about a job and the job search process, polish your interviewing skills, and create rapport with employment contacts on-line.

Identifying Job Listings. You can use the Internet to locate job opportunities in several ways:

- Look in the employment section of a company's corporate page to see if they are advertising job openings.

- Search the electronic databases of job openings of third-party services such as the following:

Select a job ad from the newspaper classifieds. Using the Internet, locate information about that firm. Submit the located materials to your instructor.

- CareerMosaic (http://www.careermosaic.com)
- Monster Board (http://www.monster.com)
- On-line Career Center (http://www.occ.com)
- America's Job Bank (http://www.ajb.dni.us)
- Yahoo! Classifieds (http://classifieds.yahoo.com)

- Access on-line job classifieds from daily and trade newspapers. CareerPath (www.careerpath.com) runs the classifieds of a number of major newspapers.

- Subscribe to a newsgroup through Usenet that gives you access to jobs by geographic location and specific job categories.

- Subscribe to services such as America On-line that provide job-search sites and services by keying "Career."[27]

On-line and printed sources will help you learn to search particular databases. The following general suggestions will help you get started:

- Input words and phrases that describe your skills rather than job titles because not every company uses the same job title.[28]

- Use specific phrases such as "entry-level job" or "job in advertising" rather than "job search."[29]

- Start with a wider job description term, such as "pharmaceutical sales jobs," then narrow down to the specific subject, geographic region, state, and so forth.

- Don't limit yourself to just one search engine. Try several and bookmark interesting sites.

- Don't get distracted as you go.

Searching for useful career sites can be quite time-consuming; therefore, you will find it beneficial to locate and study independent ratings of the job services. Magazines such as *WebWeek* or *Internet World* review the effectiveness of job services. Richard Bolles, career expert and author of the long-time leading career guide *What Color Is Your Parachute?* continually reviews the more than 11,000 career sites on the Internet and updates his list of the most useful ones. His top ratings are published as "Parachute Picks: My Personal Rating System" on the web site for *What Color Is Your Parachute: The NetGuide* (www.washingtonpost.com/wp-adv/classifieds/careerpost/parachute/parafram2.htm). Many of the top career sites include ratings for the career services listed on their sites. Some of the career sites are The Riley Guide, JobHunt, Career Paradise, Career Resource Center, InfoSeek Guide, Yahoo! Employment, and Lycos/Point 5%—Careers.[30]

Posting an On-Line Résumé on a Job Site or an Employer's Web Site. The easiest and most common method of putting your résumé on the web is through e-mail. You may also list your résumé on a résumé-posting site. After you have identified a job you would like to pursue from a job listing or a company's web site, keep these suggestions in mind:

6 *Identify the components of an effective on-line résumé.*

- ***Understand that on-line résumés are not confidential.*** Once your résumé is on-line, anyone can read it, including your current employer. You may also begin to receive junk mail and cold calls from companies who see your résumé on-line. Before you post your résumé, you may want to identify who has access to it; some companies can lock your résumé from current employers and others.

- *Read and follow instructions carefully.* Some job banks may ask that you include spaces and not tabs as well as give other specific formatting instructions. Be especially cautious that you include your résumé in the format requested by the employer. You may be instructed to include the résumé in an e-mail message or to send it as an attachment to the message. When sending an attachment, be sure to save the résumé in **ASCII format**, a text format that all word processors and mail programs can read. Keep in mind that companies may not spend time "cleaning up" your résumé if it doesn't transmit correctly. A safeguard is to send yourself a copy of the résumé and see how it looks before sending it out to an employer. Finally, read carefully to understand how long your résumé will remain active, how to update it, and how to delete it from the site.

- *Include a keyword summary after the identification section.* Grab the employer's attention by placing the keywords—a strong list of skills employers want—on the first screen (within the first 24 lines of text). Providing this relevant information will motivate the employer to keep scrolling down to see how the keywords are supported in the body rather than to click to the next résumé.

- *E-mail a cover letter to accompany an on-line résumé.* Some companies consider this cover e-mail message to be prescreening for a job interview.[31] Send the message promptly and write a formal, grammatically correct message just as you would if you were sending an application letter in the mail.

Posting a Résumé on Your Personal Web Site. While résumés posted with commercial databases are easier to find than those on personal home pages, another option for extending your exposure to prospective employers is to include a résumé on your personal web site.[32] Your home page can contain links to other screens that expand upon the traditional résumé. Developing an elaborate, highly professional home page with a multimedia résumé gives you an opportunity to showcase your technology savvy, which will give you a competitive edge.

You will include an ASCII-version of your résumé that an employer can download into an electronic database. However, you can also present your qualifications in an elaborate style using multimedia enhancements; this version will be read by the person reviewing these computer screens.

You will need to acquire basic experience in creating a home page in other courses or on your own. You should attempt to be creative in the development of a professional multimedia résumé that highlights your qualifications and reflects your personality. However, the following general suggestions will help you get started.

- *Include the identification section (name, address, telephone number, e-mail address) and an objective statement at the top of the first screen.* This information looks just like a traditional résumé.

- *Include a link to an ASCII-version of the résumé.* An employer can download this text version directly into an electronic database.

- *Include a link to a professionally formatted version of the résumé.* Including the entire résumé as a link allows the employer to scroll the entire résumé, which some employers find more convenient than going from link to link. Also, using one link to the résumé allows the employer the ability to print the entire résumé with one command. Alternately, you can place the résumé directly on the first page of the web site. If you choose this option, be certain the employer can view any important links on the first screen (twenty-four lines). For example, if your link to the ASCII résumé or additional qualifications appeared below the résumé, the employer might lose interest and stop reading before reaching this convincing information.

- *Design an attractive set of links to additional information about your qualifications.* Name the links with words that an employer can immediately recognize as a section of a traditional résumé (e.g., education, work experience, activities, references) but that give the employer freedom to explore the information in any order he/she desires.

- *Develop screens for each link that expand on the basic information provided.* For example, the education section may include a link to scanned projects, writing samples, or multimedia presentations given in courses. The work experience may include detailed descriptions of jobs or internships you have held, photos or files displaying completed projects, writing samples, and links to corporate home pages of former employers. Using links effectively produces a type of "electronic portfolio" to highlight your accomplishments and abilities.

- *Do not include personal photos and statements that reveal your gender, age, ethnic background, marital status, or religion (characteristics protected by employment legislation).* Job seekers who reveal this information may be setting themselves up for discrimination, and many employers will not consider an application if this information is disclosed.

The on-line résumé that Jeanne Fulton posted to her personal web site begins with her name and address as shown in Figure 13-9. With a mouse click, an employer can (1) access an ASCII-version of her résumé, (2) access an attractively formatted version of her résumé that can be printed in one command, and (3) send her an e-mail message directly from the web site. Notice how these three links are grouped attractively in the left column. The right column includes the objective statement and five links to additional information about her qualifications. Review Jeanne's résumé in Figure 13-8.

> What types of information do you think Jeanne could include to showcase her education, work experience, and leadership activities? What work samples might she include?

Presently, locating résumés on a home page is somewhat difficult; however, innovations will make this process easier in the future. In the meantime, you will need to advertise your on-line résumé to maximize its exposure. List your URL address in the identification section of your traditional résumé. In your application letter, motivate the prospective employer to visit your web site by describing the types of information included. Talk enthusiastically about the detailed information included on your home page during a job interview; encourage the interviewer to view it at his/her convenience. Note the way Jeanne Fulton advertises her web site when you read her application letter later in this chapter (Figure 13-10).

Application Letters

> **7** *Write an application letter that effectively introduces an accompanying résumé.*

When employers invite you to send a résumé, they expect you to include an **application letter**. A résumé summarizes information related to the job's requirements and the applicant's qualifications. An application letter (1) seeks to arouse interest in the résumé, (2) introduces it, and (3) interprets it in terms of employer benefits. The application letter is placed on top of the résumé so it can be read first.

Because it seeks to arouse interest and to point out employer benefits, the application letter is persuasive and, thus, written inductively. It is designed to convince an employer that qualifications are adequate just as a sales letter is designed to convince

> What is the purpose of an application letter?

FIGURE 13-9
On-line résumé posted to
personal web site.

1 Begins with her name, address, and objective just as her traditional résumé.

2 Includes a link to an ASCII version of her résumé (no special formatting) that an employer can download into an electronic database.

3 Includes a link to a copy of a résumé that is formatted professionally and can be read by scrolling down the screen and printed with one command.

4 Makes it easy for an employer to communicate with her by providing a link directly to her e-mail address.

5 Includes links to additional information with titles that employers will recognize as sections typically found in a traditional résumé.

Jeanne Fulton

89 Lincoln Street
San Antonio, TX 78285-9063
(512) 555-9823

ASCII Résumé
Download a text version of my resume. Use the "Save" command in your browser to save to a disk.

Complete Résumé
View or print a fully formatted copy of my resume.

Feedback
www.netdoor/jfulton

Objective

First-year audit staff with an international accounting firm; interest in work with information systems.

5 **Additional information to support my qualifications:**

- Education
- Computer skills
- Work experience
- Leadership activities
- Work samples

Related Page 1 | Related Page 2 | Related Page 3

COMMUNICATION MENTOR

An application letter should communicate your desire to obtain a position with a company and what you think you can "bring to the table" for that company. The letter should be formal but contain some personal item that will help the prospective employer identify you more readily.

Another technique is to add a short one- or two-page biography to the employment package. This document will enable a prospective employer to learn more about you from your perspective.

Terence E. McSweeney
Director of Communications
PGA of America

---

a buyer that a product will satisfy a need. Like sales letters, application letters are either solicited or unsolicited. Job advertisements *solicit* applications. Unsolicited application letters have greater need for attention-getters; otherwise, solicited and unsolicited application letters are based on the same principles.

Unsolicited application letters are the same basic letter (perhaps with slight modifications) sent to many prospective employers. By sending unsolicited letters, (1) you increase the possibility of finding employers who have employment needs, (2) you compete with fewer applicants than you would if letters were solicited, and (3) you may alert employers to needs not previously identified. Impressed by the qualities described in an unsolicited application letter, an employer could create a job. The writer of an unsolicited application letter has demonstrated initiative, a quality most employers appreciate. However, sending unsolicited letters has some disadvantages: (1) Because the employer's specific needs are not known, the opening paragraph is likely to be more general than the opening paragraph in unsolicited letters; and (2) depending on the ratio of responses to letters sent, the process could be expensive.

> What does an application letter have in common with a *sales* letter?

Organizing a Persuasive Message

A persuasive letter is designed to persuade the reader to take action, which in this case is to get the reader to (1) read the résumé and (2) invite you to an interview. Because an application letter is a persuasive letter, organize it as you would a sales letter:

> How does a successful application letter lead the reader to the desired action?

Sales Letter	Application Letter
Gets attention	Gets attention
Introduces product	Introduces qualifications
Presents evidence	Presents evidence
Encourages action	Encourages action
(sells a product, service, or idea)	*(is granted an interview)*

Like a well-written sales letter, a well-written application letter uses a central selling feature as a theme. The central selling feature is introduced in the first or second paragraph and stressed in paragraphs that follow. Two to four paragraphs are normally sufficient for supporting evidence. Consider order of importance as a basis for their sequence, with the most significant aspects of your preparation coming first.

> What central appeal could you develop to convince an employer to hire you? How might you introduce it in the attention-getting paragraph?

When you write your application letter, be sure that the letter is a reflection of your personality and not a copy of a standard application letter. You want your letter to stand apart and identify you as a unique individual.

Gain the Receiver's Attention. To gain attention, begin the letter by (1) identifying the job sought and (2) describing how your qualifications fit the job requirements. This information will provide instant confirmation that you are a qualified applicant for a position open in that company. An employer required to read hundreds of application letters and résumés will appreciate this direct, concise approach.

How does an unsolicited application letter differ from a letter responding to an announced position? How are they similar?

If you are applying for a job that has been announced, you may indicate in the first paragraph how you learned of the position—for example, employee referral, customer referral, executive referral, newspaper advertising, or job fair. One executive stated, "It is helpful if we know how you found out about the opening, or who referred you. If I place a $5,000 ad in the *Los Angeles Times*, I want to know how many résumés I got for my money.[33] Many applicant tracking systems allow recruiters to track the sources of résumés and thus assist them in evaluating methods of attracting qualified applicant pools. Note the opening of the letter in Figure 13-10 indicates the applicant learned of the position through a referral from a professor.

An opening for an unsolicited letter must be more persuasive: You must convince the interviewer to continue to read your qualifications even though a job may not exist. As in the opening of a solicited letter, indicate the type of position sought and your qualifications but be more creative in gaining the receiver's attention. The following letter uses the applicant's knowledge of recent company developments and an intense interest in the company's future to gain the receiver's attention.

> During the past few years, TelCom has experienced phenomenal growth through various acquisitions, mergers, and market expansion. With this growth comes new opportunities, new customers, and the need for new "team players" to work in sales and marketing. While following the growth of TelCom, I have become determined to join this exciting team and am convinced my educational background, leadership abilities, and internship experience qualify me for the job.

Provide Evidence of Qualifications. For graduating students entering the world of full-time work for the first time, educational backgrounds usually are more impressive than work histories. They can benefit from interpreting their educational experiences as meaningful, job-related experiences. An applicant for acceptance into an auditor's trainee program should do more than merely report having taken auditing theory and practice:

> In my auditing theory and practice class, I could see specific application of principles encountered in my human relations and psychology classes. Questions about leadership and motivation seemed to recur throughout the course: What really motivates executives? Why are auditors feared at many levels? How can those fears be overcome? How can egos be salvaged? The importance of the human element was a central focus of many courses and my research report, "The Auditor as a Psychologist."

Because the preceding paragraph included questions discussed in a class, do not assume that your application letter should do likewise. Or because this paragraph gives the title of a term paper, do not assume the same technique is a must for your letter. The techniques illustrated are commendable because they help to portray the educational experience as meaningful and related to the job sought. Recognizing that auditors must be tactful (a point on which the person reading the letter will surely agree), the applicant included some details of a class. That technique is a basic in persuasion: Do not just say a product or idea is good; say what makes it good. Do not just say that a certain educational or work experience was beneficial; say what made it so.

By making paragraphs long enough to include interpretation of experiences on the present or previous job, you can give an employer some confidence that you are well prepared for your next job. For example, the following excerpt from an applicant whose only work experience was at a fast-food restaurant is short and general: *For three months last summer, I worked at Marketplace Bagel. Evaluations of my work were superior. While the assistant manager was on vacation, I supervised a crew of five on the evening shift.*

As the only reference to the Marketplace Bagel experience, the paragraph conveys one employer's apparent satisfaction with performance. Superior evaluations and some supervisory responsibility are evidence of that satisfaction, but added details and interpretation could make the message more convincing:

> In my summer job at Marketplace Bagel, I learned the value of listening carefully when taking orders, making change quickly and accurately, offering suggestions when customers seemed hesitant, and keeping a cheerful attitude. Supervising a crew of five while the assistant manager was on vacation, I appreciated the importance of fairness and diplomacy in working with other employees.

Apparently, the applicant's experience has been meaningful. It called attention to qualities that managers like to see in employees: willingness to listen, speed, accuracy, concern for clients or customers, a positive attitude, fairness, and tact. As a *learning* experience, the Marketplace Bagel job has taught or reinforced some principles that the employer will see can be transferred to the job being sought.

In this section, you can discuss qualifications you have developed by participating in student organizations, student government, athletics, or community organizations. Be specific in describing the skills you have gained that can be applied directly on the job—for example, organizational, leadership, oral and written communication, and budgeting and financial management. You can also use your

How can a job applicant assure that the application letter is not just a "rehash" of the résumé?

involvement in student activities as a vehicle for discussing important personal traits vital to the success of a business—interpersonal skills, motivation, imagination, responsibility, team orientation, and so forth.

> For the past year, I have served as state president of Phi Beta Lambda, a national business student organization. By coordinating various statewide meetings and leadership seminars, I have refined communication, organizational, and interpersonal skills.

Finally, end this section with an indirect reference to the résumé. If you refer to it in the first or second paragraph, readers may wonder whether they are expected to put the letter aside at that point and look at the résumé. Avoid the obvious statement *"Enclosed please find my résumé"* or *"A résumé is enclosed."* Instead, refer indirectly to the résumé while restating your qualifications. The following sentence emphasizes that references confirm the statements the applicant has made about his/her qualifications :

> References listed on the enclosed résumé would be glad to comment on my accounting education and experience.

Encourage Action. Now that you have presented your qualifications and referred to the enclosed résumé, the next move is to encourage the receiver to extend an invitation for an interview. The goal is to introduce the idea of action without apologizing for doing so and without being demanding or "pushy." If the final paragraph (action closing) of your letter is preceded by paragraphs that are impressive, you need not press hard for a response. Just mentioning the idea of a future discussion is probably sufficient. If you have significant related experience and have developed this experience as a central selling feature, mentioning this experience in the action closing would add unity and stress your strongest qualification one last time. Forceful statements about *when* and *how* to respond are unnecessary and could arouse resentment. Try to avoid some frequently made errors:

- *Setting a date.* "May I have an appointment with you on March 14?" The date you name could be inconvenient; or even if it is convenient for the employer, your forwardness in setting it could be resented.
- *Expressing doubt.* "If you agree," "I hope you will," and "Should you decide" use subjunctive words that indicate lack of confidence.
- *Sounding apologetic.* "May I take some of your time" or "I know how busy you are" may seem considerate, but an apology is inappropriate when discussing ways you can contribute to a company.
- *Sounding overconfident.* "I know you will want to set up an appointment." This statement is presumptuous and egotistical.
- *Giving permission to call.* "You may call me at 555-6543." By making the call sound like a privilege (may call) you could alienate the reader. Implied meaning: You are very selective about the calls you take, but the employer does qualify.
- *Reporting capability of response*. "You can call me at 555-6543." When a number or address is given, employers are aware they are capable of using it (can call).

The following sentences are possible closing sentences that refer to an invitation to interview. They are not intended as model sentences that should appear in *your* letter. When the time comes to write your own closing sentence, write it, analyze it carefully, and rewrite it if necessary. Because finding the right job is so important, you will be well rewarded for the time and thought invested.

- *"When a date and time can be arranged, I would like to talk with you."* The statement does not indicate who will do the arranging, and the meeting place and the subject of the conversation are understood.

- *"I would appreciate an opportunity to discuss the loan officer's job with you."* The indirect reference to action is not forceful. However, if the applicant has impressive qualifications, the reader will want an interview and will not need to be pushed.

- *"I would appreciate an appointment to discuss your employment needs and my information systems experience."* The statement asks for the interview and re-emphasizes the applicant's strong related work experience.

General Writing Guidelines

Several general guidelines will aid you in writing an effective application letter:

- *Write a concise letter that develops your qualifications.* Some human resources managers favor short application letters, pointing out that only a few seconds can be spared for reading each letter. A short letter that is *read*, they argue, will do an applicant more good than a long one that is merely *skimmed*. They see brevity as a virtue that can be demonstrated in an application letter. Other human resource managers favor longer letters. They point out that good employees are hard to find and that longer letters provide more information and additional opportunity to evaluate. If the first lines arouse interest, employers will thoroughly and eagerly read additional paragraphs if doing so will possibly help resolve an employment problem. Generally, one page is sufficient for students and graduates entering the job market; yet more space is needed for developing significant experience.

  Is an employer's busy schedule a valid argument for keeping application letters short?

- *Write an original letter that reflects your personality.* A cartoon depicted an employer holding an application letter with an applicant sitting across the desk. The dialogue read, "I wish I could interview the person who wrote this letter." This scenario emphasizes an important point: the application letter and résumé must represent *you*. They should be different from any other person's. Study sample applications but write a letter that reflects your personality. Copying or paraphrasing someone else's résumé or application letter is a serious mistake, but you can benefit from studying letters in which others have applied or violated principles. In evaluating application letters written by others (and in thinking about your *own* letter to be written later), keep in mind the criteria by which any writing can be evaluated.

- *Address the letter to a specific individual.* Identify the specific person who is responsible for hiring for the position you are seeking rather than sending the letter to the "Human Resources Department" or "To Whom It May Concern." If necessary, consult the company's annual report or web site, or call the company to locate this information. Verify the correct spelling, job title, and address and send a personalized message to the appropriate individual.

- *Use the language used on the job.* If an application letter contains terminology commonly used by accountants, an applicant for an accounting job implies familiarity with the job and the language used. An applicant for a financial position would benefit from using acronyms such as ECOA for Equal Credit Opportunity Act, abbreviations, and other terms, such as *front-end load*, which are well known in the financial field but not altogether meaningful to others. Such language would communicate clearly, save space, and imply a financial background. The same principle applies to writing about other occupations. Use this specialized language only when you are confident your reader will understand.

- *Avoid overuse of "I" and writer-focused statements.* Because the letter is designed to sell your services, some use of "I" is natural and expected; but try to restrict the number of times "I" is used. "I" is especially noticeable if it is the first word of consecutive paragraphs. Instead, assume an *empathetic* attitude: Focus on providing specific evidence that you can meet the company's needs. The employer is not interested in reading about your need to earn more income, to be closer to your work, to have more pleasant surroundings, or to gain greater advancement opportunities, nor about the excitement you experienced on learning about a job opportunity.

- *Avoid overused words and obvious expressions.* Avoid words used to talk about the job search process that are overused in applicant letters: *applicant, application, opening, position, vacancy, interview.* Ideas such as "This is an application," "I read your ad," and "I am writing to apply for," are sufficiently understood without making direct statements. With the letter *and* résumé in hand, a reader learns nothing from "A résumé is enclosed." Other obvious statements that have become clichés in application letters include "Consider me an applicant for this position" and "Please grant me an interview at your earliest convenience."

- *Communicate your knowledge of the company.* A thorough job search may have identified current trends in the industry you are entering. The company to which you are applying may have had a recent stock split, announced the upcoming opening of a new branch, or introduced a new product. Sentences that *imply* your knowledge of such matters may make a favorable impression. They show that you really are interested in the field, read widely, do more than you are required to do, gather information before making decisions, and so on.

- *Communicate your knowledge of job requirements.* Direct statements such as "The requirements of this job are . . ." or "I understand that this job requires . . ." are seldom necessary because the employer assumes you have this knowledge. "An auditor should be able to . . ." and "Sales personnel should avoid . . ." seem to lecture. Although they may reveal familiarity with matters important to the job, they may be resented. If a certain job is known to place special emphasis on certain requirements, however, your awareness of that emphasis could be a point in your favor. For example, a certain accounting job requires frequent and complicated written reports. Instead of writing, "I understand the job requires frequent reports" (which is already known), you could refer to writing experiences you have had or your preference for work that requires writing (if that is true). Your understanding is revealed without a direct statement.

- *Include requested information.* For example, some ads for employment force respondents to include certain information: "Must provide own transportation and be willing to travel. Give educational background, work experience, and salary expected." Discuss these points in the responding letter. Preferably, the question of salary is left until the interview; you want your letter to focus on your contributions to the company—not what you want from the company

How would you respond to a requirement listed in a job ad that you do not meet?

(money). Until after the interview, neither the employer nor the applicant knows whether the two are compatible. If they are not, a discussion of salary is pointless. However, if an ad requests a statement about it, the letter should include that statement. You may give a minimum figure or range, indicate willingness to accept a figure that is customary for work of that type, or indicate a preference for discussing salary at the interview.

- ***Avoid insincere flattery.*** If a firm is well known for its rapid expansion, currently successful advertising campaign, competitive advantage, or superior product, conveying your awareness of these positive achievements is to your advantage. On the other hand, deliberate attempts at flattery will almost surely be detected. They are more likely to be resented than appreciated. For example, referring to the employer as "*the* leader in the field," "the best in the business," or "a company with an outstanding record" is risky. If such labels are inaccurate, they will be so recognized. If they are accurate, their use is still risky. Flattery could be taken as an attempt to get a favorable decision as a reward for making a complimentary statement.

- ***Do not discuss your current employer's shortcomings.*** Regardless of how negatively you perceive your present employer, that perception has little to do with your prospective employer's needs. Also, if you knock your present employer, you could be perceived as someone who would do the same to the next employer.

- ***Do not make self-condemning statements.*** Concentrate on reporting your strengths. Surely, you would not apply for a job you thought you could not do. Just tell the aspects of your background that have prepared you for that job. Reporting failure or lack of aptitude at some other endeavor only weakens your case. Mentioning it could raise questions about your self-esteem. Instead of apologizing for some shortcoming, look for positive aspects of your education or experience. Reporting them may be to your advantage.

- ***Avoid boastful connotations.*** Self-confidence is commendable, but overconfidence (or worse still, just plain bragging) is objectionable. Like unsupported or unsupportable superlatives in sales letters, some self-judgmental terms can do more harm than good. Instead of labeling your performance as "superior" or "excellent," give supporting facts. A manager may think of them as evidence of superiority or excellence and react favorably.

Finishing Touches

Compared with superior qualifications, physical arrangement on a page may seem insignificant. Yet, even before the letter is read, it communicates something about you. If it conveys a negative impression, it may not be read at all. The size, color, and quality of paper influence readers' reaction; so do margins, letter format, keyboarding, and paragraphing.

Use plain bond paper for this personal business letter. Using your present employer's letterhead is unacceptable because you are not representing your employer. If necessary, refer to Appendix A for letter formats and standard and special letter parts. Include your street address and city, state, and ZIP Code above the date. Include "Enclosure" a double-space below the signature block to alert the employer that a résumé is enclosed. The proper letter format is shown in the example in Figure 13-10.

FIGURE 13-10
Good example of an application letter.

1 Reveals how she learned of the position; identifies a specific job sought, and introduces her background.

2 Discusses how education relates to the job requirements.

3 Highlights skills related to the job requirements (ideas discussed come from the company/job profile where she identified the job requirements and her qualifications).

4 Introduces the résumé and a web site for additional information.

5 Encourages employer to take action without sounding pushy or apologetic.

Format Pointers

- Uses the same high-quality paper used for the résumé (neutral color, standard size).

- Includes writer's address above the date because résumé is printed on plain paper (personal business letter format).

- Addresses the letter to a specific person using the correct name and title. Includes a salutation to a specific person.

- Includes enclosure notation to alert the employer that a résumé is included.

Inductive Outline for an Application Letter

1. Gain the employer's attention by identifying the job sought and describing how qualifications fit the job requirements.
   Solicited letter: May indicate how applicant learned of position (ad or referral).
   Unsolicited letter: Must be persuasive enough to convince an employer to read the letter. Could begin by showing intense interest in and knowledge of recent company developments.
2. Provide convincing evidence of qualifications.
3. Refer to the résumé indirectly while restating qualifications. Mention the availability of a web site or portfolio for additional information (optional).
4. Encourage the employer to extend an invitation for an interview.

P.O. Box 2407
Nashville, TN 37202-2407
October 15, 1998

Mr. Bryce Gowan
Tatum & Bayne, CPAs
1000 Plaza Court
Austin, TX 78710-1000

Dear Mr. Gowan:

1 Dr. Martin, an accounting professor at Central State University, told me that Tatum & Bayne has an auditing position available. An auditing emphasis in accounting and my related job experience qualify me for this auditing position.

2 Because of my interest in auditing, I chose the majority of my accounting electives from the auditing course offerings. I especially enjoyed Auditing Practice. Unstructured, often ambiguous problems that require creative solutions are among my favorite assignments. After completing Accounting Information Systems and other computer courses, I can proficiently operate the Microsoft Office 97 Suite and several general ledger programs. I gained valuable experience using this software while working for Smith & Lewis, CPAs.

3 My experience at Smith & Lewis also gave me countless opportunities to interact with practicing auditors, often assisting them on site with clients. I learned to appreciate the need to work long, irregular hours; function effectively in groups; and develop positive relationships with clients and staff. My rating on the written and oral communication skills component of my performance evaluation was consistently "excellent," solid evidence of my ability to write and deliver clear, concise, and ethical messages—primarily planning memos, letters, and audit reports.

4 References listed on the enclosed résumé would be glad to comment on my accounting education and experience. You can also review samples of my work and more detailed information related to my degree program and work experience by visiting my home page at jfulton@netdoor.com. **5** Please call or write so we can discuss the possibility of my joining the audit staff at Tatum & Bayne.

Sincerely,

Jeanne Fulton

Jeanne Fulton

Enclosure

Paper used for the application letter, the résumé, and the envelope must match in color, weight, cotton fiber content, texture, and size. The watermark should be readable across the sheet in the same direction as the printing. Refer to the résumé format and layout guidelines on pages 499-501 for exact paper and high quality printing requirements.

Errors in grammar, spelling, and punctuation could imply that you pay little attention to detail, do your work hastily, have shortcomings in basic education, or lack pride or respect. Because the letter represents you and will be thought of as the best you can do, allow yourself time to do it well. Get opinions from others and make revisions where necessary.

Examples of Application Letters

Jeanne Fulton wrote the letter in Figure 13-10 to accompany a chronological résumé she prepared after completing the company/job profile of an entry-level auditor shown in Figure 13-2. The time Jeanne devoted to analyzing the job, the company, and her qualifications was well spent. Notice how Jeanne discusses qualifications that correspond closely with the job requirements listed in the company/job profile: intellectual skills, computer skills, interpersonal skills, knowledge of work environment, ethical standards, and communication skills.

Before writing a résumé and application letter, study carefully the overall suggestions in the "General Writing Guidelines" placed before the summary in Chapter 5. Then study the specific suggestions in the "Check Your Writing" checklist that precedes this chapter's summary. Compare your work with this checklist again after you have written a rough draft and make any necessary revisions.

TRADITIONAL RÉSUMÉ

Content

- Base on self-, career, and job analyses.
- Include qualifications compatible with job requirements.
- Include only relevant ideas.
- Present qualifications truthfully and honestly.

Organization

- Arrange headings in appropriate sequence.
- Place significant ideas in emphatic position.
- List experiences consistently, either in time sequence or in order of importance.

Style

- Omit personal pronouns.
- Use action verbs.
- Use past tense for previous jobs; present tense for present job.
- Place significant words in emphatic positions.
- Use parallelism in listing multiple items.
- Use positive language.
- Use simple words (but some jargon of the field is acceptable).

Mechanics

- Assure there are *no* keying, grammar, spelling, or punctuation errors.
- Print on high-quality (24-pound, 100-percent cotton-fiber content), neutral-colored paper.
- Use clear, sharp print.
- Balance on the page.
- Use ample margins even if a second page is required.
- Include a page number on all pages except the first.
- Position headings consistently throughout.
- Use an outline format or a bulleted list to emphasize multiple points.
- Use indention, underlining, capitalization, font changes, and graphic lines and borders to enhance overall impact.

ELECTRONIC RÉSUMÉ

Content

- Position name as the first readable item on the page.
- Include "Objective" section to identify the job sought (same as a traditional résumé).
- Include "Keyword Summary" section listing qualifications that match the job description.

- Support the keywords with specific facts; use as many nouns as possible that might match those in the job description.
- Use synonyms of the keywords in the body to ensure a match with the database.

Format

- Use nondecorative font with font range of 10 to 14 points.
- Omit design elements that could distort the text (italics, underline, open bullets, graphic lines and borders, two-column or other complex formats, and so on.)
- Allow ample white space, especially between sections.
- Print on one side of white, standard-size paper with sharp laser print.
- Mail unfolded and unstapled with an application letter.

ON-LINE RÉSUMÉ

- Begin with name, address, and objective just as a traditional résumé.
- Include links to the following:
  - ASCII version of the résumé that an employer can download into an electronic database.
  - A copy of a fully formatted résumé that can be read by scrolling down the screen and printed with one command.
  - E-mail address so a prospective employer can easily communicate with the applicant.
  - Additional information to supplement the résumé. Label the links with titles that employers will recognize as sections of a traditional résumé.

APPLICATION LETTER

Content

- Include valid ideas (statements are true).
- Identify the letter as an application for a certain job.
- Exclude nonessential ideas.
- Emphasize significant qualifications.
- Make reference to enclosed résumé.
- End with action closing that is neither apologetic nor pushy.

Organization

- Begin by revealing the job sought in the attention-getter.
- Present paragraphs in most appropriate sequence (order of importance is possibly best).

- End with a reference to action employer is to take (call or write and extend an invitation to an interview).

Style

- Use simple language (no attempt to impress with a sophisticated vocabulary; some professional jargon is justified).
- Use relatively short sentences with sufficient variety.
- Place significant words in emphatic positions.

Mechanics

- Assure that there are *no* keying, grammar, spelling, or punctuation errors.
- Include writer's address above the date.
- Include equal side margins (approximately one inch).
- Balance on the page.
- Print on plain paper that matches the résumé.
- Keep first and last paragraphs relatively short; hold others to fewer than six or seven lines.

SUMMARY

1. **Complete systematic self-, career, and job analyses.** A job candidate should complete systematic self-, career, and job analyses. Because life's enjoyment is strongly influenced by success on the job, planning and preparing for a career are vital. Like other important decisions, you must gather information to make wise career decisions and preferably record it in a career notebook or computer file for easy reference. Ask questions about yourself, about a possible career, and about a specific job in the chosen field. Interview people already working at the job. Recording and analyzing this information will assist you in selecting a satisfying career and preparing an effective résumé.

2. **Prepare an effective chronological, functional, or combination chronological/functional résumé.** The most effective résumé for a particular candidate could be a chronological, functional, or combination chronological/functional résumé. A résumé includes identification, objective, summary of achievements, qualifications, personal information, and references. To compete favorably for a job, exploit computer technology to develop an appealing, easy-to-read design and print a high-quality copy. Like other written documents, résumés and application letters should reflect high standards of content, organization, style, and mechanics.

   Chronological résumés have "Education" and "Experience" as headings and list experiences in reverse chronological order; they are appropriate for applicants who consider themselves qualified for the job. Functional résumés show qualifications the applicant possesses as headings; this format is especially effective for applicants who lack the appropriate education and experience. The combination chronological/functional résumé lists education and experience and uses functional headings that emphasize qualifications.

3. **Prepare a résumé that can be scanned and processed by an electronic applicant-tracking system.** The ability to prepare an electronic résumé that can be scanned and processed by an applicant-tracking system will enhance employment opportunities for the job candidate. To prepare an electronic résumé that can be read and processed by a computer, use popular 10- to 14-point nondecorative fonts, omit special print effects (italics, underline) and confusing graphic enhancements, use a traditional résumé format, and print on white paper with sharp laser print. Send an unfolded, unstapled original copy of the résumé. Position your name as the first readable item, insert a keyword summary section after the identification section, and support your keywords with specific facts in the body of the résumé. The keywords are nouns that describe required and desired skills for a specific position.

4. **Identify employment tools other than the résumé that can enhance employability.** The résumé may be supplemented with other employment tools that include a professional portfolio and a videotape of the applicant. The portfolio, whose use is broadening to include many career fields, showcases your projects, creative activities, and accolades. A videotape transmits a visual impression about you that may help convince the potential employer of your competence but may also lead to stereotyping and discrimination. Content for a portfolio or videotape should be carefully chosen to reflect skills necessary for effective job performance and should complement that in the printed résumé.

5. **Locate employment opportunities using traditional and electronic methods.** The job candidate can widen employment opportunities by using traditional and electronic methods for the employment search. Names and addresses of possible employers may be obtained from networks, career services centers at schools, employers' offices, employment agencies and contractors, help-wanted ads, on-line databases and printed sources, and

professional organizations. Information is available via the Internet about how to conduct a successful electronic job search. Company web sites can be accessed that provide information about the organization and list job vacancies. The job seeker can also network with prospective employers through electronic job fairs, news groups, and chat sessions. General job listings are available by career field through a variety of on-line sources.

6. **Identify the components of an effective on-line résumé.** The applicant can post a résumé to a prospective employer's web site or to a personal home page. Providing an elaborate, highly professional home page with a multimedia résumé gives you an opportunity to highlight your technical ability and possibly gain a competitive advantage for being hired. You should provide an ASCII version of the file so that an employer can download it into an electronic database. Links in the file may be used to expand on the basic information, thus providing an electronic portfolio of accomplishments that the employer can explore as desired. The applicant who posts an on-line résumé should be aware that such documents are not confidential and that inclusion of photos or visual images may lead to discrimination because they reveal gender, age, and ethnicity .

7. **Write an application letter that effectively introduces an accompanying résumé.** An application letter effectively introduces an accompanying résumé. The purposes of the application letter are to introduce the applicant and the résumé, arouse interest in the information given on the résumé, and assist an employer in seeing ways in which the applicant's services would be desirable. As such, it is a persuasive letter—beginning with an attention-getter, including a central appeal and convincing evidence, and closing with an indirect reference to the enclosed résumé and desired action (invitation to an interview). Use terminology that will be used on the job to indicate your familiarity with the field and avoid using words and expressions overused in application letters. Encourage the reader to extend an interview without apologizing or being too demanding. Prepare the application letter, résumé, and envelope on plain, high-quality bond paper, and proofread carefully to ensure your employment credentials are error free, an example of your best work.

REFERENCES

[1]Croal, N. (1997, June 9). Want a job? Get on-line. *Newsweek*, 81.

[2]Barnum, C. M. (1987, September–October). Writing résumés that sell. *Management World*, 10–13.

[3]Holley, W. H., Jr., Higgins, E., & Speights, S. (1988, December). Résumés and cover letters: What do HR managers really want? *Personnel*, 49–51.

[4]Marlow, G. (1997, May 5). On résumés, applicants telling more than little white-collar lies. *Star Tribune*, p. 3D.

[5]Jacobs, D. L. (1996, June 3). When tempted to stretch résumé, remember high price of lies. *The San Diego Union-Tribune*, p. C–2.

[6]Smith, K. (1996, September 11). Don't stretch truth on job application: Employers verify all information. *The Patriot Ledger*, p. 19E.

[7]Smith, K. (1996, September 11). Don't stretch truth on job application: Employers verify all information. *The Patriot Ledger*, p. 19E.

[8]Backler, C. J. (1995). Résumé fraud: Lies, omissions, and exaggerations. *Personnel Journal*, 74(6), 50.

[9]Griffin, M. A., & Anderson, P. L. (1994). Résumé content. *Business Education Forum*, 48(3), 11–14.

[10]Barnum, C. M. (1987, September–October). Writing résumés that sell. *Management World*, 10–13.

[11]Write a résumé that works: It's simple: Custom tailor each one to the job. (1990, June). *Changing Times*, 91, 93, 95.

[12]Charles, P. J. (1988, September-October). Résumés without clutter. *Management World*, 19–20.

[13]Hutchinson, K. L., & Brefka, D. S. (1997). Personnel administrators' preferences for résumé content; ten years after. *Business Communication Quarterly*, 60(2), 67.

[14]Baxter, N. (1987, Spring). Résumés, application forms, cover letters, and interviews. *Occupational Outlook Quarterly*, 17–23.

[15]Cesare, S. J. (1996). Subjective judgment and the selection process: A methodological review. *Public Personnel Management*, 25(3), 291–306.

[16]Kennedy, J. L. (1996, March 17). Put profile keywords on résumé. *The Des Moines Register,* Job Market, p. 1.

[17]Kennedy, J. L., & Morrow, T. J. (1994). *Electronic résumé revolution: Create a winning résumé for the new world of job seeking.* New York: John Wiley.

[18]Kennedy, J. L., & Morrow, T. J. (1994). *Electronic résumé revolution: Create a winning résumé for the new world of job seeking.* New York: John Wiley.

[19]Kennedy, J. L., & Morrow, T. J. (1994). *Electronic résumé revolution: Create a winning résumé for the new world of job seeking.* New York: John Wiley.

[20]Robinson, K. (1997, March 24). How to keep from sticking your mouse in your mouth, *The Idaho Statesman,* p. 1D.

[21]Kay, A. (1997, June 9). Portfolios add more substance to your résumé, display your work skills in a more tangible package. *The Cincinnati Enquirer*, p. B14.

[22]Szadkowski, J. (1996, September 24). Going high-tech on your job search. *The Washington Times*.

[23]King, J. (1997, July 28). Point-and-click career service: Recruitingware does more than track résumés. *Computerworld*, p. 37.

[24]Robinson, K. (1997, March 24). Job search engine. *The Idaho Statesman*, p. 1D.

[25]Cafasso, R. (1996, August 12). Struttin it on-line. *Computerworld*, p. 84.

[26]Riley, M. F. *The Riley guide: Employment opportunities and job resources on the Internet*. [On-line]. Available http://www.dbm.com/jobguide/ [1997, September 2].

[27]Cafasso, R. (1996, August 12). Struttin it on-line. *Computerworld*, p. 84.

[28]Cafasso, R. (1996, August 12). Struttin it on-line. *Computerworld*, p. 84.

[29]La Ganga, M. (1997, March 21). Application yourself: Jobs can be found via computer, but don't trade keystrokes for legwork, *Los Angeles Times*, p. D1.

[30]Bolles, R. N. *The Net Guide*. [On-line]. Available http://www. washingtonpost.com/wp-adv/classifieds/career-post/parachute/parafram2.htm [1998, March 13].

[31]Coolidge, S. D. (1997, June 10). Surf's up! Job hunters catch an Internet wave. *The Christian Science Monitor*, p. 8.

[32]Smullin, R. (1997, June 23). Job-seekers tap the net—A load of help-wanted listings, tips, employer profiles, résumés go on-line. *The Seattle Times*, p. E1.

[33]Kennedy, J. L. & Morrow, T. J. (1994) *Electronic resume revolution: Create a winning resume for the new world of job seeking*. New York: John Wiley.

[34]Kimball, D. (1997, May 28). Internet job searching. [On-line]. Available http://titan.iwu.edu/~ccenter/nettips. htm/#now [1997, August 20].

REVIEW QUESTIONS

1. What steps can a person take to increase the likelihood of making the correct career choice? (Obj. 1)

2. What are several good sources for learning about the duties and responsibilities of a certain job? (Obj. 1)

3. What is the purpose of a résumé? List its standard parts. (Obj. 2)

4. What are the consequences of inflating your qualifications on a résumé? (Obj. 2)

5. What is the purpose of the "Summary of Achievements" section? What analogy is used to describe this résumé section? Must it be included in every résumé? Explain. (Obj. 2)

6. What are the advantages of using subject-understood sentences in résumés? Action verbs? Crisp phrases? Descriptive but not overly strong adjectives? Provide one example of your own. (Obj. 2)

7. Under what conditions might you choose to include or not include references on a résumé? Is obtaining permission from references necessary? (Obj. 2)

8. Describe the three organizational patterns of résumés and tell under what circumstances each would be effective. (Obj. 2)

9. How does the format and content of a scannable (electronic) résumé differ from a traditional résumé? (Obj. 3)

10. What should a professional portfolio include? (Obj. 4)

11. List five sources from which prospective employers' names and addresses may be obtained. (Obj. 5)

12. How can a job applicant conduct a successful job search without ever leaving home? (Obj. 5)

13. What are the advantages to the applicant of posting an on-line résumé to a personal web page? (Obj. 6)

14. List techniques for writing effective persuasive letters that should be applied in application letters. Refer to Chapter 8 to answer this question if necessary.

15. Why should you avoid words frequently used in application letters? List some of these words. (Obj. 7)

EXERCISES

1. **Document for Analysis: Planning a Résumé for an Outplaced Employee (Obj. 1–4)**
Assume that as director of the Outplacement Center for Baker Mortgage Corporation you help outplaced employees prepare professional résumés that reflect their abilities. Review the narrative of qualifications provided by Shane Austin, who is seeking a position as a senior loan officer in a major banking firm. Be prepared to discuss the answers to the following questions in class: (a) What information is relevant to Shane's career objective? (b) Has essential information been omitted? (Supply fictitious information if needed.), (c) Which résumé type do you think would present Shane's qualifications most effectively: chronological, functional, or

combination chronological/functional? (d) Would a "Summary of Achievements" section strengthen Shane's résumé? (e) Should Shane list his references on the résumé or state that a list is available? Should he prepare a separate references page? Which of the references are the most appropriate (assuming that all will provide positive recommendations)? (f) What should Shane do to assure that his résumé is scannable? (g) Should Shane prepare a portfolio or videotape to supplement the résumé?

If directed by your instructor, prepare Shane's résumé (and references page if necessary) referring to the analysis you prepared and following the guidelines presented in this chapter. Incorporate the valid comments made by at least two others competent in proofreading and résumé design. Use the desktop publishing capability available to you to produce a highly effective, professional document.

EMPLOYMENT INFORMATION

Shane W. Austin, 8901 Brookdale Road, Pueblo, CO 81002-8901.

Personal data: 38 years old, divorced, two children (John 8, Jeanne 5), 6'4" tall, in excellent health (wear glasses) Exercise regularly, primarily racquetball and lifting weights. Also enjoy golf.

I received a Bachelor of Science in Business at Westbrook University in May of 1980. My major was Finance and Real Estate; my overall grade-point average was 3.6. While in college, my activities included: Phi Kappa Phi, Beta Gamma Sigma, Dean's list for four semesters, recipient of the Du Bois Foundation Scholarship (awarded to outstanding finance majors), intramural football and tennis, president of the Student Association, Who's Who Among Students in American Colleges and Universities, Hall of Fame, president of the Banking and Finance Association. I graduated in the top 10 percent of a class of 100 at Blair High School in Pueblo, Colorado, in 1976.

My employment history includes the following: (1) Teller at Saguaro Bank during summers of 1977-79. I worked 20 hours a week and was promoted from Teller I to Teller III. (2) Completed a one-semester internship (gained three hours' credit toward degree) at Sunbelt Bank from September to December, 1979. Selection process was very competitive. My primary responsibilities were to assist the branch manager and approve small consumer loans. (3) Commercial Loan Officer, Baker Mortgage Corporation from June, 1980 to November, 1997. My duties included managing a $25 million loan portfolio, making substantial credit decisions for loans averaging $800,000 each, and striving to achieve realistic lending goals. I also arranged loans for various types of clients (importers and exporters, wholesalers, and manufacturers) with tremendous sales. Completed Baker's intensive training program for commercial loan officers, which required me to pass an intermediate accounting examination before being admitted and to pass an arduous loan officer's examination when I finished.

Currently I volunteer as a Little League baseball coach (ages 6-8) and as a Boy Scout troop leader (ages 10-12).

The following individuals have agreed to provide additional information about my qualifications: (1) Paul J. Bryant, Head Teller, Saguaro Bank, 905 Courtland Drive, Pueblo, CO 81002-0905; (2) Ellyn Broome, Vice President, Sunbelt Bank, 3900 Central Avenue, Ft. Collins, CO 80521-3900; (3) James L. Hawthorne, Vice President of Commercial Loans, Baker Mortgage Corporation, 2500 North Mesquite Drive, Pueblo, CO 81002-3728; (4) Cynthia M. Buntyn, Baker Mortgage Corporation, same address as given above; (5) Rev. Joseph E. Kerns, Faith Church of Pueblo, 3710 Friar Lane, Pueblo, CO 81002-3710; and (6) Richard G. Rueter, President, Chamber of Commerce, 9310 Commerce Street, Pueblo, CO 81002-9310.

2. **Locating Employment Opportunities (Obj. 5, 6, 7)** Jennifer Simms, a graduating senior in Computer Information Systems, has sought your advice as to how to locate job opportunities in her field. Outline a course of action for her that includes traditional and electronic methods that may help her locate the right job.

3. **Document for Analysis: Application Letter (Obj. 7)** Analyze the following letter. Pinpoint its strengths and weaknesses and then revise the letter as directed by your instructor.

September 5, 1999

Nolan Stores, Ltd.
New Brunswick, NJ 08902-7543

Dear Sirs:

Please consider me as an applicant for the buyer's position you advertised in last nights issue of the Times Meridian. The primary advantage I would have as a buyer is my heavy educational background. Among the courses I have taken are buyer behavior, retailing, marketing, public relations, and advertising. I am sure you realize the many ways in which these courses can prepare one for a career in marketing.

In addition to my classes, my educational background includes work in the university bookstore, service on the school yearbook, and president of my fraternity. I will be receiving my degree on May 5, 2000. If you can use an energetic young man with my educational background, I will appreciate you studying the résumé which you will find inclosed. May I have an interview at your earliest convenience. So I can put my educational background to work for you.

Sincerely,

Yuan Chiang

E-MAIL APPLICATION

Your instructor will distribute a sample résumé to the class or may ask you to exchange a rough draft of your résumé with another class member. You are to critique its effectiveness using the guidelines and the examples provided in the chapter. Send an e-mail message to your instructor (or the student if you evaluated a class member's résumé) giving your overall impression of the résumé and specific suggestions for improving it. Printscreen to obtain a copy of your message and submit it to your instructor. Submit a copy of the résumé if you critiqued a student's résumé.

APPLICATIONS

1. **Getting Essential Information to Make a Wise Career Decision (Obj. 1)**

   Prepare a self-analysis, career analysis, and job analysis, and conduct an interview with a career person. Add when necessary to the lists of questions provided in the text for each part of the analysis. Answer each question appropriately. Select a person currently working in your career field. To validate information you receive, you may wish to interview two people. A person who has worked in a particular field but is not currently involved might be more objective (for instance, an accountant in public accounting now working in private industry or teaching accounting).

2. **Preparing a Company/Job Profile (Obj. 1)**

   Use information obtained from completing Application 1 to prepare a company/job profile for the company/job in which you expect to be interviewing. Using Figure 13-2 as a guide, complete these steps:

   a. Review the completed profile and note the degree of compatibility between your qualifications and the company and job requirements.

   b. Compile a list of strengths and weaknesses (lack of a match between your qualifications and job requirements) as they relate to the job requirements.

   c. Consider carefully the deficiencies you must overcome before your qualifications fully match the job requirements. What are possible strategies for overcoming these deficiencies? Are any of these strategies feasible, or is overcoming these deficiencies out of your control?

   d. Analyze the final comparison and decide whether interviewing for this job would be wise.

3. **Preparing a Traditional and an Electronic Résumé and an Application Letter for a Job of Your Choice (Obj. 2, 3, 7)**

   a. Write a résumé and an application letter for a job you would like to have. Use information compiled in Applications 1 and 2 to identify information that should be included in the résumé and application letter. Make the assumption you prefer:

      • You are applying for an immediate part-time job.

      • You are applying for a full-time job for next summer.

      • You are applying for a cooperative education assignment or internship.

      • You are applying for a full-time job immediately after you graduate. Look at the list of courses you plan to take and write as though you had taken them and satisfied the requirements for a degree.

      Follow the guidelines presented in this chapter for preparing a résumé. As a minimum, incorporate the valid comments of at least two others competent in proofreading and résumé design. Use the desktop publishing capability available to you to produce a highly effective, professional document.

   b. Prepare an electronic résumé from the traditional résumé you just designed.

4. **Preparing an Effective Application Letter for a Scholarship (Obj. 7)**
   Assume that a $1,500 scholarship for students in your major field of study has been advertised in *Business Week*. The money comes from a national honor society in your discipline. The recipient must (a) have a B or higher grade average, (b) have more than 60 hours of college credit, (c) be free to attend a week-long, expenses-paid convention in Houston during the second week of May, and (d) write a satisfactory letter of application. Address your application letter to The Scholarship Foundation, 301 Skinner Boulevard, St. Louis, MO 63155-3038.

5. **Designing an On-line Résumé (Obj. 6)**
   Sketch the information you would include on the first page of a personal web site containing your résumé. Brainstorm about the types of information you might include in links to additional qualifications. Use a template in a high-level word processing program to create your web site if your instructor directs you to do so.

6. **Conducting an Electronic Job Search (Obj. 5)**
   Complete the "Real-Time Internet Case" for this chapter to explore job opportunities in your field.

REAL-TIME INTERNET CASE

Harnessing the Power of the Net to Locate a Job

Many reasons exist for harnessing the "power of the Net" for job searching.

1. *Networking.* The Internet is the world's largest network, so use its reach to your advantage. Get to know people both locally and distant to you. Spend time in e-mail and develop personal relationships with people in your field of interest. Once you have made contacts, they become good sources of job leads.

2. *Free information access.* Why wait for the information you need to make it into print? You can access hundreds of free resources with thousands of job listings, help for writing résumés and cover letters, and powerful interview tips. Although some services charge a fee, a massive volume of free materials is available on-line.

3. *Round-the-clock availability.* Many job seekers cannot search for work during regular business hours because of current work schedules or other responsibilities. The Internet is available to you when you are ready to use it.

4. *World-wide access.* If you desire to locate in another city or state, or even another country, you do not need to wait until you actually arrive in your new location to begin your search for employment, housing, and services. The cost of long-distance telephone calls and subscriptions to out-of-town newspapers can be saved by browsing the Internet.

   An effective Internet job search will start out broad and narrow as you progress. Bear in mind that part of

Internet job searching is having the patience and persistence to drill down through a series of web links to find the information you want.[34]

Internet Exploration and Evaluation

1. Locate the web page of an organization for whom you would like to work. Print the page. Does the web page provide information about job vacancies? Does it invite résumé postings? How effectively is the company using its web page for recruiting applicants? Report your findings to the class.

2. Locate a web site for posting employment résumés. Print the page. How much help is provided to the job applicant in designing the résumé and preparing it for posting? What is the cost of the posting? How long is the posting maintained? Send an e-mail message to your instructor reporting what you found.

3. Locate the on-line résumé of a job applicant in your chosen field. Print it out. Is the résumé effectively designed? Are linked files used, and if so, do they enhance the candidate's appeal? Write a one-page critique of the résumé, pointing out the strengths and weaknesses.

4. Visit one of the career sites such as the Riley Guide or What Color Is Your Parachute. What types of career guidance information are available? Print the page of a resource that you believe will be beneficial to you as you search for a job. Outline a plan for utilizing electronic means of job searching.

CHAPTER FOURTEEN

Interviewing for a Job and Preparing Employment Messages

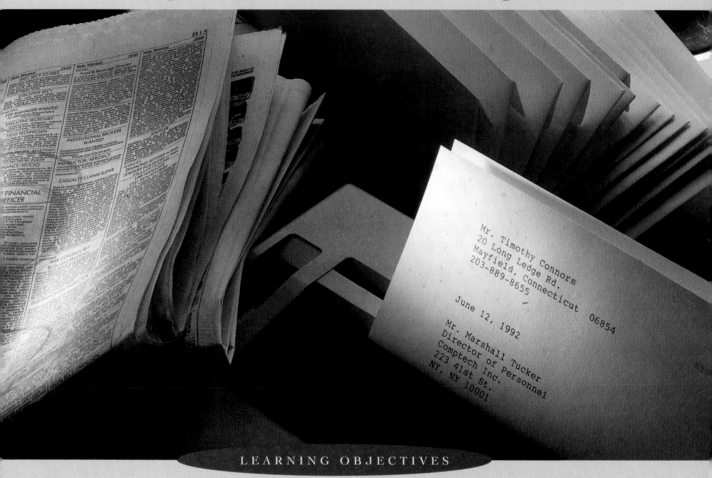

When you have completed Chapter 14, you will be able to:

1 *Explain the nature of structured, unstructured, computer-assisted, group, and stress interviews.*

2 *Explain the steps in the interview process.*

3 *Prepare effective answers to questions often asked in job interviews and questions that will communicate initiative to an interviewer.*

4 *Recognize and bypass illegal interview questions.*

5 *Write effective letters related to employment (follow-up, thank-you, job-acceptance, job-refusal, resignation, and recommendation request) and complete application forms accurately.*

6 *Write positive and negative recommendations that are legally defensible.*

*Q*uestions race through your mind as you prepare for your on-site interview. How can I convince them that I am the best person for the job? Should I ask this or that question? What about the interview and evaluation process? Do the same rules and procedures apply at the corporate office that applied on campus, and will the same techniques work there? The following corporate officers share some of their ideas for what you should do before, during, and after the interview to improve your chances at this phase of the selection:

Ramona Frazier, corporate manager of human resources for the Woolworth Corporation, suggests that for the second interview with an employer you should continue to research the company, even more thoroughly than you did for your campus interview. She further cautions that one of the biggest stumbling blocks to interview success is overconfidence. "You are now up against the cream of the crop, so prepare for the competition."[1] James J. Howard, manager of human resources administration for the Ford Foundation, advises researching your company in *The Wall Street Journal*, *Business Week*, *Fortune*, *Moody's* and *Standard and Poor's* for answers to such questions as, Is the company expanding abroad? Are they downsizing, and if so, in what geographic or professional areas? What are the current "hot issues" in the organization that may affect you in the long run?

Cassandra Bivens, IBM's program director for executive recruiting, emphasizes the importance of enthusiasm in the interview. When advising candidates, she says: "Don't downplay the importance of the on-site interview, and don't relax too much. You should be just as pumped up for the second interview as you were for the first."[2]

Corporate interviewers universally agree that the old saying "You never get a second chance to make a first impression" is certainly true. And standard advice concerning conservative business dress, impeccable grooming, honesty, and courtesy certainly still applies. No matter how friendly or open the interviewer may seem, remember that you are constantly being assessed. Remember also your role in assessment: The interview is your opportunity to form an impression of the company, its culture, and your future supervisors and coworkers.[3]

① *Explain the nature of structured, unstructured, computer-assisted, group, and stress interviews.*

Types of Employment Interviews

Most companies conduct various types of interviews before hiring a new employee. The number and type of interviews vary among companies. Typically, however, applicants begin with a screening interview, an in-depth interview, an on-site interview with multiple interviewers, and sometimes a stress interview. Depending on the goals of the interviewer, interviews may follow a structured or an unstructured approach.

Structured Interviews

In a **structured interview**, generally used in the screening process, the interviewer follows a predetermined agenda, including a checklist of items or a series of questions and statements designed to elicit the necessary information or interviewee reaction. Because each applicant answers the same questions, the interviewer has comparable data to evaluate. A particular type of structured interview is the behavior-based interview, in which applicants are asked to give specific examples of occasions in which they demonstrated particular behaviors or skills. The interviewer already knows what skills, knowledge, and qualities successful candidates must possess. The examples you provide will allow him or her to determine whether you possess them.[4]

Companies are finding computer-assisted interviews to be a reliable and effective way to conduct screening interviews. Applicants use a computer to provide answers to a list of carefully selected questions. A computer-generated report provides standard, reliable information about each applicant that enables an interviewer to decide whether to invite the applicant for a second interview. The report flags any contradictory responses (e.g., an applicant indicated he was terminated for absenteeism but later indicated that he thought his former employer would give him an outstanding recommendation), highlights any potential problem areas (e.g., an applicant responded that she would remain on the job less than a year), and generates a list of structured interview questions for the interviewer to ask (e.g., "Lorna, you said you feel your former employer would rate you average. Why don't you feel it would be higher?").

Research has shown that applicants prefer computer interviews to human interviews, respond more honestly to a computer, and are less likely to provide polite, socially acceptable responses.[5] Because expert computer systems can overcome some of the inherent problems with traditional face-to-face interviews, the overall quality of the selection process improves. Typical human errors include forgetting to ask important questions, talking too much, being reluctant to ask sensitive questions, forming unjustified negative first impressions, obtaining unreliable and illegal information that makes an applicant feel judged, and using interview data ineffectively. Regardless of whether the interview is face-to-face or computer assisted, you will need to provide objective, truthful evidence of your qualifications as they relate to specific job requirements.

Unstructured Interviews

An **unstructured interview** is a freewheeling exchange and may shift from one subject to another, depending on the interests of the participants. Some experienced interviewers are able to make a structured interview seem unstructured. The goal of many unstructured interviews is to explore unknown areas to determine the applicant's ability to speak comfortably about a wide range of topics.

Why have unstructured interviews decreased in popularity in recent years?

Stress Interview

A **stress interview** is designed to place the interviewee in an anxiety-producing situation so an evaluation of the interviewee's performance under stress may be made.

In all cases, interviewees should attempt to assess the nature of the interview quickly and adjust behavior accordingly. Understanding that interviewers sometimes deliberately create anxiety to assess your ability to perform under stress should help you handle such interviews more effectively. As the following discussion of different interviewer styles reveals, you, as an interviewee, can perform much better when you understand the interviewer's purpose.

Group Interviews

As organizations have increased emphasis on team approaches to management and problem solving, selecting employees who best fit their cultures and styles has become especially important. Involving key people in the organization in the candidate selection process has led to new interview styles. In a series interview, the candidate meets individually with a number of different interviewers. Each interviewer will likely ask questions from a differing perspective; for instance, a line manager may ask questions related to the applicant's knowledge of specific job tasks while the vice president of operations may ask questions related to the applicant's career goals. Some questions will likely be asked more than once in the process. A popular trend in organizations that desire a broad range of input in the hiring decision but want to avoid the drawn-out nature of series interviews is to conduct team interviews. The accompanying Strategic Forces box provides additional information about group interviews.

Video Interviews

Why is a face-to-face interview preferred for the final selection interview?

Many companies, ranging from IBM, Microsoft, Nike, and Hallmark Cards, are now screening candidates through video interviews from remote locations and saving money and time in the process. Video interviews (also referred to as *virtual interviews*) conducted via videoconferencing technology is a more productive use of a recruiter's valuable time. Positions are filled quickly after interviewing applicants from around the world and achieved with a 15 to 20 percent reduction in travel costs.[6] Many companies replay the taped interviews to "take another look at a candidate."[7] The general consensus is that the video interview is excellent for screening applicants, but a "live interview" is appropriate for the important final interview.

Many companies have direct hookups with the career services centers of colleges and universities to interview students. These virtual interviews allow students to meet large companies who typically would not visit colleges with small applicant pools and to interview with companies who could not travel because of financial constraints or other reasons.[8] Students simply sit in front of a camera, dial in, and interview with multiple interviewers; in some cases, several applicants are interviewed simultaneously. Some photocopy stores are now equipped for video interviews. Companies and executive search firms use higher quality systems set up in specially equipped rooms for middle-level and senior management jobs.

As you would imagine, some candidates that would interview well in person may fail on camera. Because of the additional pressure of functioning under the glare of a camera, videoconferencing is an excellent method to screen out candidates who cannot work under pressure. Likewise, a candidate who can't operate the controls would likely be eliminated from a highly technical position.[9]

Strategic Forces: Team Environment

The Team Interview: What to Do When the Interviewer Turns Out to Be a Team

Today, the hiring process is often a team effort. Once a hiring manager has identified a need, it is likely that Human Resources (HR) will pull together a team to fill it. Seven is a common number, but these teams are often larger, depending on the position to be filled. A team usually has an HR facilitator, employees who will work with the individual, the hiring manager, a peer of the hiring manager, subordinates of the position, and experts in the position's field. After the job description is developed, the team meets to discuss other attributes of the job, such as leadership and interpersonal skills. While HR screens the résumés using the job description and the desired attributes, the team develops questions to use in one or more of the team interviews. HR circulates the résumés to the hiring team that best match the job requirements; the team reviews them individually and collaboratively to identify the candidates to be invited for a team interview.

As the interview begins, the facilitator explains the interview process to the candidate; then the team spends several hours asking the questions that had been determined earlier. After the interview, the group discusses the candidate's performance and makes notes before moving to the next candidate. After all candidates have completed the interview, the group discusses the results and determines to whom, if any, to offer the job or to ask back for an additional interview. Using the group selection process, the "right" person for the job usually emerges quickly.[10]

In groups of three as assigned by your instructor, visit the following web sites to learn more about the team interview; then complete the application below.

http://www.occ.com/occ/NBEW/Interviewer
   Techniques.html
http://www.espan.com/docs/intdiff.html
http://www.dnai.com/~career/ccpan.htm

Application

Working with your group, compare and contrast the team interview and the traditional interview with one interviewer. Outline advice for the applicant for (a) pre-interview preparation, (b) interview behaviors, and (c) the post-interview follow-up.

You should prepare for a video interview differently than you would for a traditional interview. First, suggest a preliminary telephone conversation with the interviewer to establish rapport. Arrive early and acquaint yourself with the equipment; know how to adjust the volume, brightness, and other camera functions so you can adjust the equipment for optimal performance after the interview begins. Second, concentrate on projecting strong nonverbal skills: speak clearly but do not slow down; be certain you are centered in the frame, sit straight; look up, not down; and use gestures to communicate energy and reinforce points, but avoid excessive motion that will appear blurry. Third, realize voices may be out of step with the pictures if there is a lag between the video and audio transmissions. You will need to adjust to the timing (e.g., slow down voice) to avoid interrupting the interviewer.[11]

2 *Explain the steps in the interview process.*

Preparing for an Interview

College students generally schedule on-campus interviews with representatives from various business organizations. Following the on-campus interviews, successful candidates often are invited for further interviews on the company premises. The purpose of the second interview is to give executives and administrators other than the personnel interviewer an opportunity to appraise the candidate. Whether on campus or on company premises, interview methods and practices apply to the situation. When the interview is with company executives, the candidate will probably encounter a wide variety of interview styles. Preliminary planning can pay rich dividends.

Pre-interview planning involves learning something about the company or organization, doing some studying about yourself, and making sure your appearance and mannerisms will not detract from the impression you hope to make.

Study the Company

Nothing can hurt the candidate more than knowing little about the organization. No knowledge probably indicates insincerity, and the interviewer does not want to waste precious interview time providing the candidate with information that should have been gathered long before.

Companies that have publicly traded stock are required to publish annual reports. Many business school libraries have a file of annual reports and several financial service reports. Other information can be obtained from the printed and electronic sources you consulted when preparing the company/job profile discussed in Chapter 13. Employees of the company or other students who have been interviewed may be of help to the interviewee. Some universities have prepared videotape interviews with various company recruiters and make the tapes available to students. Pertinent information needed to be prepared for an interview includes the following about the company and the job sought:

Company Information. Be sure to research the following on the companies with whom you interview:

- *Name.* Know, for example, that *Exxon* was a computer-generated name selected in the 1970s to identify the merged identity of an old, established oil company.
- *Status in the industry.* Know the company's share of the market, its Fortune 500 standing if any, its sales, and its number of employees.
- *Latest stock market quote.*
- *Recent news and developments.* Read current business periodicals for special feature articles on the company, its new products, and its corporate leadership.
- *Scope of the company.* Is it local, national, or international?
- *Corporate officers.* Know the names of the chairperson, president, and chief executive officer.
- *Products and services.*

Job Information. Be sure to know the following about the job you are seeking:

- *Job title.* Know the job titles of typical entry-level positions.
- *Job qualifications.* Understand the specific knowledge and skills desired.

- ***Probable salary range.***
- ***Career path of the job.*** Are opportunities for advancement available?

Study Yourself

When you know something about the company, you will also know something about the kinds of jobs or training programs the company has to offer. Next, review your answers to the company/job profile (Figure 13-1). This systematic comparison of your qualifications and job requirements helped you identify pertinent information (strengths or special abilities) to be included in your résumé. If you cannot see a relationship between you and the job or company, you may have difficulty demonstrating the interest or sincerity needed to sell yourself.

What three points could you use to persuade an interviewer you are right for the job? Refer to the company/job profile information presented in Chapter 13.

Plan Your Appearance

An employment interviewer once said that if the job applicant did not meet her *extremities* test, the interview might as well not take place. The applicant's personal appearance is critical; fingernails must be clean and neat, shoes shined, or at least clean, and the hair clean and well groomed. This interviewer felt that if the candidate did not take care of those items, the candidate could not really be serious about, or fit into, her organization. General guidelines include being clean and well groomed and avoiding heavy makeup and large, excessive jewelry. Select conservative clothes, and be certain clothing is clean, unwrinkled, and fits properly. Additionally, avoid smoking, drinking, or wearing heavy cologne prior to the interview.

You can locate a wealth of information on appropriate interview dress from the numerous electronic and printed sources (many are listed in Chapter 13). Additionally, talk with professors in your field, professors of professional protocol (business etiquette), personnel at the career services center, and graduates who have recently acquired jobs in your field. Research the company dress code—real or implied—ahead of time. If you *look* and *dress* like the people who already work at the company, the interviewer will be able to visualize your working there.

Plan Your Time

One of the worst things you can do is be late for an interview. If something should happen to prevent your arriving on time, telephone an apology. Another mistake is to miss the interview entirely. Plan your time so that you will arrive early so you can unwind and review mentally the things you plan to accomplish. Be sure to bring a professional portfolio that contains everything you will need during the interview. These items might include copies of your résumé, a list of references and/or recommendations, a professional-looking pen, paper for taking notes, highlights of what you know about the company, a list of questions you plan to ask, and previous correspondence with the company.

Practice

The job interview may be the most important face-to-face interaction you ever have. You will be selling yourself in competition with others. How you listen and how you talk are characteristics the interviewer will be able to measure. Your actions, your mannerisms, and your appearance will combine to give the total picture of how you are perceived. Added to the obvious things you have acquired from your education, experience, and activities, your interview performance can give a skilled interviewer an excellent picture of you. Practicing for an interview will help you learn to handle the nervousness that is natural when interviewing. Practice is what you want to do; do not memorize verbatim answers that will sound rehearsed and insincere. Instead, think carefully about how your accomplishments match the job requirements and practice communicating these ideas smoothly, confidently, and professionally. The section "Presenting Your Qualifications" that appears later in this chapter will provide suggestions for preparing for standard interview questions and other interview issues. Once you are satisfied you have identified your key selling points, have a friend ask you interview questions you have developed and surprise you with others. Participate in mock interviews with a friend or someone in Career Services, alternating roles as interviewer and interviewee. Then follow each practice interview with a constructive critique of your performance.

Conducting a Successful Interview

The way you handle an interview will vary somewhat depending on your stage in the hiring process. Regardless of whether you are being screened by a campus recruiter or have progressed to an on-site visit, an interview will have three parts: the opening formalities, an information exchange, and the close.

The Opening Formalities

Larry Hayes, president of Hayes Marketing Communication, emphasizes that skills missing during the interview are important because he assumes these same deficiencies will carry over during employment. "The good and the bad are obvious in the first five to ten seconds,"says Hayes.[12] Clearly, if the impression created during the first few seconds of an interview often determines the outcome, you cannot afford to take time to warm up in an interview. You must come in the door selling yourself!

Common courtesies and confident body language can contribute to a favorable first impression in the early few seconds when you have not yet had an opportunity to talk about your qualifications:

- ***Use the interviewer's correct name and pronounce it correctly.*** Even if the interviewer calls you by your first name, always use the interviewer's surname unless specifically invited to do otherwise.

- ***Apply a firm handshake.*** Usually, the interviewer will initiate the handshake, although you may do so. In either case, apply a firm handshake. You do not want to leave the impression that you are weak or timid. At the same time, you do not want to overdo the firm grip and leave an impression of being overbearing.

- ***Wait for the interviewer to ask you to be seated.***

- ***Maintain appropriate eye contact, and use your body language to convey confidence.*** Sit erect and lean forward slightly to express interest. Avoid slouching, chewing gum, and fidgeting in order to convey a professional image.

- ***Be conscious of nonverbal messages.*** If the interviewer's eyes are glazing over, end your answer, but expand it if they are bright and the head is nodding vigorously. If the interviewer is from a different culture, be conscious of subtle differences in nonverbal communication that could affect the interviewer's perception of you. For example, a North American interviewer who sees eye contact as a sign of trust may perceive an Asian female who keeps her eyes lowered as a sign of respect to be uninterested or not listening. Women should also be aware of typical "feminine behavior" during the interview. For instance, women nod more often than men when an interviewer speaks. Women are also likely to smile more and have a rising intonation at the end of sentences; such behaviors can convey a subservient attitude.[13]

Following the introductions, the interviewer will begin the conversation with nonbusiness talk to help you relax and to set the stage for the information exchange portion of the interview. Other interviewers may bypass these casual remarks and move directly into the interview.

The Information Exchange

Much of the information about you will appear on your résumé or application form and is already available to the interviewer. Thus, the interviewer most likely will seek to go beyond such facts as your education, work experience, and extracurricular activities. He or she will attempt to assess your attitudes toward work and the probability of your fitting successfully into the organization.

Presenting Your Qualifications. Your preparation pays off during the interview. Like a defense attorney ready to win a case, you are ready to present evidence that you should be hired. According to Kennedy & Morrow, leading career consultants, your case will have three major points: You must convince the interviewer that you (1) can do the job, (2) will do the job, and (3) will not stress out everyone else while doing the job.[14] That's an overwhelming task. Where do you begin? You learned during your study of persuasive writing that saying you're the best salesperson (supply other skills) is not convincing. To convince an interviewer to allow you to continue to the next interview or to extend you a job offer, you must provide specific, concrete evidence that your qualifications match the job description. Use the following guidelines to help you relate your skills and knowledge to the job.

③ *Prepare effective answers to questions often asked in job interviews and questions that will communicate initiative to an interviewer.*

- ***List five or six key points that you want to emphasize.*** Likely, you will want to present your education as a major asset. You should point out its relationship to the job for which you are being considered. Even more important, the fact that you have succeeded in academics indicates that you have the ability to learn. Because most companies expect you to learn something on the job, your ability to learn and thus quickly become productive may be your greatest asset. So your most important response to the interviewer's questions may be about your ability to learn. Even lack of work experience may be an asset: You have acquired no bad work habits that you will have to unlearn.

  Additionally, be sure to provide evidence of your interpersonal skills. Communicate that you can get along with others and are sensitive to diversity.

What personal abilities and skills would you emphasize in a job interview?

  - What did you do in college that helped you get along with others?
  - Were you a member, an officer, or president of an organization?
  - In regard to your organization, what did you accomplish? How did others perceive you? Were you a leader? How did your followers respond to your leadership style?
  - Can you organize projects?

  The extracurricular activities listed on your résumé give an indication of these traits, but how you talk about them in your interview helps. "I started as corresponding secretary and was subsequently elected to higher office for four semesters, eventually becoming president" may be a statement that proves your leadership qualities. If you can show your organization moved to greater heights, all the more power to you. You can also use questions about your extracurricular activities to show that you have broad, balanced interests rather than a single, time-consuming avocation that could lead to burnout and stress if carried to the job.

What are other skills that graduating students need to succeed in a cross-cultural, interdependent workforce? When Andersen Consulting learned that its top consultants did not have the firm's highest grade-point averages and SAT scores, they changed their long-time emphasis on grades. The ability to juggle a complicated schedule was found to be very important in their study of job-success factors. Now applicants who hold a part-time job and take part in at least two extracurricular activities while maintaining good grades are rated most highly.[15] While participating in a focus group, CEOs generated the following list of job success traits:[16]

Is it possible for a candidate to interview too well?

- People skills (friendly, clean, proper attitude, willingness to respond quickly, interested in people).
- Leadership communication skills (written and oral).
- Team player.
- Ability to see the clients'/customers' perspective.
- Computer and Internet proficiency.
- High degree of motivation, innovation/creativity, flexibility, and adaptability.

Consider these general job success traits and then use your knowledge of the job requirements and your own strengths to develop your "central selling features." These key points targeted to your audience is the central element of a winning argument: *You are able and willing to add value to a company.*

- *Be prepared to answer standard interview questions.* These questions are designed to show (a) why you want the job, (b) why you want to work for this organization, and (c) why the company should want you. Many of the career sites and printed sources discussed in Chapter 13 include lists of frequently asked interview questions; some sources provide suggested answers to the more difficult questions. Research these sites thoroughly. The following samples illustrate the general nature of the questions.

  - Tell us about yourself.
  - What are your career plans (long-term and short-term)? What do you see yourself doing in five years?
  - What are some of the factors that led you to choose your college major? Your college/university? When did you choose your college major? What courses did you like least? Best? Explain.
  - How do you spend your spare time? What are your hobbies? What do you do to keep in good physical condition?
  - What are your greatest strengths? Weaknesses?
  - Describe the characteristics of an individual whom you especially admire.
  - What is important to you in a job? What interests you most about this job?
  - What do you know about opportunities in the field in which you are trained? What do you think determines a person's progress in an organization?
  - What do you know about our company? Why do you want to work for us?
  - Why should we hire you? What qualifications do you have that make you feel that you should be hired over others?

Projecting a confident, mentally alert impression through your speech and appearance from the moment you walk into an interview is vital because most interview decisions are made in the first four minutes. Be prepared to provide *quick, intelligent* responses to questions about your education and experiences that require you to apply skills learned in the classroom.

- What do you think are the real qualifications for this job? How do your qualifications compare to the job requirements?
- What are your salary expectations?

- ***Be prepared to answer behavioral questions.*** These questions are designed to challenge you to provide real evidence of your skills or the behaviors required to perform the job. More and more interviewers are finding that asking for specific examples to illustrate their answers is a more objective way for evaluating an applicant's skills. Asking "feel-good" questions help an interviewer decide how they feel about an applicant, but such questions cannot show whether the applicant can perform the job, or work well with difficult people, lead teams, or organize projects.[17] Examples of behavioral questions follow:

  - Describe a time when you (a) worked well under pressure, (b) worked effectively with others, (c) organized a major project, (d) motivated and led others, (e) solved a difficult problem, and (f) accepted constructive criticism.
  - What was the most difficult problem you had to overcome in your last job (or an academic or extracurricular activity)? How did you cope with it?
  - Tell me about a time you had difficulty working with a supervisor or co-worker (professor, peer in a team in a class setting). How did you handle the situation?
  - Describe something you have done that shows initiative and willingness to work.
  - How have your extracurricular activities, part-time work experience, or volunteer work prepared you for work in our company?
  - Tell me about a time you hit a wall trying to push forward a great idea.

  To prepare for answering behavioral questions, brainstorm to identify stories that illustrate how your qualifications fit the job requirements. These stories should show you applying the skills needed on the job. Career counselors recommend using the STAR method (**S**ituation or **T**ask/**A**ction/**R**esult) as a consistent format to help you present a complete answer to these open-ended questions. You first describe a situation or task you were involved in, the action you took, and finally the result of your effort.[18] Even if the interviewer doesn't ask behavioral questions, you can use this approach when answering standard interview questions.

Select one of the listed behavioral questions and structure your personal response to it, using the STAR method. Share your response with a classmate.

- **Be prepared to demonstrate logical thinking and other characteristics.**
  Many companies ask applicants to solve brainteasers and riddles, create art out
  of paper bags, solve complex business problems, and even spend a day acting as
  managers of fictitious companies. These techniques are used to gauge an applicant's ability to think quickly and creatively and observe an emotional response
  to an awkward situation. For example, when asked to calculate how long it
  would take to move Mount Fuji, an applicant asked for the height and diameter
  of the mountain, calculated the volume of a cone (she knew the formula), estimated how many cubic tons of rocks make up Mount Fuji, continued to make
  guesses about her pertinent variables. She finally told the interviewer she felt
  the math calculations were too complex to work without a calculator. The important point is that she didn't have to provide the right answer. Her brave and
  imaginative attempt to answer the question took her to the next round of interviews.[19] You cannot anticipate this type of interview question, but you can familiarize yourself with mind teasers that have been used. Most importantly,
  however, recognize the interviewer's purpose, relax, and do your best to showcase your logical reasoning, creativity, or your courage to even try.

- **Display a professional attitude.** First, communicate your sincere interest
  in the company; show that you are strongly interested in the company and not
  just taking an interview for practice. Reveal your knowledge of the company
  gained through reading published information and refer to the people you
  have talked with about the working conditions, company achievements, and
  career paths.

  Second, focus on the satisfaction gained from contributing to a company
  rather than the benefits you will receive. What's important in a job goes beyond
  financial reward. All applicants are interested in a paycheck; any job satisfies
  that need—some will pay more, some less. Recognize that the paycheck is a
  part of the job and should not be your primary concern. Intrinsic rewards such
  as personal job satisfaction, the feeling of accomplishment, and making a contribution to society are ideas to discuss in the interview. You should like what
  you are doing and find a challenging job that will satisfy these needs.

  Third, display humility. If you are being interviewed by a representative of a
  successful company, do not suggest that you can turn the company around.
  Similarly, telling an interviewer you have no weaknesses could make you sound
  shallow and deceptive. Instead, mention a weakness that can be perceived as a
  strength, preferably a "weakness" that a company wants. Indicate that you occasionally become overcommitted to extracurricular activities (assuming your
  résumé includes a high level of extracurricular participation *and* a strong academic record). If you're applying for a job that involves detail, confess that you
  are a perfectionist or that you are a workaholic.[20]

- **Be prepared to discuss salary and benefits.** For most entry-level positions,
  the beginning salary is fixed. However, if you have work experience, excellent
  scholarship records, or added maturity, you may be able to obtain a higher
  salary. The interviewer should initiate the salary topic. What you should know is
  the general range for candidates with your qualifications so that your response
  to a question about how much you would expect is reasonable. If your qualifications are about average for the job, you can indicate that you would expect to
  be paid the going rate or within the normal range. If you have added qualifications, you might say, "With my two years of work experience, I would expect to
  start at the upper end of the normal salary range."

What weaknesses do you have that you could share with an interviewer? How would you word your remarks?

If you have other job offers, you are in a position to compare salaries, jobs, and companies. In this case, you may suggest to the interviewer that you would expect a competitive salary and that you have been offered X dollars by another firm. If salary has not been mentioned, and you really want to know about it, simply ask courteously how much the salary would be for someone with your qualifications. In any case, though, if you really believe the job offers the nonmonetary benefits you seek, do not attempt to make salary a major issue.

Typically, an interviewer will introduce the subject of benefits without your asking about them. In some cases, a discussion of total salary and "perks" (perquisites) is reserved for a follow-up interview. If nothing has been said about certain benefits, you should take the liberty of asking, particularly when an item may be especially important to you. Health insurance, for example, may be very important when you have children. Retirement planning, however, is less appropriate for a new graduate to discuss.

- ***Be knowledgeable of interview questions that might lead to discriminatory hiring.*** The types of illegal (or potentially illegal) interview questions and ways to handle them are described in the Strategic Forces box that follows.

4 *Recognize and bypass illegal interview questions.*

Asking Questions of the Interviewer. Both the interviewer and interviewee must know as much as possible about each other before making a commitment in order to increase the likelihood that the relationship will be lengthy and mutually beneficial. A good way to determine whether the job is right for you is to ask *pertinent* questions.

Good questions show the interviewer that you have initiative and are interested in making a well-informed decision. For that reason, be certain not to say, "I don't have any questions." Focus on questions that help you gain information about the company and the job that you could not learn from published sources or persons other than the interviewer. Do not waste the interviewer's time asking questions that show you are unprepared for the interview (for example, questions about the company's scope, products/services, job requirements, new developments). Having committed a block of uninterrupted time to talk to you, the interviewer will resent this blatant lack of commitment and respect for the company. Avoid questions about salary and benefits that imply you are interested more in money than in the contribution you can make.

To show further initiative, introduce questions throughout the interview whenever appropriate rather than waiting until you are asked whether you have questions. This approach will promote positive two-way interaction and should create a relaxed, unintimidating atmosphere. Just remember that the *interviewer* is in charge of the interview. Add your own questions to the typical interviewee questions that follow:

- What is a typical day like in this job?
- What type of people would I be working with (peers) and for (supervisors)?
- Why do you need someone for this job (why can this job not be done by a current employee)?
- What circumstances led to the departure of the person I would be replacing? What is the turnover rate of people in this job? (or, How many people have held this job in the past five years?)
- To an interviewer who has worked for the company for an extended time: Why do you continue to work for this company?
- Would you describe the initial training program for people in this position?

Strategic Forces: Legal and Ethical Constraints

Handling Illegal Interview Questions

The Equal Employment Opportunity Commission (EEOC) and Fair Employment Practices Guidelines have made it clear that an employer cannot legally discriminate against a job applicant on the basis of race, color, gender, age (40 to 70), religion, national origin, or disability. As an interviewee, you must be aware of interview questions that may directly or indirectly seek information that could promote discriminatory hiring. Interviewers must restrict questions to an applicant's ability to perform specific job-related functions essential to the job sought. Generally, the following topics should *not* be introduced during an interview or during the small talk that precedes or follows an interview:

- **National origin and religion.** "You have an unusual accent; where were you born?" "What religious holidays will require you to miss work?"

- **Age.** "I see you attended Central State University; what years were you there?" "Could you provide a copy of your birth certificate?"

- **Disabilities, health conditions, and physical characteristics not reasonably related to the job.** "Do you have a disability that would interfere with your ability to perform the job?" "Have you ever been injured on the job?" "Have you ever filed workers' compensation?" Specific questions about health are improper because an employer may conclude that an applicant has a disability. Thus, an interviewer cannot ask, "What is your general state of health?" "How many days were you sick last year?" "Have you ever had a major illness?" "Have you ever been treated by a psychiatrist?" "How much alcohol do you drink each week?" "What prescription drugs are you currently taking?"

- **Marital status, spouse's employment, or dependents.** "Are you married?" "Who is going to watch your children if you work for us?" "Do you plan to have children?" "Is your spouse employed?" "Do you realize that this job requires a great deal of travel and may require you to relocate?" Employers may not

ask the names or relationships of people with whom you live.

- **Arrests or criminal convictions that are not related to the job.** "Have you ever been arrested other than for traffic violations? If so, explain." Keep in mind that the arrest/conviction record of a person applying for a job as a law enforcement officer or a teacher could be highly relevant to the job, but the same information could be illegal for a person applying for a job as an engineer.

Because some interviewers ask illegal interview questions because of a lack of training or an accidental slip, you must decide how you will handle potential illegal questions. You can refuse to answer and inform the interviewer that the question is improper (e.g., "You can't ask me if I have young children"). Of course, you risk offending or embarrassing the interviewer. A second option is to answer the question knowing it is illegal and your answer is not related to the job requirements. This response is more likely to keep you in the running for the job; but you may feel that you have compromised important principles.

Rather than answer an illegal question directly or bluntly refuse to answer, provide a low-key response such as "How does this question relate to how I will do my job?" or simply answer the legitimate concern that probably lies behind the illegal question. For example, an interviewer who asks, "Do you plan to have children?" is probably concerned about how long you might remain on the job. An answer to this concern would be "I plan to pursue a career regardless of whether I decide to raise a family." The interviewer who asks, "Have you ever been arrested other than for traffic violations?" is probably concerned about employee dishonesty. An appropriate answer to this concern is "Nothing I have ever done would give you any concern that I would breach your company's trust." If you can see no legitimate concern in a question, such as "Do you own your own home, rent, or live with your parents?" answer, "I'm not sure how that question relates to the job. Can you explain?"[21]

---

continued

Application

In small groups discuss illegal interview questions that your group may have been asked during a job interview, or discuss several of the questions mentioned in your text (e.g., "Do you have small children?" "How many days were you sick last year?" "Do you have a current or past medical problem?"). How did the group member handle the illegal question and what were the consequences of the answer? What suggestions can the group offer for handling the question more effectively? Do you think managers ask illegal questions purposely or accidentally (question just came out, or manager lacked training or knowledge of legalities)? What consequences does a company face when applicants believe illegal interview questions led to discriminatory hiring? Discuss examples of real companies involved in this dilemma.

- What types of ongoing employee in-service training programs do you provide?
- How much value does your firm place on a master's degree?
- How do you feel this field has changed in the past ten years? How do you feel it will change in the next ten years?
- What advice do you wish you had been given when you were starting out?
- Do you have any questions about my qualifications?
- When can I expect to hear from you about your decision?

The Closing

The interviewer will provide cues indicating that the interview is completed by rising or making a comment about the next step to be taken. At that point, do not prolong the interview needlessly. Simply rise, accept the handshake, thank the interviewer for the opportunity to meet, and close by saying you look forward to hearing from the company. The neatness with which you close the interview may be almost as important as the first impression you made. Be enthusiastic. If you really want the job, you might ask for it.

Preparing Other Employment Messages

Preparing a winning résumé and application letter is an important first step in a job search. To expedite your job search, you may need to write other employment letters: send a follow-up letter to a company that does not respond to your résumé, send a thank-you letter after an interview, complete an application form, accept a job offer, reject other job offers, and communicate with references. A career change will require a carefully written resignation letter.

5 *Write effective letters related to employment (follow-up, thank-you, job-acceptance, job-refusal, resignation, and recommendation requests) and complete application forms accurately.*

Follow-Up Letters

When an application letter and résumé do not elicit a response, a follow-up letter may bring results. Sent a few weeks after the original letter, it includes a reminder that an application for a certain job is on file, presents additional education or

Be clean, polished, and well presented when you arrive for your interview, at least ten minutes early. When answering questions, be brief but make sure to get your point across. Sometimes a yes or no answer will suffice. Always be upbeat, bright, cheerful, and never tired. Smile when possible, as personality counts a great deal in a job interview.

Ask questions. Asking questions about an area in which you have limited knowledge is a sure sign of intelligence. Remember, any prospective employer would probably like to hire you for life,

not the next 18 months. Therefore, asking long-range questions enhances your qualifications as a good candidate for a position.

Even if it becomes apparent that you are not the person for the job or the company is not you, be cordial, interested, and positive. Although you may not be the right candidate for Company A, you may be just the person for Company B. An interviewer recommending a job candidate to a competitor for possible hiring is not uncommon.

Terence E. McSweeney
Director of Communications
PGA of America

experience accumulated, points out its relationship to the job, and closes with a reference to desired action. In addition to conveying new information, follow-up letters indicate persistence (a quality that impresses some employers). Figure 14-1 shows a good example of a follow-up letter.

Thank-You Letters

After a job interview, a letter of appreciation is a professional courtesy and should be sent promptly. For maximum impact, send a thank-you letter the day of the interview or the following day. Even if during the interview you decided you do not want the job or you and the interviewer mutually agreed that the job is not for you, a thank-you letter is appropriate. As a matter of fact, if you've made a positive impression, interviewers may forward your résumé to others who are seeking qualified applicants.

After an interview has gone well and you think a job offer is a possibility, include these ideas in the letter of appreciation: express gratitude, identify the specific job applied for, refer to some point discussed in the interview (the strength of the interview), and close by making some reference to the expected call or letter that conveys the employer's decision. Specific points to cover are outlined in Figure 14-2.

The résumé, application letter, and thank-you letter should be stored in a computer file and adapted for submission to other firms when needed. Develop a database for keeping a record of the dates on which letters and résumés were sent to certain firms, and answers were received, names of people talked with, facts conveyed, and so on. When an interviewer calls, you can retrieve and view that company's record while you are talking with the interviewer.

Application Forms

Before going to work on a new job, you will almost certainly complete the employer's application and employment forms. Some application forms, especially for applicants

What purposes are served in sending a thank-you letter, even though you expressed thanks after the interview?

FIGURE 14-1
Good example of a
follow-up letter.

98 Lincoln Street
San Antonio, TX 78285-9063
October 23, 1999

Mr. Bryce Gowan
Tatum & Bayne, CPAs
1000 Plaza Court
Austin, TX 78710-1000

Dear Mr. Gowan:

① Recently I applied for an audit staff position at Tatum & Bayne's and now have additional qualifications to report.

② The enclosed, updated résumé shows that I have passed the Auditing and Practice and Law sections of the CPA exam; I will take the final section at the next sitting. In addition, I have finished my last semester of cooperative education experience with Smith & Lewis, CPAs. This realistic work experience has added value to my formal education and confirmed my interest in working as an auditor.

③ Mr. Gowan, I would welcome the opportunity to visit your office and talk more about the contributions I could make as an auditor for Tatum & Bayne. Please write or call me at (512) 555-9823.

Sincerely,

Jeanne Fulton

Jeanne Fulton

Enclosure

① States main idea and clearly identifies the position being sought.

② Refers to the enclosed résumé; summarizes additional qualifications.

③ Assures employer that Jeanne is still interested in the job.

who apply for jobs with a high level of responsibility, are very long. They may actually appear to be tests in which applicants give their answers to hypothetical questions and write defenses for their answers. Increasing numbers of companies are designing employment forms to identify applicants' written communication skills. Review the following guidelines for completing application forms.

- ***Read the entire form before you begin completing it.*** This procedure will prevent you from making careless mistakes caused by not understanding the form. Preparing a rough draft on a photocopy of the form is an excellent idea.
- ***Follow instructions.*** If the form calls for last name first and you write your first name first, the damage could be fatal. If instructions clearly say "Print" and you write cursively instead, you could be stereotyped immediately as a bungler.

FIGURE 14-2
Good example of a thank-you letter.

Deductive Outline for a Thank-You Letter

1. Express appreciation for the interview; identify the interview date and the specific position.
2. Refer to some point discussed in the interview to personalize the letter and to help the interviewer remember this particular interview. Ideally this point should reinforce a notable job-related skill.
3. Submit any information that may have been requested at the interview.
4. Close by referring to the expected call or letter that conveys the interviewer's decision.

98 Lincoln Street
San Antonio, TX 78285-9063
October 23, 1999

Mr. Bryce Gowan
Tatum & Bayne, CPAs
1000 Plaza Court
Austin, TX 78710-1000

❶ States the main idea: appreciation for the interview and information gained.

❶ Thank you for taking the time to talk with me about the auditing position at Tatum & Bayne.

❷ Includes specific points discussed during the interview, increasing the sincerity of the letter and the likelihood the interviewer will remember the applicant.

❷ Our discussion of the diversity of your clients and your plan to open an office in Mexico City was especially appealing. Thus, as you recommended, I have purchased the multimedia culture series and am familiarizing myself with the geography, culture, and economic factors of Latin America.

❸ Assures the employer Jeanne is interested in the job and politely reminds the employer she is awaiting a reply.

❸ Mr. Gowan, I would welcome the opportunity to work with your international clients and to be involved in an exciting and challenging new international venture. I am eager to receive a call from your office next week.

Sincerely,

Jeanne Fulton

Jeanne Fulton

Format Pointers

● Is prepared as a business letter rather than a handwritten note to show that the applicant understands how to communicate in the workplace.
● Is printed with a laser printer on paper that matches the résumé and application letter.

COMMUNICATION IN ACTION

Pamela M. Plager, Allen & Company Incorporated

Pam Plager is someone who knows how to move up in business and has the experience to prove it. Many graduates fresh out of college have several notions about their careers that may be well intended but fall short of being applicable to the real world. Ms. Plager offers advice to students and recent graduates through presentations and lectures. But perhaps more powerful than the advice she gives regarding interview skills, personal appearance, and other practical matters is her own success story.

Pam graduated from college in 1981 with a degree in communication. Because she lived in the small university town of Starkville, Mississippi, she did not immediately find a job in her career field. She began working at her family's department store while contributing photographs for advertisements in the local newspaper. One day, a woman at the newspaper told Pam about her daughter, who had left Starkville for a job in New York as a receptionist, and who had enjoyed her time there and found opportunity for growth in her career. The woman told Pam she should get out of the small town and give New York a try. Immediately, Pam says she had a "gut feeling" that New York was her ticket. So she followed her instincts, took some money out of savings, and flew to New York, not knowing anything about the city, the potential job, or any contacts other than the potential employer.

Pam's instincts were true, and she accepted the modest job. Over the years, she has moved from that position as a receptionist earning $12,500 a year to an executive position at Allen & Company. She learned on the job and on her feet things about business that no class can teach. She states that most of these fundamentals of business are "common sense," but if you are not exposed to the realities of the business climate on a daily basis, they can seem rather alien. For instance, she says that when you accept a position, learn tasks that few other people know how to do and don't want to learn. That way, you have gained a new skill, and others in the company quickly know who you are and come to you for assistance. Another thing she learned and passes on

to others is that you should go beyond your official job description as often as possible. She relates the story of a colleague who frantically appealed to Plager's assistant for help securing coffee for a meeting she was hosting. The assistant refused, stating that it was not in her job description. Pam herself jumped in to help the colleague, serving coffee to top company executives in the meeting, who were impressed with and grateful for Pam's willingness to help out. Besides, she says, you never know when you may be in a similar position one day.

Many times, the real world is different from what we imagine. Students and recent graduates assume that their academic background will secure them a mid- to upper-level position. "Wrong," says Plager. Most graduates can expect stiff competition for entry-level positions. But Plager says that this is not necessarily bad. Having been a receptionist and secretary herself, she believes starting out at that level gave her a strong business foundation to build on. And remember, she says, "You make the job; the job doesn't make you." After starting in an entry-level job, keep your eyes and ears open. Learn the environment and the politics, which are present in every company. Trust your instincts and intuition; learn all you can, and then move from there. Pam adds that the average American worker spends about four years at a job, and that today's college graduates can expect to have four to five careers throughout their working lives. By remembering the "small things"—developing good interviewing skills, networking, remembering people's names, having a good firm handshake, writing thank-you notes—your career can be as successful as you make it.

Applying What You Have Learned

1. According to Plager, what are some things you can do to make an entry-level job a positive step on the ladder to career success?

2. Why does Plager say "small things" are important? List some "small things" you can start working on now.

3. How many careers, according to Plager, can the average college graduate expect to have over a lifetime?

When the form has multiple copies, place the form on a hard surface and put enough pressure on the pen to make the last copy clear. If instructions say, "Do not fold," honor them.

- *Complete forms neatly.* If erasing is necessary, do it cleanly. Such techniques as marking through an original answer and squeezing another, or printing in all-capital letters in some blanks and in capital-and-lowercase letters in others may imply indecisiveness, carelessness, disrespect, or haste. Unless instructions or circumstances forbid, key your answers for a neat, legible document.

- *Answer all questions.* For any questions that do not apply, write "N/A" in the blank. If the form provides space for you to add additional information or make a comment, try to include something worthwhile. Competitors, especially those who habitually do no more than is required of them, will probably leave such spaces blank.

- *Answer questions accurately.* Carry information about courses taken, employment dates, and related experiences in a briefcase or portfolio and take it with you to employment offices and interviews. With a copy of your résumé and application letter in hand, you can make sure all factual statements are consistent with statements on the form. Providing false information would be unethical and impractical. It could result in your being hired for a job you cannot do well or termination in disgrace when the misrepresentation is discovered.

- *Keep a copy.* Save a copy of the application form for future reference. If you complete the application form before the interview, reviewing it prior to the interview could be to your advantage.

Job-Acceptance Letters

A job offer may be extended either by telephone or by letter. If a job offer is extended over the telephone, request that the company send a written confirmation of the job offer. The confirmation should include the job title, salary, benefits, starting date, and anything else negotiated.

Often companies require a written acceptance of a job offer. Note the deductive sequence of the letter shown in Figure 14-3: acceptance, details, and closing (confirms the report-for-work date).

FIGURE 14-3
Good example of a job-acceptance letter.

❶ Begins by stating the main news: job offer is being accepted.

❷ Continues with any necessary details.

❸ Confirms the beginning employment date.

❶ I accept your employment offer as a market analyst. Thank you for responding so quickly after our discussion on Thursday.

❷ As you requested, I have signed the agreement outlining the specific details of my employment. Your copy is enclosed, and I have kept a copy for my records.

❸ If you should need to communicate with me before I report for work on May 14, please call me at 555-6543.

Job-Refusal Letters

Like other messages that convey unpleasant news, job-refusal letters are written inductively: a beginning that reveals the nature of the subject, explanations that lead to a refusal, the refusal, and a pleasant ending. Of course, certain reasons (even though valid in your mind) are better left unsaid: questionable company goals or methods of operation, negative attitude of present employees, possible bankruptcy, unsatisfactory working conditions, and so on. The applicant who prefers not to be specific about the reason for turning down a job might write this explanation:

> After thoughtfully considering job offers received this week, I have decided to accept a job in the actuarial department of an insurance company.

You may want to be more specific about your reasons for refusal when you have a positive attitude toward the company or believe you may want to reapply at some later date. The letter in Figure 14-4 includes the reasons for refusal.

Should the job-refusal letter include the reason for refusing the job?

Resignation Letters

Resigning from a job requires effective communications skill. You may be allowed to "give your notice" in person or be required to write a formal resignation. Your supervisor will inform you of the company's policy. Regardless of whether the resignation is given orally or in writing, show empathy for your employer by giving enough time to allow the employer time to find a replacement.

Because your employer has had confidence in you, has benefitted from your services, and will have to seek a replacement, your impending departure *is* bad news. As such, the letter is written inductively. It calls attention to your job, gives your reasons for leaving it, conveys the resignation, and closes on a positive note (see Figure 14-5).

The memorandum format is appropriate for a resignation because the message is communicated between people *within* a company. However, some writers prefer the letter format to convey this formal message. Hence, this message is commonly referred to as a **resignation letter**.

A resignation letter is not an appropriate instrument for telling executives how a business should be operated. Harshly worded statements could result in immediate termination or cause human relations problems during your remaining working days. Remember, too, that your supervisor may subsequently review the resignation letter just before writing a recommendation letter for you.

❶ I appreciate your spending time with me discussing the loan officer's job.

❷ Thank you for your candid comparison of my background and opportunities in finance and insurance. Having received job offers in both fields, I am now convinced that a career in insurance is more consistent with my aptitudes and goals. Today, I am accepting a job in the actuarial department of States Mutual.

❸ Thank you for the confidence demonstrated by the job offer. When I receive reports of Lincoln's continued success, I will think of the dedicated people who work for the company.

FIGURE 14-4
Good example of a job-refusal letter.

❶ Begins with a neutral but related idea to buffer the bad news.

❷ Presents reasons that lead to the refusal diplomatically.

❸ Ends letter on a positive note that anticipates future association with the company.

FIGURE 14-5
Good example of a resignation letter.

❶ Begins with appreciative comments about job to buffer the bad news.

❷ Presents reasons that lead to the main idea, the resignation.

❸ States the resignation. Includes additional details.

❹ Conveys genuine appreciation for the experience gained at Covin and ends on a cordial note.

SUBJECT: PLEASURE OF SERVING COVIN STORES

❶ My job as manager of Juniors' Apparel for the last two years has been a rewarding experience. It has taught me much about the marketing of clothing and changing preferences in style.

❷ Predicting public acceptance of certain styles has been fascinating. From the time I declared a major in fashion merchandising, I have wanted to become a buyer. Before I accepted my present job in management, that goal was discussed. ❸ Now, it is becoming a reality; I have accepted a job as a buyer for Belton beginning one month from today. If satisfactory with you, I would like May 31 to be my last day as manager here.

❹ This job has allowed me to grow professionally. Thanks to you and others, I have had the privilege of trying new ideas and selecting sales personnel who get along well with one another and with customers. Thank you for having confidence in me, for your positive rapport with the sales staff, and for your expressions of appreciation for my work. As I continue my career in fashion merchandising, I will always recall pleasant memories of my job at Covin.

Recommendation Letters

When a former employee applies for a position with a new firm, the previous employer is frequently called upon to give a recommendation. Letters of recommendation are usually written in response to a request from either the applicant or the company to whom the applicant has applied.

Requesting a Recommendation Letter and Sending a Thank-You Letter. Companies seek information from references at various stages. Some prefer talking with references prior to an interview, and others, after a successful interview. Specific actions on your part will ensure that your references are treated with common courtesy and that references are prepared for the employer's call.

- *Remind the reference that he/she had previously agreed to supply information about you.* Identify the job for which you are applying, give a complete address to which the letter is to be sent, and indicate a date by which the prospective employer needs the letter. Sharing information about job requirements and reporting recent job-related experiences, you may assist the reference in writing an effective letter. Indicate your gratitude, but do not apologize for making the request. The reference has already agreed to write such a letter and will likely take pleasure in assisting a deserving person.

- *Alert the reference of imminent requests for information, especially if considerable time has elapsed since the applicant and reference have last seen each other.* Enclosing a recent résumé and providing any other pertinent information (for example, name change) may enable the reference to write a letter that is specific and convincing. If the job search becomes longer than anticipated, a follow-up letter to references explaining the delay and expressing gratitude for their efforts is appropriate.

- **Send a sincere, original thank-you letter after a position has been accepted.** This thoughtful gesture will build a positive relationship with a person who may continue to be important to your career. The letter in Figure 14-6 is brief and avoids clichés and exaggerated expressions of praise but instead gives specific examples of the importance of the reference's recommendation.

Writing Negative Recommendations. As an employer, you will be asked to write recommendation letters for former employees or others you know in a professional capacity. Almost everyone who asks permission to use your name as a reference will expect your recommendation to be favorable. For a person whom you could not favorably recommend, you have the following options:

1. **Saying "No" when asked for permission to use your name.** Refusing permission may be difficult; but, for you, it is easier than writing a negative letter. For the applicant, your refusing to serve as a reference may be preferable to your accepting and subsequently sending a negative letter.

2. **Letting the request go unanswered.** Failure to answer a request for information is in effect a negative response, even though the employer does not know whether you received the request. Nonresponse is legal and requires no effort; but (recognizing your responsibility to the applicant, the employer, and yourself) this option would probably be totally unacceptable to you.

3. **Responding with an objective appraisal.** Responding with an objective appraisal will give you the satisfaction of having exercised a responsibility to both the applicant and the employer. Because of your letter, an employer may escape some difficulty encountered after hiring an unqualified person. Your letter could spare an applicant the agony of going to work on a job that leads to failure. Figure 14-7 is an example of a well-written negative recommendation.

4. **Responding by letter and inviting a telephone call.** Responding by letter and inviting a telephone call enable a reference to avoid putting negative

6 *Write positive and negative recommendations that are legally defensible.*

Which option would you likely choose? Why?

1 Thank you so much for the letter of recommendation you prepared for my application to Tatum & Bayne. Today, I learned that I have been hired and will begin work next month.

2 Because the position is in auditing, I believe your comments about my performance in your auditing and systems classes carried a great deal of weight. Mr. Gowan commented he was impressed with the wealth of evidence and examples you provided to support your statements unlike the many general recommendations he frequently receives.

3 Dr. Herring, I appreciate your helping me secure an excellent position in a highly competitive job market. Thanks for the recommendation and your outstanding instruction. I look forward to talking with you about how I am faring in the real world when I return to campus for fall homecoming.

FIGURE 14-6
Good example of a thank-you letter to a reference.

1 States the main idea—appreciation for the recommendation. Informs reference of success in locating a job.
2 Communicates sincere appreciation for the reference's assistance; uses specific examples and avoids strong exaggeration.
3 Restates the main idea and anticipates a continued relationship; is original and sincere.

FIGURE 14-7
Good example of a
negative recommendation.

❶ Identifies clearly the
nature of the letter in the
subject line.
❷ States the main
idea—request for
employment information.
❸ Provides specific,
objective information that
can be verified easily.
❹ Provides additional
objective information;
omits opinions or value
judgments. Can be easily
verified.
❺ Describes Foster's
past performance but
does not project how he
will perform on other
jobs.

❶ PAUL FOSTER'S EMPLOYMENT RECORD

❷ Bingham Grocery provides the confidential employment information
about Paul Foster you requested in your June 1 letter.

❸ He worked from October 1 to December 13 as a courtesy clerk in our
Greenwood store. He had above-average skills at packing groceries, and
he seemed to have good rapport with customers.

❹ On three occasions (each on a Monday morning), he did not report to
work as scheduled; and he had not given the shift supervisor any notice
of his absence. He left the store at Bingham Grocery's request.

❺ While he was on the job, his work was satisfactory.

ideas in writing. The letter is short, positive, and easy to write as shown in the
following example:

> *Travis Kelley worked as a systems analyst for JEMCO from August 15, 1996,
> to December 30, 1998. The confidential information you requested will be
> provided by telephone: (601) 555-5432.*

Recognizing the possibility of negatives, which the reference did not want
to state in written form, the recipient might not call. In response to such a
call, abide by the same precautions that apply to writing letters of recommendation.

Because of the threat of possible litigation, recommendation letters must be
written carefully. Here are basic guidelines for writing a legally defensible recommendation:

What is the advantage of
labeling your letter "confidential" and reminding the
reader that the information
was requested?

- *Respond only to requests for specific information and indicate that your
  letter is written in response to a request.* Furthermore, do not provide
  information that was not requested.

- *Label your letter as confidential.* These legal precautions indicate that your
  intent was not to defame but to give an honest answer to a legitimate request
  for information. In addition, studies show that employers prefer confidential
  letters rather than open letters that allow the applicant access to the letter.
  Employers perceive the letters to be a more honest evaluation of the applicant's
  employability.[22]

- *Provide only job-related information.* If you are not familiar with the
  requirements of the job applied for, ask the requester to send you a job
  description. Use this document to include information that is *directly* relevant to the future job and to eliminate irrelevant information that could be
  defamatory.

- *Avoid vague, general statements of the applicant's personal ability.*
  Instead, provide specific examples of performance and the situation in which
  the performance occurred. Include information such as the difficulty and

When you must include negative information in a recommendation letter, be sure that you separate fact from opinion. Including only objective facts that can be supported is a foolproof safeguard against litigation and the temptation to retaliate for problems and losses caused by an employee's poor performance.

complexity of the task, degree of applicant's control in the task, and the consequences of the performance, particularly rewards.[23]

- ***Provide specific facts for any negative information.*** For example, the number of workdays missed without prior communication with the supervisor is a verifiable fact. To label it as "a terrible record" or "irresponsible" is to pass judgment (which is best left to the reader). Avoid such defaming and judgmental words as *corrupt, crook, dishonest, hypocrite,* and *incompetent.*

Other writing techniques important to writing a recommendation letter follow:

- ***Include some positives, even if your overall recommendation is negative.*** A balanced approach of positives and negatives will make the letter appear more credible to the reader.

- ***Use an inductive sequence and stylistic techniques of de-emphasis (unless your feelings are strong and you think emphasis of the negative is justified).*** Typically, the inductive sequence with de-emphasis techniques will seem considerate.

Refer to the Real-Time Internet Case at the end of the chapter for other legal implications of negative recommendations.

Writing Positive Recommendations. Fortunately, most people who invite you to write a recommendation are confident you will report positive information. Before requesting a recommendation, the employer has almost certainly seen the applicant's résumé, application letter, and (possibly) application forms. Although the effect of your letter may be to *confirm* some of the information already submitted, do not devote all your space to *repeating* it. Instead, concentrate on presenting information the employer probably does not have. Your statements about proficiency and capacity to interact with others will be of special interest. Avoid unsupported superlatives and overly strong adjectives that may cause the employer to question your credibility. Regardless of whether a recommendation is for a promotion within the firm or for work in another firm, the same principles apply. Figure 14-8 shows a recommendation for an employee who is seeking a promotion within a company.

How can strong adjectives in a positive recommendation letter be detrimental?

FIGURE 14-8
Good example of a recommendation memorandum.

1 Introduces the main idea.

2 Emphasizes each reason the promotion is deserved. Each short sentence following the bullet has high impact.

3 Restates the main idea.

1 Murray Laughlin would be an ideal senior loan officer. For the following reasons, I recommend his promotion:

2 • **He is efficient.** Beginning with a $14 million loan portfolio, he now manages $25 million. In three years, the number of clients has grown from 16 to 26. Clients are astonished at the speed with which he completes paperwork.

• **He stays informed.** Daily, he spends time on the financial monitor and financial journals. Because of his knowledge, he has frequently made loans that would otherwise have gone to competitors.

• **He works well with the staff.** Colleagues communicate easily with him. His friendly, positive disposition contributes to our pleasant office atmosphere.

• **He helps maintain Southland's public image.** Active in Kiwanis and in fund-raising for the needy, he has frequent contacts with clients, prospective clients, and competitors in social situations. To me, he is an ideal person for reflecting the bank's image.

3 A promotion would reward Murray for the part he has played in expanding our loans and would help us to keep him on our team.

INTERVIEWS

Planning Stage

- Learn as much as you can about the job requirements, range of salary and benefits, and the interviewer.
- Research the company with whom you are interviewing (products/services, financial condition, growth potential).
- Identify the *specific* qualifications that are compatible with the job requirements and any other information you learned about the company. Be prepared to discuss them clearly and concisely.
- Plan your appearance—clean, well groomed, and appropriate clothing.
- Plan to arrive early to communicate promptness and to prepare mentally for the interview.
- Try to identify the type of interview you will have (structured, unstructured, computer-assisted, group, or stress).

Opening Formalities

- Greet the interviewer by name with a smile, direct eye contact, and a firm handshake.
- Wait for the interviewer to ask you to be seated.
- Sit erect and lean forward slightly to convey interest.

Body of the Interview

- Identify the type of interview situation and adapt your responses accordingly.
- Be ready to explain how your qualifications relate to the job requirements using multiple specific examples.
- Identify illegal interview questions; address the concern behind an illegal question or avoid answering the question tactfully.
- Ask pertinent questions that communicate intelligence and genuine interest in the company. Introduce questions throughout the interview where appropriate.
- Allow the interviewer to initiate a discussion of salary and benefits. Be prepared to provide a general salary range for applicants with your qualifications.

Closing the Interview

- Watch for cues the interview is ending; rise, accept the interviewer's handshake, and communicate enthusiasm.
- Express appreciation for the interview and say you are eager to hear from the company.

OTHER EMPLOYMENT MESSAGES

Follow-Up Letters

- Remind receiver that your application is on file and you are interested in the job.
- Present additional education or experience gained since previous correspondence; do not repeat information presented earlier.
- Close with courteous request for an interview.

Thank-You Letters

- Express appreciation for the interview and mention the specific job for which you have applied.
- Refer to a specific point discussed in the interview.
- Close with a reference to an expected call or letter conveying the interviewer's decision.

Application Forms

- Read the entire form before completing it and follow instructions precisely.
- Complete the form neatly and accurately.
- Respond to all questions; insert N/A for questions that do not apply.
- Retain a copy for your records.

Job-Acceptance Letters

- Begin by accepting the job offer; specify position.
- Provide necessary details.
- Close with a courteous ending that confirms the date employment begins.

Job-Refusal Letters

- Begin with neutral, related idea that leads to the explanation for refusal.
- Present the reasons that lead to a diplomatic statement of the refusal.
- Close positively, anticipating future association with the company.

Resignation Letters

- Begin with positive statement about the job to cushion the bad news.
- Present explanation, state the resignation, and provide any details.
- Close with appreciative statement about experience with the company.

Recommendation Request

- Begin with the request for the recommendation.
- Provide necessary details including reference to an enclosed résumé.
- End with an appreciative statement for the reference's willingness to aid in the job search.
- Require a follow-up letter explaining delays and expressing appreciation for extended job searches.

Thank-You for a Recommendation

- Begin with expression of thanks for the recommendation.
- Provide specific examples of the value of the recommendation to convey sincere tone; avoids exaggerated comments.
- End courteously, indicating future association with the reference.

Negative Recommendation

- Begin by stating *confidential* information *requested* by the receiver is being provided.
- Provide *specific, objective* information that can be verified; omit opinions and value judgments. Invite receiver to telephone to avoid including negative statements in writing.
- End with courteous statement.

Positive Recommendation

- Begin with a statement of recommendation.
- Provide *specific, objective* information that the interviewer likely has not received already.
- Avoid unsupported superlatives and overly strong adjectives and adverbs that destroy credibility.
- End by restating the positive recommendation.

SUMMARY

1. ***Explain the nature of structured, unstructured, computer-assisted, group, and stress interviews.*** Interviewers and interviewees can be considered as buyers and sellers: Interviewers want to know whether job candidates can meet the needs of their firms before making a "purchase"; interviewees want to sell themselves based on sound knowledge, good work skills, and desirable personal traits. Structured interviews follow a preset, highly structured format; unstructured interviews follow no standard format but explore for information. Computer-assisted interviews provide standard, reliable information on applicants during the preliminary interview stages. Group interviews involve various personnel within the organization in the candidate interview process. Stress interviews are designed to reveal how the candidate behaves in high-anxiety situations.

2. ***Explain the steps in the interview process.*** Successful job candidates plan appropriately for the interview so that they will know basic information about the company, arrive on time dressed appropriately for the interview, and present a polished first impression following appropriate protocol. During the interview, the candidate presents his or her qualifications favorably and obtains information about the company to aid in deciding whether to accept a possible job offer.

3. ***Prepare effective answers to questions often asked in job interviews and questions that will communicate initiative to an interviewer.*** The successful job candidate effectively discusses key qualifications and skillfully asks questions that show initiative and genuine interest in the company.

4. ***Recognize and bypass illegal interview questions.*** Refusing to answer an illegal question could be detrimental to your chances to secure a job, but answering the question may compromise your ethical values. An effective technique is to answer the legitimate concern behind the illegal question rather than to give a direct answer.

5. ***Write effective letters related to employment (follow-up, thank-you, job-acceptance, job-refusal, resignation, and recommendation request) and complete application forms accurately.*** A follow-up letter is sent a few weeks after an applicant does not receive a response from an application. It includes a reminder that an application has been made, presents additional education or experience, and asks for action. Instructions on application forms should be followed carefully. Neatness, completeness, and accuracy are expected. Written deductively, job-acceptance letters include the acceptance, details, and a closing that confirms the date the employee will

begin work. Job-refusal letters are written inductively and include a buffer beginning, reasons that lead to the refusal, and a goodwill closing. Resignation letters usually satisfy a company's requirement that resignations be submitted in writing; they confirm that termination plans are definite. Assuming resignations are usually bad news for an employer, they are written inductively, with emphasis on positive aspects of the job.

6. **Write positive and negative recommendations that are legally defensible.** Requests for recommendation should include specific information about the job requirements and the applicant's qualifications to assist the reference in writing a convincing recommendation. Letters thanking a reference for a recommendation and providing an update on the status of a job search are a professional courtesy. For job seekers with good qualifications, recommendation letters are written deductively; otherwise, inductively. Because of the threat of possible litigation, special attention must be directed at writing legally defensible recommendations. General advice is to (1) provide only information that is requested; (2) indicate the information is confidential; (3) provide specific, job-related facts; (4) avoid vague, general statements; and (5) stick to the facts.

REFERENCES

[1]Vertreace, W. C. (1997, February). The on-site interview: Making it work for you. *The Black Collegian*, 56–60. [p. 57].

[2]Vertreace, W. C. (1997, February). The on-site interview: Making it work for you. *The Black Collegian*, 56–60. [p. 58].

[3]Vertreace, W. C. (1997, February). The on-site interview: Making it work for you. *The Black Collegian*, 56–60.

[4]Washington, T. (1997). Are you prepared for interviewers' new techniques? [On-line]. Available http://www.occ.com/occNBEW/InterviewerTechniques.html [1997, September 20.]

[5]Mitchell, B. (1990). Interviewing face-to-interface. *Personnel*, 67(1), 23–25.

[6]Vicers, M. (1997, April 14). Video interviews cut recruiting costs for many firms. *International Herald Tribune*, p. 15.

[7]Ralston, G. (1997). Using videoconferencing for recruiting and training. *Telemarketing & Call Center Solutions*, 15(10), 68–69.

[8]Marion, L. C. (1997, January 11). Companies tap keyboards to interview applicants. *The News and Observer*, p. B5.

[9]Vicers, M. (1997, April 14). Video interviews cut recruiting costs for many firms. *International Herald Tribune*, p. 15.

[10]Bhasin, R. (1997, January). The group interview: A new selection process. *Pulp and Paper*, 47.

[11]Vicers, M. (1997, April 14). Video interviews cut recruiting costs for many firms. *International Herald Tribune*, p. 15.

[12]Mueller, S. (1996). What skills will graduating students need to make it in the business world? *Business Journal–San Jose*, 14(8), 8.

[13]Austin, N. K. (1996, March). The new job interview. *Working Woman*, 23–24.

[14]Kennedy, J. L,. & Morrow, T. J. (1994). *Electronic résumé revolution: Create a winning résumé for the new world of job seeking.* New York: John Wiley.

[15]Siegel, P. J., & Bryant, M. R. (1997). A hiring checklist. *HR Focus*, 74(4), 22.

[16]Mueller, S. (1996). What skills will graduating students need to make it in the business world? *Business Journal–San Jose*, 14(8), 8.

[17]Eng, S. (1997, June 1). Handling "behavioral interviews." *The Des Moines Register*, p. 1.

[18]Eng, S. (1997, June 1). Handling "behavioral interviews." *The Des Moines Register*, p. 1.

[19]Munk, N., & Oliver, S. (1997, March 24). Think fast! *Forbes,* 146-151.

[20]Nelson, M., & Dauten, D. (1996, May 5). Your greatest weakness? Try your greatest strength: Candidates should be ready for the tough questions during job interviews. *Star Tribune*, p. 3D.

[21]Smith, K. S. (1996, March 24). Interviewing tips for job seekers, managers. *Rocky Mountain News*, p. 6W.

[22]Knouse, S. B. (1987). Confidentiality and the letter of recommendation: A new approach. *Bulletin of the Association for Business Communication*, 50(3), 6–8.

[23]Knouse, S. B. (1987). Confidentiality and the letter of recommendation: A new approach. *Bulletin of the Association for Business Communication*, 50(3), 6–8.

EXERCISES

1. How do structured and unstructured interviews differ? How is computer-assisted interviewing being used to screen applicants? (Obj. 1)

2. How do team interviews differ from interviews with a single interviewer? (Obj. 1)

3. List some possible sources of information about a company and three important facts you should locate. (Obj. 2)

4. Write a brief statement discussing the potential value of your education to an employer. Add information about your work experience, involvement in student organizations, and other experience. (Obj. 3)

5. What posture and body movements can the interviewee use to impress an interviewer favorably? (Obj. 2)

6. How do responses to direct and indirect questions differ? (Obj. 3)

7. Discuss three ways an interviewee can handle illegal interview questions. What are the advantages and disadvantages of each? (Obj. 4)

8. What is a good strategy to use when you are asked about your major weakness? Provide a specific example you might use. (Obj. 3)

9. What ideas are included in a follow-up letter? (Obj. 5)

10. In a thank-you letter, what is the advantage of referring to some point discussed in the interview? (Obj. 5)

11. List some suggestions for completing employment forms. (Obj. 5)

12. Which would be written deductively: (a) an acceptance letter, (b) a refusal letter, or (c) a resignation letter? What ideas should be included in each of these letters? (Obj. 5)

13. Professor Ulmer agreed to serve as one of your employment references, but you have not talked with her for two years. Today, you listed her name on an application form. Should you write to her? Explain. (Obj. 5)

14. An employee whom you fired last year has given your name as a reference. In the responding letter, would you include some positives and negatives? Discuss guidelines for writing a recommendation that you can legally defend. (Obj. 6)

E-MAIL APPLICATION

Your instructor will divide the class into groups of two. One member will send an e-mail message; the other will respond. The sender will compose an e-mail message to the other member asking for a thoughtful response to five tough interview questions. At least one of the questions should be sensitive in nature (possibly illegal or quite close). Printscreen to obtain a copy of the original message to submit to your instructor. The team member receiving the message will e-mail answers to the five questions. The instructor may ask that you reverse roles so that each of you has experience composing and answering difficult interview questions.

APPLICATIONS

1. **Researching a Company and Asking Questions of an Interviewer. (Obj. 2, 3)**
   Form small groups and research a company of your choice. Use the information on page 542 as a guide for your research. Generate a list of ten questions to ask an interviewer from the company you researched. Write original questions that communicate initiative, intelligence, and genuine interest in the company and the job. Submit your research in a memo to your instructor.

2. **Preparing to Answer Interview Questions Effectively. (Obj. 1, 3)**
   Working with another student with the same or similar career goals, compose a list of potential questions you might be asked in an interview. As directed by your instructor, complete one or more of the following:

   a. Be prepared to discuss appropriate answers to the questions in class.

   b. Divide into small groups to discuss your answers. Revise your answers, incorporating relevant feedback and being sure that the answers are truthful and reflect your individual personality.

   c. Set up a mock interview with a friend serving as the interviewer.

3. **Bypassing Illegal Interview Questions. (Obj. 4)**
   Refer to the text discussion of illegal interview questions. In pairs, practice your responses to such questions.

4. **Practicing a Job Interview. (Obj. 3)**
   Form groups of four to practice job interviews. Each person should have available a copy of his or her résumé. Alternatively play the roles of interviewer and interviewee, with the two additional people serving as critical observers. Change places until all four have had an opportunity to serve as interviewer and interviewee. You may assume that the jobs being applied for are the ones for which you have selected and designed applications. Alternatively, use one of the following positions:

   a. A part-time job visiting high schools to sell seniors on the idea of attending your school.

   b. A full-time summer job as a management intern in a local bank.

   This activity may be adapted for videotaping and review.

5. **Following Up on a Job Offer. (Obj. 5)**
   Assume that you are offered the job (or internship) for which you have applied. Make the assumption you prefer:

   a. You applied for an immediate part-time job.

   b. You applied for a full-time job for next summer.

   c. You applied for a cooperative education assignment or internship.

   d. You applied for a full-time job immediately after your graduation. Look at the list of courses you plan to take and write as though you had taken them and satisfied the requirements for a degree.

   Write a follow-up letter for the job (internship) for which you have applied.

6. **Saying "Thank-You" for an Interview. (Obj. 5)**
   Assume that you were interviewed for the job for which you applied in Application 4. Write a thank-you letter to the interviewer. Supply an address.

7. **Accepting a Job Offer. (Obj. 5)**
   Write a letter of acceptance for the job (internship) for which you applied in Application 4. Supply an address.

8. **Refusing a Job Offer Diplomatically. (Obj. 5)**
   Assume that the job search identified in Application 4 was very successful; you were offered two positions. Write a letter refusing one of the job offers. Because you want to maintain a positive relationship with the company for whom you are refusing to work, provide specific reasons for your decision. Supply an address.

9. **Resigning from a Job. (Obj. 5)**
   Write a letter resigning from your current job. If you are not currently employed, supply fictitious information.

10. **Requesting a Letter of Recommendation. (Obj. 6)**
    Write a letter requesting a reference to provide information to prospective employers. Provide specific information about how your qualifications relate to the job requirements and enclose a résumé. Supply an appropriate name and address.

11. **Informing a Reference of an Extended Job Search. (Obj. 6)**
    Your job search is taking much longer than you had hoped. Because your references have been providing recommendations for six months now, you must write expressing your gratitude and updating them on the status of your job search. If your qualifications have changed, include an updated résumé. Address a letter to one of your references. Supply an appropriate name and address.

12. **Writing a Negative Recommendation Letter. (Obj. 6)**
    In your position as sales manager with V-Tech, you recently had to dismiss a sales trainee during her probationary employment period. While the trainee, Justine Simms, was pleasant and cooperative, her sales presentations were lackluster and unproductive. Ms. Simms has now applied with Consolidated Technology, and they have contacted you for a written reference. Write a letter that is legally defensible, providing an appropriate address.

To Tell or Not to Tell: The Implications of Disclosing Potentially Damaging Information in an Employment Reference

Until recently, the rule for employers for responding to reference checks about their employees was fairly simple: The less said, the better. The risk of providing employment references to prospective employers is that former employees may sue if your references are unfavorable and lead to job rejection. The employers may be liable to a former employee for defamation if the employer communicates to a prospective employer or other person a false statement that results in damage to the former employee's reputation. Defamation is commonly referred to as "slander" if the communication is verbal and as "libel" if the communication is written. Employers have traditionally been cautioned about relating information that is not formally documented or for which no objective evidence exists. Thus, the more information provided, the greater the likelihood of a defamation suit by the former employee. Awards in successful defamation suits may include damages for lost earnings, mental anguish, pain and suffering, and even punitive damages.

Recent court decisions may have changed all of that or at least created confusion for employers about what to disclose. In situations where the employer knows that a former employee has a history of criminal violence or extremely aggressive behavior, the employer may have a legal obligation to provide such information to a prospective employer. Questions arise as to what to do if you are not sure that the information about the previous employee is true. The risk of remaining silent is that you could be sued for negligently failing to disclose the information if the former employee were to harm someone on the next job. On the other hand, you could be sued for defamation if you do disclose the information and the former employee can successfully establish that it is not true.

Locate the following Internet sites and complete the activities as directed by your instructor:

Internet Sites

http://www.toolkit.cch.com/text/p05_8640.htm
http://www.toolkit.cch.com/text/p05_8610.htm
http://research.badm.sc.edu/research/bereview/be43_1/employ.htm

Activities

1. Make a list of types of statements that a former employer should generally avoid making when giving employment references.

2. Write an organizational policy that addresses the appropriate guidelines for giving employee references. Include statements concerning appropriate content and the manner in which such information should be issued.

3. Formulate a legal argument that presents the conflict between the potential employer's right to know and the previous employer's right to avoid possible defamation charges. Present both sides of the issue in a five-minute oral report.

Team Building Projects

During the Performing stage, a group of individuals becomes a truly collaborative team. Members share a vision and work together to accomplish their objectives. Team members feel inspired to go the extra mile, and enjoy the fulfillment that comes from achieving objectives together. Typical feelings in the Performing stage include:

- Joy at being a member of the team.
- Desire to assist other team members.
- Admiration of other members' skills.
- Satisfaction with the team's progress.

Typical behaviors include:

- Majority of effort directed toward task completion.
- Accomplishment of tasks through collaborative work.
- Effective decision making.
- Maximization of team members' skills.
- Problem solving efforts that result in creative and effective solutions.
- Open, direct, and businesslike communications.

Unfortunately, many teams in the real world never achieve high performance. High-performance teams result from a blend of individual performances, teamwork, and leadership. Team development requires careful, on-going facilitation that incorporates clear behavior standards, ongoing diagnosis, team critique and appraisal, and proper training in how to improve on strengths and shore up weak spots. High-performance team essentials include the following:

- **Shared vision.** All team members share and support a common vision that the team is working to achieve. Team members are highly focused on objectives.
- **Time orientation.** The team operates under specific deadlines, often self-imposed, for achieving results.
- **Effective communication.** The team takes extraordinary efforts to make certain that everyone understands the plan and progress toward the plan.
- **Concern zone.** The team works outside its comfort zone, so that they are not always sure how they are going to achieve the desired results.

- **Quality reviews.** The team stops at appropriate times to check the quality of its recent work for the purpose of determining how the process could be improved and what learning can be shared with other members.
- **Unanimous involvement.** Team members work to make sure every member is involved. "Watchers" and "wonderers" are employed in progress toward the goals.
- **Distributed leadership.** Team leadership changes according to expertise required. Individual members jump into the breach as weaknesses or gaps are discovered.
- **Celebration of success.** The team takes time to celebrate small victories toward goal achievement. Team members work to build each other up and avoid zinging each other, because they care deeply about each other's development and personal growth.

For a team to function optimally, each member must share responsibility for team results. Companies utilizing team structure have found that performance appraisals should reward team achievements, not just individual contributions. The company should have systems in place to measure and evaluate the effectiveness of team performance at the onset of team development. When team members are given only individual performance rewards, they often develop a "look out for myself" approach despite encouragement to practice teamwork. Performance appraisals and raises should reward team achievements, not just individual contributions, which means that some form of peer evaluation must be used.

A recommendation for peer evaluation that has emerged from work-world team evaluation is to use weighted reviews, with a portion of the review coming from team members and the other portion coming from the manager or supervisor. For instance, team-member reviews might count for 50 percent, with manager review accounting for the remainder. This method can compensate for personality conflicts and grudges that can reflect in peer evaluations. If team members think a different ratio between team and manager evaluations is important, they should be able to propose and justify the idea. Rating forms and processes must be clear and give peer reviewers adequate opportunity to respond completely concerning the effort, quality, and quantity of member contributions; all observations must be supported by examples.

In addition to individual performance appraisal, high-performing teams periodically evaluate their team progress toward established goals. Reasons for successes are noted, so that they can be repeated in the future. Reasons for shortfalls are also discussed to determine alternate ways to approach issues or deal with challenges so that success can be achieved.

Exploration

Read the following article that provides the results of research with 61 U.S. companies concerning the effectiveness of work teams:

Fitz-enz, J. (1997, August). Measuring team effectiveness. *HR Focus*, 74(8), 3.

Summarize the results of the study; end your summary with your own conclusions concerning team success and how it can be maximized.

Application

Complete the following activities individually:

- As an individual team member, complete a performance appraisal for each member of your team, including yourself. Your instructor will provide you with a form.

- As an individual team member, compose a "debriefing memo" to your instructor about the success of your completed team project. Include the following in your discussion: (1) how you would rate the overall effectiveness of your team, with reasons; (2) the overall strengths and weaknesses of your team; (3) what you learned about working in teams; and (4) what you would do differently the next time you are assigned to a team project.

Sources:

Kennedy, M. M. (1993, September). Where teams drop the ball. *Across the Board*, 30(7), 9–10.

Bodwell, D. J. (1996, October). High performance teams essential elements. [On-line]. Available http: rampages,onramp.net/~bodwell/tsld002.htm [1998, February 5].

VIDEO CONNECTION

Every job seeker desires to be effective in employment communication. The stakes are obvious and high. Preliminary analysis of one's strengths and weaknesses and careful planning of arrangement and format are essential to the development of an effective résumé and application letter. In addition to the planning and organization, originality is a plus, as the job seeker must somehow distinguish his or her résumé from the countless others with which it competes. Success at this stage means that an interview is granted, at which time a candidate has the opportunity to sell him or herself to the company as well as to take a closer look at what the company has to offer.

Interviewing involves the use of numerous interpersonal communication skills, both verbal and nonverbal. The challenge of the interview is to relax, while realizing that every word, action, and response is being scrutinized. No small task!

Discussion Questions

1. Hyman Albritton suggests that a job seeker should prepare two résumés. Explain the two and tell the purpose of each.

2. List three "do's" and three "dont's" for résumé preparation.

3. What is the "call for action" John Cripe mentions as essential for the application letter?

4. What advice does Marie Mulvoy have concerning dress for the interviews?

5. Conducting a self-awareness activity is suggested as a helpful prelude to the employment search process. What is involved? How does it benefit the job seeker?

Application

Interview a businessperson who is involved in employment interviewing. Prepare a written summary that includes answers to the following questions: (1) What strategies are used for "weeding out" résumés of job applicants? (2) What are five questions most commonly asked by the interviewer? (3) What is the interviewer looking for in terms of the candidate's nonverbal communication skills?

Document Format and Layout Guide

First impressions are lasting ones, and the receiver's first impression of your letter is its appearance and format. Preparing an error free, attractive document is a basic requirement for maintaining credibility with your receiver. This section presents techniques for producing an appealing document. In addition, you will learn the standard letter formats, punctuation styles, the standard and special parts of a letter, and envelope-addressing formats.

Appearance

To convey a positive, professional image, a letter should be proofread carefully, prepared on high-quality paper, and balanced attractively on the page. Other factors that affect the overall appearance of your document are justification of margins, spacing after punctuation, abbreviations, and word division. Review the following guidelines to ensure that your documents are accurate in these areas.

Proofreaders' Marks

Carefully proofread for three overall factors: (1) organization, content, and style; (2) grammatical errors; and (3) format errors. In addition, check your document with the electronic spellcheck. Refer to Chapter 4 for a detailed explanation of systematic proofreading procedures. Become familiar with the standard proofreaders' marks shown in Figure A-1.

Paper

The quality of paper reflects the professionalism of the company and allows a company to control communication costs effectively. Paper quality is measured in two ways: cotton-fiber content and weight.

High-cotton bond paper has a crisp crackle, is firm to the pencil touch, is difficult to tear, and ages without deterioration or chemical breakdown. The weight of paper is based on the weight of a ream consisting of approximately 500 sheets of 17-by 22-inch paper (equivalent to 2,000 sheets of 8½- by 11-inch paper). If the ream weighs 20 pounds, the paper is said to be 20-pound weight. The heavier the paper, the higher the quality. Most business letters are produced on company letterhead that is printed on 16- or 20-pound bond paper.

Extremely important external documents such as reports and proposals may be printed on 24-pound bond paper with 100-percent cotton content. Memorandums, business forms, and other intercompany documents may be printed on lighter-weight paper with lower cotton-fiber content. Envelopes and plain sheets to be used for the second and successive pages of multiple-page letters should be of the same weight, cotton-fiber content, and color as the letterhead.

The standard paper size for business documents is $8^1/_2$ by 11 inches. Some top executives use executive-size ($7^1/_4$ by $10^1/_2$ inches) letterhead printed on 24-pound bond paper with 100-percent cotton content. However, this smaller size could easily be misfiled and may require special formatting that adds to the document cost.

Another characteristic of high-quality paper is the watermark, a design imprinted on the paper. The paper must be held up to the light to see this mark clearly. The watermark may be the trademark of the company using the paper or the brand name of the paper. Watermarked paper has a right side and a top edge; therefore, it must be placed in the printer correctly. The watermark is positioned so that it can be read across the sheet in the same direction as the printing.

Proofreaders' Mark	Draft Copy	Final Copy
‖ Align type vertically	**Date:** May 21, 1999 **Subject:** International Assignments Available	**Date:** May 21, 1999 **Subject:** International Assignments Available
☰ Capitalize	The intern is enrolled in marketing research this term.	The intern is enrolled in Marketing Research this term.
◡ Close up	Staff meetings begin at 9 a. m.	Staff meetings begin at 9 a.m.
][Center	]Proofreading Procedures[	Proofreading Procedures
Change	Responsible for work crews of six-to-ten employees	Supervised work crews of six-to- ten employees . . . .
No ¶ Combine paragraphs	No ¶ The manager approved	The manager approved . . . .
ℯ Delete	Presentation graphics software available today is capable	Presentation graphics software is capable . . . .
ⓓⓢ Double-space copy	About two thirds of the consumers preferred to	About two thirds of the consumers preferred to . . . .
=/ Hyphenate	Follow these easy to understand instructions.	Follow these easy-to-understand instructions.
∧ Insert	This system can accomodate	This system can accommodate . . . .
Insert apostrophe	The managers perspective	The manager's perspective . . . .
Insert comma	Clear concise messages save time and money.	Clear, concise messages save time and money.
Insert em dash	Additional equipment--video camera and microphone--is needed	Additional equipment—video camera and microphone—is needed . . . .
Insert quotation mark	Reread e-mail messages written in anger to avoid flaming.	Reread e-mail messages written in anger to avoid "flaming."
# Insert space	Managers address this problem everyday.	Managers address this problem every day.
⊙ Insert period	The agenda will be released on Friday	The agenda will be released on Friday.
[Move left	[1. Use the default margins	1. Use the default margins . . . .
] Move right	Indent paragraphs in double-spaced text.	Indent paragraphs in double-spaced text.
/ Lowercase	Jill Cox, Assistant Manager of . . . . U.S. WORKFORCE	Jill Cox, assistant manager of . . . . U.S. Workforce

FIGURE A-1 Standard Proofreaders' Marks.

Proofreaders' Mark	Draft Copy	Final Copy
Move copy as indicated	Today your June payment was received.	Your June payment was received today.
SS Single-space copy	About two thirds of the consumers preferred	About two thirds of the consumers preferred . . . .
Start a new line	Ms. Kelly Chen, Manager	Ms. Kelly Chen Manager
Start a new paragraph	Experts suggest students pursue electronic and traditional job search strategies.	Experts suggest students pursue electronic and traditional job search strategies.
Spell out	8 boxes of colored markers	Eight boxes of colored markers
Transpose	The Japanese beleive	The Japanese believe . . . .
Stet (let original text stand)	A memo template includes	A memo template includes . . . .
ital Use italics	Business Horizons *ital*	*Business Horizons*
bf Use boldface	Site Selection for New Plant *bf*	**Site Selection for New Plant**

FIGURE A-1 Standard Proofreaders' Marks (continued).

Placement of Text on the Page

Letters should be balanced on the page with approximately equal margins. Companies using word processing software set standard line lengths. To increase efficiency, the standard line length is often the same as the default margins set by the software. One-inch side margins, which produce a $6\frac{1}{2}$-inch line of writing, is a typical standard line. The dateline position varies depending on the length of the letter. Generally, begin a short letter (one or two paragraphs) three inches from the top of the page; an average letter (three or four paragraphs), 2.7 inches from the top of the page; and a long letter (four or more paragraphs), 2.3 inches from the top of the page. Side margins are usually adjusted to improve the appearance of extremely short letters.

Many software programs will allow you to center a page of text vertically with one simple command; in that case, execute the center page command. This placement, which creates approximately equal margins on all sides of the letter, is often referred to as fitting the letter into a picture frame. With the proper equipment, the exact centering process is simple and creates a highly professional effect.

Justification of Margins

Word processing software makes justified margins possible; that is, all lines start at the left margin and end flush at the right margin. Extra spaces are added between words so that the line ends exactly on the right margin. These extra spaces are visually distracting and make the document difficult to read. Research has shown that receiver comprehension is reduced when the copy is justified. In addition, justified margins give the document a computer-generated appearance, as if it were just another form letter. For these reasons, use the unjustified right margin as shown in the examples throughout this text. The three sample paragraphs that follow illustrate the appearance of justified and unjustified margins using proportional and monospaced (nonproportional) fonts.

Justified documents look very professional when they are printed with proportional spacing (the size of the letters varies and the extra space between words is minimized). Proportional printing and scalable fonts (different print styles whose size and appearance can be altered) are available with many laser printers. These enhancements increase your ability to prepare highly professional letters, reports, and proposals.

Justified Margins (Left and Right) Without Proportional Print

```
                 ESSENTIAL COMPUTER SKILLS

Currently  employees  at  all  levels  of  our  organization
are   using   primary   computer   applications   to  increase
their  productivity  and  are  eager  to  expand  their  knowl-
edge  to  other  more  advanced  areas.  A  primary  need  is  to
implement  a  telecommunications  system  that  will  allow
our  staff  to  transmit  reports  from  the  field  to  the  home
office.  Other  areas  of  interest  include  desktop  pub-
lishing  and  electronic  mail.
```

Jagged Right Margin (Left Justified)

ESSENTIAL COMPUTER SKILLS

Currently employees at all levels of our organization are using primary computer applications to increase their productivity and are eager to expand their knowledge to other more advanced areas. A primary need is to implement a telecommunications system that will allow our staff to transmit reports from the field to the home office. Other areas of interest include desktop publishing and electronic mail.

Justified Margins Using Proportional Print with Scalable Font

ESSENTIAL COMPUTER SKILLS

Currently employees at all levels of our organization are using primary computer applications to increase their productivity and are eager to expand their knowledge to other more advanced areas. A primary need is to implement a telecommunications system that will allow our staff to transmit reports from the field to the home office. Other areas of interest include desktop publishing and electronic mail.

Special Symbols

To give documents the appearance of a professional typeset document, use the following special symbols in computer-generated material:

En dash	Use to separate words indicating a duration (May–June).
Em dash	Use instead of a dash (--) to indicate an abrupt change in thought (statement—that is,).
Hyphen	Use to indicate word division (nega-tive).
Quotation marks	Use instead of the inch (″) and foot (′) symbols ("Today" or 'today').
Fractions	Create $\frac{1}{2}$ and $\frac{1}{4}$ rather than key 1/2 and 1/4. Special symbols are available for other common fractions.
Bullets	Use a variety of special symbols to highlight enumerated items (○, ●, □, ■, ♦, ✔, ∅).
Other symbols	Learn the codes for printing symbols: ©, ®, ¢, £, ‰, ¶, and others.

Spacing

Proper spacing after punctuation is essential in preparing a professional document.

1. Space *once* after a period, question mark, or exclamation point (terminal punctuation) when using a proportional font. The proportional font automatically adjusts the white space; therefore, adding an extra space to separate the sentences as traditionally done is not necessary. However, space *twice* after terminal punctuation if you use a monospaced font (a "typewriter-like" font with characters of *one* width) or a typewriter.

   Proportional: When will he arrive? Regardless of the time. . . .
   Monospaced: Step two was completed.   Then. . . .

   One space follows the terminal punctuation in the examples in this text. Because some writers advocate that extra space aids readability regardless of the font used, you should learn your instructor's preference before submitting documents.

2. Space twice after a colon except in the expression of time:

   We have three questions: (1) When is . . . .
   Please cancel my 9:15 a.m. meeting with Charlotte Gaines.

3. Space once after a comma or a semicolon.

   When the end of the month comes, we will be prepared.
   The operator left at three o'clock; he was ill.

4. Space once after a period following an initial and abbreviations.

   No. Co. Corp.   Mr. Watson A. Reynolds

Word Division

Often word division is necessary to avoid extreme variations in line length. Word processing software automatically wraps words that will not fit within the margins to the next line. If a long word is wrapped to the next line, the previous line will be extremely short (jagged right margin) or will have large spaces between words (justified right margin). In either case, the result is distracting. A divided word at the end of the line would be less distracting.

Try to avoid dividing words at the ends of lines. If words must be divided, follow acceptable word-division rules. Word processing software will allow you to make hyphenation decisions. In addition, upgrades to the industry's most popular word processing programs are now capable of automatic hyphenation based on accepted word-division rules. Apply the following word-division rules:

1. Divide words between syllables only. (Words with only one syllable cannot be divided: *through, hearth, worked*).

2. Avoid dividing a word containing six or fewer letters. (Lines on a printed page can vary as much as six or seven letters in length; therefore, dividing short words such as *letter* or *report* is pointless.)

3. Do not separate the following syllables from the remainder of a word:
   a. A syllable that does not include a vowel (e.g., contractions): *would/n't*.
   b. A first syllable that contains only one letter: *a/greement*.
   c. A last syllable that contains only one or two letters: *pneumoni/a, apolog/y, complete/ly*.

4. Divide a word between two single-letter syllables: *situ-ation, extenu-ate*.

5. Divide a word after a single-letter syllable except when the vowel is part of a suffix:

   Single vowel: *clari-fication, congratu-lations.*

   Suffix vowel: *accept-able, allow-able.*

6. Divide hyphenated words after the hyphen: *self-employed, semi-independent*.

7. Do not divide proper names, abbreviations, or most numbers: *George Martin, AICPA, 3,189,400.*

8. Do not divide the last word in more than two consecutive lines.

9. Do not divide the last word on a page.

Punctuation Styles and Letter Formats

Page layout (format) affects the effectiveness of the message. Many companies have policies that dictate the punctuation style and the letter format used.

Mixed and Open Punctuation

Two punctuation styles are customarily used in business letters: mixed and open. Letters using **mixed punctuation style** have a colon after the salutation and a comma after the complimentary close. Letters using **open punctuation style** do not have a colon after the salutation and a comma after the complimentary close.

Mixed punctuation is the traditional style; however, cost-conscious companies are increasingly adopting the open style (and other similar format changes), which eliminates unnecessary keystrokes.

Mixed Punctuation	**Open Punctuation**

SALUTATION

June 12, 1999

June 12, 1999

COMPLIMENTARY
CLOSE

Mr. Parker F. Baxter
1938 South Pines Avenue
Livingston, CA 95334-1938

Dear Mr. Baxter:

Mr. Parker F. Baxter
1938 South Pines Avenue
Livingston, CA 95334-1938

Dear Mr. Baxter

Sincerely,

Marla Vanderbilt

Marla Vanderbilt
Vice President

Sincerely

Marla Vanderbilt

Marla Vanderbilt
Vice President

Letter Formats

The three letter formats that are commonly accepted by business include block, modified block, and simplified block.

Block. Companies striving to reduce the cost of producing business documents adopt the easy-to-learn, efficient block format. All lines (including paragraphs) begin at the left margin; therefore, no time is lost setting tabs and positioning letter parts. Study carefully the letter in block format with open punctuation shown in Figure A-2.

Modified Block. Modified block is the traditional letter format still used in many companies. The dateline, complimentary close, and signature block begin at the horizontal center of the page. Paragraphs may be indented five spaces if the writer prefers or the company policy requires it; however, the indention creates unnecessary keystrokes that increase the cost of the letter. All other lines begin at the left margin. Study carefully the letter in modified block format with block paragraphs and mixed punctuation shown in Figure A-3.

Simplified Block The simplified block format is an efficient letter format. Like the block format, all lines begin at the left margin; but the salutation and complimentary close are omitted, and a subject line is required. Place the subject line a double space below the letter address and a double space above the body. Study carefully the letter in simplified block format with block paragraphs shown in Figure A-4.

FIGURE A-2
Block format with open punctuation.

July 24, 1999

QS

DATELINE

Mr. Bert A. Pittman
1938 South Welch Avenue
Northwood, NE 65432-1938

DS

LETTER ADDRESS

Dear Mr. Pittman

DS

SALUTATION

Your recent article, "Are Appraisers Talking to Themselves?" has drawn many favorable comments from local real estate appraisers.

DS

BODY

The Southeast Chapter of the Society of Real Estate Appraisers has felt a strong need for more information about appraisal report writing. About 200 members will attend our annual seminar dinner meeting. They would be glad to meet you and are interested in hearing you discuss "Appraisal Report Writing." By accepting this invitation, you will be able to assist the appraisal profession. You will meet several new members of our group. The meeting will be at the Tilton Hotel on Thursday, August 23, at 7 p.m. We promise you a pleasant evening and an attentive audience.

DS

We would appreciate having, with your acceptance, a photograph to be printed in the program.

DS

Sincerely

QS

Jennifer Malley

COMPLIMENTARY CLOSE

Jennifer Malley
Program Chair

SIGNATURE BLOCK

tw

REFERENCE INITIALS

Open punctuation omits the colon after the salutation and the comma after the complimentary close.

Standard Letter Parts

Business letters include seven standard parts. Other parts are optional and may be included when necessary. The standard parts include (1) heading, (2) letter address, (3) salutation, (4) body, (5) complimentary close, (6) signature block, and (7) reference initials. The proper placement of these parts is shown in Figures A-2, A-3, and A-4; a discussion of each standard part follows.

FIGURE A-3
Modified block format
with mixed punctuation.

STEPHEN'S SMALL ENGINES   *158 Cedar Bluff Road / Montgomery, AL 36119-0158 / Tel. (334) 555-1497*

DATELINE

February 4, 1999

QS

LETTER ADDRESS

Mr. Shannon Gholson
984 Northgate Street
Montgomery, AL 36119-8328

DS

SALUTATION

Dear Mr. Gholson:

DS

BODY

Johnson Motors are among the most dependable small electric motors manufactured in the United States today. Here at Stephen's Small Engines, we believe that the right size Johnson engine for the particular job is critical.

DS

The three-month warranty with the Johnson motors applies only if the motor is used under normal operating conditions. Your pipe size (3/15 inch), the large distance between your pool and the filtering system (100 feet), and the size of your pool (50 by 60 feet) placed undue stress on the 2.5-horsepower motor. Your sales receipt indicates that a 3.5-horsepower motor was recommended based on our evaluation of your needs.

DS

Our sales force will be happy to show you the 3.5-horsepower Johnson motor. This powerful motor should provide clear, sparkling water for outdoor enjoyment for your family.

DS

COMPLIMENTARY CLOSE

Sincerely,

QS

SIGNATURE BLOCK

Lance Danovsky

Lance Danovsky
Manager

DS

REFERENCE INITIALS

ms

Mixed punctuation requires a colon after the salutation and a comma after the complimentary close.

Heading

When the letterhead shows the company name, address, telephone and/or fax number, and logo, the letter begins with the dateline. Use the month-day-year format (September 2, 19—) unless you are preparing government documents, writing to an international audience who uses the day-month-year format, or company policy requires another format. Abbreviating the month or using numbers (9/2/—) may portray a hurried attitude.

If a letter is prepared on plain paper, the writer's address must be included. Otherwise, the recipient may be unable to respond if the envelope is discarded. The

FIGURE A-4
Simplified block format.

 PROSSER CABLE TELEVISION

8310 McCrary Road
Arvada, CO 80001-8310
(303) 555-6540   Fax: (303) 555-0943

April 15, 1999

QS

Ms. Allana Cruz
870 Bristol Court
Denver, CO 80202-8871

DS

Changes in Cable Service

DS

Some important changes in your cable television service will begin May 1, 1999. We will rearrange our channel line-up and institute a rate change. These changes are necessary to maintain quality service and to meet new federal guidelines for programming selection.

DS

Our new monthly rates are as follows:

Basic Service. $26.50
Expanded Service $31.00
Premium Service $42.00

With these changes, the cost of our expanded package (all channels except premium) is still only a dollar a day—less than the cost of a cup of coffee and a doughnut. Our employees are committed to providing you with the best quality and variety of cable television, including education, sports, religion, and public affairs programming. Please call us if we can be of additional service to you.

QS

Eleanor D. Mixon

Eleanor D. Mixon
Systems Manager

yc

DATELINE

LETTER ADDRESS

SUBJECT LINE
(Replaces salutation)
BODY

(Complimentary close is omitted)

SIGNATURE BLOCK

REFERENCE INITIALS

writer's address can be keyed immediately above the dateline. The **heading** consists of three single-spaced lines: (1) the writer's street address; (2) the writer's city, two-letter state abbreviation, and nine-digit ZIP Code; and (3) the dateline. The writer's name is omitted because it appears in the signature block. Alternately, a personal letterhead can be designed using the desktop publishing capabilities of word processing software (varied fonts and graphic enhancements).

Letter Address

The **letter address** includes a personal or professional title (e.g., Mr. or Ms.), the name of the person and company to whom the letter is being sent, and the complete address. It begins a quadruple space after the dateline. Refer to Figure A-5 for appropriate formats for letter addresses.

Heading on Letterhead	**Heading on Plain Paper**
W🌐RLD Travel Unlimited 1390 Central Avenue Bridgeton, NJ 08302-1390 (908) 555-8765	
July 26, 1999	1800 Brookdale Road Albuquerque, NM 87102-1800 July 26, 1999
Ms. Donna Henson Wyatt Enterprises 245 Southern Oaks Road Corpus Christi, TX 78469-2988	Ms. Donna Henson Wyatt Enterprises 245 Southern Oaks Road Corpus Christi, TX 78469-2988
Dear Ms. Henson:	Dear Ms. Henson:

Salutation

The **salutation** is the greeting that opens a letter and is placed a double space below the letter address. The salutation is omitted in the simplified block format shown in Figure A-4.

To show courtesy for the receiver, include a personal or professional title (Mr., Ms., Dr., Senator). Refer to the *first line* of the letter address to determine an appropriate salutation; use the *second* line if the letter includes an attention line as shown in Figure A-5. In the previous example, "Dear Ms. Henson" is an appropriate salutation for this letter addressed to Ms. Donna Henson (first line of letter address). If the first line of the letter address were "Wyatt Enterprises," "Ladies and Gentlemen" would be an appropriate salutation. To avoid use of the impersonal salutation, "Ladies and Gentlemen," format the letter in simplified block format that omits the salutation. Use the examples shown in Figure A-5 as a guide when selecting an appropriate salutation.

Body

The **body** contains the message of the letter. It begins a double space below the salutation. Paragraphs are single-spaced with a double space between paragraphs. Because a double space separates the paragraphs, indenting paragraphs, which requires extra startup (setting tabs) and keying time, is not necessary. However, some companies may require paragraph indention as company policy. If so, you must use the modified block style (Figure A-3) with indented paragraphs.

Complimentary Close

The complimentary close is a phrase used to close a letter in the same way that you say good-bye at the end of a conversation. To create goodwill, choose a complimentary close that reflects the formality of your relationship with the receiver. Typical examples are "Yours truly," "Sincerely yours," "Sincerely," "Cordially," and "Cordially yours." "Sincerely" is considered neutral and is thus appropriate in a majority of business situations. Capitalize only the first word of the complimentary

Letter address	Appropriate Salutation	Explanation
A Specific Person Mr. Chris Carlisle, President Merchant's Bank of Tampa P.O. Drawer 512 Tampa, FL 33630-9006	Dear Mr. Carlisle:	If the person is a business associate, use a courtesy title and the last name.
	Dear Chris:	If you know the person well, use the person's first name or the name you would use greeting the person face-to-face.
	Dear Chris Carlisle: or use the simplified block format (Figure A-4) that omits the salutation.	If you do not know whether the person is male or female, use the whole name or omit the salutation to avoid offending the receiver.
A Company Merchant's Bank of Tampa P.O. Drawer 512 Tampa, FL 33630-9006	Ladies and Gentlemen: or use the simplified block format (Figure A-4) that omits the salutation.	This salutation recognizes the presence of men and women in management. Do *not* use "Dear Ladies and Gentlemen." You may use "Ladies" if you are sure that management is all female or "Gentlemen" if you are sure that management is all male.
A Company and Directed to a Specific Individual Attention Mr. Chris Carlisle Merchant's Bank of Tampa P.O. Drawer 512 Tampa, FL 33630-9006	Ladies and Gentlemen: or use the simplified block format (Figure A-4) that omits the salutation.	The letter is officially written to the company; therefore, "Dear Mr. Carlisle" is *not* acceptable. The salutation matches the second line of the letter address when you direct attention to a specific person.
A Specific Position Within a Business Purchasing Officer United Brokerage Firm 716 Jefferson Road Toledo, OH 43692-1645	Dear Purchasing Officer: or use the simplified block format (Figure A-4) that omits the salutation.	Because the name of the person is unknown, the simplified block format would be especially useful. A subject line replaces the salutation.
A Group of People Institute of Public Accountants 2958 Central Avenue Baltimore, MD 21233-2958	Dear Accounting Professionals: Form letter to potential customers or policyholders (letter address may be omitted) Dear Customer	When form letters are merged with available databases, the letter is personalized by inserting the recipient's letter address and a specific salutation, such as "Dear Mr. Baxter." This automated procedure eliminates the need for less personal salutations.

FIGURE A-5 Appropriate formats for letter addresses and salutations.

A Public Official		
Honorable (first and last name of U.S. Senator)	Dear Senator (last name):	
Honorable (first and last name of U.S. Representative)	Dear Mr. or Ms. (last name):	This form is also used for state senators and representatives.
Honorable (first and last name of state governor or lieutenant governor)	Dear Governor (last name): Dear Lt. Governor:	
Refer to an up-to-date reference manual when writing other public officials.		

FIGURE A-5 Appropriate formats for letter addresses and salutations (continued).

close and position it a double space below the body. The complimentary close and the salutation are omitted in the simplified block format (Figure A-4).

Signature Block

The **signature block** consists of the writer's name keyed a quadruple space (three blank lines) below the complimentary close (or body in the simplified block letter). The writer's name is signed legibly in the space provided. A woman may include a courtesy title to indicate her preference (e.g., Miss, Ms., Mrs.), and a woman or man may use a title to distinguish a name used by both men and women (e.g., Shane, Leslie, or Stacy) or initials (E. M. Goodman). A business or professional title may be placed on the same line with the writer's name or directly below it. Use the following examples as guides for balancing the writer's name and title:

Title on the Same Line	Title on the Next Line
Ms. Leslie Tatum, President	Ms. E. M. Goodman Assistant Manager
Perry Watson, Manager Quality Control Division	Richard Creelman Human Resources Director

Reference Initials

The **reference initials** consist of the keyboard operator's initials keyed in lowercase a double space below the signature block. The writer's initials are not included because the name appears in the signature block. The reference initials and the signature block identify the persons involved in preparing a letter in the event of later questions. Reference initials are omitted when a letter is keyed by the writer—a common practice now that many executives compose documents at a computer terminal both in the office and at remote locations. However, company policy may require that the initials of all people involved in writing a letter be placed in the reference initials line to identify accountability in the case of litigation. The reference line might also include department identification or other information as required by your organization.

Special Letter Parts

Other letter parts may be added to a letter depending on the particular situation. These parts include (1) mailing notation, (2) attention line, (3) reference line, (4) subject line, (5) second-page heading, (6) company name in signature block, (7) enclosure notation, (8) copy notation, and (9) postscript.

Mailing Notation

A **mailing notation** provides a record of how a letter was sent. Examples include FACSIMILE, OVERNIGHT, SPECIAL DELIVERY, or REGISTERED. Other mailing notations such as CONFIDENTIAL or PERSONAL give instructions on how a letter should be handled. Key a mailing notation in all capitals at the left margin a double space below the dateline. Key the letter address a double space below the mailing notation.

Attention Line

An **attention line** directs a letter to a specific person (Attention Ms. Laura Ritter), position within a company (Attention Human Resources Director), or department (Attention Purchasing Department). An attention line appears as the first line of the letter address, and the company name appears on the second line. The appropriate salutation in a letter with an attention line is "Ladies or Gentlemen" as shown in Figure A-5. Because the envelope format also requires the attention line to appear on the first line of the letter address, the word processing block-print function can be used to prepare the envelope without rekeying the address.

Reference Line

A **reference line** (Re: Contract No. 983-9873) directs the receiver to source documents or to files. Key a reference line a double space below the letter address.

Subject Line

A **subject line** tells the receiver what a letter is about and sets the stage for the receiver to understand the message. The simplified block format requires a subject line; in other letter formats, the subject line is optional. Key the subject line a double space below the salutation as shown in Figure A-6. Use either lowercase and capitals or all capitals for added emphasis. If modified block format is used, a subject line can be centered for added emphasis. To increase efficiency, the word *subject* is omitted because its position above the body clearly identifies its function. Note the difference between the subject line and the reference line that directs the receiver to source documents.

The mailing notation, attention line, reference line, and subject line are illustrated in Figure A-6.

Second-Page Heading

The second and successive pages of multiple-page letters and memorandums are keyed on plain paper of the same quality as the letterhead. A **second-page heading** is used on the second and successive pages to identify them as a continuation of

FIGURE A-6
Special letter parts.

HARRISON & PEARSON, LTD, CPAs

7601 Faulkner Building, Suite 350   Billings, MT 59101-7601   Telephone: (406) 555-3400 Fax: (406) 555-6874

January 19, 1999
DS

MAILING NOTATION

FACSIMILE
DS

ATTENTION LINE

Attention Ms. Margaret Daniel
Communication Systems, Inc.
Mitchell Building, Suite 250
Atlanta, GA 30311-5309
DS

REFERENCE LINE

Re: Engagement No. 39-29-3773
DS

Ladies and Gentlemen:
DS

SUBJECT LINE

ENGAGEMENT AGREEMENT FOR COMMUNICATION SYSTEMS, INC.
DS

Harrison & Pearson is pleased to confirm arrangements to audit the financial statements of Communication Systems, Inc., for the year ended June 30, 1999.

the first page. A three-part heading includes (1) the name of the person or company to whom the message is sent (identical to the first line of the letter address), (2) the page number, and (3) the date.

Place the heading one inch (six lines) from the top edge of the paper. Double-space after the heading to continue the body of the letter. Both vertical and horizontal formats are acceptable.

With all three lines beginning at the left margin, the vertical format is compatible with all letter formats. The horizontal format is more complex to keyboard but looks attractive with the modified block style and is especially effective when using the vertical heading would force the letter or memorandum to additional pages:

Vertical Format

1-inch or default set by software
Communication Systems, Inc.
Page 2
January 19, 1999
DS
We at Harrison & Pearson look forward to providing these and other quality professional services to you.

Sincerely,

Patrick L. Numez

Patrick L. Numez
Audit Partner

Horizontal Format

1-inch or default set by software

Communication Systems, Inc.   2   January 19, 1999

DS

We at Harrison & Pearson look forward to providing these and other quality professional services to you.

Sincerely,

Patrick L. Numez

Patrick L. Numez
Audit Partner

Company Name in Signature Block

Some companies prefer to include the **company name** in the signature block. However, often the company name is not included in the signature block because it appears in the letterhead. The company name is beneficial when the letter is prepared on plain paper or is more than one page (the second page of the letter is printed on plain paper). When the writer wishes to emphasize that the document is written on behalf of the company, a company name may be useful. For example, the company name might be included when the nature of the letter is a contract such as an engagement letter to a newly acquired client. Key the company name in all capitals a double space below the complimentary close and a quadruple space (three blank lines) above the signature block as shown in Figure A-7.

Enclosure Notation

An **enclosure notation** indicates that additional items (brochure, price list, résumé) are included in the same envelope. Key "Enclosure" a double-space below the reference initials (or the signature block if no reference initials appear) as shown in Figure A-7. Key the plural form (Enclosures) if more than one item is enclosed. You may identify the number of enclosures (Enclosures: 3) or the specific item enclosed (Enclosure: Bid Proposal). Avoid the temptation to abbreviate (Enc.) because abbreviations may communicate that you are in a hurry or that a thorough job is not necessary for this particular person. Some companies use the word "Attachment" on memorandums when the accompanying items may be stapled or clipped and not placed in an envelope.

Copy Notation

A **copy notation** indicates that a copy of the document was sent to the person(s) listed. Include the person's personal or professional title and full name, after keying "c" for copy. Key the copy notation at the left margin a double-space below the enclosure notation, reference initials, or signature block (depending on the special letter parts used) as shown in Figure A-7.

SECOND-PAGE
HEADING

1-inch or default set by software
Communication Systems, Inc.
Page 2
January 24, 1999
DS

Sharon Hampton has been assigned as the audit manager in charge of
your audit examination. Please review the enclosed preliminary time schedule she has developed and direct your questions to her at (406) 555-3400,
extension 25.
DS

We at Harrison & Pearson look forward to providing these and other quality
professional services to you.
DS

Sincerely,
DS

COMPANY NAME

HARRISON & PEARSON, LTD, CPAS
QS

Patrick L. Numez
Patrick L. Numez
Audit Partner

REFERENCE
INITIALS

ek
DS

ENCLOSURE
NOTATION

Enclosure: Audit Agreement
DS

COPY NOTATION

c Mr. David Banks
DS

POSTSCRIPT

Our annual tax update has been scheduled for March 5–6, 2000. You will
receive an agenda from the tax department just as soon as all details have
been finalized.

FIGURE A-7 Special letter parts.

Postscript

A **postscript**, appearing as the last item in a letter, is commonly used to emphasize
information. A postscript in a sales letter, for example, is often used to restate the central selling point; for added emphasis, it may be handwritten or printed in a different
color. Researchers have noted an increased trend toward handwritten postscripts of a
personal nature as individuals attempt to keep in touch with people in our high-tech
society. Postscripts should not be used to add information inadvertently omitted from
the letter. Instead, edit the document and reprint an effectively organized letter.

Key the postscript a double-space below the last notation or signature block if no
notations are used, as shown in Figure A-7. Treat the postscript as any other paragraph; indent only if the other paragraphs in the letter are indented. Because its position clearly labels this paragraph as a postscript, do not begin with "PS."

The second-page heading, reference initials, company name, enclosure notation,
copy notation, and postscript are illustrated in Figure A-7.

Memorandum Formats

Memorandums are messages sent to offices or individuals *within* a business. To increase productivity, companies use formats that are easy to input and will save time. Memorandums (or memos for short) may be printed on preprinted memorandum forms, plain paper, or letterhead depending on the preference of the company. A preprinted form identifies the document as a memorandum and contains the basic information: *TO, FROM, DATE, SUBJECT*.

Memo templates, available with word processing software, increase the efficiency of producing a memo. A template includes preset margins, the memo heading, a code for inserting the data automatically, and other special formatting (fonts, graphic lines and objects). As illustrated in the memo template from Microsoft Word shown in Figure A-8, the writer simply follows on-line prompts to click and input specified information (the recipient's name, the subject line, the body). Needed notations are keyed after the body (e.g., enclosures, copy, etc.). Templates are also available for letters, fax cover sheets, and other frequently formatted documents. Writers can edit a template or create new templates that fit their needs exactly.

Regardless of whether the memo is created with a template or simply keyed in a word processing file, memos begin with a heading that contains the writer's name, recipient's name, date, and subject. When preparing the heading, follow these guidelines as illustrated in Figure A-9.

1. Omit personal and professional titles (Mr., Mrs., Dr.) on the *TO* and *FROM* lines because of the informality of this intercompany communication. Include job titles or department names.

2. Include a subject line in all memos to facilitate quick reading and filing. Key the subject line in all capitals for added emphasis or begin the first word and all other words except articles, prepositions, or conjunctions with capital letters.

3. Sign the writer's initials to the right of the writer's name.

   Also, follow these general formatting guidelines if you are not using a template:

1. Set one-inch margins or the default set by your word processing software.

2. Determine the starting line:
   Plain paper: $1^1/_2$ inches (add three hard returns from the default top margin).
   Letterhead: A double-space below the letterhead.

3. Single-space paragraphs and double-space between paragraphs. Do *not* indent paragraphs.

4. Handle reference initials, enclosure and copy notations, and postscripts just as you would in a letter.

5. Include a second-page heading on the second and successive pages of a memorandum just as you would in a multiple-page letter.

Place memos in special envelopes designated for intercompany mail or in plain envelopes. If you use plain envelopes, key COMPANY MAIL in the stamp position so that it will not be inadvertently stamped and mailed. Key the recipient's name and department in the address location and any other information required by company policy. Large companies may require use of office numbers or other mail designations to expedite intercompany deliveries.

FIGURE A-8
Memo template in
Microsoft Word.

Company Name Here
Memo

To:

From:

CC:

Date:

Re:

How to Use This Memo Template

Select text you would like to replace, and type your memo. Use styles
such as Heading 1-3 and Body Text in the Style control on the Formatting toolbar. To save changes to this template for future use,
choose Save As from the File menu. In the Save As Type box, choose
Document Template. Next time you want to use it, choose New from
the File menu, and then double-click your template.

Envelopes

The U.S. Postal Service recommends a specific format for addressing envelopes so
that the address can be read by optical character readers used to sort mail efficiently.
The recommended format requires that the envelope address be keyed in all capital
letters with no punctuation (all caps, no punctuation). Proper placement of the
address on a large envelope (No. 10) is shown in Figure A-10. Additionally, to create
a highly professional image, business writers should fold letters to produce the fewest
number of creases. The proper procedures for folding letters for small (6 3/4) and
large (No. 10) envelopes appear in Figure A-11.

WATT'S
FABRIC & SUPPLY   763 East Commerce Street   Toledo, OH 43601-7530   (419) 555-3310   Fax: (419) 555-1037

DS

TO: Erin W. Lutzel, Vice President

FROM: Isako Kimura, Marketing Director *I.K.*

DATE: March 31, 1999

SUBJECT: Marketing Activity Report, June 1999

DS

The marketing division reports the following activities for June.

DS

Advertising

Three meetings were held with representatives at the Bart and Dome agency to complete plans for the fall campaign for Fluffy Buns. The campaign will concentrate on the use of discount coupons published in the Thursday food section of sixty daily newspapers in the Pacific states. Coupons will be released on the second and fourth Thursdays in June and July.

Estimated cost of the program is $645,000. That amount includes 2.2 million redeemed coupons at 20 cents each ($440,000).

A point-of-sale advertising display, shown on the attached sheet, was developed for retail grocery outlets. Sales reps are pushing these in their regular and new calls. The display may be used to feature a different product from our line on a weekly basis.

Sales Staff

We have dropped one sales rep from the northern California section and divided the area between the southern Oregon and Sacramento reps.

Call me should you wish to discuss the information presented.

Attachment

Note these specific points related to keying an envelope correctly:

- The address matches the letter address, including a personal or professional title (Mr., Ms., Dr.).
- The address contains at least three but no more than six lines.
- All lines of the return (writer's) address and the letter (receiver's) address are keyed in block form (flush at the left) and are single-spaced.
- The last line contains *only* three items of information: (1) city; (2) two-letter abbreviation for state, territory, or province; and (3) nine-digit ZIP Code.
- One space appears between the two-letter abbreviation for state, territory, or province and the ZIP Code.

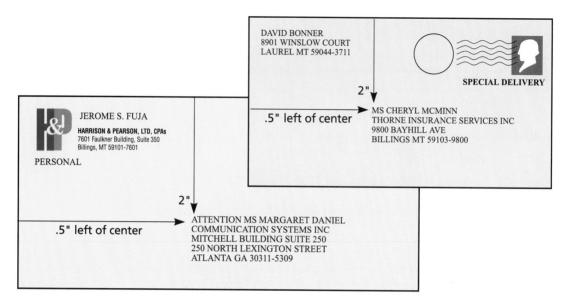

FIGURE A-10 Addressing procedures for envelopes.

Folding and Inserting Procedures for Large Envelopes

Step 1
With letter face up, fold slightly less than 1/3 of sheet up toward top.

Step 2
Fold down top of sheet to within 1/2 inch of bottom fold.

Step 3
Insert letter into envelope with last crease toward bottom of envelope.

Folding and Inserting Procedures for Small Envelopes

Step 1
With letter face up, fold bottom up to 1/2 inch from top.

Step 2
Fold right third to left.

Step 3
Fold left third to 1/2 inch from last crease.

Step 4
Insert last creased edge first.

FIGURE A-11 Folding and inserting procedures for envelopes.

- The writer's name is keyed in the half-inch of space above a preprinted company letterhead.
- Special notations for the addressee (PLEASE FORWARD, HOLD FOR ARRIVAL, PERSONAL) are placed a double-space below the return address. Mailing notations for postal authorities (OVERNIGHT and REGISTERED) are placed a double-space below the stamp position. Special notations are keyed in all capitals.

Many businesses use word processing software to print envelopes and mailing labels using the letter address in the letter. To eliminate the need to key the address twice—once for the letter and again for the envelope (all caps, no punctuation)—some authorities recommend keying the letter address in the all-caps, no-punctuation format. Obviously, if a letter is to be inserted into a window envelope, this format will assist the U.S. Postal Service in processing and delivering it quickly. The all-caps, no-punctuation format would also be appropriate for quantity mailings of a routine nature. However, because this format may make documents look like form letters and is only beginning to gain acceptance, the traditional upper- and lower-case letters with appropriate punctuation should be used for the letter address in nonroutine business letters.

Routine Letter with Letter Address Keyed in All Caps, No Punctuation

---

Northside Insurance Co.
1249 Heritage Drive
Norfolk, VA 32511-1249
(804) 555-3700

January 19, 1999

MS MAJORIE VAN DYKE
215 NORTH THIRD STREET
NORFOLK VA 23511-3100

RE: Life Insurance Policy No. 89-392-12

The two-letter abbreviations for states, territories, and Canadian provinces (see Figure A-12) and the nine-digit ZIP Code assigned by the U.S. Postal Service should be used for all letters. The first digit in a ZIP Code represents one of ten national areas. Within these areas, each state is divided into an average of ten smaller geographic areas, identified by the second and third digits. The fourth and fifth digits identify a local delivery area. The U.S. Postal Service now uses an extended ZIP Code called *ZIP+4*, which adds a hyphen and four additional numbers to the existing five-digit ZIP Code. These "+4" digits permit automated equipment to sort mail for faster delivery. The first two of the "+4" digits denote a delivery section of blocks, streets, several office buildings, or a small geographic area. The last two numbers denote a delivery "segment," which might be one floor of an office building, one side of a street, a firm, a suite, or a group of post office boxes.

State or Territory	Two-Letter Abbreviation	State or Territory	Two-Letter Abbreviation
Alabama	AL	North Carolina	NC
Alaska	AK	North Dakota	ND
Arizona	AZ	Ohio	OH
Arkansas	AR	Oklahoma	OK
California	CA	Oregon	OR
Canal Zone	CZ	Pennsylvania	PA
Colorado	CO	Puerto Rico	PR
Connecticut	CT	Rhode Island	RI
Delaware	DE	South Carolina	SC
District of Columbia	DC	South Dakota	SD
Florida	FL	Tennessee	TN
Georgia	GA	Texas	TX
Guam	GU	Utah	UT
Hawaii	HI	Vermont	VT
Idaho	ID	Virginia	VA
Illinois	IL	Virgin Islands	VI
Indiana	IN	Washington	WA
Iowa	IA	West Virginia	WV
Kansas	KS	Wisconsin	WI
Kentucky	KY	Wyoming	WY
Louisiana	LA		
Maine	ME	**Canadian Province**	**Two-Letter Abbreviation**
Maryland	MD	Alberta	AB
Massachusetts	MA	British Columbia	BC
Michigan	MI	Labrador	LB
Minnesota	MN	Manitoba	MB
Mississippi	MS	New Brunswick	NB
Missouri	MO	Newfoundland	NF
Montana	MT	Northwest Territories	NT
Nebraska	NE	Nova Scotia	NS
Nevada	NV	Ontario	ON
New Hampshire	NH	Prince Edward Island	PE
New Jersey	NJ	Quebec	PQ
New Mexico	NM	Saskatchewan	SK
New York	NY	Yukon Territory	YT

FIGURE A-12   Abbreviations of states, districts, and provinces.

Documentation Formats

In-Text Parenthetical Citations

Footnote or Endnote Citations

References (or Works Cited)

Electronic Citation Methods

A number of widely used reference styles are available for documenting the sources of information used in report writing. Popular style manuals for business writing include the following:

> *Publication Manual of the American Psychological Association,* 4th ed., Washington, DC: American Psychological Association, 1994.
> Joseph Gibaldi, *MLA Handbook for Writers of Research Papers,* 4th ed., New York: Modern Languages Association of America, 1995.
> *The Chicago Manual of Style,* 14th ed., Chicago: University of Chicago Press, 1994.

These three sources, commonly referred to as the APA, MLA, and CMS styles, present general rules for referencing and give examples of the citation formats for various types of source materials. Occasionally, you may need to reference something for which no general example applies. Choose the example that is most like your source and follow that format. When in doubt, provide more information, not less. Remember that a major purpose for listing references is to enable readers to retrieve and use the sources. This appendix illustrates citation formats for some common types of information sources and refers you to various electronic sites that provide further detailed guidelines for preparing electronic citations.

In-Text Parenthetical Citations

The *APA Manual, MLA Handbook,* and *The Chicago Manual of Style* use **in-text citations**. Abbreviated information within parentheses in the text directs the reader to a list of sources at the end of a report. The list of sources at the end contains all bibliographic information on each source cited in a report. This list is arranged alphabetically by the author's last name or, if no author is provided, by the first word of the title.

The in-text citations contain minimal information needed to locate the source in the complete list. In-text citations prepared using the *APA Manual* include the author's last name and the date of publication; the page number is included only if referencing a direct quotation. The *MLA Handbook* includes the author's last name and the page number, for both quotes and paraphrases, but not the date of publication. *The Chicago Manual of Style* includes the author's name and the year of publication. Note the following in-text parenthetical citations shown in APA and MLA styles.

One author not named in the text, direct quotation

APA: "A recent survey . . . shows that more and more companies plan to publish their annual reports on the Internet" (Prinn, 1998, p. 13).

Include page number only when referencing a direct quotation. Precede page numbers with p. (one-page) or pp. (multiple pages).

MLA: "A recent survey . . . shows that more and more companies plan to publish their annual reports on the Internet" (Prinn 13).

Multiple authors or sources not in the text wording

APA: Globalization is becoming a continuous challenge for managers . . . (Tang & Crofford, 1997).

MLA: Globalization is becoming a continuous challenge for managers . . . (Tang and Crofford 29).

APA: "For all its difficulty, teamwork is still essential . . ." (Nunamaker et al., 1997, p. 163).

MLA: "For all its difficulty, teamwork is still essential . . ." (Nunamaker *et al.* 163).

For sources by more than six authors, use et al. after the name of the first author. For works by fewer than six authors, cite all authors the first time the work is referenced; use et al. for subsequent references. Do not underline et al.

For sources by more than three authors, use et al. after the name of the first author.

More than one source documenting the same idea

APA: . . . companies are turning to micromarketing (Heath, 1996; Roach, 1997).

MLA: . . . companies are turning to micromarketing (Heath 48; Roach 54).

More than one source by the same author documenting the same idea

APA: Past research (Taylor, 1995, 1997) shows . . .

MLA: Past research (Taylor, "Performance Appraisal" 6), ("Frequent Absenteeism" 89) shows . . .

Reference to author(s) or date in the text wording

APA: Spalding and Price (1996) documented the results . . .

MLA: Kent Spalding and Brian Price documented the results . . .

In 1998, West concluded . . . .

In 1998, West concluded . . . . (E2).

Omit a page number when citing a one-page article or nonprint sources.

No author provided

APA: . . . virtues of teamwork look obvious ("The trouble with teams," 1995).

MLA: . . . virtues of teamwork look obvious ("The Trouble with Teams" 61).

One of two or more works by the same author(s) in the same year

APA: Zuidema and Kleiner (1996a) advocated . . .

MLA: Zuidema and Kleiner ("New Developments in Self-Directed Work Groups" 57) advocated . . .

Footnote or Endnote Citations

Placing citations at the bottom of the page on which they are cited is the **footnote citation** method. It is often referred to as the **traditional method** because of its long use. Quotes and paraphrases are marked in text with numbers that are keyed in superscript or parentheses and correspond to full citations at the bottom of the appropriate page. Those who prefer to cite references using the footnote method may follow *The Chicago Manual of Style* (CMS). (Neither *APA* or *MLA Handbook* permit footnote citations.) Examples of traditional footnotes documenting a direct quotation and a paraphrase in CMS style follow:

Footnote Citation—Chicago Manual of Style (CMS)

"In a Total Quality Management context, the standard for determining quality is meeting customer requirements and expectations the first time and every time."[1] Groupware can enable organizations to achieve their TQA goals by equipping teams with new communication abilities.[2]

[1]V. Daniel Hunt, *Managing for Quality* (Homewood, Ill.: Business One Irwin, 1993), 15.

[2]Jay F. Nunamaker, Robert O. Briggs, and Daniel Mittleman, "Electronic Meeting Systems: Ten Years of Lessons Learned," In D. Coleman and R. Khanna (eds.), *Groupware: Technology and Applications* (Englewood Cliffs, NJ: Prentice-Hall, 1995), 107.

Full-feature word processing programs have changed the tedious task of preparing footnotes to a simple matter of instructing the computer to create a footnote. The software inserts the superscript number identifying the footnote and provides a special footnote-entry screen for keying the footnote. The software calculates how much space is needed at the bottom of each page for the footnotes and paginates each page automatically. The software also renumbers the notes automatically any time you add, delete, or move footnotes.

The **endnote citation** method lists all citations in a list called "Endnotes" at the end of a report, instead of at the bottom of each page of text where the citations occur. A list of citations at the end of a report is obviously easier to prepare than footnotes. However, readers will be forced to turn to the end of a report rather than glance at the bottom of the page to locate a source. Endnotes are listed in the order in which citations appear in a report and correspond to the numbers keyed within the text in superscript or parentheses. The endnote page is then followed with a bibliography page that lists all sources alphabetically.

As with footnotes, word processing software can assist in the preparation of endnotes. The process is similar to that of preparing footnotes except that you instruct the software to print the endnotes in the correct sequence on a separate page rather than at the bottom of each page. Additionally, word processing shortcuts can be used to convert endnotes (and footnotes) into a properly formatted reference list. Simply use the block command to make another copy of the endnotes page. By inputting the necessary revisions on the copy (change the title to "References," reverse the order of the authors' names, add page numbers, and so on), you avoid having to re-key all the publication information. Finally, use the sort feature to put the entries in alphabetical order by author's last name or the first word of the title if no author is provided.

References (or Works Cited)

The **references** or **works cited** is an alphabetized list of the sources used in preparing a report, with each entry containing publication information necessary for locating the source. In addition, the bibliographic entries give evidence of the nature of sources the author consulted. *Bibliography* (literally "description of books") is sometimes used to refer to this list.

A researcher often uses sources that provide information but do not result in citations. To acknowledge that you may have consulted these works and to provide the reader with a comprehensive reading list, include these sources in the list of sources. The APA and MLA styles use different terms to distinguish between these types of lists:

	APA	**MLA**
Includes only sources cited	References	Works Cited
Includes works cited and consulted	Bibliography	Works Consulted

Your company guidelines or authoritative style manual may specify whether to list works cited only or works consulted. If you receive no definitive guidelines, use your own judgment. If in doubt, include all literature cited and read, and label the page with the appropriate title so that the reader clearly understands the nature of the list.

To aid the reader in locating sources in lengthy bibliographies, include several subheadings denoting the types of publications documented; for example, books, articles, unpublished documents and papers, government publications, and nonprint media. Check your reference manual to determine if subheadings are allowed.

Bibliographic styles for a variety of publications prepared using the APA style are shown in Figure B-1. The same entries prepared using the MLA style appear in Figure B-2. Note that the APA and MLA formats have several distinct variations:

	APA	**MLA**
Indention and Spacing	Indent the first line of each entry five to seven spaces, the same as paragraphs in text. Double space within and between entries.	Use hanging indention with the second and subsequent lines indented five spaces. Single space within and double space between entries.
Author Names	List the last names first for all authors. Use initials for first and middle names. Use an ampersand (&) rather than "and" before the name of the last author.	List the last name first for the first author only. Use "and" before last author name.
Date	Place date in parentheses after the author name(s).	Place date at end of book references or after title of periodical articles.
Capitalization	In titles of books and articles, capitalize only the first word of the title, the first word of the	In titles of books, periodicals, and article titles, capitalize all main words.

	APA	MLA
	subtitle, and proper names. All other words begin with lowercase letters. In titles of journals and newspapers, capitalize all significant words.	
Underlining and Quotation Marks	Underline the titles of books, journals, and other periodicals. Do not use quotation marks around the titles of articles.	Underline the titles of books, journals, and periodicals. Place titles of articles within quotation marks.
Page Notations	Use p. or pp. with page numbers for newspapers only.	Omit the use of p. or pp. on all citations.

FIGURE B-1
Guide to Preparing References in APA (4th Edition) Style.

Guide to Preparing References in APA (4th Edition) Style

A book reference with two authors and edition

Levine, J., & Baroudi, C. (1997). <u>The Internet for dummies</u>, (3rd ed.). Southlake, TX: IDG Books Worldwide.

An edited book

Webster, S., & Connolly, F. W. (Eds.). (1993). <u>The ethics kit</u>. New York: McGraw Hill.

A chapter in a book or section within a reference book

Nunamaker, J. F., Briggs, R. O., & Mittleman, D. (1995). Electronic meeting systems: Ten years of lessons learned. In D. Coleman and R. Khanna (Eds.), <u>Groupware: Technology and applications</u> (pp. 42–61). Englewood Cliffs, NJ: Prentice-Hall.

Standard & Poor's. (1997). Northland Cranberries, Inc. In <u>Standard & Poor's corporation records</u> (p. 3093). New York: Standard & Poor's.

A report, brochure, or book from a private organization, corporate author

Wal-Mart Stores, Inc. (1997). <u>Annual report</u>. Bentonville, AR: Wal-Mart Stores.

Asahi Japan Collectibles. (1997). <u>Communication habits of Americans and Japanese</u>. [Brochure]. Kensington, CT: Asahi Japan Collectibles.

A journal article with volume and issue

Thomas, J. (1997). Discourse in the marketplace: The making of meaning in annual reports. Journal of Business Communication, 34(1), 47-66.
Note: 34(1) signifies volume 34, issue 1.

A periodical article without an author

The trouble with teams. (1995, January 14). Economist, 61.

An article in a newspaper

Hirschfeld, J. (1997, June 14). Regulators worldwide struggle with online issues. The Dallas Morning News, pp. F1, F3.

A government publication

Equal Employment Opportunity Commission. (1996). Minorities and women in institutions of higher education. (Report No. NCTRL-RR-96-4). Washington, DC: EEOC.

Unpublished interviews and letters

Tabb, J., administrative director, Nibco, Inc. (1998, January 13). Interview by author. Nacogdoches, TX.
Cite letters in text as personal communications; do not include in references list.
Example: K. W. Shaie (personal communication, April 18, 1997)

Computer software

Microsoft Word 7.0 [Computer software]. (1996). Redmond, WA: Microsoft Corporation.

Films, filmstrips, slide programs, and videotapes

Coaching the team [Videocassette]. (1997). Princeton: Films for the Humanities and Sciences.

FIGURE B-1
Guide to Preparing References in APA (4th Edition) Style (continued).

Guide to Preparing Works Cited in MLA (4th Edition) Style

A book reference with two authors and edition

Levine, John and Carol Baroudi. The Internet for Dummies, 3rd ed. Southlake, TX: IDG Books Worldwide, 1997.
Note: For more than three authors, use et al. (meaning "and others") after the name of the first author.

An edited book

Webster, Sally and Frank W. Connolly, eds. The Ethics Kit. New York: McGraw Hill, 1993.

FIGURE B-2
Guide to Preparing Works Cited in MLA (4th Edition) Style.

FIGURE B-2
Guide to Preparing Works Cited in MLA (4th Edition) Style (continued).

A chapter in a book or section within a reference book
Nunamaker, Jay F., Robert O. Briggs, and Daniel Mittleman. "Electronic Meeting Systems: Ten Years of Lessons Learned." Groupware: Technology and Applications. Eds. D. Coleman and R. Khanna. (Englewood Cliffs: Prentice-Hall, 1995). 107.

"Northland Cranberries, Inc." Standard & Poor's Corporation Records, vol. 4. New York: Standard & Poor's, 1997.

A report, brochure, or book from a private organization, corporate author
Wal-Mart Stores, Inc. Annual Report. Bentonville: Wal-Mart Stores, 1997.

Asahi Japan Collectibles. Communication Habits of Americans and Japanese. Kensington, CT: Asahi Japan Collectibles, 1997.

A journal article with volume and issue
Thomas, Jane. "Discourse in the Marketplace: The Making of Meaning in Annual Reports." Journal of Business Communication 34.1 (1997): 47-66.
Note: 34.1 signifies volume 34, issue 1.

A periodical article without an author
"The Trouble with Teams." Economist 14 Jan. 1995: 61.

An article in a newspaper
Hirschfeld, Julie. "Regulators Worldwide Struggle With Online Issues." The Dallas Morning News 14 June 1997: F1, F3.

A government publication
Equal Employment Opportunity Commission. Minorities and Women in Institutions of Higher Education. Washington: EEOC, 1996.

Unpublished interviews and letters
Wang, Richard L. Personal interview. 27 June 1998.

Kline, M. Allen. Letter to D. Carlson. 30 Nov. 1997.

Computer software
Microsoft Word 7.0. Computer software. Redmond: Microsoft Corporation, 1996.

Films, filmstrips, slide programs, and videotapes
Coaching the Team. Videocassette. Princeton: Films for the Humanities and Sciences, 1997.

Electronic Citation Methods

Citing Internet and other electronic sources can be particularly complicated. Many of the style guides were written before such resources became so incredibly popular and diverse and, therefore, do not give clear guidelines for citing such sources. A good starting point for learning how to reference electronic citations is the following book:

Electronic Style: A Handbook for Citing Electronic Information, 2nd ed. by Xia Li and Nancy B. Crane, Medford, NJ: Information Today, Inc., 1996.

Li and Crane include guidelines for both "APA embellished style" and "MLA embellished style" citations, as well as a few examples of footnotes and endnotes. Citation formats for CD-ROM and dial-up information service databases are illustrated, along with Internet citation formats. Scholars in various fields have applied the recommendations of Li and Crane and extended them for particular disciplines. Janice Walker has developed a referencing style based on MLA which is endorsed by the Alliance for Computers and Writing. She has also added guidelines for adaptation to APA referencing format. Walker's site can be visited as follows:

http://www.cas.usf.edu/english/walker/mla.html

Another valuable website is the following one, which offers a summary of sites with formatting guidelines for APA, MLA, and CMS:

http://www.wtamu.edu/library/websites/citation.html

The various referencing styles are fairly standardized as to the elements included when citing documents retrieved electronically. Include the following items:

1. Author (if given)
2. Date of publication
3. Title of article and/or name of publication
4. Electronic medium (such as on-line or CD-ROM)
5. Volume, series, page, and path (Uniform Resource Locator or Internet address)
6. Date you retrieved or accessed the resource

Examples of referencing formats for various electronically retrieved documents are illustrated in Figure B-3 (APA style) and B-4 (MLA style).

For additional information on citing print and other types of resources in CMS style, visit Citing Electronic Information in History Papers at

http://www.people.memphis.edu/~mcrouse/elcite.html

Online sources of information can include graphics, sounds, and video, as well as text. An informative site that contains links to other sites that provide citation guidelines for the various referencing styles is the Classroom Connect Resource Station page on Citing Internet Addresses, located at the following address:

http://www.classroom.net/resource/CitingNetResources.html

Whenever you are not required to use a particular documentation style, choose a recognized one and follow it consistently. You will find that the formatting particulars become easier with repeated use.

FIGURE B-3
Guide to Preparing Electronic Citations in APA (4th Edition) Style.

Guide to Preparing Electronic Citations in APA (4th Edition) Style

Article from World Wide Web site

Weir, W. (1997, Winter). Year 2000, are you ready? <u>UNCSN Computing</u>

<u>News,</u> [On-line] 11(1) (1 page). Available:http://csn.uneb.edu/year2000/Year2000

AreYouReady.htm [1998, January 8].

Article from on-line periodical

Johnson, T. (1994, December 5). Indigenous people are now more combat-

ive, organized. <u>Miami Herald</u>. [On-line], p. 29SA(22 paragraphs). Available

Gopher://summitt.fiu.edu/Miami Herald Summit Related Articles/12/05/95.

Indigenous People Now More Combative, Organized [1997, July 16].

Article on CD-ROM

Microsoft Corporation. (1996). Fiber optics. <u>Encarta 96 Encyclopedia</u>
[CD-ROM]. [1997, July 10].

Discussion list message

RRECOME. (1997, August 1). <u>Top ten rules of international communica-</u>

<u>tion. Discussions on International Business Communication</u> [Online]. Available E-

mail: LISTSERV@american.edu/Get international-1 log 9804A [1997, August 1].

E-mail message

DuFrene, D. D. (ddufrene@sfasu.edu). (1998, January 14). Netiquette

guidelines. E-mail to C. M. Lehman (clehman@cobilan.msstate.edu).

For additional information on citing resources in APA style, visit
http://www.english.uiuc.edu/cws/wworkshop/apamenu.htm

FIGURE B-4
Guide to Preparing Electronic Citations in MLA (4th Edition) style.

Guide to Preparing Electronic Citations in MLA (4th Edition) Style

Article from World Wide Web site

Weir, Walter. "Year 2000, Are You Ready?" <u>UNCSN Computing News</u> 11.1 (Winter 1997): 1 page. Online. Available: http://csn.uneb.edu/year2000/Year2000AreYouReady.htm. 8 Jan. 1998.

Article from on-line periodical

Johnson, Tim. "Indigenous People Are Now More Combative, Organized." <u>Miami Herald</u> 5 Dec. 1994: 29SA. Online. Available: gopher://summitt.fiu.edu/Miami Herald—Summit Related Articles/12/05/95. Indigenous People Now More Combative, Organized. 16 July 1997.

Article on CD-ROM

Microsoft Corporation. "Fiber Optics." <u>Encarta 96 Encyclopedia</u>. 1996. CD-ROM. 10 July 1997.

Discussion list message

RRECOME. "Top ten rules of international communication. Discussions on International Business Communication" 1 August, 1997. Online posting. Discussions on International Communication. Available E-mail: LISTSERV@american.edu/Get international-1 log 9804A. 1 Aug. 1997.

E-mail message

DuFrene, Debbie D. (ddufrene@sfasu.edu). "Netiquette Guidelines." E-mail to Carol M. Lehman (clehman@cobilan.msstate.edu). 14 Jan. 1998.

For additional information on citing resources in MLA style, visit MLA Format (UIUC Writers Workshop at http://www.english.uiuc.edu.cws/wworkshop/mlamenu.htm

Language Review and Exercises

Self-Check

Nouns

Pronouns

Verbs

Adjectives and Adverbs

Sentence Structure

Punctuation

Numbers

Capitalization

Abbreviations

Words Frequently Misused

Self-Check

Review Quiz

If messages do not meet high standards of grammar and mechanics, they have negative consequences. The receiver may (1) misunderstand the message, (2) lose time by stopping to review the message, (3) think more about the error than the message, or (4) think negatively about the sender's background or lose respect for the sender.

The following pages review some of the common problems that confront business writers. Regardless of job level (from the lowest entry level to the highest managerial level), a knowledge of basics is beneficial. The rules and principles on the following pages should be mastered by personnel at all these levels.

The following review of basics seeks to answer frequently encountered questions about word usage, grammar, spelling, and punctuation. For more thorough reviews, consult standard reference books on grammar or transcription.

✓ Self-Check

To measure your knowledge of grammar, spelling, and punctuation, follow these steps: Cover the answer that appears below each numbered sentence. Identify the grammatical error(s) in the numbered sentences. Then, slide the cover sheet down and check your answer against the correct sentence.

1. Only 1 of the applicants have completed the employment tests; but 3 have submitted résumés.

   Only <u>one</u> of the applicants <u>has</u> completed the employment tests<u>,</u> but <u>three</u> have submitted résumés.

2. Neither vice president Cox nor secretary Perez are ready to present their recommendations.

   Neither <u>Vice President</u> Cox nor <u>Secretary</u> Perez <u>is</u> ready to present_ recommendations.

3. One applicants' employment test was postponed for two hours, this may have effected the test score.

   One <u>applicant's</u> employment test was postponed for two hours<u>;</u> this <u>delay</u> may have <u>affected</u> the test score. (Nouns other than "delay" can be used.)

4. Stephen's grin and bear it attitude is his fundamental principal of survival.

   Stephen's <u>grin-and-bear-it</u> attitude is his fundamental <u>principle</u> of survival.

5. Supervisors discussed one criteria for promotion during annual performance interviews with full time personal.

   Supervisors discussed one <u>criterion</u> for promotion during annual performance interviews with <u>full-time</u> <u>personnel</u>.

6. I appreciate you writing a proposal, and sending it directly to the controller and I.

   I appreciate <u>your</u> submitting a proposal_ and sending it directly to the controller and <u>me</u>.

7. A short intensive review will be conducted on April 14, 1999 at 10:00 A.M.

   A short<u>,</u> intensive review will be conducted on April 14, <u>1999</u>, at 10 <u>a.m.</u>

8. If you can complete the survey before July 1, 1999 please proceed, otherwise ask the superintendent for a new set of questionnaires.

   If you can complete the survey before July 1, <u>1999</u>, please <u>proceed</u>; otherwise<u>,</u> ask the superintendent for a new set of questionnaires.

9. Did the Controller really use the words "get out of my office?"

   Did the <u>controller</u> really use the words<u>,</u> "<u>Get</u> out of my office"<u>?</u>

10. Please try to quickly review these documents, it's to be returned before October 21st.

    Please try <u>to review</u> these documents <u>quickly</u>; <u>they</u> must be returned before October <u>21</u>.

After completing the "Self-Check," identify your problem areas and complete the pertinent sections of this review. For best results, follow these suggestions for studying Appendix C:

1. Read the principle and examine the illustrations that follow. Reread the principle to reinforce learning.

2. Complete the exercises positioned throughout this review. They are designed to test your understanding of the principles.

3. Complete the "Self-Check" exercise and "Review Quiz" designed to assess how well you have mastered the grammar principles presented in Appendix C. Analyze any questions you may have answered incorrectly to identify specific areas in which you need further study. Then reread these principles.

Nouns

Nouns are words that name people, places, things, or ideas.

1. **Use *specific* nouns for most business writing because they let a receiver see exactly what is meant.** "The dean objected" gives a clearer picture than "An administrator objected"; "A 212-ton truck is missing" is clearer than "One vehicle is missing."

   Use *general* words when you do not want (or need) to convey a vivid mental picture. "I appreciated your letting me know about the accident" is less vivid (and better) than ". . . about your sprained ankle, your broken ribs, and the smashed-up car."

2. **Use *concrete nouns* as sentence subjects normally because they help to present ideas vividly.** "Joe explained the procedure" is more vivid than "Explanations were given by Joe." Because "explanations" are harder to visualize than "Joe," the idea in the second sentence is more difficult to see. *Concrete* nouns are word labels for that which is solid—something that can be seen, touched, and so on. *Abstract* nouns are word labels for that which is not solid—something that cannot be seen, touched, and so on. *Tree* is a concrete noun. *Thought*, *confrontation*, and *willingness* are abstract nouns.

   Use an abstract noun as the subject of a sentence if you do not want an idea to stand out vividly. "His weakness was well known" is less vivid than "He was known to be weak."

Exercise 1

Write the letter for the better sentence and provide a reason for your answer.

1. a. Mr. Phillips called me yesterday.
   b. A man called me yesterday.
2. a. Mallory was driving 40 mph in a 25-mph zone.
   b. Mallory was exceeding the speed limit.
3. a. We appreciate the explanation of your financial circumstances.
   b. We appreciate the information you gave about your losses from bad debts and your shrinking markets.

> 4. a. An explanation of the procedures was presented by Jim Lewis.
>   b. Jim Lewis explained the procedures.
> 5. a. Authorization of payment is the responsibility of the controller.
>   b. The controller authorizes all payments.

Pronouns

Pronouns (words used in place of nouns) enable us to make our writing smoother than it would be if no pronouns were used. For example, compare these versions of the same sentence:

Without pronouns: Mr. Smith had some difficulty with Mr. Smith's car, so Mr. Smith took Mr. Smith's car to the corner garage for repairs.

With pronouns: Mr. Smith had some difficulty with his car, so he took it to the corner garage for repairs.

1. **Make a pronoun agree in number with its *antecedent* (the specific noun for which a pronoun stands.)**

   a. Use a plural antecedent when a pronoun represents two or more singular antecedents connected by *and*.

   The secretary <u>and</u> the treasurer will take <u>their</u> vacations.

   ["The" before "treasurer" indicates that the sentence is about two people.]

   The secretary <u>and</u> treasurer will take <u>his</u> vacation.

   [Omitting "the" before "treasurer" indicates that the sentence is about one person who has two sets of responsibilities.]

   b. Parenthetical remarks (remarks that can be omitted without destroying the basic meaning of the sentence) that appear between the pronoun and its antecedent have no effect on the form of the pronoun.

   Daniel Brown, <u>not the secretaries</u>, is responsible for <u>his</u> correspondence.

   [Because "his" refers to Daniel and not to "secretaries," "his" is used instead of "their."]

   c. Use a singular antecedent with *each*, *everyone*, *no*, and their variations.

   <u>Each</u> student and <u>each</u> teacher will carry <u>his or her</u> own equipment.

   <u>Everyone</u> is responsible for <u>her or his</u> work.

   d. Use a singular antecedent when two or more singular antecedents are connected by *or* or *nor*.

   <u>Neither</u> David <u>nor</u> Bill can complete <u>his</u> work.

   Ask <u>either</u> Mary <u>or</u> Sue about <u>her</u> in-service training.

   e. Use a singular antecedent when a noun represents a *unit* composed of more than *one* person or thing.

   The <u>company</u> stands behind <u>its</u> merchandise.

   The <u>group</u> wants to retain <u>its</u> goals.

f. Use pronouns that agree in number with the intended meaning of collective nouns.

The accounting <u>staff</u> has been asked for <u>its</u> contributions.

["Staff" is thought of as a unit; the singular "its" is appropriate.]

The accounting <u>staff</u> have been asked for <u>their</u> contributions.

["Staff" is thought of as more than one individual; the plural "their" is appropriate.]

2. **Use the correct case of pronouns.** *Case* tells whether a pronoun is used as the subject of a sentence or as an object in it.

a. Use nominative-case pronouns (*I, he, she, they, we, you, it, who*) as subjects of a sentence or clause.

<u>You</u> and <u>I</u> must work together. **["You" and "I" are subjects of the verb "work."]**

Those <u>who</u> work will be paid. **[Who is the subject of the dependent clause "who work."]**

b. Use objective-case pronouns (*me, him, her, them, us, you, it, whom*) as objects of verbs and prepositions.

Mrs. Kellum telephoned <u>him</u>. **["Him" is the object of the verb "telephoned."]**

The increase in salary is for the manager and <u>her</u>. **["Her" is the object of the preposition "for."]**

To <u>whom</u> should we send the report? **["Whom" is the object of the preposition "to."]**

Tip: Restate a subordinate clause introduced by who or whom to determine the appropriate pronoun.

She is the type of manager <u>whom</u> we can promote. **[Restating "whom we can promote" as "We can promote her (whom)" clarifies that "whom" is the object.]**

She is the type of manager <u>who</u> can be promoted. **[Restating "who can be promoted" as "She (who) can be promoted" clarifies that "who" is the subject.]**

Tip: Change a question to a statement to determine the correct form of a pronoun.

<u>Whom</u> did you call? **[You did call *whom*.]**

<u>Whom</u> did you select for the position? **[You did select *whom* for the position.]**

c. Use the nominative case when forms of the linking verb *be* require a pronoun to complete the meaning.

It was <u>he</u> who received credit for the sale.

It is <u>she</u> who deserves the award.

["It was he" may to some people sound just as distracting as the incorrect "It was him." Express the ideas in a different way to avoid the error and an expletive beginning.]

He was the one who received credit for the sale.

She deserves the award.

d. Use the possessive form of a pronoun before a gerund (a verb used as a noun).

We were delighted at <u>his</u> (not *him*) taking the job.

["Taking the job" is used here as a noun. "His" in this sentence serves the same purpose it serves in "We are delighted at <u>his</u> success."]

3. **Place relative pronouns as near their antecedents as possible for clear understanding.** A *relative* pronoun joins a subordinate clause to its antecedent.

Ambiguous	Clear
The <u>members</u> were given receipts <u>who</u> have paid.	The <u>members</u> <u>who</u> have paid were given receipts.
The agreement will enable you to pay <u>whichever</u> is lower, <u>6 percent or $50</u>.	The agreement will enable you to pay <u>6 percent or $50</u>, <u>whichever</u> is lower.

Restate a noun instead of risking a *vague* pronoun reference.

Vague	Clear
The patrolman captured the suspect even though he was unarmed.	The patrolman captured the suspect even though the patrolman was unarmed.

4. **Do not use a *pronoun* by itself to refer to a phrase, clause, sentence, or paragraph.** A pronoun should stand for a noun, and that noun should appear in the writing.

Incorrect	Correct
He expects to take all available accounting courses and obtain a position in a public accounting firm. This appeals to him.	He expects to take all available accounting courses and obtain a position in a public accounting firm. <u>This plan</u> appeals to him.

Exercise 2

Select the correct word.

1. The president and the chief executive officer reported (his, their) earnings to the employees.
2. Everyone was asked to share (his, their) opinion.
3. The production manager, not the controller, presented (his, their) strongly opposing views.
4. Stephen and Helen were recognized for (her, their) contribution.
5. Neither Stephen nor Helen was recognized for (her, their) contribution.
6. Our company is revising (their, its) statement of purpose.
7. The committee presented (its, their) recommendation to the president yesterday.
8. The instructor asked Dan and (I, me) to leave the room.

9. Lucille requested that proceeds be divided equally between Calvin and (her, she).

10. It was (she, her) who submitted the recommendation.

11. The speaker did not notice (me, my) leaving early.

12. (Who, Whom) is calling?

13. She is an employee in (who, whom) we have great confidence.

14. He is the one (who, whom) arrived twenty minutes late.

15. Mr. Smith forgot to retain his expense vouchers; (this, this oversight) caused a delay in reimbursement.

Verbs

Verbs present problems in number, person, tense, voice, and mood.

1. **Make subjects agree with verbs.**

   a. Ignore intervening phrases that have no effect on the verb used.

      Good material <u>and</u> fast delivery <u>are</u> (not *is*) essential.

      <u>You</u>, not the carrier, <u>are</u> (not *is*) responsible for the damage. [**Intervening phrase, "not the carrier," does not affect the verb used.**]

      The <u>attitude</u> of these people <u>is</u> (not *are*) receptive. [**The subject is "attitude"; "of these people" is a phrase coming between the subject and the verb.**]

      <u>One</u> of the clerks <u>was</u> (not *were*) dismissed. [**"One" is the subject.**]

   b. Use a verb that agrees with the noun closer to the verb when *or* or *nor* connects two subjects.

      Only one or <u>two</u> questions <u>are</u> (not *is*) necessary.

      Several paint brushes or one paint <u>roller</u> <u>is</u> (not *are*) necessary.

   c. Use singular verbs with plural nouns that have a singular meaning.

      The <u>news</u> <u>is</u> good.

      <u>Economics</u> <u>is</u> a required course.

      <u>Mathematics</u> <u>is</u> to be reviewed.

   d. Use a singular verb with plural subjects that are thought of as singular units.

      Twenty <u>dollars</u> <u>is</u> too much.

      Ten <u>minutes</u> <u>is</u> sufficient time.

   e. Use a singular verb for titles of articles, firm names, and slogans.

      "Understanding Computers" <u>is</u> an interesting article.

      Stein, Jones, and Baker <u>is</u> the oldest firm in the city.

      "Free lunches for all" <u>is</u> our campaign slogan.

2. **Choose verbs that agree in *person* with their subjects.** *Person* indicates whether the subject is (1) speaking, (2) being spoken to, or (3) being spoken about.

First person: I am, we are. **[Writer or speaker]**

Second person: You are. **[Receiver of message]**

Third person: He is, she is, they are. **[Person being discussed]**

She <u>doesn't</u> (not *don't*) attend class regularly.

They <u>don't</u> attend class regularly.

3. **Use the appropriate verb tense.** *Tense* indicates time. Tenses are both simple and compound.

Simple tenses:

Present: I <u>see</u> you. **[Tells what is happening now.]**

Past: I <u>saw</u> you. **[Tells what has already happened.]**

Future: I <u>will see</u> you. **[Tells what is yet to happen.]**

Compound tenses:

Present perfect: I <u>have seen</u> you. **[Tells of past action that extends to the present.]**

Past perfect: I <u>had seen</u> you. **[Tells of past action that was finished before another past action.]**

Future perfect: I <u>will have seen</u> you. **[Tells of action that will be finished before a future time.]**

  a. Use present tense when something *was* and *still* is true.

     The speaker reminded us that Rhode Island <u>is</u> (not *was*) smaller than Wisconsin.

  b. Avoid unnecessary shifts in tense.

     The carrier <u>brought</u> (not *brings*) my package but left without asking me to sign for it.

     Verbs that appear in the same sentence are not required to be in the same tense.

     The contract that <u>was prepared</u> yesterday <u>will be signed</u> tomorrow.

4. **Use active voice for most business writing.** *Voice* is the term used to indicate whether a subject *acts* or whether it *is acted upon*. If the subject of a sentence acts, the verb used to describe that action is called an *active verb*.

The keyboard operator <u>made</u> an error.

The woman <u>asked</u> for an adjustment.

If the subject of the sentence is acted upon, the verb used to describe that action is called a *passive verb*.

An error <u>was made</u> by the keyboard operator.

An adjustment <u>was asked</u> for by the woman.

Active voice is preferred for most business writing. Refer to Chapter 3 for a discussion of appropriate uses of passive voice.

5. **Use subjunctive mood when speaking of conditions that do not necessarily exist, suggesting doubt, supposition, probability, wishfulness, or sorrow.**

   a. Use <u>were</u> for the present tense of <u>to be</u> in the subjunctive mood.

      I wish the story <u>were</u> (not *was*) true.

      If I <u>were</u> (not *was*) you, I would try again.

   b. Consider the subjunctive mood for communicating negative ideas in positive language.

      I wish I <u>were</u>. **[More tactful than "No, I am not."]**

      We <u>would</u> make a refund if the merchandise had been used in accordance with instructions. **[Implies "we are *not* making a refund" but avoids negative words.]**

Exercise 3

Select the correct word.

1. If he (was, were) over 18, he would have been hired.
2. Only one of the graphs (was, were) usable.
3. The typesetters, not the editor, (was, were) responsible for these errors.
4. Neither the coach nor the players (was, were) invited.
5. Both John and Steven (was, were) promoted.
6. The news from the rescue mission (is, are) encouraging.
7. *Ten Steps to Greatness* (has, have) been placed in the company library.
8. A child reminded me that the earth (rotates, rotated) on its axis.
9. Tim (don't, doesn't) ask for favors.
10. The president studied the page for a minute and (starts, started) asking questions.

Change each sentence from passive to active voice.

1. The booklet was edited by Susan Woodward.
2. The figures have been checked by our accountant.
3. Ms. Jackson was recommended for promotion by the supervisor.
4. The applications are being screened. (When revising, assume that a committee is doing the screening.)
5. Your request for a leave has been approved. (When revising, assume the manager did the approving.)

Adjectives and Adverbs

Adjectives modify nouns or pronouns. *Adverbs* modify verbs, adjectives, or other adverbs. Although most adverbs end in *ly*, some commonly used adverbs do not end in *ly*: *there, then, after, now, hence,* and *very*. Most words that end in *ly* are adverbs, but common exceptions are *neighborly, timely, friendly, gentlemanly*. Some words are both adjective and adverb: *fast, late,* and *well*.

1. **Use an adjective to modify a noun or pronoun.**

   Doug developed an <u>impressive</u> slide show.

   I prefer the <u>conservative</u> presentation design template.

2. **Use an adjective after a linking verb when the modifier refers to the subject instead of to the verb.** (A linking verb connects a subject to the rest of the sentence. "He <u>is</u> old." "She <u>seems</u> sincere.")

   The applicant seemed <u>qualified</u>. [**The adjective "qualified" refers to "applicant," not to "seemed."**]

   The president looked <u>suspicious</u>. [**The adjective "suspicious" refers to "president," not to "looked."**]

3. **Use an adverb to modify a verb, an adjective, or another adverb.**

   The salesperson looked <u>enthusiastically</u> at the prospect. [**The adverb "enthusiastically" modifies the verb "looked."**]

   The committee was <u>really</u> active. [The adverb "really" modifies the adjective "active."]

   Worker A progressed <u>relatively faster</u> than did Worker B. [**The adverb "relatively" modifies the adverb "faster."**]

4. **Use comparatives and superlatives carefully.**

   She is the <u>faster</u> (not *fastest*) of the two workers.

   He is the <u>better</u> (not *best*) of the two operators.

   Exclude a person or thing from a group with which that person or thing is being compared.

   He is older than <u>anyone else</u> (not *anyone*) in his department. [**As a member of his department, he cannot be older than himself.**]

   "The XD600 is newer than <u>any other machine</u> (not *any machine*) in our department." [**The XD600 cannot be newer than itself.**]

Exercise 4

Select the correct word.

1. Our supply of parts is replenished (frequent, frequently).
2. Marcus looked (impatient, impatiently).
3. The server moved (quick, quickly) from table to table.
4. Of the two people who were interviewed, Jane made the (better, best) impression.
5. Benito is faster than (any, any other) keyboarder in his department.

Sentence Structure

1. **State the subject of each sentence (unless the sentence is a command).**

   I received (not *Received*) the supervisor's request today.

   Return the forms to me. [**The subject (*you*) is understood and can be omitted in this imperative sentence.**]

2. **Rely mainly on sentences that follow the normal subject-verb-complement sequence.**

   Jennifer and I withdrew for three reasons.
     (subject)   **(verb)**   **(complement)**

   People are accustomed to sentences stated in this sequence. Sentences that expose the verb *before* revealing the subject (1) slow down the reading, (2) present less vivid pictures, and (3) use more words than would be required if the normal sequence were followed.

Original	Better
There are two reasons for our withdrawal.	Two reasons for our withdrawal are . . . .
	Jennifer and I withdrew for two reasons.
It is necessary that we withdraw.	We must withdraw.

   There, it, and *here* are called *expletives*—filler words that have no real meaning in the sentence.

3. **Do not put unrelated ideas in the same sentence.**

   The coffee break is at ten o'clock, and the company plans to purchase additional parking spaces. [**These ideas have little relationship.**]

4. **Put pronouns, adverbs, phrases, and clauses near the words they modify.**

Incorrect	Correct
Belinda put a new type of gel on her hair, which she had just purchased.	Belinda put a new type of gel, which she had just purchased, on her hair.
He only works in the electronics department for $5.25 an hour.	He works in the electronics department for only $5.25 an hour.
The clerk stood beside the fax machine wearing a denim skirt.	The clerk wearing a denim skirt stood beside the fax machine.

5. **Do not separate subject and predicate unnecessarily.**

Incorrect	Clear
He, hoping to receive a bonus, worked rapidly.	Hoping to receive a bonus, he worked rapidly.

6. **Place an introductory phrase near the subject of the independent clause it modifies.** Otherwise, the phrase dangles. To correct the dangling phrase, change the subject of the independent clause, or make the phrase into a subordinate clause by assigning it a subject.

Incorrect	Correct
When a little boy, my mother took me through a pineapple-processing plant. **[Implies that the mother was once a little boy.]**	When I was a little boy, my mother took me through a pineapple-processing plant. When a little boy, I was taken through a pineapple-processing plant by my mother.
Working at full speed every morning, fatigue overtakes me in the afternoon. **[Implies that "fatigue" was working at full speed.]**	Working at full speed every morning, I become tired in the afternoon. Because I work at full speed every morning, fatigue overtakes me in the afternoon.
To function properly, you must oil the machine every hour. **[Implies that if "you" are "to function properly," the machine must be oiled hourly.]**	If the machine is to function properly, you must oil it every hour. To function properly, the machine must be oiled every hour.

7. **Express related ideas in similar grammatical form (use parallel construction).**

Incorrect	Correct
The machine operator made three resolutions: (1) to be punctual, (2) following instructions carefully, and third, the reduction of waste.	The machine operator made three resolutions: (1) to be punctual, (2) to follow instructions carefully, and (3) to reduce waste.
The human resources manager is concerned with the selection of the right worker, providing appropriate orientation, and the worker's progress.	The human resources manager is concerned with selecting the right worker, providing appropriate orientation, and checking the worker's progress.

8. **Do not end a sentence with a needless preposition.**

   Where is the plant to be located (not *located at*)?

   The worker did not tell us where he was going (not *going to*).

   End a sentence with a preposition if for some reason the preposition needs emphasis.

   I am not concerned with what he is paying for. I am concerned with what he is paying with.

   The prospect has everything—a goal to work toward, a house to live in, and an income to live on.

9. **Avoid split infinitives.** Two words are required to express an infinitive: *to* plus a *verb*. The two words belong together. An infinitive is split when another word is placed between the two.

Incorrect	Correct
The superintendent used to occasionally visit the offices.	The superintendent used to visit the offices occasionally.
I plan to briefly summarize the report.	I plan to summarize the report briefly.

Exercise 5

Identify the weakness in each sentence and write an improved version.

1. It is essential that you sign and return the enclosed form.
2. When a small girl, my brother taught me to play basketball.
3. I am submitting an article to *Presentations*, which I wrote last summer.
4. Almost all of my time is spent in planning, organizing, and the various aspects of control.
5. The work team wants to quickly bring the project to a conclusion.

Punctuation

Review basic rules for the use of the following punctuation marks in business writing.

Comma

1. **Use a comma**

   a. Between coordinate clauses joined by *and, but, for, or,* and *nor.*

      He wanted to pay his bills on time, <u>but</u> he did not have the money.

   b. After introductory dependent clauses and certain phrases (participial, or infinitive, or prepositional with five or more words). Sentences that begin with dependent clauses (often with words such as *if, as, since, because, although,* and *when*) almost always need a comma. Use a comma after prepositional phrases with fewer than five words if the comma is necessary for clarity.

Dependent clause:	<u>If you can meet us at the plane</u>, please plan to be there by six o'clock. [**The comma separates the introductory dependent clause from the independent clause.**]
Infinitive:	<u>To get the full benefit of our insurance plan</u>, just fill out and return the enclosed card. [**A verb preceded by "to" ("to get").**]
Participial:	<u>Believing that her earnings would continue to increase</u>, she sought to borrow more money. [**A verb form used as an adjective: "believing" modifies the dependent clause "she sought."**]
Prepositional phrase:	<u>Within the next few days</u>, you will receive written confirmation of this transaction. [**Comma needed because the phrase contains five words.**]
	Under the circumstances we think you are justified. [**Comma omitted because the phrase contains fewer than five words and the sentence is clear without the comma.**]

   c. To separate words in a series.

      You have a choice of gray, green, purple, and white.

Without the comma after "purple," no one can tell for sure whether four choices are available, the last of which is "white," or whether three choices are available, the last of which is "purple and white."

You have a choice of purple and white, gray, and green. [**Choice is restricted to three, the first of which is "purple and white."**]

d. Between coordinate adjectives (two separate adjectives that modify the same noun).

New employees are given a long, difficult examination. [**Both "long" and "difficult" modify "examination."**]

We want quick, factual news. [**Both "quick" and "factual" modify "news."**]

Do not place a comma between two adjectives when the second adjective may be considered as part of the noun that follows.

The supervisor is an excellent public speaker. [**"Excellent" modifies the noun phrase "public speaker."**]

e. To separate a nonrestrictive clause (a clause that is not essential to the basic meaning of the sentence) from the rest of the sentence.

Mr. Murray, who is head of the collection department, is leaving for a vacation. [**The parenthetical remark is not essential to the meaning of the sentence.**]

The man who is head of the collection department is leaving for a vacation. [**Commas are not needed because "who is head of the collection department" is essential to the meaning of the sentence.**]

f. To separate parenthetical expressions from the rest of the sentence.

Ms. Watson, <u>speaking in behalf of the entire department</u>, accepted the proposal.

g. Before and after the year in month-day-year format.

On <u>July 2, 1999</u>, Mr. Pearson made the final payment.

h. Before and after the name of a state when the name of a city precedes it.

I saw him in <u>Kansas City, Missouri</u>, on the 12th of October.

i. After a direct address.

<u>Jason</u>, I believe you have earned a vacation.

j. After the words *No* and *Yes* when they introduce a statement.

<u>Yes</u>, you can count on me.

<u>No</u>, I will have to decline.

k. To set off appositives when neutral emphasis is desired.

The group heard a speech from Mr. Kyle Welch, <u>a recruit</u>.

Mr. Herbert Jackson, <u>former president of the Jackson Institute</u>, spoke to the group.

l. Between contrasted elements.

We need more money, <u>not less</u>.

The job requires experience, <u>not formal education</u>.

m. To show the omission of words that are understood.

   Ms. Rent scored 96 percent on the employment examination; Mr. Mehrmann, 84 percent.

n. Before a question that solicits a confirmatory answer.

   It's a reasonable price, <u>isn't it</u>?

   Our bills have been paid, <u>haven't they</u>?

o. Between the printed name and the title on the same line beneath a signature.

   Roy Murr, President

   No comma is used if the title is on a separate line.

   Cathryn W. Edwards
   President of Academic Affairs

p. After an adverbial conjunction.

   The check was for the right amount; however, it was not signed.

Exercise 6

Insert needed commas. Write "correct" if you find no errors.

1. The man who came in late has not been interviewed.
2. Ammonium sulfate which is available at almost all home supply stores is ideal fertilizer for citrus.
3. Margie Harrison a new member of the board remained silent during the long bitter debate.
4. Primary qualifications for graduates seeking a first job are education work experience and activities.
5. We surveyed the entire population but three responses were unusable.
6. If you approve of the changes in paragraph three please place your initials in the margin.
7. To qualify for the position applicants must have two years of work experience.
8. John was awarded $25; Bill $40.
9. We have lost our place in the production line haven't we?
10. We should be spending less money not more.
11. On November 20 1999 all related documents were submitted.
12. Yes I agree that the meeting in Oxford Tennessee should be scheduled in April.

Semicolon

2. **Use a semicolon**

   a. To join the independent clauses in a compound sentence when a conjunction is omitted.

      Our workers have been extraordinarily efficient this year; they are expecting a bonus.

b. To join the independent clauses in a compound-complex sentence.

As indicated earlier, we prefer delivery on Saturday morning at four o'clock; but Friday night at ten o'clock will be satisfactory.

We prefer delivery on Saturday morning at four o'clock; but, if the arrangement is more convenient for you, Friday night at ten o'clock will be satisfactory.

c. Before an adverbial conjunction.

Adverbial conjunction: The shipment arrived too late for our weekend sale; <u>therefore</u>, we are returning the shipment to you.

Other frequently used adverbial conjunctions are *however, otherwise, consequently,* and *nevertheless.*

d. Before words used to introduce enumerations or explanations that follow an independent clause.

Enumeration with commas: Many factors affect the direction of the stock market; <u>namely</u>, interest rates, economic growth, and employment rates.

Enumeration without commas: Several popular Internet browsers are available, <u>for example</u>, Netscape and Internet Explorer. [**A comma, not a semicolon, is used because the enumeration contains no commas.**]

Explanation forming a complete thought: We have plans for improvement; <u>for example</u>, we intend . . . .

The engine has been "knocking"; <u>that is</u>, the gas in the cylinders explodes before the pistons complete their upward strokes.

Explanation forming an incomplete thought: Many companies have used nontraditional methods for recruiting applicants, <u>for instance</u>, soliciting résumé postings to company web sites. [**A comma, not a semicolon, is used because the explanation is not a complete thought.**]

e. In a series that contains commas.

Some of our workers have worked overtime this week: Smith, 6 hours; Hardin, 3; Cantrell, 10; and McGowan, 11.

Exercise 7

Insert a semicolon where needed.

1. Expense tickets were not included, otherwise, the request would have been honored.

2. The following agents received a bonus this month: Barnes, $400, Shelley, $450, and Jackson, $600.

3. The proposal was not considered it arrived two days late.

4. This paint does have some disadvantages for example a lengthy drying time.

5. Soon after the figures have been received, they will be processed, but a formal report cannot be prepared before June 15.

Colon

3. **Use a colon**

   a. After a complete thought that introduces a list of items. Use a colon following both direct and indirect introductions of lists. Do not use a colon after an introductory statement that ends with a preposition or a verb (*are, is, were, include*). The list that follows the preposition or verb finishes the sentence.

Direct introduction:	The following three factors influenced our decision: an expanded market, an inexpensive source of raw materials, and a ready source of labor. [**The word "following" clearly introduces a list.**]
Indirect introduction:	The carpet is available in three colors: green, burgundy, and blue.
Incomplete sentence:	We need to (1) expand our market, (2) locate an inexpensive source of materials, and (3) find a ready source of labor. [**A colon does not follow "to" because the words preceding the list is not a complete sentence.**]
	Examples of leading presentation graphics software include Corel Presentations, PowerPoint, and Aldus Persuasion. [**A colon does not follow "include" because the words preceding the list are not a complete sentence.**]

   b. To stress an appositive (a noun that renames the preceding noun) at the end of a sentence.

   His heart was set on one thing: promotion.

   Our progress is due to the efforts of one person: Mr. Keating.

   c. After the salutation of a letter (when mixed punctuation is used).

   Dear Dr. Gorga:

   d. After a word or phrase followed by additional material in ads or signs.

   No Parking: Reserved for executives

   For Rent: Two-bedroom apartment

   e. Between hours and minutes to express time in figures.

   5:45 p.m.   11:05 a.m.

Exercise 8

Correct the use of colons. Write "correct" if you find no errors.

1. The program has one shortcoming: flexibility.
2. Our meetings are scheduled for: Monday, Tuesday, and Friday.
3. We liked this car because of: its price, durability, and appearance.
4. We liked three features of Ms. Cole's résumé: her experience, her education, and her attitude.
5. We are enthusiastic about the plan because: (1) it is least expensive, (2) its legality is unquestioned, and (3) it can be implemented quickly.

Apostrophe

4. **Use an apostrophe to form possessives.**

   a. Add an apostrophe and *s* ('s) to form the possessive case of a singular noun or a plural noun that does not end with a pronounced *s*.

Singular noun:	Jenna's position	firm's assets
	employee's benefits	

Plural noun without a pronounced *s*:	men's clothing	children's games
	deer's antlers	

   b. Add only an apostrophe to form the possessive of a singular or plural noun that ends with a pronounced *s*.

Singular noun with pronounced *s*:	Niagara Falls' site
	Ms. Jenkins' interview

Plural noun with pronounced *s*:	two managers' decision
	six months' wages

   Exception: An apostrophe and *s* ('s) can be added to singular nouns ending in a pronounced *s* if an additional s sound is pronounced easily.

Singular noun with additional *s* sound:	boss's decision	class's party,
	Jones's invitation	

   c. Use an apostrophe in an expression that indicates ownership. The apostrophe shows omission of a preposition.

   Last year's reports. . . . **(Reports of last year. . . .)**

   d. Use an apostrophe with the possessives of nouns that refer to time (minutes, hours, days, weeks, months, and years) or distance in a possessive manner.

eight hours' pay	today's schedule	a stone's throw
two weeks' notice	ten years' experience	a yard's length

   e. Use an apostrophe in a possessive noun that precedes a gerund.

   Ms. Bowen's receiving the promotion caused . . . .

   The manager appreciated Mitzi's working overtime to complete the order.

   f. Use an apostrophe to show whether ownership is joint or separate.

   To indicate joint ownership, add an 's to the last name only.

   Olsen and Howard's accounting firm.

   To indicate separate ownership, add an 's to each name.

   Olsen's and Howard's accounting firms.

5. **Do not use an apostrophe**

   a. In the titles of some organizations. Use the name as the organization uses its name.

   National Sales Executives Association

   b. To form the possessive of a pronoun (most pronouns become possessive through a change in spelling; therefore, an apostrophe is not used).

   Yours [**Not your's**]

   Ours [**Not our's**]

Exercise 9

Correct the possessives.

1. This companies mission statement has been revised since it's recent merger.
2. The workers earned a bonus of three weeks wages for last months overtime.
3. The banks' had been negotiating a merger for several months time.
4. Two service stations were cited: West and Johnson's.
5. The manager will appreciate you completing the review before the auditors arrive.

Hyphen

6. **Use a hyphen**

   a. In such compound words such as *father-in-law* and *attorney-by-law*, words beginning with *ex* (ex-mayor) and *self* (self-analysis).

   b. Between the words in a compound adjective. (A *compound adjective* is a group of adjectives appearing together and used as a single word to describe a noun.) Hyphenate compound adjectives that appear before the nouns or pronouns they describe.

      An <u>attention-getting</u> device

      A technical, <u>hard-to-follow</u> lecture

      A <u>two-thirds</u> interest

      Do not hyphenate a compound adjective in the following cases:

      (1) When the compound adjective follows a noun.

         A device that is <u>attention getting</u>.

         A lecture that was <u>hard to follow</u>.

      (2) An expression made up of an adverb that ends in *ly* and an adjective is not a compound adjective and does not require a hyphen.

         <u>commonly accepted</u> principle

         <u>widely quoted</u> authority

      (3) A simple fraction and a percentage.

         Simple fraction: Two thirds of the respondents

         Percentage: 15 percent sales increase

   c. To prevent misinterpretation.

      A small-business executive **[An executive who operates a small business]**
      A small business executive **[An executive who is small]**

      Recover a chair **[To obtain possession of a chair once more]**
      Re-cover a chair **[To cover a chair again]**

      Eight inch blades **[Eight blades, each of which is an inch long]**
      Eight-inch blades **[Blades eight inches long]**

d. When spelling out compound numbers from 21 to 99.

<u>Thirty-one</u>   <u>Ninety-seven</u>

e. To avoid repetition of a word in a series of hyphenated adjectives that has a common ending.

<u>Short-</u>, <u>medium-</u>, and <u>long-range</u> missiles

"Short-range, medium-range, and long-range missiles" have the same meaning; but repetition of "range" is not necessary. The hyphens after "short" and "medium" show that these words are connected to another word that will appear at the end of the series (called *suspending hyphens*).

f. To divide words at the end of a line. (See the discussion of word division in Appendix A.)

g. In a nine-digit zip code.

83475-1247

Exercise 10

Add necessary hyphens. Write "correct" if you find no errors.

1. The employee's self confidence was damaged by the manager's harsh reprimand.

2. State of the art computers provide us quick access to accurate information needed to manage our business effectively.

3. Surveys indicate that a majority of today's consumers are convenience driven.

4. A two thirds majority is needed to pass the 5 percent increase in employee wages.

5. Sixty five of the respondents were female; nearly one half were highly educated professionals.

6. Print résumés and cover letters on 8½ by 11 inch bond paper.

Quotation Marks and Italics

7. Use quotation marks

a. To enclose direct quotations.

Single-sentence quotation:	The supervisor said, "We will make progress."
Interrupted quotation:	"We will make progress," the supervisor said, "even though we have to work overtime."
Multiple-sentence quotation:	The president said, "Have a seat, gentlemen. I'm dictating a letter. I should be through in about five minutes. Please wait." **[Place quotation marks before the first word and after the last word of a multiple-sentence quotation.]**
Quotation within a quotation:	The budget director said, "Believe me when I say 'A penny saved is a penny earned' is the best advice I ever had." **[Use single quotation marks to enclose a quotation that appears with a quotation.]**

Note: Periods and commas appear within the quotation marks. Other punctuation marks appear outside—unless the punctuation mark is part of the quotation.

"Take your time," she said, "and the work will be easier." [**Periods and commas *inside* the quotation marks.**]

The manager said, "That's fine"; his facial expression conveyed an entirely different message. [**Semicolons *outside* quotation marks.**]

The contractor asked, "When will we begin?" [**Question marks *inside* quotation marks when the question is within the quotation.**]

Did the contractor say, "We will begin today"? [**Place question marks *outside* quotation marks when the question is not within the quotation.**]

b. To enclose titles of songs, magazine and newspaper articles, and themes within text.

"Candle in the Wind"

"Progress in Cancer Research"

c. To enclose a definition of a defined term. Italicize the defined word.

The term *downsizing* is used to refer to "the planned reduction in the number of employees."

d. To enclose words used in humor, a word used when a different word would be more appropriate, slang expressions that need to be emphasized or clarified for the reader, or nicknames. These words can also be shown in italics.

Humor/Different Word: Our "football" team. . . . [**Hints that the team appears to be playing something other than football.**]

Our football "team" . . . . [**Hints that "collection of individual players" would be more descriptive than "team."**]

. . . out for "lunch." [**Hints that the reason for being out is something other than lunch.**]

Slang: With negotiations entering the final week, it's time "to play hardball."

Nicknames: And now for some comments by Robert "Bob" Johnson.

8. **Use italics** (Underscore is not used in computer-generated copy but can be used in typewritten copy.)

a. To indicate words, letters, numbers, and phrases used as words.

The word *effective* was used in describing his presentation.

He had difficulty learning to spell *recommendation*.

b. To emphasize a word that is not sufficiently emphasized by other means.

c. To indicate the titles of books, magazines, and newspapers.

Managing for Quality   *The New York Times*   *Reader's Digest*

Underscore or italicize the titles of books, magazines, and newspapers within text. Refer to documentation style manuals for correct treatment of these titles in citations and bibliographic references.

Exercise 11

Add necessary quotation marks and italics.

1. Goleman presents an interesting theory of intelligence in his book Emotional Intelligence.
2. The article 11 Tips for Using Flip Charts More Effectively appeared in the October 1997 issue of Presentations.
3. His accomplishments are summarized on the attached page. [Indicate that a word other than *accomplishments* may be a more appropriate word]
4. Nick said the firm plans to establish a sinking fund. [direct quotation]
5. The term flame is online jargon for a heated, sarcastic, sometimes abusive message or posting to a discussion group.
6. Read each e-mail message carefully before you send it to avoid flaming.

Dash, Parentheses, Brackets, Ellipses, and Period

9. **Use a dash**

   a. To place emphasis on appositives.

   His answer—the correct answer—was based on years of experience.
   Compare the price—$125—with the cost of a single repair job.

   b. When appositives contain commas.

   Their scores—Mary, 21; Sally, 20; and Jo, 19—were the highest in a group of 300.

   c. When a parenthetical remark consists of an abrupt change in thought.

   The committee decided—you may think it's a joke, but it isn't—that the resolution should be adopted.

   Note: Use an em dash (not two hyphens) to form a dash in computer-generated copy.

10. **Use parentheses**

    a. For explanatory material that could be left out.

    Three of our employees (Mr. Bachman, Mr. Russo, and Mr. Wilds) took their vacations in August.

    All our employees (believe it or not) have perfect attendance records. [**Note a parenthetical sentence within a sentence neither begins with a capital letter nor ends with a period.**]

    Use commas before and after parenthetical material for neutral emphasis; use dashes for added emphasis.

    b. For accuracy in writing figures.

    For the sum of three thousand five hundred dollars ($3,500). . . .

    c. To enclose numbers or letters used to enumerate lists of items within a sentence.

Incorrect	Correct
. . . authority to 1) issue passes and 2) collect fees.	. . . authority to (1) issue passes and (2) collect fees.

d. *After* a period when an entire sentence is parenthetical; *before* a period when only the last part of a sentence is parenthetical.

> The board met for three hours. (The usual time is one hour.)
>
> Success can be attributed to one person (Earl Knott).

11. **Use brackets**

a. To enclose words that are inserted between words or sentences of quoted material.

> "How long will the delay be? No longer than this: [At this point, the speaker tapped the lectern three times.] That means no delay at all."

b. As required in certain mathematical formulas.

c. To enclose parenthetical material within parentheses.

> The motion passed. (The vote [17 for and 4 against] was not taken until midnight.)

d. To explain, clarify, or correct words of the writer you quote.

> "To [accounting] professionals, the ability to express themselves well is more than a hallmark of educated persons," was quoted from a study conducted by the American Institute of Certified Public Accountants.

12. **Use an ellipsis to indicate words have been omitted from a quotation or to add emphasis in advertising material.** Insert a space between the three periods. Use four periods in ellipses at the end of a quotation; one period indicates the end of the sentence.

Omission:	Mr. Thomas said, "We believe . . . our objectives will be accomplished."
	Mr. Thomas reported, "The time has come when we must provide our employees with in-service training. . . ."
Emphasis:	Don't be left out in the cold . . . order your cost-efficient Premier gas logs today.

13. **Use a period after declarative and imperative sentences and courteous requests.**

We will attend. **[Declarative sentence.]**

Complete this report. **[Imperative sentence.]**

Will you please complete the report today. **[Courteous request is a question but does not require a verbal answer with requested action.]**

Exercise 12

Add necessary dashes, parentheses, brackets, ellipses. or periods.

1. Our accountant said, "Such expenses are not justified." [Show that words have been omitted in the middle of the sentence.]

2. Our accountant said, "Such expenses are not justified." [Show that words have been omitted at the end of the sentence.]

3. Additional consultants, programmers and analysts, were hired to complete the computer conversion.[Emphasize the appositive.]

4. The dividend will be raised to 15 cents a share approved by the Board of Directors on December 1, 1999. [Deemphasize the approval.]

5. The following conclusions were presented for the plan: 1) it is least expensive, 2) its legality is unquestioned, and 3) it can be implemented quickly.

6. Has your work team developed recommendations for expanding our customer base

Numbers

Businesspeople use quantitative data often, so numbers appear frequently in business writing. *Accuracy* is exceedingly important. The most frequent problem in expressing numbers is whether to write them as figures or spell them out as words.

1. **Use figures**

   a. In most business writing because (1) figures should get deserved emphasis, (2) figures are easy for readers to locate if they need to reread for critical points, and (3) figures can be keyed faster and in less space than spelled-out words.

      Regardless of whether a number has one digit or many, use figures to express dates, sums of money, mixed numbers and decimals, distance, dimension, cubic capacity, percentage, weights, temperatures, and chapter and page numbers.

May 10, 1999	165 pounds
$9 million	Chapter 3, page 29
5 percent (use % in a table)	
over 200 applicants (or two hundred) **[an approximation]**	

   b. With ordinals (*th, st, rd, nd*) only when the number precedes the month.

      The meeting is to be held on <u>June 21</u>.

      The meeting is to be held on the <u>21st of June</u>.

   c. With ciphers but without decimals when presenting even-dollar figures, unless the figure appears in a sentence with another figure that includes dollars and cents.

      He paid <u>$30</u> for the cabinet.

      He paid <u>$31.75</u> for the table and <u>$30.00</u> for the cabinet.

   d. Numbers that represent time when a.m. or p.m. is used. Words or figures may be used with o'clock.

      Meet me at <u>10:15 p.m.</u>

      Please be there at <u>ten o'clock</u> (or 10 o'clock).

      Omit the colon when expressing times of day that include hours but not minutes, unless the time appears in a sentence with another time that includes minutes.

      The reception began at <u>7 p.m.</u>

      The award program began at <u>6:30 p.m.</u> with a reception at <u>7:00 p.m.</u>

2. **Spell out**

   a. Numbers if they are used as the first word of a sentence.

   Thirty-two people attended.

   b. Numbers one through ten if no larger number appears in the same sentence.

   Only three people were present.

   We need five machines.

   Send 5 officers and 37 men.

   c. The first number in two consecutive numbers that act as adjectives modifying the same noun; write the second number in figures. If the first number cannot be expressed in one or two words, place it in figures also.

   The package required four 17-cent stamps. [**A hyphen joins the second number with the word that follows it, thus forming a compound adjective that describes the noun "stamps."**]

   We shipped 250 180-horsepower engines today. [**Figures are used because neither number can be expressed in one or two words.**]

   d. Numbers in legal documents, following them with figures enclosed in parentheses.

   For the sum of Five Thousand Four Hundred Ninety-five Dollars ($5,495), . . .

3. **Use symbols**

   For convenience in completing forms such as invoices and statements, but not in letters and reports. The dollar sign ($), in contrast with such symbols as %, ¢, @, and #, should be used in letters and reports.

   Spell out terms rather than use symbols in sentences of letters and reports.

   31 percent (**not "31%"**)

   80 cents a foot (**not "80¢ a foot"**)

   21 cases at $4 a case (**not "21 cases @ $4 a case"**)

   Policy No. 468571 (**not "Policy #468571"**)

Exercise 13

Correct the number usage in the following sentences taken from a letter or a report.

1. The question was answered by sixty-one percent of the respondents.
2. The meeting is scheduled for 10:00 a.m. on February 21st.
3. These 3 figures appeared on the expense account: $21.95, $30, and $35.14.
4. Approximately 100 respondents request a copy of the results.
5. We ordered five sixteen-ounce hammers.
6. The MIS manager ordered 150 3-GB hard drives.
7. 21 members voted in favor of the motion.
8. The cost will be approximately $8,000,000.00.
9. Mix two quarts of white with 13 quarts of brown.
10. Examine the diagram on page seven.

Abbreviations

Avoid abbreviations because they are visually distracting to the reader, are difficult to understand, and may send the mistaken message that you are too hurried to do a complete job. Follow these guidelines when abbreviating is appropriate:

1. **Abbreviate**

   a. Titles that come before and after proper names and academic degrees

      Dr., Mr., Mrs., Ms.

      M.B.A.., Esq., Jr., M.D., Ph.D., R.N., Sr.

      [Periods are not used in the abbreviations of CPA (Certified Public Accountant), CPS (Certified Professional Secretary), and CLU (Chartered Life Underwriter).]

   b. Commonly known government agencies, organizations or businesses, and institutions.

      Government agencies: SEC, FBI, FDA, FDIC, FCC, FHA, SBA, USDA, VA

      Business and educational organizations: GE, IBM, TWA, UPS, MIT

      Other organizations: AMA, BBB, NBC, WLOX, YMCA, UN, NASDAQ,

   c. Commonly used business expressions:

      ATM, EDP, COD/c.o.d, FIFO or LIFO, FOB/f.o.b., CD-ROM, CEO, CFO, MHz, LAN, RSVP, TQM, VCR, WWW, time zones (EST, CDT), a.m., p.m.

      (Note: Use a.m. and p.m. only when a specific time is mentioned. Small letters—a.m. and p.m.—are preferred.)

      Come to the office at 10:15 <u>a.m.</u> (**not <u>this a.m.</u>**)

   d. The words *Co.*, *Corp.*, *Inc.*, *Ltd.*, and *Mfg.* in the names of businesses when their own letterheads contain abbreviations:

      J. C. Penney Company, Inc.   S & A Restaurant Corp.
      Microsoft Corporation   C. Thames & Co.

   e. The word *number* when a numeral directly follows the term unless the term begins the sentence.

      Ship a gross of <u>No.</u> 10 envelopes.

      Refer to Policy <u>No.</u> 384862.

      <u>Number</u> 89-9-1 bolts will be replaced with an improved part on March 1.

   f. The word extension (*Ext.*) when it appears with a telephone number.

      Please call our regional sales rep at (404) 555-9620, <u>Ext.</u> 139.

   g. The names of states when they appear as parts of envelope addresses or inside addresses. Use the two-letter abbreviations recommended by the U.S. Postal Services shown in Appendix A, Figure A-12.

2. **Do not abbreviate**

   a. The names of cities, states (except in an envelope and letter address), months, and days of the week. They may be abbreviated in lists, tables, graphs, charts, illustrations, or other visuals where space is limited.

b. Points on the compass.

> Tom has lived in the <u>West</u> for seven years.
>
> Go <u>east</u> one block and turn <u>south</u>; then continue to 650 <u>North</u> Cypress Street.

Capitalization

Capitalize

1. **Proper nouns (words that name a particular person, place, or thing) and adjectives derived from proper nouns.** Capitalize the names of persons, places, geographic areas, days of the week, months of the year, holidays, deities, specific events, and other specific names.

Proper nouns	Common nouns
Lynn Claxton	An applicant for the management position
Bonita Lakes	A land development
Centre Park Mall	A new shopping center
Veteran's Day	A federal holiday
Information Age	A period of time

    Proper adjectives: Irish potatoes, Roman shades, Swiss army knife, Chinese executives, British accent, Southern dialect.

    Do not capitalize the name of the seasons unless they are personified.

2. **The principal words in the titles of books, magazines, newspapers, articles, compact disks, movies, plays, television series, songs, and poems.**

    Seven Habits of Highly Effective People [**Book**]

    "Add Dimension to Presentations with Document Camera" [**Article**]

    Video Producer [**Magazine**]

    Encarta '98 [**Compact disk**]

3. **The names of academic courses that are numbered, are specific course titles, or contain proper nouns. Capitalize degrees used after a person's name and specific academic sessions.**

    Thomas Malone is enrolled in classes in <u>French</u>, <u>mathematics</u>, <u>science</u>, and <u>English</u>.

    Students entering the MBA program must complete <u>Accounting 6093</u> and <u>Finance 5133</u>.

    Ms. Sheila O'Donnell, <u>M.S.</u>, will teach <u>Principles of Management</u> during <u>Spring Semester 1999</u>.

    Ms. O'Donnell earned a <u>master's</u> degree in business from Harvard.

4. **Titles that precede a name.**

Mr. Ronald Smith	Editor Franklin	Uncle Fred
Dr. Sarah Hobbs	President Lopez	Professor Senter

Do *not* capitalize titles appearing alone or following a name unless they appear in addresses.

The manager approved the proposal submitted by the editorial assistant.

Susan Morris, executive vice president, is responsible for that account.

Dean has taken the position formerly held by his father.

Address all correspondence to Colonel Michael Anderson, Production Manager, 109 Crescent Avenue, Baltimore, MD 21208.

5. **The main words in a division or department name if the official or specific name is known or the name is used in a return address, a letter address, or a signature block.**

Official or specific name known:	Return the completed questionnaire to the Public Relations Department by March 15.
Official or specific name unknown:	Employees in your information systems division are invited . . . .
Return or letter address, signature block:	Mr. Owen Rowan, Manager, Public Relations Department . . .

6. **Most nouns followed by numbers (except in page, paragraph, line, size, and verse references).**

Policy No. 8746826	Exhibit A	Chapter 7
page 97, paragraph 2	Figure 3-5	Model L-379
Flight 340, Gate 22	size 8, Style 319 jacket	

7. **Only the first and last words in salutations and only the first word in complimentary closes.**

My dear Sir:	Sincerely yours,

8. **The first word of a direct quotation.**

The sales representative said, "<u>We</u> leave tomorrow."

Do *not* capitalize the first word in the last part of an interrupted quotation or the first word in an indirect quotation.

"We will proceed," he said, "with the utmost caution." **[Interrupted quotation]**

He said that the report must be submitted by the end of the week. **[Indirect quotation]**

9. **The first word following a colon when a formal statement or question follows.**

Here is an important rule for report writers: Plan your work and work your plan.

Each sales representative should ask this question: Do I really look like a representative of my firm?

Exercise 14

Copy each of the following sentences, making essential changes in abbreviation and capitalization.

1. The first question asked of me during interviewing 101 was "why do you want to work for us?"
2. The summer season is much slower than the rest of the year according to the Sales Manager.
3. We paid for *Awaken the Giant Within* with check no. 627 on Dec. 10.
4. The N.C.A.A. meeting, moderated by president Marla Stanton, will be held in N.Y.
5. A retirement ceremony is being planned for president Sims at 9 P.M. E.S.T.
6. Inform the marketing department of the temporary shortage of Model Y-139.
7. We recently purchased corel stock music gallery, an excellent source of copyright-free music clips.
8. Bill Gates, President of Microsoft, was interviewed on a national television program last week.

Words Frequently Misused

1. *Accept, except. Accept* means "to take what is offered," "to accede," "to assent"; *except* means "to exclude," or "with the exclusion of."

   I <u>accept</u> your offer.

   All columns have been added <u>except</u> one.

2. *Advice, advise. Advice* is a noun meaning "suggestions or recommendations about a course of action." *Advise* is a verb meaning "to give advice; to caution or warn."

   The supervisor's <u>advice</u> to John was to abide by safety rules.

   Supervisors <u>advise</u> employees of the consequences of safety rules violations.

3. *Affect, effect. Affect* is a verb meaning "to influence"; *effect* is a noun meaning "result"; *effect* is also a verb meaning "to bring about."

   The change does not <u>affect</u> his pay.

   What <u>effect</u> will the change have?

   The manager wants to <u>effect</u> a change in the schedule.

4. *Among, between.* Use *among* to discuss three or more; *between* to discuss two.

   Divide the earnings <u>among</u> the six workers.

   Divide the earnings <u>between</u> the two workers.

5. *Amount, number.* Use *amount* when speaking of money or of things that cannot be counted; use *number* when speaking of things that can be counted.

   The <u>amount</u> of grumbling has been troublesome to the supervisors.

   The <u>number</u> of workers has been increased.

6. *Capital, capitol. Capital* is money, property, or a city in which state or national government is located. A *capitol* is a building in which the government meets.

> One business partner provided the <u>capital</u>; the other provided the expertise.
>
> The <u>capitol</u> is at the intersection of Jefferson Street and Tenth Avenue.

7. *Cite, sight, site. Cite* means to quote or mention. *Sight* refers to the sense of seeing, the process of seeing, or a view. *Site* is a location.

> Marianne <u>cited</u> several authorities in her report.
>
> Working at the computer is affecting her <u>sight</u>.
>
> Market Avenue is the <u>site</u> of the new store.

8. *Complement, compliment. Complement* means "to complete" or "that which completes or suits another." *Compliment* means "words of praise."

> This shipment is a <u>complement</u> to our latest series of orders.
>
> The clerk was <u>complimented</u> for his success.

9. *Continual, continuous.* If an action is *continual* it will have planned-for breaks in continuity; if an action is *continuous*, it will be constant, without breaks.

> The mechanism for raising and lowering the garage door has given <u>continual</u> service for four years.
>
> The clock has run <u>continuously</u> for four years.

10. *Council, counsel. Council* means "an advisory group." *Counsel* means "advice," "one who gives advice," or "to advise."

> <u>Council</u> members will meet today.
>
> First, seek legal <u>counsel</u>.
>
> The defendant and his <u>counsel</u> were excused.
>
> An attorney will <u>counsel</u> the suspect.

11. *Credible, creditable. Credible* means "believable." *Creditable* means "praise-worthy" or "worthy of commercial credit."

> The explanations were <u>credible</u>.
>
> Mr. Fulton did a <u>creditable</u> job for us.

12. *Criteria, criterion.* A *criterion* is a standard for judging, a yardstick by which something is measured. The plural form is *criteria*.

> The most important <u>criterion</u> was cost.
>
> Three <u>criteria</u> were developed.

13. *Data, datum. Datum* is a singular noun meaning "fact," "proposition," "condition," or "quantity" from which other facts, and so forth, may be deduced. *Data* is the plural form.

> This <u>datum</u> suggests . . .
>
> These <u>data</u> suggest . . .

Use of *data* as a singular form is gaining some degree of acceptance. Some people use the word in the same way they use *group*. Although composed of more than one, *group* is singular.

> The group has decided.

Until *data* becomes generally accepted as singular, the word should be used carefully. Instead of "This data is" or "These data are" such expressions as "This *set* of data is" or "These facts are" can be used to avoid the risk of alienating certain readers or listeners.

14. *Different from, different than*. *Different from* is correct; *different than* is to be avoided.

> That machine is different from mine.

15. *Each other, one another*. Use *each other* when referring to two people; use *one another* when referring to more than two.

> The two employees competed with each other.
>
> The members of the group helped one another.

16. *Eminent, imminent*. *Eminent* means "well known." *Imminent* means "about to happen."

> An eminent scientist will address the group.
>
> A merger seems imminent.

17. *Envelop, envelope*. *Envelop* is a verb meaning "to surround" or "to hide." *Envelope* is a noun referring to a cover for a letter.

> A fog was about to envelop the island.
>
> Just use the enclosed envelope for your reply.

18. *Farther, further*. Use *farther* when referring to distance. Use *further* when referring to extent or degree.

> Let's go one mile farther.
>
> Let's pursue the thought further.

19. *Fewer, less*. Use *fewer* with items that can be counted; use *less* with items that cannot be counted.

> Fewer than half the employers approved the proposed pay plan.
>
> Maria spent less time writing the report than Michael because she had spent more time organizing her data.

20. *Formally, formerly*. Use *formally* when discussing that which is ceremonious or done according to an established method. Use *formerly* in discussing that which has preceded in time.

> The award will be formally presented at tomorrow's convocation.
>
> Tom formerly worked for the department of revenue.

21. *Infer, imply*. *Infer* means "to draw a conclusion"; readers or listeners infer. *Imply* means "to hint" or "to set forth vaguely"; speakers and writers imply.

   I <u>infer</u> from your letter that conditions have improved.

   Do you mean to <u>imply</u> that conditions have improved?

22. *Insure, ensure*. To *insure* is to contract for payment of a certain sum in the event of damage or loss. To *ensure* is to make certain that a specified event or result will occur.

   We plan to <u>insure</u> the house for $80,000.

   To <u>ensure</u> a passing score, study systematically.

23. *Irregardless*. Avoid using this word. Use *regardless* instead.

24. *Its, it's*. *Its* is a possessive pronoun; *it's* is a contraction for "it is."

   The phrase has lost <u>its</u> meaning.

   <u>It's</u> time to quit.

25. *Lend, loan*. *Lend* is a verb meaning to let another use something temporarily. *Loan* is a noun referring to the thing given for the borrower's temporary use.

   The bank has agreed to <u>lend</u> us the money.

   The bank has approved our <u>loan</u>.

26. *Lose, loose*. *Lose* means "to fail to keep"; *loose* means "not tight."

   Don't <u>lose</u> the moneybag.

   The cap on the fountain pen is <u>loose</u>.

27. *Media, medium*. A *medium* is a means for transmitting a message. Letter, telephone, radio, newspaper, and telegraph are examples. The plural form is *media*.

   The best <u>medium</u> for advertising this product is the radio.

   The news <u>media</u> are very objective in their coverage.

28. *Personal, personnel*. *Personal* means "concerned with a person" or "private." *Personnel* means "people" or "employees."

   Omit the questions about family background and musical preference; they're too <u>personal</u>.

   All advertising <u>personnel</u> are invited to participate in the workshop.

29. *Principal, principle*. *Principal* means "a person in a leading position," "main," or "primary"; *principle* means "rule" or "law."

   The <u>principal</u> scheduled an all-day faculty meeting.

   The <u>principal</u> purpose is to gain speed.

   The <u>principal</u> plus interest is due in thirty days.

   The theory is based on sound <u>principles</u>.

30. *Reason is because. Because* means "for the reason next presented"; therefore *reason is because* is a redundancy.

    Not: The reason is because losses from bad debts tripled.

    But: The reason is that losses from bad debts tripled.

    Or: Profits decreased because losses from bad debts tripled.

31. *Stationary, stationery. Stationary* means "without movement" or "remaining in one place." *Stationery* is writing paper.

    The machine is to remain <u>stationary</u>.

    Order another box of <u>stationery</u>.

32. *That, which.* Use *that* when a dependent clause is essential in conveying the basic meaning of the sentence. Use *which* when a dependent clause is not essential in conveying the basic meaning of the sentence.

    The books <u>that</u> were on the shelf have been sent to the bindery. [**The clause identifies certain books sent to the bindery; therefore, it is essential**].

    Multigrade oil, <u>which</u> is only slightly more expensive than one-grade oil, will serve your purpose better. [**Purpose of sentence is to convey the superiority of multigrade oil; therefore, "which is only slightly more expensive than one-grade oil" is not essential.**]

33. *Their, there, they're. Their* is the possessive form of "they." *There* refers to "at that place" or "at that point." *They're* is a contraction for "they are."

    The president accepted <u>their</u> proposal immediately.

    The final copy must be <u>there</u> by May 1.

    <u>They're</u> eager to complete the renovation in time for the spring selling season.

34. *To, too, two. To* is a preposition or the beginning of an infinitive. *Too* is an adverb meaning "also" or "excessive." *Two* is a number.

    José organized the campaign <u>to</u> initiate flexible scheduling.

    Twenty percent overtime is <u>too</u> demanding.

    The entire department shares the <u>two</u> laser printers.

35. *While. While,* meaning "at the same time that," should not be used as a synonym for such conjunctions as *but, though, although, and,* and *whereas.*

    You complete the appendixes <u>while</u> I key a transmittal letter. [**Concurrent activities**]

    One man likes his work, <u>but</u> the other does not.

    <u>Although</u> we realize your account is overdue, we think you should not pass up this opportunity.

Exercise 15

Select the correct word.

1. All questionnaires were returned (accept, except) one.
2. Exactly how will the change (affect, effect) us?
3. The consultants' (advice, advise) is to downsize the organization.
4. The commission is to be divided equally (among, between) the three sales agents.
5. We were astonished by the (amount, number) of complaints.
6. The (cite, sight, site) of Jim's receiving the service award was exhilarating.
7. I consider that remark a (compliment, complement).
8. Because the suspect's statements were (credible, creditable), no charges were filed.
9. The three panelists were constantly interrupting (each other, one another).
10. The issue will be discussed (further, farther) at our next meeting.
11. Limit your discussion to five or (fewer, less) points.
12. From his statements to the press, I (infer, imply) that he is optimistic about the proposal.
13. (Regardless, Irregardless) of weather conditions, we should proceed.
14. The storm seems to be losing (its, it's) force.
15. Please, (lend, loan) me a copy of today's *The Wall Street Journal*.
16. Employees are entitled to examine their (personal, personnel) folder.
17. The system's (principal, principle) advantage is monetary.
18. (Their, There, They're) planning to complete (their, there, they're) strategic plan this week.
19. The supervisor expects us (to, too, two) complete (to, too, two) many unnecessary reports.
20. (Although, While) my findings are similar, my conclusions are dissimilar.

Complete the "Self-Check" and the "Review Quiz" to test your understanding of grammar, spelling, and punctuation principles.

✓ Self-Check

Cover the answer that appears below each numbered sentence. Identify the error(s) in a sentence; then, slide the cover sheet down and check your answer against the correct sentence. Refer to the pages listed in parentheses to review the reasons for each correction. The first number is a page number in Appendix C; the second number or letter identifies a certain place on the page.

1. While Jan's request for promotion had been denied three times her self esteem was high.

   <u>Although</u> Jan's request for promotion had been denied three times<u>,</u> her <u>self-esteem</u> was high. (33) (13b) (19, a)

2. I will appreciate you sending next months report too my home address, 9 S. Maple St.

   I will appreciate <u>your</u> sending next <u>month's</u> report <u>to</u> my home address, <u>Nine</u> <u>South</u> Maple <u>Street</u>. (6, d) (18, 4a) (33) (25, b) (27, b; 27, 1)

3. Only one of the participant's were willing to ask what do you think? **[direct quote]**

   Only one of the <u>participants</u> <u>was</u> willing to ask<u>,</u> <u>"</u>What do you think?<u>"</u> (18, 4) (7, a) (20, a; 28, 8) (21, 7a)

4. On March 1st, 1999 we moved to a five room suite, it was formally occupied by Woodson Travel Agency.

   On March <u>1, 1999,</u> we moved to a <u>five-room</u> suite<u>;</u> it was <u>formerly</u> occupied by Woodson Travel Agency.

   On March <u>1, 1999,</u> we moved to a <u>five-room</u> <u>suite, which</u> was <u>formerly</u> occupied by Woodson Travel Agency. (14, g) (19, a) (15, a; 11, e) (31)

5. The box, which was in room 12, has been prepared for mailing, all other boxes are to be wrapped with heavy paper, and returned to room 5.

   The box <u>that</u> was in <u>Room 12</u> has been prepared for mailing<u>;</u> all other boxes are to be wrapped with heavy paper and returned to <u>Room 5</u>. **[or . . . mailing, but . . . .]** (14, e) (28; 24) (15, a) (28)

6. I am willing to complete this long complicated questionnaire but I lack the required experience.

   I am willing to complete this long<u>,</u> complicated questionnaire<u>;</u> but I lack the required experience. (14, d) (13, 1a)

7. Although the company has lost their first place position the next six months predictions are promising.

   Although the company has lost <u>its</u> <u>first-place</u> position, the next six <u>months'</u> predictions are promising. (32) (19, a) (18, 4a)

8. That price seems reasonable for you and I, however, it probably seems very high for a recently-hired assistant.

   That price seems reasonable for you and <u>me;</u> <u>however,</u> it probably seems very high for a <u>recently hired</u> assistant. (5, 2b) (16, c) (19, 2)

9. The spellcheck was not able to detect all errors, for example, derive was keyed incorrectly as drive.

   The spellcheck was not able to detect all errors<u>;</u> for example, <u>*derive*</u> was keyed incorrectly as <u>*drive*</u>. (16, d) (21, 8a) (21, 8a)

10. The following employees have worked 7 hours of overtime this week; Welch, 4, Redford, 6, and Woods, 11.

    The following employees have worked <u>seven</u> hours of overtime this week<u>:</u> Welch, 4<u>;</u> Redford, 6<u>;</u> and Woods, 11. (25, 2b) (17, a) (16, e)

11. Helen made a higher score than any one in her work unit but her promotion was denied because of habitual tardiness.

    Helen made a higher score than <u>anyone else</u> in her work unit<u>,</u> but her promotion was denied because of habitual tardiness. (10, 4) (13, a)

12. Spamming is considered improper on-line behavior by most netiquette experts.

    <u>*Spamming*</u> is considered improper on-line behavior by most netiquette experts. (21, 8a)

Review Quiz

To test your understanding of the grammar, spelling, and punctuation principles presented in Appendix C, identify the error(s) in each sentence.

1. Less than 25% of the questionnaires mailed on June 21st have been returned.

2. George was once in charge of security at the capital building, he is not impressed with our firms security system.

3. Lin Daniel, President of Haneman Industries has written an article that will appear in "Newsweek".

4. Will you please find out whether first and second year students are eligible too receive that scholarship.

5. Although the committee agreed with the plant managers' conclusions; several members raised serious questions about the survey instrument.

6. John has submitted more suggestions than anyone in his department but he has yet to receive an award.

7. The procedure has been highly successful; however, is not popular in the advertising department.

8. The man, who came late to the meeting, is the new Sales Manager for the southwest region.

9. The 3 applicants were waiting to interview for the same job, therefore they had little to say to each other.

10. Only one of my recommendations were considered, this was very disappointing to the superintendent and I.

11. Most of the discussion was devoted to personal policy but that topic has not been listed on the agenda.

12. After you have completed your Management class, write to me, we have some highly-important matters to discuss.

13. When you rewrite the final draft please change the word charge to debit.

14. Each of our assistants are required to take a short intensive Internet course.

15. 13 respondents thought the company was losing site of it's objectives.

16. One June 3, 1999 the Carlisle Pennsylvania location was officially approved.

17. John insisted on us listening to his play by play recap of the game.

18. No the bicycle comes in these styles only, 1) road, 2) mountain and 3) Y-frame.

19. The sight for the new plant is 5 blocks East of N. Lampkin St.

20. While presenting the proposed change in distribution, an emergency call required the manager to leave abruptly.

Grading Symbols

Organization and Development

Word Choice and Style

Punctuation

Mechanics

Format

Your instructor may use the following grading symbols to mark corrections on your writing assignments. The instructor may write the abbreviation (highlighted to the right of the numbers) to identify the major area needing improvement. To provide additional feedback on all or selected errors, the instructor may write the number and letter designating the *specific* principle violated. To review the principles marked on your paper, refer to the pages indicated within the parentheses.

Organization and Development

1. **seq**   Organizational Sequence
   a. Deductive approach to convey good news (Chapter 5, 159)
   b. Inductive approach to convey bad news (Chapter 6, 199-200)
   c. Memos and e-mail messages (Chapter 7, refer to specific document)
   d. Persuasive approach if reader must be persuaded (Chapter 8, 264-268)

2. **ss**   Sentences
   a. Normal subject-verb-complement sequence (107; C-11,#2)
   b. Related ideas in sentence (C-11,#3)
   c. Avoid expletive beginnings (132; C-11,#2)
   d. Avoid clumsy split infinitives (C-12,#9)

3. **¶**   Paragraphs
   a. Topic sentence presents central idea (113-114)
   b. Coherence; ideas connect logically (114-115)
   c. Unity; has beginning, middle (systematic sequence), and ending (115)

4. **trans**   Transition

   Transition between sentences and paragraphs so that ideas connect; avoid choppy sentences (114-115)

Word Choice and Style

5. **read**   Readability
   a. Use plain, simple words; use jargon only if reader will understand (129-131)
   b. Use short sentences (134-138)
   c. Avoid long, complicated paragraphs (116-117)

6. **clear**   Clarity
   a. Include relevant ideas; develop logically (102-104)
   b. Specific vs. general word choice (127; C-3,#1)
   c. Concrete vs. abstract nouns—word choice (127; C-30,#2)
   d. Active voice for vivid writing (109; C-8,#4)
   e. Plain, simple language (129-131)
   f. Action-oriented ending paragraph (see example of specific document)
   g. Cite reference for source (323-326; B-2 to B-4)
   h. Verify accuracy of names, places, dates, amounts, etc. (see case problem)

7. **concise**   Conciseness
   a. Redundancies (134)
   b. Clichés (127-128)
   c. Brevity (unnecessary words and ideas) (134-136)

8. **tone**   Tone
   a. Reader's viewpoint; overuse of first person—I (83-88)
   b. Emphasize positive ideas: use active voice (109; C-8, #4) second person (96), and positive words (95)
   c. De-emphasize negative ideas: use passive voice (96) and avoid second person (96), positive words (95), and subjunctive mood (96-97; C-9,#5)
   d. Use bias-free language (88-91)
   e. Condescending (91-92) and demeaning tone (93)
   f. Misuse of euphemistic tone (92-93) and connotative tone (93-94)
   g. Expressions of surprise, doubt, and judgment (94-95)

9. **agr**   Agreement
   a. Number: subject and verb (C-7,#1)
   b. Person: subject and verb (C-7,#2)
   c. Tense (C-7,#3)
   d. Mood (C-7,#5)
   e. Pronoun and antecedent (C-4,#1; C-6,#3-4)

10. **case**   Case
    a. Nominative (C-5,#2a,c)
    b. Objective (C-5,#2b)
    c. Before a gerund (C-6,#2d)
    d. Relative pronouns—who, whom (C-6,#3)
    e. Possessives (C-18,#4-5)

11. **adj or adv**   Adjectives and Adverbs
    a. Adjectives; use correct degree, avoid superlatives and overly strong adjectives (128-129; C-10,#1,2,4)
    b. Adverbs; use correct degree, avoid superlatives, and overly strong adverbs (128-129;C-10,#3)
    c. Double negatives

12. **frag**   Sentence Fragments (107; C-9,#1)

13. **ro**   Run-on Sentences
    Review the punctuation of sentence types (104; 107-108)

14. **ref**   Pronoun Reference
    a. Ambiguous pronoun reference (C-6,#3)
    b. Misuse: using a pronoun to refer to phrase, clause, sentence or paragraph (C-6,#4)
    c. Use of *you* when the meaning is not clear

15. **shifts**   Shifts
    a. Person and number (See agreement)
    b. Tense and mood (See agreement)

16. **mm/dm**   Misplaced and Dangling Modifiers
    a. Misplaced and dangling modifiers (131-132; C-11,#6)
    b. Relative pronouns (C-6,#3)
    c. Do not separate subject and verb unnecessarily (C-11,#5)

17. **//**   Parallelism (133-134; C-12,#7)

18. **emph**   Emphasis
    a. Sentence structure (109-110)
    b. Position: first and last positions for emphasis (110)
    c. Numbers or tabulated enumerations (111-113)
    d. Include positive idea in sentence (97)

19. **var**   Variety
    a. Sentence length (116)
    b. Sentence structure (116)
    c. Paragraph length (116)

Punctuation

20.   . ? !   Terminal Punctuation (C-23,#13a)

21 .   ,   Comma
    a. Coordinate conjunction—*and*, *but*, and *for* (107-108; C-13,#1a)
    b. Introductory clause or phrase (C-13,#1b)
    c. Items in a series (C-13,#1c)
    d. Coordinate adjectives (C-14,#1d)
    e. Nonrestrictive clauses and parenthetical expressions (C-14,#1e)
    f. Parenthetical expressions (C-14, 1f)
    g. Date, city, and state (C-14,#1g-h)
    h. Direct address (C-14,#1i)
    i. Yes and No (C-14,#1j)
    j. Appositive (C-14,#1k)
    k. Adverbial conjunction (C-15,#1p)
    l. Other rules (C-14,#1)

22.   ;   Semicolon
    a. Omitted conjunction (C-15,#2a)
    b. Compound-complex sentence (108; C-16,#2b)
    c. Adverbial conjunctive (C-16,#2c)
    d. Within series that contains a comma (C-16, #2e)
    e. Before words used to introduce enumerations or explanations that follow an independent clause (C-16,#2d)

23.   '   Apostrophe
    a. Rules for using apostrophes (C-18,#4)
    b. Rules for not using apostrophes (C-18,#5)

24.   [ ] : — . . . - ( ) " "   Other Marks
    a. Brackets (C-23,#11)
    b. Colon (C-17,#3)
    c. Dash (C-22,#9)
    d. Ellipses (C-23,#12)
    e. Hyphen (C-19,#6); compound adjective (C-19,#6b)
    f. Parentheses (C-22, C23,#10)
    g. Quotation Marks (C-20,#7)

Mechanics

25. **caps**
    a. Capitals (C-27,#1-9)
    b. Envelope address: all caps and no punctuation (A-20 to A23)

26. **ital**   Italics (Underline if software does not support italics.)
    a. Words named as words (C-21,#8a)
    b. Emphasis (C-21,#8b)
    c. Titles of books, magazines, and newspapers (C-21,#8c)

27. **ab**   Abbreviations
    a. Abbreviate (C-26,#1)
    b. Do not abbreviate (C-26,#2)
    c. Two-letter ZIP code abbreviation (A-24)

28. **num**   Numbers
    a. Use figures (C-24,#1)
    b. Spell out (C-25,#2)
    c. Use symbols (C-25,#3)

29. **div**   Word Division (A-7,#1-7)

30. **sp**   Spelling
    a. Use a spellchecker or proofread carefully for omitted or repeated words
    b. Frequently misused words. Locate the correct usage from text pages or a dictionary. (C-29 to C33
    c. Verify names, places, dates, amounts, etc. (see case problem)

31. **# or >**   Spacing
    a. Once after terminal punctuation, a comma, a semicolon, and an initial (A-6,#1, 3, 4)
    b. Twice after a colon (A-6,#2)
    c. Proper vertical spacing in letters (A-4)

Format

32. **App**   Appearance
    a. Poor print quality
    b. Not balanced attractively on page
    c. Unprofessional (submitted with perforated edges; crumpled, etc.)

33. **fmt**   Format
    Letters and Memos
    a. Letter style: block (A-8, A-9), modified block (A-8, A-10), simplified block (A-8, A-11)
    b. Punctuation style: open (A-7, A-8), mixed (A-7, A-8)
    c. Include return address on letter if plain paper is used (A-10 to A-12)
    d. Appropriate salutation (A-12 to A-14)
    e. Acceptable memo style: traditional (A-19, A-21), template (A-19, A-20)
    f. Second-page heading for letters/memos (A-15 to A-17)
    g. Appropriate special parts—enclosure, copy, etc. (A-15 to A-18)
    h. Envelope format (A-20, A-21)
    i. Letters signed and memos initialed legibly

    Reports
    j. Report title page (see sample report)
    k. Contents and list of figures (see sample report)
    l. Executive summary (see sample report)
    m. Report text (see sample report)
    n. Citations: In-text parenthetical (B-2, B-3)
    o. Citations: Footnote or endnote (B-4)
    p. Electronic citations (B-9 to B-11)
    q. Bibliography or references page (B-5 to B-8)

    Other Documents
    r. Traditional résumé (502; 504-506)
    s. Electronic résumé (510-511)
    t. On-line résumé (520)
    u. References Page—employment credentials (503)

Index